THE OR
THE WORLD WAR

II
AFTER SARAJEVO
IMMEDIATE CAUSES OF THE WAR

BY

SIDNEY BRADSHAW FAY

PROFESSOR OF HISTORY IN HARVARD UNIVERSITY

Volume Two

Illustrated

ISHI PRESS
INTERNATIONAL

The Origins of the World War
Volume II
After Sarajevo
Immediate Causes of the War

by Sidney Bradshaw Fay

First Published in 1928
by The MacMillan Company

Revised Edition Published in 1930
by The MacMillan Company

Third Printing in February, 2010
by Ishi Press in New York and Tokyo

with a new foreword by Sam Sloan

ISBN 4-87187-878-3
978-4-87187-878-4

Ishi Press International
1664 Davidson Avenue, Suite 1B
Bronx NY 10453-7877
1-917-507-7226

Printed in the United States of America

Foreword by Sam Sloan

The Origins of the World War

Volume II

After Sarajevo
Immediate Causes of the War

by Sidney Bradshaw Fay

This is a **two volume work**. Volume 1 is *"Before Sarajevo –
Underlying Causes of the War"*. Volume 2 is *"After Sarajevo -
Immediate Causes of the War"*.

By *"Before Sarajevo"*, it is meant before the assassination in
Sarajevo on **28 June 1914** of **Archduke Franz Ferdinand** of
Austria, the heir to the throne of **Austria-Hungary**.

This volume two starts with the **Serbian Plot** to Assassinate the
Archduke and continues to the **mobilizations** in **France** and
Germany on **August 1, 1914**. Unlike some other authors, Sidney
Fay believes that the assassination of the Archduke was part of the
plot by the **Black Hand**. Others, however, state that the
assassination was a coincidence caused by a wrong turn by a driver
and that there is no proof that the assassin was part of the **Black
Hand**.

This book deals with the incredible series of events in which in
only **37 days** after the assassination of the Archduke and his wife
Sophie, Germany invaded both Belgium and France. These
events have ever since been studied by career diplomats, seeking to
learn the reasons for this so as to try to prevent another pointless
war like this one from happening.

This is the authoritative work on the causes of **World War One**.
The author, **Sidney Bradshaw Fay (1876–1967)**, was an

Foreword by Sam Sloan

American historian. He was **Professor of History** at **Dartmouth College (1902–14), Smith College (1914–29),** and **Harvard University (1929–46)**.

This is a book on the causes of the war, not on the war itself. Sidney Fay reaches a different conclusion than almost every other researcher on the **Causes of the War**. Whereas others state that the War was the fault of **Germany**, who attacked **France** through **Belgium** on **August 4, 1914**, Sidney Fay asserts that Germany was forced to attack because of the circumstances it faced at the time. Sidney Fay says that **Austria, Serbia, and Russia** were primarily to **blame** for the war.

Few agree with him but, on one point, all authorities agree. At the beginning, all sides believed that the war would be swift and successful. None of the countries had any idea that the war would last four years with **15 million people killed**.

Ishi Press has published several books on the origins of **World War One**. Each of these books reaches a different conclusion on the cause of the war. Sidney Fay primarily blames *"secret alliances"*. He even casts some blame on **Sir Edward Grey** of **England**. He says that Sir Edward Grey should have declared that England would support France in the event of a war, or else Grey should have stated that England would remain neutral in the event of a war.

By straddling the fence and not informing either side what it would do in the event of a war, Grey caused tensions that led to the war.

Another war book by **Ishi Press** is *Fateful Years 1909-1916 The Reminiscences of Serge Sazonov G.C.B., G.C.V.O. Russian Minister for Foreign Affairs: 1914* **ISBN 0923891323**. In this book, **Serge Sazonov** defends his decisions and refuses to take any blame for his actions that led to the war.

Foreword by Sam Sloan

Another book by Ishi Press is *The Making of a State - Memories and Observations 1914-1918* by **Thomas Masaryk, President of Czechoslovakia ISBN 0923891331.**

Yet another **Ishi Press** book is *Source Records of the Great War Vol I How the Great War Arose* **ISBN 4871878732** by **Charles Francis Horne.** The author, editor and compiler of those documents finds that the Assassination of Archduke Franz Ferdinand of Austria merely provided the pretext for the war, that was going to happen anyway. He concludes: *"The Great War could no more have been avoided than an earthquake or any other cataclysm of Nature's Unknown Forces"*.

Sam Sloan
New York NY
February 9, 2009

PREFACE TO THE SECOND EDITION
REVISED

Since the publication of the first edition nearly two years ago, the stream of new documentary material on the origins of the war has continued to flow very freely. Dr. G. P. Gooch and Professor H. W. Temperley have pushed forward with energy their admirable collection of *British Documents*, so that the sixth volume carries the story of Anglo-German relations through the failure of the Haldane Mission in 1912. Austrian scholars took everyone by surprise last Christmas by presenting the world with eight closely packed volumes on *Oesterreich-Ungarns Aussenpolitik*, containing nearly 12,000 documents from their archives covering the years 1908 to 1914. This collection runs parallel to the German *Die Grosse Politik*, and is of especial value for the additional light that it throws on Balkan problems in general and on Austro-Serbian relations in particular. The French Government has published three initial volumes of *Documents Diplomatiques Français*, a monumental series which will eventually illuminate French foreign policy from 1871 to 1914 in the same detail as has been done for German policy in the same period by *Die Grosse Politik*.

In addition to these official publications there have also appeared many valuable private publications containing important new documents or based on unpublished first-hand material. Dr. Bogitchevitch's unofficial collection, *Die Auswärtige Politik Serbiens 1903-1914*, partly compensates for the Serbian Government's persistent failure to follow the example of other states in disclosing fully and frankly their secret pre-war archives. Interesting light on leading English personalities and their psychology is contained in charming biographies, like Lord Newton's *Lord Lansdowne*, Mr. Harold Nicolson's *Lord Carnock* (better known as Sir Arthur Nicolson), and in Lord Morley's remarkable *Memorandum on Resignation*. In *La Politique Russe d'avant Guerre* Baron Taube has stated in no uncertain terms what he knew of Izvolski and certain episodes in Russia's pre-war policy. The present writer has also been privileged to read the advance pages of the first volume of Professor B. E. Schmitt's scholarly and detailed forthcoming work, *The Coming of the War, 1914.*

These and many other recent publications of source material, as well as innumerable secondary monographic studies, can usefully be drawn upon to add an infinite amount of new detail to the story of the main outline of the origins of the war which I have tried to give within the compass of two volumes. But I do not find that they so essentially modify the chief thread of my narrative or my general conclusions that it is necessary in a revised edition to recast the whole form of the book. I have therefore mainly confined the revision to rewriting several passages, to calling attention in the footnotes to important new material, and to adding a few supplementary notes at the end of the first volume. This has made possible the retention of the paging of the first edition, which it is hoped will be a convenience to students. Many of these revisions have already been made in the German and French editions.

Sidney B. Fay

Harvard University,
June 28, 1930.

PREFACE

WHEN the World War suddenly set Europe aflame and American public opinion, soon under the influence of propaganda and war prejudice, began to denounce Germany and the Kaiser as being guilty of causing it, the present writer refused to join in the chorus. His historical sense told him that in this present case, as in the past, no one country or no one man was solely, or probably even mainly, to blame. A little study of the documents in the Blue, Yellow and Orange Books which were early issued by the English, French and Russian Governments quickly convinced him that these documentary publications were by no means so complete and reliable (though more so than the White and Red Books, issued by Germany and Austria) that one could safely base sound and final conclusions upon them, as seemed to be believed by the millions of men and women who read such facile and superficial arguments as those of Mr. James M. Beck, and others who followed his cue. Therefore the present writer during the War remained silent, except for his discussions of the subject in college class rooms.

When, however, the new socialist governments of Germany and Austria published in 1919 a very complete collection of documents from the secret archives relating to the diplomatic crisis of July, 1914, this seemed to provide material for reaching at last some tentative opinion about the immediate causes of the War. These the present writer ventured to express in "New Light on the Origins of the War" published in the American Historical Review in

1920-1921. This called to the attention of scholars in this country the desirability of reconsidering opinions formed during the heat of the battle as to the immediate responsibility of causing it. With the publication of more documents, especially from the Russian sources, and with the refusal of the French and British Governments to issue any such convincingly complete documentary record of their conduct in July, 1914, there soon arose a group of writers who demanded a "revision" of that clause in the Treaty of Versailles declaring that Germany and her allies were solely responsible. With some of these writers— especially with some of the anti-Poincaré revisionists in France—the pendulum of opinion has been in danger of swinging nearly as far away from the golden mean of historical truth as in the case of those who formerly followed in the propagandist path of Mr. Beck.

The present writer is no more inclined to accept the arguments of the former than of the latter. In the pages which follow he has no political motive, either to justify the Treaty of Versailles or to demand its revision but simply to carry out what a great master has defined as the proper task of the historian—to tell how it really came about. He has written, he hopes, *sine ira ac studio*. If he has made infrequent citations from the mass of controversial literature which has grown up in regard to the origin of the war, this is not because he has not read a very considerable part of it, but because he wishes to avoid controversy and reach his conclusions as far as possible from documentary evidence. The mass of documentary and autobiographical material is now so great that it affords either of two possibilities. On the one hand, a writer by centering attention on the acts of any one man or country, and by picking out passages in the documents to support his contention, can easily make a seemingly convincing argument for the uninitiated, that this or that man or country was altogether angelic or devilish in motives and methods. On the other hand, a writer may conscientiously try to look fairly at all sides of the question, explain acts from the point of view of the actors themselves instead of from that of their champions or enemies, and try to reach an unbiassed judgment. Needless to say it is the latter possibility which is attempted in the present volume. With what success, the reader must judge.

In the troublesome matter of transliterating Slavic proper names the best practice of American libraries has been followed, so far as is possible, without the use of diacritical marks. But in the case of some Russian names of German origin, like Schilling for Shilling, and in a few Serbo-Croat names, such as Princip for Printsip, popular usage has been allowed to prevail over proper practice.

Quotations from the documents and foreign works are usually made from direct translations from the original, rather than from translations into English which have been made by others. This is because the latter are sometimes abridged, or because the present writer made his translation prior to the publication of other translations, or because he prefers his own rendering to that of others. If the quotations from the documents are often tediously long, it is because he wishes to avoid as far as possible picking out phrases or sentences which might give a *suggestio falsi* or *suppressio veri*. In some cases, for the sake of brevity, prolix phrases and titles have been curtailed or omitted; "Austria," for instance, has been commonly used in place of "Austria-Hungary."

No formal bibliography is included in these volumes, because reference to all the more important recent literature of the subject has been made either in the List of Abbreviations, in the text, or in the numerous bibliographical footnotes in connection with each topic in the text; most of those which contain several titles are cited in the Index under "Bibliography."

Among the various bibliographies which include references to the less recent literature, the most helpful are the following: G. W. Prothero, *Subject Index of the Books relating to the European War, 1914-1918, acquired by the British Museum, 1914-1920* (London, 1922); A. von Wegerer, *Literatur zur Kriegsschuldfrage* (Berlin, 1923, new ed., 1926); J. L. Kunz, *Bibliographie der Kriegsliteratur* (Berlin, 1920); *Die Kriegsschuldfrage: Ein Verzeichnis der Literatur des In- und Auslandes, hrsg. vom Börsenverein der Deutschen Buchhändler* (Leipzig, 1925); A. Lumbroso, *Bibliografia ragionata della guerra delle nazioni* (Roma, 1920); H. H. B. Meyer, *Check List of the Literature and Other Material in the Library of Congress on the European War* (Washington, 1918); and the valuable *Catalogues Méthodiques* (Paris, 1921 ff.), issued by the *Bibliothèque et Musée de la Guerre*, and edited by J. Dubois, C. Appuhn, C. Bloch, and others.

For keeping abreast with current literature on the origins of the War there are two excellent periodicals largely devoted to the subject: *Die Kriegsschuldfrage*, edited by A. von Wegerer (Berlin, 1923 ff.); and *Revue d'Histoire de la Guerre Mondiale* (Paris, 1923 ff.). Articles, critical reviews, and titles of new books may be found in the various historical and political journals, such as the *American Historical Review, English Historial Review, Slavonic Review, Historische Zeitschrift, Revue Historique, Krasnyi Arkhiv, Foreign Affairs*, the New York Times *Current History, Political Science Quarterly, European Economic and Political Survey, Archiv für Politik und Geschichte, Europäische Gespräche, L'Europe Nouvelle, Evolution*, the *Bulletin of the Central Commission for Neutral Investigation of the Causes of the World War*, and many others.

To those who have kindly permitted the reproduction of

many of the illustrations the writer wishes to express his gratitude—to Mr. Hamilton Fish Armstrong for the portrait of M. Pashitch and the facsimile of the Austrian Declaration of War; to Mr. R. H. Lutz of the Hoover War Library for the Minutes of the Russian Council of Ministers; to the editors of *Current History* for the portraits of MM. Sazonov and Sukhomlinov; to the Frederick A. Stokes Company for the portraits of MM. Benckendorff, Cambon, Metternich, and Lichnowsky, which appeared in Viscount Grey's *Twenty-Five Years;* and to Herr A. von Wegerer for several of the German and Austrian portraits and for the material for the maps which appeared in *Die Kriegsschuldfrage.*

Finally, the author takes pleasure in acknowledging his indebtedness to Professor J. F. Jameson and the late Professor Coolidge, who first encouraged him to undertake this study; to Professor B. E. Schmitt, who read parts of the manuscript; and to Professors W. L. Langer and L. B. Packard, who read the proofs. But they are in no way responsible for the errors or the views expressed.

S. B. F.

July 28, 1928.
Northampton, Mass.

ABBREVIATIONS

Citations from collections in which the documents antedate July, 1914 (like "Affaires Balkaniques," "G.P.," "Siebert-Schreiner," and "Stieve") are by *volume and page*, because the documents are often long despatches extending over many pages, and a page reference is therefore more precise. But documents of July, 1914 (like those in "A.R.B.," "B.D.," etc.) are mostly short telegrams, and are cited by *serial number* of the publication in which they appear.

Affaires Balkaniques: Ministère des Affaires Étrangères, Les Affaires Balkaniques, 1912-1914, 3 vols., Paris, 1922.

A.R.B.: [Austrian Red Book of 1919] Diplomatische Aktenstücke zur Vorgeschichte des Krieges, 1914, 3 vols., Wien, 1919. (Eng. trans., 1920.)

B.B.B.: [British Blue Book] Great Britain and the European Crisis, Correspondence, and Statements in Parliament, together with an Introductory Narrative of Events. London, 1914. (Cd. 7467).

B.D.: British Documents on the Origins of the War, 1898-1914. Edited by G. P. Gooch and Harold Temperley. Vols. I-VI, XI. London, 1926-1930. (Vol. XI, Foreign Office Documents, June 28th-August 4th, 1914, cited merely as "B.D." and by serial number).

Bogitchevitch: M. Boghitschewitsch, Kriegsursachen. Zurich, 1919. (Eng. trans., 1919; 2nd ed. in French, 1925.)

Bourgeois et Pagès: E. Bourgeois et G. Pagès, Les Origines et les Responsabilités de la Grande Guerre. Paris, 1921.

Brandenburg: E. Brandenburg, Von Bismarck zum Welkriege, Berlin, 1924. (Eng. trans. of 2nd ed., 1927.)

Conrad: Feldmarschall Conrad von Hötzendorf, Aus meiner Dienstzeit. 5 vols., Wien, 1921-25.

D.D.F.: Ministère des Affaires Étrangères, Documents Diplomatiques Français, 1871-1914. Paris, 1929 ff.

Deutschland Schuldig?: Deutsches Weissbuch über die Verantwortlichkeit der Urheber des Krieges. 3rd ed., Berlin, 1919. (Eng. trans., 1924.)

Dirr: Dr. P. Dirr, Bayerische Dokumente zum Kriegsausbruch und zum Versailler Schuldspruch. Dritte erweiterte Auflage. Munich and Berlin, 1925.

Dobrorolski: S. Dobrorolski, Die Mobilmachung der russischen Armee, 1914. Berlin, 1921.

Frantz: Gunther Frantz, Russlands Eintritt in den Weltkrieg. Berlin, 1924.

F.Y.B.: [French Yellow Book] Ministère des Affaires Étrangères, La Guerre Européenne, 1914. Paris, 1914.

Gooss: Dr. Roderich Gooss, Das Wiener Kabinette und die Entstehung des Weltkrieges, Wien, 1919.

G.P.: Die Grosse Politik der Europäischen Kabinette 1871-1914, Sammlung der Akten des Deutschen Auswärtigen Amts, 40 vols. Berlin, 1922-27.

Grey: Viscount Grey of Fallodon, Twenty-five Years, 1892-1916, 2 vols. New York, 1925.

Investigating Commission: Die Deutsch Nationalversammlung: Beilagen. . . . über die Oeffentliche Verhandlungen des [ersten] Untersuchungsausschusses; Heft I, Zur Vorgeschichte des Weltkrieges; Heft II, Militärische Rüstungen und Mobilmachungen. Berlin, 1920-21 (Eng. trans. of Heft I, 1923.)

Jevtitch: B. Jevtitch, Sarajevski Atentat. Sarajevo, 1922.

K.A.: Kasnyi Arkhiv, 34 vols. Moskva, 1923-30.

K.D.: [Kautsky Documents] Die deutschen Dokumente zum Kriegsausbruch, edited by Karl Kautsky, Graf Max Montgelas and Prof. Walter Schücking, 4 vols. Berlin, 1919; new enlarged edition, 1927. (Eng. trans., 1924.)

KSF.: Die Kriegsschuldfrage: Berliner Monatshefte für internationale Aufklärung, hrsg. von der Zentralstelle für Erforschung der Kriegsursachen; ed. by Alfred von Wegerer. 8 vols. Berlin, 1923 ff.

L.N.: Un Livre Noir: Diplomatie d'avant-Guerre d'après les Documents des Archives Russes, 1910-1914, ed. R. Marchand, 2 vols. Paris, 1922-23.

Montgelas, Leitfaden: Graf Max Montgelas, Leitfaden zur Kriegsschuldfrage, Berlin and Leipzig, 1923. (Eng. trans., 1925.)

M.F.R.: [Materials for the History of Franco-Russian Relations] Materialy po Istorii Franko-Russkikh Otnoshenii za 1910-1914. Moskva, 1922.

Nicolson: Harold Nicolson, Sir Arthur Nicolson, Bart., First Lord Carnock. London, 1930.

Oe.-U.A.: Oesterreich-Ungarns Aussenpolitik von der Bosnischen Krise 1908 bis zum Kriegsausbruch 1914. Edited by L. Bittner, A. F. Pribram, H. Srbik and H. Uebersberger. 9 vols. Vienna and Leipzig, 1930.

Paléologue: M. Paléologue, La Russie des Tsars pendant la Grande Guerre, 3 vols. Paris, 1922. (Eng. trans., 1924-1925.)

Pharos: Professor Pharos [pseud.], Der Prozess gegen die Attentäter von Sarajewo. Berlin, 1918.

Poincaré: R. Poincaré, Au Service de la France, 5 vols. Paris, 1926-28. (Abridged Eng. trans., 1927 f).

Pribram: A. F. Pribram, Die politischen Geheimverträge Oesterreich-Ungarns 1879-1914. Wien, 1920. (Eng. trans., 1920.)

Renouvin: P. Renouvin, Les Origines Immédiates de la Guerre. 2nd ed. Paris, 1927. (Eng. trans., 1928.)

R.O.B.: [Russian Orange Book] Ministère des Affaires Étrangères: Recueil des Documents Diplomatiques, Négociations ayant précédé la Guerre, 10/23 Juillet-24 Juillet/6 Aout 1914. Petrograde, 1914.

Romberg: G. von Romberg, Falsifications of the Russian Orange Book. New York, 1923.

Schilling's Diary: How the War Began in 1914: Being the Diary of the Russian Foreign Office . . . of July, 1914; translated from the original Russian by Major W. Cyprian Bridge. London, 1925.

Schwertfeger: Zur Europäischen Politik: Unveröffentlichte [Belgische] Dokumente, herausgegeben unter Leitung von Bernhard Schwertfeger, 5 vols. Berlin, 1919; 2nd ed., 6 vols., 1925.

Seton-Watson: R. W. Seton-Watson, Sarajevo: A study in the Origins of the Great War. London, 1925.

Siebert-Schreiner: G. A. Schreiner, Entente Diplomacy and the World. New York, 1921. (Eng. trans., re-arranged with annotations of Diplomatische Akten-stücke zur Geschichte der Ententepolitik der Vor-kriegsjahre, hrsg. B. von Siebert. Berlin and Leipzig, 1921. New enlarged ed., 3 vols. Berlin and Leipzig, 1928.)

S.B.B.: [Serbian Blue Book] Les Pourparlers Diplo-matiques 16/29 Juin-3/16 Aout. Paris, 1914.

Stieve: F. Stieve, Der Diplomatische Schriftwechsel Is-wolskis, 1911-1914, 4 vols. Berlin, 1924.

Taube: Baron M. de Taube, La Politique Russe d'Avant-Guerre et la Fin de l'Empire des Tsars, 1904-1917. Paris, 1928. (Enlarged German edition, Berlin, 1929.)

TABLE OF CONTENTS

ILLUSTRATIONS

I

II

II
AFTER SARAJEVO
IMMEDIATE CAUSES OF THE WAR

CHAPTER I

THE ARCHDUKE FRANZ FERDINAND

ARCHDUKE FRANZ FERDINAND, who became Heir-Presumptive to the Austrian throne after the death of his father, Karl Ludwig, in 1896, has remained, both living and dead, one of the most enigmatic of political personages. Even Austrians themselves held the most contradictory views as to the supposed purposes and influence of this sphinx. By many he was regarded as the chief of the Austrian militarists, eager for a "preventive war" against Italy or Serbia. Others, however, believed that he had little active influence on Austrian policy. Still others even thought the Heir to the Throne was almost a pacifist. There was the same wide divergence of opinion as to his views on domestic politics. He was commonly believed to hate the Magyars and to favor the Serbs. He was credited with having in mind a regeneration of the Monarchy by giving to the Slavic nationalities an equal political recognition with that enjoyed by the Germans in Austria and by the Magyars in Hungary—that is, he was thought to favor a federalistic "triple" organization of the Monarchy known as "Trialism" in place of the existing "Dualism." By fanatical Serbs, however, he was blindly hated as being a powerful and determined enemy and oppressor, as a man who might well be assassinated in the interests of a Greater Serbia. In fact at the trial of the Sarajevo assassins in October, 1914, Chabrinovitch, who threw the bomb, frankly declared, "The Heir-Presumptive was a man of action—I knew that at the Ballplatz there existed a clique, the so-called war-party, which wanted to conquer Serbia. At its

1

head stood the Heir-Presumptive. I believed that I should take vengeance on them all in taking vengeance on him." And Princip, who fired the fatal shots, defiantly asserted, "I am not at all sorry that I cleared an obstacle out of our path. He was a German and an enemy of the South Slavs." [1] By Russians likewise he was regarded as an enemy, of whom the Tsar was fortunately rid by the crime of Sarajevo. "Not only in the press, but also in society, one meets almost nothing but unfriendly judgments concerning the murdered Archduke, with the suggestion that Russia has lost in him an embittered enemy," reported the German Ambassador at St. Petersburg. The German Kaiser, on the other hand, in one of those marginal notes which unrestrainedly expressed his inmost thoughts and first impressions, wrote in comment on this report, "The Archduke was Russia's best friend. He wanted to revive the League of the Three Emperors." [2]

The misconceptions and conflicting views current about the Archduke alive, were as nothing to those which circulated upon his death. It was said that he had plotted to displace his uncle; and was planning to break up the Dual Monarchy in alliance with Emperor William by seizing Poland and Venice and by creating two new states over which his sons might ultimately rule, while German Austria was to be added to the German Empire as Emperor William's reward. It was darkly hinted that his tragic death was due to the connivance of Austrian officials, who wanted to prevent these suspected designs, or at least wanted to throw the blame on Serbia and so have a pretext for the annihilation of this neighboring kingdom. Other rumors alleged that his assassination was due to the fact that, as a

[1] Pharos, *Der Prozess gegen die Attentäter von Sarajevo* (Berlin, 1918), pp. 11, 13, 30. The idea that Franz Ferdinand headed the militarist clique and was an enemy of the Serbs was, as will be seen below, wholly incorrect.

[2] Pourtalès to Bethmann, July 13, 1914; K.D., 53.

ARCHDUKE FRANZ FERDINAND

Roman Catholic, he was planning to attack Italy and restore the Temporal Power of the Pope. One widely-read German author devotes half a chapter to showing that the Scottish-Rite Masons had decreed his death and worked for that purpose through the Masonic Lodge at Belgrade.[3] Amid this mass of conflicting gossip and rumor, where lies the truth about this mysterious man whose death served as the spark which lit the conflagration in Europe? [4]

Franz Ferdinand of Austria-Este, born on December 18, 1863, was the eldest son of Karl Ludwig, brother of Emperor Francis Joseph. His consumptive mother, a daughter of the late Bourbon King of the Two Sicilies, Ferdinand II, died while he was a child, but he was affectionately cared

[3] Reventlow, *Politische Vorgeschichte des grossen Krieges,* Berlin, 1919, pp. 28-38. See below, p. 111, note 103.

[4] There is no satisfactory complete biography of Franz Ferdinand. Of the older biographies written during his lifetime, Paul von Falkenegg, *Erzherzog Franz Ferdinand von Oesterreich-Este* (Vienna, 1908), and H. Heller, *Franz Ferdinand* (Vienna, 1911), deserve mention. In celebration of his fiftieth birthday on December 18, 1913, the *Oesterreichische Rundschau* published a special illustrated edition containing interesting, though superficial, articles by Chlumecky, Sosnosky, Admiral Mirtl, Professor Mycielski and others on Franz Ferdinand as soldier, sailor, traveler, hunter and collector, etc. *Franz Ferdinands Lebensroman* (Stuttgart, 1919), purports to be based on the diary of one of the Archduke's instructors and intimate friends; the anonymous author has a romantic touch, but appears to give much reliable and solid fact. Conrad von Hôtzendorf, *Aus Meiner Dienstzeit,* (5 vols., Vienna, 1921-1925), throws much light on the Archduke from the pen of one of those who knew him best. Freiherr von Margutti, personal adjutant to Francis Joseph, was in a position to know intimately the relations between the old Emperor and his imperial nephew; in his interesting reminiscences, *Vom Alten Kaiser* (Vienna, 1921), the chapter on the Archduke reflects unfriendly Vienna gossip. It needs to be corrected by the loyal devotion and intimate personal account of the Archduke's private secretary for a dozen years, Paul Nikitsch-Boulles, *Vor dem Sturm: Erinnerungen an Erzherzog Thronfolger Franz Ferdinand* (Berlin, 1925); and by the affectionate appreciation of his military adjutant, Karl Freiherr von Bardolff, "Franz Ferdinand," in KSF, V, 599-608, July, 1927. See also the fair-minded and friendly accounts by Count Czernin, *In the World War* (New York, 1919), ch. ii; and the more complete life by Horstenau, in the *Neue Oesterreichische Biographie;* the references in G.P., XL, 45; and the less favorable accounts by R. W. Seton-Watson, *Sarajevo* (London, 1926), ch. iv; and by Eugene Bagger, *Francis Joseph* (New York, 1927). p. 524 ff

for by a Portuguese stepmother. In his youth he had not been seriously thought of as a possible successor to the throne, until the tragic death of Crown Prince Rudolph at Meyerling in 1889 left Francis Joseph without a direct male heir. Franz Ferdinand had not therefore at first been given any special training in politics, but, like Austrian Archdukes generally, had been placed in the army for a military career. His health had never been robust, owing perhaps to tubercular tendencies inherited from his mother. This tendency at times became so threatening that he often had to spend months at Brioni or Miramar on the warm shores of the Adriatic, where he came to have an intense interest in the creation of an Austrian navy; at other times he sought better health in the dry air of Switzerland at Davos, or in a ten months' trip around the world in 1892-1893. In the fatal spring of 1914 there were those who prophesied that the old Emperor at eighty-four would actually outlive his nephew who had just passed fifty.

Franz Ferdinand's lung trouble appears to have influenced somewhat his life and character. It had not sweetened his temper; it had made him feel that fate had been unfair to him, and had developed in him a tendency to shun society life. The undisguised haste with which many people, especially those connected with the Court, deserted him when he was seriously ill and seemed unlikely ever to come to the throne, hardened the Archduke's character, which was not naturally gentle, increased his distrust of the men who surrounded him, and heightened his contempt for mankind in general. His ill health may also have contributed somewhat to his intense zeal for the Catholic Church, especially after his marriage to a strict Catholic; and it strengthened his iron determination to overcome obstacles and fit himself for the task of ruling the Hapsburg dominions. He learned the languages of the nations over which he seemed likely some day to rule. He also took instruction from men of science in special branches of knowledge; his later collections in natural science and in art formed a notable museum. To the organization and improvement of the army, and later to the creation of a navy, he began to devote himself with persistent energy and more than average ability.

Since the Archduke had a family to provide for, he spent a considerable part of each year on his estate at Konopischt, where he established a model farm, which, like Wallenstein, he managed very profitably. This determination to live may actually have contributed toward the more vigorous health which he enjoyed in his last years. But he never outgrew his tendency toward aloofness from society and from the public. He had, in fact, very few intimate friends. He did not try to make them. Quite characteristic of his aloofness is a remark which he once made to Conrad von Hotzendorf; they had been discussing the proper basis for the promotion of officers in the army, and the Chief-of-Staff had said that it was his own tendency to think well of a man until he knew something against him, and that he had therefore been sometimes too quick in advancing new officers. The Archduke replied, "We hold opposite views. You think every man is an angel at the outset, and have unfortunate experiences afterwards. I regard every one whom I meet for the first time as a cheap fellow (*gemeiner Kerl*) and wait until he does something to justify a better opinion in my eyes." [5] This was hardly an attitude of mind to make friends, and partly accounts for the hostile and malicious tittle-tattle which circulated so freely about him and his wife at Vienna, and which has found its way into many accounts of him in the Entente countries. But the few friends whom he did admit to his intimacy, who saw him sitting on the floor playing with his children, like his secretaries or like Emperor William, were affectionately devoted to him.

[5] Conrad, I, 338.

FRANZ FERDINAND AND THE ARMY

Franz Ferdinand's chief interests in life, aside from his hobbies as a hunter and collector and gentleman farmer, were the army, the navy and his wife and children.

In 1906, with the appointment of Major Brosch as his personal adjutant, the Archduke began to exercise a more direct influence on the army. Brosch was an extremely intelligent and able officer, anxious to increase his own influence and also that of the Archduke in military matters. After long opposition he was able to bring it about that the Archduke was given a military chancery (*Militärkanzlei*) of his own, similar to that of the Emperor. Henceforth all the important military documents, as well as the reports of the military attachés, were made out in duplicate so that Franz Ferdinand received a copy at the same moment that the Emperor received his, and the nephew was kept as fully informed as his uncle. In fact he soon came to take a more active part in military reforms and reorganization than the Emperor himself. His activity is indicated by the fact that his military chancery quickly grew from a personnel of two to one of fourteen persons—only two less than the Emperor's own chancery.[6]

Franz Ferdinand regarded the Austro-Hungarian army as a potentially important unifying political instrument for counteracting the disintegrating elements in the Dual Monarchy, as well as for defending it in case of foreign war. He wanted one language of command—German—to be the tongue of at least all the officers, though those who commanded non-German regiments should also be masters of the tongue spoken by the rank and file under their command. It was one of his main aims in life to strengthen and increase the army. It was this aim that lay at the bottom of his hatred of the Magyar politicians who refused

[6] Nikitsch-Boulles, p. 60 f.

to vote the military credits asked for, and who insisted that
Magyar should be the language of command in the Hungarian half of the army.[7] How strongly Franz Ferdinand
felt this need for an increase in the army is seen in the
characteristic letter to Conrad, complaining of the Magyar
refusal to vote taxes for an increase in the number of Hungarian recruits: "You can imagine, dear Conrad, what I
have had to go through in the way of rage and desperation,
especially on account of the attitude of the Minister of
War [Schönaich] and the two [Austrian and Hungarian]
Governments! On the one hand they proclaim to all the
world that there is a surplus of 200 million kroner, give the
civilian officials 20 million here and the railroad employees
the same there, and yet do not even grant the paltry nine
million for the poor army officers. And all this because of
a few traitorous Hungarian political wind-bags. This
means that this is only a pretext; the fundamental reason
is that the Monarchy has fallen into the hands of Jews, Free
Masons, Socialists and Hungarians, and is ruled by them;
and all these elements make the army and its officers discontented and injure it so that at the moment when I need
the army, I can no longer count upon it. . . . Do you know
what I would do if I were Emperor? I would summon
Weckerle, Beck, Sieghart and Schönaich and say to them:
'I'll send you all to the devil if I don't get the increased
number of the recruits and the officers' pay for my army
within a week,' and I wager that I should have it all within
24 hours!" [8]

The most important step in Franz Ferdinand's energetic
efforts for improvement of the army was his insistence in
1906 upon the appointment of a new Chief-of-Staff. Beck,
the officer who held this position at the time, was generally

---

[7] *Cf.* his Memorial to the Emperor, Jan. 5, 1909, summarized by
Conrad, I, 134; and Conrad's own similar views, pp. 135-138, and 327-334.
[8] Conrad, I, 565.

recognized by experts as totally unfit for the place. He was a shrivelled-up old man belonging to the same generation as the aged Emperor. His days of usefulness were long outlived, and yet the kindly heart of Francis Joseph had hated to dismiss him. "One might see him any day going for a walk in Vienna, looking like a good-natured little monkey, a living picture of military inefficiency." [9] Beck was, however, an honest and upright officer and a thoroughly likable, easy-going personality, and enjoyed a certain popularity. He and the corps of officers whom he had carefully selected represented the chivalry, the dignity, and the *esprit de corps* of the best old Vienna society. They were regarded by Francis Joseph as one of the main supports of his ancestral throne. "Efficiency" had not been born to disturb their quiet routine; their ideal was "the development of Austria's defensive force gradually along the line of natural evolution." Owing to the terms of mutual confidence and intimacy on which he stood with the Emperor, Beck had been allowed to continue at the head of the Austrian Staff for twenty-four years. In spite of his excessive age—one might even say senility—Beck was still a painstaking official. At his home in Baden he had been trained in German "thoroughness." With his cautious, conservative, do-nothing policy, he had to a certain extent been an influence in favor of European peace. So no one had had the courage to insist on the retirement of the genial old chief, until Franz Ferdinand urged a new appointment. The Emperor finally gave way, and in November, 1906, a new Chief-of-Staff took up his quarters at the war office in Vienna—Conrad von Hötzendorf.

Conrad's appointment to the highest position in the Austrian army coincided with a change at the Foreign

---

[9] Kanner, *Kaiserliche Katastrophen-Politik,* p. 153. For a kindly but just estimate of Beck's qualities and deficiencies see Margutti, *Vom Alten Kaiser,* pp. 282-291.

Office. The timid Pole, Count Goluchowski, was replaced by the ambitious aristocrat, Baron Aehrenthal. A new era in Austrian policy was soon manifested. It was the beginning of a more aggressive and reckless activity in foreign affairs. Men came into control who felt that Austria was gradually disintegrating, and that desperate eleventh-hour efforts must be made to infuse fresh life and vigor into the body politic, and to check the tendencies to dissolution arising from the hot ambitions of the subject nationalities. Austria, it was said, was decaying like Turkey. Not the Ottoman, but the Hapsburg, ruler was now the "sick man of Europe." Conrad and Aehrenthal were the doctors who should try strong remedies to keep their patient from collapse. Unfortunately for the sick man, the doctors differed radically in their views and remedies, and they loved each other about as little as bedside specialists often do.

Conrad's appointment as Chief-of-Staff, urged by the Heir to the Throne and acquiesced in by the Emperor, never, however, really commended itself to Francis Joseph. The aged Monarch, who had taken the greatest pride in the old army at whose head he had fought so many years, now found himself importuned by Conrad to make sweeping changes and reforms. With impulsive self-confidence Conrad urged that the army maneuvers be speeded up to approximate war conditions as closely as possible, and that an early opportunity be seized for "preventive wars" against Italy and Serbia. At Christmas, 1906, scarcely a month after Conrad's appointment, the old Emperor remarked ruefully: "Conrad is a restless organizer! He is lacking in experience; one sees this from everything he puts his hand to! And moreover his hand does not look to me like a lucky one!" [10]

The Emperor's distrust of the new régime tended, as years went on, to estrange him from the army with which

[10] Margutti, p. 293.

he had grown up. It was one of the things which added
loneliness and sadness to the last years of the loneliest and
saddest of the Hapsburgs. Conrad's policy of conducting
the great annual maneuvers, "under conditions like actual
war" without carefully prepared plans, with the aim of developing initiative and self-reliance among his officers,
often had the most distressing results. All emphasis was
placed on a hasty offensive; the soldiers were totally exhausted by the forced marches; they often arrived at the
objective completely worn out and in greatest confusion,
too tired and hungry to have ears and eyes for anything,
even for their King and Emperor. As he rode about the
field, Francis Joseph would see hundreds of soldiers lying
dead-tired in the ditches along the road, and cavalry and
guns were strewn over fields where the horses had fallen
from exhaustion. This was the Conrad régime, very different from the decorous and dignified ways of old Beck, when
the Emperor had been greeted by the well-formed lines
of troops standing at a respectful salute as he rode down
the front. The old Emperor was terribly distressed by what
he saw. Though very slow to find fault and criticize, he
did give expression to his feelings on a visit to the German
Emperor in 1909. A German regiment had just passed in
review in perfect order and discipline. Francis Joseph
turned to one of his own officers and said sharply: "Why is
this kind of thing totally impossible with us?" The officer
shrugged his shoulders, whereupon the Emperor continued
more bitterly, "Well, owing to the misguided practices which
have now become the fashion with us, any such parade is
beyond even my dreams." [11]

Conrad had in fact alienated the Emperor and his army
from one another. After 1909 Francis Joseph ceased to
take pleasure in the maneuvers which had been one of the
delights of his life. He allowed himself to be represented

[11] Margutti, p. 298.

at them instead by his nephew. It was as his representative that Franz Ferdinand went to Sarajevo in 1914 to attend the maneuvers of a couple of army corps.[12]

The fact that it was Franz Ferdinand who selected Conrad, secured his appointment, and remained intimately associated with him, was one of the reasons for the lack of cordiality between the Emperor and the Heir to the Throne. It was also one of the reasons that it was commonly believed, especially among Austria's enemies, that Franz Ferdinand held the same militaristic views which Conrad so freely proclaimed in memorials, interviews and coffeehouses. It is true that the Heir remained Conrad's staunchest supporter, except for occasional bursts of irritation, in spite of all the criticism and jealous opposition directed against the new Chief-of-Staff. When Conrad was forced to resign in November, 1911, because of his conflicts with Aehrenthal and Schönaich on foreign and military matters, it was Franz Ferdinand who secured his re-appointment the following year.[13]

---

[12] For many evidences and anecdotes of the Emperor's distrust of Conrad's system and his consequent distress of mind and gloomy forebodings, both before and during the war, see Margutti, *Vom Alten Kaiser,* pp. 291-306, 391-452. Alfred Krauss, *Die Ursachen unserer Niederlage* (Munich, 1912), *passim,* is a severe but not unjust estimate of Conrad by a high military expert in the Austrian General Staff. Kanner's sharp portrait of Conrad, (*Kaiserliche Katastrophen-Politik,* pp. 151-173) loses nothing in vigor because of the fact that Conrad's agents tried to suppress Kanner's Vienna newspaper, *Die Zeit.* Conrad's best defense, though not convincing, are his own five bulky volumes *Aus meiner Dienstzeit,* which contain invaluable documents of every sort. Nowak, who is one of his admirers and claims to have had access to his papers, writes panegyrics of him: *Der Weg zur Kastastrophe* (Vienna, 1920) and *Hötzendorf's Lager* (Vienna, 1921). See also friendly biographies by Ludwig Pastor, *Conrad* (Vienna, 1916); François, *Conrad, Baron de Hötzendorf* (Berne, 1916); and *Unser Conrad, Von einem Oesterreicher* (Vienna, 1915). *Cf.* also General Auffenberg-Komarów, *Aus Oesterreichs Höhe und Niedergang,* Munich, 1921, *passim.*

[13] G.P., XXX, 525 ff.; Margutti, p. 302; Kanner, 157 ff.; Conrad, II, 218 ff., 373 ff.; Pribram, "Der Konflikt Conrad-Aehrenthal," in *Oest. Rundschau,* August, 1920.

Lacking authentic information, the public naturally tended to identify protector and protégé. But it is incorrect to regard Franz Ferdinand as one of the Austrian militarists, holding the same views as to strenuous maneuvers, preventive wars, and aggressive foreign policy as the Chief-of-Staff. The Archduke certainly disapproved the extreme strenuousness of Conrad's exhausting army maneuvers. He used his influence to moderate them after the distressing experiences at the Meseritz maneuvers in 1909, where he had exclaimed: "It is not necessary to teach death to the troops; least of all is that what the maneuvers are for!" [14] When the Annexation Crisis reached its height, and Austria and Serbia were preparing for war, the more cautious Heir to the Throne opposed the Austrian militarists who favored immediate war with Serbia, which involved the possibility of war with Russia. He approved the peaceful settlement of the crisis.[15] Later on, during the First Balkan War, when the Pan-Slav and militarist elements in Russia appeared very threatening to Austria, Conrad, as always, urged a final reckoning with Serbia, even at the risk of war with Russia; but Franz Ferdinand was absolutely opposed to it and insisted on the reduction of the Austrian forces in the interest of peace. "Under no circumstances did he want war with Russia, nor would he consent to it. He will not take from Serbia a single plum-tree, not a sheep. He will not hear of it." [16] He told the German Military Attaché that a war against Russia would be "absolutely nonsense," because there was no reason for it and no gain worth the price; that he was also opposed to a conflict with Serbia; and that in his opinion the internal

---

[14] Margutti, p. 303; cf. also Conrad, II, 323-328.

[15] Conrad, I, 146, 153, 155; Nikitsch-Boulles, p. 118 ff.

[16] Statement of Col. Bardolff, the Archduke's confidential secretary, to Conrad, Feb. 22, 1913; Conrad, III, 127; and Berchtold to Conrad, Feb. 22, 1913; "I cannot lend my name to a war with Russia; the Archduke Franz Ferdinand is absolutely opposed to a war;" *ibid.*, p. 129.

problems of Austria-Hungary were more pressing than the external ones.[17]

In conversation with Conrad, "the Archduke emphasized that their guiding star must be coöperation between Germany, Russia and Austria-Hungary, primarily out of regard for monarchical interests, and added, 'Possibly it may come to some action against Serbia, merely to chastise her, but under no conditions must a square kilometer be annexed! . . . War with Russia must be avoided, because France is stirring it up, especially the French Freemasons and anti-monarchists, who want to bring about a revolution by which monarchs will be cast down from their thrones.' He called attention to a letter of the German Emperor which represented the same views; hence his determination: 'No war!' "[18]   One sees that both the Archduke and the German Emperor were altogether opposed to war with Russia and inclined toward the old policy of the League of the Three Emperors for protection against France and the safeguarding of monarchical interests.

A month later Franz Ferdinand sent Col. Bardolff to warn Conrad to stop trying to influence Berchtold in favor of war.   Conrad's reply shows how incorrect is the common notion that the German Kaiser was always backing Austrian aggression in the Balkans: "I wish the Archduke would not let himself be so much influenced by the German Emperor; he held us back in 1909, and now he is staying our hand again.   This is the result of our wholly unsuccessful Turkish policy.   I have the conviction that the Germans are indifferent to our interests, but we have to think of them.   Germany calmly uses us, while she sees that she is better secured against France, which is her chief fear, but

[17] Reports of Count Kageneck, Dec. 17, 1912, and Feb. 26, 1913; Brandenburg, p. 372; cf., G.P., XXXIII, 473 ff., XXXIV, 229, 250 f., 309 ff., 318 ff., 323, 415 ff., 426 f.

[18] Conversation of Feb. 27, 1913; Conrad, III, 155 f. Cf. also pp. 236, 324, 329.

will eventually sacrifice us." [19]   In consequence, Conrad
even thought of resigning his position as Chief-of-Staff,
rather than be responsible for letting slip another opportunity to settle with Serbia.

In the fall of 1913, when Serbia and Montenegro were
defying the Powers by refusing to respect the Albanian
frontier established by the London Conference, Conrad
again urged military action on the part of Austria for the
defense of Albania.   Berchtold hesitated.   Conrad then
talked with Forgach.   "Count Forgach agreed that a strong
intervention would be the best thing, but he had lost hope
that it could be brought about.   The Emperor and the Heir
to the Throne were opposed to it, and Berchtold would not
force them to it." [20]

Toward Italy Franz Ferdinand always had a strong an-
tipathy and deep distrust, based partly on political hatred
for the country which had seized his family lands in Modena
and Este, partly from bigoted religious dislike for the state
which had dispossessed the Pope and seemed to be ruled by
Freemasons and anti-clericals, and partly on a shrewd
suspicion of the duplicity of Italian diplomacy.   Nevertheless, he refused to support Conrad in his repeated efforts to
let loose a preventive war against Italy in 1907 and again in
1911, when Italy was involved in war with Turkey.

The idea that Franz Ferdinand is to be wholly identified
with the reckless fire-eating militarists of Austria is unsound.   It is a legend which grew up later after the War
began.   He was one of those who thoroughly believed in
the maxim, *Si vis pacem, para bellum.*   But he was not the
kind of a man to be swept away, as so many worshipers of
this maxim are, by the desire to engage in war and put into

[19] *Ibid.,* 169.
[20] October 6, 1913; *ibid.,* p. 462.   A few days later Czernin also told
Conrad: "Here in Austria we have to reckon with the Emperor and the
Heir to the Throne, who are not in favor of war, least of all the Heir;
he clings blindly to peace;" *ibid.,* 464.   See also p. 597.

actual use the military machine which has been created to preserve the peace. Baron Szilassy, a liberal-minded Hungarian magnate, who went as Austrian Minister to Athens in December, 1913, writes: "Two days before my departure, Archduke Franz Ferdinand invited me to visit him and discussed with me the whole international situation. He appeared to be even as pacifistic as his imperial uncle, and desired an entente with Russia. He regarded the realization of South Slav aspirations within the framework of the Monarchy as altogether possible later, and criticized severely Tisza's policy, which was making better relations with Serbia and Rumania impossible." [21] If he had been alive in July, 1914, it is quite possible that Franz Ferdinand would have used his influence and authority to check Conrad and Berchtold in the mad policy which led to the World War.

FRANZ FERDINAND AND THE NAVY

There was another subject on which Franz Ferdinand and Conrad did not see eye to eye. This was the Austrian navy. At the close of the nineteenth century the Austrian navy was almost negligible. It was Franz Ferdinand who, by his great energy and interest, virtually created the new navy, hoping it would be a counterweight to that of Italy in the Adriatic and Mediterranean. Before his day the view had prevailed that Austrian interests were purely continental; that any conflict with a foreign power would ultimately be decided by land armies; that the army therefore was the branch on which money should be spent, not the navy; a navy was merely a luxury. The Dual Monarchy, it had been thought, did not possess sufficient resources to maintain a proper army and at the same time to create a navy which could ever face that of Italy, to say nothing of opposing the great naval forces of France and England in

[21] Baron J. von Szilassy, *Der Untergang der Donau-Monarchie* (Berlin, 1921), p. 259. *Cf.* Czernin, *In the World War*, p. 43.

the Mediterranean. Conrad adhered to this older way of thinking. With his endemic suspicion of Italy, he naturally would have been glad to see the Austrian navy developed, but only if this could be done without detriment to the interests of the army. When, therefore, the legislatures drew the purse strings tight, and one was faced with the alternative of choosing between the absolutely necessary demands of the army, as he saw them, and the laudable desire of creating a navy, he used all his influence in favor of the former. With equal jealousy he opposed recruiting for the navy at the expense of the army.[22]

Emperor Francis Joseph had still less understanding for, or interest in, the navy. In his last years he did, to be sure, visit the ship-yards and witness naval evolutions, but he did it in a perfunctory way, merely to do his duty as a sovereign. He would stand on the bridge by the hour, almost never taking the marine glasses from his eyes. He gave an appearance of following the evolutions with intelligent interest. But it was remarked by those close to him that he never asked an intelligent question on naval matters, never showed any enthusiasm for the fleet, and never wore the naval uniform; in fact, he never even possessed one, though he had a large and very expensive wardrobe of military uniforms. The mighty battleship of the twentieth century, with its complicated mechanism of steel, steam and electricity, was a thing strange and new to him. He and Bismarck belonged to the older generation who felt at home in a general's uniform and knew what armies were good for. Emperor William and Franz Ferdinand were of the new age, who believed that "the future lies on the water." Interest in naval matters was in fact one of the common bonds which tended to draw the German Emperor and the Austrian Heir together.[23] In spite of this opposition, or lack of enthusiasm, from Conrad and the Em-

[22] Conrad, I, 357-360.   [23] Margutti, 125 f.; 306-311.

peror, Franz Ferdinand had succeeded by 1914 in raising the Austrian navy to a respectable size; though scarcely half as strong as that of Italy, it gave a good account of itself during the War and showed that the spirit of Admiral Tegetthoff was not dead.

FRANZ FERDINAND'S POLITICAL VIEWS

In his views on foreign affairs Franz Ferdinand was at one with his uncle in regarding the Dual Alliance with Germany as the corner stone of Austrian policy. This conviction was strengthened by his strong personal regard for William II, whose great tact in the matter of the Archduke's wife had won his heart. With Rumania Franz Ferdinand sought to strengthen the ties of loyalty and alliance. He and his wife were charmed with the visit they paid to King Carol and Carmen Sylva in July, 1909. They adored the simplicity of life of the Rumanian royal family at their summer castle at Sinaia, which was so different from the stiff ceremonial and stifling court atmosphere at Vienna. His heart was touched at the genuineness and friendliness with which the Queen of Rumania entertained his Countess, took her to ride, and served her tea at a rustic farm house. He long remembered it as one of the happiest visits of his life.[24]

Italy, however, the Archduke regarded with deep distrust, but not to the point of thinking it wise to unmask her suspected disloyalty to the Triple Alliance by a preventive war. On the contrary, he wanted to remain at peace with Italy and maintain as firm relations as possible with her. As heir of Francis V, Duke of Modena, he had inherited in 1875 the fortune of the Este family, but he had no notion of attempting to restore the ducal power which had been overthrown in 1859. In fact, in order to avoid giving offense to the ruling house of Savoy in Italy, he never

[24] *Cf.* Nikitsch-Boulles, p. 129 ff.

wore the insignia of the Este Black Eagle Order, the grand-mastership of which he had inherited as Francis V's heir.

With Russia Franz Ferdinand wanted to be on terms of friendly understanding. Autocratic himself by nature, he had admired the autocratic government of Russia before the Russo-Japanese War and the Russian Revolution of 1905 had begun to shake the Tsar's throne. But later he was disillusioned as to Nicholas II's stability. This may have been one of the reasons he sought more close personal relations with Emperor William and King Carol. The French he frankly disliked. He never forgot the humiliation imposed upon Austria by Napoleon I, and he regarded Napoleon III as responsible for Austria's downfall in the nineteenth century. Great Britain, on the other hand, he held in respect, and there had even been rumors at one time that he might marry Princess Mary.

Such are the views on foreign affairs ascribed to Franz Ferdinand by men who knew him well. There is no reason to doubt their substantial accuracy.[25]

Of Franz Ferdinand's views on the internal nationality problems of the Hapsburg Empire it is less possible to speak with certainty. It was the conviction of those who stood close to him, like Major Brosch,[26] and his private-secretary, Nikitsch-Boulles,[27] that if the Archduke had come to the Throne, he would have come to the rescue of the oppressed nationalities and attempted a federal organization of the Monarchy, substituting "Trialism" for the existing "Dualism." This was also the commonly expressed opinion in the Austrian and German obituary notices of the Archduke.[28] There are also several signs which point in this direction:

---

[25] Margutti, pp. 126-138; Conrad, I-IV, *passim;* Czernin, *In the World War,* ch. ii.

[26] Cf. Seton-Watson, *Sarajevo,* p. 83 ff.

[27] *Vor dem Sturm,* p. 58, 62 ff.

[28] The *Vossische Zeitung* was an exception; cf. *Belgian Documents,* IV, 97 ff.

the Archduke's energetic reforming temperament, his relations with Emperor Francis Joseph, the study he gave to the subject, and various draft projects which have come to light.

Though in many respects conservative, as one might expect from his Roman Catholic traditions, there is no doubt that Franz Ferdinand possessed qualities of character which indicate that he was quite the kind of man to undertake a reorganization of the Monarchy. He had no sympathy with preserving an institution simply because it had long existed. On the contrary, he looked to the future rather than to the past, and was inclined to reform in accordance with modern conditions rather than to conserve that which was old. Possessed of restless energy and an iron will, he had no patience with the traditional ceremonial of the Vienna Court or the antiquated methods of the old Austrian administrative machine which was managed in large part by old men who belonged to Francis Joseph's generation rather than to the twentieth century. His influence in substituting Conrad for the aged Beck as Austria's Chief-of-Staff, and in building up the army and navy, was typical of his reforming tendencies. Wherever he had authority, he showed his executive ability in modernizing and improving the arrangements which he found in existence. This is seen notably in his transformation of the Konopischt estate, which he built up into a flourishing landed property with rose gardens famous throughout Europe. He believed in dispatching business rapidly, making large use of the telephone and the telegraph. He was impatient with his secretaries if any business was left unfinished on his desk for more than twenty-four hours. In all this he was the exact opposite of his aged uncle.

Francis Joseph was a Monarch by the Grace of God in the old sense. He still ruled or wanted to rule in patriarchal fashion. One of his greatest faults was his insistence on dealing himself with all matters of minutest detail. His mind was so occupied with these minor matters that he had no breadth of view for the wider interests of the Monarchy. As was natural in his old age, he was inclined to live in the past rather than to look to the future. He was extremely conservative and hesitated to make any changes in the red tape of the old Hapsburg machine, even when it was pointed out to him what advantages could be secured by modern methods.

The contrast in attitude between the uncle and nephew is seen in an incident of 1911 concerning the administration of some Hapsburg family property left by the Empress Maria Theresa. This was still being administered under provisions a century and a half old, which were no longer adapted to modern conditions. The Archduke looked into the question carefully and ventured to hand the Emperor a long memorandum in which he pointed out how the administration of this family property needed reorganization. There were too many officials handling the property and they were often incapable and sometimes dishonest. He showed in detail how the Göding beet-root sugar factory was losing 200,000 crowns a year as a result of a foolish contract. Another estate was being rented for 47 crowns an acre when it might easily bring 70 to 80 crowns an acre, thus causing another loss of about 100,000 crowns a year. "A great part of the domains of the family are mostly leased for a long term of years for a rent which may have been suitable 40 or 50 years ago, but which today is simply ludicrous," he wrote. He therefore begged the Monarch to examine the question with a view to economic reforms corresponding to the twentieth century. The Emperor left the letter unanswered for weeks. After his attention had been called to it several times, he finally replied in characteristic fashion: "I have fully considered the question in its various aspects and come to the conclusion that as the responsible guardian of this family property, I cannot bring myself to permit an experiment which would so destroy a long tried administrative system which has worked without criticism for so many years for the advantage of our property." [29] This is a good example of Emperor Francis Joseph's opposition to innovation, and of his nephew's readiness for energetic administrative and political reforms.

Franz Ferdinand was very keenly aware, much more so than the Emperor, of the violent discontent among the subject nationalities of the Empire. He had one characteristic which is of great value in a ruler—he was ready and anxious to know the facts, even if they were unpalatable. Though he had a very violent temper, it was far more likely to be vented upon any one whom he suspected of trying to deceive him, than on one who told him disagreeable truths. He took pains to read opposition newspapers, with the result that he was well informed of the public feeling on the part of the Czechs, Transylvanians, Croats, and Serbs within the Dual Monarchy, and realized the danger which they constituted for the future unless something was done to satisfy them. His strong disapproval of the oppressive policy of the ruling Magyar magnates in Hungary was notorious, and will be indicated a few pages further on in connection with the Konopischt interview. He was criticized by the Magyar and German dominant factions for wishing to favor the small nationalities. It was a reproach which did honor to his wisdom and sense of justice. Here again he differed from the aged Emperor. Francis Joseph was inclined to half-measures and compromise. He regarded himself as the author of the Austro-Hungarian Compromise of 1867 and had no thought of modifying it. Franz Ferdinand, however, seems to have regarded this dual organization of the Empire as an unfortunate mistake, because it gave in practice so much power into the hands of

29 Letters of Franz Ferdinand and Francis Joseph, quoted in Nikitsch-Boulles, pp. 49-57.

the Magyar magnates. He therefore seems to have been quite ready to see the "Dualism" of 1867 replaced by some kind of "Trialism" when he himself should come to the throne. He had given much study to the question of a possible constitutional reorganization along federal lines. He had pondered the proposals of noted Austrian writers like Lammasch, Tezner and Steinacker. He had heard with great interest expositions of the American federal system by Professor J. W. Burgess of Columbia University; Professor Burgess had been invited to return to Vienna to give further information on the subject and was on the point of again sailing for Europe to do so at the moment the Archduke was assassinated.

A further indication of Franz Ferdinand's intention of making constitutional reforms in the direction of curbing the power of the Hungarian magnates and extending political rights to the minor nationalities is seen in various draft proposals which have been published from his papers.[30] One of the most recent of these is the draft Manifesto which he had prepared for publication in case the old Emperor's periodical bronchial trouble should sometime suddenly cause his death and open the way for a new régime. Though expressed in somewhat vague and general terms, it indicates that the Heir to the Throne was a true friend to the Croats and Bosnian Serbs and that he intended important constitutional reforms in the interests of all the minor nationalities before taking the oath to the Hungarian Constitution. The Manifesto runs in part as follows:

> Since it has pleased Almighty God to call out of this life after a long and richly blessed reign, My exalted Uncle, . . .
>
> We hereby solemnly announce to all people of the Monarchy Our accession to the Crown. . . .
>
> To all peoples of the Monarchy, to all ranks, and to

[30] *Cf.* Seton Watson, *Sarajevo*, p. 84, note 1.

everybody that does his duty in the work of the nation, no matter what his race or creed, We return equal love. In high station, or low, poor or rich, all shall be equal before Our Throne.

The established constitutional arrangements and the judicial system of the state, in which every citizen has equal rights according to the laws, We will honor and protect with a strong hand. For the well-being and prosperity of all peoples in all parts of the Monarchy, We deem it Our first duty to bring about a concentration into a great unit and a harmonious coöperation according to just principles. . . . In the Constitution of the Empire all contradictions must be removed which exist in the laws of Austria and those of Hungary in regard to the common affairs of the Monarchy, and which make the giving of the prescribed oath on the Constitution impossible through the incompatibility of these laws. As pledge of Our most sacred duties as ruler, We shall thereupon confirm by solemn oath of coronation the unambiguous provisions of the Constitution together with the fundamental rights and privileges of all those who belong to the Monarchy. In order to create the possibility for this, Our Governments will inaugurate without delay the necessary measures. . . .

Since all peoples under Our scepter shall have equal rights in regard to participation in the common affairs of the Monarchy, this equality of rights demands that to every race be guaranteed its national development within the frame of the common interests of the Monarchy, and that to all races, ranks, and classes the preservation of their just interests be made possible through just laws of suffrage —wherever this has not yet been carried through.[31]

It is doubtful, however, whether Franz Ferdinand had come to any definite decision in his own mind as to the exact form which the reorganization should take. Count

[31] Published by J. A. Freiherr von Eichhoff in the *Berliner Tageblatt* No. 152 of Mar. 31, 1926, and reprinted in translation in the New York *Nation*, May 26, 1926.

Czernin, who was more intimately acquainted with Franz
Ferdinand's ideas than most men, says: "The Archduke
was a firm partisan of the Great-Austria program. His idea
was to convert the Monarchy into numerous more or less
independent National States, having in Vienna a common
central organization for all important and absolutely necessary affairs—in other words, to substitute Federalism for
Dualism. . . . However, it had many opponents who
strongly advised against dissecting the State in order to
erect in its place something new and 'presumably better,'
and the Emperor Francis Joseph was far too conservative
and far too old to agree to his nephew's plans. This direct
refusal of the idea cherished by the Archduke offended him
greatly, and he complained often in bitter terms that the
Emperor turned a deaf ear to him as though he were the
'lowest serving man at Schönbrunn.' . . . There was a
widely spread but entirely erroneous idea in the Monarchy
that the Archduke had drawn up a program of his future
activities. This was not the case. He had very definite
and pronounced ideas for the reorganization of the Monarchy, but the ideas were never developed into a concrete
plan—they were more like the outline of a program that was
never completed in detail." [32]

Two projects closely connected with the federalization
idea had been much discussed. One of them is suggested
in Conrad's letter to the Archduke of December 14, 1912:
"The unification of the South Slav race is one of those
nation-moving phenomena which cannot be denied nor ar-
tificially prevented. The only point is whether this unification shall take place *within* the control of the [Dual] Monarchy—that is at the expense of Serbia's independence—or
whether it shall be accomplished under the aegis of Serbia
at the cost of the Monarchy. This cost for us would con-
sist in the loss of our South Slav lands and thereby of nearly

[32] *In the World War*, pp. 41 f., 49.

all our coast. This loss in territory and prestige would depress the Monarchy into a Small State." [33]

This peaceful incorporation of all South Slavs into the Hapsburg Empire was often dwelt upon by Conrad. In June, 1913, on the eve of the Second Balkan War the Austrian Military Attaché in Belgrade reported that there was a party in Serbia in favor of it. The idea was that Austria-Hungary should cede to Serbia the South Slavs, and to Rumania her kindred populations in Transylvania, and that the Serbian and Rumanian Kingdoms, thus enlarged, should be incorporated into a federal Hapsburg Empire and have somewhat the same constitutional position as the Kingdoms of Saxony and Bavaria in the German Empire. But it was generally agreed that this peaceful incorporation of Serbia and Rumania was impracticable, because the two kindoms would never consent to give up their complete independence. The analogy with Saxony and Bavaria was hardly apt, since their population was solidly of the same nationality as the rest of the German Empire, while Rumania and Serbia were not only of absolutely different nationality from the Germans in Austria and the Magyars in Hungary, but had come to regard them with deep hostility. Moreover, Vienna and Budapest looked down in aristocratic contempt upon Belgrade and Bucharest as representing totally different and inferior civilizations. Doubtless also the Triple Entente would have raised strenuous objections to any such apparent strengthening of Austria and consequently of Germany.

A second scheme, which was regarded as more practical and hopeful by many, was altogether different and was in flat contradiction to Conrad's view of the inevitability of Jugoslav unification. It had long been favored by Count

[33] Conrad, II, 380. Baron Conrad reiterated frequently this view (III. 343 f., 362 ff., 419 ff., 456. 461. 729 ff.).

Aehrenthal.[34]   It consisted in a policy of playing off the
Croats against the Serbs and thus splitting the Jugoslavs
apart according to the old maxim of *divide et impera.*   It
contemplated the creation of a "Greater Croatia" as a third
unit with Austria and Hungary in a *regnum tripartitum.*
Franz Ferdinand was very favorably inclined toward the
Croats.   They were Roman Catholics and had helped preserve Hapsburg authority in the revolutions of 1848.   A
"Greater Croatia," composed of the Slav elements in
Croatia, Slavonia, Dalmatia, and Bosnia-Herzegovina, and
given equal political federal rights with the remaining parts
of Austria and Hungary, would form a valuable bulwark
against the "Greater Serbia" propaganda.   The plan had
had many staunch adherents among the Croats themselves,
and in view of the unhappy conflicts between the Serbs and
Croats since the War can hardly be regarded as altogether
Utopian if it had been adopted seasonably.   But during
the years just before the War this antagonism between Serb
and Croat had been rapidly disappearing owing to the oppressive rule of the German and Magyar authorities on the
one hand, and the active propaganda of Jugoslav intellec-
tuals on the other.   Baron Musulin, an observant Austrian
diplomat and Foreign Office Secretary, who was born in
Croatia, visited his old home in 1913 and noted with alarm
the change which was rapidly taking place from Croat
loyalty to Jugoslav agitation.   He believed the Croatian
peasantry were still true to the Hapsburgs and that a
strengthening of the Croatian sentiment could still be used
to offset the Jugoslav movement for uniting Croats and
Serbs into a "Greater Serbia." [35]   An incident in the trial
of the Sarajevo assassins which moved the court to mirth

[34] Musulin, *Das Haus am Ballplatz,* Munich, 1924, p. 205 ff.   *Cf.*
also G.P., XXVI, 28, 47.

[35] Musulin, pp. 195-210.   *Cf.* also Stephan Count Burián, *Austria in
Dissolution,* New York, 1924, pp. 358-371 on the conflict between the
Croatian and the Jugoslav tendencies.

seems to confirm Baron Musulin's view, and shows how the superficial Jugoslav agitation had not overcome the older inherent Croat dislike of Serbs. A certain Sadilo was being questioned:

> Question: What are you according to your political convictions?
> Sadilo: I belong to the Croatian Right Party.
> Question: Do you like the Serbs?
> Sadilo: Yes, when I don't see them. (Laughter.) [36]

This creation of a "Greater Croatia," perhaps under the historic name of "Illyria," offered possibly the nearest approach to a peaceful solution of the Austro-Serbian conflict. Austria-Hungary would then have been transformed into a federation of at least three component parts, instead of a kind of Siamese-twin state, in which one of the twins insisted on oppressing all the non-Magyar elements. But it would have amounted to a constitutional revolution and would have certainly provoked bitter opposition from Germans and Magyars. Whether Franz Ferdinand would have actually attempted to replace "Dualism" by "Trialism" had he come to the throne, and whether he would have been successful, must remain among the great unanswered questions of history.

Certain it is, however, that he was commonly credited with wide-reaching plans for reorganizing and strengthening the Dual Monarchy, as was stated by Count Czernin and in most of the obituary notices. The dread of what he might do was one of the factors which led fanatical Serbs to plot his assassination. It also unquestionably caused many Viennese and Budapest officials to heave a sigh of relief when they heard the news of Sarajevo.

[36] Pharos, p. 154. The preceding paragraphs were written prior to the Serbian assassination of Croatians in the Serbian Parliament on June 20, 1928. On Croatian desires, see [Dr. Pilar], *Die Südslawische Frage und der Weltkrieg,* Vienna, 1918.

FRANZ FERDINAND'S MARRIAGE

One of the most fateful influences on the Archduke's life was his marriage. In the early 'nineties it was rumored at Vienna that he was paying attention to the Archduchess Marie Christine, eldest daughter of the Archduke Frederick and the Archduchess Isabella. He paid such frequent visits to them in Pressburg, sometimes twice a week, that the parents began to flatter themselves that their daughter would one day be Empress. But in reality Franz Ferdinand had fallen deeply in love with one of the ladies-in-waiting in their household—Countess Sophie Chotek. She was a handsome, proud, tall woman with flashing eyes and an eager step. She belonged to an ancient but impoverished Czech family. For nearly a year their love ran on in secret and unsuspected. When absent from one another they exchanged letters weekly through one of the Archduke's trusted officers. But then came a catastrophe. After a tennis party at Pressburg Franz Ferdinand changed his clothes, but forgot his watch. A servant brought it to the Archduchess Isabella. She opened the locket, expecting perhaps to find a photograph of her daughter—and found instead that of her lady-in-waiting. One can imagine the feelings of a disappointed mother! Countess Sophie was instantly dismissed in disgrace and had to leave the house that very night.[37]

The tongues of the gossips at the Austrian capital began to wag vigorously. But Franz Ferdinand, with his usual determination and obstinacy, declared that he would marry her. All his Hapsburg relatives objected. She was not a princess and did not belong to a ruling family. She was only a countess and therefore debarred from an "eligible" (*ebenbürtige*) marriage with an Archduke. To the old Emperor, Francis Joseph, the announcement of his neph-

[37] Nikitsch-Boulles. p. 26 ff.

ew's determination came as a terrible blow. It was a disgrace unworthy of the family. It seemed like the last drop in his cup of bitterness and family sorrows. His brother, Maximilian, had been shot against a wall in Mexico, and Maximilian's wife had gone insane with grief. His own and only son, Rudolph, had died by violence under the most suspicious circumstances—very probably by suicide. His wife, the Empress Elizabeth, was assassinated by an Italian anarchist in 1898. His wife's insane nephew, Louis of Bavaria, escaping from his guardian, strangled his pursuer and together the two were drowned in the Starnbergersee. His younger nephew, Otto, Franz Ferdinand's brother, living a riotous life and weakened by the disease which he had contracted, caused frequent shocks to the old Emperor's sense of dignity and decency. And now his own heir insisted on defying European traditions and Spanish etiquette by marrying a mere impoverished countess with a possible taint of insanity in her blood. "Was I not to be spared even this?" the Emperor was heard to murmur.[38]

For months Francis Joseph remained absolutely opposed to the marriage. But when he saw that this only increased the obstinate determination of his nephew, and that Franz Ferdinand would sooner give up the right to the throne than the hand of the woman he loved, the old formalist sadly gave his final consent to a compromise. The marriage might take place, but it was to be only a morganatic alliance. On June 28, 1900, the marriage declaration was solemnly registered in the small council room of the Vienna Hofburg in the presence of the Emperor, the Archdukes, and the leading government officials. At the same time the Archduke made a solemn Oath of Renunciation, signed and sealed in German and Magyar copies, declaring:

> "Our marriage with the Countess Chotek is not an eligible but a morganatic marriage, and is to be considered

[38] Margutti, p. 139.

as such for now and all time; in consequence whereof neither Our wife nor the issue to be hoped for with God's blessing from this Our marriage, nor their descendants, will possess or be entitled to claim those rights, titles, armorial bearings, privileges, etc., that belong to the eligible wives and to the issue of Archdukes from eligible marriages. And in particular we again recognize and declare that inasmuch as the issue from Our aforesaid marriage and their descendants are not members of the Most High Arch-House, they possess no right to succeed to the Throne."

The Act of Renunciation was to be the source of untold unhappiness and bitterness in the days to come, since those whom he held dearest were deprived of rights and honors which would have been theirs except for the restrictions of feudal law and Spanish etiquette. June 28, fatal day! Precisely fourteen years later on another June 28 the assassin's revolver, which made no distinctions of birth, united in death the two human beings whose life in matrimony had been clouded by the morganatic bond. June 28! Nineteen years later, on another anniversary of the Archduke's renunciation, was signed the Treaty of Versailles which registered the tragic results from the War of which the Archduke's death was made the immediate occasion!

After the marriage Countess Chotek was raised in rank with the title of Duchess of Hohenberg through the graciousness of Francis Joseph. Yet notwithstanding this elevation in rank, she was still regarded as inferior in position to the youngest Archduchess. Her lot was far from happy. "Greatness is dearly bought," she is said to have confessed to an intimate friend a year before her death. The members of the Imperial family often inflicted cruel humiliations upon her, and there were stories of violent scenes between Franz Ferdinand and his relatives because of the slights which were put upon his wife. Ultimately things came to such a pass that the Heir Presumptive and the Duchess of Hohenberg preferred to absent themselves from Court functions altogether.[39]

As Franz Ferdinand found that his wife was slighted and rebuffed at Vienna, he was all the more grateful for the more generous attitude which Emperor William displayed towards her. This explains in part the increasingly close relations which developed in the years before the War between the German Kaiser and the Archduke. On his first visit to Berlin Franz Ferdinand had been captivated, as had been so many others, by the Kaiser's vivacity, intellectual interests, and efforts to please. In November, 1908, the German Emperor stayed for two days with Franz Ferdinand for hunting at Eckartsau on the Danube, and their relations grew more intimate. A year later the Archduke was invited to Potsdam and the Duchess of Hohenberg was included in the invitation. There she was received with all the honors due to an Archduchess. The Kaiser's tact was in striking contrast to the galling etiquette at Vienna. At dinners at the Austrian Court, the Duchess of Hohenberg had been compelled to sit far removed from her husband at the foot of the table, below all the Austrian Archduchesses. At Potsdam the embarrassment of having her sit at a long table above others who were of higher

[39] *Cf.* the clerical *Reichpost,* a journal regarded as the personal organ of Franz Ferdinand, Jan. 17, 1911: "We are not acquainted with the reasons for the absence of the exalted couple, but we should find it comprehensible if the position assigned to the Consort of the Heir to the throne by the present Court ceremonial should have been thought unnecessarily painful. According to this ceremonial, the wife of the Heir Presumptive is preceded not only by the married ladies of the Imperial House, but even by the youngest Princesses. We remember the disagreeable scene at the Court Ball two years ago, when the members of the Imperial House appeared in the Ballroom, each Imperial Prince with a lady on his arm according to rank, whereas the wife of the Heir to the Throne was obliged to enter the room last, alone and without escort. As several young Archduchesses appear this year at the Court Ball for the first time, the rigors of the ceremonial hitherto observed would, perhaps, have been even more conspicuous. It would be very intelligible if the Duchess Sophie of Hohenberg should have wished to avoid a painful situation, if only out of regard for her exalted husband."

rank was ingeniously obviated by having many small tables. The German Emperor and Empress and the Archduke and his wife dined at one table, while the other guests dined at similar small tables. In this way no precedent could be created, and it could not be said that the German Court had given the Duchess precedence over any princess of the blood royal. On subsequent visits to Vienna the German Emperor was careful to pay personal visits to the Duchess of Hohenberg and show her every mark of esteem. Such conduct touched the heart of the Archduke and was one of the reasons for the more intimate relations and frequent visits of the two men to one another. When the Kaiser went to Corfu the Archduke would take pains to meet him and have the Austrian navy draw up to salute him, or would invite him to visit at Brioni or Miramar.[40] In the course of this interchange of visits, it so happened that the Kaiser was invited to Franz Ferdinand's beautiful villa at Konopischt in Bohemia on June 12, 1914.

THE KONOPISCHT MEETING: LEGEND AND FACT

The meeting at Konopischt, according to the official announcement in the Austrian Press, was a purely personal affair, "in order that the Kaiser might see the Archduke's wonderful roses in full bloom." Horticulture and landscape gardening were in fact one of the Archduke's most passionate hobbies. Having bought the Konopischt estate in 1886, he had spent years of thought, and sums of money which shocked his stewards, in laying out one of the finest parks in Europe. A sugar-factory, a brewery and peasants' houses had been removed, an artificial lake had been created, and rare and beautiful plants had been set out, so that from every window in the castle only the most pleasing prospect met the eye. Here at Konopischt Franz Ferdinand knew every tree and every bush. Every bed of flowers was

[40] Nikitsch-Boulles, pp. 114 ff., 143 ff.

designed according to his exact orders, and his roses were his especial delight and care.[41] But the fact that William was accompanied by Admiral von Tirpitz, and that the Austrian Foreign Minister, Berchtold, came to Konopischt the day after the Emperor left, quickly caused some newspapers at the time to suspect that this meeting had some more serious occasion than merely the viewing of roses. A few weeks later, after the Archduke's assassination and the mysterious events connected with his death and interment, the wildest rumors began to circulate about the "pact" which had been plotted at Konopischt and which had caused the World War. It is therefore worth while to examine a little more closely into this meeting and the rumors to which it gave rise.

According to the London *Times* correspondent, Mr. H. Wickham Steed, who based his account upon an anonymous informant "whose position and antecedents entitle his statements to careful examination," the German Emperor had been deliberately courting the good-will of Franz Ferdinand by attentions to his wife for political purposes, which found their expression in the "Pact of Konopischt." Mr. Steed would have us believe that "the Kaiser opened to the Archduke Franz Ferdinand a magnificent horizon, and spread out before him a grandiose plan which promised presently to place his sons, Maximilian and Ernest, at the head of two vast realms in Eastern and Central Europe." Russia was to be provoked to a war for which Germany and Austria were ready; France was to be reduced to impotence by a few vigorous strokes; and the abstention of England was considered certain. The result of the war was to be the transformation of Europe. The ancient kingdom of Poland, with Lithuania and the Ukraine, was to be reconstituted, stretching from the Baltic to the Black Sea. This was to be the inheritance of Franz Ferdinand; after

41 Nikitsch-Boulles, pp. 188-197.

his death it was to pass to his eldest son. For his younger son was reserved, under his father's direction, a new realm comprising Bohemia, Hungary, and the Jugoslav lands, including Serbia, Dalmatia, and Salonica. Franz Ferdinand, according to this story, saw great thrones prepared for his sons, and Sophie Chotek saw herself the mother of Kings. Emperor William, on his part, was to give up to the new Polish state a part of Posen, and to indemnify himself by bringing into the German Empire a new state comprised of German Austria and Trieste and ruled by Franz Ferdinand's nephew, the Archduke Charles Francis Joseph. Germany would thus acquire a coveted outlet upon the Adriatic, and would be enlarged by the addition of another state equal in importance to Bavaria. Between the enlarged German Empire, the reconstituted kingdom of Poland, and the new Bohemian-Hungarian-Jugoslav realm, a close and perpetual military and economic alliance was to be formed. This alliance would become the arbiter of Europe, and would command the Balkans and the route to the East.

Such, according to Mr. Wickham Steed, were the terms of the agreement. Knowledge of it, he thinks, came to the ears of the Austrian Imperial family, and herein lies the explanation of the shabby way in which Franz Ferdinand and his wife were unceremoniously hurried to their graves after being murdered at Sarajevo. He darkly hints that the Austrian Court itself was guilty of complicity in the murder. He then goes on to exaggerate or distort in sensational newspaper fashion a number of other circumstances calculated to leave the reader with the impression that the assassination of the Archduke was brought about through the complicity of Austrian officials and that Serbia was in no way responsible. "General Potiorek, who was sitting in the archducal car, escaped injury. Neither he nor any other military or civil dignitaries were punished for their failure to protect the visitors. General Potiorek remained Governor and presently commanded the Bosnian army through the first campaign against Serbia. After the defeat of his troops he was deprived of his command, was reported to have lost his reason, and was placed in a lunatic asylum. . . . When the Emperor Francis Joseph visited Sarajevo in June, 1910, the number of police available exceeded a thousand; probably double that number of secret agents were employed; yet when the Heir to the Throne visited the city the police were warned off! No evidence proving the complicity of the Serbian Government in the plot to assassinate the Archduke has ever been adduced. . . . It would certainly not be beyond the power of the Austro-Hungarian secret service agents to work up a plot at Belgrade or at Sarajevo . . . to 'remove' obnoxious personages or to provide a pretext for war." [42]

After describing at length the indignity of the funeral arrangements made for the murdered couple which "were hardly less astonishing than had been the circumstances of the assassination," Mr. Steed adds as a further incriminating circumstance the fact that it was at first announced that the German Emperor would attend the funeral, but "on the 2nd of July it was announced in Berlin that owing to a slight indisposition, the German Emperor had abandoned his journey to Vienna. He nevertheless gave audiences as usual on that day." He implies that the German Emperor and the other sovereigns were instructed from Vienna not to attend the funeral and that this is a further indication that the Archduke's death was contrived by Austrian officials because of his having plotted at Konopischt a partition of the Hapsburg lands to provide crowns for his sons. But as a matter of fact the failure of the Kaiser to attend the funeral was not due to any hint from the authorities in Vienna who wanted to deprive the Archduke and his wife

[42] Steed, "The Pact of Konopischt," pp. 265 ff.; see below, note 45.

of due honors even after death. He abandoned his intention of going to Vienna because a warning had come from the German consul at Sarajevo that the Serbs might make an attack on his life also, and because his Chancellor declined to assume the responsibility of allowing the Emperor to risk his life by going to Vienna. As we learn from Bethmann-Hollweg's telegram to the German Ambassador at Vienna on July 2:

> As a result of warnings which have been received from Sarajevo, of which the first, in fact, dates back to April of this year, I have been obliged to request His Majesty the Emperor to give up the visit to Vienna. What confirmed me in the determination was the fact that the journey was not an act of national or political necessity, but one concerned with the voluntary announcement of friendly feelings beyond a point required by etiquette; that there is apparently a wide-spread conspiracy at the bottom of the Sarajevo crime; and that assassinations are well known to exercise a suggestive influence on the criminal elements. On the strength of these considerations, I was unable to undertake the responsibility of exposing His Majesty unnecessarily in a foreign land.
>
> For public purposes, the giving up of the visit will be laid to the physical indisposition of His Majesty. His Majesty wishes, however, that the true reason be communicated to His Majesty the Emperor Franz Joseph personally.[43]

Similarly all the other circumstances with which Mr. Steed and his followers have built up the theory of Austrian complicity are really to be explained quite simply and naturally on altogether different and less sensational grounds, as will be indicated below. There is not a shred of evidence that the Archduke was plotting at Konopischt, or that Austrian officials conspired for his assassination.

[43] K.D., 6 B; and the warning telegram from Sarajevo, K.D., 6 A.

Nevertheless Mr. Steed's astounding theory received wide acceptance among Austria's late enemies. Serbians naturally are glad to adopt it because it would remove all responsibility for the crime from their country.[44] It has been widely circulated with some reservations or amplifications by many over-suspicious French writers: by M. Raymond Recouly, a popular newspaper correspondent and magazine writer; by M. Alfred Dumaine, who was French Ambassador to Vienna, but who at the time appears to have known nothing of all this; by M. Chopin in his monograph on the Sarajevo murder; and even by such a sober historian as Professor Debidour.[45]

Fortunately for the cause of truth, documents have re-

[44] Mr. A. V. Seferovitch, Jugoslav Consul-General at Montreal, quotes Mr. Steed at length to prove "that the plot to murder the Archduke originated in Austria and served a twofold purpose, namely, the elimination of the Archduke as heir presumptive and a pretext for the long-desired attack on Serbia by Austria;" see his article, "The blame for the Sarajevo murder plot" in New York Times *Current History*, Dec., 1925, p. 385.

[45] H. Wickham Steed, "The Pact of Konopischt," in *Nineteenth Century and After*, Vol. 79, pp. 253-273 (Feb., 1916). Many months later Mr. Steed is said to have admitted in private conversation that he no longer believed in this fantastic story. Nevertheless he repeats it in abbreviated form in his interesting but unveracious work, *Through Thirty Years*, London, 1924, I, 396-403, where it will doubtless continue to deceive thousands of unsophisicated readers like Mr. Seferovitch. Among the French writers who have swallowed and broadcasted with variations his theory are Jean Pozzi, "Les Roses de Konopischt," in *Le Correspondant*, June 10, 1921; Recouly, *Les Heures Tragiques d'Avant-Guerre* (Paris, 1922), pp. 173-194; and also in *La Revue de France*, April 1, 1922, pp. 598-610; Dumaine, *La Dernière Ambassade de France en Autriche* (Paris, 1921), p. 126 ff.; Debidour, *Histoire Diplomatique de l'Europe* (Paris, 1918), II, 229; Jules Chopin (pseudonym of J. E. Pichon, a lecturer at the University of Prague who shares the characteristic Czech attitude of hostility towards the Hapsburgs) "La préméditation austro-hungroise," in *Mercure de France*, Vol. 115 (1916), pp. 577-599. In his much-quoted little book, *Le Complot De Sarajevo* (Paris, 1918), p. 82, Chopin sums up: "Il est certain que l'entrevue de Konopischt avait un tout autre but que celui d'échanger des politesses et de mettre à mal le gibier des parcs archiducaux. Nous croyons donc que son seul objet était justement de trouver le prétexte d'une guerre qui manquait en 1914, et de minutieusement régler la marche diplomatique et militaire de toute cette entreprise belliqueuse

cently been published which give precise and trustworthy accounts of what really took place at Konopischt and which will lead all serious students to consign Mr. Steed's amazing theory to the limbo of propagandist war myths.[46] One of these documents is the official report sent to the German Foreign Office the day after the interview by Baron von Treutler, the Minister in attendance upon William II.[47]

This gives a good account of the conversations between William II and Franz Ferdinand. They first touched upon the Balkan situation, in view of an alarming telegram from Athens that the Greeks had called up their marine reserves and were rumored to be planning an attack on Turkey. Franz Ferdinand and his guest agreed to sound King Carol of Rumania, to see whether he would use his influence in favor of peace and the preservation of the *status quo* as fixed by the Treaty of Bucharest. Both expressed their dislike of Ferdinand of Bulgaria. Franz Ferdinand gave vent to his suspicions of Italy's *mala fides* in Albania and in general. The German Emperor tried to allay his suspicions, and hoped that when Franz Ferdinand should meet the King of Italy at the German routine maneuvers later in the year, there would be an opportunity for establishing more cordial personal relations between Victor Emmanuel and the Heir to the Hapsburg throne.

The main topic of conversation at Konopischt, however, like that between William II and Francis Joseph at

---

[46] Even Mr. Seton-Watson, whom no one will accuse of being over lenient toward Austria, has at last acknowledged (*Sarajevo*, p. 111): "Nothing which even remotely deserves the name of evidence has ever been adduced in proof [of the theory of official complicity on the part of Vienna and Budapest] and each of the many suspicious details is susceptible of a simpler and less sensational explanation;" similarly also pp. 114, 287.

[47] In *Deutsche Politik*, May 14, 1920; G.P., XXXIX, 365 ff.; and reprinted by Montgelas, *The Case for the Central Powers*, pp. 232-235. Treutler's accuracy as to the first point discussed in the interview is confirmed by the telegram sent by the Austrian Minister in Athens on June 12, printed in Conrad, III, 660 f.

Vienna three months previously,[48] dealt with internal Austrian politics—Tisza's treatment of the Rumanians in Transylvania and its dangerous effect on public feeling in the Kingdom of Rumania. Franz Ferdinand assailed the medieval and anachronistic Magyar oligarchy, with Tisza at its head, which dominated Hungary and was trying to dominate Austria as well. "Already Vienna begins to tremble when Tisza starts for the city; everyone lies flat on his stomach when Tisza steps out at Vienna." Emperor William, on the other hand, urged that Tisza was such a powerful and unusual man that he "ought not to be thrown overboard, but be kept under a firm hand, and then used for his valuable qualities." The Archduke complained that "it was precisely Tisza who was to blame, if the interests of the Triple Alliance were badly looked after, since it was Tisza who, in contradiction with his own promises at Schönbrunn, had been maltreating the Rumanians in Hungary. The Archduke finally begged His Majesty whether he would not instruct Tschirschky [the German Ambassador at Vienna] to remind Tisza at every opportunity that he should not lose sight of the necessity of winning over the Rumanians through moderation in the treatment of their brothers who were living in Hungary. His Majesty promised that he would instruct Tschirschky continually to repeat to Tisza, 'Sir! Remember the Rumanians!' The Archduke greatly approved of this." Treutler gathered the impression from the Archduke's secretary that Franz Ferdinand felt that the Kaiser and the Berlin Foreign Office were too inclined to look at conditions in Austria-Hungary through Hungarian spectacles, owing to the fact that for decades the Dual Monarchy had been represented at Berlin by a Hungarian Ambassador. Franz Ferdinand in fact told William II confidentially that it was planned to replace Szögyény, a Hungarian, by Prince Hohenlohe, an Austrian.

[48] G.P., XXXIX, 333 ff., 358 ff.; Montgelas, pp. 229-231.

At the close of the conversation Franz Ferdinand expressed the opinion that Russia was not to be feared; her internal difficulties were too great to allow her to follow an aggressive foreign policy.

Treutler's report, showing that the main topic of conversation at Konopischt was Tisza's Rumanian policy, is further corroborated from the Austrian side. The day after the German Emperor left Konopischt, Berchtold was summoned thither, and upon his return to Vienna gave the German Ambassador a résumé of the conversations which Tschirschky reported as follows:

> After His Majesty the Kaiser left, Count Berchtold was invited to Konopischt by Archduke Franz Ferdinand. This Minister told me today that the Archduke expressed himself as greatly gratified at the Kaiser's visit. He had talked over in detail all possible questions with the Kaiser and was able to find that they were in complete agreement in their views.
>
> The Archduke also told Count Berchtold what he had said to the Kaiser in regard to Count Tisza's policy, especially the policy toward the non-Magyar nationalities. "Toward the Rumanians," the Archduke had remarked, "Count Tisza used fine words, but his deeds did not correspond to his words." It was one of the Hungarian Premier's cardinal mistakes that he had not given more parliamentary seats to the Rumanians in Transylvania.
>
> Count Berchtold told me that he had attempted often and emphatically to influence Count Tisza to make greater concessions to the Rumanians. But his efforts had been in vain. Count Tisza maintained that he had already conceded as much as possible to the Rumanians.
>
> For my part I will also use every opportunity, as I have been doing hitherto, in accordance with the Kaiser's directions, to point out to the Hungarian Premier the necessity of winning over the Rumanians.[49]

[49] Tschirschky to. Bethmann, June 17, 1914; K.D., 4. On this report the Kaiser made the marginal note, "He [Tisza] must not by *his internal*

In view of these precise contemporary documents, one may therefore confidently relegate to the realm of legend all the fantastic tales of Mr. Wickham Steed and the French writers, that William II and Franz Ferdinand were planning a rearrangement of the map of Europe, or plotting a European war which was to be provoked by the Archduke's maneuvers near the Serbian frontier at Sarajevo. The Magyar oppression of the Transylvanian Rumanians, and the consequent indignation that was being stirred up among King Carol's subjects, involving as it did the danger that Rumania might cease to be loyal to her secret treaties with the Triple Alliance Powers, was a sufficiently serious question, aside from the roses and personal friendship, to account for the meeting at Konopischt. In this connection it is significant that the Rumanian question, and its relation to Germany and Austrian policy, fills a large place in the documents recently published by Conrad von Hötzendorf and by the German Government.[50]

policy, which through the Rumanian question has an influence on *the external policy of the Triple Alliance*, jeopardize the latter."

For further references to the Konopischt meeting and the possible subjects discussed there see the report of the Russian Ambassador in Vienna to Sazonov (printed in *Die Kriegsschuldfrage*, III, 169, June, 1925), alleging that Franz Ferdinand had discussed the Austrian naval program with Admiral Tirpitz in view of the danger that Russia would open the Straits Question. Tirpitz's brief memorandum on the visit, written immediately upon his return to Berlin (*ibid.*, III, 561 f., Sept. 1925), is mainly a description of the society and landscape gardening at Konopischt with which he was greatly impressed; "aside from the Kaiser's talk with the Archduke, politics were hardly touched upon at all;" the Kaiser had mentioned to Franz Ferdinand the possibility of sending the German fleet into the Mediterranean in case of war, "because it had been deduced from the naval manoeuvres that in view of the submarines, etc., we could not do much in the North Sea." For the Triple Alliance Naval Convention of June 23, 1913, fixing the conditions of naval coöperation in the Mediterranean, see Pribram, I, 282 ff. Conrad, III, 36 f., reports a conversation with Francis Joseph on July 5, 1914 in which the Emperor said, "I instructed Franz Ferdinand to request from the German Emperor at Konopischt information as to whether in the future also we could reckon unconditionally upon Germany. The German Emperor had evaded the question and given no answer."

[50] Conrad, III, *passim;* G.P., XXXIII-XXXIX, *passim.*

The uncertainty as to Rumania's loyalty and the consequent advisability of a definite shift in the Balkan policy of the Triple Alliance is also, as we shall see, the main theme of a long memoir for preserving peace in the Balkans, which Tisza drew up in the spring of 1914, and which was being worked over in the Austrian Foreign Office at the moment Franz Ferdinand was assassinated.

The fact that the German Emperor was accompanied at Konopischt by Admiral von Tirpitz has caused some remark, and helped to spread the legend that great things were being plotted there. But Tirpitz's presence at Konopischt is probably sufficiently explained, as Jagow later asserted,[51] by the Archduke's interest in the upbuilding and reorganization of the Austrian navy, which he had so much at heart. Possibly it is also to be explained by the fact that the Kaiser was unquestionably greatly worried, as was the German Foreign Office, at the rumors of a naval agreement between Russia and England which was actually under discussion just at this time. France and Russia had supplemented the Military Convention of the Dual Alliance by an analogous Naval Convention in the spring of 1912. In November of the same year, France had secured from Sir Edward Grey a written promise that the French and British naval and military experts should continue to consult together in anticipation of a possible war. The British and French navies had been rearranged in such a way that the French increased their forces in the Mediterranean to protect British as well as French interests in that area, and the British on their part concentrated their fleet in the North Sea to protect the north coast of France from attack by Germany. Finally, in the spring of 1914, Poincaré, Izvolski and Sazonov were eagerly trying to arrange

[51] Jagow, *Ursachen*, p. 181, n. 2: "That Secretary of State Tirpitz accompanied the Kaiser at Konopischt was due to the express wish of the Archduke who wished to hear the Grand Admiral's views concerning the construction of types of ships."

for a naval agreement between England and Russia which would consolidate the naval forces of the Entente against Germany. Naturally the Kaiser would be anxious to consult with Franz Ferdinand and his own Grand Admiral as to the significance of these negotiations, and as to the means of averting, if possible, what looked like naval "encirclement."

Perhaps after all, however, the most important result of the meeting at Konopischt was the effect that it had on the Kaiser's psychology. On his impetuous and emotional nature the murder made all the more vivid impression inasmuch as it had struck down a friend at whose home he had been visiting so intimately only a few days previously. The pistol shots at Sarajevo followed so closely upon the roses at Konopischt that they intensified all the more the horror with which he regarded all tyrannicide. Whereas heretofore he had been restraining Austria from rash action against Serbia, now he instantly envisaged Serbia as a den of murderers, and unwisely allowed Count Berchtold complete freedom to take any steps against Serbia which should be deemed advisable at Vienna.

THE TRIP TO SARAJEVO

The Archduke's fatal trip to Bosnia and Sarajevo in June, 1914, was decided upon many months beforehand. On September 16, 1913, during the Austrian army maneuvers in Bohemia he spoke to Conrad of it. On September 29 Conrad discussed it in Vienna with General Potiorek, Governor of Bosnia, who said it was the Archduke's intention to visit Bosnia as Heir to the Throne, to attend the maneuvers of the XVth and XVIth Army Corps, and to take advantage of the occasion to bring his wife with him.[52]

[52] Conrad, III, 445. Whether the original suggestion for the trip came from the Archduke himself, as is usually assumed, or whether it was due to the request of General Potiorek, Governor of Bosnia, as I think more probable, is not clear. Conrad says (III, 702): "On whose initiative the

This conversation indicates the three-fold purpose of the visit and explains the somewhat unusual details in connection with it.

From the political point of view it was highly desirable that a member of the imperial family should show himself in the recently annexed provinces. Among the impressionable simple peasant populations of Europe, who before the War had a deep-rooted respect for royalty and a traditional feeling of loyalty to a personal ruler, nothing was better calculated to stimulate and strengthen this feeling of personal loyalty than such official visits of princes. They flattered local pride. The simple peasant liked the pageantry of princes. He liked to see his ruler and find in him a flesh and blood human being like himself, who walks and rides about and eats three good meals a day. Merely to see him or hear him speak was to renew the human bond of common understanding and interests. So throughout history, from Henri Quatre and Frederick the Great in the past to the Prince of Wales in the present, it has been a common practice for popular princes and rulers to make royal progresses, which tend to strengthen the bonds between ruler and ruled.[53] With this in view Emperor Francis Joseph had visited Bosnia in 1910. It was with this same idea that Baron Musulin in 1913 had urged that Franz Ferdinand should make himself better known in Croatia, and that members of the Hapsburg family should make

decision for the Heir's trip originated, and who fixed the measures for it, I do not know. But that an imperial prince should finally again visit Bosnia, like Crown Prince Rudolf in earlier days, seemed to me only natural and in the interests of the dynasty; especially so if it was the Heir to the Throne himself who should undertake this trip." Nikitsch-Boulles (pp. 209-216), who accompanied the Archduke's wife, indicates that the Archduke made the trip rather against his will because of his dislike of the heat, and implies that it was undertaken to please General Potiorek and the military officers.

[53] On the political importance of having princes present their traits familiarly to peasants, see the shrewd observations of Mr. H. A. L Fisher, *The Republican Tradition in Europe*, Boston, 1911, pp 322-324.

longer visits there, in order to counteract among the loyal peasantry the propaganda of Jugoslav agitators.[54] Possibly his suggestion may have had something to do with the Archduke's decision to visit Bosnia and Herzegovina. Such a visit would strengthen the Roman Catholic and other loyal elements and tend to offset Jugoslav revolutionary propaganda and the Serb agitation for "Greater Serbia." This was the political aspect of his trip, and it partly explains why he did not wish to be protected by heavy guards of soldiers and secret police, but preferred to ride about freely in an open automobile. In 1909, when he had travelled through Hungary to visit King Carol, he had been highly indignant at the way the civilian authorities had shut off the railway stations with cordons of police and kept at a distance the crowds of peasantry who had come to wave their hats and handkerchiefs to the Archducal couple.[55]

The main object of the trip, however, was that the Archduke might attend the maneuvers of the XVth and XVIth Army Corps, which were regularly stationed in Bosnia. As Inspector-in-Chief of the Army he had in recent years regularly represented the Emperor at such maneuvers. The Bosnian maneuvers of 1914 are commonly represented by Austrophobe writers as "planned as a kind of rehearsal for military operations against Serbia." [56] Mr. Jovanovitch, the Serbian Minister in Vienna, says: "The plan was to hold the **maneuvers in the district between** Sarajevo and the Romanija and Han Pisesak [to the *east* of Sarajevo]— thus just against the Serbian frontier. **With maneuvers** so planned the 'enemy' was naturally Serbia. . . . The **maneuvers** were to be held in Bosnia on the Drin just opposite to Serbia." [57] There is no truth in these assertions. All the provisions for a campaign against Serbia were taken

[54] Musulin, pp. 206-210.   [55] Nikitsch-Boulles, p. 130.
[56] Seton-Watson, *Sarajevo*, p. 115.
[57] Letter of Jovan Jovanovitch in *Neues Wiener Tageblatt*, No. 177, June 28, 1924.

care of in an altogether different way, namely by Baron
Conrad's "Mobilization B"[alkan] plan. This included not
merely the two Corps regularly stationed in Bosnia, but the
use of five more Corps from the rest of Austria-Hungary
comprising altogether about half the total army; [58] it contemplated of course a direct offensive against the Drin,
which forms the boundary between Bosnia and Serbia.
This plan had been worked out in all its details by Conrad
and his General Staff, and, like the General Staff mobilization plans of all countries, was always in readiness. But
the Bosnian maneuvers which the Archduke was to inspect
comprised merely two Army Corps and were merely part
of the routine training to which parts of the army were
regularly subjected. They had no connection with any concrete war preparations, but simply had as their main object
the practicing of considerable forces moving in a relatively
difficult and varied terrain. Nor were they to be held in
the Romanija *east* of Sarajevo "on the Drin just opposite
to Serbia," as M. Jovanovitch states. On the contrary they
were held some 30 kilometers to the *southwest* of Sarajevo
in the Tarcin district. They did not in the slightest con-
template a theoretical attack on Serbia to the eastward, but
looked in exactly the opposite direction—the theoretical
protection of Sarajevo against an attack coming from the
west from the direction of the Adriatic. The "Blue" defending army had a position southwest of Sarajevo and was
to prevent the "Red" attacking force, advancing from the
side of Mostar and the west, from capturing the Ivan
Pass which guards the road which runs up from the Adriatic to Sarajevo.[59] It was in order to become acquainted
with this region at the opposite side of Bosnia, as far away
from Serbia as possible, that the Archduke travelled to

[58] Conrad, I, 361-423; IV, 112-124. For the disposition of the Austrian forces, see below, at the end of ch. vii.

[59] For the details of the maneuvers see the *Neue Freie Presse*, Nos.
17901-2, June 27, 28, 1914.

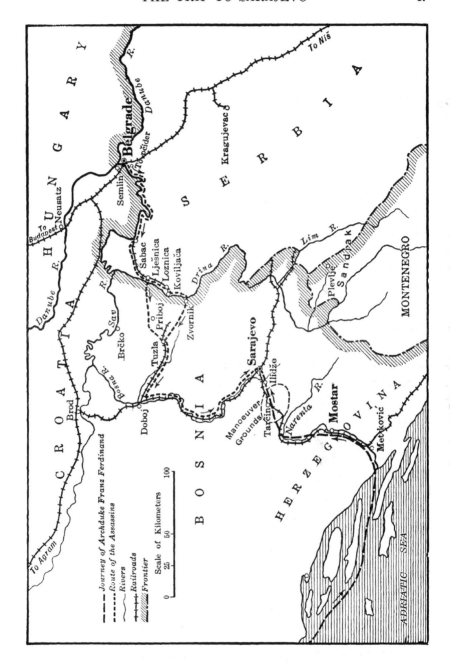

Sarajevo by way of Fiume and the Adriatic and then came up the railway via Metkovic and Mostar. His wife, however, had to come alone all the way by rail from Vienna, via Budapest, and only met him at Ilidze near Sarajevo.[60]

So far as the Bosnian maneuvers can be said to have had any practical immediate objective in view at all, they were designed to acquaint the officers, not with the *terrain* for a war with Serbia, but rather with that for a campaign for the protection of Albania or for the defense of Bosnia against troops landing on the Adriatic Coast.[61]

As the Archduke's trip was primarily a military tour of inspection, the details of it were worked out by his *Militärkanzlei* in conjunction with Baron Conrad and General Potiorek. M. Bilinski, who as Joint Finance Minister had charge of the civil administration of Bosnia, was not consulted. After the assassination recriminations took place between him and General Potiorek as to the responsibility for the tragedy.[62] M. Bilinski insists in his memoirs [63] that he was in no way responsible, since he and his officials had been systematically disregarded in regard to the preparations for the Archduke's journey. He even says he did not know "the program of the Archduke's trip to Bosnia" until he read it in the *Neue Freie Presse* about eleven o'clock on the fatal Sunday morning, before taking his carriage to go to

[60] Conrad, III, 700-702; IV, 13; Nikitsch-Boulles, pp. 209-214.

[61] As, for instance, by the Italians, whom the Archduke particularly distrusted and whose King he had refused to visit, though a return visit by a member of the Hapsburg family to the King of Italy was long overdue, as we know from Conrad, III, 502 f., 626. In 1908 the German, and presumably therefore the Austrian, authorities were informed that the Italian Military Attaché in Belgrade had worked out for the Serbian General Staff a plan of campaign for the realization of a "Greater Serbia" and had given them a plan of operations by which Italy should aid the Serbs; G.P., XXVI, 18. This was in line with the Racconigi agreement a year later.

[62] Bilinski to Potiorek, July 3; Gooss, p. 46 f. Potiorek to Bilinski, July 6; Conrad, IV, 64-67.

[63] Léon Bilinski, *Wspomnienia i Dokumenty* [Reminiscences and Documents], 2 vols., Warsaw, 1924-25, I, 273-277.

church. He had a painful shock, he says, when he then learned for the first time that the program of the Archduke's trip contained, contrary to the Emperor's original permission for a military tour, a solemn entry into Sarajevo.[64] Bilinski's denial of any prior knowledge of the Archduke's intended entry into Sarajevo can hardly be true, because the *Neue Freie Presse* does not contain on June 28 any "program of the Archduke's trip to Bosnia"; it merely gives an account of the day's maneuvers there. Moreover, three weeks earlier, on June 4, it had already printed an outline of the Archduke's trip, including the proposed visit to Sarajevo, which he can hardly have failed to see. Furthermore, on June 24 there was printed a detailed private program of the trip for the information of officials.[65] Bilinski admits that a copy of this had been brought to him by one of his assistants.[66]

The point that Bilinski was not consulted has been made much of by writers who try to explain the responsibility for the crime by emphasizing the "bevy of assassins" lying in wait for the Archduke, the "criminal negligence" of the Austrian police, the arrogance of Potiorek, and headstrong obstinacy of Franz Ferdinand in ignoring the Joint Finance Minister.[67] In thus trying to put the blame on the Austrian authorities they obscure the true conspiracy which was developed at Belgrade. One of the main reasons which they cite for putting the preparations into the hands of Potiorek instead of Bilinski was said to be the Archduke's desire to eliminate Court officials who might have placed obstacles in the way of having the Duchess Sophie go to

[64] Bilinski, I, 276.
[65] Margutti, p. 146; *cf.* Seton-Watson, p. 107, note 2.
[66] Bilinski, I, 274 f.
[67] Seton-Watson, *Sarajevo*, pp. 106-117; Wickham Steed, in *The Nineteenth Century and After*, LXXIX, 253-273; Recouly, *Les Heures Tragiques*, pp. 180-182; Chopin, *Le Complot de Sarajevo*, pp. 89-100; Margutti, pp. 145 ff., 396 f.

Sarajevo. However this may be, the Emperor appears to have made no objection to her participation in the trip when the matter was laid before him by the Archduke on June 4.[68]

The Archduke appears finally to have undertaken the trip more from a sense of duty than from the desire, as usually stated, to have an opportunity to have his wife received with royal honors by his side. As already noted they travelled to Sarajevo by different routes. In the last weeks he had some doubts about going at all, because of his health and the heat. He discussed the point with the Emperor, who said, "Do as you wish." [68a] His private secretary has noted several remarks which indicate that Franz Ferdinand was the reverse of enthusiastic about the trip. On June 23 the special railway carriage regularly reserved for him had a hot-box, so that he and his wife had to travel in an ordinary first class compartment after leaving their three children at Chlumetz. Franz Ferdinand remarked sarcastically, "Well, the journey is beginning in a right promising fashion!" [69] A little later, when told that the train by which he and his wife intended to leave Sarajevo on June 29 would have to start at 5 A. M. instead of 6 A. M. as originally planned, he exclaimed, "Tell Colonel Bardolff that if he continues daily to make the Bosnian trip still more disgusting with new difficulties and unpleasantnesses he can hold the maneuvers alone, and I will not go down there at all." The secretary adds that the idea "that

[68] Conrad, III, 700. Bilinski had an audience with the Emperor on this same day (*Neue Freie Presse*, No. 17878, June 4, p. 2) and had plenty of opportunity to raise objections to the Archduke's proposed trip, but there is no indication that he did so. It was *after* the tragedy that he and his officials emphasize how worried they had been and how much they had disapproved of the plans. Mr. Seton-Watson, to be sure (*Sarajevo*, p. 106) quotes a second-hand statement by A. Mousset to the effect that Bilinski did instruct Sarajevo to sound the local authorities, who declined to take responsibility; but Mousset, though he passes for an authority on Serbian history, is strongly Austrophobe and not an altogether reliable writer.

[68a] Conrad, III, 700.   [69] Nikitsch-Boulles, p. 210.

the Archduke himself wanted the trip to Bosnia in order to provide a triumphal journey is a pure invention." [70]

However, in spite of these annoyances, and the fact that the electricity gave out in the train in which he rode from Vienna to Trieste, the rest of the journey passed off excellently and the Archduke was in the best of humor. He was greeted with enthusiasm at the railway stations on the way from the Adriatic to Sarajevo, and joined his wife on the afternoon of June 25 at the pleasant little resort of Ilidze, a dozen miles from Sarajevo, where they were to stay. The maneuvers passed off very satisfactorily in spite of heavy rain, and the Archduke complimented General Potiorek on the spirit and training of the troops.[71]

On Friday afternoon, June 26, after returning from the first day's maneuvers, Franz Ferdinand and his wife motored in to Sarajevo to do some shopping in the bazaars. The Mayor of the town had already issued a proclamation expressing the loyalty of the population to Francis Joseph and their pleasure that he had sent his Heir to visit Bosnia; he urged the people to decorate the stores and houses with flags and flowers, and this was done; everywhere his picture was in the windows.

On this afternoon Franz Ferdinand was in uniform and was continually recognized and acclaimed with loyal shouts of "*Zivio*." The crowd was so dense that the officers accompanying him had some difficulty in making way for him from one shop to another.[72] Had there been really a "bevy of assassins" waiting to do away with him, here was ample opportunity. But the visit passed off without any incident, and the Archducal pair returned to Ilidze, much pleased with the town and the way they had been received.

On Sunday morning the Archduke telegraphed to his

---

[70] Nikitsch-Boulles, p. 211.   [71] Conrad, IV, 13-15.

[72] Nikitsch-Boulles, p. 213; Conrad, IV, 14 f.; Jevtitch, *Sarajevski Atentat*.

children at Chlumetz that everything was going well with "Papi" and "Mami," and that they were looking forward to seeing them again on Tuesday. These were the last words he ever wrote.[73]

[73] Nikitsch-Boulles, p. 215

CHAPTER II

THE ASSASSINATION PLOT

THE immediate occasion of the World War was the murder of the Austrian Archduke at Sarajevo. Had it not occurred, there would have been neither an Austro-Serbian War, nor a World War, in the summer of 1914. In spite of the increasing tension between the Triple Alliance and the Triple Entente, it is probable that European diplomacy would have succeeded for months, perhaps for years, in averting a conflict which all statesmen foresaw as unspeakably terrible, and for which the Franco-Russian forces planned to be better prepared in 1917 than in 1914. The murder of the Archduke ignited material which would not otherwise have taken fire as it did, or perhaps not at all. It is, therefore, of importance to trace the origins of the plot to which he fell a victim and to determine the responsibility for the deed which was to have such awful and world-racking consequences.

What are the true details of the Sarajevo plot? What were the motives of the assassins? Who were their instigators or accomplices? These are dark and difficult questions which have remained more mysterious and baffling than most of the problems relating to the immediate causes of the War. Serious historians have devoted relatively little attention to them. Fantastic rumors and persistent misstatements, born of hatred and war propaganda, have passed current for a longer time on this subject than on any other aspect of those tragic days which set Europe aflame. There are many reasons for this. Historians have been mainly

occupied with the question of the relative responsibility of
the Great Powers. Information from Serbian sources was
not only very meager, but such as there was consisted of
contradictory assertions. Another reason was the fact that
the official Austrian version of the plot, which laid the blame
largely on the Serbian agitation for a "Greater Serbia,"
and especially on the subversive activities of the Serbian
patriotic association known as the "Narodna Odbrana,"
was set forth in Austria's ultimatum to Serbia, and in the
dossier offered to the Powers, containing the results of Austria's Sarajevo investigation and justifying the ultimatum.[1]
But this Austrian version never inspired much confidence
—to put it mildly—among most people in the Entente or
neutral countries. The investigation at Sarajevo had necessarily been very hurried and had been carried on in strict
secrecy. The *dossier* seemed to read like a hasty patch-
work; appended to it are a couple of "supplements after
the close of the printing." As the *dossier* did not reach the
Powers until after they had begun seriously to suspect that
Austria was bent on war against Serbia in any event, the
statesmen of Europe were already so entirely absorbed with
apprehension of a general European war that they had no
time, in their hot, sleepless days and nights, to give any
serious attention to what they suspected might be fabricated accusations.[2] There was fresh in everyone's mind

---

[1] *Austrian Red Book* of 1914, Nos. 7-9, 19.

[2] The *dossier*, in German, was dispatched by mail or messenger to
twenty-two Austrian diplomatic representatives abroad on July 25, (A.R.B.,
II, 48). As there had been no time to translate it into French, as was
usually done with Austro-Hungarian communications to the Powers, it
was sent in the original German. It was delivered to Bienvenu-Martin
in Paris on July 27 (F.Y.B., 75), but only the first part of it was printed
in the French Yellow Book. It was not offered to Sir Edward Grey in
London until July 29, and not printed at all in the English Blue Book.
It is doubtful whether Sir Edward even read it at the time; *cf.* Grey
to Bunsen, July 29 (B.D., 282): "The Austrian Ambassador told me today
he had ready a long memorandum, which he proposed to leave and which
he said gave an account of the conduct of Serbia toward Austria, and

the memory of the disgraceful Agram and Friedjung trials, in which Austrian officials had been detected in using forged documents in their efforts to incriminate Serb sympathizers. Was it not very probable that the *dossier* of 1914 was equally dishonest? People prejudiced against the Central Powers, therefore, were inclined to consign Berchtold's *dossier* to oblivion or incredulous ridicule, and to accept instead the Serbian Government's explicit denial of the Austrian charges and its sweeping assertion that it was in no way guilty of any complicity.

Later on, in November, 1914, the assassins and other suspects were brought to a formal trial at Sarajevo. A stenographic report of the essential part of it, translated into German from the Croatian original, was published in Berlin in 1918.[3] It is a fascinating human document, full

an explanation of how necessary the Austrian action was. I said I did not wish to discuss the merits of the question between Austria and Serbia." To Sazonov in St. Petersburg the *dossier* was apparently never shown at all, and is not printed in the Russian Orange Book. On July 24, when informed of the ultimatum, Sazonov told the Austrian Ambassador that he "was really not curious at all to see the *dossier;* the fact is, you want war and have burned your bridges." But on July 29, "Sazonov begged again urgently for the transmission of the *dossier,* which had been promised to the Powers, but had not yet been produced. One would like to see it before the war with Serbia should have begun. If war once broke out, it would be too late to examine the *dossier;*" Szápáry to Berchtold, July 24, 29; A.R.B., II, 19; III, 16.

The author of the *dossier,* Dr. Wiesner, has recently given an interesting account of the way it was compiled and the reasons for the delay in presenting it to the Powers; "Die unwiderlegt gebliebene Begründung für das Ultimatum Oesterreichs an Serbien vom Juli, 1914," in *Die Kriegsschuldfrage,* V, 492-503, June, 1927. He has recently summed up the responsibility of Serbia in an article, "Die Schuld der serbischen Regierung am Mord von Sarajevo", *ibid.,* VI, 307-395, April, 1928.

[3] Professor Pharos, *Der Prozess gegen die Attentäter von Sarajevo: nach dem amtlichen Stenogram der Gerichtsverhandlung aktenmässig dargestellt; Einleitung von Josef Kohler.* Berlin, 1918, pp. 165. "Pharos" is said to be a pseudonym. The fact that he was evidently personally present at the trial, giving a personal description of each defendant and showing a strong bias against Free-Masonry, suggests that the pseudonym covers the identity of Father Puntigam, the Archduke's Jesuit Confessor. Pharos does not attempt in his German translation to reproduce all the evidence from the lesser defendants and the witnesses; he gives

of pathos and humor. It seems to indicate that the trial was full and fair. In contrast to the preliminary judicial investigation in July preceding, it was less strictly secret; in addition to the twenty-two defendants, more than a hundred witnesses, several soldiers and the judicial officials themselves, a small select "public" was admitted into the crowded, stuffy little court room. Several times the Judge had to suspend the session for five minutes to open the windows for fresh air. Twice he had to instruct feeble-voiced persons, "Speak louder! Because this is a public proceeding, and the rest, as well as I, want to hear what you say." [4] The report of the trial also throws much valuable light on the dark preparations within Serbia which culminated in the assassination. Yet few persons outside Germany appear ever to have given it any serious attention. This is partly because, at the time of its publication in 1918, Germany was cut off from communication with much of the world; and it is partly because war hatred and moral blindness condemned it in advance as another German

only the part of the record concerning the leading prisoners. A condensed summary of the whole trial, including some portions omitted by Pharos, was published anonymously at Berne in 1917: *Serajevo; La Conspiration Serbe contre la Monarchie Austro-Hongroise,* pp. 62-150. Mr. Seton-Watson gives no proof of his assertion (*Sarajevo,* p. 295) that these versions are "very incomplete and unreliable," and that they "were published by the Austro-Hungarian Government." A carbon copy of the original stenographic report is said (according to the Vienna paper, *Der Tag,* No. 84, April 7, 1925) to have come into the hands of the editor of the Sarajevo newspaper, *Vetchernje Posta* (Evening Post), and to have been placed by him at the disposal of the Jugoslav Government. It is significant that the Jugoslav authorities have been unable to extract from it anything for their own exculpation, or to publish a single word of evidence beyond what is contained in the two volumes just mentioned. Brief extracts, to be sure, were published by Mr. P. Slijepchevitch (*Nova Evropa,* June, 1925) and reprinted in translation by Mr. Seton-Watson in *The Slavonic Review,* IV, 645-656, March, 1926. There are significant (but unindicated) omissions in these extracts. Their aim is to conceal references to Serbia and to emphasize the idea that the murderers did not receive external prompting from Serbia, but were crude Bosnian fanatics, attempting to bring about Jugoslav unity.

[4] Pharos, pp. 120, 144, and photographs of court, defendants, exhibits, etc.

"falsification" or "piece of propaganda." Even so distinguished a historian as Sir Charles Oman thought "the whole evidence is falsified. . . . The record of the trial has been so much tampered with that no confidence can be placed in any word of it." [5] Yet the fact is, as we shall see below, that Austria's charges against Serbia in 1914, confirmed by the evidence at the trial, are really an understatement, rather than an overstatement, of Serbia's responsibility. So, for nearly a decade, the truth about the Sarajevo plot remained mysterious and unknown. The Austrian evidence was neglected, discredited, or ridiculed. Serbian writers, on the other hand, were careful to publish nothing in conflict with the attitude of injured innocence which their Government had assumed in 1914.

RECENT REVELATIONS

Within the last five years, however, there have come numerous Serb revelations, whose authors appear to be moved by various motives: simply to tell the truth and see that justice shall replace injustice; to play party politics; or, strangely enough, to claim the doubtful honor of being among those who planned the murder of the Archduke, which ultimately resulted in the establishment of the glorious Jugoslav Kingdom.

The first of these revelations to attract attention beyond the frontiers of Serbia [6] came from the pen of a well-known professor of history at Belgrade, Stanoje Stanojevitch.[7] He

[5] C. Oman, *The Outbreak of the War of 1914-1918*, London, 1919, p. 9.

[6] Among well-informed Serbians themselves it has long been an open secret that higher Serbian officials than those charged in the Austrian ultimatum shared in the preparation of the plot to murder Franz Ferdinand; see below the discussion of the "Black Hand" and the Salonica Trial of 1917.

[7] S. Stanojevitch, *Ubistvo Austriskog Prestolonaslednika Ferdinanda* [The Murder of the Austrian Heir to the Throne Ferdinand], Belgrade, 1923; German trans. by H. Wendel, *Die Ermordung des Erzherzogs Franz Ferdinand*, Frankfurt, 1923; summarized in English by M. Edith Durham, *The Serajevo Crime*, pp. 96-117. Stanojevitch's statements, though not

gives no references to his authorities, but, according to his preface, gathered much of his information at first hand from surviving Serbian conspirators with whom he was personally acquainted. In seeking to minimize the responsibility of the *Narodna Odbrana* (National Defense), and thus to discredit the Austrian version of the plot, he throws the blame on the leader of a less well-known secret Serbian revolutionary society, *Ujedinjenje ili Smrt* (Union or Death), commonly known as the "Black Hand." This was composed of a powerful clique of military officers who had plotted and carried out the murder of King Alexander and Queen Draga in 1903, and had since then played a sinister rôle in Serbian domestic politics and foreign relations. Its organizer, and its leader and moving spirit in 1914, was no less a person than the Chief of the Intelligence Department [including spy service] of the Serbian General Staff, Col. Dragutin Dimitrijevitch. Of this remarkable arch-plotter, who was put to death by the Pashitch Party in 1917, but who has become a hero in the eyes of a large part of the Serbian people, Professor Stanojevitch gives the following edifying picture:

> Gifted, cultured, personally brave, honest; full of ambition, energy, and willingness to work; and a convincing talker, Dragutin Dimitrijevitch had an extraordinary influence on those about him, especially on his companions and the younger officers, who were altogether inferior to him in feeling and character. He had the qualities which fascinate men [in Serbia]. His reasoning was always thorough and convincing; he understood how to make the worst deeds appear trifles, and the most dangerous schemes innocent and harmless. At the same time, he was in every respect a splendid organizer; he always kept everything in his own hands, and even his most intimate friends knew

free from inaccuracies, are in large part supported by the pro-Serb German writer, H. Wendel, *Die Habsburger und die Südslawenfrage,* Belgrade-Leipzig, 1924.

only what was on foot at the moment. But Dragutin Dimitrijevitch was also extraordinarily conceited and quite affected. Being very ambitious, he loved secret activity. He loved also that men should know that he was engaged in this secret activity, and kept everything in his own hands. Doubts about what was possible or impossible, or about the reciprocal relation of power and responsibility, never troubled him. He had no clear conception of political life and its limitations. He saw only the goal immediately before his eyes, and went straight at it, without hesitation and regardless of consequences. He loved danger, adventure, secret trystings, and mysterious doings. . . .

Restless and adventuresome, he was always planning conspiracies and assassinations. In 1903 he had been one of the chief organizers of the plot against King Alexander. In 1911 he sent someone to murder the Austrian Emperor or Heir to the Throne. In February, 1914, in concert with a secret Bulgarian revolutionary committee, he agreed upon the murder of King Ferdinand of Bulgaria. In 1914 he took over and organized the [Sarajevo] plot against the Austrian Heir to the Throne [Franz Ferdinand]. In 1916 he sent someone from Corfu to murder King Constantine of Greece. And in the same year he was apparently seeking to have dealings with the enemy, and organized a plot against the then heir to the Serbian throne, Prince Alexander. For this reason he was condemned to death and shot at Salonica in June, 1917.[8]

Stanojevitch goes on to describe in detail how this Serbian General Staff officer helped organize the plot in

[8] Stanojevitch (German ed.), pp. 50-51. This is the orthodox Pashitch version of the Salonica affair. There is some reason to believe, however, that this alleged plot against Prince Alexander was in part a mere pretext, trumped up as a convenient means of getting rid of a powerful political opponent. Another reason for closing his mouth forever may very probably have been the fear on the part of the Pashitch Party that he might reveal to the world the truth about his own part in the murder-plot which gave rise to the World War, and thus reveal the Serbian Government's own guilty knowledge of that plot. On the Salonica Trial, see below, notes 32, 33.

Belgrade and provide the Bosnian youths with the bombs and Browning revolvers actually used at Sarajevo. He gives a naïve motive for Dimitrijevitch's crime: when Dimitrijevitch heard, in addition to other rumors, that the Austrian Archduke was coming to hold manoeuvres in Bosnia, "he was thoroughly convinced that Austria-Hungary intended to carry out an attack upon Serbia," and, "after long consideration, came to the conclusion that the attack on Serbia and war itself could only be prevented by killing Franz Ferdinand."[9]

Some months after Stanojevitch made these admissions, which went far beyond the Austrian charges of 1914, a Jugoslav journalist, Borivoje Jevtitch, came forward with an interesting pamphlet.[10] It explains the rise of the new terrorist movement, with its fanatical "cult of assassination," which developed among the Bosnian youth in the decade before the War. It minimizes the influence of Serbia, and throws light mainly on the execution of the plot in Sarajevo, rather than on its preparation in Belgrade. Jevtitch had been one of the witnesses at the trial of the murderers in 1914. At that time he admitted frankly that he was a contributor to such Sarajevo newspapers as *Srpska Rijetch* (The Serbian Word) and *Narod* (Nation), and also that he was a member of the *Srpska Omladina* (Serbian Youth), an association devoted to fostering Serb nationalism in Bosnia. He even admitted having corresponded intermittently with the principal assassins, but stoutly denied that he knew anything of the plot to murder the Archduke, and managed to appear innocent. Such was

9 Stanojevitch, 55.

10 Jevtitch, *Sarajevski Atentat*, Sarajevo, 1924; some of his conclusions are summarized by Albert Mousset, "L'Attentat de Sarajevo," in *Revue d'Histoire Diplomatique*, XXXI, 44-68, 1925; in the Paris *Figaro*, May 23, 1924; and in the New York *Times*, June 22, 1924, E, p. 5. The first seven chapters are published in German translation in KSF, III, 657-686, Oct., 1925.

his testimony in 1914.[11]   But in 1924, when his life was no longer in jeopardy at the hands of the Austrian police, and when his hopes for Jugoslav unity had been realized as a result of the assassination and the World War, he declared that he knew all about the plot.   He even gives a vivid description of how he spent Saturday night, the eve of the crime, in company with Princip, who fired the fatal shots next morning.   He claims that there were no fewer than ten ambuscades for the Archduke; that, if Franz Ferdinand had escaped Princip's bullet as he did Chabrinovitch's bomb, so many others were prepared to slay him that he could scarcely have left Sarajevo alive.

The most sensational revelation, important because made by a distinguished Serbian official who was Minister of Education in the Pashitch Cabinet in July, 1914, is that of M. Ljuba Jovanovitch.   To celebrate the tenth anniversary of the outbreak of the World War, there was published in the summer of 1924, under the editorship of a Russian, a book of short articles by leading Serbians under the title, "The Blood of Slavdom." [12]   The opening article, "After Vidov Dan, 1914," is by M. Jovanovitch.   In it he suddenly lets the cat out of the bag in the most extraordinary fashion.   The very thing that M. Pashitch and the Serbian Government had been concealing for years, he admits in the most matter-of-fact way:

[11] *La Conspiration Serbe*, p. 133; Mousset, p. 59 f.

[12] *Krv Slovenstva*, Belgrade, 1924.   Mr. Jovanovitch's article is of such importance that it has several times been reprinted in English translation; in the *Journal of the Institute of International Affairs* for March, 1925; in the *National Review* for April, 1925; and in *The Living Age*, May 9, 1925.   English attention was first called to it by the Balkan traveller and specialist, M. Edith Durham, in an address before the British Institute of International Affairs in Dec., 1924, and in an article, "Fresh Light on the Crime of Serajevo," in the *Contemporary Review*, 1-11, Jan., 1925, which is reprinted in *The Living Age*, March 7, 1925, pp. 532-539.   She discusses it at length in her recent volume, *The Serajevo Crime*, pp. 127-147.   "Vidov Dan" (St. Vitus' Day), June 28, was the anniversary of the Battle of Kossovo in 1389 A. D. and a national Serb festival: it was also the day of the Archduke's assassination.

At the outbreak of the World War I was Minister of Education in M. Nikola Pashitch's Cabinet. I have recently written down some of my recollections and some notes on the events of those days. For the present occasion I have chosen from them a few extracts, because the time is not yet come for everything to be disclosed.

I do not remember whether it was at the end of May or the beginning of June, when one day M. Pashitch said to us (he conferred on these matters more particularly with Stojan Protitch, who was then Minister of the Interior; but this much he said to the rest of us) that certain persons [neki] were making ready to go to Sarajevo to murder Franz Ferdinand who was to go there to be solemnly received on St. Vitus' Day. As they told me afterwards, this plot was hatched by a group of secretly organized persons and by patriotic Bosno-Herzegovinian students in Belgrade. M. Pashitch and the rest of us said, and Stojan agreed, that he should issue instructions to the frontier authorities on the Drina to prevent the crossing over of the youths who had already set out from Belgrade for that purpose. But the frontier "authorities" themselves belonged to the organization, and did not carry out Stojan's instructions, but reported to him (as he afterwards told us) that the instructions had reached them too late, because the youths had already crossed over.[13]

From this it appears that members of the Serbian Cabinet knew of the plot a month or so before the murder took place, but took no effective measures to prevent it. The Serbian Government was thus criminally negligent, to say the least. Not having nipped in the bud the plot prepared

[13] *Krv Slovenstva*, p. 9 f. In an explanatory letter in the *Novi Zivot* (New Life) and the Belgrade *Politika* of March 28, 1925, Jovanovitch makes it clear that by this phrase he meant the "Black Hand": [upon the news of the Austrian annexation proclamation in 1908] "private initiative founded the association *Narodna Odbrana,* and other elements, which were irreconcilably dissatisfied with the activity of official Serbia, later founded, under the name *Ujedinjenje ili Smrt* ['Union or Death,' commonly known as the 'Black Hand'] that 'group of secretly organized persons' which I mentioned in my article."

in their capital by one of their own General Staff officers, and not having prevented the youths from crossing over into Bosnia, either because Protitch did not give his instructions in time, or more probably, because "the frontier 'authorities' themselves belonged to the organization" of the "Black Hand," the Serbian Government should at once have notified the Austrian authorities, giving the names of the criminals and all other details which might have led to their arrest before their execution of the plot. But M. Pashitch and his Cabinet did nothing of the kind. Furthermore, after the crime had been committed, they should have made a searching inquiry into the incriminated secret organizations in Serbia, and arrested all the accomplices who had helped hatch or carry out the plot. Instead, as we shall see, they sought to conceal every trace of it, and denied all knowledge of it, in the hope that Austria would be unable to discover their complicity. No wonder that M. Jovanovitch, with his guilty conscience, was "overwhelmed with grave anxiety," when he heard the fatal news at his country house on Sunday afternoon, June 28. It was not regret for the crime, but fear of its consequences, which filled him with "terrible thoughts":

About 5 P.M. an official from the Press Bureau rang me up on the telephone and told me what had happened that morning at Sarajevo. Although I knew what was being prepared there, yet, as I held the receiver, I felt as though someone had dealt me an unexpected blow; and a little later, when the first news was confirmed from other quarters, I began to be overwhelmed with grave anxiety.

I did not doubt for a moment that Austria-Hungary would make this the occasion for a war on Serbia. I saw that the position of our Government and our country in regard to the other Powers would now become very difficult, in every way worse than after May 29, 1903 [N. S. June 11, the date of King Alexander's assassination], or than at the time of our later conflicts with Vienna and Budapest. I

was afraid that all the European Courts would feel themselves the targets of Princip's bullets, and would turn away
from us, with the approval of the monarchist and conservative elements in their countries. And even if it did
not come to that, who would dare to defend us? I knew
that neither France, nor, still less, Russia, was in a position
to match herself with Germany and her ally on the Danube,
because their preparations were not to be complete until
1917. This especially filled me with anxiety and fear.

The most terrible thoughts crowded in upon me. This
began at 5 P.M. on the Sunday of *Vidov Dan*, and continued day and night, except during a few fitful moments of
sleep, until Tuesday forenoon. Then there came to see me
a young friend, Major N—— (in the Ministry of Education). He was uneasy, but not in despair as I was. I
poured out to him my apprehensions without restraint or
reflection. He at once said to me, in the tone usual to him
on such occasions, that is to say, pleasantly and quietly,
but with real inspiration: "My dear Minister, I think it
is quite unnecessary to despair. Let Austria-Hungary
attack us! It must come to that sooner or later. The
present is a very inconvenient moment for us for settling
the account. But it is not now in our power to choose the
moment. And if Austria chooses it,—well, so let it be! It
may possibly end badly for us, but who knows? It may
also be otherwise!" [14]

These words· of Major N——, which suggest that the
Serbian military circles did not take so gloomy a view, but
felt sure, or speedily received assurances, of Russian protection, "quite pulled me together," M. Jovanovitch continues; "Happily, from the St. Petersburg Press—and so
far as it was concerned we could assume in advance that
it represented the Government view—we received the first
favorable reports; it began to take up our defense against
the Austro-Hungarian accusations. Russia would not deny
us nor withdraw her hand from us. After Russia would

[14] *Krv Slovenstva,* p. 11.

come her friends. And so it was." M. Jovanovitch therefore braced himself to the idea of an attack on Serbia and a European War. He noted as favorable circumstances the anti-Serb "pogroms" in Bosnia and the violence of the Austrian Press, which would turn European opinion against Austria. His colleagues, however, believed that war could be avoided. In the expectation "that Vienna would be unsuccessful in establishing any connection between official Serbia and the deed on the Miljacka" [the river flowing through Sarajevo near which the Archduke was murdered], it was decided to conceal everything, to pose as unconcerned and innocent, to make a demonstration of sorrow, and to try to get off as cheaply as possible in giving satisfaction to the country whose royal couple had been murdered:

M. Pashitch therefore hoped that we should somehow pull ourselves through this crisis, and he made efforts, in which all the rest of us supported him, to preserve as far as possible the relations which we had so far established, in order that Serbia might get off as cheaply as possible with the unhappy task of giving satisfaction to Austria-Hungary, and that she might recover as quickly as possible from the blows which in such an affair were bound in any case to fall upon her.

As is well known, the Government did not fail to do all it could to show their friends and the rest of the world how far removed we were from the Sarajevo conspirators. Thus, on the very same evening upon which it was known what Princip had done, Stojan gave orders that the Belgrade police should forbid all music, singing, and merry-making in public places; everything was suspended, and something like official mourning began. M. Pashitch expressed to the Vienna Government our regret at the loss which a great neighboring Power had suffered and his execration at the deed itself. At the Requiem in the Catholic Church of the Legation on June 20 [July 3], on the day when the funeral of the murdered Heir to the Throne and his wife took place in Vienna, the Government was represented by several Ministers. I, too, was among them. I wished to show that even I, who more than any of the others might have been thought to have approved of Princip's deed,[15] was on the contrary entirely in agreement with what our Cabinet were doing. Nevertheless, this occasion and the short stay in the church were unpleasant to me. I felt myself among enemies, who did not desire peace with us.[16]

What a study in the psychology of the guilty conscience! Knowing of the plot a month beforehand, doing nothing effective to forestall it, terrified at first that Serbia will be isolated and attacked, then hopeful that the truth could be concealed, the Minister of Education goes to church in pretended mourning for the murdered victim for the sake of the good impression it will make. No wonder he felt "unpleasant"!

Many more interesting details of these tragic days M. Ljuba Jovanovitch gives in his recent revelations, but they are too long to reprint here. So far as the present writer is able to judge them in the light of other evidence, the Minister's account is substantially accurate and trustworthy —in fact remarkably so, when compared with the memoirs of other politicians written ten years after the events. To persons not blinded by prejudice or propaganda, it will not come as such a total surprise that the serious historian can no longer maintain the theory that the war-guilt was all on the side of Austria, and that Serbia was an innocent victim. But among many Serbians and champions of Serbia, M. Jovanovitch's revelations have roused mixed feelings of surprise and sorrow, indignation and incredulity. M. Mousset, who passes for a leading French authority on Serbia, still writes in 1925: "Without doubt certain diplo-

15 M. Jovanovitch was one of the founders and active members of the *Narodna Odbrana,* and, in a paragraph which we have omitted, tells of his personal acquaintance with Princip at Belgrade.

16 *Krv Slovenstva,* p. 15.

matic archives [he does not name them] have been opened.
They have made it possible to wash the Belgrade Government of the charge of complicity which Austria, without
herself giving it much credence, brought against it." [17]

A more thorough English scholar and prolific writer on
the Balkans, and long a stout champion of the Jugoslavs,
Mr. R. W. Seton-Watson, has been much disturbed at M.
Jovanovitch's revelations, but cannot bring himself to
accept them as trustworthy and literally true. In 1925 he
declared: "The whole article [of Jovanovitch] is written
in a careless, naïve and reminiscent vein, and its author
seems to be blissfully unaware how damning are his admissions if they are to be taken literally. . . . There thus rests
upon Belgrade the onus of proving, either that the information at its disposal was much more vague than Ljuba
Jovanovitch would have us believe, or that it conveyed an
adequate warning of the danger in some way of which no
record has yet reached us. The matter can hardly rest
here. Public opinion in Europe and America is more interested than ever in the problem of responsibility for the
Great War, and is entitled to demand a full and detailed
explanation from Ljuba Jovanovitch and from his chief, M.
Pashitch." [18]   A little later Mr. Seton-Watson went in
person to Serbia to demand this explanation—to make M.
Jovanovitch eat his words on the spot or explain them away

[17] "L'Attentat de Sarajevo," in *Revue d'Histoire Diplomatique*, **XXXI**,
p. 44. M. Alfred Mousset is the author of *Le Royaume des Serbs,
Croates, et Slovenes*, Paris, 1921 (Bossard).

[18] *Foreign Affairs* (N.Y.), III, 507-9, April, 1925; *cf.* also Mr. Seton-
Watson's recent volume, *Sarajevo* (London, 1926), pp. 153-159. In articles
in the London *Times* of Feb. 16, 1925, the *Post* of April 7, the Zagreb
Obzor of April 12 and May 13, and the Belgrade *Politika* of April 13,
Mr. Seton-Watson admitted the seriousness of Ljuba Jovanovitch's statements for Serbia's good name, but still refused to believe they were to
be taken literally at their face value; see the quotations and comments
by A. von Wegerer, "Der ungläubige Seton-Watson," in K.SF, III, 287-
292, May, 1925; and "Der Anlass zum Weltkrieg," *ibid.*, 394-395, June,
1925.

in some fashion if possible, or failing in that to force the Serbian Government to clear its reputation by making a clean breast of all it knew about the plot in 1914. But he appears to have succeeded in neither the one effort nor the other, judging by a justly impatient open letter which was published in the Zagreb *Obzor* (Observer) of May 13, 1925:

> It is now more than two months since I requested the Belgrade Government to clear up those statements which Mr. Ljuba Jovanovitch made some time ago in the pamphlet, *Krv Slovenstva*, concerning the Sarajevo murder. But I have never yet received any answer. . . .
>
> A few weeks ago, to be sure, Ljuba Jovanovitch published some articles on responsibility for the war, but in them he evades the main issue and accuses me of an incorrect reproduction of his former statements. [Mr. Seton-Watson therefore put the two concrete questions, "Does Ljuba Jovanovitch stand by his statement, that *at the end of May or the beginning of June . . . one day M. Pashitch said . . . that certain persons were making ready to go to Sarajevo to murder Franz Ferdinand?*" And, second, "Does he actually mean it, when he says, in describing how he received the telephone news of the murder at Sarajevo, *although I knew what was being prepared there?*"]
>
> I can understand very well Mr. Ljuba Jovanovitch's hesitation in giving a downright answer. If he denies it, one must wonder how a responsible statesman could write in so frivolous a fashion. And if he admits it, then his colleague and Minister-President at the time, Mr. Pashitch, is placed under the unpleasant duty of speaking out clearly and frankly, and setting forth the facts in their true light.[19]

To this strong and clear letter of Mr. Seton-Watson's, M. Pashitch and the Serbian Government made no answer. The Belgrade Press, however, announced that the Jugoslav Government had decided to publish a new *Blue Book* on

[19] Zagreb *Obzor*, No. 126, May 13, 1925; *cf.* KSF, III, 394 f., June, 1925.

the origins of the War. Mr. Seton-Watson then wrote a second letter to the London *Times,* begging its readers to suspend judgment until these documents could appear. But, as he has to admit in his recent volume,

> Eight months have passed, and nothing more has been heard of the *Blue Book;* and it seems probable that the announcement was merely tactical, intended to appease the critics until the whole agitation should die down. Unfortunately the Jugoslav Government, instead of demonstrating its innocence by a detailed statement of the facts, shrouded itself in mystery.[20]

M. Ljuba Jovanovitch's revelations attracted at first little attention in Serbia, where well-informed persons apparently saw in them nothing really new. Neither M. Pashitch nor anyone else thought of taking him to task for them. He was elected President of the Serbian Skupshtina, President of the Election Committee, and President of the Legislative Committee. But when it was learned how great attention was being given to them in England and America, where people began to wake up to the extent of Serbia's responsibility for the War, some Serbian newspapers began to attack M. Jovanovitch as a liar and a traitor. In self-defense, he wrote a series of long articles in the magazine *Novi Zivot* (New Life) setting forth and justifying his part in Serbian history for more than thirty years, from the time he first came to Belgrade in 1881 as an emigré from Herzegovina.[21] "I have made no revelations," he said, "the way people are now trying to make out. I only wrote what was essentially already known to everyone in 1914." [22] This may have been true enough as regards Serbia, which was well acquainted with the do-

[20] Seton-Watson, *Sarajevo,* p. 156.

[21] *Cf.* the Belgrade *Politika,* March 22, 29; April 6, 12, 17, 1925; and KSF, III, 211-220, 270-287, April, May, 1925.

[22] Interview in the *Politika,* April 17, 1925; KSF, III, 395, June, 1925.

ings of the "Black Hand" and its powerful leader, Dimitrije-vitch, but it was not true of the Entente countries which had been taught to believe in Serbia's innocence.

But Mr. Seton-Watson, in spite of the stony silence of M. Pashitch and the Government, the non-appearance of any new *Blue Book,* and M. Jovanovitch's explanatory articles, still cannot bring himself to believe in the truth of M. Jovanovitch's revelations which we have quoted above. He devotes an appendix of several pages to them, conclud-ing that "Mr. Jovanovitch, for reasons of his own, has misrepresented the true facts, and his former colleagues, for reasons of their own, have refrained from giving him the lie publicly." His line of argument is that Jovanovitch "is one of those politicians who like to exaggerate their own importance"; that in the struggle for increased political influence "he was making a bid for the support of the Bosnian youth by showing that the Belgrade Government had sympathized with the revolutionary movement," and "probably hoped to strengthen his own position in the Radical Party, as against those whose outlook is more nar-rowly identified with the old Serbian Kingdom"; that he feels on the defensive on account of the part he took in the Salonica Trial; and that M. Pashitch has made no pub-lic denial, because "he has always shown an astonishing indifference to public opinion, especially to foreign public opinion." [23]

The question of M. Jovanovitch's veracity, however, roused a storm of passionate discussion in the Serbian Press, where it is mixed up with questions of party politics and leadership. Some Serbian leaders demanded that M. Pashitch speak out and deny the truth of M. Jovanovitch's revelations. On February 26, 1926, M. Jovan Jovanovitch,

[23] *Sarajevo,* pp. 156-159. These hypotheses have been subjected to severe criticism by A. von Wegerer in KSF, IV, 767-785, Oct., 1926. See also above, note 18.

of the Peasant Party and former Serbian Minister in
Vienna, at a meeting of the Budget Commission of the
Skupshtina, called attention to the injury done to Serbia's
reputation in Entente countries by the fact that Ljuba
Jovanovitch's revelations were being widely circulated and
received no official contradiction. He therefore earnestly
begged M. Pashitch, in the interests of Serbia's good name,
to speak out, lest otherwise Serbia should suffer eventually
in the matter of foreign credits and Reparation Payments.[24]

Others, like Professor Jelenitch, formerly private secretary of Crown Prince Alexander, bitterly denounced Ljuba
Jovanovitch as a traitor to Serbia and his revelations as
"a lie, a most perfidious, Levantine lie." He went on with
a fantastic development of Mr. Wickham Steed's legend
that the assassination was the work of Austro-Hungarian
authorities. His assertion that the deed was prepared in
Berlin, developed at Konopischt, and "carried out through
the coöperation of the Vienna and Budapest Camarilla with
the 'Black Hand' in Belgrade" is so naïve and preposterous
that it hardly needs comment. The notion that it was
developed at Konopischt is tantamount to saying that
Franz Ferdinand plotted his own assassination. M. Jelenitch appealed to Pashitch and the other surviving members
of his Cabinet of 1914 to denounce Ljuba Jovanovitch.[25]

It is interesting to observe that Professor Jelenitch has
not the slightest doubt that the "Black Hand" had an
important part in the assassination plot, though he denies
that M. Pashitch knew of it. But his insinuation that the
"Black Hand" had coöperated with the hated Vienna
authorities in the assassination instantly brought forth an

[24] Cf. KSF, IV, 260 ff., 343 ff.
[25] Cf. the Belgrade Politika, March 26, 1926; and KSF, IV, 345,
400-403. On Mr. Wickham Steed's legend, see above, pp. 32-43, "The
Konopischt Meeting: Legend and Fact." It is naturally a favorite theme
with Serbian writers and was again set forth in 1926 by Dr. Leo Pfeffer,
of Sarajevo, and by others (cf. KSF, IV, 661, 722).

indignant denial from two surviving "Black Hand" members, Milan G. Milanovitch and C. A. Popovitch. They declared that they would be glad to see Jelenitch's alleged proofs of his assertions; "then we also shall produce all that we know about the Sarajevo murder, on the basis of facts at our disposal. The attack upon our dead companions whose patriotism has hitherto never been challenged in circles of earnest and impartial men releases us, in our opinion, for the future, from all considerations by which we have hitherto been bound." [26]

This press campaign rose to such a pitch that finally, at a committee meeting of the Radical Club on April 25, 1926, M. Pashitch spoke out against Ljuba Jovanovitch and tried to drive his former friend and colleague out of the party. According to the report of this speech in his party newspaper, he said,

> Foreign correspondents had asked him whether he had known that the Austrian Heir to the Throne would be murdered. He repudiated the idea. He had begged M. Jovanovitch to contradict it, because it was not true that he [M. Pashitch] had said this in a Cabinet Meeting. . . . M. Pashitch had waited for M. Jovanovitch's denial. M. Jovanovitch had delayed to make one, and had not made one. M. Pashitch repeated and maintained that he had not said what M. Jovanovitch ascribed to him [in the pamphlet *Krv Slovenstva*]. He also asked his ministerial colleagues: "Friends, have I perhaps not forgotten that I said that?" They all confirmed the fact that he had really not.
>
> It has not been contradicted, and now this question is alive. I must contradict it. Why M. Ljuba Jovanovitch said it, I do not know. But he said what was not true. . . . I have given evidence that I can keep still, but if Ljuba Jovanovitch wants to act independently, let him separate

[26] *Politika*, March 31, 1926; KSF, IV, 406. For a summary of many other articles, see *ibid.*, 403-408.

himself from us and work independently. That is a mistake of M. Jovanovitch's which cannot be pardoned.[27]

In reply to this attack, M. Ljuba Jovanovitch declared that he had never said in his pamphlet that M. Pashitch had given certain information in regard to the preparation of the assassination *at a Cabinet Meeting*. It was *in a private conversation*. To substantiate the truth of what he had written, he offered to bring forward documents and proofs, but demanded that the Prime Minister and Minister of Foreign Affairs assume the responsibility for his doing so. Thereupon these two responsible Ministers, MM. Uzunovitch and Nintitch, refused his offer, apparently in fear lest he might reveal more unpalatable secrets concerning the Serbian Government of 1914 and the origin of the World War.[28]

Many Serb newspapers at once proclaimed that at last M. Pashitch had spoken out and denied the truth of the charges, but on examining his carefully phrased statement it appeared that he denied a charge which had not been made. He denied that he had given the information about the assassins *in a Cabinet Meeting*, which M. Jovanovitch had never asserted.[29] As will be pointed out below, and as M. Jovanovitch had indicated in one of his articles in 1925, the truth of his assertion that M. Pashitch knew of the plot beforehand is indicated, among other things, by the fact that an order was actually given to stop the assassins from crossing over from Belgrade into Bosnia, but the order was not carried out because the Serbian frontier guards belonged to the "Black Hand" organization and did not obey the order. This is confirmed by the diary and papers of the

[27] Belgrade *Politika*, April 26, 1926, KSF, IV, 408-9.
[28] Belgrade *Politika*, April 26, 1926; *Obzor*, April 27, 1926; *cf.* KSF, IV, 408-413, 780-783; and the New York *Times*, April 30, 1926.
[29] See Jovanovitch's own words, quoted above at note 12.

frontier guard, Todorovitch, which the Austrians captured during the War.

One may conclude, therefore, that there is no good reason to doubt the accuracy of M. Ljuba Jovanovitch's revelations of 1924. Mr. Seton-Watson's argument, that they were written in a "careless, naïve, reminiscent vein," is really an argument in favor of their genuineness. M. Jovanovitch evidently made no effort to elaborate them carefully as a political pamphlet to gain adherents or to show his own personal importance. As he explained in 1925, he had promised in the spring of 1924 to M. Ksjunjin, a Russian journalist and emigré, that he would write an article for a pamphlet on the tenth anniversary of the outbreak of the World War. Occupied with other matters, he did not write the article at once. Some months later, being asked for it and not wishing to disappoint M. Ksjunjin, he took some material from a manuscript of recollections and notes which he had already written down.[30] The fact that the MM. Uzunovitch and Nintitch intervened to prevent M. Jovanovitch from bringing forward his proofs, and that the "Black Hand" survivors also threatened to make revelations, seems to indicate that there are things which the Serbian Government still prefers to conceal. Until M. Jovanovitch's revelations are definitely proved to be untrue, impartial historians will conclude that M. Pashitch and members of the Serbian Government had a guilty knowledge of a murder plot, but concealed it, in oblivion of the fact that "murder will out."

Another series of revelations, said to be contained in some 2,000 documents which were seized by the Austrians in Belgrade during the War, relates to the propagandist and revolutionary activities of the Serbian nationalist organizations known as the *Narodna Odbrana* and the "Black Hand." Many of these documents were found in the houses

[30] *Politika*, March 25, 1925; KSF, III, 213; IV, 768.

of M. Pashitch and Milo Pavlovitch, a leading member of the *Narodna Odbrana*. They contain lists of "serviceable people," Bosnian editors, students and spies, and the amounts of money with which they were subsidized from Belgrade.[31]

Much new information concerning the "Black Hand" has also recently been brought to light by a careful examination of the official record of the famous Salonica Trial of 1917.[32] This thick volume, published officially in Salonica in 1918, was later withdrawn from circulation and suppressed so far as possible, apparently because it contained so much material damaging to the reputation of the Serbian Government of 1914. It is now almost impossible to get a copy. But it has been studied by students of Serbian affairs and the causes of the War, and is found to contain a great deal of information about the activities of the "Black Hand" before 1914, and about those of its members who participated in the plot to assassinate the Archduke Franz Ferdinand.[33]

[31] *Cf.* M. Edith Durham, in *Current History*, XXV, 661 f., Feb., 1927.

[32] *Tajna Prevratna Organisacija: Izvestaj sa pretresa u vojnom sudu zu offizire u Solunu, po beleskama vodjenim na samom pretresu.* Solun Stamparija "Velika Srbija," 1918 (A Secret Revolutionary Organization: Report of the Trial at the Court Martial of Officers at Salonica, from Notes Taken at the Trial Itself. Salonica Press "Great Serbia," 1918, pp. 638). Mr. Seton-Watson (*Sarajevo*, p. 295) incorrectly translates the title of this "strange book" as a secret "pre-war," instead of a secret "revolutionary," organization.

[33] *Cf.* M. Bogitchevitch's numerous articles: "Bemerkungen zum Saloniki Prozess, 1917," in KSF, II, 112-113; "Weitere Einzelheiten über das Attentat von Sarajevo," in KSF, III, 15-21, 437-444, Jan. and July, 1925; "Nouvelles dépositions concernant l'attentat de Sarajevo," in KSF, IV, 21-28, 87-95, Jan.-Feb., 1926; "La Société 'Union ou Mort' dite la 'Main Noire,'" in the French periodical *Evolution*, No. 7, 16-30, July 15, 1926, and in German and English trans. in KSF, IV, 664-689, Sept., 1926; M. Bogitchevitch has now collected much of this material and other new information on the "Black Hand" and Salonica Trial in his recent volume, *Le Procès de Salonique, juin, 1917* (Paris, 1927). See also M. Edith Durham, *The Serajevo Crime*, London, 1925, pp. 44-74, 158-201; "The Serajevo Murder Plot," in *Current History*, XXV, 656-662, Feb., 1927; S. B. Fay, "The Black Hand Plot that led to the World War," in

On the basis of this material, we may now outline briefly the main threads of the assassination plot, and the three factors which largely contributed to it: the *Narodna Odbrana*, the "Black Hand," and the revolutionary movement in Bosnia.

THE *NARODNA ODBRANA*

In the 'sixties and 'seventies of the nineteenth century many Serbian revolutionaries gathered in Switzerland and came under the influence of Russians like Bakunin, Kropotkin, and Herzen. They adopted a revolutionary program which was to be brought about by anarchist deeds of violence and terrorism. They were responsible for the Zajecar revolt against King Milan in Serbia in 1883. Their tendency toward revolution by violence and assassination has continued to exert an influence over a certain group of Serbs ever since. But not all the young Serbians studying in Switzerland adopted these views completely. Among the latter was M. Nikola Pashitch. He believed in the gradual building up of the moral and material forces of Serbia as a means for the eventual liberation and union of all Serbs

Current History, XXIII, 196-207, Nov., 1925; and Dr. Wiesner in KSF, VI, 362-395, April, 1928.

Some information on the "Black Hand" may also be found in the following: *Carnegie Report of the International Commission to Inquire into the Causes and Conduct of the Balkan Wars.* Washington, 1914, pp. 169 ff.; D. R. Lazarevitch, *Die Schwarze Hand.* Lausanne, 1917; Seton-Watson, "Serbia's Choice," in *The New Europe*, Aug. 22, 1918; *Sarajevo*, pp. 143, 158, 295; Pharos, pp. 14 f., 81 f.; Stanojevitch, pp. 49-56; Wendel, pp. 48-62; A. von Wegerer, "Der Anlass zum Weltkrieg," in KSF, III, 353-405, June, 1925; "Neue Ausschnitte zum Attentat von Sarajewo," in KSF, IV, 400-414, June, 1926; L. Mandl, "Ein düstere Gedenktag," in the Vienna *Neues 8 Uhr-Blatt*, Nos. 2906-2909, June 27-July 1, 1924; N. Nenadovitch, "Les secrets de la camarilla de Belgrade," in *La Fédération Balkanique*, Dec. 1, 1924; the articles by M. Vladimirov, N. Mermet, and V. Nikolitch, *ibid.*, May 31, 1925, and by N. Obarov, *ibid.*, July 15, 1925; and the statements of Colonel Bojin Simitch printed by Victor Serge in the Paris Periodical, *Clarté*, No. 74, May, 1925. The statements made at the Salonica Trial and by "Black Hand" members later, however, are often contradictory and inspired with animus against M. Pashitch. and must therefore be used with great caution.

in a powerful state, after the manner in which Italy had accomplished her unification in the generation immediately preceding. Serbia should be "the Piedmont of the Balkans." With this aim in view, M. Pashitch founded in Serbia in 1881 the Radical Party, which under his venerable leadership long preserved its original name, though in character it is today the very opposite of radical.

The program of the Radical Party, as stated in the first issue of its organ, *Samouprava*, on January 8, 1881, was: "The people's welfare and freedom at home, and the country's independence and unification with the other parts of Serbdom abroad." A special section was devoted to the importance of organizing and training the Serbian army; but until the time should come for the army to fulfil these tasks, the program provided, under the heading "Foreign Policy," that "there must be organized, in the field of intellectual development, a way of helping the divided and unliberated parts of Serbdom, as well as of keeping alive the sense of our national unity in the Serb provinces which, being far away, are exposed to the influence of foreign elements." In other words, discontent must be kept alive in the Serb districts of the Turkish and Hapsburg Empires until the future war of liberation should join them to a Greater Serbia.

These two political ideals—individual acts of assassination practiced by immature half-baked students and by military cliques on the one hand, and national unification by a well-prepared movement and eventual war with Turkey and Austria as advocated by the Radical Party—dominated Serb political leaders until the triumph of the latter in the World War. Sometimes the leaders of the two tendencies have been in harmony, as in the palace assassinations of 1903; at other times they have been in bitter opposition, as in the so-called "priority question" in the spring of 1914. This dualism of ideals is the key to the

obscure and much disputed problem of the origin and relations of the *Narodna Odbrana* and the "Black Hand" with
one another, as well as to the notorious "Salonica Affair"
of 1917 which stirred political fury in Serbia much as did
the Dreyfus Affair in France.

M. Pashitch and the Radicals soon became the implacable enemies of King Milan, on account of the brutal and
bloody severity with which he had taken vengeance on the
Zajecar rebels, his disgraceful neglect of Serbia's national
interests, and his scandalous private life, much of which
was spent in questionable society in Vienna. Later the
same hostile attitude was assumed toward his successor,
King Alexander, especially after the latter's marriage to the
notorious woman who became Queen Draga. Being child-
less, Queen Draga was suspected by many of intending to
secure the succession to the throne for one of her brothers.
Fear and disgust gradually united many Radicals and revolutionary army officers against the existing régime. In the
words of a Serbian historian:

> What went on at Court and outside of it was justly
> regarded as a shame to the State and the Nation. Every
> moment grave scandals became public, and by these scan-
> dals Serbia and the Serbian people were becoming notorious
> and in bad repute. . . . The finances were in a pitiful state,
> and for months officials and officers received no salary.
> After the King's marriage every thing was still worse in
> every respect. Fickle changes were the order of the day,
> and likewise scandals. The fabricated story of the Queen's
> pregnancy, and the overbearing, provocative behavior of
> her brothers, roused the public and especially the military
> officers still further. All this brought it about that some
> eighty officers and several civilians formed a conspiracy
> with the purpose of murdering the King, the Queen, and
> her brothers. The greater part of the conspirators con-
> sisted of young officers inspired by upright patriotism. They
> saw their country given over to decay and shame under

the rule of a bad and unscrupulous monarch. They came to the conviction that Serbia was neglecting or abandoning her ideals and tasks because of the bad administration. The deep conviction that they must save the State and the Nation brought these people to a wicked deed which they believed justified by their patriotic duty.[34]

On the night of June 11, 1903, these patriotic assassins suddenly forced their way into the palace, murdered the King and Queen cowering in hiding, shot down the Queen's brothers in cold blood, and killed several Ministers. One of the chief leaders in organizing this brutal palace revolution was a young army captain, Dragutin Dimitrijevitch, who received incidentally three bullets which he carried in his body the rest of his days. Another—the man who ordered the murder of the Queen's brothers—was a young lieutenant, Voja Tankositch. These two were the later leaders of the "Black Hand," and, as another "patriotic duty," helped to prepare the Sarajevo plot against the Austrian Archduke.[35]

After the tragic night in 1903, which placed Peter I. Karageorgevitch upon the blood-stained throne of Alexander Obrenovitch, the conspirators who had carried out the palace revolution remained bound together as a protection against a possible counter-revolution, and also for the sake of personal interests and political advantages. They met together often and intervened in party politics whenever they believed their own interests were concerned. But when the country regained its balance and the new régime they had inaugurated seemed to be fairly established, their organization was no longer needed for safety, and their interference in politics was resented by the Radicals and the public. So the military conspirators as an organized group gradually retired until a new crisis arose.

[34] S. Stanojevitch, *Die Ermordung des Erzherzogs Franz Ferdinand,* pp. 45-46.　　　　[35] *Ibid.,* 54-56.

In 1908, on the day Austria proclaimed her annexation of Bosnia and Herzegovina, Dr. Milovan Milovanovitch, then Serbian Minister of Foreign Affairs, called together in the evening several ministers and notables, including Pashitch, Ljuba Stojanovitch, Professor Ljuba Jovanovitch, the Burgomaster of Belgrade, and others, to consider what action to take in the face of the Austrian "provocation." It was decided that the Burgomaster should summon next morning at the Town Hall a larger group of representative Serbians which included the historian, Stanojevitch.[36] In the course of this meeting next day, there was founded the *Narodna Odbrana* (National Defense). This association was to enrol and train volunteers and strengthen Serbia in other ways for an armed struggle to prevent Austria from carrying out her annexation program.

The universal indignation in Serbia at Austria's breach of the Berlin Treaty and incorporation of coveted Serb lands had again brought together in harmonious coöperation leading representatives of both the dualistic tendencies noted above. Thus, at its foundation, the *Narodna Odbrana* included political leaders of the Radical Party, as well as military officers like Dimitrijevitch, Tankositch, and General Bozo Jankovitch. It also included Zivojin Dashitch, Director of the Government Printing Office, in which Chabrinovitch was employed just before setting out to murder Franz Ferdinand; and Milan Pribichevitch, whose brother, Svetozar, was one of Austria's most bitter opponents in the Croatian Landtag, and who is said to have received from Sarajevo on the day of the assassination of the Archduke and his wife, a telegram, with apparent reference to the crime, "Both horses well disposed of." [37]

[36] S. Stanojevitch, p. 47.

[37] Conrad, IV, 73. Milan Pribichevitch remained active in the *Narodna Odbrana;* it was to him that Princip first thought of applying for the means to carry out the Sarajevo plot, which he later received from the "Black Hand" leaders. Pribichevitch fought as a colonel in the Serbian

The organization and the activity of the *Narodna Odbrana* began immediately. Its Central Committee, sitting at Belgrade, directed the work of the District Committees which were established in the chief towns and divided into sections for cultural work, physical training, collection of money, and in some cases relations with neighboring lands. Below the District Committees were "divisional committees," "local committees," and, at the bottom, "confidential men," "located in those places in the interior of the country where the establishment of a Committee is not necessary." In Serbia these committees and "confidential men" were rapidly organized everywhere. The *Narodna Odbrana* affiliated with itself and aided financially the existing patriotic associations like the Sokols, Riflemen's Clubs, and Horsemen's Clubs. It began its task of enrolling *comitadjis* and training them in bomb-throwing, the blowing up of railways and bridges, and similar activities to be carried on in a guerilla war against Austria. It collected funds and stirred the people to hatred against Austria by an active propaganda of fervid nationalism.[38] This activity was not limited to Serbian subjects. Bosnian émigrés in Serbia were similarly enrolled, trained for treasonable activity upon their return to Bosnia, and provided with funds.[39]

Army at the beginning of the World War, but the story that he was murdered by his own soldiers in the woods on Jastrebac Mountain (*cf.* Pharos, 8. 161-2), is incorrect; he disappeared to America to enlist Serbian recruits. *Cf.* also Wiesner's telegram of July 13. 1914 (*Austrian Red Book*, I, 17), and Krstanovitch's deposition in the Austrian *dossier*, appendix 5.

38 *Cf. Narodna Odbrana Izdanje Stredisnog Odbora Narodne Odbrane,* Belgrade, 1911, ch. i, "Origin and activity of the first Narodna Odbrana." This pamphlet and annual report, "issued by the Central Committee of the Narodna Odbrana," was read at the trial of the murderers in 1914, and a summary of it is printed in the Austrian *dossier*, appendix 2. The complete pamphlet, giving a vivid and full picture of the propagandist agitation of the *Narodna Obdrana,* is printed in German translation in KSF, V, 192-225, March, 1927.

39 *Cf.* the deposition of Trifko Krstanovitch in the Austrian *dossier*, appendix 5; he tells how he went from Bosnia to Belgrade in 1908, was given food and lodging by Voja Tankositch, trained in bomb-throwing,

Gatchinovitch, the chief leader of the terrorist wing of the revolutionary movement in Bosnia, was at first closely associated with the *Narodna Odbrana* in Belgrade and worked in its interests in Bosnia,[40] though he later joined the "Black Hand," and, in accordance with its ideals, instigated assassination plots in Bosnia. Princip, the Archduke's murderer, was, according to his own admissions at the trial, enrolled in the *Narodna Odbrana* in 1912, given money, and trained as a *comitadji*.[41]

Within Bosnia itself similar committees and "confidential men" were recruited to form a net-work of spies and serve as a "tunnel," or "underground railway," for conveying propagandist literature, weapons, and conspirators across the frontier from Serbia into Bosnia.[42] This is also evident from the subsequent report of a Serbian frontier officer, Kosta Todorovitch, to the commander of the Drin Division. His report, along with his diary and accounts, was captured by the Austrians in the first weeks of the War, and gives detailed evidence of the way the "tunnel" was originally established in the Annexation Crisis by the *Narodna Odbrana*, and later continued by the "Black Hand" military authorities. Todorovitch's report was, of course, unknown to the authors of the Austrian *dossier*, but it was read at the trial in October, 1914, and its trust-

and then became a paid spy and secret carrier of letters between the leaders of the *Narodna Odbrana* in Serbia and its agents in Bosnia. Some doubt, to be sure, has been cast upon the trustworthiness of this man (*cf.* Wendel, p. 46; Chopin, pp. 12-17; Conrad, IV, 83, where the Governor of Bosnia, Potiorek, speaks of him as "keine integre Persönlichkeit").

40 Jevtitch, p. 6.

41 Pharos, pp. 22-25. For other evidences of the activity of the *Narodna Odbrana*, see Pharos, pp. 5, 8, 14 f., 19, 21 ff., 34, 43, 55, 81-101, 108, 132, 162.

42 This "tunnel" still existed in 1914, and is several times referred to by the Archduke's murderers in their conversations with their accomplices in Belgrade; *cf.* Pharos, pp. 9, 16, 34, 91.

worthiness is incidentally vouched for by Ljuba Jovanovitch.[43] After referring to an enclosed letter from a "confidential man" in Bosnia, Todorovitch's report continues:

> The plan which I have begun to carry out and to which
> I have devoted the greatest care is the winning of "confi-
> dential men" [in Bosnia]. They had all belonged to the
> time of the Annexation Crisis, but have all been dropped,
> with the exception of the one mentioned [in the letter] and
> two or three others. Some have moved away to other
> districts. The *Narodna Odbrana* in Shabats has also found
> some "confidential men," as for example in Tuzla and
> Sokolac. The connection has hitherto been weak and in-
> sufficient, since it has been in the hands of people who
> devoted themselves to it but little and did not give it enough
> attention. In accordance with the wish of the Minister of
> War, I have tried to carry out as conscientiously as possible
> the tasks and directions sent to me, especially the organizing
> work on the ground. . . . In the Drin region the connection
> has been sufficiently restored; it goes *via* Zvornik and
> Dabovje. In the other places the connection formerly ex-
> isting has broken down, because it is now superfluous since
> the garrisons have been removed from the points in ques-
> tion. The connection by way of the Bosnian Islands and
> Draljatcha Vrata is favorable. There are people here who
> are admirably fitted for smuggling across. The tunnels do
> not yet have their full numbers; but I hope soon to be able
> to send you information and news.[44]

[43] Jovanovitch wrote in the *Politika*, April 17, 1925: "It is known
exactly how it was . . . about the measures which M. Pashitch took to
prevent the crossing over of those who took part in the murder, about
whom it was heard that they had obtained the weapons in Belgrade and
gone over the Drin to Bosnia. Of these measures the Austrians found
positive traces when they crossed the Drin for the first time in 1914,
took Lozhnica, and found the diary of our frontier officer, the late
Kosta Todorovitch, who recorded from day to day the orders received,
and among them a strong order given by the then War Minister, Dushan
Stepanovitch, that the youths from Bosnia who were mentioned were
to be prevented from crossing the frontier."   [44] Pharos, pp. 91-92.

The report further states that the activity of these "confidential men" consists ostensibly in spreading education and the *Pobratimstvo* (an anti-alcohol brotherhood), "because thus they are splendidly masked" in their real work of spying, smuggling, and conspiring.[45]

After the settlement of the Annexation Crisis in March, 1909, when Serbia, deserted by Russia, had to promise to cease her subversive agitation and to maintain in the future friendly relations with the Hapsburg Monarchy, the *Narodna Odbrana* made a show of transforming itself from an aggressive and subversive organization into a society which emphasized more laudable "cultural" aims, such as education, physical training, and the fostering of national ideals. Though its official report still proclaimed that "Austria is our greatest enemy," it added by way of recapitulation: "While the *Narodna Odbrana* works in conformity with the times according to altered conditions, it also maintains all connections made at the Annexation Period; today therefore it is the same as at the Annexation Period. . . . Then the cry was for war; now the cry is for work. Then meetings, demonstrations, volunteers, weapons, and bombs were asked for; today steady, fanatical tireless work and again work is required to fulfil the tasks and duties to which we have drawn attention by way of present preparation for the fight with gun and cannon which will come." [46] Though there was undoubtedly some change in the character of the *Narodna Odbrana* after 1909 in the direction here indicated, it never became so completely innocent and "cultural" as

[45] Pharos, p. 94. *Cf.* map, at p. 47 above. Some of the "favorable" places here mentioned are precisely the ones actually used by the Sarajevo assassins; Chabrinovitch was smuggled over at Zvornik, and Princip and Grabezh with the bombs and revolvers, at the Bosnian Islands, the three meeting again at Tuzla; *ibid.*, 16, 19, 25-27, 36-40, 48-52, 56-58, 86-108, 126-151.

[46] Extract from the pamphlet report issued by the *Narodna Odbrana* Central Committee in 1911, printed in the Austrian *dossier*, appendix 2; and complete reprint in KSF, V, 223-225, March, 1927.

is often asserted.[47]   Nor did it cease its propagandist work in the Hapsburg territories.

On the other hand, it is true that the direct connection of the *Narodna Odbrana* with the Sarajevo plot was exaggerated in the Austrian ultimatum and *dossier*, because the Austrians centered their attention more on its earlier and more aggressive, rather than its later and more "cultural" activity, and particularly because, in their ignorance of the secret work of the Serbian military authorities, they failed to distinguish sufficiently between the *Narodna Odbrana* and the "Black Hand." It is nevertheless clear that the *Narodna Odbrana* secretly continued its work of maintaining "tunnels" and smuggling revolutionary literature from Belgrade into Bosnia. It kept in touch with the "confidential men" who were later used by the "Black Hand" and who actually assisted the Archduke's murderers on their journey. And it inspired and assisted Bosnian emigrants who came to Belgrade. It thus helped to develop the revolutionary movement in Bosnia and to prepare the ground for the Sarajevo crime. The original membership of the *Narodna Odbrana* and the measures which the Radical Government took to give it the appearance of a "cultural" organization show that M. Pashitch and his colleagues were perfectly acquainted with its work of propaganda, espionage, and the recruiting of "confidential men" on Austrian soil. Even after 1909, M. Pashitch evidently did not regard the association as purely "cultural," because he himself has said, "as soon as he came back from Bucharest [in August, 1913] he advised the *Narodna Odbrana* not to undertake anything against Austria, because it would be dangerous." [48]

[47] E. g., Stanojevitch, pp. 49-54; Ljuba Jovanovitch, *Politika* articles, March 22-April 17, 1925; Wendel, pp. 46-49, 59-61; Seton-Watson, in *Foreign Affairs*, III, 499-500.

[48] M. Pashitch's speech against Ljuba Jovanovitch at the Radical Club as reported in *Politika*, April 26, 1926; KSF, IV, 409, June, 1926.

THE "BLACK HAND"

By 1911 the old divergence of views between the Radical
political leaders and the more restless and reckless military
officers began to show itself again. The Radicals, in view
of Russia's attitude and the existing diplomatic situation
in Europe, believed that Serbians must preserve correct and
peaceful relations with Austria-Hungary and confine their
work for the present to strengthening the State for the
future struggle which would realize their ultimate aim—the
creation of a Greater Serbia. This, as we have seen, was
now the ostensible policy of the *Narodna Odbrana*. But
some [49] of the more hot-headed and zealous military clique
which had carried out the palace revolution of 1903 were
impatient of the more moderate Radical policy. They
wanted "deeds." They therefore revived their old organization of 1903 in a new secret association known in its statutes
as *Ujedinjenje ili Smrt* (Union or Death), but commonly
referred to as the "Black Hand."

The most authoritative information about the "Black
Hand" is contained in its Rules and By-Laws. These were
published in a mutilated form in *Tajna Prevratna Organisacija*, the report of the Salonica Trial printed in 1918,
which has already been mentioned.[50] At this later time the
Serbian Government, wishing to make it appear that the
"Black Hand" was a revolutionary organization exclusively
within Serbia aiming to overthrow the power of the Radical
Party and even the reigning dynasty, deleted certain passages which referred to the subversive and terrorist activity

[49] Some, not all; several of the former conspirators of 1903 refused
to enter the new "Black Hand" organization on the ground that, though
the murder of King Alexander was necessary, there was no need to
plunge into new adventures which could only harm the State; these
officers followed the Radical Party and were eventually rewarded after
the crushing of the "Black Hand" in 1917 by being given the places of
their rivals; they were commonly known as the "White Hand."

[50] *Cf.* above, note 32.

of the Society outside Serbia. But M. Bogitchevitch, from information supplied by two surviving members of the "Black Hand," has been able to establish the complete text of its Rules and By-Laws.[51] He has also been able to establish the identity of a large number of its members and the secret numbers by which they were known, showing that they included many Serbian civilian officials, as well as military officers. It is from his text of the Rules that the following quotations are made.

The aim of the "Black Hand" was (Art. 1): "The realization of the national ideal: the union of all Serbs." "Art. 2. This organization prefers terrorist action to intellectual propaganda, and for this reason must be kept absolutely secret from non-members." To accomplish its aim, it brings influence to bear on Government circles and on the various social classes of the Kingdom of Serbia, which is regarded as "Piedmont." Then follow the clauses which were deleted in 1918, but which show clearly its terrorist activity in the Hapsburg lands:

Art. 4. (b) It organizes revolutionary activity in all the lands inhabited by Serbs.

(c) Beyond the frontiers of Serbia, it fights with all means those who oppose this idea.

(d) It maintains friendly relations with all States, peoples, organizations, and private individuals who are friendly toward Serbia and the Serb element.

(e) It lends help and support in every way to all peoples and all organizations struggling for national liberation and unity. . . .

Art. 7. The Central Committee in Belgrade includes, besides the members of the Kingdom of Serbia, one delegate for each of the Serb lands abroad [Pokraine]: (1) Bosnia

---

[51] Bogitchevitch, "La Société 'Union ou Mort' dite la 'Main Noire,'" in the French periodical *Evolution*, No. 7, 16-30, July 16, 1926; in German and English trans. in KSF, IV, 664-689, Sept., 1926; and in his recent interesting volume, *Le Procès de Salonique* (Paris, 1927), pp. 41-53.

and Herzegovina, (2) Montenegro, (3) Old Serbia and Macedonia, (4) Croatia, Slavonia and Syrmia, (5) the Voivodina, (6) the Coast Lands [Primorje, i.e. Dalmatia]. . . .

Art. 18. The Central Committee in Belgrade is in touch with the committees of Serb territory abroad by authorized delegates, who are usually members of the Central Committee, or, in exceptional cases, are special delegates.

Art. 19. Liberty of action is left to the Committees in the Serb lands abroad; but the execution of more extensive revolutionary movements shall depend upon the approval of the Central Committee in Belgrade.

To enlarge the society and yet secure absolute secrecy, obedience, and devotion among its members, it was provided (Arts. 23-33) that it was the duty of each new member to enrol new members and pledge his own life for those whom he introduced. Members were not generally known to each other personally, but were designated by secret numbers. Only the Central Committee at Belgrade was to know their names. "The interests of the organization are to be put above all others. Every member on entering the organization must realize that by this act he forfeits his own personality and that he can expect within it neither glory nor personal profit." "When the Central Committee at Belgrade has pronounced penalty of death, the only matter of importance is that the execution shall take place without fail. The method of execution employed is a matter of indifference." The initiation of a new member took place in a darkened room, lighted only by a wax candle, before a small table covered with a black cloth on which lay a crucifix, a dagger and a revolver. The candidate took an oath "by the Sun that warms me, by the Earth that nourishes me, before God, by the blood of my ancestors, on my honor and on my life, that I will from this moment till my death be faithful to the laws of this organization, and that I will always be ready to make any sacrifice for it." The seal of the "Black Hand," with ominous significance, bore an unfurled flag, skull and cross-bones, dagger, bomb, and

Facsimile of the last page of the Rules of the Serbian Secret Society. *"Ujedinjenje ili Smrt"* ("Union or Death"), commonly known as the "Black Hand." Signature No. 6 is that of Dragutin Dmitrijevitch, the most influential leader in the Society. The Society's seal shows symbolically a skull and cross-bones, hand-bomb, dagger, and bottle of poison.

bottle of poison, with the inscription *Ujedinjenje ili Smrt*.

The inspirer and leader of this singular association, which seems to belong to the spirit of the sixteenth rather than of the twentieth century, was that reckless, generous, idolized, childish Renaissance figure, whose portrait by

Stanojevitch was given above,[52] Colonel Dragutin Dimitrijevitch—head of the espionage department of the Serbian
General Staff. On the last page of the statutes, dated
"Belgrade, May 9, 1911," his name appears on the membership list as "No. 6." His chief aide was Major Voja
Tankositch, "No. 7." He also had taken a leading part in
the royal murders of 1903. He had organized later a
comitadji school, in which he trained Bosnian émigrés who
came to Belgrade and on whom he exerted a large influence
between 1908 and 1914. He is described as "quiet, calm
and gentle in private life, giving the impression of a retir-
ing, almost timid man; but he had a rough, wild, undis-
ciplined spirit; . . . as a *comitadji* leader in Macedonia,
notorious for his wild severity toward his followers, his
personal heroism and bravery and his presence of mind;
without doubt an honest and upright patriot; the conviction that he was doing a patriotic duty justified in his eyes
many of his horrible deeds." [53] Another member of the
"Black Hand," more mysterious and enigmatic, was Milan
Ciganovitch, "No. 412." Coming originally as an émigré
from Bosnia to Belgrade, he served under Tankositch as a
comitadji in the Balkan War against Turkey. In 1914 he
was enjoying a sinecure as a subordinate official in the
Serbian State Railways. He is believed by many to have
joined the "Black Hand" in order to keep M. Pashitch informed of its doings.[54] Tankositch and Ciganovitch were
the two men who directly helped prepare the assassination
plot in Belgrade, giving the three youths who were to
murder Franz Ferdinand bombs, Browning pistols, and

---

[52] See quotation at note 8. For further characterizations of Dimitrijevitch, see Bogitchevitch, *Le Procès de Salonique*, pp. 61-69.

[53] Stanojevitch, p. 52. Jevtitch, p. 23, speaks of Tankositch as "an
officer greatly beloved among the émigrés" from Bosnia in Belgrade.

[54] *Cf.* N. Mermet, "L'Agent Provocateur Milan Ciganovitch," in
La Fédération Balkanique, pp. 270-272, May 31, 1925; Durham, *The Serajevo Crime*, pp. 80 ff., 174 ff., 182; and the obituary notice by Dr. Wiesner,
in KSF, V, 1041-1048, Nov., 1927.

poison to be swallowed as soon as their deed was accomplished.

Another early member of the "Black Hand" was Vladimir Gatchinovitch, who appears as "No. 217" in the list of members published in *Tajna Prevratna Organisacija*. This interesting man, as we shall see a little later, carried on an active terrorist propaganda in Bosnia, both by his writings and by his organization of secret terrorist groups.

Among the other members of the "Black Hand" identified by M. Bogitchevitch were Dushan Obtrkitch, "No. 166," an intimate friend of M. Ljuba Jovanovitch; Michel Givkovitch, "No. 442," Secretary of the Serbian Court of Cassation; Demetrius Novakovitch, "No. 471," Secretary of the University of Belgrade; Dr. Milan Gavrilovitch, "No. 406," Secretary at the Ministry of Foreign Affairs and afterwards editor of the *Politika*; M. A. Jovanovitch, "No. 401," Secretary of the Railway Department; Bogoljub Vutchitchevitch, "No. 407," Commissioner of Police; and Stanoje Simitch, "No. 467," an employee at the Ministry of Foreign Affairs.[55] These names indicate that the "Black Hand" was not so exclusively a military organization as it has often been represented. Nor was it so divorced from, and opposed by, the *Narodna Odbrana,* as is often stated. While it is true, as pointed out above, that the *Narodna Odbrana* professed to work for Greater Serbia by "cultural" preparation, and the "Black Hand," more impatient, preferred terrorist action by assassination, the two Societies had the same ultimate goal and even had many members in common. Milan Vasitch, who was one of the ten members of the Supreme Central Committee of the "Black Hand" at Belgrade, was at the same time mentioned by the Archduke's murderers as "Secretary of the *Narodna Odbrana*," and as having provided them with funds and revolutionary literature.[56] The two organiza-

[55] Bogitchevitch, in KSF, IV, 675, 688.　　　[56] Pharos, pp. 5, 22.

tions also made use of the same "confidential men" in
Bosnia and the same "tunnels" of communication. Radé
Malobabitch, for instance, who was one of the Austrian
Serbs condemned for treason at Agram, and became a "confidential man" for the *Narodna Odbrana* in 1911, was introduced to Col. Dimitrijevitch in 1913 by Todorovitch,
the frontier guard at Lozhnica, and thereupon became one
of the chief spies for the "Black Hand" and the Intelligence
Department of the Serbian General Staff.[57]   So close was
the connection between the two Societies that the members
of the Carnegie Commission of Inquiry on the Balkan Wars
failed to distinguish between them.[58]   The three youths
who planned to murder the Archduke sought to give the
impression at their trial that their relations in Belgrade
had been rather with the *Narodna Odbrana* than the "Black
Hand." They declared that they knew of the latter only
by hearsay or what they had read in the newspapers; but
they admitted that they were aware that Tankositch and
Ciganovitch were on bad terms with the *Narodna Odbrana,*
and were perhaps providing the bombs and Browning pistols
"because they were members of another society." [59]

THE REVOLUTIONARY MOVEMENT IN BOSNIA

For more than half a century before the World War,
there had been an increasing antagonism between the
Austro-Hungarian ruling authorities and the subject nationalities within the Dual Empire. This arose partly
from the new feeling of nationality, which was an ever
stronger force in the course of the nineteenth century, and
partly from the oppressive rule of the Hapsburg Government and its disregard of the aspirations of its Slav and
Rumanian subjects. This antagonism was particularly

[57] *Tajna Prevratna Organisacija,* p. 201, quoted by Durham, *The
Serajevo Crime,* p. 162.
[58] Carnegie Report, p. 169.
[59] Pharos, p. 82; *cf.* also pp. 14, 43, 47, 55, 80 f.

sharp in Bosnia and Herzegovina after the Austrian occupation of these provinces in 1878, and especially after their annexation in 1908. The unrest was heightened by the suspension of the Bosnian Landtag and by the repressive "Exceptional Laws" introduced during the popular ferment caused by the Serbian victories and the great extension of Serbian territory in 1912. But in 1913-14, under the administration of Count Bilinski, the Landtag was reopened, the Exceptional Laws withdrawn, wide freedom given to the Press, and great efforts were made to improve the political and economic conditions in Bosnia. Bilinski, being a Slav himself (a Galician Pole), had more sympathy with Serb aspirations than his German and Magyar colleagues. By a policy of conciliation in Bosnia, he hoped to win from the Serb population something of the same loyalty to Hapsburg rule which was found in the Croatian and Mohammedan elements of the recently annexed provinces.

In Bosnia and Herzegovina, according to the census of 1910, the population consisted, according to religion, which was the most vital factor, of Greek Orthodox, Mohammedans, and Roman Catholics, approximately in the proportion of 4, 3, and 2: 825,000 Greek Orthodox, mainly Serbs; 612,000 Mohammedans, mainly Serbs and Turks; and 442,000 Roman Catholics, mainly Croats; altogether, with Jews and a sprinkling of Protestants and gypsies, nearly 1,900,000. Generally speaking, the Greek Orthodox sympathized with the Serbians in the neighboring kingdom; the Roman Catholics were divided between loyalty to Austria and their higher cultural connections with the West on the one hand, and, on the other, their nationalistic desires for a national Serb-Croat union, either as a self-governing unit in a federalized "trialistic" Hapsburg state, or as part of a "Greater Serbia, or of an independent Jugoslav Federation; the Mohammedans were generally loyal to the Hapsburg Monarchy. These four political tendencies were represented respectively by the four main political parties: (1) *Srbska Rijec* (Serbian Party led by G. Ievtanovitch and Sola) and the *Narodna Stranka* (Nationalist Party), both in bitter opposition to Austrian rule; (2) the loyalist Serb minority led by Dr. Dimovich; and the loyalist Croats, formerly a part of the Starcevitch Party, but in 1914 having an anti-Serb tendency and known as the *Frankovacka Stranka* after their leader, a Hungarian Jew, Dr. Frank; (3) the *Starcevicanjka Stranka,* founded half a century earlier by the Croatian patriot Starcevitch; (4) the loyal Mohammedan Party.[60] But Bilinski's conciliatory efforts met with little or no response. On the contrary, they were interpreted as signs of Austrian weakness and decay. They were taken advantage of for further open newspaper attacks and secret subversive movements against Austrian authority.[61]

In 1914, however, the Bosnian parties and movements just mentioned represented what M. Jevtitch calls the "older generation." [62] They represented the politicians and

[60] *Cf.* Conrad, *Aus meiner Dienstzeit,* I, 13-28; and the interesting memorials presented to the Russians in December, 1914, by the Jugoslav agents, MM. Supilo and Salviati and printed by Stieve, *Iswolsky im Weltkriege* (Berlin, 1925), pp. 136-161.

[61] Leon Bilinski, *Wspomnienia i Dokumenty* (Reminiscences and Documents), 2 vols., Warsaw, 1924-25, I, 227-332; Bilinski, as Austro-Hungarian Joint Finance Minister from Jan., 1912, to the War, had supreme charge of the administration of Bosnia. See also the interesting views of his predecessor, Count Burián, *Austria in Dissolution,* N. Y., 1925, pp. 244-310, 358-371. Bilinski's conciliatory policy was not favored by Conrad nor by Gen. Potiorek, the military Governor of Bosnia (*cf.* Conrad, III, 95 ff., 157 ff., 370 ff., 442 ff.; IV, 13-124), nor by the Bosnian police officials (*cf.* Baron Carl Collas, "Auf den bosnischen Wegspuren der Kriegsschuldigen," in KSF, V, 11-27, Jan., 1927.

[62] Jevtitch, *Sarajevski Atentat,* p. 3 ff.; *cf.* also Pharos, *passim;* and Seton-Watson, *Sarajevo,* ch. iii, "The Jugoslav Revolutionary Movement," in many respects an excellent and informing account, except that he minimizes the influence exerted from Belgrade upon the movement in Bosnia, as has been pointed out by M. Bogitchevitch, "Nouvelles dépositions concernant l'attentat de Sarajevo," in KSF, IV, 21-28, 87-95. Mr. Seton-Watson fails to note such significant points as the fact that the

the bourgeoisie who had been educated in the universities. Though they formed an opposition party in the Bosnian Landtag, they were content for the most part to follow legal means of action and counted on exacting larger political concessions from the Austrian authorities. They were the elements which Austria hoped to divide against one another. Hapsburg authority was to be maintained by the policy of *divide et impera.*

In contrast to this older generation was an altogether different "new generation." This arose in Bosnia in the early years of the twentieth century. It was known as *Mlada Bosna* (Young Bosnia). It was impatient with the politicians, the bourgeoisie, and all legal forms of opposition. It repudiated all notions of "trialism" as a solution of Serbo-Croat national aspirations. It was recruited from the youth of the "small and insignificant classes"—peasants, journeymen, school teachers, and sons of priests and young students.[63] Its members were impatient and "desperate." They had begun to feed upon Russian revolutionary and anarchistic literature, especially the writings of Herzen and Kropotkin. They were fired with the success of violence in the Russian revolution of 1905. They developed the "cult of the individual deed," that is, they believed that terrorist acts of assassination were the best means of putting a speedy end to the temporizing methods of Bosnian politicians and of throwing off all Austrian control to prepare the way for a new "Jugoslav" nationalism. Deeds of revo-

chief leader of the new movement, Gatchinovitch, was a member of the *Narodna Odbrana* and later of the "Black Hand," and that nearly all of the attempted assassinations of Austrian officials between 1910 and 1914 were made by youths who had just come from spending some months in Belgrade.

[63] *Cf.* the Bosnians directly connected with the preparation and execution of the plot to murder the Archduke: Chabrinovitch was a typesetter; Mehmedbashitch, a cabinet-maker; Mishko Jovanovitch, a merchant and cinema director; Ilitch, an ex-school teacher; Pushara, a town-clerk; the Kerovichi, peasants; Jakov Milovitch, a fisherman on the Drin; and Princip and Grabezh were students; *cf.* Jevtitch, p. 23.

lutionary terrorism served two great purposes: they created panic among the ruling authorities; and they uplifted the national spirit of the masses.[64]

The first most notable expression of this new cult was the "deed" of Bogdan Zherajitch, a Herzegovinian Serb. After being trained in revolver practice at Vranja by a Serbian officer, Bojin Simitch, who soon became a "Black Hand" member, "No. 111," [65] Zherajitch returned to Bosnia in 1910 and at Sarajevo fired five shots at the Governor, General Vareshanin. Zherajitch then committed suicide on the spot. The story of the General's contemptuous spurning of the corpse with his foot, as Zherajitch still lay sprinkled with mud and blood upon the bridge at Sarajevo, and his burial in the part of a cemetery where only suicides and criminals were interred, spread throughout the land, and did much to inflame Bosnian youths to imitate and avenge him.[66] He was speedily hailed as a hero and "first martyr" by the Serbs of Bosnia and Serbia. Two months later, on the occasion of Emperor Francis Joseph's birthday, August 18, 1910, the Belgrade *Politika* published a large portrait of Zherajitch, with an incendiary poem and laudatory article saying, "Today, we too light a candle at his grave and cry, 'Honor to Zherajitch.'" [67] His grave was. kept fresh with flowers and became a place of pilgrimage for Bosnian youths filled with nationalistic fanaticism and a desire for the notoriety which would come to anyone who should follow his example. Thus, Princip, on the evening before he shot the Archduke, is said to have placed flowers on Zherajitch's grave and to have sworn by it that his hand should not waver next day.[68] Among Bosnian youths,

[64] *Cf.* Jevtitch's chapter (pp. 17-21) on "The Cult of Individual Action."

[65] Bogitchevitch, in KSF, IV, 24, 675, 688.

[66] *Cf.* Jevtitch, pp. 5, 20; Pharos, pp. 21, 30, 40.

[67] Austrian *dossier*, appendix 1.

[68] Jevtitch, p. 20; Pharos, p. 40.

whose mental balance had been unsteadied by a mixture of anarchism, socialism, and nationalism, it was not unnatural that the force of mental suggestion, in an act of political assassination like that of Zherajitch, should exercise a strong psychological influence.

The man most influential in developing the revolutionary movement in Bosnia and in inspiring the Bosnian students who carried out the plot against the Archduke was Vladimir Gatchinovitch.[69]   He was the son of an orthodox priest in Herzegovina.   His father wished him to follow the priesthood and sent him to school for the purpose, but he threw up his studies and began reading revolutionary Russian literature.   In the spring of 1909, during the Annexation Crisis, he went to Belgrade, where he came in contact with the leaders of the newly organized *Narodna Odbrana* and also with the more violent spirits who favored "direct action" and later organized the "Black Hand."   He remained in Serbia for a couple of years and came under the influence of Skerlitch, an active propagandist of anti-Austrian revolutionary ideas.   Later he returned to Bosnia on behalf of the *Narodna Odbrana* and, in the words of one of his followers, "speaks, wakes people up, and again disappears like a shadow, as if he were swallowed up by the earth, feeling himself followed by the foot-falls of Austrian agents among whom were to be found some Serbians also." [70]

Gatchinovitch attended the University of Vienna; but

[69] The best source of information of this arch-conspirator is to be found in *Spomenica Vladimira Gatchinovitch,* Sarajevo, 1921. This contains his famous pamphlet, *Smrt Jednog Heroja* (The Death of a Hero), glorifying Bogdan Zherajitch's attempt on General Vareshanin's life in 1910; it was published at Belgrade in 1912 by the "Piedmont" Press, the organ of the "Black Hand." It also includes some of his other writings and some interesting biographical notes by his friends and fellow conspirators. On Gatchinovitch, see also Jevtitch, pp. 5, 13, 15, 19-21; Seton-Watson, *Sarajevo,* pp. 69-79; and M. Edith Durham in *Current History;* XXV, 657-661, Feb., 1927.

[70] Jevtitch, p. 6.

he spent more time in organizing a revolutionary movement among the Slav students than in study. Here also
he wrote his famous eulogy on the murderer Zherajitch,
which, as Mr. Seton-Watson well says, "by its strange,
perverted idealism and high-falutin style gives a clear insight into the revolutionary movement which is now com-
mencing." Gatchinovitch complained that Serbian public
opinion did not pay due attention to "those who are coming," whose aim is "to kindle revolution in the minds and
thoughts of young Serbs, so that they may be saved from
the disastrous influence of anti-national ideas and prepare
for the breaking of bonds and for the laying of healthy
foundations for the shining national life that is to come."
After quoting the example of Orsini, who tried to murder
Napoleon III, and after lauding the Russian terrorists, he
sang the praises of Zherajitch, as "a man of action, of
strength, of life and virtue, a type such as opens an epoch,
proclaims ideas and enlivens suffering and spell-bound
hearts." He urged young Serbs to avenge Zherajitch's
martyrdom by imitating his example.[71] This pamphlet
was published anonymously at Belgrade at the office of
Piedmont, the newspaper organ of the Greater Serbia
movement and the "Black Hand" group. It was smuggled
from Belgrade into Bosnia and circulated widely among
young students upon whom it had a profound and decisive
effect.

In 1912 Gatchinovitch was again in Belgrade, probably
in connection with the printing of his pamphlet. Finding
the *Narodna Odbrana* too mild, he joined the newly organized "Black Hand." His name appears as "No. 217" in
the list of members published by the Serbian Government
at the Salonica Trial. He is said to have received funds
from both societies, and also a "scholarship" from the
propagandist department of the Serbian Ministry of For-

[71] *Spomenica,* pp. 41, 47-8; see below, ch. iii, at notes 5-7.

eign Affairs. This enabled him to go to Lausanne for further study.[72] Here he came into direct touch with various Russian revolutionists, including Trotsky, who wrote an introduction, signed "L. T.," to a selection of Gatchinovitch's French articles.

Meanwhile Gatchinovitch had also found time to travel in Bosnia and organize the radical youth of *Mlada Bosna* into secret revolutionary "circles" known as *Kruzhoci*, "small groups of trustworthy persons, who do not know each other, but are in touch with one another through intermediaries." [73] This method of organization was also characteristic of the "Black Hand," from which Gatchinovitch got the idea. It gave the "Black Hand" a network of affiliated groups spread throughout Bosnia and the other Serb districts of Austria-Hungary. The students, peasants, and workmen who largely composed these *"Kruzhoci"* outside of Serbia were probably not regular members of the "Black Hand," but they could be used by the "Black Hand" for revolutionary agitation and terrorist action in Bosnia.[74] It is impossible to estimate the number of these *Kruzhoci*, but it is certain that they existed in all the towns with

[72] Bogitchevitch, in KSF, IV, 25 ff, 92 ff.; *Le Procès de Salonique*, p. 157 f. His statement is based on the deposition of two revolutionists, Mustapha Golubitch and Paul Bastaitch, who shared with Gatchinovitch in the plot against the Austrian authorities which prepared at Toulouse. That Gatchinovitch was one of the many Bosnian students subsidized by the Belgrade authorities seems also to be indicated by the documents seized by the Austrian authorities during the War in the houses of MM. Pavlovitch and Pashitch; Durham, in *Current History*, XXV, 661, Feb., 1927.

[73] Jevtitch, pp. 6-7.

[74] One of the chief Serbian authorities on the "Black Hand," however, M. Boghitchevitch, *Le Procès de Salonique*, pp. 2-4, seems to regard the men in these *Kruzhoci* as regular "Black Hand" members. But I do not find proof of this. The evidence at the trial of the Sarajevo assassins appears to show a pretty general and probably genuine ignorance of the real and more restricted "Black Hand" in Serbia on the part of the suspects arrested in Bosnia after the assassination. He is undoubtedly correct, however, in contrasting the relatively humble social composition of the *Kruzhoci* in Bosnia with the "Black Hand" members in Serbia who were drawn mainly from the professional and especially the military class.

secondary schools—Banja Luka, Tuzla, Mostar, Trebinje, and especially in Sarajevo. One of the most active and alert groups, which gave directions to the others, was the one organized by Gatchinovitch at the house of Danilo Ilitch in Sarajevo. "Through it passed all that was most revolutionary. It was, in a way, the leading organ of all the nationalistic currents in the country. Its relations, direct and indirect, with the émigrés in Belgrade were very close." [75]

The revolutionary ferment among the Bosnian youth, which arose from exasperation at Austrian oppression, from a desire for Serbo-Croat national unity, and from the influence of Russian anarchistic writings and Serbian propaganda, manifested itself also in the widespread practice of young Bosnians migrating back and forth between Serbia and their own country. These "émigrés" liked to escape from the stifling atmosphere of Hapsburg control and roam about in the freer and more congenial air of Belgrade. Here they were well received, and it was easy for them quickly to secure a certificate of education. Princip, for instance, with the personal approval of M. Ljuba Jovanovitch, the Serbian Minister of Education, passed off three years' work in less than two years, in spite of the fact that meanwhile he was spending much of his time in political discussions and in travelling back and forth.[76] This practice of "emigration" is well illustrated by the case of the three youths who carried out the plot to assassinate Franz Ferdinand.

Gavrilo Princip was born at Grahovo, in Western Bosnia in the wild mountains near the Dalmatian border. Though at first diligent in school, his periods of application to study were frequently interrupted by excursions into po-

---

[75] Jevtitch, p. 23; *cf.* also Seton-Watson, *Sarajevo,* pp. 74-77.

[76] Pharos, pp. 22-24; Jevtitch, p. 71. Ljuba Jovanovitch describes his personal acquaintance with Princip in *Krv Slovenstva,* p. 10. Princip's fellow conspirator, Grabezh, also passed off examinations rapidly in Belgrade; Pharos, p. 44.

itical propaganda, so that he was often suspended, and finally came to Sarajevo, where he stayed for a month. In May, 1912, he went to Belgrade, ostensibly to study; but when asked at the trial why he went there, he replied, "That is my affair." [77] As this was just about the time that Gatchinovitch was organizing the *Kruzhoc* at Sarajevo and impressing upon the youth there the need of revolutionary agitation, it is probable that Princip's journey to Belgrade was inspired by him.[78] At any rate, Princip quickly came into touch with the "Black Hand" *comitadjis* in the Belgrade coffee-houses, and, according to his own declaration, was taken into the *Narodna Odbrana* by its secretary, Major Vasitch, who was also a leading member of the "Black Hand." When the Balkan War broke out, he went to the Turkish frontier to receive military training with *comitadjis* under Major Tankositch, another leading "Black Hand" terrorist and agitator. But being only sixteen years old, with a small weak body, he was sent home by Tankositch.[79] He had, however, become filled with the "Black Hand" ideas of terrorist action by political assassination, and spent the next fifteen months in plotting with Gatchinovitch and Ilitch, and in journeys between Belgrade and Hadzhici, a village half a dozen miles west of Sarajevo. At this village he passed the winter of 1913-14, and then returned to Belgrade in February, 1914.[80]

Nedjelko Chabrinovitch, who later threw the bomb at

[77] Pharos, p. 22. For the details of Princip's early life, see Jevtitich, p. 35 ff.; and Princip's own interesting confessions, made in prison to the Austrian psychiatrist, Dr. Pappenheim, and published in English translation by Mr. H. F. Armstrong in *Current History*, August, 1925, pp. 701-707; and in an anonymous pamphlet, *Gavrilo Princips Bekenntnisse*, Vienna, 1927.

[78] For Gatchinovitch's strong influence on Princip, see Jevtitch's biography of the former in *Spomenica*, p. 104 ff., and Miss Durham's summary of it in *Current History*, XXV, 657 f., Feb., 1927.

[79] Pharos, pp. 22-23; Jevtitch, p. 13.

[80] Pharos, p. 23; Princip's "Confessions," in *Current History, Aug.*, 1927, p. 705.

the Austrian Archduke, left school because he made no progress and quarreled with his father.[81] He turned from one trade to another, and finally took up type-setting. After quarrelling with various employers, he went to Belgrade, where he found work in a shop which printed anarchist literature, and where he himself drank in anarchist views. But he fell sick and returned to Sarajevo, bringing anarchist books with him—some of which his mother burned. Here he worked for a couple of months in 1912, until his activity in a type-setters' strike and other complaints against him caused the Sarajevo authorities to order his banishment from the town, when he again sought refuge in Belgrade. Here he was in touch with Princip, though at this time they held somewhat different political views. Here also he came into contact with the *Narodna Odbrana*. Desiring travelling money to enable him to return to Sarajevo, he was advised by a friend to apply to this Serbian society which often secretly helped Bosnian émigrés. He did so, and the same Major Vasitch, who was also an active "Black Hand" member and who had befriended Princip, gave him fifteen dinars, a quantity of *Narodna Odbrana* literature, and the advice, "Be always a good Serb." [82] He then returned to Sarajevo in December, 1912. But after quarrelling with his friends there, he left the city and worked for a while on a newspaper in Trieste. From there he went to Abbazia in October, 1913, where, according to a recent statement,[83] he told a friend of his intention to assassinate the Archduke Franz Ferdinand. The friend aided him to go again to Belgrade, where he was given employment in the Serbian Government Printing Office, by its Director, Zhivojin Dachitch, one of the founders of

---

[81] His father, who is said to have been an Austrian spy, committed suicide in 1924, near the tenth anniversary of his son's attempt on the Archduke.   [82] Pharos, pp. 4-5.

[83] By Dr. Orlitch, in the Zagreb *Rijetch* of July 10, 1927; quoted by Dr. Wiesner in KSF, V, 884, Sept., 1927.

the *Narodna Odbrana*. It was while there that he received
from one of the members of the Sarajevo *Kruzhoc* at Easter,
1914, a newspaper clipping announcing the Archduke's
coming visit to Bosnia. He at once determined to take
advantage of this favorable opportunity to carry out his
intention of assassinating Franz Ferdinand, and quickly
found that "Black Hand" officers were ready to supply him
and two fellow émigrés with the necessary bombs and
revolvers.[84]

The third member of the student trio who conspired at
Belgrade to go to Sarajevo to murder Franz Ferdinand was
Trifko Grabezh. He was expelled from the Tuzla high
school for slapping a teacher in the face during the fall of
1912, and went home for six months to his father's house at
Pale, a dozen miles to the east of Sarajevo. Then he went
to Belgrade to finish his studies, and managed to pass the
fifth, sixth and seventh classes at Easter, 1914. Here he met
Princip and other émigrés, and became fired with Serbian
nationalism and an eagerness to participate in political
assassination.[85]

Meanwhile, at Lausanne and Toulouse, Gatchinovitch
was plotting the assassination of Austrian officials, though
there is disagreement as to the details in the accounts left
by his fellow conspirators. The version given by Mr.
Seton-Watson, on the basis of what he learned from persons
now living in Sarajevo is as follows. In January, 1913,
Gatchinovitch invited certain young Bosnians—among
them two Moslems, Mehmedbashitch and Mustapha Golubitch—to meet him at Toulouse. Here he provided them
with weapons and poison, for the purpose of attempting
the life of General Potiorek, the Governor of Bosnia, and

[84] Pharos, pp. 7 ff. For the false allegation of the Serbian authorities
after the assassination that they had wished to expel Chabrinovitch but
that he had been protected and vouched for by the Austrian Consulate
in Belgrade, see the article by A. von Wegerer, in KSF, IV, 330-332, May,
1926.   [85] Pharos, pp. 24, 44 ff.

forestalling their own capture by suicide. But the youth·
ful conspirators' nerve failed them; fearing a customs ex·
amination on their return across the Austrian frontier,
they threw their weapons out of the railway carriage window, and nothing further came of this design.[86] A year
later, "early in 1914, Danilo Ilitch set himself to collect
youths ready for some desperate outrage," but without any
clear idea against whom they were to act, until the announcement of the Archduke's intended visit to Bosnia.
This was clipped from a newspaper by Ilitch's friend,
Pushara, at Sarajevo, pasted on a piece of paper without
comment, and mailed to Chabrinovitch at Belgrade. This
news suggested to him and to Princip, whose "heads were
already full of terrorist ideas," the idea of assassinating
Franz Ferdinand. While they were winning over a third
youth, Grabezh, and obtaining weapons from Tankositch
and Ciganovitch, "Ilitch continued his preparations in Sarajevo quite independently of them, and armed three other
youths, Cvetko Popovitch, Vaso Chubrilovitch, and Muhamed Mehmedbashitch, none of whom had any connection with Belgrade. . . . The initiative lay, not with those
who so recklessly provided arms to the three in Belgrade,
but with Ilitch and Pushara in Sarajevo, and above all with
Gatchinovitch in Lausanne." [87]

Thus, according to Mr. Seton-Watson's version, the
initiative for the assassination plot "came from Bosnia, not
from Serbia," [88] and Danilo Ilitch took a very prominent
part in it.

[86] Seton-Watson, *Sarajevo,* p. 74.   [87] Seton-Watson, p. 77 f.

[88] Seton-Watson, p. 78. Lest his readers may not be convinced by his
evidence, he again twice repeats (pp. 144, 145) his view that "the real initiative for the crime came from within Bosnia itself." It is natural that
the Jugo-Slavs now living in Sarajevo or Jugoslavia, from whose statements
he has largely drawn his information, should seek to magnify the Jugoslav
Movement before 1914 and the oppression of the Austrian authorities in
Bosnia, and to minimize the activity of Serbian officers in Belgrade, as the
responsible causes of the crime.

According to another version, told to M. Bogitchevitch by two Serbs, Paul Bastaitch and Mustapha Golubitch, the latter of whom was himself present, the Toulouse meeting took place in January, 1914 (not January, 1913), in the Restaurant St. Jerome, Rue St. Jerome. Only Golubitch, Mehmedbashitch, and Gatchinovitch were present. The idea of the meeting came from Voja Tankositch in Belgrade. Its purpose was to prepare the assassination of the Archduke Franz Ferdinand and other important Austrian officials, with a view to rousing the Slav elements in the Hapsburg lands. After the meeting at Toulouse, Gatchinovitch wrote to Princip asking him to come to Lausanne with Danilo Ilitch to arrange the details of these assassinations. At the end of January, 1914, Mehmedbashitch returned from Toulouse to Herzegovina and soon afterwards went to see Ilitch at Sarajevo to put himself at his disposition for the murder of General Potiorek. But Ilitch at once said it was unnecessary to assassinate Potiorek because it had been decided to murder the Archduke, which was much more important. In fact, as soon as Ilitch and Princip had received Gatchinovitch's letter asking them to come to Lausanne, Princip had departed for Belgrade to ask authorization to make this journey. But Tankositch, who executed Dimitrijevitch's orders, said the journey was not necessary, as it had also been decided at Belgrade that the Archduke should be murdered. For this reason Princip was kept at Belgrade till the end of May, and trained by Ciganovitch in pistol practice.[89]

Several facts appear to confirm this second version, according to which there was already on foot an intention to murder the Archduke prior to the announcement of his intended visit to Bosnia; and the initiative for it came not from Bosnia but from Belgrade from Major Tankositch, a

[89] Bogitchevitch, in KSF, IV, 26-28, 93-95; reprinted in *Le Procès de Salonique,* pp. 151-163.

Serbian officer and one of the most active "Black Hand" leaders.

In the first place, there is every indication that the Toulouse meeting took place in January, 1914, and not in 1913. In view of the fact that Gatchinovitch fought in the First Balkan War at Scutari in the winter of 1912-13 and sent interesting reports of the fighting to the Sarajevo nationalist newspaper *Narod*,[90] it is hardly likely that he would have been at Toulouse in January, 1913. But a year later, when Serb nationalism and ambitions had been enormously swollen by the victories over Turkey and Bulgaria, would be the natural time for him to be plotting to assassinate Austrian officials as a means of hastening the further realization of Serb or Jugoslav nationalist aspirations. Furthermore, it is true that Princip went from Sarajevo to Belgrade in February, 1914;[91] this accords with the statement of M. Bogitchevitch's two informants that he departed from Sarajevo for Belgrade upon the receipt of a letter from Gatchinovitch shortly after the Toulouse meeting in January, 1914.

In the second place, the testimony concerning Danilo Ilitch at the trial of the assassins in many respects corroborates M. Bogitchevitch's version and contradicts that of Mr. Seton-Watson. Ilitch was one of the more active members of the Sarajevo *Kruzhoc*. He was some five years older than the other conspirators, who were mostly youths not out of their teens. He had been a schoolmaster, then worked in a bank, and in July, 1913, went to Belgrade.

Ilitch stayed there two months, frequented the coffeehouses used by Bosnian émigrés and "Black Hand" members like Ciganovitch and Tankositch, and "saw how indi-

<hr>

90 Jevtitch, p. 13.

91 Princip's own testimony at his trial; Pharos, p. 23; and "Confessions," p. 705.

vidual *comitadjis* knew how to get hold of bombs." [92]   Like other Bosnians who went to the Serbian capital, he drank in there the ideas current among the *comitadjis* of political agitation by terrorist acts like the assassination of high officials.   Returning to Sarajevo, he devoted his time to writing articles for nationalist Serb newspapers, to spreading revolutionary propaganda among the Bosnian youth, and to plotting with Gatchinovitch at Lausanne and Toulouse.   Having no regular livelihood, he lived at his mother's house, depending on the money she received from lodgers.[93]   Though his statements after his arrest and at the trial in October, 1914, are often confused and contradictory, evidently with the aim to escape conviction, he admitted that he had talked with Mehmedbashitch early in 1914 about the need for a political assassination as the best means for realizing the Jugoslav ideal.   This was evidently just after Mehmedbashitch had returned from Toulouse and before the news of the Archduke's intended visit to Bosnia.   Ilitch relates that as a result of his talk with Mehmedbashitch: "We were completely agreed on the idea that an assassination must be executed.   This was before they came upon the idea of carrying out an attempt against the Heir to the Throne. . . . Since we had no weapons, we decided to go to Serbia for them because here [in Bosnia] one cannot get them, and in Serbia they are cheaper.   We did not decide which of us should go to Serbia, but whoever should first decide to make the journey should tell the other he was going to get the weapons." [94]   But a little later he received a letter from Princip which made it unnecessary for either him or Mehmedbashitch to go to Serbia after weapons: "It was by chance about our Easter time, that one day—I no longer remember the date—I received a letter from Princip from Belgrade, in which he said he had the

---

[92] Ilitch's own testimony at the trial; Pharos, p. 62; *cf.* also Jevtitch, pr 22-24   [93] Pharos, 59 f.   [94] Pharos, p. 60.

intention of carrying out an assassination, and that he would have the weapons for it, and that I was to collect some fellow assassins. Later I did collect some. . . . When I received the letter from Princip, I wrote to Mehmed-bashitch [at Mostar] and told him that the weapons would come." [95] Princip likewise stated at the trial: "I wrote to him [Ilitch] from Belgrade in very indefinite terms that I would carry out the assassination. . . . [After arriving in Sarajevo about three weeks before the crime] I said to him [Ilitch] that he should collect some other serviceable participants in the assassination, people who could be relied on." [96]

The independent testimony of these two conspirators against the Archduke's life makes it clear that Ilitch had no weapons except those which Princip and his two companions were to bring from Serbia; and furthermore, that the idea of recruiting more participants came from Princip and not from Ilitch; whether this suggestion was contained in Princip's letter, however, or whether it was made by him in person after his arrival at Sarajevo, is not clear. The leading spirit was not Ilitch but Princip, and the active impulse came from Serbia and not from Bosnia. The testimony of these two men clearly contradicts Mr. Seton-Watson's version, quoted above, that "early in 1914 Danilo Ilitch set himself to collect youths"; and that while Princip, Chabrinovitch and Grabezh were obtaining arms in Belgrade, "Ilitch continued his preparations in Sarajevo quite independently of them, and armed three other youths, Cvetko Popovitch, Vaso Chubrilovitch and Muhamed Mehmedbashitch, none of whom had any connection with

[95] Ilitch's testimony; *ibid.*, pp. 60-62.

[96] Ilitch's testimony, *ibid.*, p. 28 f. Similarly, in his "Confessions" in prison, Princip says he wrote in cipher to Ilitch, who "was under his [Princip's] influence though he was five years older and formerly a teacher," saying that "he himself would also take part," and "would procure five or six weapons" (*Current History*, Aug., 1927, p. 706).

Serbia." In reality Ilitch did not set himself to collect youths until after Easter, after receiving Princip's letter, and very probably not until Princip's arrival at Sarajevo about three weeks before the crime.[97] Nor can it be true that Ilitch, while Princip and his two companions were still in Belgrade, "continued his preparations in Sarajevo quite independently of them" and "armed three other youths," because he had no arms until Princip brought them. Incidentally it may be noted that neither Ilitch nor his Sarajevo recruits appear to have had the nerve or determination to do the deed. None of them raised a finger on the fatal day. Had it not been for the fixed purpose with which Princip and Chabrinovitch had come from Belgrade it is probable that the Archduke would have come and gone unharmed. More will be said on this point later in connection with the responsibility for the crime.

Furthermore, though there is no doubt that Mr. Seton-Watson's version is correct in so far as it relates to the newspaper clipping sent at Easter from Sarajevo to Chabrinovitch in Belgrade,[98] it is to be noted that Princip declared energetically that even before this clipping was received, he had formed the determination to carry out the deed: "I know positively that before Chabrinovitch received the clipping I said to him that I would carry out the assassination." [99]

As between these two accounts of Mr. Seton-Watson and M. Bogitchevitch, one may say that the latter is in many

[97] The testimony at the trial concerning Popovitch and Vaso Chubrilovitch seems to indicate that they were recruited by Ilitch for the deed only a few days before it was to be committed, and that they really lacked the nerve and determination for the actual deed (cf. Pharos, pp. 52 f., 64 f., 69 ff., 76 ff.). The idea of having a number of assassins armed was to make the demonstration of protest against Austria's rule appear to be as wide as possible; as Grabezh testified, "we wished to be as many as possible in order in this way more to show the discontent" (ibid., p. 55).

[98] Cf. Pharos, pp. 7, 23; Jevtitch, p. 25 f.

[99] Cf. Pharos, p. 40, Chabrinovitch, however, claimed the doubtful honor of first suggesting it to Princip.

respects nearer the truth.   Both contain certain statements which it is difficult to accept.   But there seems to be
no doubt that the effective impulse to the plot came from
Princip at Belgrade and not from Ilitch at Sarajevo.   Evidently the idea of carrying out a political assassination had
been plotted in the winter of 1913-14 by Princip, Gatchinovitch and Ilitch, and this was the purpose of the Toulouse
meeting, but probably these plotters had not yet definitely
decided whether the victim should be the Austrian Archduke
or General Potiorek, who was hated as being immediately
responsible for the severity of the Austrian régime in
Bosnia; the preference appears at first to have been to take
vengeance on the Governor of Bosnia rather than on the
Heir to the Throne.[100]   At the same time, it is likely that
Princip had, as he says, "formed the determination" to kill
the Archduke.   It is probable that he had been strengthened
in this determination, if indeed it was not suggested to him
by Ciganovitch in Belgrade, who was an intimate associate
of Major Tankositch, and who later secured from Tankositch the Browning revolvers to be used against the Archduke.   Both Princip and Chabrinovitch declared at the trial
that Ciganovitch had told them that the Freemasons had
already decreed in 1913 that the Archduke must be killed,
but the decree had not been executed because no assassins
had yet been found to do the deed.[101]   All three youths
asserted that both Ciganovitch and Tankositch were members of a Masonic Lodge in Belgrade, and Chabrinovitch
mentioned their dealings with a mysterious "man," who
came and went and finally gave the word that it was time
for them to cross over from Serbia to Bosnia to carry out
the plot against Franz Ferdinand.[102]   Whether the Freemasons had actually passed any such decree, or whether
this idea arose from the fact that Franz Ferdinand was

---

[100] Pharos, p. 8; Jevtitch, pp. 15 ff., 22; Princip's "Confession," p. 705.
[101] Pharos, pp. 14, 33, 162.   [102] Pharos, pp. 11 f., 14, 33 f., 58, 162.

known to be a zealous Roman Catholic and hence obnoxious to Freemasons, or whether Ciganovitch and his friends used "Freemasons" as a convenient screen for hiding the activities of the "Black Hand," cannot be determined with certainty.[103] But the statements of the youths in Belgrade concerning Ciganovitch, Tankositch, and the Freemasons indicates that there had been discussion by them of the question of the Archduke's assassination.

On the whole, one may conclude that at a Toulouse meeting in January, 1914, Gatchinovitch, in collaboration with Princip and Ilitch, plotted to terrorize the Austrian authorities by assassinating either Franz Ferdinand or Potiorek, probably the latter; but the plot came to nothing either because the assassins lost their nerve, or because it had meanwhile been decided at Belgrade to make the Archduke the victim. Princip then went to Belgrade in February, 1914, having formed the decision to assassinate the Archduke, and got into touch with Ciganovitch, and through him with Major Tankositch. When the newspaper clipping arrived with the announcement of the Archduke's intended visit to Bosnia, this visit was at once seized upon

---

[103] "Pharos," judging by his preface, footnotes, and care in reproducing passages relating to Freemasonry at the trial of the assassins, evidently suspected the Freemasons of having contributed to the crime. *La Conspiration Serbe,* p. 33, quotes a prophecy alleged to have been made by a high Masonic official and published in the *Revue internationale des sociétés secrètes,* II, 788 (1912) to the effect that the Archduke made a good appearance and it was too bad that he had been condemned and that he would die upon the steps to the throne. The responsibility of the Freemasons has been a favorite theme of many writers: Karl Heise, *Die Entente-Freimaurerei und der Weltkrieg: ein Beitrag zur Historie des Weltkrieges und zum Verständnis der wahren Freimaurerei* (Basel, 1919); Ernst Reventlow, *Politische Vorgeschichte des Grossen Krieges* (Berlin, 1919), pp. 29-38; H. Gruber, *Der deutsche Katholizismus im Weltkriege.* But much of their evidence concerning the Freemasons seems to be fantastic. The present writer believes it very doubtful whether they had any responsibility for the plot, but thinks it very probable that their name may have been used as a means of throwing dust in the eyes of the Austrian authorities and of covering up the real activities of the "Black Hand."

by the three youths as offering an excellent occasion for
carrying out an assassination which had already been discussed. Princip wrote to Ilitch at Sarajevo that he had
determined to do the deed, and would come bringing
weapons. In any case, the inspiration for the plot sprang
from the group of Bosnian revolutionaries—Gatchinovitch,
Princip, Ilitch, and others—all of whom had been in Belgrade and in close touch with "Black Hand" members. The
idea of murdering the Archduke had certainly been discussed before his trip to Bosnia was announced. It would
have been quite in keeping with the character of Major
Tankositch and with the fact that he later procured the
revolvers, as well as in keeping with the purposes and
methods of the "Black Hand," that the idea should have
originated with him or with his associate, Ciganovitch; but
whether it really did originate with Tankositch, as asserted
by M. Bogitchevitch's two informants, may be regarded as
uncertain until further evidence confirms their assertion.

PREPARATION OF THE PLOT IN BELGRADE

In March, 1914, the Zagreb newspaper *Srbobran* published the announcement that the Austrian army would
hold summer manoeuvres in Bosnia and that the Archduke
Franz Ferdinand would be in command. This news at first
greatly alarmed the little revolutionary group in the Sarajevo *Kruzhoc,* because it was well known that the Archduke was friendly to the Roman Catholic Croats and was
believed to favor some form of "trialism." They feared
that his visit would strengthen the Croatian bourgeoisie and
political leaders who were ready to accept political concessions from the Hapsburgs, and that it would deal a blow
at Jugoslav aspirations for national unity and independence. The Archduke's presence and the army manoeuvres
would seem to be a demonstration of Hapsburg strength
which might weaken the Orthodox Serb elements and the

irredentist movement for a Greater Serbia. But the alarm of *Kruzhoc* members was only momentary. They at once saw that here was the opportunity for the best possible political assassination of the kind which Gatchinovitch had long been preaching. But in the temporary absence of Ilitch they did not have the courage to think of planning to commit the murder themselves. Instead, they bethought them of the more reckless and fanatical Bosnian émigrés at Belgrade with their *comitadji* friends in Serbia, and decided to inform them of the Archduke's intended visit. One of their number, Pushara, clipped the announcement from the newspaper, pasted it on a card without any commentary except "Greetings," and typewrote the address to Chabrinovitch at his coffee-house in Belgrade. In order not to draw any suspicion to themselves in case the letter was opened, Pushara took the letter to Zenica and mailed it there.[104]

When Chabrinovitch received the news clipping from Sarajevo, he showed it to Princip at the coffee-house where they were in the habit of meeting. In the evening they went to walk in the park to discuss it, and Princip invited Chabrinovitch to join him in murdering the Archduke. Chabrinovitch, according to his statement at the trial, had not hitherto thought of an attempt on Franz Ferdinand. He would have preferred to assassinate General Potiorek, as the personification of the Austrian system of oppression. But he now fell in with Princip's proposal.[105]   Princip, however, claimed that he had had the idea of assassinating Franz Ferdinand even before Chabrinovitch received the clipping. "By myself alone I had already previously formed the decision to do the deed. When I was in Sarajevo earlier I had already determined upon it." [106]   When confronted with one another at the trial, both claimed priority

104 Jevtitch, pp. 25-26.   105 Pharos, pp. 7 ff., 23 f.; Jevtitch, p. 27.
106 Pharos, p. 40.

for the idea, and a curious wrangle took place between them. Grabezh also claimed that he had already formed the idea independently during a brief visit to his home in Pale at Easter, 1914, when he read in *Istina* that Franz Ferdinand was coming to Bosnia. When he returned to Belgrade he showed the clipping to Princip, and the latter told him that he and Chabrinovitch were ready for the deed. "So am I," replied Grabezh, and from that moment the three youths discussed the ways and means for realizing their project.[107]

Among the Serbian *comitadjis* who frequented the coffee-houses with the Bosnian émigrés was Milan Ciganovitch, a Bosnian by birth, who had come to Belgrade some years before. He had been trained as a *comitadji* by Major Tankositch and fought under him during the Balkan Wars. He had joined the "Black Hand" as "No. 412," and in 1914 enjoyed a subordinate position on the Serbian State Railways. He had often talked with Princip about the oppressive conditions in Bosnia before this time,[108] fully approved the idea of murdering Franz Ferdinand, and offered to provide the weapons and other means. A little later he took Grabezh to his room, and showed him a chest full of bombs which he had either secured from the Serbian arsenal or saved from the Balkan Wars. But since bombs were somewhat uncertain, only exploding after a few seconds, it was agreed that the murderers ought also to be provided with revolvers.[109]   To secure these, Ciganovitch turned to his fellow members in the "Black Hand"—to Major Tankositch, who got from Dimitrijevitch the money with which to buy them.[110]   Ciganovitch also told the youths of the

107 Pharos, pp. 45 ff.; Princip's "Confessions," p. 706.

108 Pharos, p. 24.   109 Pharos, pp. 9, 24, 47.

110 Chabrinovitch testified at the trial, on being asked where Ciganovitch got the money and the Browning revolvers: "I do not know. He [Ciganovitch] got the money from Tankositch. This man endorsed a check with one of his colleagues [presumably Dimitrijevitch], cashed it, and bought the weapons. In our name Grabezh went to Tankositch

"tunnel," or underground railway, by which Serbian officials would help them over the frontier and put them in touch with "confidential men" on the Bosnian side. At the suggestion of Tankositch, who wanted to make sure that there would be no failure, Ciganovitch also gave the students revolver practice in a shooting park near Belgrade.[111]

So far during the preparations it was Ciganovitch with whom the students dealt chiefly. But Ciganovitch evidently was acting with the approval of Major Tankositch and Col. Dimitrijevitch, who were leading members of the Supreme Central Committee of the "Black Hand." Ciganovitch, in talking with the students, several times spoke of Tankositch. Shortly before the students left Belgrade, Ciganovitch took one of them—Grabezh—to the lodgings of Tankositch, who wanted to convince himself that the youths were determined in their purpose and knew how to use the weapons.[112]   Tankositch, however, judging at least by the statements made at the trial, kept himself for the most part carefully in the background. Grabezh declared: "Ciganovitch had an understanding with Major Tankositch. But he was a side-figure. The man mainly guilty, if one wants to speak of guilt at all, is Ciganovitch."[113]   The students denied knowing whether Tankositch was a member of the "Black Hand," but asserted that "he had a conflict" with the *Narodna Odbrana,* and was on bad terms with the Serbian civilian officials.[114]

Tankositch asked him: 'Are you ready?' When Grabezh answered 'Yes,' he asked him about us, whether we were reliable fellows. Grabezh assured him that he could guarantee us. What further dealings he had with Tankositch I do not know at all;" Pharos, p. 10. On Grabezh's visit to Tankositch's lodgings and talk with him, see *ibid.,* pp. 24, 47 f. Chabrinovitch's testimony about the money and revolvers coming from Tankositch and Dimitrijevitch is confirmed by Bogitchevitch who says (KSF, III, 440, note 1) that Dimitrijevitch actually showed him and others the receipted bill for the purchased revolvers.

[111] Pharos, pp. 9 ff., 24 f., 47 f.   [112] Pharos, p. 24.   [113] Pharos, p. 47.

[114] Pharos, pp. 14, 43, 55, 82. In the latter part of the preparations for the secret journey, with the aid of the frontier military officers, they

Dimitrijevitch kept himself even more completely in the background. The students declared that Ciganovitch had merely referred mysteriously to "a man" whom he had to consult about procuring the weapons, and that he seemed to get his instructions as to the time for their departure and other matters only after consulting some other important person.[115] Whether the students at their trial were really as ignorant of Tankositch and Dimitrijevitch and the "Black Hand" as they appeared to be, or whether they were carefully concealing from the Austrian authorities the real connection of these high Serbian military officers with the plot, one cannot say. In the first case, one must admire the secrecy with which the "Black Hand" leaders worked, or, in the second, the skill with which the students managed to throw the Austrian officials off the right track.

In order to avoid suspicion more easily and escape ar-

admitted that Tankositch took a direct and active part (ibid., 47, 82).

In this connection may be noted the improbable story of Jovan M. Jovanovitch, in the Politika, December 4, 1926. When the plotters had first applied to Tankositch, he had disapproved of the idea of murdering the Archduke. Thereupon the youths had applied directly to Col. Dimitrijevitch, and he had sanctioned the plot, but without telling anyone else. There were at first five conspirators who got as far as Shabats, but before crossing over the frontier one of them turned traitor. The civil authorities got wind of it, and upon the order of Protitch, the Minister of Interior, the conspirators were brought back to Belgrade; so the first effort failed. But it contributed to the antagonism between the Radical Party and the "Black Hand" just at this time. Tankositch was not informed of this first effort, but after it he was importuned by Princip and Chabrinovitch to help them cross over into Bosnia; he then changed his attitude and did so. Such is the story told by the former Serbian minister at Vienna.

The three youths nowhere make any mention of this first arrest, which, if true, would be certain evidence that the Serbian Government had knowledge beforehand of the plot. And it would confirm the statement of Ljuba Jovanovitch, quoted above, at note 13, that, at the end of May or beginning of June, Pashitch learned of a plot. Jevtitch, p. 30, says: "Three weeks before Vidov-Dan [June 28th] these young people came through 'tunnels' to Bosnia. Probably due to someone's indiscretion, something was known about the movements of the émigrés. The Belgrade police immediately made several raids, but without any apparent success."

[115] Pharos, pp. 33 f., 162.

rest, the three assassins finally left Belgrade for Sarajevo some three weeks before the Archduke's arrival in Bosnia. Before their departure, Ciganovitch provided them with six bombs from his room, four Browning pistols and ammunition, 150 dinars in cash, and some cyanide of potassium with which they were to commit suicide immediately after killing the Archduke, in order to lessen the possibility of any confessions or statements which might incriminate the Serbian officers in Belgrade who had helped to prepare the plot.[116] They were also provided with a map of Bosnia showing the roads which they were to follow and the Austrian gendarmerie stations which they were carefully to avoid.

Meanwhile at Sarajevo, Danilo Ilitch, who had been in correspondence with Princip, soon recruited a number of local men who would be armed with the extra weapons which the three assassins from Belgrade would bring with them.

JOURNEY OF THE ASSASSINS FROM BELGRADE TO SARAJEVO

From Belgrade to Shabats, the three assassins went up the Save by boat. They carried a note from Ciganovitch to the frontier commander at Shabats, Major Popovitch, and were to say to him that they were being sent by Major Tankositch. But they were carefully warned not to make themselves known to the civilian authorities, lest they should be arrested and sent back.[117] Arriving at Shabats,

---

116 This precaution, as it turned out, was not successful: Princip swallowed the poison, but threw it up immediately in great pain before it had taken effect. Chabrinovitch took his dose, but it did not work. Grabezh did not have any because Ilitch mislaid the dose which he was to take; Pharos, pp. 17, 18, 35, 55; Princip's "Confessions," in *Current History,* Aug., 1927, p. 702; Jevtitch, p. 29, is incorrect in saying that Chabrinovitch alone took the poison.

117 Chabrinovitch testified: "Ciganovitch had expressly told us that we were to take care that none of the civilian authorities should learn anything of our journey and purpose. If it became rumored about the Ministry of Interior would have us at once arrested;" Pharos, p. 80 f.

they easily found Major Popovitch at a coffee-house, and told him that they were journeying secretly to Bosnia. He seemed to be already well acquainted with their mission, having probably learned of it directly from Tankositch during a visit to Belgrade a couple of days previously.[118] He conducted the three students to the guard-house and secured an order for them for buying half-fare tickets on the railway for the next stage of their journey from Shabats to Lozhnica, where they were to cross the frontier. He also gave them a card to the frontier authorities: "The officials concerned are requested to assist these people." [119] Finally, he filled out for them a false pass, making it appear that one of them was a Serbian exciseman and the other two his colleagues. With the half-fare railway tickets, they went by train to Lozhnica and delivered to the frontier captain the card from Major Popovitch. He immediately telephoned to the excisemen's watch-house directly on the border, but could get no connection. He therefore told the youths to return in the morning. Next day it was arranged that Chabrinovitch should take the false pass and go on to Zvornik, where he was helped over the frontier by a Serbian exciseman and later driven across Bosnia to Tuzla. Meanwhile Princip and Grabezh, with the bombs and revolvers, were driven back a few miles to a watch-house near Ljeshnica, where they were met by prearrangement by another Serbian exciseman who smuggled them over the Drin by way of the Bosnian Islands. There he handed them over to a peasant in whose hut they spent the night. Next day they were passed on to another peasant, who conducted them safely along by-paths in Bosnia toward Priboj until they were met by Veljko Chubrilovitch.[120]

Veljko Chubrilovitch was an Orthodox Serb school-

---

[118] Pharos, pp. 15 f., 48, 82.   [119] Pharos, p. 36 f.
[120] Pharos, pp. 15 ff., 34 ff., 48 ff., 80 ff.; cf. Dr. Wiesner, in KSF, VI, 332 ff., April, 1928. For this region, see the sketch-map, above, p. 47.

master at Priboj and the "confidential man" of the *Narodna Odbrana* for this region. He had made trips to Serbia, had become a member of the *Narodna Odbrana,* and then chairman of the Priboj *Sokol,* one of the apparently harmless and "cultural" Serb organizations which were a medium, however, for active Serbian propaganda. He was in touch with *Narodna Odbrana* officials in Serbia and other "confidential men" in Bosnia and with local peasants who appeared to be in the habit of smuggling letters and information across the frontier.[121] He now took Princip and Grabezh to the house of another peasant, Jacob Kerovitch, and arranged that the latter's son should drive the two conspirators and their weapons on to Tuzla, where they would find another "confidential man," the cinema director, Mishko Jovanovitch. Princip and Grabezh accordingly set out that night in the peasant's cart. On approaching Lopare, where Austrian gendarmes were stationed, they let the peasant drive on alone with the weapons well hidden, while they made a detour on foot and mounted the cart again on the other side of the village. Arriving at Tuzla early in the morning, they went to the cinema director, Mishko Jovanovitch, as the Priboj school-master had directed, and found a ready reception.[122]

As Princip and Grabezh had just come from Serbia and had no travelling passes for Bosnia, they feared that they might be stopped and searched on entering Sarajevo at a time when the police might be expected to be keeping an especially sharp eye out for suspicious characters in view

[121] Pharos, pp. 83 ff.

[122] Mishko Jovanovitch was a middle-aged, well-to-do business man in Tuzla, being chairman of the Serbian parish school board, director of a local Serbian bank, and manager of a cinema. In 1912, at the urging of his relative, Chubrilovitch, he had gone to Shabats, become a member of the *Narodna Odbrana,* and then distributed its literature in Bosnia, for which his position in the Serb school gave him an excellent opportunity. Letters found in his house spoke of "working for beloved Serbia" and "risking one's life for Serbia;" Pharos, p. 83 ff.

of the Archduke's coming visit. They did not think it was
safe that they should carry the bombs and revolvers any
further. They therefore begged Jovanovitch to hide the
weapons in his house until some safer person should come
from Sarajevo to fetch them. He agreed, and hid them in
his attic. It was arranged that the person who came for
them should identify himself by offering a half-open package of Stephanie cigarettes. The three youths then went
on safely by train from Tuzla to Sarajevo. Princip at once
sought out Ilitch, took lodgings with him, and told him of
the weapons at Tuzla. Grabezh went to his home in Pale.
All three lived as quietly and inconspicuously as possible
until the time for the deed. Thus, the "tunnel," often mentioned by Ciganovitch, which Serbian officials had long
prepared, had worked to perfection.[123]

A few days later Ilitch went to Tuzla and identified
himself to Mishko Jovanovitch in the agreed-upon way
with the package of cigarettes. Fearful, however, that he
might be arrested if seen carrying a large package in Tuzla
where he was not known, he begged Jovanovitch to bring
the weapons to Doboj on the way to Sarajevo, and hand
them over to him there. This was finally agreed upon.
Jovanovitch concealed the bombs and revolvers in an inno-
cent-looking paste-board sugar box, and took them to
Doboj. Not finding Ilitch at once as he had expected, he
left the explosives under his raincoat in the railway waiting-
room and later in a friend's shop in care of a child; in either
place they might easily have been discovered. Finally
Ilitch turned up, took charge of the precious package, carried it safely to Sarajevo by train, and hid it under a couch
in his room. A few days before the crime he gave some of
the weapons to two of his own Sarajevo recruits, and took
them to a suburb to show them how to shoot.[124]

123 Pharos, pp. 28 ff., 51 ff., 103 ff.; Jevtitch, p. 30 ff.
124 Pharos, pp. 63 ff., 70 ff., 76 f., 105 ff.

Early on the morning of the day Franz Ferdinand and his wife were to make their formal visit to Sarajevo, Princip and Chabrinovitch met Ilitch at the back of the Vlajinitch pastry shop and received again from him some of the weapons they had brought from Belgrade—Princip took one of the Browning revolvers, Chabrinovitch a bomb, and Grabezh both a revolver and a bomb. Then they dispersed to take their stand at various places, as agreed upon, along the route which the Archduke was to pass.

THE ASSASSINATION, JUNE 28, 1914

Sarajevo, for some five hundred years, had been the capital of Bosnia and is still its principal city. It is crowded into a narrow valley at the foot of high hills. Through its center runs a little river, the Miljachka, half dry in summer. In the older parts of the city toward the cathedral the streets are crooked and narrow. But the Appel Quay, now known as the Stepanovitch Quay, is a fairly wide straight avenue lined with houses on one side, and with a low wall on the other, where the Quay follows the Miljachka. It leads towards the Town Hall, and is connected by several bridges with the other side of the town, where one of the principal mosques and the Governor's residence or Konak are situated. Along the Appel Quay, which was the route the Archduke and his wife were to follow, Ilitch had placed the various murderers to whom he had distributed the bombs and revolvers a few hours before the assassination. Mehmedbashitch, Vaso Chubrilovitch and Chabrinovitch were on the river side near the Cumurja Bridge. Ilitch and Popovitch were across the street, near the Austro-Hungarian Bank. Further along the Quay Princip at first stood near the Latin Bridge; after Chabrinovitch's attempt, while the Archduke was at the Town Hall, he crossed over the Quay to the corner of the narrow winding Franz Josef Street, now King Peter Street. where the actual assassination finally took place. Further on toward the Town Hall Grabezh was walking up and down, looking for a good place where he would not be interfered with by the police or bystanders.[125]

On Vidov-Dan, Sunday, June 28, 1914, the day opened with glorious summer weather. The streets, at the request of the Mayor, had been beflagged in the Archduke's honor. His portrait stood in many windows. Considerable crowds were abroad in the streets to see him pass. No effort was made to keep them back, by forming a line of soldiers, as had been done in 1910 when Francis Joseph visited the city. Several of the loyal newspapers welcomed the Archduke's presence, but the leading Serb newspaper, *Narod*, contented itself with the bare announcement of his visit, and devoted the rest of its issue to a patriotic account of the significance of Vidov-Dan, an account of the Battle of Kossovo, and a picture of King Peter of Serbia framed in the national Serbian colors.

Franz Ferdinand and his party reached Sarajevo from Ilidze about 10 A. M. After reviewing local troops, they started in autos toward the Town Hall for the formal reception in accordance with the announced program. The Heir to the Throne was in full uniform, wearing all his decorations. His wife, in a white gown and large hat, sat beside him. On the seat facing them was General Potiorek, the

[125] For various details of the assassination, see the testimony of the accused and the witnesses at the trial in Pharos, and *La Conspiration Serbe, passim,* and especially the accounts of General Potiorek and Count Harrach. One of the most trustworthy contemporary accounts is the report of the Archduke's military secretary, Col. Bardolff, to Conrad on July 3 (Conrad, IV, 19-22). Of the newspaper accounts that by René Gourdiat, the local correspondent of the Paris *Matin*, is the best; *Sarajevo, 28 juin, 1914* (Thionville, 1920); it appears to have attracted little notice, until largely drawn upon by R. Recouly, *Les Heures Tragiques d' avant Guerre* (Paris, 1923), ch. vii. Jevtitch, *Sarajevski Atentat,* exaggerates the part played by the local Sarajevo conspirators and the certainty of success of their arrangements. His account is largely followed by Seton-Watson, *Sarajevo,* ch. x, and by Clair Price, *N. Y. Times Magazine,* June 22, 1924, p. 2. Jules Chopin [J. E. Pichon], *Le Complot de Sarajevo* (Paris, 1918) is full of fantastic errors.

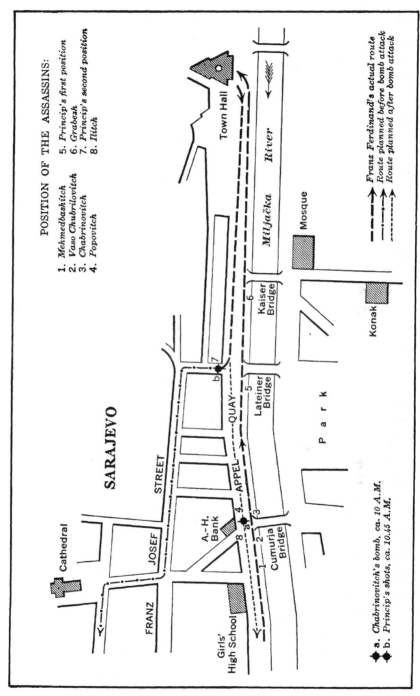

POSITION OF THE ASSASSINS:

1. Mehmedbashitch 5. Princip's first position
2. Vaso Chabrilovitch 6. Grabezh
3. Chabrinovitch 7. Princip's second position
4. Popovitch 8. Ilitch

SARAJEVO

Cathedral

FRANZ

JOSEF STREET

A.-H. Bank

Girls' High School

Cumurja Bridge

Lateiner Bridge

Kaiser Bridge

APPEL QUAY

Miljačka River

Town Hall

Park

Mosque

Konak

● a. Chabrinovitch's bomb, ca. 10 A.M.
◆ b. Princip's shots, ca. 10.45 A.M.

- - - → Franz Ferdinand's actual route
—·—·→ Route planned before bomb attack
- - - -→ Route planned after bomb attack

123

military Governor of Bosnia, who pointed out the objects of interest as they drove along. In front of them, in another car, the Mayor and Chief of Police led the way. Then followed two other autos bearing various persons belonging to the Archduke's suite or General Potiorek's staff.

Just as they were approaching the Cumurja Bridge and Potiorek was calling the Archduke's attention to some new barracks, Chabrinovitch knocked off the cap of his bomb against a post, stepped forward, and hurled it at the Archduke's car. The chauffeur, observing him, put on speed, so that the missile fell onto the folded hood of the uncovered car and bounced off; or, according to another account, Franz Ferdinand, with extraordinary coolness, seized it and threw it back of him into the road. There it exploded with a heavy detonation, partly wrecking the following auto and seriously wounding Lieut.-Col. Merizzi and several bystanders. Chabrinovitch sprang over the wall into the river-bed, which was nearly dry at this season of the year, and tried to escape; but police agents quickly seized him and marched him off for examination. Meanwhile the fourth auto, uninjured except for a broken windshield, passed the wrecked car and closed up quickly to that of the Archduke, none of whose occupants had been hurt, except for a scratch on the Archduke's face, probably caused by the flying cap of the bomb. The Archduke ordered all the cars to stop, in order to learn what damage had been done. Having seen that the wounded men were dispatched to a hospital, he remarked with characteristic coolness and courage: "Come on. The fellow is insane. Gentlemen, let us proceed with our program." [126]

So the party drove on to the Town Hall, at first rapidly, and then, at the Archduke's order, more slowly so that the people could see him better. The Archduke's wife met a

[126] Recouly, p. 183; and accounts of Potiorek, Harrach, and Bardolff cited in preceding note.

deputation of Mohammedan women, while the Archduke was to receive the city officials. The Mayor, who had written out his speech of welcome, started to read it, as if nothing had happened. But it hardly suited the occasion. It dilated upon the loyalty of the Bosnian people and the overwhelming joy with which they welcomed the Heir to the Throne. Franz Ferdinand, by nature quick-tempered and outspoken, roughly interrupted the Mayor, saying: "Enough of that. What! I make you a visit, and you receive me with bombs." [127] Nevertheless, he allowed the Mayor to finish his address. This terminated the formalities at the Town Hall.

The question then arose whether the party should still follow the prearranged program which provided for a drive through the narrow Franz Josef Street in the crowded part of the city and a visit to the Museum; or whether, in view of another possible attack, they should drive straight to the Governor's residence on the other side of the river for luncheon. The Archduke insisted that he wanted to visit the hospital to inquire after the officer who had been wounded by Chabrinovitch's bomb. General Potiorek and the Chief of Police thought it very unlikely that any second attempt at murder would be made on the same day. But as a punishment for the first, and for the sake of safety, it was decided that the autos should not follow the prearranged route through the narrow Franz Josef Street, but should reach the hospital and Museum by driving rapidly straight along the Appel Quay. Therefore the Archduke and his wife and the others entered the cars in the same order as before, except that Count Harrach stood on the left running-board of the Archduke's car, as a protection from any attack from the Miljachka side of the Quay. On reaching the Franz Josef Street the Mayor's car in the lead turned to the right into it, according to the original

[127] Recouly, p. 184; cf. Jevtitch, p. 38.

program. The Archduke's chauffeur started to follow it, but Potiorek called out. "That's the wrong way! Drive straight down the Appel Quay!" The chauffeur put on the brakes in order to back up. It happened that it was precisely at this corner, where the car paused for a fatal moment, that Princip was now standing, having crossed over from his original position on the river side of the Quay. These chance occurrences gave him the best possible opportunity. He stepped forward and fired two shots point blank. One pierced the Archduke's neck so that blood spurted from his mouth. The other shot, aimed perhaps at Potiorek,[128] entered the abdomen of Sophie Chotek.

The car turned and sped over the Latin Bridge to the Konak. The Archduke's last words to his wife were: "Sophie, Sophie, do not die. Live for our children." But death overtook them both within a few minutes. It was about 11:30 A. M., St. Vitus's Day, Sunday, June 28, 1914.[129]

[128] At his trial and in prison Princip maintained that his second shot was intended for Potiorek and that he had not meant to kill the Archduke's wife; Pharos, p. 30; Nikitsch-Boulles, p. 227.

[129] Accounts of Potiorek, Harrach and Bardolff in Pharos, pp. 155-159, and Conrad, IV, 19-22.

CHAPTER III

THE RESPONSIBILITY FOR THE SARAJEVO ASSASSINATION

THE preceding chapters on Balkan Problems, Franz Ferdinand, and the Assassination Plot have given a brief narrative of the events and an account of the conditions which contributed to the fatal tragedy at Sarajevo. They will also have indicated to some extent the responsibility for it. But they left aside several much-disputed questions which can now be best dealt with separately, before one attempts to draw any final conclusions concerning the relative responsibility for the crime which was the immediate occasion of the World War. Chief among these disputed points are the motives of the assassins, the lack of Austrian police protection, the part played by Dimitrijevitch and the "Black Hand," M. Pashitch's cognizance of the plot and failure to prevent it, and the alleged Serbian warning to Austria.

MOTIVES OF THE ASSASSINS

A man's motives are ordinarily mixed, and often not even fully understood by himself. This is particularly true in the case of a political murderer, who has every reason to expect that one of the consequences of his act will be his own death. One would naturally expect to find each assassin assigning various reasons for his deed, and to find that the different conspirators differed somewhat from one another in the emphasis which they placed on their various motives. This is in fact the case with the half dozen youths who conspired against Franz Ferdinand. Princip and Chabrinovitch, however, may conveniently be considered together, not only because they may be regarded as the ringleaders, and because they had the courage of their convictions to make the actual attempts on the Archduke's life, but also because their motives were much the same.

The best materials for judging their motives are their statements after their arrest and at their trial, if due allowance is made for the fact that they were speaking as prisoners under indictment for murder and treason, and were trying to shield each other and their accomplices in Serbia. Of this attempt to shield each other and their accomplices among the Serbian officers in Belgrade there is abundant evidence. When first arrested, Princip declared that he alone was guilty, that he had acted as an anarchist, "convinced that there is nothing so fine as to commit a political assassination," and that his attempt had no connection with that of Chabrinovitch. "I have nothing in common, I repeat, with the author of the first attempt. When the bomb exploded, I said to myself, that there is someone else who thinks as I do." [1]   This, of course, was totally false, as soon appeared when Chabrinovitch and Grabezh were arrested and their confessions made it clear how the three had conspired together at Belgrade and came to Sarajevo with the common purpose of murdering Franz Ferdinand. Even at their trial in October, 1914, when much of the truth was known about their activities and that of the *Narodna Odbrana,* all three students sought to shield the Belgrade authorities by asserting that the *Narodna Odbrana* was "purely cultural," that it did not extend to Bosnia, and that it had nothing to do with their preparations.[2]   But these assertions were shown to be untrue, both by their own admissions, and by the evidence of the "confidential men" of the *Narodna Odbrana* in Bosnia, as to the way the three

---

[1] Princip's first confession, as published in the Budapest *Az Est* of July 1, 1914.   [2] Pharos, pp. 15, 34, 43, 55, 82, 162.

youths had been helped forward by the "tunnel" on their journey from Belgrade to Sarajevo.[3] Similarly Princip and Chabrinovitch denied knowing much of anything about the "Black Hand" except what they had read in newspapers, and denied having met Major Tankositch; they admitted, however, that he had procured the weapons and money, and that he had asked Grabezh to come to his room so that he could convince himself that the three youths were to be relied on.[4] How far these denials of knowledge of the "Black Hand" and its leaders were true, in which case the youths would be acting as the more or less ignorant tools of this secret Serbian terrorist organization, and how far the denials were purposely concocted to shield it and deceive the Austrians, one cannot at present say with certainty. Probably the latter hypothesis is closer to the truth than the former.

Making allowance for this tendency in their statements, one may say that the motives of Princip and Chabrinovitch were mainly of three kinds.

In the first place, there was a personal motive—a feeling of discontent with their own lives, of the desire to be martyrs and heroes after the fashion of Bogdan Zherajitch, who fired five shots at the Governor of Bosnia and then committed suicide at Sarajevo. Both Princip and Chabrinovitch had been unhappy at home, and received little or no financial support from their parents. Chabrinovitch had quarrelled often with his father and with his fellow Socialists at Sarajevo. Both youths had early left school but had not become established in any occupation. They drifted to Belgrade where they came under the influence of anarchist and terrorist propaganda, and heard the coffee-house talk about Austria's oppression and Serbia's future rôle as the "Piedmont" which would bring liberation to the Bos-

[3] See preceding chapter, at notes 40-48.
[4] Pharos. pp. 10, 24, 47 ff.; see also preceding chapter, note 110.

nian Serbs. Both, but especially Chabrinovitch, suffered from ill health and lack of proper food, and were probably already tubercular. Both died in prison not long afterwards, Chabrinovitch in January, 1916, and Princip in the spring of 1918. Life seemed to hold out little for either of them, but they could at least secure the glory of a martyr's crown by imitating the example of Zherajitch.

Princip declared, after being at Belgrade but before hearing of the Archduke's coming visit to Bosnia: "I often used to go out to the grave of Zherajitch. I often passed whole nights there, pondering over our conditions and our miserable situation and over him [Zherajitch], and then I determined upon the assassination. On his grave I made an oath to myself to carry out an assassination at some time or other." [5] Later, in prison, he told Dr. Pappenheim that, "in Sarajevo he used to dream every night that he was a political murderer, struggling with gendarmes and policemen; that he had read much about the Russian revolution, about the fightings; and that this idea had taken hold of him." [6]

Chabrinovitch also stated: "I too went to the grave of the late Zherajitch, when I came to Sarajevo. There I fixed upon the firm determination to die as he had done. I knew moreover that I had not long to live. I was continually occupied with the idea of suicide, because I was indifferent to everything." [7] His psychopathic thirst for notoriety is suggested by the fact that he had his photograph taken an hour or so before he threw the bomb and attempted suicide,[8] and also by his boast a moment after his

[5] Pharos, p. 40. Jevtitch, p. 21 f., adds that on the eve of the assassination, Princip again went to the grave as to a holy shrine "to bid good-bye to Zherajitch with a big wreath."

[6] Current History, August, 1927, p. 706.

[7] Pharos, p. 40 f. He also said Gatchinovitch's eulogy of Zherajitch, "The Death of a Hero," had made a great impression upon him (ibid., p. 21).

[8] The photograph is reproduced in Pharos, p. 165.

attempt on the Archduke, "Yes, I am a Serb, a hero." [9]
Both youths were clearly psychopathic, maladjusted by
personal suffering, discontent and failure, and easily open
to suggestive influences toward murder by the example of
"heroes" and the talk of Belgrade *comitadjis*.

A second motive was to take vengeance on Austria for
the oppressive régime in Bosnia, arouse opposition to it,
and prepare the way for a revolution which should put an
end to it. "What moved me primarily," declared Chabrinovitch, "was revenge for the oppression which the Serbs in
Bosnia and Herzegovina had had to suffer, especially the
'Exceptional Laws' which last year continued for two full
months. . . . I regarded revenge as the holy duty of a
moral civilized man, and therefore I planned to take vengeance. . . . I knew that there existed at the Ballplatz
[the Austro-Hungarian Foreign Office] a clique, the so-
called war-party, which wanted to conquer Serbia. At its
head stood the Heir to the Throne. I believed that I should
take vengeance on them all in taking vengeance on him.
. . . I hated him because he was an enemy of Serbia. . . .
All the injustices of which I read in the newspapers—all
this had collected in me until it burst forth on St. Vitus's
Day." [10]

[9] Testimony of Josef Mitro, who helped arrest him; *La Conspiration
Serbe*, p. 121.

[10] Pharos, p. 13 f. This declaration shows incidentally how the Serb
Nationalist Press stirred up hatred and opposition against Austria by
misrepresenting the facts. The "Exceptional Laws" were indeed very
repressive and objectionable, but they had been cancelled in 1913 in
accordance with Bilinski's policy of conciliation (see above, ch. ii, note
61). Franz Ferdinand, though a friend of Baron Conrad who headed the
war-party in Vienna, was not a member of any Vienna war clique himself;
on the contrary, he had often used his influence against it in favor of
peace; he represented a friendly, rather than hostile, policy toward the
Serbs; his policy of "trialism" would have favored them at the expense
of the Germans and Magyars in the Dual Monarchy (see above, ch. i,
passim).

At the close of the trial, giving his final defense, Chabrinovitch said
the idea of killing Franz Ferdinand had not been a spontaneous idea with

Princip likewise, on being asked if he was sorry that he had killed the Archduke replied: "No, I am not sorry. I have cleared an evil out of the way. He [Franz Ferdinand] is a German and an enemy of the South Slavs. He treated them badly. . . . Every day a high treason trial. Every day it went worse with our people. They are impoverished. I have seen how our people fall more and more into decay. I am a peasant's son, and so I can convince myself of the misery of our people. I killed him and I am not sorry. I knew that he was an enemy of the Slavs. . . . I regarded him as an energetic man who as ruler would have carried through definite ideas and reforms which stood in our way." [11] "For union [of the South Slavs] one must sacrifice many lives, and it was for this reason that Franz Ferdinand fell. Nevertheless, the main motive which guided me in my deed was: the avenging of the Serbian people." [12]

A third motive was to kindle further opposition and hatred toward the Hapsburg rule, cause a revolution among the Serbs in Bosnia and Herzegovina, and so prepare the way for tearing these two provinces away from the Dual Monarchy and uniting them with Serbia in some kind of a national South Slav state. Princip had hinted at this in the passage just quoted, where he expressed the fear that Franz Ferdinand on coming to the throne might make some energetic reforms—such as the carrying out of his "trialistic" plan to unite the South Slavs, not by union with Serbia

himself and his two associates, but had been suggested to them by the milieu in which they lived in Belgrade, where the assassination was represented as a noble enterprise. The men with whom they associated had kept repeating that the Archduke ought to be done away with, because he was an obstacle to the realization of the Jugoslav idea. Although Princip remained defiant and unrepentant, the other defendants regretted what they had done. They had not known that the Archduke had children, and begged the forgiveness of these orphans; *La Conspiration Serbe,* p. 147.

[11] Pharos, p. 30 f. Similarly Chabrinovitch: "People said that he [Franz Ferdinand] wanted to establish a federal monarchy including Serbia;" *ibid.,* p. 10.   [12] Pharos, p. 36.

but by giving them an organic position under the Hapsburgs comparable to that enjoyed by the Germans in Austria and by the Magyars in Hungary. Asked if that was the kind of union he wanted, Princep exclaimed, "God forbid!", thereby causing laughter in the court room.[13] On the contrary, he believed unification would come through the action of Serbia: "I am a nationalist. I aimed to free the Jugoslavs. For I am a Jugoslav. This is to come from intimidation—from above. . . . As far as Serbia is concerned, it is her duty to free us, as Italy freed her Italians."[14]

This accords also with his later "Confessions" in prison: "The ideal of the young people was the unity of the South Slav peoples, Serbs, Croats, and Slovenes, but not under Austria. In a kind of state, republic or something of that sort. Thought that if Austria were thrown into difficulties then a revolution would come. But for such a revolution one must prepare the ground, work up feeling. Nothing happened. By assassination this spirit might be prepared."[15] "He considered that if he prepared the atmosphere, the idea of revolution and liberation would spread first among men of intelligence and then later in the masses. Thought that thereby attention of the *intelligentsia* would be directed upon it. As, for instance, Mazzini did in Italy at the time of the Italian liberation."[16] "Could not believe that a World War would break out as a result of an act like his. Did indeed think that a World War might break out, but not at that moment."[17] This was precisely the trend of opinion which was set forth at Belgrade in much

[13] Pharos, p. 29.

[14] Pharos, p. 23. Similarly Chabrinovitch: "We said we must organize the Serbs [in Bosnia], provide them with means, dynamite and bombs, so that they could make a revolution before the war, and so that Serbia could just come over and establish order;" *ibid.*, p. 11.

[15] *Current History*, August, 1927, p. 703.

[16] *Current History*, p. 706.

[17] *Current History*, p. 704.

of the *Narodna Odbrana* propagandist literature and in the "Black Hand" newspaper *Piedmont* which inspired Princip and his companions.

Chabrinovitch agreed with Princip in working like Mazzini to prepare a revolution in Bosnia which should open the way for a reunion of all the Serb lands which had once formed the Empire of Stephen Dushan. But his political evolution had been somewhat different. He had at first held anarchist and social revolutionary opinions, but after living in Belgrade and mixing with *comitadjis* he had become more nationalist—"anarchistic with a mixture of nationalism," as he defined his position in 1914.[18]

His ideal was a Jugoslav republic, not a monarchy with a Serbian dynasty. The unification of the Serb peoples was to be accomplished, "after Mazzini's fashion. The ideal was to tear Bosnia away from the Dual Monarchy. We were all agreed in that. Some were for the [Karageorgevitch] dynasty; I was a republican. We could therefore have made a compromise, that King Peter should be king during his lifetime, and that after his death a republic should be proclaimed." [19]

Such were the three chief motives of the two principal plotters. But which was the strongest of the three—their personal psychopathic condition, or their desire for vengeance on Austria, or their Serb nationalism—it would be difficult to say. Jugoslav writers and sympathizers of today, like M. Jevtitch and Mr. Seton-Watson, emphasize Jugoslav nationalism as the main motive. But in 1914 the accused themselves hardly knew. Princip, being asked whether he had acted primarily from revenge or from the idea of national unity—i.e., whether the personal or the political motive predominated, replied, "The personal. But the other was also strong. They were evenly balanced." [20]

[18] Pharos, p. 6.   [19] Pharos, p. 7.   [20] Pharos, p. 41.

It is often urged in mitigation or explanation of the crime that it was a wanton provocation on the Archduke's part to hold maneuvers in Bosnia, that the Serbs feared he meant to attack Serbia, and that they resented his visiting Sarajevo precisely on a Serb national anniversary like Vidov Dan. This has been stressed since the event by writers hostile to Austria and friendly to Serbia.[21] But Princip's and Chabrinovitch's own statements do not indicate that such considerations had any considerable influence upon them. They had in fact begun to organize their plot when they heard of the Archduke's coming trip to Bosnia but *before they were aware that he would visit Sarajevo on Vidov Dan.* They had decided to assassinate him in Bosnia, not because they resented the visit or feared an attack on Serbia, but because his presence in Bosnia afforded an excellent opportunity for giving effect to the three motives which have been sketched above.

THE "BEVY OF ASSASSINS" AND THE AUSTRIAN "NEGLIGENCE"

Most Jugoslav sympathizers, and most critics of Austria who follow the fantastic insinuations of Mr. H. Wickham Steed, like to represent the assassination of the Archduke as virtually inevitable, both because of the Austrian oppression, the wide-spread nationalist movement in Bosnia, and the "bevy of assassins" lying in wait for him, and also because of the "criminal negligence" of the Austrian authorities in not taking adequate precautions to protect him.[22]

[21] E.g., Seton-Watson, *Sarajevo,* p. 110; Jevtitch, pp. 32-34; and Jovan Jovanovitch in his letter of 1924, concerning his "warning," quoted below at note 68. Fear of an Austrian attack under the Archduke's leadership is also often given as the motive for Dimitrijevitch's share in the plot (*cf.* Stanojevitch, p. 55 f.; Wendel, *Die Habsburger und die Südslawenfrage,* p. 50 ff.); but it is very unlikely that any such fear was really one of his motives (*cf.* Wegerer, in KSF, III, 385 f., June, 1925).

[22] H. Wickham Steed, "The Pact of Konopischt," in *The Nineteenth Century and After,* LXXIX, p. 265 ff.; *Through Thirty Years,* I, 401; Recouly, *Les Heures Tragiques,* p. 108 ff.; Chopin, *Le Complot de Sarajevo,* pp. 89-100; Dumaine, *La Dernière Ambassade de France en Autriche,* p.

After the crime, in the recriminations of Austrian officials as to the responsibility for not averting it, and in the boasts of Jugoslav survivors at having participated (or intended to participate) in a glorious deed which has ultimately resulted in the creation of a Jugoslav state, it is easy to collect many expressions of opinion which seem to bear out these views. Thus, Mr. Wickham Steed quotes the Archbishop of Sarajevo as saying that "the Archduke could not have escaped, because he would have had to pass through 'a regular avenue of bomb-throwers.' " [23]   Mr. Seton-Watson also quotes this, and unhesitatingly accepts all the stories which have been told to him of heroes who would have assassinated the Archduke had not Princip done so.[24]   He even speaks of "a whole bevy of assassins on the streets of the capital." [25]

At the same time, both these writers blame the Austrian authorities for their lack of police protection. Says Mr. Steed: "When the Emperor Francis Joseph visited Sarajevo in June, 1910, more than one thousand uniformed police and probably double the number of 'plain clothes men' were employed to protect him. In June, 1914, when the Heir Presumptive went there the police were warned off." [26]   Similarly Mr. Seton-Watson: "Every street [at the Emperor's visit in 1910] along which he passed was

147; Seton-Watson, pp. 77-79, 106-114, 144-152; Jevtitch, *passim;* Clair Price, in *N. Y. Times Magazine,* June 22, 1924, p. 2.

On Wickham Steed's fantasies concerning the Konopischt Meeting, see above, ch. i, pp. 32-43. Recouly and Dumaine intimate that at Sarajevo the Austrian authorities, instead of detailing proper police, assisted in placing the assassins at favorable points; and Chopin attempts to show that Chabrinovitch was an Austrian *agent provocateur* who had been sent to Belgrade before the crime in order to give the impression of Serbian complicity! Such intimations are pure fiction. Nor has there been any confirmation of the story of the Croatian, Rudolph Bartulitch, that the assassination was the result of Magyar connivance (*cf.* G. Beck, *Ungarns Rolle im Weltkriege,* Lausanne, 1917, pp. 215-218).

[23] Steed, *Through Thirty Years,* I, 401.

[24] Seton-Watson, *Sarajevo,* pp. 77-79, 147 f.

[25] Seton-Watson, p. 110.   [26] Steed, *Through Thirty Years,* I, 401.

lined with a double cordon of troops, and the town swarmed with special police and detectives from headquarters in Vienna and Budapest"; but in 1914 the police "showed itself strangely remiss or inefficient." "The contrast between 1910 and 1914 amply justifies us in speaking of criminal negligence on the part of those Austro-Hungarian authorities with whom the care of the Archduke lay." [27] But to assert that the assassins were so numerous that the Archduke could not have escaped, and at the same time to blame the police for negligence in not saving him, is illogical. As a matter of fact, neither was the danger to him from residents in Bosnia so great, nor the conduct of the Austrian authorities so strangely negligent, as these writers would have us believe.

On the Archduke's journey up through Bosnia from the Adriatic to Ilidze, and at the maneuvers, he was received with demonstrations of loyalty and there were no signs of danger. Soon after his arrival at Ilidze he and his wife motored in to Sarajevo, visited some of the shops, and were everywhere recognized and acclaimed. So great was the crowd about them that a passage had to be cleared for them. Here would have been an excellent opportunity for assassins.[28] On the fatal Sunday morning it is noteworthy that only those conspirators who had just come from Belgrade had the courage of their convictions. Chabrinovitch and Princip acted, and perhaps Grabezh would have done so also, if he had not had an uneasy feeling that he was being shadowed by police.[29] There was something about the atmosphere in Belgrade and the talk of the *comitadjis*

[27] Seton-Watson, *Sarajevo*, p. 109 f.; for his repeated assertions of "criminal negligence," see also pp. 129, 287.

[28] Conrad, IV, 14 f., 65 f.; Nikitsch-Boulles, p. 213; Jevtitch, p. 33, adds the piquant detail that, as the Archduke stopped in front of one of the bazaars, he came almost face to face with Princip; "Princip saw him, but did not move; behind him a stranger, undoubtedly a police agent, had carefully spread his hands. The same evening in the *kruzhok* Princip told us about the meeting." [29] Pharos, p. 53.

there which bred a firm determination to assassinate Austrian officials. It is significant that it was directly after being trained in Serbia by one of the officers of the later "Black Hand" group that Bogdan Zherajitch came to Sarajevo to assassinate the Governor of Bosnia in 1910. It was directly after a visit to Belgrade where he received a bomb from a Serbian major and a Browning revolver from a comrade, that Lukas Jukitch used this revolver to shoot the Commissioner of Croatia in 1912. Similarly Princip, Chabrinovitch and Grabezh had come straight from Belgrade with the firm determination to execute the plot prepared there.

But the resident youths who were recruited by Ilitch in Sarajevo and who had not been in Belgrade were a less robust sort of conspirators. Mr. Seton-Watson ascribes much importance to this Sarajevo group, in his effort to emphasize the Bosnian, and to minimize the Serbian, aspects of the plot. But he is in error, as has been pointed out above, in saying that the Sarajevo recruits were already being armed by Ilitch while Princip and his two companions were still in Belgrade. They had no arms until the Belgrade conspirators brought them.[30]

Ilitch himself appears to have lost his nerve, and to have advised abandoning the attempt. He asserted at the trial that he had tried to dissuade the Belgrade conspirators from carrying out their purpose. If his assertion stood alone and unsupported, one might well discount it as a fiction intended to exculpate himself. But it is confirmed

---

[30] See above, p. 107 ff. Nor can one accept his view that "the entire initiative came from Bosnia" and that the murder would have been committed anyway even without the bombs brought from Belgrade, because, "after all, it was a 'Browning' that did the mischief, and there were plenty of Brownings available without importing them from Serbia" (*Sarajevo*, p. 147). All the evidence at the trial shows that the youths had no money with which to buy revolvers, that Brownings were very difficult to get in Bosnia, and that Ilitch had planned to go to Serbia as the only place where he could secure them (*cf.* Pharos, pp. 9 f., 19, 23 f., 47 f., 61).

separately by Princip, Chabrinovitch, and Grabezh.[31]
Asked why he had not destroyed the weapons, if he was
really opposed to the assassination, Ilitch replied: "I did
not dare. Princip had told me that he had received the
bombs from *comitadjis*, and therefore I did not dare to
throw them away, in view of my going to Serbia." [32]
Shortly before the crime Princip told Chabrinovitch that he
did not regard Ilitch as "reliable." [33] Certain it is that
Ilitch himself did not raise a finger against the Archduke
on Vidov Dan, nor did any of his three recruits. Mehmedbashitch let the procession of autos pass without taking any
action, but, after hearing Chabrinovitch's bomb, fled pre-
cipitately to Montenegro—the only one of the seven armed
men who was not speedily apprehended by the police
Similarly Popovitch and Vaso Chubrilovitch watched the
Archduke's party go by—and did nothing; after the crime
the latter, "all pale and trembling in his whole body," came
to one of his friends and got him to take and hide his
weapons.[34] Such was the "bevy of assassins"—three determined conspirators who had come from Belgrade, and

[31] Pharos, pp. 20, 29, 41 f., 52 f., 60, 62, 64, 66 f. 83.

[32] Pharos, p. 83. This fear of vengeance from Serbians, which arose
from the "Black Hand" secret vows and terrorist methods, is also vividly
given by several of the "confidential men" who formed the "tunnel' as their
excuse for assisting the three conspirators on their journey from Belgrade
to Sarajevo (*ibid.*, pp. 87 f., 95 f., 98, 104, 138). Thus, the Priboj school-
master, Chubrilovitch, declared: "I feared the annihilation of my family.
Our house is only five miles from the frontier, and so we could be ruined
in a night—all destroyed and murdered. . . . I had heard what horrors the
secret organizations in Serbia had committed in Macedonia. Now I
feared that Princip might be a member of one of those organizations,
and so I was apprehensive about my head. I thought there must be
some one standing behind Princip; because otherwise how would he have
gotten the bombs? I had heard of a landowner in Old Serbia whose whole
family had been annihilated" (p. 95). For actual examples of *comitadji*
terrorist intimidation, see *ibid.*, p. 81, quoted below at note 46; and Miss
Durham, *The Serajevo Crime*, pp. 55-74.

[33] Statements of both men; Pharos, pp. 20, 42. Grabezh also, on
hearing the bomb explosion, at once concluded that it was Chabrinovitch's
bomb, because he regarded Ilitch and his recruits as "of poorer quality
as assassins" (*ibid.*, p. 53). [34] Kranjchevitch's testimony, *ibid.*, p. 115.

a hesitating and "unreliable" Sarajevo ex-schoolmaster with three weak-kneed local recruits. If it had not been for the first three, and for the excellent chance opportunity afforded by the mistake of the Archduke's chauffeur in turning into the Francis Josef Street and stopping just at the point where Princip happened to be standing, it is altogether probable that there would have been no assassination.

MR. PASHITCH, THE *NARODNA ODBRANA* AND THE "BLACK HAND"

Some indication has already been given in the preceding chapter of the activity of the *Narodna Odbrana* and the "Black Hand," and of the probable cognizance of a plot on the part of Mr. Pashitch and some members of his Cabinet. But to understand more adequately the responsibility of Serbia something further must be said concerning the relation of these two Serbian organizations to one another and to the Serbian Government.

The Serbian Government may be regarded as responsible for the activities of the *Narodna Odbrana*. This society was publicly organized by prominent Serbians, including some members of the Serbian Cabinet of 1908. Its central committee sat in the Serbian capital and its president was General Jankovitch. Its statutes were published, and its activities, alleged to be "cultural," were publicly approved by members of the Serbian Government, with which it remained on intimate and friendly terms. It was organized originally to prepare forcible means for preventing Austria from carrying through her policy of annexing Bosnia and Herzegovina. But after the crisis of March, 1909, when Russia failed to back up Serbian hopes, and Serbia was forced to make to Austria her promise to live on good and neighborly terms, the *Narodna Odbrana* ostensibly changed its aims from the use of force against Austria to the "cultural work" of stimulating national feeling within the King-dom of Serbia.

As a matter of fact, it continued a secret subversive work of propaganda in Bosnia: smuggling in nationalist Serb literature and recruiting "confidential men" who should organize ostensibly harmless local societies for edu-cation, physical training, and the anti-alcohol movement, but who in reality were to rouse Serbian nationalism and prepare the ground for the eventual unification with Serbia of the Serb populations in the Dual Monarchy. It had also given assistance and encouragement to Bosnian youths who came to Belgrade to study or to plot assassina-tions and revolution against the Hapsburg authorities. Though the *Narodna Odbrana* probably had no knowledge officially of the plot to assassinate Franz Ferdinand, its net-work of "confidential men" and its "tunnel" for secret communications between Serbia and Bosnia were certainly used by "Black Hand" officials and by the three youths who went from Belgrade to Sarajevo to commit the crime.[35] This interlocking activity between the two Serbian socie-ties, which otherwise had somewhat different ostensible aims and were not altogether friendly, was facilitated by the fact that the Secretary of the *Narodna Odbrana,* Milan Vasitch, and other members of it were also members of the "Black Hand." Thus the Serbian Government may be re-garded as responsible for an organization whose secret agents in Bosnia were preparing the way for the disruption of Austria-Hungary and were actually made use of to assist the Archduke's assassins on their journey to Sarajevo. Austria was therefore justified in her demand in the ulti-matum to Serbia that the *Narodna Odbrana* be dissolved.

The relations of the Serbian Government to the "Black Hand" were quite different. This secret society had "budded itself off" from the *Narodna Odbrana,* in the words of one

[35] See above, ch. ii. at notes 56-59 and 117-123.

of the witnesses at the trial of the Sarajevo assassins,[36]
being formed in 1911. The clique of military officers, who
had murdered King Alexander and Queen Draga in 1903,
had become impatient at the ostensibly "cultural" activities of the *Narodna Odbrana* and at the policy of the
Pashitch Radical Party of postponing the final struggle
with Austria until Serbia had liberated Serbians under
Turkish rule, greatly consolidated her internal resources
and strength, and made more certain of the support of
Russia and France. The "Black Hand" was a very secret
terrorist organization; its members were designated by
numbers instead of by their names; and its curiously
medieval statutes were never published until the famous
Salonica Trial of 1917. The Serbian Government was well
aware of the existence of this organization, which was a
matter of common knowledge in Belgrade and was discussed
in the newspapers,[37] but probably did not know at first
in any detail its membership and all its subterranean
activities.

At first the relations between the Serbian Government
and the "Black Hand" leaders were tolerably harmonious.
This Society included Dimitrijevitch, who was advanced
in June, 1913, to the position of Chief of the Intelligence

[36] Stanarinchitch; in *La Conspiration Serbe,* p. 109; see also above,
ch. ii. p. 85 ff.

[37] Chabrinovitch, being asked at the trial if he knew of a secret
fraternity at Belgrade known as the "Black Hand," replied, "Yes, I
know from my reading that the "Black Hand" exists in military circles";
Pharos, p. 14. *Cf.* also Potiorek to Bilinski, July 14, 1914 (Conrad, IV,
83): "There exists in Serbia by the side of the official Government a
military secondary government [eine militärische Nebenregierung]. It
is proven that active Serbian officers coöperated in the plot and in the
whole propaganda in a preëminent way, and therefore are to be counted
among the originators of the treasonable agitation stirred up in our
country. To be sure the army is not part of the Government. But to
try to maintain that the official Serbian Government does not know what
the army is doing, is not at all allowable." For further evidence that the
"Black Hand" was a matter of common knowledge in Belgrade and well
known to the Serbian Government, see Bogitchevitch, *Le Procès de Salonique,* p. 31 ff.

Department of the Serbian General Staff, Major Tanko-sitch, who was one of the most famous *comitadji* leaders, and a large number of other officers. It was regarded primarily as a group of military men, but it also included a considerable number of civilian officials, among whom were at least three employees in the Serbian Ministry of Foreign Affairs.[38]   Prince Alexander at the outset favored it.   He is said to have contributed 26,000 dinars toward the support of its newspaper organ, *Piedmont,* to have made various presents to the officers, and to have paid the expenses of Dimitrijevitch's illness in the fall of 1912.   But when he intimated that he would like to be made head of it, the officers for various reasons did not take the hint; this rebuff wounded the Prince's pride and was the beginning of an estrangement which widened when he sided with the Pashitch Radical Party against the "Black Hand" in the so-called "priority-question." [39]

This "priority-question" arose after the Balkan Wars out of a dispute between the military and civilian officials

[38] Milan Gavrilovitch, No. 406; Y. Simitch, No. 420; and S. Simitch, No. 467, according to the partial list of members identified by Dr. Bogit-chevitch, *Le Procès de Salonique,* pp. 53-58.   He includes also in the list, though without giving his number, the name of Mr. Pashitch's nephew, Milutin Jovanovitch, formerly Secretary in the Ministry of Foreign Affairs, then Serbian Chargé d'Affaires at Berlin in 1914, and later Serbian Minister to Switzerland.   For other details on the rules and membership of the "Black Hand," see above ch. ii., p. 86 ff.

[39] Bogitchevitch, *Le Procès de Salonique,* pp. 7 ff.; 34; Protocol of the Salonica Trial, p. 195.   Shortly before the assasins left Belgrade, Prince Alexander visited the Government Printing Office, with the Director, Zhi-vojin Dachitch, an ardent Serbian nationalist. Here he was made acquainted with Chabrinovitch whom Dachitch had employed as a typesetter.   Questioned after his arrest concerning this meeting, Chabrinovitch admitted it, but then suddenly refused to answer any further questions, as if fearing to incriminate Prince Alexander.   These circumstances, together with evidence collected by the Austrians in Belgrade during the War, have suggested to some writers the possibility that Dachitch and Prince Alexander may have known something of the assassination plot; *cp.* Pharos, pp. 6, 11; and the articles by A. von Wegerer and Friedrich von Wiesner in KSF, IV, 485-489, 639-661, July, Sept. 1926.   But this cannot be regarded as definitely established.

concerning the government of the territories which Serbia had conquered from Turkey. The Radical Party, headed by Mr. Pashitch, instead of extending the Serbian constitution to the new districts as demanded by the army officers, had introduced a Draconian régime which angered the inhabitants and quite surpassed in violence and oppressiveness anything which had occurred under Hapsburg rule in Bosnia.[40] The blame for this, according to the military officials and articles in *Piedmont,* lay with the selfish and incompetent civilian officials whom the Radicals placed in charge of the newly conquered districts. According to the Radicals, military officers were improperly refusing to admit the priority of authority decreed by the civilians. In this conflict the officers were supported by the Opposition political groups who demanded the resignation of the Pashitch Cabinet. The Minister of Interior tried to deal a blow to the "Black Hand" by seizing its club quarters. The conflict reached such a point at the beginning of June, 1914, that Pashitch asked King Peter to dissolve the Skupshtina and give the people an opportunity to express themselves on the matter in a new general election. The King at first refused. Pashitch thereupon actually did resign. He doubtless counted on strengthening his own hand, believing that no one else would be able to form a Cabinet in his place. At this point in the ministerial crisis Mr. Hartwig, the Russian Minister in Belgrade, is said to have intervened and helped smooth the way for the restoration of the Pashitch Cabinet as being indispensable for the policy of collaboration with Russia and France. On June 11, King Peter had to restore Pashitch to power, and a few days later, on grounds of ill health, retired from Belgrade, leaving his

[40] For the text of this Serbian decree of Oct. 6, 1913, concerning government of the "liberated" territories, see *La Conspiration Serbe,* pp. 171-180. See also Stanojevitch, *Die Ermordung des Erzherzogs Franz Ferdinand,* p. 53 ff.; and Wendel. *Die Hapsburger und die Südslawenfrage,* 54 i.

M. PASHITCH

Serbian Prime Minister 1912-1918

COLONEL DIMITRIJEVITCH

son, Alexander, as Prince-Regent.[41]

This internal party conflict between the Pashitch Radicals and the "Black Hand" military officers is often cited as proof that Dimitrijevitch and the Sarajevo assassins were in no way in league with the Serbian Government and would have tried to conceal all knowledge of the assassination plot from it. This is probably true. There are several indications at the trial of the assassins that they were warned by their Serbian military friends to avoid letting the Serbian civilian authorities get wind of what was on foot.[42]

So it may be regarded as perfectly certain that Mr. Pashitch and his Cabinet had nothing to do with the originating of the assassination. It was hatched behind their backs. They probably had no knowledge of it until the preparations were nearly complete and the youths were about ready to go from Belgrade to Sarajevo. On the other hand, the fact that the Government and the "Black Hand" group were in political conflict over the "priority-question" is no proof that no knowledge of the plot came to the ears of the Government. We have, on the contrary, the clear and explicit statements of the Minister of Education, Mr. Ljuba Jovanovitch, that at the end of May or beginning of June, Mr. Pashitch knew that certain persons were preparing to go to Sarajevo to murder the Archduke; that he told some of his Cabinet of it; and that orders were given to the frontier authorities to stop the assassins, but the orders were not carried out because the frontier authorities were members of the "Black Hand" organization, and reported afterwards that the orders had arrived too late and the youths had already crossed over. We have already

---

[41] Bogitchevitch, *Le Procès de Salonique,* p. 8 ff.; Stanojevitch, p. 54; Seton-Watson, *Sarajevo,* p. 139 f.; and London *Times* and Vienna *Neue Freie Presse,* for May and June, 1914, *passim.*

[42] Pharos, p. 80 ff

given our reasons for believing these statements of the
Minister of Education to be true.[43]

THE SERBIAN NEGLECT TO ARREST THE ACCOMPLICES

The significance of the "priority-question" does not lie
merely in the presumption that the Serbian Government
was at first ignorant of the assassination plot. Even more
important is the fact that it affords one explanation of two
of the most serious charges which have been brought
against Mr. Pashitch: his failure to give any definite warning to the Austrian authorities after he was aware that the
assassins had gone to Sarajevo, and his remissness after the
murder in failing to search for and arrest the accomplices
in Belgrade.

In fact Serbian police officials appear to have actually aided one of them, Ciganovitch, conveniently to disappear from sight. To have attempted to arrest Ciganovitch, who was a member of the "Black Hand," and to have
exposed the part taken by such prominent members of it
as Dimitrijevitch and Tankositch, would have still further
accentuated the political conflict and have strengthened the
antagonism which had already caused the temporary downfall of the Cabinet. Mr. Pashitch apparently did not dare
to take action against the leaders of such a powerful organization, and therefore adopted a purely passive attitude
hoping that Austria and Europe would not learn the truth.

Precisely when and how Mr. Pashitch learned of the
plot has not been revealed from Serbian sources. One commonly accepted theory is that he was secretly informed of
it by Milan Ciganovitch, who is believed to have played a
double rôle as a kind of *agent provocateur*, both conspiring
with the "Black Hand" leaders, and at the same time being
employed by Mr. Pashitch to spy upon them and keep him
informed in the interests of the Serbian Government and

[43] See above, ch. ii. p. 61 ff.

the Radical Party.[44] Ciganovitch was freely declared by all three of the Sarajevo plotters, both at their arrest and at their trial, to have taken a most active part in their preparations in Belgrade. He was a Bosnian Serb, who came as an émigré to Belgrade in 1908, was trained as a *comitadji* by Tankositch, and then given employment as a small official on the Serbian State Railways. In 1911 he was enrolled in the "Black Hand" as "No. 412," and fought as a *comitadji* under Tankositch in the Balkan Wars. In the preparation of the plot he served as the agent of Tankositch. He secured for Princip and his companions in Belgrade the bombs and revolvers which were to be used against the Archduke. He gave them the cyanide of potassium with which to poison themselves after the crime, and thus prevent revelations concerning Ciganovitch himself and his Serbian accomplices. Upon orders from Tankositch, Ciganovitch took the youths to a shooting park near Belgrade and gave them practice in the use of the revolvers. At the end of May, when they were ready to start, he supplied them with cards of introduction to "Black Hand" agents and "confidential men" who would help them forward on their journey to Sarajevo.[45] The reasons for believing that Ciganovitch informed Pashitch do not lie in any direct evidence prior to the assassination, but in the apparent collusion between them afterwards—in the action

[44] Bogitchevitch, *Le Procès de Salonique*, pp. 32, 131-133, 142 f.; and in KSF, III, 18 f., Jan., 1925; M. E. Durham, *The Serajevo Crime*, pp. 53, 80-85, 174-182; A. von Wegerer in KSF, III, 380-384, June, 1925; articles by Dimitrijevitch's personal friend and fellow "Black Hand" member, Col. Bozhin Simitch, in the French review *Clarté* for May, 1925, and in the Vienna publication *La Fédération Balkanique*, May 31, 1925; N. Nenadovitch, "Die Geheimnisse der Belgrade Kamarilla," *ibid.*, Dec. 1, 1924; and F. von Wiesner's obituary notice on Ciganovitch, who died Sept. 28, 1927, in KSF, V, 1041-1048, Nov., 1927. Most of these writers draw part of their conclusions from the records of the Salonica Trial, in which Ciganovitch was a prominent witness against Dimitrijevitch.

[45] Pharos, pp. 9-12, 14-17, 19, 24 f., 33 f., 37-39, 47 f., 55, 82; and Austrian *Dossier* of 1914, Appendix VIII.

of the Serbian authorities in attempting to conceal Ciganovitch and have him conveniently disappear from sight, and
in the evidence which Ciganovitch gave in 1917 to aid the
Radical Party in convicting Dimitrijevitch and in breaking
the power of the "Black Hand."

Within a couple of days after the assassination, when
rumors began to reach Belgrade of the confessions made by
Chabrinovitch and Princip, both Tankositch and Pashitch
appear to have tried to suppress all information about the
Belgrade accomplices.   On the evening of June 29 three
comitadjis "came to Mr. Svetolik Savitch, owner of the
newspaper *Balkan*, and told him in the name of Major
Tankositch that under no circumstances was he to publish
anything in his newspaper about any of the connections
and relations of the assassin Chabrinovitch with their
acquaintances here [in Belgrade].   Above everything he
was not to write anything which might in any way compromise Serbians; *otherwise it would fare badly with
him.*" [46]   This kind of intimidation—fear of violence and
vengeance from *comitadjis* like Tankositch—was frequently
mentioned by "confidential men" in Bosnia as one of their
motives for assisting the assassins.[47]   It suggests an additional reason why Mr. Pashitch did not care or dare to
make any move to arrest this popular and powerful "Black
Hand" leader, until finally forced by the Austrian ultimatum to detain him for a few days.

On June 30 the Austrian Chargé d'Affaires inquired of
the Serbian Government what police measures it had taken,
or proposed to take, "to follow up the clues to the crime
which notoriously are partly to be found in Serbia," but
was informed that "the matter had not yet engaged the

[46] Confidential report of the Belgrade Police to Protitch, Serbian
Minister of Interior, June 30, 1914; discovered by the Austrians after
the capture of Belgrade; published in the *Hrvatski Dnevnik* (Croatian
Daily), No. 132, May 12, 1916; and reprinted in Pharos, p. 81, note 45.
Italics by the present writer.   [47] See above, note 32.

attention of the Serbian police" [48]—"that up to the present nothing had been done, and that the matter did not concern the Serbian Government." [49] High words then passed between the two, as the Austrian expressed "his extreme astonishment that any Government which was continually asserting its desire to live on good terms with its neighbors should exhibit such indifference." [50]

On June 30, Zimmermann, the German Foreign Under-Secretary, gave the Serbian Chargé d'Affaires in Berlin some timely advice with a view to averting serious complications, as we know from the report of the Bavarian Minister at Berlin:

> At the Foreign Office they hope that Serbia will now neglect nothing in order to call to account those persons guilty of the conspiracy. Mr. Zimmermann immediately and seriously called the attention of the local Serbian Chargé d'Affaires to the consequences to which a Serbian refusal in this direction might lead, and, furthermore, suggested to the Russian Ambassador that he get his Government to give the same advice at Belgrade. Mr. Zimmermann offered this counsel on the ground that no one could tell what would happen should the Serbian Government fail to fulfil its obligations, considering the wrath which the Sarajevo deed had aroused in Austria-Hungary.[51]

Zimmermann also spoke to the diplomatic representatives of England and Russia in Berlin in the same sense, with the evident hope that they would give Serbia similar good advice,[52] but they do not appear to have done so. If the Serbian Government had at once taken energetic

[48] Ritter von Storck to Berchtold, June 30; *Austrian Red Book* of 1914, No. 2.

[49] Von Griesinger, German Minister in Belgrade, to Bethmann, July 2; K.D., 12; *cf.* also B.D. 27.

[50] Von Griesinger, *ibid.*

[51] Lerchenfeld to Hertling in Munich, July 2; Dirr, p. 118; K.D., IV. Anhang IV, No. 1.

[52] *Cf.* Rumbold to Grey, June 30 and July 11; B.D., 22, 44.

action to arrest the Belgrade accomplices, and given genuine evidence of its often asserted desire to live on good neighborly terms with Austria, this would have mitigated Germany's indignation at the assassination, made her less ready to follow Austria's fatal path, and increased the chances of friendly mediation. In failing to do this, and in assuming the passive and negative attitude of waiting to see what definite incriminating evidence and charges Austria might be able to bring forward, Mr. Pashitch incurred a further serious responsibility for what befell.[53]

The Serbian Government was informed on July 6 by its Minister in Vienna that the Austrian evidence from Sarajevo indicated the Belgrade origin of the plot and implicated Ciganovitch.[54] In spite of this, and of Zimmermann's warning, it not only made no move to apprehend the accomplices in Belgrade, but it apparently actually facilitated the disappearance of Ciganovitch, the chief accomplice, in order that it might not have to hand him over to the Austrian authorities. As Ciganovitch was a Bosnian by birth, Austria might have demanded that he be extradited for trial, and Austria might have then learned the whole truth. So it was better that he should disappear. On July 8 the Austrian Government learned by a cipher despatch from its Legation in Belgrade that Ciganovitch had been in Belgrade the day of the assassination, but had left the city three days later, having been granted supposedly a month's

---

[53] Musulin, p. 221. *Cf.* Seton-Watson, *Sarajevo*, pp. 133-137, for some excellent remarks on this subject. We cannot agree, however, with his explanation that this passive attitude on Pashitch's part was owing to his "truly Oriental indifference to public opinion both about himself and about his country" (p. 136). We suspect it was his fear that Austria and Europe might learn more of the truth about the complicity of Serbian officers, and also his fear of further antagonizing the "Black Hand;" Mr. Seton-Watson concedes that "a further reason for the Serbian Government's inaction at this critical time was the rôle played by the 'Black Hand'" (p. 137 ff.). On Serbian efforts to conceal the truth and deceive Europe, see also Wegerer, "Wie Serbien England täuschte," in **KSF, V,** 238-29, March, 1927.   [54] S.B.B., 16.

vacation by the railway administration in which he was employed. The Belgrade prefect of police declared that he did not know anyone of the name of Milan Ciganovitch, but it soon appeared that it was the prefect of police himself who had brought about Ciganovitch's disappearance from Belgrade.[55] It later appeared also that his name was erased from the railway books and was reëntered under the name of Milan Danilov, and as such he continued to draw pay. When Serbian mobilization took place he quickly joined Tankositch's band. Dr. Bogitchevitch says that on August 3 or 4, 1914, he was told by Commandant Srb, who was in charge of an important Serbian railway station, that he had just assisted Ciganovitch to escape to the south.[56]

The Austrian authorities, having learned from the confessions of the assassins some of the facts about the Belgrade accomplices, demanded in the ultimatum of July 23 (Point 7) that Serbia "proceed without delay to the arrest of Major Voja Tankositch and of the individual named Milan Ciganovitch, a Serbian State employee." The Serbian Government replied a couple of days later that it had arrested Tankositch as requested, but "as regards Milan Ciganovitch, who is a subject of the Austro-Hungarian Monarchy and who up to June 15 [N. S. 28, that is, the day of the assassination] was employed (on probation) by the railway administration, he has not yet been able to be found (and therefore a writ of arrest has been issued against him)."[57] It is certainly a curious fact that the Serbian Government pretended to cease to have any knowledge of

[55] Wiesner, in KSF, V, 1046, Nov. 1927; and Austrian comment on Serbian reply to the ultimatum, Point 7; A.R.B., II, 96.

[56] Bogitchevitch, *Le Procès de Salonique*, p. 143.

[57] In its embarrassment to explain why Ciganovitch had not been arrested, the Serbian Government appears to have given its reply in various forms: as given in A.R.B., II, 47, the last clause reads: "il n'a pu encore être découvert et un mandat d'amener a été lancé contre lui;" but in S.B.B., 39, and F.Y.B., 49, "joint"—and in B.B.B., 39, "arrêté"—is substituted for "découvert," and no mention is made of "un mandat d'amener."

Ciganovitch precisely from the moment of the assassination. In view of the other facts given above, one may doubt
the sincerity of their asserted ignorance of his whereabouts
and their inability to find him. This doubt is increased by
the fact that the Minister of Education, speaking of the
period just after the assassination and before the Austrian
ultimatum, when the Serbian authorities might have arrested Ciganovitch but did not do so, indicates clearly that
his colleagues were informed about this accomplice:

> When the Austrian stories arrived from Vienna to the
> effect that the assassins had been sent to Sarajevo by an
> official of the Serbian Ministry of Public Works, a certain
> Milan Ciganovitch, Mr. Pashitch asked Mr. Jotsa Jovano-
> vitch, then in charge of that department, who this official
> of his was; but Mr. Jotsa knew nothing about him, nor did
> anybody in his department. Under pressure from Mr.
> Pashitch, they at last unearthed Ciganovitch in some small
> clerical post in the railway administration. I remember
> that somebody (either Stojan or Pashitch) said, when Jotsa
> told us this: "There, you see! It is true enough what
> people say: if any mother has lost her son, let her go and
> look for him in the railway administration." After that
> we heard from Mr. Jotsa that Ciganovitch had gone off
> somewhere out of Belgrade.[58]

DID SERBIA "WARN" AUSTRIA?

This question is exceedingly important, because of the
variety of conclusions which have been drawn from the
affirmative and negative answers which have been given to
it. On the one hand, if the Serbian Government gave a
warning at Vienna, this can be interpreted either, (1) in
favor of Serbia, as showing that the Pashitch Cabinet, on
discovering the plot, did its utmost to avert a crime and
thus went far in clearing itself of all blame in the matter;
or, (2) in favor of Austria, as proving that the Serbian

[58] Ljuba Jovanovitch, *Krv Slovenstva*, p. 14.

Government was aware of a plot, and as justifying the Austrian demand that Austrian officials be allowed to coöperate with Serbian officials in discovering the Belgrade accomplices, since the Serbian officials themselves had taken no steps in this direction. On the other hand, if no warning was given, then either, (1) the Serbian Government could claim—as in fact it did claim—that it knew nothing of any plot beforehand and was therefore wholly innocent; or, (2) in justification of Austria, it could be claimed that Serbia was guilty of concealing the plot and thus of conniving at the crime. With the possibility of these various interpretations in either direction, it is not surprising to find Serbian sympathizers arguing violently against each other, and Austrian sympathizers doing the same. Nor is it surprising that a great deal of conflicting evidence has been brought forward. In sifting it, it is helpful to fix the attention especially upon three points: To whom was the warning given, if given at all? Was it given on his own initiative and unofficially by Mr. Jovanovitch, the Serbian Minister in Vienna, or officially upon instructions from Belgrade? Did it contain any hint of a definite plot, or was it merely a vague general statement about the undesirability of the Archduke's visit to a troubled province?

The first important assertion that Serbia warned Austria came from the Serbian Minister to Russia, Mr. Spalaikovitch. In an interview in the St. Petersburg *Vechernee Vremia*, within a couple of days after the assassination, he declared the Serbian Government had given a warning in Vienna in regard to the Archduke's trip to Bosnia; it had learned that a plot was being planned by Bosnians who were embittered by the Austrian oppression and believed the Archduke was responsible for it; but in Vienna the warning was left unheeded.[59] But the truth of

[59] Summarized in the Vienna *Neue Freie Presse*, July 2, No. 17906, p. 4

this assertion and others like it was officially denied at the Vienna Foreign Office on July 3.[60]

Here the matter rested for some months, being over-shadowed by the Austrian ultimatum and the excitement of the War. It was revived again by the eminent French professor of Slavic history, E. Denis, who wrote: "Mr. Pashitch attempted in a discreet way to indicate to the Ballplatz the dangers which the Archduke was incurring; on June 21 the Serbian Minister [Jovan Jovanovitch] in-formed the Minister of Foreign Affairs that his Government had reason to believe that a plot was being prepared in Bosnia. The Chancellor [Berchtold] paid no attention to this communication." [61] Professor Denis's statement was generally accepted during the War by persons outside Ger-many and Austria, though it was emphatically contra-dicted by Berchtold when eventually brought to his no-tice.[62] It was later repeated, for instance, by Stano-

[60] The London Times, July 1, p. 7, had already reported from its Vienna correspondent that he "understood on the best authority that there is no foundation for the reports that information of the existence of a plot against the Archduke was given to the Austro-Hungarian Govern-ment by the Serbian Minister in Vienna." Mr. Pashitch also, accord-ing to an interview published in the Budapest Az Est of July 7, and copied the same day in the Neue Freie Presse, No. 17811, p. 5, is reported as saying: "The statement is false that Serbia had knowledge beforehand of the preparation of the murder and that it therefore gave a warning." The Paris Temps, July 8, p. 8, printed a summary of the Pashitch inter-view of July 7 in the Az Est; but in the leading editorial of July 10 made the extraordinary statement: "M. Pashitch in an interview of day before yesterday showed in an irrefutable manner that the Serbian Government had given warning of the danger [avait signalé le peril], and that no notice had been taken of its warning [avertissement] by the Austro-Hungarian authorities."

[61] E. Denis, La Grande Serbie (Paris, 1915), p. 277. As Denis wrote largely from Serbian sources he may have had his information from Pashitch or one of the Serbian ministers, or he may have merely copied the irresponsible Temps editorial quoted in the preceding footnote.

[62] In a letter of May 9, 1917, to the Austrian historian, Leopold Mandl: "The fantastic statements of Professor E. Denis . . . are a pure invention from A to Z, both as to Jovanovitch's communication to me, as well as to my ignoring it. Whether an order of this kind was sent by Pashitch to Jovanovitch, but was ignored by the latter, I am of course

Jevitch,[63] who even claimed that its truth could be proved by a certain bundle of documents in the Austrian Foreign Office marked "Reg. B. 28 VI, 1914"; but the archivists of the present Austrian Republic have searched the records, and state that no papers with any such marking are to be found; and Professor Stanojevitch has been unable or unwilling to tell what source of information led him to think there was such a record. These Austrian denials that Jovanovitch ever gave any warning of any kind to Berchtold or the Ministry of Foreign Affairs are unquestionably correct. If he gave a "warning," all the reliable evidence indicates that he communicated his fears, not in accordance with regular procedure to Berchtold or the Ministry of Foreign Affairs, but to Dr. von Bilinski, the Joint Finance Minister; to explain the curious reason for this irregular procedure we must digress for a moment.

Mr. Jovan Jovanovitch came to Vienna as Serbian Minister at the end of December, 1912, to take the place of Dr. Simitch. The latter was an elderly, experienced

unable to say;" Mandl, *Die Habsburger und die serbische Frage* (Vienna, 1918), p. 151 ff.; *cf.* also KSF, II, 29, 108 ff., Jan., Apr., 1924.

[63] Stanojevitch, *Die Ermordung des Erzherzogs*, p. 61: "Some days before the murder, the Serbian Minister in Vienna officially informed the Austro-Hungarian Government that the Serbian Government possessed indications that something was being prepared at Sarajevo against the Heir to the Throne."

On this whole controversy see KSF, II, 28-30, 108-111, 208-9, 231-8, 282-3, Jan.-July, 1924; III, 282-287, 293-299, 393-405, 437-444, May-July, 1925; and L. Mandl, in *La Fédération Balkanique,* pp. 272-3, May 31, 1925. By the Treaty of St. Germain (Art. 93) Serbia had the right to take all documents relating to the territories which she received from the former Austro-Hungarian Monarchy and she did actually take records going back as far as 1895. *Cf.* Ludwig Bittner, "Die zwischenstaatlichen Verhandlungen ueber das Schicksal der oesterreichischen Archive nach dem Zusammenbruch Oesterreich-Ungarns," in *Archiv f. Pol. u. Gesch.,* III, 58-96, Jan., 1925). If the Serbians found any such document as Stanojevitch claims, they would doubtless have taken a copy of it and could make it public. Moreover, they have their own Legation records and the correspondence of Pashitch and Jovanovitch; if these contain anything to their advantage in this question of an alleged warning, one would expect that they would have published it. But they have not done so.

diplomat of tact and dignity, who had had fair success in what was at best a very difficult office. Even in normal times the position of the Serbian representative in Vienna was no easy one after 1903, in view of the national antagonism between the peoples of the two countries and the constantly irritating questions of alleged spying, propaganda, oppression, and incitement to treason on both sides. At the moment when Jovanovitch arrived in 1912 the situation was particularly delicate and difficult on account of the exciting consequences of the First Balkan War and the Austrian efforts in the London Conference to deprive the Serbians of the fruits of their victories. Mr. Jovan Jovanovitch, in contrast to his predecessor, was a young man of hardly forty; even according to one of his best friends and colleagues, "with his unruly, bushy hair, dark eyes, and black moustachio across his face, the new arrival presented a less reassuring appearance than his venerable predecessor. In Vienna people made no bones of affirming that he had fomented trouble in 1908 against the annexation of Bosnia and Herzegovina, and even that he had commanded bands of *comitadjis*." [64]

Upon his arrival in Vienna, therefore, Jovanovitch was not regarded altogether as a *persona grata*. In fact Austria is said to have delayed her assent when his name was first proposed, and afterwards have given hints that she would be glad to have him recalled—hints which Belgrade refused to take. His reception was far from cordial. When he was presented to Francis Joseph, the Emperor is said merely to have bowed to him, instead of extending him the handshake usual on such occasions. The Archdukes would not see him at all. Berchtold was chilly, and limited his relations to official business. Under these painful circumstances Jovanovitch appreciated all the more his cordial relations with Dr. von Bilinski. Bilinski, being recently appointed

[64] Dumaine, *La Dernière Ambassade de France en Autriche*, p. 79 f.

Joint Finance Minister, had charge of the civil administration in Bosnia and Herzegovina, and as such had much in common to discuss with the Serbian Minister. Being a Slav himself (a Galician Pole), it was easier for him, than for an Austrian-German or a Magyar, to get on amicably with a Serb like Jovanovitch. In fact, in the interest of better relations between the two countries, it was soon agreed between the two, and approved by Francis Joseph and Berchtold, that Bilinski should handle diplomatic relations with the Serbian Minister, and then report upon them to Berchtold.[65] This was, of course, wholly anomalous and irregular. But further reasons for it, in addition to those just given, are doubtless to be found in Berchtold's natural indolence, and in Bilinski's ambition to gather as much power as possible into his own hands, and increase his own importance. It explains, however, why in June, 1914, Jovanovitch might prefer to choose Bilinski, rather than Berchtold or anyone in the Austrian Ministry of Foreign Affairs, as the person to whom to make his delicate suggestion that it might be dangerous for Archduke Franz Ferdinand to go to Bosnia.

In 1924, at the tenth anniversary of the Archduke's assassination, the controversy concerning Serbia's alleged "warning" to Austria was revived. A letter to a Vienna newspaper signed "X.Y.," but attributed to Mr. Josimovitch, secretary to the Serbian Legation in Vienna in 1914, declared: "On June 18, 1914, Mr. Jovanovitch received a cipher despatch from Pashitch directing him to dissuade the Archduke from his trip to Sarajevo, or at least to warn him of the dangers threatening him;" Jovanovitch then

[65] Bilinski, I, 258 f.; Paul Flandrak, "Bilinski's Eingreifen in die Auswärtige Politik," in *Neues Wiener Journal*, No. 11289, April 26, 1925; Mandl, "Zur Warnung Serbiens an Oesterreich" in KSF, II, 108-111, April, 1925; Ljuba Jovanovitch, "Sketches from the history of the relations between Vienna and Belgrade" in the Belgrade daily *Politika*, No. 6095, April 12, 1925, quoted *ibid.*, III, 281-287, May, 1925.

informed Bilinski of this "at noon on June 21." [66]   At first
sight this seems to confirm the allegations of Denis and
Stanojevitch as to an official warning from the Belgrade
Government. But this letter is of such doubtful authentic-
ity that no reliance can be placed upon it.[67]   It is also
contradicted in several particulars by Mr. Jovanovitch himself, who a week later made to another Vienna newspaper
the following interesting communication (slightly condensed):

> I am glad to give you an authentic account of the
> warning given to the Archduke which came from me and
> arose from my own initiative. I was at that time Minister
> Plenipotentiary and Envoy to Vienna. And I learned that
> the Heir to the Throne intended to be present at manœuvres
> in Bosnia. [After mentioning—incorrectly—some of the
> details of Franz Ferdinand's proposed visit to Bosnia, and
> asserting that it would be regarded as a "provocation" by
> Serbs, he continues:] After I had duly weighed all these
> circumstances, I resolved to visit Dr. von Bilinski, who was
> then Finance Minister and Minister for Bosnia. So far as
> I remember, my visit took place about June 5—thus 23 days
> before the assassination. I explained quite openly to the
> Minister what I had learned, namely, that the manœuvres
> were to be held in Bosnia on the Drin just opposite to
> Serbia, and that the Archduke himself would take com-
> mand.[68]   I said to Minister von Bilinski: "If this is true,

66 *Wiener Sonn- and Montagszeitung*, No. 25, June 23, 1924; *cf.* KSF,
II, 234, 282, June, 1924.

67 Mr. Josimovitch is said to have denied that he wrote it (Seton-
Watson, *Sarajevo*, p. 154). The statement that Jovanovitch informed
Bilinski "at noon on June 21" is contradicted by the fact that Bilinski
did not return to Vienna from a holiday at Lemberg until the *afternoon*
of June 21 (*Neue Freie Presse*, No. 17896, June 22, p. 8). And a further
assertion contained in the letter, that Bilinski then informed the Archduke's *Hofmeister*, Baron Rummerskirch, has been emphatically denied by
the latter, KSF, II, 233, note 6).

68 His information in 1914, or his remembrance of it in 1924, was not
accurate: The maneuvers were not to be held "on the Drin just opposite
Serbia," but the southwest of Sarajevo, in the Tarcin district toward

I can assure your Excellency that it will arouse the greatest discontent among the Serbs who must regard this as an act of provocation. Manœuvres under such circumstances are dangerous. Among the Serb youths there may be one who will put a ball-cartridge in his rifle or revolver in place of a blank-cartridge, and he may fire it, and the bullet might strike the man giving provocation. Therefore, it would be good and reasonable that the Archduke should not go to Sarajevo; that the manœuvres should not be held on Vidov Dan [St. Vitus's Day, June 28, a Serb holiday]; and they should not be held in Bosnia."

To these clear words Dr. von Bilinski replied that he took note of them, and would inform me what result they had with the Archduke, although he himself could not believe in any such result of the manœuvres as I foresaw· and that moreover, he was in possession of information that Bosnia was completely quiet. A few days later I again called on Minister von Bilinski about this matter. But nevertheless had shortly to learn that the original program would be followed and nothing changed in spite of my warning. The Archduke was certainly informed, but would heed none but himself.[69]

the Adriatic (about as far away as possible from the Drin and the Serbian frontier), as was clearly stated in the announcement in the *Neue Freie Presse*, No. 17878, June 4, 1914, p. 9. Nor was it true that "the Archduke himself would take command;" General Potiorek was in command, and the Archduke was merely an official onlooker.

[69] *Neues Wiener Tageblatt*, No. 177, June 28, 1924.

In a private letter to Dr. Bogitchevitch, the Serbian Chargé d' Affaires at Berlin in 1914 but later a severe critic of Mr. Pashitch and Entente diplomacy, Mr. Jovan Jovanovitch had given a shorter account which says nothing about his having acted on his own initiative, and is less definite as to the date: "In the month of May, the end of May, 1914, I said to the Joint Finance Minister, von Bilinski, when I heard that the Archduke Franz Ferdinand was going to go to the Sarajevo manoeuvres in Bosnia on the very day of Vidov Dan, 14/15 [27/28] June, 1914, that it would be undesirable [nezgodno] that the Archduke should conduct manoeuvres there on Vidov Dan. This would mean a provocation to the Serbs, and something untoward [rgjavo] might happen, because at manoeuvres some real shots might often occur in shooting with blank cartridges;" Bogitchevitch, "Die Warnung vor dem Attentate in Sarajevo," in KSF, II, 235, July, 1924.

This account of Mr. Jovan Jovanovitch appears to be the closest approximation to the truth hitherto made from the Serbian side. It is in some respects confirmed, and in others contradicted, in a valuable statement by Mr. Paul Flandrak, who was Chief of the Press Section in Bilinski's Finance Ministry in 1914, and since the war the director of the Vienna *Depositenbank*. This evidently responsible and trustworthy man wrote recently:

"In May, 1914, when the first announcements about the Archduke Franz Ferdinand's trip to Dalmatia and Bosnia began to spread among the public, Jovanovitch appeared for the last time at the office of the Joint Finance Minister. Upon his arrival he began to speak at once about the proposed manœuvres and expressed the fear that the Serbian Government might regard them as a provocation. Furthermore he would like to bring to the serious consideration of the Joint Finance Minister whether the patriotic demonstrations inevitable at the appearance of the future ruler of the Monarchy would be likely to arouse bad feeling on both sides of the [Austro-Serbian] frontier. He begged Bilinski not to regard his remarks as an official communication. He was moved only by the desire to prevent everything which might possibly, even though only temporarily, disturb the negotiations which had begun for the improvement of the mutual relations [of Austria and Serbia].

Bilinski did not pay these declarations any sort of special attention, and I believe that he did not inform Count Berchtold of them at all, though otherwise he used to report on all his conversations with the Serbian Minister. . . . Though at the time of this conversation he did not yet know that out of the Archduke's military tour of inspection was to grow a political tour, yet he was convinced that the moment was at least premature for Franz Ferdinand's trip to the southern provinces; and he also frankly expressed to the Emperor his misgivings.

From this conversation of the Serbian Minister Jovanovitch, which Bilinski told me directly afterwards quite incidentally and to a certain extent as confirming his standpoint of the untimeliness of the Archduke's trip, there has developed in the course of years a cycle of legends; some have even gone so far as to construct out of Jovanovitch's remarks a warning of the murder or a hint at the possibility of it. Bilinski himself, who during his service as Finance Minister kept no notes, does not mention at all this last interview with the Serbian Minister in his memoirs written from memory—an evidence that he saw in it neither an open nor a hidden warning." [70]

It would be interesting to hear what the person who received the "Warning" has to say about it. But curiously enough, the late Dr. von Bilinski's two volumes of memoirs, though they deal fully with his public life otherwise, say nothing of this. From this fact some writers have drawn the conclusion that he never received any warning, as otherwise he would have surely mentioned it because of its crucial interest. But more probably he avoided recalling the painful fact that he did not dissuade the Archduke from his fatal trip, or that at least, as the Minister officially responsible for the administration of Bosnia, did not make sure that adequate arrangements were made for his protection and that Sarajevo was carefully combed for potential murderers. In view of the terrible consequences to Austria and the world, this neglect must have haunted him as the most dreadful nightmare of his life.[71] While the War was still raging, an Austrian historian applied to him for any light he could throw upon the alleged Serbian Warning

[70] P. Flandrak, "Bilinski's Eingreifen in die Auswärtige Politik," in *Neues Wiener Journal,* No. 11289, April 26, 1925.

[71] In the days following the assassination he tried to shove the blame upon General Potiorek, Governor of Bosnia, upon the military authorities, and even upon the Archduke himself for the irregular and headstrong way in which the trip had been planned. Margutti, *Vom Alten Kaiser,* pp. 45 ff., 397; Conrad, IV, 37, 41, 64-70, 82-85; Musulin, *Das Haus am Ballplatz,* p. 215; Seton-Watson, *Sarajevo,* pp. 106 ff., 154; and also the sentence from Bilinski's own memoirs to be quoted below.

concerning the Sarajevo plot. Bilinski's brief letter of reply is significant: he would gladly talk about every other aspect of this sad affair, except precisely this point, over which he "wished to draw the veil of oblivion." [72] In his memoirs he merely complains that he was not consulted about the arrangements because the Archduke had expressed the wish "that on this occasion the matter should be handled exclusively by the *Landeschef* [Gen. Potiorek, Governor of Bosnia and Herzegovina] as commanding general, without involving the Joint Finance Ministry in any arrangements. Against this I could raise no objections, because I did not interfere in regard to the organization of the province in affairs of military administration—with the exception of summoning recruits and paying the costs of this." [73] "The rumor that I warned the Emperor before the trip is not true, for I had no right to interfere in a purely military tour, and the extension of the trip into a political affair was permitted without my being asked or informed." He explained these facts, he says, in an audience with the Emperor two days after the assassination, and the Emperor exonerated him from all responsibility; except for this audience he "never talked about the Archduke's trip, never, either before, or after." [74]

From all this evidence, we may venture to draw the following conclusions:

1. On or about June 5 the Serbian Minister in Vienna, Mr. Jovan Jovanovitch, made a communication to Bilinski, the Austro-Hungarian Joint Finance Minister, but not to Berchtold or the Austrian Foreign Office as he should properly have done according to regular diplomatic procedure. His irregular diplomatic procedure on this occasion may

[72] L. Mandl, "Zur Warnung Serbiens an Oesterreich," in KSF, II, 108 ff., April, 1924; and "Ein düsterer Gedenktag," in the Vienna *Neues 8 Uhr Blatt,* No. 2907, June 28, 1924.

[73] Bilinski, I, 273.

[74] Bilinski, I, 277; *cf.,* however, Flandrak's statement to the contrary

have been unwise as matters turned out, but it was not unnatural, because it had been a practice for many months. Jovanovitch also doubtless realized that what he had to say was of a very delicate and difficult character, and that it would be far easier to say it to the cordial Bilinski than the chilly and suspicious Berchtold. He also did not want to give his communication a formal or official character; a communication to his friend Bilinski would seem less official than one to the Minister of Foreign Affairs. Bilinski, who was not especially alarmed about conditions in Bosnia, and was intending soon to make a trip there himself with his wife,[75] did not take Jovanovitch's communication very seriously and probably did not mention it either to the Emperor, to Franz Ferdinand, or to Berchtold.[76] The repeated denials of the Austrian Foreign Office officials of receiving any official warning from Serbia are therefore wholly correct.

2. It is possible that Jovanovitch, as he himself alleges, made his communication "on his own initiative." But it is to be observed that in his earlier letter to Dr. Bogitchevitch he says nothing of this. Moreover, it seems strange that he should take such an important step without authorization or instructions from the Serbian Minister of Foreign Affairs. If he really acted on his own initiative in suggesting that there was danger of the Archduke's being shot at the maneuvers through the disloyalty of his own troops—by the substitution of a ball-cartridge for a blank-cartridge—why did he wait until the beginning of June? As the trip had been announced in the papers in March—Jovanovitch himself says, "This was already fixed in March"—he would have known of it for some two months. He would have known as much concerning the general loyalty or

75 Bilinski, I, 273.

76 Possibly he may have communicated it to the local authorities in Sarajevo; cf. Mandl, in KSF, II, 109, April, 1924; and Seton-Watson, *Sarajevo*, p. 106.

disloyalty of the Bosnian troops earlier as later. One would have expected him to have pointed out this danger at a much earlier date, if he had been acting only on his own initiative.

Is it a mere coincidence that his "warning" was given very soon after Mr. Pashitch, "at the end of May or the beginning of June," told Ljuba Jovanovitch and others of his Cabinet that "there were people who were preparing to go to Sarajevo to kill Franz Ferdinand"? [77] May there not after all be some truth in Mr. Denis's statement that "Mr. Pashitch attempted in a discreet way" to indicate the danger the Archduke was incurring and therefore instructed his Minister at Vienna to take steps to avert the tragedy if possible. The venerable Serbian Prime Minister was a shrewd enough man to realize perfectly well the odium which would fall upon Serbia if any of the facts concerning the Dimitrijevitch and "Black Hand" complicity should leak out. Ljuba Jovanovitch's revelations are eloquent enough as to this "terrible" possibility. Serbia's record was already too spotted with blood to be able to stand the disgrace of another political murder of a prince of such rank. Serbia would be ostracized by Europe. Worse than that. Mr. Pashitch was well enough acquainted with Austro-Serbian tension in the past to realize that Austria would make very stiff demands on Serbia if the assassins should be successful, and perhaps even seize upon the crime as a pretext for war with her troublesome neighbor. But Mr. Pashitch did not want war at this time, and least of all a war occasioned by such an event. He knew that Serbia needed peace for many more months at least before the final life and death struggle with Austria, in order that his country might recover from the Balkan Wars and consolidate the new territories which she had just acquired. And he was doubtful whether Russia or France would sup-

[77] Ljuba Jovanovitch, *Krv Slovenstva*, p. 9.

port him in a conflict with Austria, if the truth should leak out that the murder had been hatched in the capital of Serbia with the aid of a high officer in the Serbian General Staff and other members of a secret Serbian society notorious for their political assassinations in the past. He was certainly in a very difficult and embarrassing position. He wanted to avert the murder because of its potential terrible consequences. But to have warned Austria of the facts, in the only way which would have been effective, would have been to reveal his own cognizance of a plot and to confess one more to the long list of assassinations plotted in Serbia against the Dual Monarchy. Under these circumstances may he not have sent the Serbian Minister in Vienna some hint which led the latter to express to Bilinski his doubts about the loyalty of Bosnian troops and the general undesirability of the Archduke's proposed trip? In such a case Jovanovitch would of course have sought to give the impression that he was speaking unofficially and merely on his own initiative. This is a very common practice in diplomacy. Innumerable examples of it may be seen in the recent publications from the German, Russian, and English archives. When one government desires to sound another, or to give a hint, on an especially delicate subject, it is a well-recognized ruse to instruct its ambassador to bring up the subject for discussion, but to preface it with the assurance that he is merely "expressing his own private personal opinion," or simply "acting on his own initiative."

The fact that Spalaikovitch in St. Petersburg could also issue so quickly after the assassination the statement that Belgrade had "warned" Vienna, suggests that Pashitch had hinted to him, as well as to Jovanovitch, something of the danger impending and the indirect step which had been taken to try to avert it. Furthermore, it was scarcely within the bounds of diplomatic etiquette and propriety for the Serbian Minister in Vienna to assume to interfere

in such purely domestic affairs of another country as
manoeuvres and journeyings of princes; it is therefore
difficult to believe that Jovanovitch would have taken such
an important step, infringing on diplomatic propriety, unless he had received some instructions from Belgrade.
Until the Serbian authorities see fit to publish in full the
correspondence exchanged between Pashitch and Jovanovitch in the weeks before the assassination, or at least the
document in which Jovanovitch must have reported to
Pashitch his interview with Bilinski, one may doubt
whether he really acted "on his own initiative."

3. The "warning" was given in the most general
terms; it contained no hint of the possibility of assassination by civilian conspirators or of any plot such as was
actually on foot; of this there is complete agreement in all
the accounts, otherwise so divergent. It referred only to
the possible danger of disloyalty among the troops. It is
therefore small wonder that Bilinski paid so little attention
to it. Nor does it in any way relieve the Serbian Government of the guilt of withholding information concerning a
plot to commit murder, connived at by its own officers—a
crime known in private life as "compounding a felony."

CHAPTER IV

THE LEGEND OF THE "POTSDAM COUNCIL"

AFTER the publication of the *Kautsky Documents* and the report of the Reichstag Investigating Committee on the preliminaries of the War, it may seem superfluous again to refute the legend that, "This greatest of human tragedies was hatched by the Kaiser and his imperial crew at this Potsdam conference of July 5, 1914." [1] It may seem like "flogging a dead horse." But as it was cited by the Commission of the Peace Conference, presided over by Mr. Lansing as justification for Art. 231 of the Treaty; as it has been accepted by MM. Bourgeois and Pagès and appears to be endorsed by President Poincaré,[2] in spite of the full documents available to them when they wrote; and as the legend is still largely believed by those who have not kept abreast with recent investigations into the causes of the War, it is perhaps worth while to examine again this wide-spread legend, as a typical example of the way myths grow up and flourish during war-time hatred and propaganda.

The most interesting and picturesque account of the alleged "Crown Council" at Potsdam on July 5, as well as the one which had received widest currency, is that given by Mr. Morgenthau, in the volume just quoted, in a chapter entitled, "Wangenheim Tells the American Ambassador How the Kaiser Started the War:"

[1] Henry Morgenthau, *Ambassador Morgenthau's Story*, N. Y., 1918, p. 86. This book, which first appeared serially in *The World's Work*, beginning May, 1918, was also published in England under the title *Secrets of the Bosphorus*, and widely circulated in French and other translations.

[2] *Les Origines et Les Responsabilités de La Grande Guerre*, Paris, 1921, p. 76; Poincaré, IV, 196-199.

I shall always keep in my mind the figure of this German diplomat, in those exciting days before the Marne. . . . The good fortune of the German armies so excited him that he was sometimes led into indiscretions, and his exuberance one day caused him to tell me certain facts which, I think, will always have great historical value. . . .

The Kaiser, he told me, had summoned him to Berlin for an imperial conference. This meeting took place at Potsdam on July 5th. The Kaiser presided and nearly all the important ambassadors attended. Wangenheim himself was summoned to give assurance about Turkey and enlighten his associates generally on the situation in Constantinople, which was then regarded as almost the pivotal point in the impending war. In telling me who attended this conference Wangenheim used no names, though he specifically said that among them were—the facts are so important that I quote his exact words in the German which he used—"*die Häupter des Generalstabs und der Marine*"— (the heads of the general staff and of the navy) by which I have assumed that he meant Von Moltke and Von Tirpitz. The great bankers, railroad directors, and the captains of German industry, all of whom were as necessary to German war preparations as the army itself, also attended.

Wangenheim now told me that the Kaiser solemnly put the question to each man in turn: "Are you ready for war?" All replied "yes" except the financiers. They said that they must have two weeks to sell their foreign securities and to make loans. At that time few people had looked upon the Sarajevo tragedy as something that would inevitably lead to war. This conference, Wangenheim told me, took all precautions that no such suspicion should be aroused. It decided to give the bankers time to readjust their finances for the coming war, and then the several members went quietly back to their work or started on vacations. The Kaiser went to Norway on his yacht, Von Bethmann-Hollweg left for a rest, and Wangenheim returned to Constantinople.

In telling me about this conference Wangenheim, of

course, admitted that Germany had precipitated the war. I think that he was rather proud of the whole performance, proud that Germany had gone about the matter in so methodical and far-seeing a way, and especially proud that he himself had been invited to participate in so epoch making a gathering. I have often wondered why he revealed to me so momentous a secret, and I think that perhaps the real reason was his excessive vanity—his desire to show me how close he stood to the inner counsels of his emperor and the part that he had played in bringing on this conflict. Whatever the motive, this indiscretion certainly had the effect of showing me who were really the guilty parties in this monstrous crime. The several blue, red, and yellow books which flooded Europe during the few months following the outbreak, and the hundreds of documents which were issued by German propagandists attempting to establish Germany's innocence, have never made the slightest impression on me. For my conclusions as to the responsibility are not based on suspicions or belief or the study of circumstantial data. I do not have to reason or argue about the matter. I know. The conspiracy that has caused this greatest of human tragedies was hatched by the Kaiser and his imperial crew at this Potsdam conference of July 5, 1914. One of the chief participants, flushed with his triumph at the apparent success of the plot, told me the details with his own mouth. Whenever I hear people arguing about the responsibility for this war or read the clumsy and lying excuses put forth by Germany, I simply recall the burly figure of Wangenheim as he appeared that August afternoon, puffing away at a huge black cigar, and giving me his account of this historic meeting. Why waste any time discussing the matter after that?

Why discuss the matter any further? Because the contemporary documents now available prove conclusively that there is hardly a word of truth in this whole narrative, either as to (1) the persons present, (2) the Kaiser's attitude toward delay, (3) the real reason for delay, or, finally, (4) the alleged selling of securities in anticipation of war.

THE PERSONS ALLEGED TO BE PRESENT

Let us examine the narrative, taking the statements one by one.

"Nearly all the important ambassadors attended." The most important ambassadors would be those stationed at London (Lichnowsky), Vienna (Tschirschky), Paris (Schoen), and St. Petersburg (Pourtalès).

Lichnowsky at London was not at this Potsdam Council, because he himself says in his pamphlet that he learned of it "subsequently." [3]

It is also equally certain that Tschirschky at Vienna was not present, for otherwise Bethmann would not have telegraphed him as he did on July 6, giving an account of an important interview at Potsdam on July 5 between Emperor William and the Austrian Ambassador, Szögyény.[4] This interview and its significance will be described in detail later. Nor is there the slightest indication that Schoen and Pourtalès came from Paris or St. Petersburg.

Perhaps, however, the "important ambassador" whom Wangenheim referred to was no other than Wangenheim himself. Now it is true that Baron Wangenheim left Constantinople on July 2, arrived in Berlin on July 4 at 4:25 P. M., and was back again at Constantinople on July 15. But it is not true that "the Kaiser summoned him for an imperial conference." On the contrary, he did not see the Kaiser at all, but only reported to the Foreign Office. In fact, he was much irritated that in these uneasy days the Kaiser had not thought it worth while to arrange for an

---

[3] *My London Mission,* p. 323.
[4] K.D., 15.

interview with such an important person as his Ambassador to Turkey during the latter's visit to Berlin.[5]

"The heads of the General Staff and of the Navy." General von Moltke, the Chief of Staff, certainly was not at Potsdam on July 5. On April 15, 1914, Moltke went to Karlsbad for the "cure" which he had been in the habit for some years of taking there with members of his family.[6] Here he was visited on May 12 by the Austrian Chief of Staff, Baron Conrad, who came in civilian clothes, and talked with Moltke two or three hours on the general political situation. Conrad pointed out the unreliability of Rumania, the possible ways of employing Italian troops north of the Alps, and the desirability of Moltke's adopting a strategic plan which would send more German troops against Russia in case of war, and so relieve Russian pressure on the Austrians in Galicia. Neither General had any expectation of an immediate war. The whole conversation was merely a general one as to political conditions and military coöperation between the Central Powers, such as was natural between the Chiefs of Staff of two allied Powers,—such as the two men had carried on before, and such as the French and Russian Staff Officers had been carrying on for years. When Conrad left Moltke, to take the midnight train back to Vienna, it was understood that Conrad should attend the ordinary German manoeuvres later in the year.[7] Neither of the Generals had

[5] Private letter from Baroness von Wangenheim in the author's possession.

[6] Photographs of the police registration records at Karlsbad, which the writer has secured, show that Moltke was at Karlsbad in 1911, April 8-May 12; in 1912, April 15-May 8; in 1913, April 13-May 9; and in 1914, April 15-May 14; and again June 28-July 25; the latter record reads: "Angemeldet Stadtrath Karlsbad. 28 Juni 1914. No. 23673. Name: *Excellenz Helmuth v. Moltke.* Beruf: *Offizier.* Wohnsitz: Berlin. Angekommen in Karlsbad am 28, 6, 1914, und wohnt *Haus Bremen*, Abgereist 25. 7 nach *Berlin*."

[7] For a detailed summary of this interview see Conrad, *Aus Meiner Dienstzeit*, III, 667-674, 701.

the slightest idea that they were never to see each other again.[8]

On May 14 Moltke left Karlsbad to accompany one of the routine General Staff observation trips in the Vosges Mountains. At the close of this he had a talk with Eckardstein in Baden-Baden on June 1.[9] He was not a well man at this time—he died a few months later after his failure at the Battle of the Marne—and upon the advice of his physician, returned again to Karlsbad on Sunday, June 28, before he heard the news of Franz Ferdinand's assassination which occurred on the same day. He stayed in Karlsbad, as he had planned to do, until July 25, arriving in Berlin again July 26.[10] The evidence from the Karlsbad police register indicates that Moltke, even after the Sarajevo murder, was pursuing his normal routine life, and was living quietly at Karlsbad on July 5, instead of plotting war in a Council at Potsdam. A further proof that Moltke was not at Potsdam on July 5 is the interesting letter which Falkenhayn, the Prussian Minister of War, sent to him on July 5 at Karlsbad, giving him an account of the interview between the Austrian Ambassador and Emperor William on that day at Potsdam.[11]

Perhaps the author of the legend had in mind not Moltke, but the Acting Chief of Staff, Count Waldersee. But neither was he at Potsdam on July 5. Because of a death in his family he had gone to Hanover on July 4, leaving word to call him on the telephone if anything of importance arose. If there had really been an important Conference, such as the Potsdam Council myth describes, Waldersee would certainly have returned to Potsdam for it; but he did not come back from the funeral until July 7.

[8] Private letter of Conrad's in author's possession.

[9] Eckardstein, *Lebenserinnerungen*, III, 184-187.

[10] Confirmed by K.D., 74, 197; by Moltke's letters to his wife in his *Erinnerungen*, p. 381; and by Tirpitz, *Erinnerungen*, p. 227.

[11] Published by Montgelas, *Leitfaden zur Kriegsschuldfrage*, p. 196.

He learned from a subordinate, General Bertrab, of the interview between the Austrian Ambassador and Emperor William which had taken place on July 5 in his absence; but he considered it of so little importance that he again left Berlin on a short furlough which had been previously arranged. If any military plans were to have been made, or if war had been "plotted" and was thought to be impending, he certainly would not have left his post.[12]

The head of the Navy, Admiral von Tirpitz, was likewise absent from Berlin. He was enjoying a vacation at Tarasp in Switzerland from July 2 to July 27, and could not, therefore, have been at the famous council as the legend represents.[13]

What of the other notables, vaguely referred to by Wangenheim, "who were as necessary to German war preparation as the army itself"? Krupp v. Bohlen-Halbach, the head of the great Krupp munition works, was not at Potsdam on July 5, but saw the Kaiser at Kiel on the latter's way to his Northern cruise. There at Kiel he learned of the Kaiser's interview with the Austrian Ambassador on July 5, but did not believe that, because of it, his firm need make any special preparations.[14] One of Krupp's directors, who has been much quoted, Dr. Mühlon, himself admits that he heard nothing of the Austrian communication until the "middle of July" in a conversation with Dr. Helfferich, the Director of the Deutsche Bank. And in 1919 when invited to tell what he knew of the alleged meeting at Potsdam and of the consequent military preparations, Mühlon stated that he had nothing to say which would throw any more light on the matter.[15] Dr. Helfferich has vigorously denied that any war council took place at Potsdam, or that he received any official hint before the Aus-

---

[12] *Investigating Commission,* I, 63-64.

[13] Tirpitz, *Erinnerungen,* pp. 204 ff., 208 ff.; *Investigating Commission,* I, 60, 67, 72.

[14] *Investigating Commission,* I, 87.   [15] *Ibid.*

trian ultimatum was delivered to Serbia that he ought to take any financial or economic measures preparatory to war. He suggests that the whole rumor may have started with a waiter in a Berlin hotel who overheard some mention of the interview between the Kaiser and the Austrian Ambassador.[16]

Herr Ballin, the head of the Hamburg-American Line, who had been absent from Berlin the early part of July at a health resort, was asked on July 15 if he would go to England and try to find out from Haldane what truth there was in the rumor as to an Anglo-Russian naval agreement. Neither he nor the director of the North German Lloyd could have been present at the "Potsdam Council," because they do not appear to have had any information until July 20 that there was a possible danger of warlike complications.[17] Von Jagow, the Secretary of State, did not return from his honeymoon in Switzerland until July 6.[18]

As a result of this evidence it appears that the very persons who would have been most likely to have been present at any such council, had it really taken place, can be proved to have been elsewhere on July 5, and to have taken no measures toward "plotting war." Finally, it is worth noting that neither Sir Horace Rumbold, who was in charge of the British Embassy in Berlin during the early days of July, nor any of his diplomatic colleagues, had at the time any inkling of such a conference as the Wangenheim story represents. If it had really taken place it is almost certain that they would have heard some rumor of

16 *Ibid.*, p. 88. Helfferich, *Vorgeschichte*, I, 175-186.

17 K.D., 56, 80, 90.

18 Jagow, *Ursachen und Ausbruch des Weltkrieges*, p. 97. The first document from his hand is of July 8; K.D., 18, note 2. Lichnowsky says (*My London Mission*, p. 323 f.) that soon after "the decisive conference at Potsdam on July 5 . . . von Jagow was in Vienna to talk over everything with Count Berchtold." There is not a shadow of evidence for this statement. In the hundreds of telegrams from the Berlin and Vienna archives now published, there is not the slightest hint of such a visit.

it within a few days or weeks. Later, in 1917, when the legend spread, Sir Horace was rightly inclined to believe that the newspapers had found a mare's nest.[19]

THE KAISER'S ATTITUDE TOWARD DELAY

Baron Wangenheim, according to the story above, represents the Kaiser and the Council as deciding to delay action for two weeks in order to give the bankers time to sell their foreign securities. This is the opposite of the truth. There is much contemporary evidence in the *Kautsky Documents* that the Kaiser wished that, whatever action Austria took against Serbia, *she should not delay.* She should take it as quickly as possible, while the sentiment of Europe, shocked by the horrible crime at Sarajevo, was still in sympathy with the Hapsburgs and indignant at regicide Serbs. When he read that the German Ambassador at Vienna, two days after Sarajevo, had "used every opportunity to warn [Austria] calmly but very energetically and earnestly against overhasty steps," the Kaiser made the marginal note: "Now or never! Who authorized him to do this? It is very stupid! It's none of his business, for it is purely Austria's affair to consider what to do in this matter, for it will be said afterwards, if things go wrong, that Germany was not willing!! Tschirschky will please drop this nonsense! Matters must be cleared up with the Serbs, *and that soon.* That's all self-evident and the plain truth."[20] The Austrian Ambassador at Berlin similarly reported that the Kaiser said to him that "he would be sorry if we left unused the present moment which was so favorable to us."[21] When Tschirschky reported on July 14 that Berchtold himself was at last convinced that the "speediest action was desirable," the Kaiser underlined the words twice; and when he heard that the ultimatum was

---

[19] Oman, *The Outbreak of the War of 1914-1918,* p. 16 ff.

[20] K.D., 7.   [21] Szögyény to Berchtold, July 5; A.R.B., I. 6.

to be delayed for more than two weeks, until after President Poincaré had left St. Petersburg, he noted, "A pity." [22] No, instead of urging delay, according to the Wangenheim story, the Kaiser, with his natural impetuosity, wanted Austria's action, whatever it might be, to be taken as quickly as possible.

THE REAL REASONS FOR DELAY

Equally without foundation is Wangenheim's alleged reason for the two weeks' delay in sending the ultimatum: "The financiers said they must have two weeks to sell their foreign securities and to make loans." The real reasons for the delay came wholly from Vienna and not at all from Berlin. They were mainly two, and are repeatedly referred to in the German and Austrian documents which were published in 1919. The first was that Berchtold, the Austro-Hungarian Minister of Foreign Affairs, could not act against Serbia until he had secured the consent of Tisza, the Premier of Hungary. It took two weeks to win Tisza over from his original opposition to violent action against Serbia. The second, and by far the more important, reason for the final delay, was the fact that Berchtold did not want to present the ultimatum to Serbia until it was certain that President Poincaré and the French Premier, Viviani, had left St. Petersburg and were inaccessible upon the high seas returning to France. For otherwise Russia, under the influence of the "champagne mood" of the Franco-Russian toasts and the chauvinism of Poincaré, Izvolski, the Grand Duke Nicholas and the others gathered at St. Petersburg, would be much more likely to give Serbia military support, and thereby thwart Austria's plans for "localizing" the conflict with Serbia.[23]

[22] K.D., 40, 50.
[23] For delay on account of Tisza, cf. A.R.B., I, 2, 8, 9, 10, 19, 26; K.D., 18. 19. 29. 40. 49. 50; and on account of Poincaré's presence in

THE ALLEGED SELLING OF SECURITIES IN
ANTICIPATION OF WAR

Following upon the narrative as quoted from the lips of Baron Wangenheim, there appears in Mr. Morgenthau's volume a paragraph, which does not increase one's confidence in his account of "how the Kaiser started the War." As if to confirm the truth of Wangenheim's story this paragraph asserts:

> This imperial conference took place on July 5th, and the Serbian Ultimatum was sent on July 22nd [sic]. This is just about the two weeks' interval which the financiers had demanded to complete their plans. All the great stock exchanges show that the German bankers profitably used this interval. Their records disclose that stocks were being sold in large quantities and that prices declined rapidly. At that time the markets were somewhat puzzled at this movement, but Wangenheim's explanation clears up any doubts which may still remain. Germany was changing her securities into cash for war purposes. If anyone wishes to verify Wangenheim, I should suggest that he examine the quotations of the New York Stock Market for these historic weeks. He will find that there were astonishing slumps in prices, especially in the stocks that had an international market. Between July 5th and July 22nd Union Pacific dropped from 155½ to 127½, Baltimore and Ohio from 91½ to 81, United States Steel from 61 to 50½, Canadian Pacific from 194 to 185½, and Northern Pacific from 111⅜ to 108. . . . How little the Wall Street brokers and financial experts realized that an imperial conference which had been held in Potsdam and presided over by the

Russia A.R.B., I, 19, 21, 26, 39, 57, 62; K.D., 50, 65, 93, 96, 108, 112, 127. Two further but minor reasons for the two weeks' delay were Berchtold's desire to wait till the harvest had been gathered and to await the results of the judicial investigation at Sarajevo which was expected to afford grounds of accusation against Serbia; cf. Conrad IV, 72; and Dirr, p. 129.

Kaiser, was the real force which was then depressing the market.[24]

Now if one follows Mr. Morgenthau's suggestion and examines the quotations of the New York Stock Market for these weeks, and reads the accompanying articles in the New York *Times*, one does not find very much evidence, either in the price of stocks or the volume of sales, that large blocks of German holdings were being secretly unloaded and thereby depressing the New York market during these two weeks. The stocks that he mentions declined only slightly or not at all; such declines as did take place were only such as were to be naturally expected from the general trend downward which had been taking place since January, or are quite satisfactorily explained by local American "bearish" influences, like the publication of a very depressing report by the Interstate Commerce Commission. Here are the facts. The "astonishing slump" in Union Pacific from 155½ to 127½, alleged by Mr. Morgenthau, represented in fact *an actual rise* of a couple of points in the value of this stock. Union Pacific sold "ex-dividend" and "ex-rights" on July 20; the dividend and accompanying "rights" were worth 30⅝, which meant that shares ought to have sold on July 22 around 125. In reality they sold at 127½; that is, at the end of the two weeks' period, during which it is asserted that there was depressing "inside selling" from Berlin, Union Pacific, instead of being depressed, was actually selling two points higher.[25]

Baltimore and Ohio, Canadian Pacific, and Northern

---

[24] *Ambassador Morgenthau's Story*, p. 86 f.

[25] *Cf.* article "Taking off U. P. Dividend" in New York *Times* July 18: 8:3: "It will be some time before experienced traders become accustomed to Union Pacific stock as an 8% issue. Disregarding other factors over Sunday which may affect all stocks, Union Pacific should open Monday morning [July 20] ex-dividend around 125¾. The shares closed yesterday at 156⅞, and the value of the warrants, 30⅝, will be deducted after today's trading."

Pacific did in fact slump on July 14, and there was evidence of selling orders from Europe. But this is to be explained partly by the fact that Baltimore and Ohio had been already falling steadily since January, and partly to the very depressing influence exercised on all railroad shares by the sharply adverse report on the New York, New Haven, and Hartford Railroad which was made by the Interstate Commerce Commission. The comment of the New York *Times* of July 15 is significant: "Stocks which had lately displayed a stable character in the face of great weakness of particular issues, could not stand up under such selling as occurred in New Haven and some others today. There were times when it looked as though the entire market was in a fair way to slump heavily, and only brisk short covering toward the close prevented many sharp net declines. . . . For its own account, or on orders from this side, Europe was an unusually large seller of stocks in this market. The cable told that a very unfavorable impression had been created abroad by the Commerce Commission's New Haven report. The European attitude toward American securities is naturally affected by such official denunciations of the way in which an important railway property had been handled." [26]

Most extraordinary is the striking assertion concerning United States Steel Common. It states that between July 5 and 22 it fell from 61 to $50\frac{1}{2}$. The real fact, as any one may verify from the Stock Market reports for himself, is that Steel during these two weeks never fell below $59\frac{5}{8}$, and on July 22 was almost exactly the same as two weeks earlier. [27]

When the facts are examined, therefore, it does not appear that the New York Stock Market affords any confirmation of the widespread story of German bankers

[26] New York *Times*, July 15: p. 12, cols. 2, 3.

[27] July 5th, the date given by Mr. Morgenthau, was Sunday; the true quotation for Steel Common on Monday, July 6, was $61\frac{7}{8}$; on July 22, $61\frac{3}{8}$.

demanding a two weeks' respite in which to turn American securities into gold in preparation for a war already decided upon. A real and violent decline on the New York Market did begin, of course, *after July 23,* when universal alarm was caused by the publication and character of the Austrian ultimatum to Serbia.[28] Within a week it approached panic conditions and the Governors of the Stock Exchange, following the example already taken by all the European stock exchanges, decided to close the doors to all further trading until conditions again became more normal.

In this connection there is another bit of interesting evidence. Sir William Plender, Comptroller of "Enemy Banks, London Agencies" during the War, made a report to the Chancellor of the Exchequer on December 16, 1916, which was presented to the House of Commons. Among other things, he had been directed by the British Government to ascertain whether the London branches of German banks had executed any unusual sales of securities for foreign account during the weeks immediately preceding the outbreak of War; and also whether there had been any unusual shipments of gold or silver. He reported that, after a very thorough examination of the books of these German banks, he "did not find any unusual transactions nor anything to suggest that the banks shipped securities or bullion from London" during the weeks just before the War. On the contrary, the Deutsche Bank alone held assets of nearly $50,000,000 in London when War broke out, which it might have easily transferred by cable to Holland or Germany, if it had any anticipation of the war which the Kaiser is supposed to have plotted at the "Potsdam Council."

[28] It is also true that the Vienna and Budapest markets, if not that at New York, had begun to show a disquieting decline before July 23, due, no doubt, to an inkling of the action which Berchtold was about to take.

CONCLUSIONS

It is clear that the "Potsdam Council" was a myth. It is an interesting example of the way a legend will grow up, flourish, and receive the widest currency in an atmosphere of war propaganda and readiness to believe anything about an enemy. There remain, however, several interesting questions. How did the legend first start? How did it reach the complete form in which it was cited by Mr. Lansing and his associates at the Paris Peace Conference as proof of Germany's guilt?

As will be indicated in the next chapter, the Kaiser had interviews separately with the Austrian Ambassador and various German officials on July 5 at Potsdam. It is quite possible, as Dr. Helfferich suggests, that the legend started with a waiter in a Berlin hotel who overheard mention of these conversations, and exaggerated them as he passed them on. In September, 1914, there appeared in a Dutch newspaper, the *Nieuwe Rotterdamsche Courant*, the tale of a meeting at Potsdam on July 5, attended by the leading German and Austrian officials, including even Berchtold, Tisza, Conrad and the Archduke Frederick, at which the outline of the fatal ultimatum was drawn up. The tale passed almost unnoticed at the time, owing to the fact that the Battle of the Marne was then engrossing the attention of the world. It was forgotten until revived again in 1917 and given great publicity by Socialists in Germany, by the allusion to it made by Prince Lichnowsky, and by the general discussion it attracted in the European Press. It was shortly after this that Mr. Morgenthau's books was written, and then cited in 1919 at the Peace Conference in assigning responsibility for the War.

Is it not extraordinary that Baron Wangenheim should have given to Mr. Morgenthau so many picturesque details which are in flat contradiction with the facts? How could he have dared to make such an important revelation so prejudicial to the interests of his Government? Germany at this time, in the early weeks of the War, was trying hard to win the good-will of the United States and make the world believe that she was fighting for self-defense in a war forced upon her. A statement such as Wangenheim's would have done Germany infinite damage.

And is it not difficult to understand why the American Ambassador did not report to Washington what was perhaps the most important thing he ever heard at Constantinople? Yet a careful search through the files of the State Department at Washington shows that there is no despatch or telegram recounting this interesting conversation with Baron Wangenheim; nor does Mr. Morgenthau in his book say anything about having made a report on the subject to Washington.

CHAPTER V

THE PREPARATION OF THE AUSTRIAN ULTIMATUM

THE assassination of Franz Ferdinand and his wife shook Berchtold out of his undecided hesitating attitude of the past. It determined him to use the crime as a good excuse for clearing up the unsatisfactory situation with Serbia and for putting an end once and for all to danger to the Dual Monarchy from the Greater Serbia propaganda and the Russian intrigues against Austrian influence in the Balkans. For months and years past there had been a growing conviction among certain groups at Vienna that the political situation was becoming dangerous and intolerable for Austria in the Balkans. Serbia, as a result of the Balkan Wars, had grown greatly in territory, population, and pretensions. The Greater Serbia movement was gathering strength and received support from the growing nationalist movement among all the South Slavs living under Hapsburg rule. In the spring of 1914 there were rumors that Serbia and Montenegro were to be fused together. This would give Serbia an outlet on the Adriatic and threaten the existence of the struggling infant Albanian State, and so endanger the arrangements by which Austria had sought to protect herself against the Slav danger on her southern borders. Rumania could no longer be counted upon as a reliable ally, and the Rumanian irredentist agitation in Hungary was as violent as ever. It was suspected that a Serbo-Rumanian-Greek Balkan League was being secretly encouraged by Russia, and was only waiting for the favorable opportunity afforded by the death of the aged Francis Joseph or by a European War to disrupt Austria by liberating her oppressed nationalities, while Russia possessed herself of the long-sought control of the Straits and a free outlet to the Mediterranean. Russian armaments, military railway construction, and trial mobilizations were proceeding apace. France was loaning Russia millions of francs for these purposes, while at the same time increasing her own military establishment. Albania, Austria's pet creation to check Serbia, was in the throes of disorder and revolt against the weak prince who had finally been selected as its ruler. Prince William of Wied's flight had led to the sarcastic pun, "Les caisses sont vides; le trône est Wied; tout est vide." [1] The ever-latent irritation between Italy and Austria, arising from Italian irredentist aspirations for Trieste and the Trentino and from Austro-Italian jealousy and rivalry in the Balkans, had again become recently acute because of an Austrian decree excluding persons of Italian birth from holding municipal office at Trieste. Even Germany was felt to betray an irritating disregard for her Austrian ally's Balkan interests and dangers; the best way to make Germany respect Austria as a worthy ally— as *bündnisfähig*—would be to adopt a more vigorous policy, show that she was capable of decisive action, and prove that she was really an asset and not a liability in the Triple Alliance.

Thus, even before Sarajevo, there was a general feeling on the part of many officials at Vienna that something must be done to prevent the decaying Hapsburg structure from crumbling to pieces, either from its own internal weaknesses and hesitating indecisions, or from being violently thrown down before long by its enemies. The news of the Archduke's assassination enormously strengthened this feeling. If Austria accepted this blow to her dynasty without actively resenting it and taking vigorous measures to put

[1] Dirr, p. 13; K.D., IV, p. 130.

an end to the Greater Serbian danger once and for all, her prestige in the Balkans and in Europe would be gone forever. The currently expressed Serb opinions that she was "worm-eaten," would soon be dismembered like Turkey, and find a place only in a "historical museum," would gain strength. Her enemies would be all the more ready to disregard her interests or even fall upon her. She must therefore show that she had vitality to restore her prestige and build new buttresses. It was better to do this instantly, for the situation would only grow worse with the future, as Russian armaments reached completion and nationalist ambitions grew stronger. Austria's existence as a Great Power was at stake. As Conrad, the Chief of Staff and head of the militarist party at Vienna, has put it:

> Two alternatives stood sharply out against one another: either the preservation of Austria-Hungary as a conglomerate of various nationalities which should stand together as a whole toward the outside and find their common well-being under a single ruler; or the rise of separate independent national states which would seize upon the Austro-Hungarian territories inhabited by their co-nationals and so bring about the destruction of the Monarchy.
>
> The conflict between these two alternatives, long foreseen, had reached an acute stage through Serbia's procedure; its decision could not longer be postponed.
>
> For this reason, and not as vengeance for the assassination, Austria-Hungary must draw the sword against Serbia. . . .
>
> Austria-Hungary could no longer remain coolly indifferent, suffer this provocation quietly, and observe the Christian humility which demands that, after a blow, one shall turn the other cheek also. It was not a question of a knightly duel with "poor little" Serbia, as she liked to call herself, nor of punishment for the assassination. It was much more *the highly practical importance of the prestige of a Great Power,* and indeed of a Great Power

which, by its continual yielding and patience (herein lay its fault), had given an impression of impotence and made its internal and external enemies continually more aggressive, so that these enemies were working with increasingly aggressive means for the destruction of the old Empire.

A new yielding, especially now after Serbia's act of violence, would have unloosed all those tendencies within the Empire which were already gnawing at the old structure anyway, in the shape of South Slav, Czech, Russophil, and Rumanian propaganda, and Italian irredentism. . . .

The Sarajevo assassination had torn down the house of cards erected by diplomacy in which Austria-Hungary had thought herself safe. The Monarchy had been seized by the throat, and had to choose between allowing itself to be strangled, and making a last effort to prevent its destruction.[2]

So Conrad, convinced that Austria must make war on Serbia as an act of self-preservation, urged Berchtold to approve immediate mobilization against Serbia. But Berchtold replied that there were difficulties: public opinion must be prepared; the grounds for war must first be established as a result of the investigation at Sarajevo; Francis Joseph was opposed to any immediate action; and Count Stephan Tisza, Minister-President of Hungary, was opposed to any war at all against Serbia, fearing that Russia would attack Austria and that Germany and Rumania would leave her in the lurch. Conrad was forced to admit that it was unsafe to make war on Serbia until they had made sure that Germany would protect Austria's rear from a Russian attack.[3] Berchtold had, however, like Conrad, become convinced of the necessity of a local war against Serbia. During the following days he proceeded to scheme to secure Germany's support, to build up a case against Serbia, and to overcome the two chief domestic obstacles to an imme-

[2] Conrad, IV, 31 f.; cf. Berchtold, in *Current History*, July, 1928, p. 626 f.

[3] Conrad, IV, 33 f.; interviews of June 29 and July 1.

diate local war against Serbia—the hesitation of Francis
Joseph and the opposition of Count Tisza.

EMPEROR FRANCIS JOSEPH

Emperor Francis Joseph at the time of the Sarajevo
assassination had hardly recovered from the illness of the
preceding winter, which many observers had thought might
prove fatal to the aged monarch. All the wars which he
had waged in the past had resulted in defeat, or loss of
territory, or generally both. He was not enthusiastic for
Conrad as Chief of Staff, nor optimistic about the changes
which had been made in the Austrian army. There is little
doubt that he wanted to end his days in peace. But now,
with the news of Hartwig's Pan-Slav intrigues at Belgrade,
the Greater Serbia propaganda, and this final tragedy to
his family, he had begun to fear that the Serbian situation
might at last become intolerable. "I see a very dark
future," he said to the German Ambassador on July 2;
"what is particularly disquieting to me is the Russian
practice mobilization which is planned for the fall, just
at the time when we are shifting our recruit contingents.
Hartwig is master at Belgrade, and Pashitch does nothing
without consulting him." "Every one is dying around me,"
he added mournfully, referring to the sudden death of the
Italian Chief of Staff, General Pollio, who was one of the
few loyal adherents of the Triple Alliance in Italy. But
though very sad and pessimistic, Francis Joseph evidently
had no immediate expectation of even a local war with
Serbia, for he spoke of his plans for the summer and the
prospects for the stag-hunts.[4]

Three days later, on July 5, when Conrad urged mobilization measures, Francis Joseph refused to approve them.
"No, that is impossible," he said, pointing out the danger
of an attack from Russia and the doubtfulness of German

[4] Tschirschky to Bethmann, July 2; K.D., 9, 11.

support; before the Konopischt meeting he had asked Franz Ferdinand to get from Emperor William an unconditional declaration that Austria could count on Germany, but William II had avoided committing himself.[5] On July 7 the sad old man returned to his summer rest and repose at Ischl, having been unwilling to make any decision which might involve war. Some of the most important documents which Berchtold laid before him during the following days are pencilled in trembling hand with his signature as having been read, but they no longer bear the searching annotations of his earlier and more vigorous years. It is quite possible that the aged sovereign did not fully grasp the consequences of the policies which Berchtold was now pursuing.[6] We have no satisfactory accounts of the interviews which took place between him and his Minister of Foreign Affairs, but Berchtold seems not to have met with great difficulty in persuading his sovereign to approve the measures placed before him. Tisza, however, was a more difficult person.

TISZA'S PEACE PROGRAM

Count Stephan Tisza,[7] the famous son of a famous father, was perhaps the ablest and most striking political figure at this time in the whole Dual Monarchy. With close-cropped hair, square dark face, and flowing Hungarian cloak, he was like a little giant among the Magyar nobles, when he led the majority party as his father had done before him. He saw clearly the dangers ahead on all sides, and had the ability to reason coolly concerning them. He knew

[5] Conrad, IV, 36 f.

[6] Wilhelm Fraknói, *Die ungarische Regierung und die Entstehung des Weltkrieges* (Vienna, 1919), p. 34; Gooss, p. 40; Margutti, p. 391 ff.

[7] Tisza's own lips were sealed with blood when he was murdered on the threshold of his own hall at the very end of the War. It was the general impression that he was one of those primarily responsible for its origin. For the meager references in his papers to the July Crisis of 1914 and for articles in defense of his memory, see below at notes 77, 78.

exactly what he wanted, and having become Hungarian Minister-President in June, 1913, he was in an official position to compel attention to his views. He had already worked out, in the spring of 1914, as will be explained in detail, a diplomatic *"politique de longue main,"* which was to win Bulgaria to the side of Germany and Austria and secure peace in the Balkans for a few years at least. This peace program had been adopted with some changes by Berchtold, and made the basis for a long memorandum to Berlin—just before the news from Sarajevo made him suddenly change to Conrad's war program. Tisza, however, was not the kind of man to allow his matured judgments to be overturned in a moment, even by such a crime. On June 29, the day after the assassination, he hastened to Vienna to express his country's sympathy to Francis Joseph, but with no idea that the Monarchy's policy was to be altered because of what had occurred. After condoling with the Emperor, Tisza visited the Ballplatz, little suspecting the sudden change in the attitude of the Minister of Foreign Affairs. But here at the Foreign Office he learned with painful surprise of Berchtold's "intention of making the horrible crime of Sarajevo the occasion for the final reckoning with Serbia." [8]

Tisza thereupon told Berchtold frankly that the provoking of such a war with Serbia would be "a fatal mistake"; it would pillory Austrians "before the whole world as disturbers of the peace, besides beginning a great war under the most unfavorable circumstances." But he apparently made little impression on Berchtold. At any rate, upon his return to Budapest, Tisza considered it his duty to inform Francis Joseph of Berchtold's reckless plans and warn him against them. Since it was expected that Emperor William was about to come to Vienna to express his personal sympathy for his brother monarch, Tisza begged Francis Joseph

[8] Tisza to Francis Joseph, July 1; A.R.B., I, 2.

to take advantage of the opportunity "to induce him to support us in our Balkan policy as intended," [9] i.e., winning Bulgaria and preserving peace in the Balkans. In his conflict with Berchtold, Tisza wanted to play German influence in favor of his own diplomatic peace program against Berchtold's new and reckless war program. But Berchtold proceeded to take this very arrow out of Tisza's quiver, and use it, as we shall see, against Tisza himself.

In view of the unreliability of Rumania as an ally, and the increasing dangers to the Dual Monarchy after the Balkan Wars, Tisza had drawn up a memoir in March, 1914. In this he set forth a program of peace, recuperation, and diplomatic readjustment in the Balkans, which he laid before Francis Joseph and Berchtold, and which he hoped would be adopted as the basis of a well-considered.Austrian and German policy in the Balkans. It may be summarized as follows.[10]

The Balkan Wars and the Peace of Bucharest have created for Austria-Hungary an intolerable situation. Until this is improved there can be no real lasting peace. On the other hand, the general exhaustion and dismay have been too great to allow any advantageous military action in the immediate future. Hatreds and passions lie in the way of a sound, correct judgment of one's own interests, as well as of those of one's neighbors. The over-confidence of the victor impairs correct judgments, just as much as the bitterness of the vanquished. Austria cannot come to a correct appreciation of her own worth nor command a corresponding respect for her interests and advice among the Balkan States until the smoke has cleared away and

[9] Tisza to Francis Joseph, July 1; A.R.B., I, 2. *Cf.* also the post-War statements of Berchtold, Hoyos, Wiesner, Jagow, and Zimmerman, in *Current History*, July, 1928, pp. 626-636.

[10] Fraknói, pp. 7-13, gives the German text, which Tisza sent to Vienna. A German and English translation of the Tisza's original Magyar text is given by Marczali in *Am. Hist. Rev.*, XXIX. 303-310, Jan., 1924

cool reason holds sway. It would be a great mistake to precipitate matters, or to try to force a premature development which can only come as a result of time, patience, and a well-considered policy. Nevertheless one must not sink into apathetic resignation or passive inactivity. On the contrary, one must adopt a carefully thought out *"politique de longue main"* which shall gradually smooth away the internal difficulties and bring about a more favorable situation in the Balkans. "With this aim we must consider not only our own interests, but also come to a clear understanding with Germany. Our task is a difficult one. There can be no talk of success unless we have complete assurance of being understood, respected, and supported by Germany. Germany must see that the Balkans are of decisive importance not only for us but for the German Empire."

As to Russia, Tisza did not believe that she intended to make war immediately. Her aggressive attitude and saber-rattling was meant to impress the Balkan States and was encouraging the nationalist movement in Rumania and Serbia. It might even win Ferdinand of Bulgaria to the Tsar's side. Bulgaria, Tisza believed, could and ought to be deflected to the side of the Central Powers. Undoubtedly, Ferdinand had fallen into his desperate position after the Second Balkan War because of his own crazy policy and his failure to follow Austrian advice. Nevertheless, clamped in between Rumania, Serbia, and Greece, and still threatened by Turkey, Bulgaria would certainly throw herself into the arms of Russia, unless Austria came strongly to her support. Such a combination, in which Bulgaria should be reconciled with the other Christian States under Russian patronage, would lead to a successful war against Austria, Bulgaria being rewarded with Macedonia. Austria would be surrounded by the iron ring which Russia was so persistently forging, and the military superiority of the Triple Entente on the Continent would be complete. The

long-sought moment would then have arrived in which
Russia and France could attack Germany with overwhelming forces and begin the World War with a prospect of
success.

The Triple Entente would not attack Germany, however, Tisza believed, until Russia had won over Bulgaria
and so threatened Austria with a war on three fronts.
The crux of the European situation lay, therefore, in the
Balkans and particularly in attaching Bulgaria to the Central Powers. This was of just as much vital interest to
Germany as to Austria. Therefore the Dual Monarchy
should strive to oppose Russia's Balkan policy by a well-
considered harmonious German-Austrian policy. The best
way to win Bulgaria, Tisza believed, was to hold out to
Ferdinand the prospect of acquiring Macedonia. This
could not be accomplished at once. Bulgaria would need
several years to recover strength and heal the wounds of
war. Meanwhile the Central Powers must assure Bulgaria
protection against attack from Turkey or Greece. Rumanian public feeling was very strong against Hungary, but
an effort must be made to keep King Carol firm in his
alliance and assure him that Rumania was in no danger of
an attack from Bulgaria. Germany and Austria must
henceforth coöperate together to effect a favorable grouping
of the Balkan States; Rumania and Greece must be wooed
away from Serbia, and reconciled with Bulgaria on the basis
of an enlargement of Bulgaria at Serbia's expense.

Such, in outline, was the policy which Tisza thought
ought to be urged upon Germany, so that the two Central
Powers would support one another at Sofia, Bucharest, and
Constantinople. At the end of his Memoir he again repeats
that this is a policy of peace for the present, and that "it
is only in a relatively distant future that Bulgaria can com-
pensate herself with Macedonia." And in closing, he
again says with emphasis: "In the Balkans we must first

preserve the peace and prepare a favorable development. There is no time to be lost."

Tisza's program apparently met with the approval of Francis Joseph and Berchtold, who had Baron Flotow, the Foreign Office specialist on Balkan affairs, draw up a much longer memoir developing Tisza's ideas in more detail. Flotow emphasized the critically dangerous position in which Austria found herself. Rumania, in spite of King Carol's undoubted personal loyalty, could not be depended upon in view of the strong tide of anti-Austrian feeling among the Rumanian people. Austria must therefore compel Rumania to declare herself openly either for or against Austria. The best way to put pressure on Rumania for this purpose was for Austria to enter into an alliance with Bulgaria, and to make Sofia, instead of Bucharest, the pivot of Austria's Balkan policy. Bulgaria would guarantee to Rumania the existing boundary between Bulgaria and Rumania, so that King Carol would not be antagonized or alarmed. In fact he would then see the wisdom of holding to the Triple Alliance; he might even be induced to use his great influence with Serbia "to draw Serbia closer to the Dual Monarchy; in which case the Dual Monarchy, within the bounds of such a political situation, would meet Serbia most loyally half-way." [11] But if King Carol should not consent to make a satisfactory public declaration of his loyalty to the Triple Alliance, then Austria must revise her military arrangements, and seek to bring Turkey into alliance with Bulgaria, so that both would support the Triple Alliance.

Flotow's memorandum, somewhat amplified by Matscheko and Pogascher, was put before Berchtold about the middle of June. Whether it was shown to Franz Fer-

[11] Gooss, p. 5. Berchtold later went over Flotow's draft and deleted this clause contemplating mediation by Rumania for a possible friendly settlement between Austria and Serbia.

dinand during the visit which Berchtold paid to Konopischt the day after Emperor William's interview with the Heir to the Throne is not clear. At any rate it was decided that it should be worked out in greater detail and laid before the Berlin authorities as a memorandum for guidance of the two allies in Balkan affairs. Accordingly, an elaborate draft to this effect was completed by June 24. Berchtold then went over the draft, and gave it the final gentle form, which he hoped would prove unobjectionable and persuasive to the Berlin Foreign Office.[12]

Beginning with an analysis of the results of the Balkan Wars, Berchtold pointed out the dangers to Germany and Austria of the existing situation. "Turkey, which has a natural community of interests with the Triple Alliance and has formed a strong counter-weight against Russia and the Balkan States, has been almost entirely driven out of Europe and largely lost its position as a Great Power. Serbia, whose policy for years has been hostile to Austria-Hungary, and is now wholly under Russian influence, has gained unexpectedly in population and territory. Her proximity to Montenegro and the general spread of the Greater Serbia idea makes imminent the possibility of her further aggrandizement by a union with Montenegro. Finally, the relations of Rumania with the Triple Alliance have essentially altered during the crisis." Omitting for obvious reasons all Austria's own responsibilities for the bad situation, Berchtold emphasized the dangerously aggressive intrigues of Russia and France. "The idea of liberating the Christian peoples of the Balkans from the Turkish yoke in order to use them as a weapon against the Triple Alliance has long been the political main-spring of Russia's traditional interest in these peoples. Recently [i.e., in 1912] this idea, which has been sympathetically taken up in France, developed into a plan for uniting all

[12] Printed in A.R.B., I, 1; K.D., 14; cf. Gooss, pp. 6-26.

the Balkan States into a Balkan League in order in this way to put an end to the superiority of the Triple Alliance. . . . But [the Second Balkan] War caused the Balkan States to split into two almost equally strong opposing groups: Turkey and Bulgaria on the one hand, and Serbia, Montenegro, Greece and Rumania on the other. To heal this split, in order to use all the Balkan States, or at least a decisive majority of them, to shift the balance of power in Europe, is the present task which Russia, aided by France, is attempting to accomplish. Since Serbia and Greece are already in alliance, and Rumania has declared herself in harmony with them, at least as far as the Treaty of Bucharest is concerned, France and Russia are anxious to remove the rancor which exists between Bulgaria and Greece and especially between Bulgaria and Serbia on account of Macedonia. They are anxious to find a basis on which Rumania would be willing to come over completely to the side of the Entente, and even to coöperate in a po-litical combination with Bulgaria, whom she regards with suspicion; and they are anxious finally, if possible, to bring about a peaceful solution of the Aegean Islands question that would lead Turkey to approach or even to join the Balkan States. The basis on which Russian and French diplomacy intends to accomplish an adjustment of all this hostility and rivalry and build up a new Balkan League is undoubtedly founded upon a program directed against Austria-Hungary, at whose expense all the members of the League could be promised a successive extension of boundaries westwards."

After detailing all the intrigues by which Russia and France were seeking to build up this new Balkan League, aimed at the territorial dismemberment of the Dual Monarchy, Berchtold dealt as tactfully as possible with the Rumanian problem, pointing out Austria's embarrassments and hinting that Germany might use pressure to make

Rumania see the error of her ways. As the best method of thwarting Russia's projected Balkan League and compelling Rumania to return to the fold of the Triple Alliance, Berchtold then urged Tisza's program for an alliance with Bulgaria, adding that Turkey also might be included in it eventually. "Austria must accept the offer of a definite alliance made by Bulgaria a year ago and repeated several times since then. At the same time she must aim to bring about an alliance between Bulgaria and Turkey; both these states were recently so favorably disposed to this, that a draft treaty was worked out, though not signed afterwards. This is another instance in which the Dual Monarchy, if it continued delaying action out of consideration for Rumania, which is moved by no such reciprocal feelings, might cause itself serious and irreparable injury. Further delay and failure to begin a countervailing activity at Sofia would give Russia and France free scope for their intensive and wide-reaching plans. Rumania's attitude simply forces Austria to give Bulgaria that support which she has long been seeking, and which will frustrate Russia's otherwise unavoidable encirclement policy. And this must be done at once, while the road to Sofia and also to Constantinople is still open."

"The treaty with Bulgaria, the details of which will have to be examined more fully, must naturally be so framed as not to be in conflict with Austria's treaty obligations to Rumania. It also ought not to be kept secret from Rumania, since there is no hostility against Rumania in this step, but simply a serious warning to the authorities in Bucharest of the consequences of a persistent partisan dependence on Russia on their part."

Berchtold closed with an appeal to Germany for support for Tisza's program for a diplomatic shift in the Balkans, pointing out that Germany, no less than Austria, was threatened by Russia's aggressive policy. "Before Austria takes the step in question, she is most anxious to establish a full understanding with the German Empire, not only in consideration of old traditions and of what is due to a close ally, but more especially because grave interests of Germany and the Triple Alliance are at stake, and because its common interests can be successfully safeguarded only if the joint action of Russia and France is opposed by an equally joint counter-action of the Triple Alliance, and especially of Austria-Hungary and the German Empire. . . . While France aims to weaken the Dual Monarchy with the hope of promoting her plans for *revanche*, the intentions of Russia are much more comprehensive. If one considers the development of Russia during the last two centuries, the steady extension of her territory, the enormous increase of her population, exceeding so much that of all the other European Great Powers, and the vast progress of her economic resources and military strength, as well as the fact that this great Empire is as good as cut off from the sea by its geographical position and treaty obligations, one sees why Russia's policy has necessarily always had an inherently aggressive character. . . . For these reasons the Austrian Foreign Office is convinced that it is for the common interests of Austria no less than of Germany to oppose a timely and energetic counter-action to the development which is being pushed by Russian intrigues, and which perhaps at a later time could never be undone."

In this form the memorandum was complete and ready for transmission to Berlin. It was to "open Germany's eyes" to the need of supporting Austria more energetically in this diplomatic wooing of Bulgaria.[13]

Then on Sunday afternoon, June 28, came the terrible

[13] Hoyos at Vienna to Pallavicini at Constantinople, June 26: "Unterdessen wird ein langes Memorandum für Berlin ausgearbeitet, das demnächst abgehen soll, und der Minister [Graf Berchtold] tut sein Mögliches, Tschirschky die Augen zu öffnen." Gooss, p. 6. *Cf.* Berchtold's article in *Contemporary Review*, April, 1928, pp. 422-432.

telephone message that Franz Ferdinand and his wife had been murdered at Sarajevo. The news appears to have had a stimulating effect upon the ordinarily rather indolent and undecided mind of Count Berchtold. Many historians, and several Viennese with whom the present writer has talked, speak of Berchtold as a minister who allowed himself to be managed by others, especially by a number of Serb-haters in the Austrian Foreign Office, like Hoyos, Forgach, Macchio, and by Baron Conrad, the Austrian Chief of Staff. The Foreign Minister has been regarded as a mere "rubber stamp," approving what others urged upon him. While this view may be more or less true for the period before Sarajevo, it does not appear equally so for the crisis of July, 1914. The contemporary evidence seems to show that however much Berchtold may have been guided by his subordinates at the Ballplatz, and by the militarists, he took a very active and sinister part in the events which led directly to the World War. Hitherto he had vacillated between the two opposing groups of opinion represented respectively by Conrad and by Tisza. But now, after Sarajevo, he decided to use this crime as the final justification for clearing up, once and for all, Austrian relations with Serbia.

BERCHTOLD'S APPEAL FOR GERMAN SUPPORT

Berchtold was now finally converted to Conrad's desire for immediate war against Serbia. But owing to Francis Joseph's hesitation and Tisza's opposition he could not adopt it at once. Moreover, he realized that it would be madness to embark on any such hare-brained action without first getting from Berlin an assurance of German support. Germany during the last few years had been constantly restraining Austria from aggressive action in the Balkans which might involve the Triple Alliance in conflict with the Triple Entente. Two days after Sarajevo, when even serious people in Vienna "were expressing frequently the hope that Austria had now the excuse for coming to a final reckoning with the Serbians," the German Ambassador, Tschirschky, used every opportunity to warn calmly but very energetically and earnestly against any overhasty steps. He pointed out above all else that Austria must be clear as to exactly what she wanted, and remember that she did not stand alone in the world; she must consider her allies and the entire European situation, and especially the attitude which Italy and Rumania would take in regard to Serbia.[14] On July 2, Berchtold set forth to him all the dangers from the Greater Serbia propaganda. News had just come that twelve assassins were on the way to assassinate Emperor William. It was as much to Germany's, as to Austria's, interest to put an end to the Belgrade plottings. Tschirschky admitted this, but observed confidentially to the Austrian Minister that the reason Berlin had not given more definite promises of support in the past was that Austria "had talked much theoretically but had never formulated a fixed and definite plan of action"; only when such a plan was formulated, could Berlin promise full and complete support; and he again warned Berchtold of the danger of alienating Rumania and Italy.[15] Similarly from Berlin came expressions of sympathy, but they were accompanied with advice to be cautious. The Austrian Ambassador in Berlin telegraphed:

> Zimmermann [German Under-Secretary of State for Foreign Affairs] assured me that he would consider decisive action on the part of Austria, with whom the whole civilized world today was in sympathy, quite comprehensible, but still he would recommend the greatest caution, and advise that no humiliating demands be made upon Serbia.[16]

[14] Tschirschky to Bethmann, June 30, K.D., 7.
[15] Berchtold's summary, July 3, A.R.B., I, 3; Gooss, 37 ff.
[16] Szögyény to Berchtold, July 4; A.R.B., I, 5.

In view of this attitude of caution and moderation on the part of Francis Joseph, Tisza, and Germany, Berchtold feared that an immediate mobilization against Serbia might result in Austria being left without German backing and the consequences might be disastrous. He saw that he must first gain an assurance of support from Berlin for whatever policy he should ultimately adopt. To secure this he decided to send Count Hoyos on a special mission to Berlin. Berchtold intended to have two strings to his bow. He would not openly abandon Tisza's peace program for winning over Bulgaria to the side of Austria and Germany, to which Berlin would probably assent; but at the same time he would do all he could to bring Germany as far as he could in the direction of approving energetic and immediate military action against Serbia. For this purpose he would exploit to the utmost the horror of Sarajevo; he would emphasize the fact that the threads of conspiracy certainly led to Belgrade, that the crime was merely the culmination of the series of intolerable Serbian outrages which must now at last be forcibly dealt with. Accordingly, with this double program in view, he decided to send at once to Berlin the long memorandum on policy mentioned above; but to it he added the postscript:

"The above memorandum had only just been completed, when the terrible events of Sarajevo happened. The full significance of the villainous murder can hardly be estimated today. Most certainly, if a proof was needed that the gulf between the Monarchy and Serbia is beyond bridging over, or that the ambition of Greater Serbia in its intensity and recklessness does not stop at anything, that proof has been given. Austria-Hungary has not been lacking in good-will and readiness to bring about tolerable relations with Serbia. But it has recently been shown that all these efforts are in vain, and that the Monarchy must in future look to the persistent, implacable and aggressive enmity of Serbia. It is all the more necessary for the Monarchy to tear asunder with a determined hand the threads which its enemies are weaving into a net over its head." [17]

Berchtold also drew up an ambiguous double-faced letter for Francis Joseph to sign and send to Emperor William. The greater part of it, like the memorandum on policy, was devoted to Tisza's pacific program for a diplomatic shift in the Balkans to strengthen the hold on Rumania, win Bulgaria, and isolate Serbia. But the beginning and the end of the letter, like the postscript above, were calculated to convince the two imperial Monarchs of Serbia's responsibility for the Sarajevo crime, and so to lay the foundation on which Berchtold might base military action. Military action, however, was not actually mentioned, for he did not want to alarm the Monarchs unduly and brusquely at first. But if he found that they accepted his view of Serbian responsibility, they might be willing to take the next step of approving armed invasion of Serbia; and if they did not, he could at any rate fall back on Tisza's diplomatic program. The royal missive ran as follows:

> . . . I am sending you a memorandum, drawn up by my Minister of Foreign Affairs prior to the frightful catastrophe at Sarajevo, which after that tragic event now appears especially noteworthy. The attack on my poor nephew is a direct result of the agitation of the Russian and Serbian Pan-Slavs, whose single aim is the weakening of the Triple Alliance and the disruption of my Empire. According to all indications, the crime of Sarajevo is not the deed of a single individual, but the result of a well-arranged plot whose threads reach to Belgrade; and though presumably it will be impossible to prove the complicity of the Serbian Government, there can be no doubt that its policy of uniting all the South Slavs under the Serbian flag promotes such crimes, and that a continuation of this situa-

[17] A.R.B., I, 1; K.D., 14; Gooss, p. 4.

tion spells lasting danger for my dynasty and for my territories.

This danger is heightened by the fact that Rumania, in spite of its existing alliance with us, is in close friendship with Serbia and permits in its own territory just as hateful an agitation against us as does Serbia. [In spite of Carol's loyalty and because of **popular feeling**] I **fear** that Rumania can only be rescued for the Triple Alliance in case we do two things: prevent the establishment of a new Balkan League under Russian protection by joining Bulgaria to the Triple Alliance; and give it clearly to be understood in Bucharest that Serbia's friends cannot be our friends, and that Rumania can no longer count upon us as allies, unless she cuts loose from Serbia and suppresses with all her power her own agitation in Rumania which is directed against the existence of my Empire.

The aim of my Government must henceforth be to isolate and diminish Serbia. The first step in this direction must be to strengthen the present Government of Bulgaria whose real interests tally with ours, and prevent her return to a Russophil policy. When Rumania realizes that the Triple Alliance does not hesitate to ally with Bulgaria and yet is ready to compel Bulgaria to guarantee Rumania's territorial integrity, Rumania will then perhaps retreat from the dangerous path into which she is led by her friendship with Serbia and her *rapprochement* with Russia. If this should succeed, a further attempt could be made to reconcile Greece with Bulgaria and Turkey, and so form a new Balkan League under the protection of the Triple Alliance; its purpose would be to set a dam to the Pan-Slav flood and assure peace to our lands.

This will only be possible when Serbia, which at present forms the pivot of the Pan-Slav policy, is eliminated as a political factor in the Balkans. After the last frightful events in Bosnia, you too will be convinced that a friendly settlement of the antagonism which divides Austria from Serbia is no longer to be thought of, and that the peace policy of all European monarchs is threatened so long as

the source of criminal agitation in Belgrade lives on unpunished.[18]

THE POTSDAM CONVERSATIONS, JULY 5 AND 6

This royal letter, together with Berchtold's completed
memorandum and postscript, were dispatched to Berlin
by Berchtold's confidential Foreign Office Secretary, Alexander Hoyos, and then presented to the Kaiser by the
Austrian Ambassador, Count Szögyény, at Potsdam on Sunday, July 5. According to Szögyény's report of what took
place:

> After I had brought it to the knowledge of Emperor
> William that I had an autograph letter to deliver, I re-
> ceived Their Majesties' invitation to lunch today at noon
> in the New Palace. I gave His Majesty the letter and the
> accompanying memorandum. He read both documents in
> my presence with the greatest attention. At first he assured
> me that he had expected an earnest action on our part
> against Serbia, but at the same time he must confess that
> the statements of Our Majesty raised the prospect of a
> serious European complication, and he therefore, wished to
> give no definite answer until he had consulted with the
> Chancellor.
>
> After luncheon, when I again emphasized the serious-
> ness of the situation, His Majesty authorized me to report
> that in this case also we could reckon on Germany's full
> support. He must, as he said before, first hear what the
> Imperial Chancellor had to say, but he did not doubt at
> all that Bethmann-Hollweg would agree with him com-
> pletely. As regards any action on our part against Serbia,
> he thought such action ought not to be delayed. Russia's
> attitude would doubtless be hostile, but he had been pre-
> pared for that for years, and even if it should come to a
> war between Austria and Russia, we could be convinced
> that Germany would stand by our side with her accustomed

[18] Francis Joseph to William II, drafted by Berchtold July 2, and
presented by Szögyény July 5, K.D., 13; A.R.B., I, 1; Gooss, pp. 26-29.

faithfulness as an ally. Russia, furthermore, he thought, as things stand today, was in no way ready for war and would certainly ponder very seriously before appealing to arms. But she would stir up the other Powers of the Triple Entente against us and blow upon fire in the Balkans.

His Majesty said he understood how hard Francis Joseph, with his well-known love of peace, would find it to invade Serbia; but if we had really decided that military action against Serbia was necessary, he would be sorry if we left unused the present moment which was so favorable for us.

As to Rumania he would take care that King Carol and his counsellors should observe a correct attitude. He could not sympathize with the idea of concluding an alliance with Bulgaria; he had never trusted King Ferdinand, nor his former or present counsellors, and he did not trust him now. Still he would make no objections to a treaty between Austria and Bulgaria, but care must be taken that the treaty contained nothing to offend Rumania and it must, as the memorandum proposes, be communicated to Rumania.

Early tomorrow morning Emperor William intends to go to Kiel to start from there on his northern cruise. But first he will talk with the Chancellor, and for this purpose he has summoned him from Hohenfinow for this evening to the New Palace. In any case, I shall find an opportunity to speak with the Chancellor sometime tomorrow morning.[19]

What were Emperor William's feelings at the time of this interview? His emotional nature had been deeply shocked at the horrible news of the assassination of Franz Ferdinand and his wife, whom he had just been visiting at Konopischt. While yachting on the preceding Sunday afternoon at Kiel he espied a little launch steaming at full speed as if to board his boat. He made a peremptory gesture to her to keep off. But, instead, Admiral Müller, who was at the helm, made a sign that he had something to commu-

---

[19] Szögyény to Berchtold July 5, 7:35 P. M.; A.R.B., I, 6; Gooss, pp. 30-32.

nicate. Holding up to view a piece of paper, he folded it into his cigarette case, and tossed it carefully on board. A sailor picked it up and handed it to the Emperor. William II opened the case, took out the paper, and turned pale as he read the fatal news from Sarajevo. He at once gave orders to tack about and give up the regatta.[20] He intended to go to Vienna to attend the Archduke's funeral and show his respect to the aged Francis Joseph in his latest bereavement. But when it was reported to him that a dozen Serb assassins were on their way from Belgrade to Vienna to bring about his own assassination, he allowed himself to be persuaded by his Chancellor to abandon his visit.[21] It was officially announced that the reason for his change of purpose was an attack of lumbago and not at all considerations for his personal safety,[22] but his sudden decision not to go to Vienna to pay the last honors to his late friend gave rise to all sorts of contradictory statements and fantastic rumors.[23]

[20] J. Cambon's account of what he heard a few days later direct from "a personage who was beside the Kaiser at this moment;" Recouly, pp. 19 f. Recouly adds that the Kaiser remarked, as he turned pale, "Tout est à recommencer!" He deduces from this, wholly without proof, that the Kaiser had persuaded Franz Ferdinand to some great project at Konopischt—he is careful not to be very definite as to just what this project was—and that now the whole plan was spoiled by the Archduke's death.

[21] K.D., 6a, 6b, 9, 13; cf. also Berchtold's statement to Tschirschky, July 2, that "today's news from Semlin, according to which twelve assassins are on their way with the intention of murdering Emperor William, will perhaps at last open people's eyes in Berlin to the danger which is threatening from Belgrade;" A.R.B., I, 3.

[22] Dirr, p. 120; B.D., 24.

[23] B.D., 11, 12, 18, 24, 26, 29; Wickham Steed, *Through Thirty Years*, I, 401; Seton-Watson, *Sarajevo*, p. 105. According to the British Ambassador in Vienna (B.D., 18; cf. also B.D., 26; and Dirr, p. 117) Berchtold had expressed the hope on June 29 that no missions of foreign princes would be sent to the Archduke's funeral, in order to spare Francis Joseph fatigue and to shorten the ceremonies as much as possible. Possibly he feared that a meeting of sovereigns at Vienna would exercise a moderating influence and tend to thwart him in his plan of making war on Serbia. That such a gathering of sovereigns might have perhaps have led to advice which would have found some other solution than war is the post-

It would be rash for any writer to attempt to give an adequate analysis of the Kaiser's psychology on July 5, 1914, or at any other time. Karl Kautsky, the German Socialist leader, thinks he was already something of a madman. Herman Lutz has made an elaborate study to show that the Emperor had long suffered from periods of maniacal depression, each of which coincided with one of the insensate bellicose gestures with which he had continually alarmed Europe.[24] Other writers, having read the Kaiser's emotional speeches during the War, alternating between exaltation and tearfulness, or his futile "Comparative Tables" and Memoirs composed after the War, think of him variously as a dangerous paranoiac, an incurable megalomaniac, or an egotistical simpleton; but they forget that to judge leaders, even in the Entente countries, by what they said under the stress of War or for political propaganda, is no fair indication of their pre-War views or mental condition. They forget, in reading the historically inaccurate effusions from Doorn, the disintegrating effect upon an emotional and excitable mind of the strain of years of war. To estimate the Kaiser's attitudes in July, 1914, there is no better material than the marginal notes which he jotted down on the despatches which were laid before him. This was a practice which he had long since adopted in imitation of Bismarck, who found it a great saving of time to indicate his wishes by marginal notes, rather than by writing out or dictating long instructions. Bismarck and William II supposed that these *verba privatissima* would always remain

War opinion of two high Austrian officials: General Auffenberg, *Aus Oesterreichs Höhe und Niedergang* (Munich, 1921), p. 255 f.; and A. Hoyos, *Der deutsch-englische Gegensatz und sein Einfluss auf die Balkanpolitik Oesterreich-Ungarns* (Berlin, 1922), p. 77, note.

[24] Kautsky, *Wie der Weltkrieg Entstand* (Berlin, 1919); Herman Lutz, *Wilhelm II periodisch geisteskrank* (Leipzig, 1919). For a hostile but excellent brief study of the Kaiser's mentality, with a full bibliography, see [F. C. Endres], *Die Tragödie Deutschlands*, (Leipzig, 1922, 3rd ed. 1924).

secret in the archives; both would have been exceedingly astonished if they could have foreseen that they were so soon to be published to the world.[25] But while Bismarck's notes were carefully pondered and usually intended as instructions, the Kaiser's marginalia are more often merely the hasty emotional reaction to the document before him. In using them it must be remembered that they are often merely the first impressions of the moment, rather than the conclusions of mature reflections; that they are often contradictory and exaggerated; and that they frequently had no influence upon the actual course of events, because they were commonly made several days late on documents upon which the Foreign Office had already taken decisions. Nevertheless they do give some indication of the trend of his mind and the decisive impression made by the assassination of his friend.

Before Sarajevo Emperor William had been inclined to think that Austria was unnecessarily nervous about Serbia, and ought to try to come to some friendly understanding with her. In the spring of 1914, when Austria was greatly alarmed at rumors that Serbia, instigated by Russia, might attempt some union with Montenegro,[26] the Kaiser appeared to be pro-Serbian rather than pro-Austrian. Austria's efforts during the Balkan Wars to exclude Serbia from access to the Adriatic he regarded as "nonsense"; her new effort to prevent Serbia from reaching the Adriatic by union with Montenegro he pronounced "Unbelievable! This union is absolutely not to be prevented. And if Vienna attempts it, she will commit a great stupidity, and stir up the danger of a war with the Slavs, which would leave us quite cold." [27] He agreed with Tisza, who calmly accepted the union as imminent, rather than with Berch-

[25] In *Die Grosse Politik* and *Kautsky Documents, passim.*

[26] *Cf.* G.P., XXXVIII, 325-358; Conrad, III, 661-665.

[27] Marginalia on Griesinger's despatch from Belgrade, Mar. 11, 1914; G.P., XXXVIII, 335. Similarly on a despatch of May 12; "One must

told and Franz Joseph who were declaring it unacceptable. He telegraphed from Corfu to Bethmann on April 5:

> It is absolutely necessary that the people in Vienna should face the possibility [of union of Serbia and Montenegro] seriously, and be clear in their minds whether under all circumstances they would stand by the position taken by the Emperor and Count Berchtold, or whether they adopt Tisza's view. The first would only be possible in case they were absolutely firmly determined to prevent the planned union by force of arms. In any case Austria must not put her prestige at stake, and publicly declare unacceptable things which she will ultimately be willing to permit. If they will agree to the sensible views of Tisza, Austrian policy will without further ado be able to adapt itself to the changed conditions in the direction which we have been preaching for years. There must be found a *modus vivendi* with the Dual Monarchy which will be attractive to Serbia.[28]

While the German Kaiser had hitherto generally inclined to protect Serbia from dangerously excessive demands by Austria and hoped for a peaceful settlement of their difficulties,[29] now, after the murder of one of his best friends, whom he had just been visiting, by assassins who had admittedly come from Belgrade, his indignation against the Serbians was thoroughly roused. His marginal notes excoriate them as "murderers," "regicides," and "bandits." He sincerely felt that the monarchical principle was in danger; that the spirit which led them to murder their own king and queen in 1903 still dominated the country; that

realize that in the long run Serbia and Montenegro will come together anyway, just as Tisza said;" G.P., XXXVIII, 352.

[28] G.P., XXXVIII, 337 f.

[29] Tisza in his letter of July 1 to Francis Joseph had spoken of "the Kaiser's preference for Serbia" (A.R.B., I, 2). Bethmann wrote to the German Chargé d'Affaires at Bucharest, July 6: "The Kaiser, as King Carol is aware, has always intervened at Vienna in favor of an understanding with Serbia" (K.D., 16).

all monarchs, Nicholas II most of all, ought to support, instead of opposing, any action on Austria's part which aimed at the suppression of the unscrupulous agitation which had been going on for years among Serbians and which, as he was now informed by Berchtold, threatened the very existence of his Austrian ally, and had made his own personal friend its victim. When therefore he read that Tschirschky, his Ambassador at Vienna, was "using every opportunity to warn [Berchtold] calmly but energetically and earnestly against any overhasty steps," he noted in the margin, as already pointed out in the preceding chapter: "Now or never! Who authorized him to this? That is very stupid! It's none of his business, for it is purely Austria's affair to consider what to do in this matter, for it will be said afterwards, if things go wrong, that Germany was not willing!! Tschirschky will please drop this nonsense! Matters must be cleared up with the Serbians, *and that soon*. That's all self-evident and the plain truth." [30] With his natural impetuosity he wanted Austria to take action in regard to the Serbians as quickly as possible, while the whole civilized world, still under the vivid impression of the terrible assassination, sympathized with her.

What this action of Austria's was to be, the Kaiser did not know definitely on July 5, and did not care to advise. But neither he nor Bethmann thought it at all probable on that day that the Austro-Serbian dispute would lead to a European war. He could therefore quite safely depart on his northern cruise early next morning, as he had long planned, and as Bethmann advised. This he would hardly have done, if he had thought that the action, which he wished Austria to take at once instead of delaying more than two weeks, would probably involve a European conflagration. It is significant that the moment he heard the kind of ultimatum Berchtold had presented to Serbia, he

[30] K.D., 7; *cf.* also 29, 120, 288, 290, 335, 337.

started in a hurry to return to Berlin. The "Potsdam Council" legend represents him as leaving the scene of action with the Machiavellian intent of lulling Europe into unsuspecting security before his sudden attack on France and Russia; but such a notion he characterized at the time as "childish," in a marginal note on a despatch from Vienna reporting that this was exactly what the Austrian Chief of Staff and Minister of War were doing.[31] Furthermore, the Kaiser was not the kind of man to leave Berlin if he seriously expected European complications. And to have suddenly given up the northern cruise, which he had been accustomed for years to take at this season, and which had been long announced in the papers, would have been the very thing which would have excited uneasy comment abroad and played into the hands of the militarists everywhere. Therefore the Kaiser decided to carry out previously made arrangements, in spite of the Sarajevo assassination—precisely as Poincaré decided to carry out his previously arranged visit to Russia.

Nevertheless, the Kaiser realized that, while it was not probable that Austria's action would kindle a European war, it was possible. It was likely at any rate to give rise to rumors of war during his absence, and therefore he deemed it prudent quietly to inform representatives of the army and navy who happened to be in Berlin, as well as Bethmann, of his interview with Szögyény.

Accordingly, on Sunday afternoon or early Monday, before taking the auto from Potsdam for Kiel on July 6 at 9:15 A.M., the Kaiser had brief interviews with representatives of the army and navy. He informed each of his con-

---

[31] Tschirschky to Bethmann, July 10: "Der Kriegsminister wird morgen auf *Urlaub gehen,* auch Freiherr Conrad von **Hötzendorf** Wien zeitweilig verlassen. Es geschieht dies, wie Graf Berchtold mir sagte, absichtlich, um *jeder Beunruhigung vorzubeugen,*" on which the Kaiser noted "kindisch!" and underlined the words italicized; K.D., 29. See below, pp. 243 f., 249.

versation with the Austrian Ambassador. He told them privately to inform their chiefs who were absent on vacation, but added that they need not cut short their vacations to return to Berlin, and that no orders for military preparations need be given, as he did not expect any serious warlike complications.[32]

On Sunday afternoon the Kaiser also telephoned to Falkenhayn, the Prussian Minister of War, to come to Potsdam. Upon his arrival he received him at once, read him the communications from Szögyény, and suggested the

[32] The officers whom he saw were General Falkenhayn, Prussian Minister of War, and Captain Zenker of the Navy Staff on Sunday afternoon; and Lieut. Gen. Bertrab of the Army Staff and Admiral Capelle, Acting Secretary of the Navy, on Monday morning. In answer to a questionnaire sent out by the Foreign Office of the German Republic in October, 1919, they replied in letters, which were apparently written without consultation together but which are in substantial agreement, that they talked separately with the Kaiser, that he did not expect any warlike complications; that he did not order any military preparations; and that no such orders were given in the period July 5-23 covered by the questionnaire. Their letters are printed in the K.D., I, pp. xiv-xvi. The accuracy of their statements is confirmed by the results of an investigation into the responsibilities for the War undertaken by a subcommittee of the Reichstag in December, 1919; *cf. Investigating Comm.*, especially pp. 58-67, 70-72. Bertrab's letter may be cited as typical: "In reply to the Foreign Office, I respectfully state that on July 6, 1914, His Majesty personally informed me, without witnesses being present, of his view of the situation created by Austria's measures, in order that I, as the senior representative officer of the General Staff present in Berlin, might inform the Chief of the General Staff who was staying at Karlsbad. Present in the background were Her Majesty, the Empress, an adjutant, and a servant. Just before this His Majesty had been speaking apparently with the same purpose and likewise with no one in hearing with a naval officer who withdrew directly after the interview. After the Kaiser had dismissed me he entered his auto for the northern journey. No orders were given then nor as a result of the interview. In fact His Majesty emphasized the point that he did not consider it necessary to give any special orders, as he did believe there would be no serious complications as a result of the Sarajevo crime." Capelle likewise declared: "The Kaiser said he did not believe there would be any great warlike complications. The Tsar would in his opinion in this case not place himself on the side of regicides. Moreover, Russia and France were not ready for war. England was not mentioned by the Kaiser. Upon the advice of his Chancellor, in order not to create any unrest, he would go on his northern cruise. Still he wished to inform me of the strained situation so that I could weigh the future."

possibility of serious complications. When Falkenhayn asked if any military preparations ought to be made, the Kaiser said "No,"—and the short interview was at an end. No one was present except Plessen and Lyncker, two military secretaries regularly in attendance upon the Kaiser. Falkenhayn gave in consequence no orders for military preparations at this time nor until after the ultimatum had been presented to Serbia.[33] On the contrary, he left Berlin on July 8 for an official visit, then joined his family on vacation at the sea-side, and did not return to Berlin until Saturday, July 25, the day after the ultimatum had been published in the newspapers.[34]

One might object that these statements of 1919, as to events in 1914, are open to question. But they are confirmed by a noteworthy letter which Falkenhayn wrote to Moltke immediately after the interview with the Kaiser. This letter, being a private communication from one high army officer to another, deserves quoting in full as giving a fairly exact account of what the Kaiser said and thought on July 5:

> This afternoon His Majesty commanded me to the New Palace to inform me that Austria-Hungary appeared determined to tolerate no longer the intrigues stirred up against Austria in the Balkans, and with this in view to invade Serbia soon in case it should be necessary; should Russia not be willing to consent to this, even then Austria would not be willing to give in.
>
> His Majesty believed this was the view to be gathered from what the Austrian Ambassador said when he delivered today at noon a memorandum from the Government at Vienna and a letter from Emperor Francis Joseph.
>
> I did not hear their conversation, and cannot therefore permit myself any judgment in regard to it. On the other

[33] Statement of Falkenhayn in December, 1919; *Investigating Comm.*, p. 62 f.

[34] Letter of Wurtzbacher to the Foreign Office, Oct. 19, 1919; K.D., I, p. xvi.

hand, His Majesty read me the letter as well as the memorandum; and from them so far as it was possible to arrive at an opinion from hearing them read rapidly, I did not get a convincing impression that the Vienna Government had come to a firm determination. Both documents gave a very gloomy picture of the general position of the Dual Monarchy as a result of the Pan-Slav intrigues. Both also regarded it as necessary that something should be done as quickly as possible to check them. But neither of them spoke of any warlike issue; it was rather some "energetic" political steps which seemed indicated; for example, the making of a treaty with Bulgaria, for which they wished to be assured of the support of the German Empire.

This support is to be promised to them, with the statement that it is primarily and solely Austria's affair to take steps necessary for her own interests.

The Imperial Chancellor, who also came to Potsdam, does not believe any more than I do that the Austrian Government with its talk, though more decided than formerly, is in earnest. At least, not only has he raised no objections to the departure for the northern cruise, but he has even advised it. A long time will pass before the treaty with Bulgaria is signed. Your Excellency's stay at the baths will therefore hardly need to suffer any curtailment. Nevertheless, though I have no instructions to do so, I thought it proper to inform you of the strain in the situation, so that sudden events, which in the end may always occur, should not take you wholly by surprise.

With best wishes for the success of your cure, I remain with sincere devotion and high esteem, as always,

Your devoted,
v. Falkenhayn.[35]

---

[35] Falkenhayn to Moltke, July 5; Alfred von Wegerer, *Kritische Bemerkungen zu Kapitel XIII aus Vivianis "Réponse au Kaiser"* (Berlin, 1923), appendix ii; Montgelas, *Leitfaden*, p. 196. Moltke also evidently did not expect any immediate complications, for he wrote to his wife from Karlsbad on July 18; "I am looking forward a great deal to our meeting in August when you come back from Bayreuth;" Moltke, *Erinnerungen*, p. 380.

Falkenhayn's letter, it will be seen, has quite a different tone from Szögyény's report of the luncheon interview quoted above. Falkenhayn did not at all expect any immediate danger to the peace of Europe, nor "that the Austrian Government with its talk, though more decided than formerly, is in earnest." He got the impression that the main point of Berchtold's ambiguous missives was the diplomatic action to secure Bulgaria, and that even this would take "a long time."

As the Kaiser had very properly told Szögyény that he could give no definite answer until he had consulted his Chancellor, Bethmann-Hollweg also was summoned to Potsdam the same afternoon. With him went Zimmermann, Acting-Secretary of State of Foreign Affairs during Jagow's absence on a honeymoon in Switzerland.[36] The results of their conference, embodying Germany's official decision, were stated next day by Bethmann to Szögyény at Berlin, and notified to the German Ambassador in Vienna in the following telegram:

> The Austro-Hungarian Ambassador delivered yesterday to His Majesty a private letter from Emperor Francis Joseph, which describes the present situation from the Austro-Hungarian point of view and the measures contemplated by Vienna, copies of which are now being sent to you.
>
> I replied today to Count Szögyény, thanking him for Francis Joseph's letter, to which the Emperor will soon send a personal answer. In the meantime His Majesty wishes to emphasize that he is not blind to the danger threatening Austria, and consequently the Triple Alliance, from the agitation carried on by Russia and Serbian Pan-Slavs. Although His Majesty, as is known, has no great confidence in Bulgaria and its ruler, and is naturally more inclined toward his old ally Rumania and its Hohenzollern prince,

36 *Cf.* Bethmann, *Betrachtungen zum Weltkrieg,* I, 135 ff.; *Investig. Comm.,* I, pp. 9-10, 28, 31-33.

nevertheless he can understand that Emperor Francis Joseph should want to join Bulgaria to the Triple Alliance in view of Rumania's attitude and of the danger from the formation of a new Balkan League pointed directly against the Danubian Monarchy. His Majesty will therefore direct his minister in Sofia to support steps in this direction taken by Austria's representative, if requested to do so. His Majesty will also use his efforts at Bucharest, as suggested by Francis Joseph, to bring King Carol to fulfil his duties as an ally, to drop Serbia, and to suppress the agitation in Rumania against Austria-Hungary.

Finally, concerning Serbia, His Majesty naturally can not take any stand in the questions between Austria and Serbia, for they are beyond his competence, but Francis Joseph may be sure that His Majesty, in accordance with his treaty obligations and old friendship, will stand true by Austria's side.[37]

Bethmann also telegraphed immediately to the German Chargé d'Affaires in Bucharest, for King Carol's information, concerning Francis Joseph's letter to the Kaiser, the Sarajevo assassination, and Germany's resulting consent to accept Tisza's Balkan policy of winning Bulgaria:

The Kaiser, as is known to King Carol, has constantly intervened at Vienna in favor of an understanding with Serbia. In spite of this, the Austro-Serbian relations have grown steadily worse. In view of the assassination at Sarajevo, which evidently appears to be the result of a well organized plot and of the policy promoted by the Government at Belgrade for uniting all South Slavs under the Serbian flag, His Majesty understands that Emperor Francis Joseph regards an understanding with Serbia as impossible,

[37] Bethmann to Tschirschky, July 6; K.D., 15. The original draft made by Zimmermann had said Germany would stand true by Austria's side "under all circumstances;" but these last three words were stricken out by the more cautious Bethmann and not sent to Tschirschky. The Kaiser's personal reply to Francis Joseph, drawn up by the Foreign Office on July 9 and sent on July 14, after expressing condolences, is of similar tenor; K.D., 26.

and, by approaching Bulgaria, is seeking to counteract the dangers threatening his dynasty and his empire from the side of Serbia. His Majesty has therefore agreed that Francis Joseph should receive favorably Bulgaria's expressed desires for adhesion to the Triple Alliance.[38]

Szögyény also, after an interview with Bethmann on the morning of July 6, at which Hoyos and Zimmermann were present, sent a second telegram to Berchtold. The first part of this substantially reproduced what Bethmann had telegraphed to Tschirschky as Germany's decision in regard to the new diplomatic action at Sofia and Bucharest; and as to Serbia: "Austria must judge what is to be done to clear up her relation with Serbia; but whatever Austria's decision may turn out to be, Austria can count with certainty upon it, that Germany will stand behind her as an ally and friend."

Szögyény then went on to make other assertions of which there is no trace in Falkenhayn's letter or in Bethmann's telegrams as to Germany's position on July 5 and 6:

> In the course of further conversation, I made certain that the Chancellor, as well as the Emperor, regards an immediate action by Austria against Serbia as the most radical and best solution of our Balkan difficulties. From an international point of view he regards the present moment as more favorable than a later one. He is in complete agreement that we should not inform either Italy or Rumania beforehand of an eventual action against Serbia. On the other hand, Italy ought to be informed now by Germany and by us of the intention of bringing about Bulgaria's adhesion to the Triple Alliance. At the close of the interview the Chancellor asked about the state of affairs in Albania, and warned us most energetically against any plans

[38] Bethmann to Waldburg, July 6; K.D., 16. The German Minister at Sofia was also instructed to support Austrian steps to win Bulgaria; K.D., 17.

which might endanger our relations with Italy and the existence of the Triple Alliance.[39]

It is easy to see why Szögyény alleged that Bethmann was "in complete agreement" with him that Austria should not inform Italy beforehand of action against Serbia. Like most Austrian officials, he now wanted war with Serbia, and by this statement encouraged Berchtold not to inform Italy beforehand, for fear that Rome would let the cat out of the bag at Belgrade, or at least that Italy would make demands for territorial compensation which Austria had no intention of giving. But this policy of deceiving Italy, or of delaying to inform her, was so completely contrary to the German attitude just before and after July 5, that one is forced to doubt the accuracy of the Austrian Ambassador's assertion. Germany's whole effort in recent years had been to keep Italy loyal and to restrain Austria from doing things in the Balkans which would unduly offend her, and make her likely to abandon completely her treaty obligations in the Triple Alliance. On July 3 Tschirschky had expressed to Berchtold Germany's unvarying attitude, by reminding him of "Italy, which, in view of her relations as an ally, ought to be consulted before the adoption of any military action." Berchtold had replied: "If we should put this question before the Cabinet at Rome, they would probably demand Valona as compensation, but we cannot concede this." [40]

Similarly, a little later, on July 15, Jagow reiterated Tschirschky's statement that Austria should inform Italy beforehand: "It is, according to my opinion, of the *greatest* importance that Austria should come to an understanding with the Cabinet at Rome as to her aims in case of a conflict with Serbia, and that she should hold her on her side,

[39] Szögyény to Berchtold, July 6, 5:10 P. M.; A.R.B., I, 7; Gooss, p. 32. *Cf.* Berchtold to Merey in Rome, July 12; A.R.B., I, 16.
[40] A.R.B., I, 3.

or (since a conflict with Serbia alone does not give rise to the *casus foederis*) keep her strictly neutral. Italy has the right, according to her agreements with Austria, in case of any change in the Balkans in favor of the Dual Monarchy, to claim compensations." [41] Thus Szögyény's assertion that Bethmann agreed that Italy should not be informed beforehand of an eventual action against Serbia is directly contrary to the whole tenor of German policy. It even seems to be contradicted by Szögyény's own words at the end of his despatch, that Bethmann "warned us most energetically against any plans which might endanger our relations with Italy." Nothing would be more calculated to do this, as the event proved, than the presenting Italy with a *fait accompli* of which she had been told nothing by her ally. Hoyos, however, in the course of reckless conversation with Zimmermann, seems to have indicated Berchtold's intention of keeping Italy in the dark, and secured Zimmermann's assent, and so stated later in Vienna.[42] But it is doubtful whether the Kaiser or Bethmann gave any such assent. If such is the case, and if Szögyény attributed to Bethmann a concession made only by Zimmermann, this would be one of the instances in which Szögyény did not report quite accurately, and exerted an influence in the direction of encouraging Austria in her reckless policy.[43]

[41] Jagow to Tschirschky, July 15; K.D., 46. For Germany's repeated attempts to persuade Austria to come to a seasonable and reasonable understanding with Italy, see K.D., 57, 68, 87, 89, 94, 104, 119, 150, 202, 212, 244, 267, 269, 287, 326, 396, 573, 577.

[42] Stolberg to Jagow, July 18, K.D., 87; and Berchtold's statement to Tschirschky, July 20 (Journal No. 3425; A.R.B., I, 35): "I cannot make up my mind to enter at present into an exchange of views with the Italian Government concerning our action, a point moreover which was discussed between Hoyos and Zimmermann at Berlin."

[43] For other instances, *cf.* Gooss, pp. 31, note 1, 173 ff., 235 ff., 248, note 3, and 253, note 2; and below ch. ix, at notes 33-36.

CONCLUSIONS AS TO GERMANY'S ATTITUDE ON JULY 5 AND 6

If one compares the two accounts of Germany's attitude as stated by Bethmann and by Szögyény, he will find that they are somewhat different in substance and spirit. Bethmann devotes four-fifths of his attention to the innovation in German policy involved in the Austrian diplomatic project of winning Bulgaria to the Triple Alliance. He only touches briefly, at the end of his telegram, on the question of Austro-Serbian relations, and then only to repeat a principle which he and Kiderlen had stated at one of the crises in the Balkan Wars—Germany will continue to act as a loyal ally, but must leave with Austria the decision as to what her vital interests require.[44] Szögyény, on the other hand, is mainly interested in Berchtold's projected military action against Serbia, of which he had been made acquainted by Count Hoyos. His telegrams represent both the Kaiser and Bethmann as believing "an immediate action by Austria against Serbia as the most radical and best solution" and "the present moment as more favorable than a later one"; and he says Bethmann is "in complete agreement" that neither Italy nor Rumania should be informed beforehand.

What is the explanation of this divergence in the two accounts? Probably it is partly to be found, as Gooss suggests, in the fact that Szögyény was already suffering from old age, and did not always grasp and report conversations accurately. His inaptitude had been responsible for some of the diplomatic friction between Berlin and Vienna during the Balkan Wars. He was a personal favorite with Em-

[44] Cf. Kaiser's conversation with Bethmann Nov. 9, 1912 (G.P., XXXIII, 302-305), and Kiderlen to Tschirschky, Nov. 19, 1912 (ibid., p. 361); "We are not the arbiter of what Austria regards as her vital interests or as possible concessions in regard to Albania; but we have expressly supported in diplomacy what Austria has indicated to us as her necessary demands, and we shall continue to do so."

peror William, but also moved in Berlin militarist circles, whose ideas did not always accord with the more moderate and cautious policies of Bethmann. Owing to Szögyény's superannuation, and perhaps to his bellicose tendencies and Magyar sympathies, Franz Ferdinand several weeks before the Sarajevo tragedy had raised the question of replacing him by a more capable representative. His successor, Prince Gottfried Hohenlohe, had already been selected and approved in Berlin on June 12. But unfortunately, in view of the sudden development of the July crisis, the change was not made until August 19, 1914.[45] In the case of these Potsdam conversations Szögyény seems to have over-emphasized Berlin's approval of the indefinitely stated second part of Berchtold's appeal.

Probably also the divergence is partly to be explained as reflecting a slight divergence of attitude on the part of Bethmann, the Kaiser, and Zimmermann. Bethmann, more optimistic and idealistic in character, desiring better relations with England and the Triple Entente, and encouraged by the Bagdad and Portuguese colonial treaties now ready for final signature, hoped that the Austro-Serbian crisis might be sufficiently dealt with by the peaceful diplomatic plan of winning over Bulgaria. He was less affected emotionally by the Archduke's death. He had recently been alarmed at the reckless way Berchtold had antagonized Italy in connection with Montenegro and thereby endangered the increasingly tottering Triple Alliance structure. "Vienna is beginning to emancipate herself from us somewhat rudely [etwas stark]) and in my opinion needs to be reined in before it is too late," [46] he had written a few weeks earlier, and had accordingly sent a strong warning to Berchtold. So now, after Sarajevo, he did not want to encourage Berchtold to other reckless adventures; and,

---

[45] G.P., XXXIX, 362 f., 546; Dirr, p. 114.
[46] Bethmann to Jagow, May 8, 1914; G.P., XXXVIII, 349 ff.

while forced to agree with the Kaiser that Germany must promise to support Austria, he had stricken out the words "in all circumstances" from the telegram as drafted by Zimmermann.[47]

The Kaiser, with shrewder insight than Bethmann, with longer acquaintance with the Balkan question, and bound by close personal ties to Franz Ferdinand and Francis Joseph, but with less self-control and less regard for the political consequences of his acts, expressed his feelings in the marginal note, "Now or never, etc.," which has already been quoted.[48]   He was willing to assent to the Austrian plan of winning Bulgaria, though this did not accord with his past policy and his personal distrust of King Ferdinand. He was more impressed with the last part of Berchtold's memorandum and Francis Joseph's letter urging the necessity for some energetic action to put an end to the Greater Serbian danger.   In view of Austria's hesitations and vacillations in the past, he advised her to act quickly while she had the sympathy of Europe; but, as Falkenhayn's letter to Moltke indicates, it was doubted whether Berchtold really would make any immediate and decisive moves.

Zimmermann, Acting-Secretary of State until Jagow's return to Berlin after these conversations of July 5 and 6, had at first reflected Bethmann's cautious views.   Immediately after Sarajevo he "recommended the greatest caution" to Szögyény, advised Serbia "to call to account the persons guilty," and urged the Entente Ambassadors to back up this timely advice in order to avert dangerous consequences.[49]   But on July 4 the Kaiser's marginal note, "Now or never, etc.," was received at the Foreign Office, and Zimmermann thereafter took his cue from it.   He apparently made no objections when Hoyos confided to him

47 K.D., 15; see above, note 37.

48 K.D., 7; see above, at note 30.

49 A.R.B., I, 5; Dirr, p. 118; B.D., 22, 44; see above at note 16, and ch. iii, at notes 51, 52.

that "Austria had in mind a complete partition of Serbia."
Berchtold had carefully avoided saying anything of this in
the missives which Szögyény was to present to the Kaiser.
When Hoyos returned to Vienna and reported what he had
said to Zimmermann about partitioning Serbia, his remarks
were promptly disavowed: "Berchtold, and especially Tisza,
want it expressly emphasized that Hoyos was uttering
merely a purely personal opinion." [50]

Such were the views of the three leading Berlin officials
at the moment Germany had to make her decision on July
5 and 6. It would be a mistake to exaggerate the divergence
of attitudes, but it helps to explain the way in which the
"blank check" was given at Berlin, and the way it was interpreted and used at Vienna. During the following days
the Kaiser was absent on his northern cruise and Bethmann
was on his estate at Hohenfinow, so that they exerted little
influence on the course of affairs. This left the German
Foreign Office in charge of Zimmermann, and then of Jagow
who returned to Berlin and took up again his duties as
Secretary of State soon after the departure of Hoyos on
July 6. Jagow, though in general agreement with Zimmermann, soon began to adopt a more cautious attitude. He
forwarded some good advice to Vienna—which Berchtold
disregarded. In order to find out where the Austrian path
was leading, he began to offer advice and ask questions—
which Berchtold did not answer fully and frankly.[51]

Thus the Kaiser and his advisers, influenced by the

---

[50] Tschirschky to German Foreign Office, July 7, 3:25 P. M.; K.D.,
18; cf. also 61 and 361. Evidently the Kaiser was unaware on Sunday
afternoon of this reckless talk of Hoyos, which probably took place on
Monday morning after he had left for Kiel. This explains why this
passage relating to the Hoyos incident was cut out from Tschirschky's
despatch when it was forwarded by Jagow for the Kaiser's perusal; K.D.,
note 2.

[51] Cf. Jagow's despatches, July 9-18; K.D., 23, 31, 33, 36, 39, 46,
61, 67-70, 72; and the information gathered from Zimmermann and Jagow
by the Bavarian Legation in Berlin, in Dirr, pp. 4-13, 123-129.

Sarajevo assassination and confronted with Berchtold's appeal for support, made their decision. Toward Bulgaria they agreed to adopt a new policy; and in regard to Serbia, they stated, according to Szögyény: "Austria must judge what is to be done to clear up her relation to Serbia; whatever Austria's decision may turn out to be, Austria can count with certainty upon it, that Germany will stand behind her as an ally and friend." [52] They gave Austria a free hand and made the grave mistake of putting the situation outside of their control into the hands of a man as reckless and unscrupulous as Berchtold. They committed themselves to a leap in the dark. They soon found themselves involved, as we shall see, in actions which they did not approve, and by decisions which were taken against their advice; but they could not seriously object and protest—at least until the eleventh hour when it proved too late—because they had pledged their support to Austria in advance, and any hesitation on their part would only weaken the Triple Alliance at a critical moment when it most needed to be strong. The Kaiser and his advisers on July 5 and 6 were not criminals plotting the World War; they were simpletons putting "a noose about their necks" [53] and handing the other end of the rope to a stupid and clumsy adventurer who now felt free to go as far as he liked. In so doing they were incurring a grave responsibility for what happened later.

[52] Szögyény to Berchtold, July 6; A.R.B., I, 7; see above, at notes 19, 37, 39.

[53] As the Kaiser himself noted frantically on July 30, after hearing of Grey's warning, Russian mobilization measures, and Berchtold's persistent disregard of all proposed peaceful solutions: in addition to encirclement by the Entente, "the stupidity and clumsiness of our ally has been made a hangman's noose for us" [wird uns die Dummheit und Ungeschicklichkeit unseres Verbündeten zum Fallstrick gemacht]; K.D., 401.

BERCHTOLD'S EFFORTS TO CONVERT TISZA

Having been informed by Szögyény that Germany as-sented to the second part of his double-faced appeal, i.e., that Germany would stand firm as an ally in whatever Aus-tria should decide to undertake against Serbia, Berchtold no longer pretended to advocate the first part, i.e., the peace program of Tisza.[54] For he had now overcome half his difficulties. He now needed only to persuade his aged monarch and Tisza to agree to the extirpation of the Serbian danger, which Conrad had long urged,[55] and which he him-self had finally decided upon. How was this to be done?

Tisza's *"politique de longue main"* to win Bulgaria and secure peace in the Balkans for a few years at least had been adopted by Berchtold and made the basis for his memoran-dum to Berlin—until the news of Sarajevo made him sud-denly change to Conrad's war program. Tisza, however, was not the kind of man to allow his matured judgments to be overturned in a moment even by such a crime. He had told Berchtold frankly that the provoking of such a war with Serbia would be "a fatal mistake"; it would pillory Austrians "before the whole world as disturbers of the peace, besides beginning a great war under the most un-favorable circumstances." But he apparently made little impression on Berchtold. Tisza had also informed Francis

[54] In fact he not only abandoned it, but on July 8 suggested to Berlin to drop taking further steps at Bucharest and Sofia for the winning of Bulgaria; and Berlin acquiesced; A.R.B., I, 11; K.D., 19, 21, 22. This only increased Berlin's belief in the "vacillation" of the "ever timid and undecided authorities in Vienna;" Schoen's report of July 18; Dirr. p. 7; K.D., IV, Anhang iv, No. 2.

[55] Not counting the period 1906-1912, covered by the two first vol-umes of his memoirs, it may be noted that in the seventeen months from January 1, 1913 to June 1, 1914, the Chief of Staff had, according to his own statements, urged war against Serbia no less than twenty-five times; cf. Conrad, III, 12 ff., 74, 78, 82, 84, 114, 165, 178 ff., 183 f., 249, 257 f., 261, 267, 302 f., 333, 342, 354 f., 375 f., 405 f., 453 f., 457, 461, 463, 467, 477, 661, 694 ff.

Joseph of Berchtold's reckless plans and warned him against them.[56]

After Tisza had returned to Budapest, Berchtold added the postscript to the memorandum for Berlin, denouncing Serbia, and drew up the royal missive from Francis Joseph to Emperor William which, like the memorandum, set forth Tisza's peace program, but which also at its close hinted at more vigorous action against Serbia: peace "will only be possible when Serbia . . . *is eliminated as a political factor in the Balkans.* After the last frightful events in Bosnia, you too will be convinced that *a friendly settlement of the antagonism which divides Austria from Serbia is no longer to be thought of,* and that the peace policy of all European monarchs is threatened so long as this source of criminal agitation in Belgrade lives on *unpunished.*" [57]

Berchtold could not properly or constitutionally send such an important message on foreign policy, suggesting, as it did, a modification of what had already been agreed upon, without informing the Hungarian Premier. He therefore sent a copy to Tisza; but Tisza, on reading it, was not at all pleased with it. He feared it would make Berlin "shy off" from approving the peaceful diplomatic program. He suspected the truth, that Berchtold was scheming to get the backing of Germany for military action against Serbia rather than for the agreed-upon *"politique de longue main."* He therefore telegraphed at once to Berchtold urging the omission of the words printed in italics above.[58] But at the very moment he was sending this telegram, Szögyény was already putting the unmodified text of the letter into Emperor William's hands at Potsdam. Berchtold had sent

[56] Tisza to Francis Joseph, July 1; A.R.B., I, 2.

[57] Francis Joseph to William II, drafted by Berchtold July 2, and presented by Szögyény July 5; K.D., 13; A.R.B., I, 1, Gooss, pp. 26-29; see above, at note 18. Words italicized were objected to by Tisza.

[58] Tisza to Berchtold, July 5, 11:50 A. M.; Gooss, p. 28 f.; Fraknói, p. 16.

it off without waiting to hear from Tisza. He had resorted to the sharp practice, which he was to employ later in similar fashion but in far more serious matters, of making use of a *fait accompli*. Disliking argument because of his natural indolence, his ignorance of detail, and his consequent dependence on his secretaries for information,[59] he always found it easier to take a step first, and avoid argument about it until after the moment had passed when the step could not very well be undone, and argument about it would therefore be futile.

The best lever with which to pry Tisza from his firm stand, as Berchtold, Hoyos and Forgach believed, was to represent to Tisza that Berlin wanted immediate and energetic action against Serbia; to make it appear that if Austria did not take advantage of the present favorable opportunity, Germany would more than ever regard Austria as *bündnisunfähig,* i.e., as a weak, hesitating, decrepit state of little value to Germany as an ally; and that consequently Berlin would disregard Austria's interests and treat her even more cavalierly in the future than in the past. In this purpose they were assisted by, or perhaps it would be more correct to say, they made use of, Tschirschky, the German Ambassador in Vienna.[60]

On July 4, at Forgach's suggestion, Berchtold sent to Francis Joseph and Tisza a rumor, gathered by one of the press agents in the Foreign Office, that "Tschirschky is re-

---

[59] For indications of Berchtold's incompetence and aversion to the hard study necessary to master the intricate subject of foreign affairs, see H. Kanner's portrait of "Graf Berchtold, der aristrokratische Dilettant" in *Kaiserliche Katastrophen-Politik* (Vienna, 1922), pp. 87-93; and Dumaine, *La Dernière Ambassade de France en Autriche* (Paris, 1921), pp. 22, 34 ff., 99 f.

[60] *Cf.* Berchtold to Tisza, July 8: "Aus den weiteren Aeusserungen des Botschafters [Tschirschky] konnte ich ersehen, dass man in Deutschland ein Transigieren unsererseits mit Serbien als Schwächebekenntniss auslegen würde, was nicht ohne Rückwirkung auf unsere Stellung im Dreibunde und die künftige Politik Deutschlands bleiben könnte;" A.R.B. **I,** 10.

ported to have declared, with the evident intention that it should be reported in the Ministry of Foreign Affairs, that Germany would support the Dual Monarchy through thick and thin, whatever should be decided against Serbia. . . . The sooner Austria attacked the better. Yesterday would have been better than today; today would be better than to-morrow. Even if the German press, which is wholly anti-Serbian today, should preach again in favor of peace, Vienna should not allow herself to be in doubt that the [German] Emperor and Empire would stick unconditionally to Austria-Hungary. One Great Power cannot speak more clearly to another than this." [61]

Again on July 6, the moment he received from Berlin Szögyény's version of the interviews with the Kaiser and Bethmann, Berchtold had Forgach forward the news to Tisza,[62] and for Tuesday, July 7, he summoned a Ministerial Council to approve the repressive measures in Bosnia and the warlike action against Serbia which he desired. Before the Council met, he arranged for a preliminary meeting, including himself, Tisza and Stürgkh, the Premiers respectively of Hungary and Austria, Tschirschky, and also Hoyos, who had just come back from Berlin and was one of the most active instigators for war with Serbia. Hoyos read aloud the two despatches from Szögyény and a memorandum of his own talk with Zimmermann. Berchtold

[61] Austrian Foreign Office *Journal* No. 3117; Gooss, p. 40, n. 1. How far Tschirschky was correctly reported here, and how far his words were twisted by Berchtold and his agents for their own purposes does not appear. Even if correctly reported, Tschirschky was evidently giving expression merely to his own personal views, for there is no indication in any of the documents that he had at this time received from Berlin any instructions to this effect; and if he had received instructions he would certainly have stated them officially to Berchtold, who would have been only too glad to emphasize the fact to Francis Joseph and Tisza. For Tschirschky's genuine views, given on June 30, July 2 and 3,— expressions of Austro-German solidarity, coupled with warnings against any hasty and reckless steps which would disturb the general European situation, see K.D., 7, 11; A.R.B., I, 3; and above, at notes 14 and 15.

[62] Forgach to Tisza, July 6, 1:30 P.M.; Gooss, p. 65.

expressed to Tschirschky his gratitude to the Kaiser and
Bethmann "for their clear attitude which was in accordance with treaty obligations and friendship," but promptly
disavowed what Hoyos had said to Zimmermann about
Austria's intention to partition Serbia.[63]

At the Ministerial Council of July 7, Berchtold raised
the question:

> whether the time had not come to make Serbia harmless
> once for all through the use of force. Such a decisive blow
> could not be struck without diplomatic preparations. So
> he had got into touch with the German Government. The
> discussions in Berlin had led to a very satisfactory result,
> inasmuch as Emperor William, as well as Bethmann-
> Hollweg, had given emphatic assurance of unconditional
> German support in case of a warlike complication with
> Serbia.[64] Italy and Rumania must still be reckoned with;
> and here he was in accord with the Berlin Cabinet that it
> was better to act first without consulting them, and then
> await any possible demands for compensation.[65]

> He [Berchtold] was aware that a passage of arms with
> Serbia might result in a war with Russia. But Russia
> was following a policy, that, looking to the future, was
> aiming at a combination of the Balkan states, including
> Rumania, for the purpose of using them against the Mon-
> archy when the time seemed opportune. He was of the
> opinion that Austria must take into account the fact that

[63] K.D., 18; see above, at note 50.

[64] The words, "inasmuch as . . . with Serbia," were added by Berchtold afterwards to the minutes which were noted down by Hoyos; Gooss,
p. 51, n. 3. Berchtold's alteration of the record would make it easier
for him to persuade Francis Joseph to consent to war with Serbia when
the minutes of the Council were presented to him for approval.

[65] Berchtold here implies that it was the Berlin Cabinet which made
the suggestion that Italy and Rumania be not informed. In reality,
(even admitting the fact of Bethmann's assent on this point which is
doubtful; see above, at notes 39-42), it is clear from Szögyény's own
phrase, "Bethmann as well as the Emperor is in complete agreement with
us," that it was from the Austrian, and not from the German, side that
this shortsighted suggestion was first made.

her situation in the face of such a policy was bound to become increasingly worse, especially as passive toleration would be interpreted by her South Slavs and Rumanians as a sign of weakness, and would lend strength to the magnetic power of the two border states.

The logical conclusion of what he had said was that Austria should get ahead of her enemies, and, by a timely final reckoning with Serbia, put an end to the movement which was already in full swing, a thing which might be impossible later.[66]

Tisza thereupon replied, at least according to the minutes which were made by Hoyos but which were somewhat touched up afterwards by Berchtold:

He [Tisza] agreed with Berchtold that the situation had changed somewhat in the last few days as a result of the investigation [at Sarajevo] and the attitude of the Serbian press, and emphasized that he also regarded the possibility of warlike action against Serbia as nearer than he had believed just after the crime at Sarajevo. But he would never agree to a surprise attack on Serbia without preliminary diplomatic action, which seemed to be intended [by Berchtold], and which had been unfortunately mentioned by Hoyos in Berlin, because in this case we should stand, in his opinion, in a very bad position before the eyes of Europe, and in all probability would have to reckon with the hostility of all the Balkan States except Bulgaria; and Bulgaria, which is at present very weak. would be unable to give us any corresponding support.

Unquestionably demands must be made on Serbia, but

[66] This and the following quotations are from the minutes of the Ministerial Council of July 7 in A.R.B., I, 8; English translation in the N. Y. Times *Current History*, Dec., 1919, pp. 445-460; Gooss, pp. 50-62, indicates the alterations which Berchtold made in the minutes See also Conrad, IV, 43-56, who was present with an Admiral at the afternoon session from 3-5 P. M., and gave secret military information, which he records in his memoirs but which was omitted for reasons of prudence from the official minutes of the Council; Fraknói, pp. 18-27; the reports of Tschirschky (K.D., 19) and of Tucher, the Bavarian Minister in Vienna. Dirr, p. 125 f.; and *Investigating Comm*. I, p 90.

no ultimatum must be sent until Serbia had failed to comply with these demands. These demands, to be sure, must be severe, but not such as could not be complied with. If Serbia accepted them, we should be able to point to a notable diplomatic success, and have increased our prestige in the Balkans. If the demands were not complied with, he too would favor military action, but must still emphasize that we aim at the diminution, but not the complete annihilation, of Serbia, both because this would never be permitted by Russia without a life-and-death struggle, and because he, as Hungarian Premier, could never consent to have the Dual Monarchy annex any part of Serbia.

Refusing to be shaken by Berchtold's assertion that Germany was in favor of immediate military action, Tisza declared further:

It is not Germany's affair to decide whether we should attack Serbia now or not. He personally was of the opinion that it was not unconditionally necessary to make war at the present moment, and that in view of the excited state of public opinion in Rumania we should have to reckon with a Rumanian attack, and in any case should have to maintain considerable forces in Transylvania to intimidate the Rumanians. At present, when Germany had happily prepared the way for the adhesion of Bulgaria, there was opened a promising prospect for successful diplomatic action in the Balkans; by joining with Bulgaria and Turkey, and by securing their adhesion to the Triple Alliance, we could out-balance Rumania and Serbia, and so compel Rumania to return to the Triple Alliance. As to Europe, one must bear in mind that the strength of France, in comparison with that of Germany, was steadily decreasing on account of her lower birth-rate, and that Germany therefore in the future would have more troops available for use against Russia. . . . [He concluded therefore that the Bosnian situation could be improved by internal administrative reforms, and that] he could not decide unconditionally for war, but would consider a corresponding diplomatic success with the severe humiliation of Serbia as the proper means for improving Austria's position and making possible a successful Balkan policy.

Berchtold answered in reply that the last few years had shown that, though diplomatic victories had raised the prestige of the Monarchy temporarily, they had only increased the existing tension in Austro-Serbian relations. Neither the success in the Annexation Crisis, nor that in connection with the creation of Albania, nor the later backing-down on Serbia's part in October, 1913, had actually changed the situation materially. "A radical settlement of the problem raised by the Greater Serbia propaganda, systematically carried on from Belgrade, whose disruptive force could be detected as far as Agram and Zara, was only possible through an energetic intervention." The Rumanian danger he did not think serious. And as for the relative strength of the Great Powers, Russia's increasing population more than offset France's declining birth-rate.

After a long discussion through the morning and afternoon, in which all the ministers except Tisza expressed views in virtual agreement with Berchtold, and in which Conrad set forth secret military plans which he asked not to be recorded in the minutes, no complete agreement was reached. Tisza was willing that specific demands should be made upon Serbia, but insisted that they should not deliberately be made so hard that Serbia could not comply with them, and that they should not be in the form of an ultimatum. He also insisted that he should see them before they were sent, so that he should not be faced with another *fait accompli*. All the other ministers, however, agreed with Berchtold against Tisza, "that a purely diplomatic victory, even if it ended with a striking humiliation of Serbia, would be worthless, and that consequently the demands presented to Serbia must be so far-reaching that their rejection would be a foregone conclusion, and so the way would be prepared for a radical solution through a military attack." As to military preparations, Tisza made his view prevail to the extent that the others consented that there should be no mobilization until after specific demands and an ultimatum had been successively presented and rejected.

At the close of the meeting Berchtold stated that he would present its results to Francis Joseph at Ischl next day. Tisza, however, who had to return to Budapest, feared that his own views against deliberately forcing war upon Serbia might not be effectively presented by Berchtold to the aged sovereign. He therefore requested Berchtold to delay his audience until he, Tisza, could draw up a memoir to be laid before the Emperor along with Berchtold's report on the Ministerial Council. This Berchtold consented to do, and postponed his audience with the Emperor until Thursday morning, July 9.

In his memoir of July 8 Tisza still urged the advisability of his original diplomatic program to win Bulgaria; but in view of the unanimity of the opinion against him in the Council the day before, he devoted most of his long memoir to what had now become the main secret question at Vienna: should the demands on Serbia, as Tisza insisted, take the form of a polite note, humiliating but not impossible for Serbia, stating specific grievances, and asking remedies which Austria was ready, *bona fide,* to accept as satisfactory; or, should the demands, as Berchtold and the majority wished, be a general indictment of Serbia in the form of an ultimatum, deliberately worded to provoke immediate war with Serbia? In favor of the former, Tisza argued to the Emperor, as he had done in the Council:

> I [Tisza] am not pleading at all that we should swallow all these provocations [of Serbia], and I am ready to assume the consequences of a war caused by a rejection

of our just demands. But, in my opinion, it must be made possible for Serbia to avoid war by accepting a severe diplomatic defeat, and if it comes to war it will be clear to the world that we stand on the basis of justifiable self-defense. A note in moderate, but not threatening, language should be addressed to Serbia, which should set forth our specific grievances and our precise demands in connection with them. [He suggests, for example, the remarks of the Serbian Minister, Spalajkovitch in St. Petersburg, and Jovanovitch in Berlin, the fact that the bombs in Bosnia came from the Serbian arsenal at Kragujevac, that the assassins crossed the border with false passes issued by Serbian authorities; and the general attitude of the Serbian press, societies, and schools.]

Should Serbia give an unsatisfactory answer, or try dilatory tactics, an ultimatum should follow, and after its expiration, the opening of hostilities. . . . After a successful war Serbia could be diminished in area by the cession of some of the conquered districts to Bulgaria, Greece, and Rumania, but we ourselves should ask at most merely certain important boundary modifications. To be sure, we could claim a war indemnity, which would give us the chance to keep a firm hand on Serbia for a long time. . . .

Should Serbia yield, we must accept this solution *bona fide,* and not make her retreat impossible.[67]

This possible peaceful solution urged by Tisza was not at all what Berchtold wanted. Shortly after Tisza had left Vienna, he again tried to apply the German lever, by alleging in a letter to Tisza on July 8:

Tschirschky has just left me, after informing me that he has received a telegram from Berlin in which his Imperial Master directed him to declare here *most emphatically* that Berlin expects Austria to act against Serbia, and that it would not be understood in Germany if we should let this opportunity go by without striking a blow. . . . From

[67] Tisza to Francis Joseph, July 8; A.R.B., I, 12.

further things the Ambassador said, I could see that in Germany any yielding on our part toward Serbia would be interpreted as a confession of weakness, which would not fail to react on our position in the Triple Alliance and on Germany's future policy.

These statements of Tschirschky's seem to me of such importance as possibly influencing your conclusions that I wanted to inform you of them at once, and beg you, if you see fit, to send me a cipher telegram to this effect at Ischl, where I shall be tomorrow morning and could interpret your view to His Majesty.[68]

Tisza was apparently unmoved by this, and did not telegraph as requested. Accordingly, although Berchtold had gone to Ischl to get Francis Joseph's approval for such demands upon Serbia "that their acceptance would be out of the question," [69] he did not succeed, as we learn from Tschirschky's report of July 10:

. . . The Minister informed the Emperor of the two possible methods of procedure against Serbia which are in question here. His Majesty thought perhaps the difference between them could be bridged over. But in general His Majesty inclines to the view that specific demands should be addressed to Serbia. Count Berchtold likewise would

[68] Berchtold to Tisza, July 8, ca. 8 P. M.; A.R.B., I, 10; Gooss, p. 68 ff. There are serious grounds for thinking that Berchtold himself fabricated these statements which he attributed to Tschirschky, his purpose being, as stated in the second paragraph, to "influence" Tisza: (1) The *Kautsky Documents* do not contain any such telegram to Tschirschky, nor does Tschirschky make any acknowledgment of its receipt or the carrying out of its instructions, as he usually does in such cases; (2) Tschirschky, in reporting his interview with Berchtold on July 8, (K.D., 19) does not make the slightest mention of any such statements as Berchtold alleged to Tisza; (3) Berchtold speaks of "a telegram from Berlin in which his Imperial Master etc.," whereas the Kaiser had already left Berlin two days earlier to go on his northern cruise. It may be noted that Berchtold did receive a telegram from Szögyény on July 8, alleging that Berlin was waiting with impatience for a decision (Gooss, p. 39 f.); perhaps it was the contents of Szögyény's telegram which Berchtold fathered upon Tschirschky to serve his purpose of "influencing" Tisza.

[69] Tschirschky to Berlin F.O., July 8; 8:10 P. M.; K.D., 19.

not deny the advantages of such a procedure. . . . He thinks one might demand among other things the establishment of an Austro-Hungarian agency in Belgrade to watch from there the Greater Serbia machinations, and also the dissolution of societies and the dismissal of compromised officers. The time-limit for this answer ought to be made as short as possible, perhaps 48 hours. To be sure, even this short time-limit would suffice for Belgrade to get directions from St. Petersburg. Should the Serbians accept all the demands made, this would be a solution which would be "very unwelcome" to him, and therefore he was thinking how he could frame demands which would make Serbia's acceptance wholly impossible.

Finally the Minister complained again of Count Tisza's attitude, which made difficult for him an energetic action against Serbia. Count Tisza maintained that one must proceed "gentleman-like," but this was hardly appropriate, when such important interests of state were at issue, and especially toward such an opponent as Serbia.[70]

Thus, by July 9, Berchtold had secured the approval of Francis Joseph and Tisza to the idea that some demands should be presented to Serbia, but not in the form of an ultimatum, the terms of which were to be deliberately framed to make acceptance impossible. Nevertheless, he secretly proceeded with this second purpose. On July 11 he told Tschirschky that he had summoned Tisza to Vienna for a conference on July 14, when he hoped the document would be finally drafted:

So far as he [Berchtold] could say today, the chief demands on Serbia would be to request that the King should officially and publicly make a declaration, and publish it as an army order, that Serbia abandons the policy of a Greater Serbia; secondly, the institution of an Austro-Hungarian Government agency which should watch over the strict observance of this declaration. The time-limit

[70] Tschirschky to Berlin, F.O., July 10; K.D., 29.

for the answer to the note would be as short as possible, perhaps 48 hours. If the answer was not regarded in Vienna as satisfactory, mobilization would take place at once.[71]

WIESNER'S REPORT OF JULY 13

During the first two weeks after the murder of Franz Ferdinand, all action proposed against Serbia, both in Vienna and Berlin, had been based on the conviction that "the crime was the result of a well-organized plot, the threads of which reach to Belgrade." To gather proof of this Berchtold sent Dr. Wiesner, a legal counsellor of the Foreign Office, to Sarajevo on July 11 to investigate on the spot. Wiesner was a cautious and conservative lawyer who did not want to make any charges against Serbia except what were clearly established by documentary evidence and could satisfactorily stand examination in a court of law. Having to examine the material hurriedly during a couple of days and nights at Sarajevo, he learned only a small part of what we now know concerning the way the plot was organized in Belgrade.

Wiesner telegraphed from Sarajevo on July 13 that it was the prevailing conviction of all persons of influence in Bosnia that the Greater Serbia propaganda there was carried on with the knowledge and approval of the Serbian Government, but that the evidence laid before him gave "no support for the charge that this propaganda is promoted by the Serbian Government. The evidence that this

[71] Private letter of Tschirschky to Jagow, July 11; *Investig. Comm.,* I, p. 120 f. This private letter and the telegram of July 10 quoted above, were to prove important, as they evidently formed the basis of the famous despatch of Schoen, the counsellor of the Bavarian Legation at Berlin, on July 18, which was published in mutilated form by Kurt Eisner and cited at the Peace Conference as one of the proofs of Germany's war responsibility; its publication also gave rise to a famous libel suit at Munich (*cf.* Dirr *passim*). These two reports of Tschirschky were evidently the basis also of Tirpitz's statement in his polemic against Bethmann that "on July 13 the Chancellor was acquainted with the essential points of the ultimatum;" Tirpitz, *Erinnerungen,* p. 212 f.

agitation is stirred up by societies in Serbia and is tolerated
by the Serbian Government is sufficient, although scanty."
As to the crime itself, "there is nothing to prove, or even
to cause suspicion of the Serbian Government's cognizance
of the steps leading to the crime, or of its preparing it, or of
its supplying the weapons. On the contrary, there are indications that this is to be regarded as out of the question." [72]
On the other hand, there was "hardly a doubt that the
crime was resolved upon in Belgrade, and prepared with the
coöperation of Serbian officials, Ciganovitch and Major
Tankositch, who provided bombs, Brownings, ammunition,
and cyanide of potassium"; that the bombs came from the
Serbian Kragujevac arsenal; and that the three assassins,
with bombs and weapons upon them, were secretly smuggled across the frontier to Bosnia by Serbian agencies
through the assistance of Ciganovitch and the frontier-
captains at Shabats and Loznica. He also reported that
there was valuable material in regard to the *Narodna
Odbrana* which had not yet been sifted, but· which he was
bringing back to Vienna next day for further study. This
was incorporated in the Austrian *dossier* later. Meanwhile
he suggested the following demands as justified by the evidence already found:

[72] These two sentences, and these only, were cited from the Wiesner
report by Mr. Secretary Lansing and Mr. J. B. Scott, the American members of the Commission on the Responsibility of the Authors of the
War, at the Paris Peace Conference, April 4, 1919 (*German White Book
concerning the Authors of the War,* Eng. trans., N. Y., 1924, p. 28). But
in stating that these two sentences were the "essential portion" of the
Wiesner report, they gave a totally misleading impression of its true
character. Whether they did this deliberately, or whether they were supplied with the report only in this mutilated form (possibly by Mr. Ves-
nitch, the Serbian Minister in Paris, who, as they admit, supplied them
with other documents), they have never stated, so far as the writer
knows. For other cases in which the "evidence" for Germany's responsibility for the World War was later proven to be of an unsound or misleading character, thereby constituting a moral justification for a "revision" of the Versailles Treaty, see A. von Wegerer, "Die Unterlagen des
Versailler Urteils über die Schuld am Ausbruch des Weltkrieges," in
KSF, V, 1087-1106, Nov., 1927; and in *Current History,* Aug.. 1928. p. 810 ff.

A. Suppression of the coöperation of Serbian official agencies smuggling persons and goods across the frontier.

B. Dismissal of Serbian frontier-captains at Shabats and Loznica as well as the implicated customs officials.

C. Prosecution of Ciganovitch and Tankositch.[73]

Dr. Wiesner also showed General Potiorek a copy of this telegram to Berchtold absolving the Serbian Government from direct complicity in the Sarajevo crime, though not from the responsibility for the subversive agitation against Austria. Potiorek thought the report much too conservative. He at once wrote to Conrad, expressing his own convictions, which, as we now know from the activities of the "Black Hand," were very much closer to the truth. "It is downright impossible that some person or other in a democratic government in such a small country as Serbia should not have had knowledge of the preparation of the crime and the traitorous working methods of the whole propaganda. According to the investigations so far, several persons in Bosnia-Herzegovina certainly knew what was going to happen on June 28. According to one of the assassins the preparations were talked over in a tavern in Belgrade. . . . Furthermore, in Serbia, by the side of the official Government, there is a rival military government, which takes its existence from the army. That Serbian officers in active service participated in the preparation of the assassination, and also participated prominently in the whole propaganda, and are therefore among the instigators of the traitorous agitation stirred up in our country, is proven. The army, to be sure, is not part of the Government. But to try to main-

[73] Wiesner to Berchtold, July 13; 1:10 and 2 P. M.; A.R.B., I, no. 17; Gooss, p. 91 ff. For the difficulties under which Dr. Wiesner labored in drawing up this preliminary report, owing to the shortness of the time at his disposal and his desire to make no charges not fully proven, and also for Entente misrepresentations concerning it, see his two valuable articles: "Der Serajevoer Mord und die Kriegsschuldfrage," in Das Neue Reich, No. 44, August 2, 1924; and "Der verfälschte und der echte Text des 'Dokument Wiesner,'" in KSF, III, 641-657, Oct., 1925.

tain that the official Serbian Government does not know what the army is doing, is by no means tenable." Potiorek added new information which he had just received concerning the treasonable activities of the Sokol Societies in which Serbian military officers and high officials had an active part. He declared that he could not assume the responsibility of remaining in office unless vigorous measures were taken at once. Mere demands such as those suggested by Wiesner were not enough. It was necessary to crush the machine behind all this agitation, i.e., the Serbian army. "All this sort of thing would have been wholly impossible, unless it had been known and tolerated, if not furthered, by the Serbian Government." [74]

Potiorek's views, strengthened by long residence in Bosnia and close contact with Serbia, corresponded more nearly to what Berchtold and the Ballplatz officials suspected was the truth than Wiesner's more judicial and conservative preliminary conclusions. The three demands which Wiesner had suggested were incorporated in the ultimatum to Serbia, but otherwise Berchtold appears to have made little or no immediate use of his report. Wiesner was left at work sifting the material and drawing up the *dossier* of evidence to be presented to the Powers. Meanwhile Berchtold continued with the plan, desired by Conrad and Potiorek, of bringing about a localized preventive war against Serbia.

THE CONVERSION OF TISZA

On July 14 Berchtold finally succeeded in persuading Tisza to give up his opposition to an ultimatum with a short time-limit. But he had to yield to Tisza's unalterable demand that before the ultimatum was presented, a full Ministerial Council should adopt the formal resolution that "Austria, aside from slight regulations of boundary,

[74] Potiorek to Conrad, July 14; Conrad, IV, 82-85.

seeks no acquisition of territory as a result of the war with Serbia"—a resolution calculated both to safeguard what Tisza regarded as the special interests of Hungary, and to prevent Italian claims to compensation and intervention on the part of the Powers. It was also decided that the ultimatum should not be presented until it was certain that Poincaré had left Russia. For otherwise Berchtold feared that "to take such a step at the moment when the President of the French Republic was being fêted as the guest of the Tsar might conceivably be interpreted as a political affront, which we wish to avoid." Moreover, he feared it would be unwise to threaten Belgrade while "the peace-loving, hesitating Tsar and the cautious Sazonov were subject to the immediate influence of the two instigators, Poincaré and Izvolski"; then Russia, under the influence of the "champagne-mood" of the warm Franco-Russian toasts and the chauvinism of the French President, Izvolski, and the Grand Duke Nicholas, would be more likely to intervene with military action.[75] After the date had been changed several times, it was ultimately decided that if the ultimatum were not presented in Belgrade until after 5 P.M. on Thursday, July 23, the news could not reach St. Petersburg until after Poincaré and Viviani had embarked on the waters of the Baltic, and were safely out of touch with the Russian authorities.[76]

Why did Tisza change his mind and consent to an ultimatum and the idea of immediate local war with Serbia?

[75] Berchtold's report to Francis Joseph, July 14; and Berchtold to Szögyény, July 15; A.R.B., I, 19, 21; K.D., 49, 50.

[76] For the high importance of waiting until Russia had recovered from the "champagne-mood" and Poincaré's influence, see telegrams between Berchtold and the Austrian Ambassador in Paris, July 12-16, deciphered by the French and published by Poincaré, IV, 283 f.; A.R.B., I, 19, 21, 26, 36, 39, 57, 62; K.D., 50, 65, 69, 80, 93, 108, 112, 127. That Berchtold's fears were not without foundation may be seen from the accounts which Paléologue, Buchanan, and Szápáry, the French, British, and Austrian Ambassadors in St. Petersburg, have given of the Poincaré visit; see below, ch. vi.

We do not know with certainty. Probably Berchtold's use of the German lever had something to do with it. Several months later, when some recriminations were passing privately between Austrian and German officials concerning responsibility for the war, Tisza wrote to Tschirschky: "Before beginning our action against Serbia we went to Germany for advice; and upon the direct encouragement and declaration of the German Government that it regarded the present situation as favorable for the ever more threatening settlement [with Serbia], we presented our Note in Belgrade." [77] This, as we have seen, was what Berchtold had been continually urging upon Tisza as Germany's attitude and as an argument for seizing the present moment for the final reckoning with Serbia.

But a stronger influence which made Tisza change his mind, with a heavy heart, was the growing conviction that unless Austria acted now she would be throttled by her enemies later. As he wrote to his niece a month afterwards: "My conscience is clear. Already the noose had been thrown around our necks with which they would have strangled us at a favorable moment, unless we cut it now. We could not do otherwise, but it agonized me that we had to do as we did." [78] This conviction arose from the evidence collected at Sarajevo and especially from what Tisza regarded as the "downright intolerable" utterances of cer-

[77] Tisza to Tschirschky, November 5, 1914; *Gróf Tisza István összes munkái*, 4 Sorozat, II, Kötet, Kiadia a Magyar Tudományos Akademia [Count Stephan Tisza's Collected Works, 4th Series, Vol. 11, edited by the Hungarian Academy of Sciences], Budapest, 1924, p. 267.

[78] Tisza to Margaret Zeyk, Aug. 26, 1914; *Ibid.*, p. 90. These are almost the only references in his letters to his change of attitude during the July crisis. See also A. Weber, "Graf Tisza und die Kriegserklärung an Serbien," in KSF, III, 818-826. Dec., 1925; H. Marczali, "Papers of Count Tisza, 1914-1918," in *Am. Hist. Rev.*, XXIX, 301-315, Jan., 1924; Ernest Ludwig, "The Martyrdom of Count Stephan Tisza," in *Current History*, Jan., 1925, pp. 542-549; and by the French brothers, Jérome and Jean Tharaud in their articles in the *Revue des Deux Mondes*, Dec. 15, 1920, and April 15, 1921, and more at length in their recent volume, *Die Herrschaft Israels*, Zürich and Leipsig, 1927.

tain Serbian diplomatists and of the Serbian press. In his letter of July 8 to Francis Joseph he had already protested against the statements of Spalajkovitch and Jovanovitch, representing Serbia in St. Petersburg and Berlin, and of "the well-known abuses in connection with the Serbian press, societies, and schools, of which we have complained." [79] On July 14, after his conference with Berchtold, Tisza went to see Tschirschky, and told him of his change of mind:

> Count Tisza said that hitherto he had always been the person who had urged caution, but every day had strengthened him in the feeling that the Monarchy must come to an energetic action, prove its ability to exist, and put an end to the downright intolerable conditions in the south-east. The language of the Serbian press and of Serbian diplomatists was so presumptuous as simply not to be borne. "I have found it hard to decide to advise in favor of war," said Tisza, "but I am now firmly convinced of its necessity, and shall apply all my strength for the greatness of the Monarchy." [80]

Another decisive factor with Tisza was Berchtold's reiteration of Conrad's militarist argument that "everything must be avoided in the way of diplomacy which by delays or by any kind of successive application of diplomatic steps might give the enemy time to take military measures, and so put us at a military disadvantage." [81] And so, as Berchtold reported to Francis Joseph after the conference of July 14, "Count Tisza gave up the objection which he had brought forward in regard to an ultimatum with a short time-limit, because I pointed out the military difficulties which would be involved in a delayed procedure. I also used the argument that even after mobilization had taken

79 Tisza to Francis Joseph, July 8; A.R.B., I, 12.
80 Tschirschky to Bethmann, July 14; K.D., 49.
81 Conrad to Berchtold, ca. July 10; A.R.B., I, 14.

place, a peaceful settlement would still be possible, in case Serbia yielded sufficiently quickly." [82]

Thus, for various reasons—Germany's supposed attitude, the provocative tone of Serbian Ministers and newspapers, military considerations, and the general conviction that the very existence of the Dual Monarchy depended upon putting an end to Serbian propaganda—Tisza decided to abandon his attitude of opposition.

Berchtold had now overcome his main obstacles to an ultimatum with which Serbia could hardly be expected to comply. The precise form of these demands had not been fixed in the conference of July 14, but Berchtold promised Tschirschky that same evening that as soon as the precise wording had been fixed at a second Ministerial Council to be held on July 19, he would immediately show him a copy in great confidence, even before it had been submitted to Francis Joseph for approval.[83] Berchtold, however, did not keep this promise, as will appear later.

Meanwhile Berchtold and one of the Foreign Office secretaries, Baron Musulin, set to work at once on the ultimatum.

AUSTRIAN EFFORTS TO DECEIVE EUROPE

During these days while the ultimatum was being drafted and Berchtold was waiting for the Poincaré visit to Russia to run its course, he made every effort to preserve the greatest secrecy as to its contents. He alleged that he was waiting for the final results of the Sarajevo investigation before making demands on Serbia.

In order to allay all suspicions everywhere as to his real purpose, Berchtold arranged that the Austrian Chief of Staff and Minister of War should leave Vienna as if on

[82] Berchtold to Francis Joseph, July 14; A.R.B., I., 19; Gooss, p. 85 f.
[83] Tschirschky to Bethmann, July 14; K.D., 50.

vacation,[84] and all Austro-Hungarian officials adopted a more pacific and conciliatory tone in their utterances.

Tisza, on returning to Budapest and being interpellated in the Hungarian Diet next day, gave the non-committal declaration:

> "Our relations with Serbia, to be sure, need to be cleared up, but in what manner. . . . I cannot in the nature of the case state, as the question is still under discussion. I can only emphasize again that the Government is fully conscious of all the weighty interests in favor of the maintenance of peace. The Government is not of the opinion that the clearing up will necessarily involve warlike complications. In this connection, therefore, I shall not indulge in any prophecies, but merely observe that war is a sad *ultima ratio*, which one should not adopt until every possibility of a settlement has been exhausted. But every state, every nation, must be in a position to carry on war as an *ultima ratio*, if it is to continue as a state and as a nation." [85]

This Delphic utterance produced on the whole a reassuring impression. In Vienna "some people saw in it signs of an intention quietly to await the development of events and of calmness in the attitude of the Austro-Hungarian Government, while others saw in it hidden intentions for an action as yet undecided." [86] At Paris even the *Temps* had a good word to say for his moderation and for the Austrian Government, though the other French newspapers sought to contrast the tone of the Hungarian Premier's speech with the hitherto intransigent attitude of the Hungarian press

[84] Conrad, IV, 77 f., 87, 94 f., K.D., 29; and above note 31, Conrad left Vienna on July 14, returned for a few hours to take part in the Ministerial Council of July 19, left again immediately after it, and did not return until July 22, the day before the Austrian Note was delivered to Serbia.

[85] Fraknói, p. 38.

[86] J. M. Jovanovitch, Serbian Minister at Vienna, to Pashitch, July 15, S.B.B., 23; cf. however, Dumaine, French Ambassador at Vienna, to Viviani, July 15, F.Y.B., 12; and the reports of Bunsen in Vienna and Max Müller in Budapest to Grey; B.D., 70, 81-83, 85.

and the fiery speech of the opposition leader, Smrecsanyi.[87]

Fortunately for Berchtold, the Hungarian Diet was the only legislative body before which explanations had to be given. Neither the Delegations nor the Austrian Reichsrat were in session at the moment.

In order further to avoid possible embarrassing questions, Berchtold also gave up his usual weekly receptions, and ceased to discuss the Sarajevo outrage with the representatives of foreign countries; or, if discussions did arise at the Ballplatz, they were such as to dispel all apprehensions and suspicions that Austria was preparing a serious step against Serbia. The Foreign Office officials acknowledged that some step would be undertaken at Belgrade as soon as the results of the investigation in Bosnia should have established the connection between Belgrade and the Sarajevo outrage. But, at the same time, it was said that this step would not be such as to give rise to any uneasiness. Dumaine, the French Ambassador in Vienna, reported that the expected "requirements of the Austro-Hungarian Government with regard to the punishment of the outrage, and to guarantees of control and police supervision, seem to be acceptable to the dignity of the Serbians; M. Jovanovitch believes they will be accepted. Pashitch wishes for a peaceful solution, but says he is ready for a full resistance." [88]

Shebeko, Russian Ambassador at Vienna, spoke several times on the situation with Forgach, in the absence of Berchtold, but was unable to discover the true nature of Austria's intentions. He was told by Szápáry, the Austro-Hungarian Ambassador at St. Petersburg, who, for family reasons happened at the time to be in Vienna, that the step to be taken at Belgrade would be of a conciliatory character and not such as to cause Russia any dissatisfaction. In con-

---

[87] Fraknói, p. 39; Kanner, p. 246 f.

[88] Dumaine to Viviani, July 22, F.Y.B., 18. A couple of days earlier, however, Dumaine had been less optimistic (see F.Y.B., 13 and 14, quoted below at note 96).

sequence of these reassuring explanations Shebeko left for a trip to Russia, and was not at Vienna during the first days of the crisis which soon followed.[89]

At Belgrade Baron Giesl assured a Hungarian journalist on July 11 that at the conclusion of the Sarajevo inquiry "we shall take eventual steps in the most conciliatory fashion and within the bounds of international diplomatic proprieties."[90] And a week later he told his English colleague that "personally he was not in favor of pressing Serbia too hard, since he was convinced that the Serbian Government was ready to take whatever measures can reasonably be demanded of them, and that he did not view the situation in a pessimistic light."[91] Yet Giesl was the Serbophobe general whose appointment to Belgrade a few months before had been likened to the throwing of a lighted match into a powder magazine.[92] And Giesl himself, at the end of a long secret jeremiad against Serbia, reported his conviction to Berchtold on July 21, that the best thing was "to crush the enemy which has been threatening us, and so give Austria quiet after years of crisis. Half-measures, a presentation of demands, long negotiations, and finally a rotten compromise would be the worst blow which could happen to Austria-Hungary's prestige in Serbia and position in Europe."[93] Such was the Machiavellian deceit with which Berchtold and his officials sought to lull Europe into a false security before the explosion of his diplomatic bomb.

Berchtold, however, was not so successful in these efforts

[89] Dumaine to Bienvenu-Martin, July 22, 26; F.Y.B., 18, 55; Jovano-vitch to Pashitch, Aug. 16; S.B.B., 52; Szápáry also told Sazonov on July 18 that "they are convinced in Vienna that Serbia will meet our possible demands;" Szápáry to Berchtold, July 18, A.R.B., I, 25.

[90] Kanner, p. 248.

[91] Crackanthorpe to Grey, July 18; B.D., 57.

[92] Giesl, formerly Austrian Minister to Montenegro, had been an ardent champion of Austrian interests against Serbia during the Balkan Wars.

[93] Giesl to Berchtold, July 21; A.R.B., I, 37.

to deceive Europe concerning his real intentions, as has usually been assumed on the basis of the "colored books" published in 1914. At the opening of the War, Serbia and the Entente countries tried as much as possible to make it appear that they were taken totally by surprise by Austria's note to Serbia.[94] But as we know now from more recently published documents, the Great Powers suspected and knew more of Berchtold's intentions than has usually been supposed.

On July 16 the English Ambassador in Vienna telegraphed to Sir Edward Grey:

> A kind of indictment is being prepared against the Serbian Government for alleged complicity in the conspiracy which led to assassination of the Archduke. Accusation will be founded on the proceedings in the Sarajevo Court. My informant states that the Serbian Government will be required to adopt certain definite measures in restraint of nationalist and anarchist propaganda, and that Austro-Hungarian Government are in no mood to parley with Serbia, but will insist on immediate unconditional compliance, failing which force will be used. Germany is said to be in complete agreement with this procedure, and it is thought that the rest of Europe will sympathise with Austria-Hungary in demanding that Serbia shall adopt in future more submissive attitude. . . .
>
> I asked if Russia would be expected to stand by quietly in the event of force being used against Serbia.
>
> My informant said that he presumed that Russia would not wish to protect racial assassins, but in any case Austria-Hungary would go ahead regardless of results. She would lose her position as a Great Power if she stood any further nonsense from Serbia.[95]

[94] Cf. Seton-Watson, Sarajevo, ch. viii, "The Duping of Europe."

[95] Bunsen to Grey, July 16; B.D., 50 (suppressed from B.B.B.). Sir Eyre Crowe noted on this: "Count Trauttmansdorff spoke to me (quite informally) at great length to-day, giving expression to very much the same views." In a letter to Sir Arthur Nicolson at the British Foreign

Similarly, on July 21, President Poincaré at St. Petersburg, as we shall see, believing that "Austria is preparing to strike a blow," [96] undertook to give the Austrian Ambassador a rude and severe warning, saying significantly, "The Russian people are very warm friends of the Serbians, and France is Russia's ally." [97] He was trying to bluff Austria out of doing precisely what Berchtold was intending to do, and at the same time encouraging Sazonov to stand firm in support of Serbia.[98]

Italy also appears to have gotten some inkling of what was preparing at Vienna—possibly from Count Lützow or from Bunsen. On July 16 the Italian Ambassador in St. Petersburg, "having the impression that Austria was capable of taking an irrevocable step with regard to Serbia,"

Office next day Bunsen explained that he had this information from "Count Lützow, ex-Ambassador at Rome. He has a place near us in the country and we motored over to luncheon. He had seen both Berchtold and Forgach at the Ballplatz the day before, and had long conversations. He put on a serious face and said he wondered if I realized how grave the situation was. This Government was not going to stand Serbian insolence any longer. No great Power could submit to such audacity as Serbia had displayed, and keep her position in the world. . . . If Serbia did not at once cave in, force would be used to compel her. Count Lützow added that Count Berchtold was sure of German support and did not believe any country could hesitate to approve—not even Russia. . . . I expressed my doubts whether, if it really came to fighting, which I could not believe, Russia would allow Austria and Serbia to have it out in a cockpit. Count Lützow said Austria was determined to have her way this time and would refuse to be headed off by anybody" (B. D., 56).

96 Paléologue, *La Russie des Tsars*, I, 7. The French Ambassador in Vienna had already forwarded as "accurate information" a memorandum stating: "The French Government would be mistaken to have confidence in disseminators of optimism; much will be demanded of Serbia; she will be required to dissolve several propagandist societies, repress nationalism, to guard the frontier in cooperation with Austrian officials, and to keep a strict control over anti-Austrian tendencies in the schools; and it is a very difficult matter for a Government to consent to become in this way a policeman for a foreign Government. . . . The tenor of the Note and its imperious tone almost certainly ensure that Belgrade will refuse. Then military operations will begin" (Dumaine to Viviani, July 19 and 20; F.Y.B., 13, 14).

97 A.R.B., I, 45, 60; K.D., 134; and Poincaré, IV, 253 f.
98 See below, ch. vi.

advised Russia to warn Vienna that "Russia would not endure any infringement by Austria of the integrity and independence of Serbia." [99]   On the evening of July 23 a Counsellor of the Italian Embassy definitely informed Prince Trubetzkoi that "Austria-Hungary would today present to Serbia a quite unacceptable ultimatum." [100]

THE FINAL DRAFTING OF THE ULTIMATUM

The precise terms of the ultimatum, or "Note with a time-limit" (*befristete Démarche*) as it was euphemistically called,[101] were laid before a second secret Ministerial Council on Sunday, July 19. To make secrecy doubly sure, the meeting was held at 10 A.M. at Berchtold's private residence, instead of at the Foreign Office, and those who attended it came in ordinary autos instead of in their own official "unnumbered" cars. Tisza's renewed trip to Vienna was "explained" as being due to his need of getting further information—an explanation which was plausible enough since the Hungarian Diet was still in session and thirsting for news. Conrad made a brief flying trip back to the capital, which was given out as being caused by the illness of his son.[102]

Before the Joint Ministerial Council was called to order for business by the presiding officer [Berchtold], an informal discussion took place as to wording of the Note to be sent to Serbia, and its definitive text was fixed. The presiding officer then opened the Council, and requested approval for the presentation of the Note to the Serbian Government about 5 P.M. on Thursday, July 23, so that after the expiration of the 48-hour time-limit at 5 P.M. on Saturday, July 25, the mobilization orders could be sent out in the night between Saturday and Sunday. According to the

[99] Schilling's *Diary*, p. 25.

[100] Schilling's *Diary*, p. 28. As early as July 18 Berchtold suspected that Italy had learned something of his intentions; A.R.B., I, 24; Gooss, pp. 79, 117 ff.

[101] *Cf.* Berchtold to Giesl, July 23, A.R.B., I, 65, 66; and B.D., 105.

[102] Kanner, p. 250; Conrad, IV, 78, 87, 94 f.

opinion of Count Berchtold, it was not probable that our step would become known in St. Petersburg before the departure of the President of the French Republic, but even if this should happen, he would see no great disadvantage in it, as we had observed sufficient regard for courtesy in waiting for the end of his visit. On the other hand, for diplomatic reasons, he would be decidedly opposed to any further postponement, since they were already beginning to get nervous in Berlin and news of our intentions had already leaked out at Rome, so that he could not be responsible for undesirable incidents if they should postpone the matter longer.[103]

After Conrad, the Chief of Staff, had made a statement about military operations, and had reassured Tisza as to the safety of Transylvania from possible Rumanian uprisings or invasion, Tisza renewed the request which he had made on July 14, that the Council unanimously declare that "no plans of conquest by Austria were connected with the action against Serbia, and that, with the exception of rectifications of frontier necessary for strategic reasons, Austria did not wish to annex a single bit of Serbian territory." Berchtold remarked that he would accept this "only with a certain reserve":

Austria, in case of victory over Serbia, ought not to annex any of her territory, but should seek to reduce her size so that she would no longer be dangerous, by ceding as large parts of Serbian territory as possible to Bulgaria, Greece, Albania, and possibly to Rumania also. The situation in the Balkans might change; it was not at all impossible that Russia might succeed in overturning the existing cabinet at Sofia, and in bringing into power again there a government hostile to Austria; Albania also was no de-

[103] Minutes of the Ministerial Council, July 19; A.R.B., I, 26; Gooss, p. 101 ff. The date of presentation at Belgrade was later changed from 5 P.M. to 6 P.M., in order to make more certain that Poincaré should have left Russia before the news reached St. Petersburg; Berchtold to Giesl, July 23, A.R.B., I, 62; see also note 76 above.

pendable factor; as the person responsible for foreign affairs, he must reckon with the possibility that at the end of the war, on account of conditions then existing, it would no longer be possible not to annex anything, if we wanted to establish better conditions along our frontier than exist at present.[104]

Count Stürgkh, the Austrian Premier, pointed out that a public disclaimer of any intention to annex Serbian territory would not prevent "necessary strategic rectifications of the frontier" or "the bringing of Serbia into a position of dependence on Austria by overthrowing the dynasty, by a military convention, or by other appropriate measures." The Minister of War was willing to vote for such a disclaimer only on condition that it did not exclude a permanent occupation of a bridge-head over the Save into Serbia, as well as "rectifications of the frontier."

Tisza, however, made his consent and that of the Hungarian Government which he represented, inflexibly dependent upon a unanimous acceptance of his request. Whereupon it was unanimously voted:

> Immediately at the beginning of war a declaration shall be made to the Foreign Powers that the Monarchy is not waging a war of conquest, and does not intend to incorporate the Kingdom [of Serbia]. This vote naturally does not preclude rectifications of the frontier strategically necessary, nor the diminution of Serbia for the benefit of other states, nor the temporary occupation of parts of Serbia which may eventually be necessary.[105]

This solemn obligation to declare to the Powers at the beginning of war Austria's "territorial disinterestedness" was another of the promises, as we shall see, which Berchtold did not honestly live up to. Even when the declaration was finally made, its insincerity is indicated by these mental reservations of several of the Ministers, and by

[104] A.R.B., I, 26; Gooss, p. 101 ff.
[105] A.R.B., I, 26; Gooss, p. 101 ff.

Conrad's remark to the Minister of War as they were leaving the Council: "Well, we shall see; before the Balkan
War the Powers talked about the *status quo*—but after the
war no one bothered himself about it." [106]

The next day, July 20, the Note was dispatched by
courier to Giesl at Belgrade, with instructions to present
it to the Serbian Government on Thursday the 23rd.[107] It
was also sent on July 20 under the seal of strictest secrecy
to the Austro-Hungarian Ambassadors at Berlin,[108] Rome,
Paris, London, St. Petersburg, Constantinople, and the
Ministers at the lesser courts. Each was given appropriate
instructions that on Friday morning, July 24, he was to
inform the Government to which he was accredited of the
"Note" presented to Serbia the night before, make a statement of the justice of Austria's cause, and in some cases say
that a *dossier* giving fuller details of the Austrian case
against Serbia was at the disposal of the Powers for
examination.[109]

[106] Conrad, IV, 92.

[107] Berchtold to Giesl, July 20; A.R.B., I, 27, 28. It was post-dated
"July 22"; Gooss, p. 101, note 1. Berchtold perhaps thought it would
look better if it did not appear that it had been dispatched before it had
been shown to Francis Joseph and received his approval; or if the
Emperor demurred, there was the *fait accompli* that it had already
been sent out. It is dated "July 22" in the original *Austrian Red Book*
of 1915, and "July 24" in the copies presented to the Powers on the
morning of July 24; B.B.B., 4; F.Y.B., 24.

[108] Szögyény at Berlin had received it by July 21, for on that day
at 7:30 P.M. he urgently requested to be allowed to show it to the
German Government ahead of the time stated in his instructions; A.R.B.,
I, 39, 41; Gooss, p. 110 f. The Austrian representatives in Rome, Paris
and Cettinje had received their copies of the ultimatum by July 22; *ibid*,
50, 51, 55. Szápáry in St. Petersburg cannot have received the note on
July 20, as incorrectly stated by Mr. Seton-Watson (*Sarajevo*, p. 207;
and pp. 221, 227 for similar misstatements as to its reception in Paris
and London). There was deceit enough in Austria's actions without
accepting Mr. Seton-Watson's further allegation that Szápáry had "this
secret explosive in his breast" when he made "the grossly dishonest statement" to Poincaré at the reception to the diplomatic corps in St. Petersburg.

[109] Berchtold's instructions, 3401-3406, 3426-3436, July 20; A.R.B., I,
29-31. As to the *dossier* see above, ch. ii, note 2.

Berchtold had despatched the ultimatum without the knowledge or approval of Francis Joseph. The aged Emperor, who was away at Ischl and had been told that the "Note" was to be settled at the Ministerial Council of July 19, had heard nothing further of it, and therefore telegraphed on the 20th to know about it.[110] Berchtold hastened to reply that it had not been possible to complete it on July 19[!], but that it was now finished and would be sent to Ischl by a courier, and that he himself would arrive next morning, July 21, for an audience. There is no record of the explanations which he may have given to Francis Joseph in this audience on Tuesday morning, except that at its close he telegraphed to his subordinate, Baron Macchio, in Vienna: "His Majesty has approved without change the text of the Note to Serbia and that to the Powers. I beg you to inform the German Ambassador, Tschirschky, that he cannot be given the Note until early tomorrow morning since some corrections are still to be made in it." [111] Why this falsehood? Why did Berchtold here break the promise which he had made a few days before to Tschirschky that "as soon as the text [of the Note] had been fixed on Sunday [July 19, at the Ministerial Council], he would immediately communicate it to the Imperial [German] Government in great confidence, even before it had been submitted to Francis Joseph for approval"? [112] If the "definitive text was fixed" [113] on July 19, secretly forwarded to all the Austrian Ambassadors on July 20,[114] and "approved without change" by the Emperor on July 21, why did Berchtold still want to withhold it from Tschirschky and allege that "some corrections are still to be made in it"? Probably

110 Telegram from Ischl from Baron Schiessl, head of the Emperor's cabinet chancery, to Berchtold, July 20, 11 A.M.; Berchtold's reply July 20, 1:30 P.M.; Gooss, p. 101.

111 Berchtold to Macchio, July 21, 12:30 P.M.; A.R.B.,I, 46.

112 Tschirschky to Bethmann, July 14; K.D., 50; cf. K.D., 88.

113 Minutes of the Ministerial Council, July 19; A.R.B., I, 26.

114 A.R.B., I, 29-31.

because Berchtold feared that even the Berlin Foreign Office would disapprove the extreme and intransigent tone of the Note, and might, at the last moment, stretch out a restraining hand. Berlin, as he had already alleged to the Council on July 19, was becoming "nervous," and he could "not be responsible for undesirable incidents if they should postpone the matter longer." Therefore Berlin must not know the text of the Note until it was too late to do anything. Berlin must accept the *fait accompli* that a very severe ultimatum had been dispatched, and that it was practically too late to recall or modify it.[115]

AUSTRIA'S DISREGARD OF GERMAN ADVICE

In this connection, and in view of Germany's repeated statements later that she did not have foreknowledge of the Austrian ultimatum, it is important to observe the change in Berchtold's treatment of Germany before and after July 14, the day on which he finally secured Tisza's consent to a severe ultimatum. Before this date Berchtold had kept Germany quite fully informed of the plans which were developing to deliver a stiff ultimatum to Serbia, and some of the probable terms to be included in it had been indicated to Berlin. He had intimated that they would be so exacting that Serbia could hardly accept them, and that

---

[115] *Cf.* Merey to Berchtold, July 27 (Gooss, p. 114): "I have the feeling that the German Cabinet , . . is aiming and hoping in various ways, for example at Rome and Bucharest, to work against our military conflict with Serbia. In this way sufficient diplomatic and political barriers will be erected on all sides, by friend and foe, to prevent our fighting, in the period between the delivery of the Note and the outbreak of hostilities on all sides. Should Germany succeed in this, Serbia would finally be compelled to yield in the main, but as a matter of form would be spared to a certain extent in its dignity as a state. This in the end would be the outcome which Your Excellency has regarded as such a horrible contingency, and which in fact would be a situation far worse for us than that which preceded it. But Germany would again reap in Vienna a cheap and undeserved jubilation for having again stood by us 'in shining armor.'"

an acceptance would be "very disagreeable" to him.[116]   He had asked advice, and appeared ready to receive it and act upon it. Germany, having given a *carte blanche* on July 5, acquiesced in these plans. Knowing Berchtold's hesitations and indecisions in the past, and desiring that Austria should act quickly before the horror and sympathy aroused in Europe by the Sarajevo crime had died away, Germany had not only acquiesced, but encouraged Berchtold to speedy action. Not knowing the precise text of the intended note, and being still optimistic that any possible Austro-Serbian conflict could be "localized," Germany began to take steps and to offer advice which would help assure such localization. But now Berchtold, after July 14, having been promised German support and having converted Tisza, no longer showed the same consideration for Germany, and gave little heed to her advice and requests.

Jagow, for instance, advised Vienna to "assemble sufficient evidence to prove that there exists a Greater Serbia agitation in Serbia which endangers the Dual Monarchy, in order that the public opinion of Europe may be convinced as far as possible of the justice of Austria's cause. This material would best be published, not separately but as a whole, shortly before submitting to Serbia the demands, or the ultimatum, as the case may be." [117]   But Berchtold did not heed this excellent advice. The *dossier*, which set forth in detail Austria's grievances against Serbia and the results of the Sarajevo investigation, was not laid before the Powers until several days after the presentation of the ultimatum. It came so late, after a serious diplomatic crisis had begun to develop, that the Powers paid little or no

116 See Tschirschky's nine despatches, July 7 to 14; K.D., 18, 19, 27, 29, 35, 40, 41a, 49, 50; three of these have been quoted in part above at notes 69-71; see also Schoen, the Bavarian Chargé d'Affaires in Berlin, to Hertling in Munich, July 18 (Dirr, p. 4 ff.; K.D., IV, Anhang, iv, No. 2) for the fullest statement of the extent of Germany's knowledge up to that date of Austria's intentions.

117 Jagow to Tschirschky, July 11; K.D., 31

attention to it,[118] and Austria lost completely the advantage which she might have had of influencing public opinion in her favor and against Serbia.

Germany also urged Berchtold to come to a timely understanding with Italy. The Italian Government, owing to the threatening outpourings of the Austrian Press against Serbia and to the suspiciously silent attitude of the Vienna authorities, was becoming very uneasy. Baron Flotow, the German Ambassador at Rome, reported on July 14 that San Giuliano was very pessimistic as to plans which Berchtold might be hatching. The Italian Minister had said that he could not admit in international law that a Government could be made responsible for a criminal act of an individual, nor for political propaganda, if the propaganda did not amount to an overt act. He feared therefore that the Italian Government could not support the demands which he suspected Austria might make upon Serbia, especially as they would be contrary to the deep-seated feelings of the Italian people, contrary to liberal principles, and contrary to the principle of nationality, which Italy, with her traditions, could never oppose. Flotow concluded that San Giuliano "apparently wanted to warn us that Italy would not remain on Austria's side in case of further complications."[119] During the following days he sent a series of increasingly emphatic and alarming telegrams that Italy would not support Austria against Serbia, because of the prevailing popular hatred of Austria and sympathy for the Serbian nationalistic "Piedmont" movement, so similar to Italy's own struggle for national unity in the face of Hapsburg oppression half a century before. He also said that it was virtually impossible to influence the Italian Press.[120]

Jagow, realizing the importance of keeping Italy from

118 See above, ch. ii, note 2.
119 Flotow to Bethmann, July 14; K.D., 42.
120 Flotow to Bethmann, July 15, 16, 17, 19; K.D., 51, 54, 59, 60, 64, 73, 75, 78.

siding with Serbia, and the difficulty of bribing or bargaining with the Italians, sent Flotow's telegram on to Tschirschky at Vienna, and told him to discuss the Italian situation confidentially with Berchtold. He declared that any territorial extension of Austria, or even an extension of her influence in the Balkans, would absolutely horrify Italy; every time there was a question of Austria threatening Serbia, Italy became extraordinarily nervous; and Italian support to Serbia would materially increase Russia's lust for action. It was therefore of the greatest importance, he believed, that Austria should come to an understanding with the Cabinet at Rome, and hold out as a bait the prospect of some compensations, such as Valona, which formed part of Albania and would cost Austria nothing but might not satisfy Italy, or even such a fat morsel as the Trentino, which would certainly stop the mouths of Austrophobe public opinion in Italy.[121]

In accordance with these instructions, and in the absence of Tschirschky, Stolberg, a Counsellor of the German Embassy at Vienna, "asked Berchtold whether he intended to get into touch with Italy prior to a possible action against Serbia. Berchtold replied that up to now he had not breathed a word of it, and indeed intended to face the Italian Government with a *fait accompli*, because he was not quite sure whether it could keep a secret, and with its Serbophil attitude might easily let some hint leak out at Belgrade." [122] Stolberg did not press the point with Berchtold, preferring to leave the delicate question of compensations for Tschirschky to deal with. Stolberg, however, had a long talk with Berchtold's confidential agent, Hoyos, and urged conciliation toward Italy, but got little satisfaction. Hoyos suggested compensating Italy with another territory—which did not belong to Austria—namely, the Dodecanese..

---

[121] Jagow to Tschirschky, July, 15; K.D., 46.
[122] Stolberg to Jagow, July 18; K.D., 87.

Two days later, on July 20, Tschirschky had a long interview with Berchtold and set forth emphatically Jagow's arguments in regard to the importance of winning and compensating Italy before it was too late. But he too had little success. Berchtold blindly insisted that Italy had no claim to compensation; that he did not need Italian coöperation or support, but only Italy's abstention from interference; that the best way to keep Italy out was to keep intended action secret from her until after the *fait accompli*; and that he had strictly forbidden Merey, the Austrian Ambassador in Rome, to speak of the Serbian question, because he was sure that the slightest hint would be at once communicated by Italy to St. Petersburg, and be seized upon at Rome as an excuse for some counter-action or for claims to compensations. Berchtold gave such a down-right refusal to have Italy get even Valona that Tschirschky apparently refrained from the more delicate proposal that Austria give up the Trentino.[123]

Instead of acting on Germany's wise and prudent suggestion of bargaining reasonably with Italy, Berchtold sent Merey a long argument, in which he tried to contradict the interpretation held by Germany, as well as by Italy, in regard to Art. VII of the Triple Alliance, relating to compensations for Italy in case of a change in the Balkans in Austria's favor.[124] And on the same day, after sending Merey the text of the ultimatum, he instructed him to say to San Giuliano, if questioned, that "he had no precise information as yet in regard to the conclusion of the investigation at Sarajevo and the step which Austria would take at Belgrade as a result of it." [125] Merey was also to avoid, if possible, any discussion of Art. VII because "neither side would be able to bring the other to its own interpretation,

123 Tschirschky to Bethmann, July 20, K.D., 94; and report of the interview in the Austrian F.O. Journal, No. 3425, A.R.B., I, 35.
124 Berchtold to Merey, July 29, A.R.B., I, 32, 33.
125 A.R.B., I, 34.

and there was danger that the discussion of it might give rise to heated feelings and in the end endanger the whole Triple Alliance Treaty." [126]

Berchtold had promised Tschirschky that, as an act of courtesy to Italy as an ally, he would inform the Cabinet at Rome of the ultimatum before it was delivered to Serbia, so that San Giuliano and his colleagues should not have to learn of it from the newspapers, and that at the same time he would declare that Austria in her action against Serbia did not aim at any extension of territory for herself.[127] But he kept neither of these promises fully. As to giving Italy preliminary notification, he sent a series of contradictory orders to Merey, who was sorely perplexed what to do. In the end he had to take to his bed and send his secretary by automobile to San Giuliano in the country on the afternoon of July 23 at about the time the ultimatum was being handed in at Belgrade; and even then no copy of it was given to the Italian Minister, merely the meager information that the Note, with a 48-hour time-limit, contained a number of demands based on the Sarajevo inquiry and aimed to protect Austria against Greater Serbia propaganda.[128]

Berchtold likewise did not make any clear and timely declaration to Italy or to any of the Powers that Austria would not seek any extension of territory for herself at Serbia's expense, a declaration such as was desired by Tisza and by Germany.[129] Thus, after having converted Tisza on July 14, Berchtold paid no more attention to Germany's advice in regard to Italy than in regard to publishing the

[126] Berchtold to Merey, July 21; A.R.B., I, 42.

[127] Tschirschky to Bethmann, July 20; K.D., 94.

[128] A.R.B., I, 22, 30, 34, 50, 56; II, 8; Gooss, pp. 114-127.

[129] Merey did tell San Giuliano on July 21 that Austria did not intend to incorporate any territory, but refused to allow San Giuliano to publish this in the papers "because it was not to be understood as a promise;" A.R.B., I, 43. For the hesitating and unconvincing statements to Russia and the other Powers on the same subject, see below.

Sarajevo evidence simultaneously with the demands on Serbia.

WHAT FOREKNOWLEDGE DID GERMANY HAVE OF THE ULTIMATUM?

Similarly Berchtold paid little heed to Germany's requests after July 14 to be informed as to Austria's final intentions and the precise terms of her contemplated demands on Serbia. This fact, together with Jagow's repeated assertions a few days later that "he had no previous knowledge of the contents of the Austro-Hungarian Note," [130] and the new facts revealed in subsequently published German documents, have given rise to much controversy as to the extent of Germany's foreknowledge of the Austrian ultimatum.[131]

During the first week after the Potsdam Conversations, as has already been pointed out, Berchtold had kept the German Ambassador in Vienna quite fully informed of the progress of his plans, and of several of the probable demands which he intended to include in the ultimatum.[132] This information was passed on to the Bavarian Chargé d'Affaires in Berlin, who summed it up in a long despatch on July 18:

> As Zimmermann told me, the Note, so far as yet determined, will contain the following demands:
>
> 1. The issuing of a proclamation by the King of Serbia which shall state that the Serbian Government com-

---

[130] Rumbold to Grey, July 25; B.D., 122; cf. also his statement to the French Ambassador on July 24 that "the Berlin Cabinet had been entirely ignorant of Austria's requirements before they were communicated to Belgrade" (F.Y.B., 30); and on the same day Sazonov was informed by the German Ambassador in St. Petersburg that "the German Government had no knowledge of the Austrian note before it was presented" (R.O.B., 18).

[131] For a discussion of opposing views on this question, see the articles of G. von Jagow and B. E. Schmitt in *Current History*, Dec., 1927, pp. 393-398.

[132] See above, at notes 69-71 and 116.

pletely dissociates itself from the Greater Serbia movement, and disapproves of it.

2. The opening of an investigation against persons guilty of complicity in the Sarajevo assassination, and the participation of an Austrian official in this investigation.

3. Proceedings against all persons who have participated in the Greater Serbia movement.

For the acceptance of these demands a 48-hour time-limit will be granted. It is evident that Serbia cannot accept such demands, which are incompatible with her dignity as an independent state. Thus the result would be war.

Here [in Berlin] they are thoroughly willing that Austria use this favorable moment, even at the risk of further complications. But whether they will actually rise to the occasion in Vienna, still seems doubtful to Jagow as well as Zimmermann. The latter expressed the opinion that Austria-Hungary, thanks to her indecision and breaking-up, has now become really the Sick Man of Europe, like Turkey formerly, for whose partition Russians, Italians, Rumanians, Serbians and Montenegrins are now waiting. A vigorous and successful move against Serbia would have the result that Austrians and Hungarians could feel themselves once more to be a national power, would again revive the decayed economic life, and would suppress the foreign aspirations for years to come. . . .

What attitude the other Powers will take toward an armed conflict between Austria and Serbia will chiefly depend, according to the view here, on whether Austria is content to chastise Serbia, or will also demand territorial compensations for herself. In the first case, it would be possible to localize the war; in the other case, on the other hand, more serious complications would probably not be lacking.

The German Government will immediately after the presentation of the Austrian Note at Belgrade, initiate diplomatic action with the Powers, in the interest of the localization of the war. It will claim to have been just as much surprised as the other Powers by Austria's action, pointing out that the Kaiser is on his northern cruise and that the Chief of the General Staff as well as the Prussian Minister of War are absent on vacation. . . . It will emphasize that it is a matter of common interest for all monarchical Governments that "the Belgrade nest of anarchists" be rooted out once and for all; and it will try to get all the Powers to accept the view that the settlement between Austria and Serbia is a matter concerning these two states alone. The mobilization of the German Army is to be refrained from, and they are also going to work through the military authorities to prevent Austria from mobilizing her entire Army, and especially not the troops in Galicia, in order to avoid bringing about automatically a counter-mobilization on Russia's part, which in turn would cause us, and then France, to take similar measures, and thereby conjure up a European War.[133]

The first part of this famous report indicates that Germany had received only a brief outline of a part of the actual later ultimatum, namely, the issuing of a proclamation by the Serbian Government dissociating itself from the Greater Serbia agitation, the 48-hour time-limit, and two demands which roughly correspond to four of the total ten points elaborated in the ultimatum (viz. points 2, 4, 5 and 6, concerning Austrian coöperation in an investigation of persons guilty of complicity, and concerning proceedings against persons who have participated in propaganda). Beside the ten points, the eventual ultimatum contained a long introductory statement of Serbia's breach of the promises of friendly behavior made in 1909. Incidentally it may also be noted that Schoen reported that it "still seemed doubtful" to Zimmermann and Jagow whether "the always

---

[133] Schoen to Hertling, in Munich, July 18; K.D., IV, Anhang iv, No. 2; Dirr, p. 4 ff., gives in parallel columns Schoen's report in its authentic form and in its abbreviated or "forged" version as published by Kurt Eisner in 1918.

timid and undecided authorities at Vienna" [134] would actually "rise to the occasion," and take the action which had been intimated.

On the other hand, while it is true that the German Government did not know half the demands nor the actual wording of the ultimatum (which in fact had not yet been definitely drawn up even in Vienna), it knew the substance of some of the probable demands which were most important; and it knew that the ultimatum was to be so framed that Serbia would not be likely to yield to it. Jagow was therefore virtually lying when he repeatedly asserted a few days later that "he had no previous knowledge of the Austro-Hungarian Note." This is a matter to which we shall return in a moment. Though it is no justification of his lie, it may be pointed out that Sir Edward Grey, who is often extolled as an example of honesty and sincerity, lied just as deliberately in regard to his foreknowledge of the probable terms of the ultimatum. He had learned on July 16, from a friend of Berchtold's who told the English Ambassador in Vienna, that "a kind of indictment is being prepared against the Serbian Government for alleged complicity in the conspiracy which led to the assassination of the Archduke. . . . The Serbian Government will be required to adopt certain definite measures in restraint of nationalist and anarchist propaganda; the Austro-Hungarian Government are in no mood to parley with Serbia, but will insist on immediate unconditional compliance, failing which force will be used." [135] Nevertheless on July 20, Sir Edward Grey, having "asked the German Ambassador today if he had any news of what was going on in Vienna with regard to Serbia," and having received a negative reply, remarked that he also "had not heard anything

[134] Dirr, p. 4 ff.

[135] Bunsen to Grey, received July 16, 3:15 P M.; B.D., 50; quoted above at note 95.

recently," except that Count Berchtold had spoken reassuringly to the Italian Ambassador.[136]   Either Sir Edward Grey was ignorant of Bunsen's important despatch received at the British Foreign Office four days before this (such ignorance seems hardly likely), or he too was making an untrue assertion of ignorance concerning what was going on at Vienna.   This kind of diplomatic lying, unfortunately, was not the monopoly of any one country, but was indulged in all too freely by Foreign Secretaries and Ambassadors almost everywhere in July, 1914.

Though Germany possessed, within the first week or ten days after the Potsdam Conversations, such knowledge concerning the ultimatum as has just been indicated, this was still regarded at Berlin as too indefinite.   After July 14, therefore, she repeatedly requested further information as to Austria's ultimate aims and the precise terms of the ultimatum, in order to prepare public opinion in favor of "localization."   Thus, on July 17, Jagow recognized that Berchtold's "plans may be influenced or modified by the course of events," but assumed that "he has in mind a general picture of the aims to be sought, including the matter of territory;" Jagow therefore instructed the German Ambassador in Vienna to "get some information on this point," and "about where the road is likely to lead us."[137]   And again on July 20:   "For dealing with public opinion, it is of the greatest importance for us to be precisely informed beforehand, not only of the contents of the Note, but also as to the day and hour of its publication. Reply by telegraph."[138]   But now Berchtold paid little

---

[136] Grey to Rumbold, July 20; B.D., 68; *cf.* also the account of this interview by the German Ambassador, who was given the impression that Grey "was still viewing the Austro-Serbian quarrel optimistically, and believed that a peaceful solution would be reached.   He [Grey] said that he had received no information that would indicate anything to the contrary;" Lichnowsky to Bethmann, July 20; K.D., 92.

[137] Jagow to Tschirschky, July 17; K.D., 61.

[138] K.D., 83.

heed to these requests, and Germany was virtually unable to learn anything further, except as to the date when the ultimatum would be presented and Berchtold's obstinacy in rejecting German advice as to Italy.[139]

The German Foreign Office also applied for information to the Austrian Ambassador in Berlin. Szögyény's instructions were that he was not to show the ultimatum to Germany until July 24, the morning after it had been delivered in Belgrade. But Szögyény now felt himself compelled to telegraph to Berchtold, that he "considered it unconditionally necessary to inform the German Government at once, that is, before the other Powers, in a strictly confidential manner." And in a letter of the same day he wrote: "Jagow gave me clearly to understand that Germany would naturally stand behind us unconditionally and with all her strength, but for this very reason it was of vital interest to Germany to be informed betimes as to 'where our path is leading to.' " [140] Accordingly, on the following afternoon, July 22, Berchtold finally gave his consent, and Szögyény then showed the text of the ultimatum to Jagow.

After reading it on Wednesday evening, July 22, Jagow told Szögyény it was, in his opinion, "too sharp," and went too far in its demands. He reproached the Austrian Ambassador for thus communicating it only at the eleventh hour. Szögyény replied that nothing could be done about it, as it had already been dispatched to Belgrade, and would be presented there next morning, and officially published by the Vienna telegraph agency at the same time.[141]

---

[139] See the despatches from Tschirschky and Stolberg in Vienna, July 17-21; K.D., 65, 87, 88, 94, 95, 103, 104, 106.

[140] Szögyény to Berchtold, July 21; A.R.B., I, 39, 41.

[141] Jagow, *Ursachen*, p. 110, and Bethmann, *Betrachtungen*, I, 139, both state that Szögyény said it would be presented "next morning;" if they are correct, this would be another instance of Szögyény's inaccuracies tending in the direction of aggravating the situation; it would make the *fait accompli* seem even more irrevocable. Szögyény himself made no report to Berchtold on this conversation, or if he did, it has not been

While Jagow was considering the ultimatum, another copy of it was brought to him which had just arrived from Tschirschky. Curiously enough, on the preceding day at Vienna, Forgach, in ignorance of Berchtold's order to Macchio not to show Tschirschky the text of the ultimatum "since some corrections are still to be made in it," [142] actually handed it to him for transmission to Berlin. Forgach "expressly emphasized that it was for Your Excellency's strictly personal information, as the Emperor's approval is still lacking, though there is no doubt that he will give it." [143] Tschirschky sent it by mail instead of by telegraph, probably because he feared that its subsequent publication might endanger the secrecy of the German cipher. It thus did not reach Berlin until the evening of July 22, as Jagow was knitting his brows over the copy which Szögyény had just given him. Bethmann, who was at Hohenfinow at this time, apparently did not know of the text of the note until late on the night of the 22nd or the morning of the 23rd,[144] but when he saw it, he too, like Jagow, was of the opinion that it was too sharp. Emperor William, away at sea on the *Hohenzollern,* first heard the contents of the ultimatum later still, through a newspaper agency and not officially from the German Foreign Office, as we know from an irritated telegram which he sent to his "civilian Chancellor." [145]

published. The time decided upon for presenting the note at Belgrade was not "next morning," but next afternoon, July 23, at 5 P.M.; at the last moment the hour was changed, at Jagow's suggestion, from 5 to 6 P.M., to make certain that the news should not reach St. Petersburg until after Poincaré had departed; K.D., 112, 127; A.R.B., I, 62; and above at note 76.

142 See above, at note 111.

143 Tschirschky to Bethmann, July 21; K.D., 106.

144 Bethmann's telegram of July 22 at 11:40 P.M. (*ibid.,* no. 116), speaks of "the wording of the Austrian note which is not yet known to me."

145 Kaiser to Bethmann, July 26, 7:30 P.M.; K.D., 231. This telegram, together with what has been said above, shows the incorrectness of the much-quoted despatch from the English Ambassador at Vienna:

Thus it is essentially true that Germany knew the general tenor of some of the terms of the ultimatum, and was aware that they were likely to lead to a localized war with Serbia, but she did not know the text of it beforehand in time to modify or recall it. Berchtold's *fait accompli* methods had prevented that. At the time Jagow finally saw the text, on the evening of July 22, there remained less than twenty-four hours before the Austrian Minister was to present it at Belgrade. The text of it was already in his hands. Even in these modern days of the telephone and telegraph it would have been virtually impossible for the German and Austrian officials in Berlin, Vienna and Belgrade to communicate with each other within the brief time and agree upon a modification of the ultimatum. And even if Bethmann and Jagow had been informed of the text much earlier, it is not to be assumed that they would have modified or stopped it. They would have probably still adhered to the policy adopted on July 5, that the Austro-Serbian question was "beyond the competence of Germany," but that Germany must support her ally in the action she had decided upon to protect herself against the Greater Serbia danger. They felt they had to accept Berchtold's *fait accompli*. It was a consequence of their folly in giving him a free hand on July 5. To have disavowed Austria's action at the last moment, would of course, as events turned out, have been wiser. But it would have meant that the Triple Alliance would have been greatly weakened further in the face of the Triple Entente which was growing closer and stronger. The internal dissolution of Austria would have been accelerated through the encouragement to restless Slav subjects. Austria's evaporating prestige in the Balkans would have completely

"Although I am not able to verify it, I have private information that the German Ambassador [Tschirschky] knew the text of the ultimatum to Serbia before it was despatched, and telegraphed it to the German Emperor;" Bunsen to Grey, July 30; B.B.B., 95; *cf.* B.D., 307.

dried up, and Russia, with her growing population and ambitions, would have dominated the Balkans and hastened the day for controlling Constantinople and the Straits.

Bethmann and Jagow concluded that the more energetically they appeared to support Austria, the more likely they would be to succeed in "localizing" the conflict and in preventing Russia and the other Powers from interfering. Therefore on the morning of July 24, when Austria notified the Powers of Europe of the Note delivered to Serbia the night before, Germany immediately followed with declarations endorsing Austria's charges against Serbia and emphasizing the importance of localizing the conflict. Jagow made the assertions which we have quoted above as to Germany's having no foreknowledge of the contents of the ultimatum. But in pretending to be wholly ignorant of Austria's step and at the same time approving it when taken, the German Foreign Office stupidly put itself in a false and self-contradictory position which not unnaturally made the Entente Powers suspect that it was acting in bad faith; it made them suspect that the German authorities were more responsible for Austria, and were harboring more reprehensible plans of their own, than was really the case —that Germany had not only approved but had instigated Austria's action; that this action was not aimed merely at Serbia, but was the pretext for a general war which would realize the ambitions voiced by irresponsible Pan-German orators and newspapers. These suspicions were not unnatural under the circumstances, and though they were far from accurate, they were assiduously spread, especially by the representatives of France, and contributed much to the later fatal course of events. Later, when Germany perceived that it might not be possible after all to "localize" an Austro-Serbian war, and therefore made genuine efforts to restrain Austria and avoid a general European War, less credence was given to her statements because of the suspicions which had been aroused by Jagow's untrue assertions that Germany had been ignorant of the ultimatum. Reputation for good faith once weakened is difficult to restore. This is what made so serious her adding to the first blunder of giving Berchtold a blank check on July 5 the second blunder of saying what was not true in regard to foreknowledge of the ultimatum.

THE ULTIMATUM

The Note which Austria addressed to Serbia on July 23 at 6 P. M., and notified to the Powers next morning, was as follows:

On the 31st March, 1909, the Serbian Minister in Vienna, on the instructions of the Serbian Government, made the following declaration to the Imperial and Royal Government:—

"Serbia recognises that the *fait accompli* regarding Bosnia has not affected her rights, and consequently she will conform to the decisions that the Powers may take in conformity with article 25 of the Treaty of Berlin. In deference to the advice of the Great Powers, Serbia undertakes to renounce from now onwards the attitude of protest and opposition which she has adopted with regard to the annexation since last autumn. She undertakes, moreover, to modify the direction of her policy with regard to Austria-Hungary and to live in future on good neighborly terms with the latter."

The history of recent years, and in particular the painful events of the 28th June last, have shown the existence of a subversive movement with the object of detaching a part of the territories of Austria-Hungary from the Monarchy. The movement, which had its birth under the eye of the Serbian Government, has gone so far as to make itself manifest on both sides of the Serbian frontier in the shape of acts of terrorism and a series of outrages and murders.

Far from carrying out the formal undertakings contained

in the declaration of the 31st March, 1909, the Royal
Serbian Government has done nothing to repress these movements. It has permitted the criminal machinations of various
societies and associations directed against the Monarchy,
and has tolerated unrestrained language on the part of the
press, the glorification of the perpetrators of outrages, and
the participation of officers and functionaries in subversive
agitation. It has permitted an unwholesome propaganda in
public instruction, in short, it has permitted all manifestations of a nature to incite the Serbian population to hatred
of the Monarchy and contempt of its institutions.

This culpable tolerance of the Royal Serbian Government had not ceased at the moment when the events of the
28th June last proved its fatal consequences to the whole
world.

It results from the depositions and confessions of the
criminal perpetrators of the outrage of the 28th June that
the Sarajevo assassinations were planned in Belgrade; that
the arms and explosives with which the murderers were
provided had been given to them by Serbian officers and
functionaries belonging to the Narodna Odbrana; and
finally, that the passage into Bosnia of the criminals and
their arms was organised and effected by the chiefs of the
Serbian frontier service.

The above-mentioned results of the magisterial investigation do not permit the Austro-Hungarian Government to
pursue any longer the attitude of expectant forbearance
which they have maintained for years in face of the machinations hatched in Belgrade, and thence propagated in the
territories of the Monarchy. The results, on the contrary,
impose on them the duty of putting an end to the intrigues
which form a perpetual menace to the tranquillity of the
Monarchy.

To achieve this end the Imperial and Royal Government
see themselves compelled to demand from the Royal Serbian
Government a formal assurance that they condemn this
dangerous propaganda against the Monarchy; in other
words, the whole series of tendencies, the ultimate aim of

which is to detach from the Monarchy territories belonging to it, and that they undertake to suppress by every means this criminal and terrorist propaganda.

In order to give a formal character to this undertaking the Royal Serbian Government shall publish on the front page of their "Official Journal" of the 13/26 July the following declaration:—

"The Royal Government of Serbia condemn the propaganda directed against Austria-Hungary—i.e., the general tendency of which the final aim is to detach from the Austro-Hungarian Monarchy territories belonging to it, and they sincerely deplore the fatal consequences of these criminal proceedings.

"The Royal Government regret that Serbian officers and functionaries participated in the above-mentioned propaganda and thus compromised the good neighborly relations to which the Royal Government were solemnly pledged by their declaration of the 31st March, 1909.

"The Royal Government, who disapprove and repudiate all idea of interfering or attempting to interfere with the destinies of the inhabitants of any part whatsoever of Austria-Hungary, consider it their duty formally to warn officers and functionaries, and the whole population of the kingdom, that henceforward they will proceed with the utmost rigor against persons who may be guilty of such machinations, which they will use all their efforts to anticipate and suppress."

This declaration shall simultaneously be communicated to the Royal army as an order of the day by His Majesty the King and shall be published in the "Official Bulletin" of the Army.

The Royal Serbian Government further undertake:

1. To suppress any publication which incites to hatred and contempt of the Austro-Hungarian Monarchy and the general tendency of which is directed against its territorial integrity;

2. To dissolve immediately the society styled "Narodna Odbrana," to confiscate all its means of propaganda, and

to proceed in the same manner against other societies and their branches in Serbia which engage in propaganda against the Austro-Hungarian Monarchy. The Royal Government shall take the necessary measures to prevent the societies dissolved from continuing their activity under another name and form;

3. To eliminate without delay from public instruction in Serbia, both as regards the teaching body and also as regards the methods of instruction, everything that serves, or might serve, to foment the propaganda against Austria-Hungary;

4. To remove from the military service, and from the administration in general, all officers and functionaries guilty of propaganda against the Austro-Hungarian Monarchy whose names and deeds the Austro-Hungarian Government reserve to themselves the right of communicating to the Royal Government;

5. To accept the collaboration in Serbia of representatives of the Austro-Hungarian Government for the suppression of the subversive movement directed against the territorial integrity of the Monarchy;

6. To take judicial proceedings against accessories to the plot of the 28th June who are on Serbian territory; delegates of the Austro-Hungarian Government will take part in the investigation relating thereto;

7. To proceed without delay to the arrest of Major Voja Tankositch and of the individual named Milan Ciganovitch, a Serbian State employee, who have been compromised by the results of the magisterial enquiry at Sarajevo;

8. To prevent by effective measures the co-operation of the Serbian authorities in the illicit traffic in arms and explosives across the frontier, to dismiss and punish severely the officials of the frontier service at Shabats and Loznica guilty of having assisted the perpetrators of the Sarajevo crime by facilitating their passage across the frontier;

9. To furnish the Imperial and Royal Government with explanations regarding the unjustifiable utterances of high

Serbian officials, both in Serbia and abroad, who, notwithstanding their official position, have not hesitated since the crime of the 28th June to express themselves in interviews in terms of hostility to the Austro-Hungarian Government; and, finally,

10. To notify the Imperial and Royal Government without delay of the execution of the measures comprised under the preceding heads.

The Austro-Hungarian Government expect the reply of the Royal Government at the latest by 6 o'clock on Saturday evening, the 25th July.

In the light of what has been said in the preceding chapters concerning the Sarajevo assassination, the circumstances leading up to it, Serbia's failure to take prompt steps to discover and arrest the accomplices, and Austria's conviction that her very existence was at stake, one cannot say that the demands, though very severe, were excessive from the Austrian point of view. If they had been honestly calculated merely to exact punishment for those connected with the Sarajevo assassination and to obtain guarantees of security for the future, they might be regarded as justified. But having been deliberately framed with the expectation that they would be rejected, and that their rejection would lead to a localized war with Serbia, they must be condemned on both moral and practical grounds as one of the main causes of the World War. And Germany, in so far as she assented to them and endorsed them, must share in this condemnation.

CHAPTER VI

THE RUSSIAN DANGER

THE first news of the assassination of the Archduke Franz Ferdinand made a painful impression in Russia, as everywhere else in the civilized world. But the feeling of hatred toward Austria-Hungary which prevailed in Russia, and which had been steadily increasing since the Balkan crises, soon overshadowed all expressions of sympathy for the aged Austrian monarch in the latest of his many tragic bereavements. At the memorial services arranged in St. Petersburg by the Austrian Ambassador there was, to be sure, a full attendance of Russian officials, including Grand Dukes Boris and Nicholas, who had been requested by the Tsar to represent the Imperial family. But aside from this perfunctory expression of feeling, the German Ambassador, Pourtalès, did not notice any genuine sympathy with Austria's loss. Not only in the newspapers, but also in society, he heard virtually nothing but unfriendly comments on the murdered Austrian Archduke: that Russia, by his death, was now rid of a bitter enemy.[1]

At the close of the memorial service, Pourtalès took the opportunity to talk with Sazonov, the Russian Minister of Foreign Affairs. It was the first time he had seen him since the assassination. Sazonov began by sharply criticiz-ing the Sarajevo officials for their conduct after the crime: they had not only permitted attacks on the Serbs, but had

[1] Pourtalès to Bethmann, July 13; K.D., 53. The Kaiser's marginal note at this point was much nearer the truth: "He [Franz Ferdinand] in fact always wanted to renew the old League of the Three Emperors! He was the best friend of Russia!"

274

deliberately given a free rein to the popular fury. He did not believe that there was any population worth mention‑ ing in Bosnia and Herzegovina which was really loyal to the Hapsburgs—at most merely some Mohammedans and Roman Catholics. He denied Austria's assertion that the assassination was the result of a Greater Serbian plot; at least, he said, there was not the slightest proof of this so far, and it was exceedingly unjust to hold the Serbian Government responsible, as the Austro-Hungarian news‑ papers were doing. This was no more justifiable than it would have been for Russia to call the French Government to account for the crimes which were plotted on French soil and committed in Russia. Championing the official Serbian attitude, he declared that the Sarajevo crime was only the isolated act of immature young persons, and there was no proof of their connection with any deep-laid politi‑ cal plot. When Pourtalès urged "monarchical solidarity" against such dangerous anarchists and murderers, he found that Sazonov responded to this ancient theme with less warmth than usual, and concluded that Sazonov, like nearly everyone else in Russia, was blinded by his hatred of Aus‑ tria-Hungary. He noticed also everywhere in Russia a boundless contempt for the condition of affairs in the Dual Monarchy.[2]

During the middle of July, Sazonov spent several days at his country estate near Grodno. He wanted a rest before the exacting demands on his strength, which would be made by the approaching visit of the French President and Prime Minister. Such an absence from St. Petersburg seemed, at that time, quite safe. But when he returned to the Russian Foreign Office on July 18, he began to grow nervous at the ominously silent attitude of the Vienna authorities, and the heated recriminations between the Austrian and

[2] K.D., 53. Beside the last remark the Kaiser penciled, "Pride goeth before destruction!"

Serbian Press. The Italian Ambassador had told the Secretary, Baron Schilling, of his impression that Austria was about to take an irreparable step against Serbia, and that it would be well to serve a warning at Vienna.[3] To the Austrian and German Ambassadors Sazonov therefore reiterated his views, that it was unjust to make the whole Serbian people responsible for the crime of a single individual, as the Austrian newspapers were doing. "Russia," he said to the Austrian Ambassador, "would not be indifferent to any effort to humiliate Serbia. Russia could not permit Austria to use menacing language or military measures against Serbia. In short, *'La politique de la Russie est pacifique, mais pas passive!'* "[4] Szápáry, who had unexpectedly returned from his vacation the day before, said that Austria could not continue to tolerate the Serbian terrorist activities, but that his Government were convinced that Serbia would yield to any such demands as might result from the investigation going on at Sarajevo. He gave the impression in peace-loving phrases that Austria had not the slightest intention of rendering more acute her relations with Serbia. Sazonov was fully quieted, and told Schilling that there was no need to resort to threats, as the Ambassador had assured him emphatically of his Government's love of peace. *"Il a été doux comme un agneau."* [5]

Sazonov had feared that some sudden stroke might be attempted by Austria, which would humiliate Serbia

[3] Schilling's *Diary,* p. 25; on the high value of this Diary, see above, vol. I, ch. i, at notes 14 and 15. Barun Schilling was Director of the Chancellery of the Russian Foreign Office. His position corresponded to that of the Permanent Under-Secretary for Foreign Affairs in England. He was reported to be "an extraordinarily clever, skilful, and influential man", who really directed foreign policy more than Sazonov (*cf.* G. P., XXXIX, 526).

[4] Szápáry to Berchtold, July 18; A.R.B., I, 25; Pourtalès to Bethmann, July 21, K.D., 120.

[5] Schilling's *Diary,* p. 27. *Cf.,* however, Buchanan to Grey, July 18, 8:50 P.M. (B.D., 60) for evidences of Sazonov's great nervousness and anxiety.

directly, and thereby Russia indirectly. He was always very much afraid that Germany or Austria would do something to diminish Russia's prestige in the Balkans and in Europe. It was a point on which he was very sensitive, particularly in view of the strong Pan-Slav sentiment of the Russian Press and the militarists, who were not wholly friendly to him, and who might drive him from office if he suffered a diplomatic defeat. He did not want a repetition of anything like the Liman von Sanders episode. However, the main matter immediately at hand, until Austria should finally break her sphinx-like silence, was the reception of President Poincaré and M. Viviani, and the ceremonial renewal of the Franco-Russian solidarity.

POINCARÉ'S VISIT TO RUSSIA

In January, 1914, at the height of the Liman von Sanders crisis, the French had asked Sazonov when it would be convenient for President Poincaré to repeat the summer visit to Russia, which he had made in August, 1912, shortly before the outbreak of the Balkan War. It was finally arranged that he should arrive at Kronstadt at 2 P. M. on July 20, and leave at 11 P. M. on July 23.[6] When the Sarajevo assassination occurred the French Cabinet raised the question whether it was desirable for him to leave France, but decided, as did the Kaiser in going on his northern cruise, that it would seriously alarm public opinion as to the European situation, if important arrangements long announced should be abandoned.[7] Jean Jaurès, however, the veteran French Socialist and historian, distrusting the policies of Izvolski and Poincaré, refused to vote credits for the trip, declaring that it was dangerous for France to become increasingly entangled in adventurous Near East questions, and in treaty arrangements of which the French

[6] Poincaré, IV, 3-6, 221-285; K.D., 96, 108; Paléologue, I, 1-19.
[7] Poincaré, IV, 211; Les Origines de la Guerre, 197 ff.

public knew neither the text nor the consequences.[8] But the French President and his Prime Minister embarked from Dunkirk on the cruiser, *France*, on July 15, and were welcomed five days later off Peterhof by Sazonov, Paléologue, and Izvolski, and then by the Tsar. Poincaré and Paléologue in their memoirs have left elaborate and picturesque accounts of all the ceremonial occasions with which the three following days were filled, but they say very little of private conversations which were exchanged.

One of Poincaré's aims was to reduce Anglo-Russian friction over Persia, in order to secure closer coöperation between the ally and the friend of France,[9] and so perhaps pave the way for a renewal of the negotiations for an Anglo-Russian Naval Convention; these had been interrupted owing to the rumors of it which had leaked out, and to Sir Edward Grey's unwillingness to continue negotiations in secret which he had publicly denied in Parliament.[10] But among the main subjects of their discussion were certainly the strengthening of the bonds of the Franco-Russian Alliance, as well as of the Triple Entente,[11] and especially

[8] *Cf.* G. Demartial, *L'Evangile du Quai d'Orsay* (Paris, 1927), p. 11 f. Demartial has given a most penetrating analysis of the French Yellow Book, showing how French official telegrams were suppressed and altered by its editor (M. Berthelot?), to conceal the truth concerning Poincaré's visit and the Russian mobilization measures. His revelations and those of August Bach and others (*cf.* KSF, II, 129-152; IV, 879-884; V, 262-5; 1228 f.) make all the more welcome the eventual prospect of a complete and honest publication of the French diplomatic correspondence during the July crisis. Such a publication will perhaps clear M. Poincaré's reputation of the suspicions which have been leveled against him at home and abroad. *Cf.* R. Gerin et R. Poincaré, *Les Responsabilités de la Guerre* (Paris, 1930).

[9] Poincaré, *Les Origines de la Guerre*, p. 201 f; *cf.* also B.D., pp. x-xi, and Nos. 49, 75, 164.

[10] *Cf.* Benckendorff, Russian Ambassador in London, to Sazonov, July 2, 1914; Siebert-Schreiner, p. 733; see also G.P., XXXIX, 612-628.

[11] Just before Poincaré's arrival, the Tsar said to the French Ambassador: "There is one question which preoccupies me above everything else; our Entente with England. We must get her to enter our alliance. . . . It is all the more important that we should be able to count upon the English in case of a crisis;" Paléologue, I, 2 f.

the measures to be taken in view of the increasing indications that Austria was preparing to deliver a stiff ultimatum to Serbia.[12]

In all the conversations which took place in the course of the next three days it was Poincaré, as one might expect from his dominating and energetic personality, who took the lead, and sounded the key-notes. At the very outset, as the guests were leaving the *France* in a launch, Paléologue observed: "The Emperor and the President, sitting in the stern, enter at once into conversation. . . . It is Poincaré who guides the discussion. Soon it is he alone who is talking. The Emperor only acquiesces." [13] At the gala banquet at Peterhof in the evening the Tsar, in his toast of welcome, hoped the two countries "will continue to enjoy the benefits of the peace, which the fullness of their strength ensures, by constantly tying more tightly the bands which unite them." [14] Poincaré in a longer reply, which Paléologue thought had a remarkably significant force and note of authority,[15] recalled that the Franco-Russian Alliance had existed nearly twenty-five years, and added:

> Founded upon community of interests, consecrated by the peaceful desires of the two Governments, supported by armed forces on land and sea which know and value each other and have become accustomed to act as brothers, strengthened by long experience and augmented by valu-

[12] For the fact that the Entente Powers knew more of Austria's intended action than they admitted in their documentary publications of 1914, see above, ch. v, at notes 95-100. As early as July 5 the British Ambassador in Vienna had reported that, "Dumaine, my French colleague, is full of serious apprehension. His country is known to be in sympathy with the Serbian aspirations and he is in a position to know what is being said and done by Serbians in Vienna. He has repeatedly spoken to me during the past week of the dangers of the situation, which he fears may develop rapidly into complications from which war might easily arise;" Bunsen to Grey, July 5; B.D., 40, but omitted from B.B.B.

[13] Paléologue, I, 4.

[14] Schilling's *Diary*, Appendix, p. 113 f.

[15] Paléologue, I, 6.

able friendships, the Alliance to which the sublime Tsar Alexander III and the lamented President Carnot gave the initiative has ever since constantly afforded proof of its beneficial activity and its unshakable strength. Your Majesty can be assured that France in the future, as always in the past, will, in sincere and daily co-operation with her ally, pursue the work of peace and civilization for which both the Governments and both the peoples have never ceased to labour.[16]

Next morning, July 21, Poincaré and the Tsar talked over the general European situation, and especially the Persian Question. The Tsar assured him that "he would not allow Persia to cause division between England and Russia." [17] In the afternoon the French guests went to St. Petersburg to receive the French colony and the Diplomatic Corps, but were surprised that the Tsar did not accompany them. This was probably because of the severe strikes which had broken out there, the workingmen being more interested in their own grievances than in the representatives of French capitalism.[18] In the reception at the Winter Palace, Paléologue presented his diplomatic colleagues to the French President, who spoke affably to all except the Austrian Ambassador: to Pourtalès, about his French ancestors, but not a word about politics; to Motono, virtual assent to Japan's acting with the Triple Entente; to Buchanan, he repeated the Tsar's assurances about Persia; it was probably also on this occasion that he rejected emphatically Sir Edward Grey's first proposal for settling peacefully European complications which might grow out of the Austro-Serbian question by means of "direct-conversations" between Austria and Russia,[19] though

16 Schilling's *Diary*, Appendix, p. 114.

17 Buchanan to Grey, July 22, 23; B.D., 75, 164.

18 *Cf.* Pourtalès to Bethmann, July 23; K.D., 130, 291; and B.D., 164.

19 Poincaré "expressed opinion that a conversation *à deux* between Austria and Russia would be very dangerous at the present moment;'

neither Paléologue nor Poincaré mention this in their accounts. When Szápáry, the Austrian Ambassador, came forward in his turn, Poincaré seized the occasion to try to draw him out as to Berchtold's intentions, and to warn him almost threateningly against Austria's holding Serbia responsible for Sarajevo:

> After some words of condolence over the assassination of the Archduke Franz Ferdinand, the President asked Szápáry:
> "Have you any news from Serbia?"
> "The judicial investigation is advancing," replied Szápáry coldly. Poincaré went on:
> "The results of this investigation do not fail to disturb me, Mr. Ambassador; for I remember two former investigations which did not improve your relations with Serbia. You remember the Friedjung Affair and the Prochaska Affair?"
> Szápáry replied drily: "We cannot tolerate, Mr. President, that a foreign Government shall allow murderous attacks to be prepared on its soil against our sovereignty."
> Poincaré tried in a most conciliatory tone to show him that, in the present state of feeling in Europe, all Governments ought to be doubly prudent. "With a little good-will, this Serbian affair is easy to settle. But it is easy also for it to become envenomed. Serbia has very warm friends in the Russian people. And Russia has an Ally, France. What complications are to be feared here!" [20]

This description by Paléologue of Poincaré's conversation with the Austrian Ambassador is confirmed in its essentials by Szápáry himself, who concluded his long report of it with the shrewd observation:

> This action of the President, tactless, considering that it came from the head of a foreign state, who was here on a visit, sounding like a threat and so strikingly different from

Buchanan to Grey, July 22; B.D., 76. On the significance of this, see below ch. viii, at notes 27-37.   [20] Paléologue, I, 9 f.

Sazonov's reserved and cautious attitude, confirms the expectation that M. Poincaré will have anything but a calming effect here. Significant is the close resemblance between the President's juristic deductions and the arguments by Pashitch in the *Leipziger Neueste Nachrichten.* Spalajkovitch [Serbian Minister at St. Petersburg], whom Sazonov characterized to me only recently as "unbalanced" [déséquilibré], may have had a hand in this game.[21]

When Szápáry had bowed and departed, Poincaré remarked to Paléologue that the interview had made an unfavorable impression on him: Austria seemed to be preparing some sudden stroke which Szápáry was concealing; "Sazonov must be firm, and we must support him." These words sum up better than anything else the significance of Poincaré's trip to Russia. Aware of Sazonov's changeable and mercurial temperament, of his ardent Russian nationalism, alternating, however, with a genuine desire for peace and a certain timidity which made him shrink at critical moments from supporting the Serbians to the point of war,[22] Poincaré wanted to strengthen Sazonov's attitude toward Austria. He wanted him to warn Austria against making inacceptable demands on Serbia, and to prevent him, in case of need, from accepting any compromise settlement which might be regarded as a diplomatic defeat for the Triple Entente at the hands of Germany and Austria.

Poincaré's visit also greatly strengthened the militarist group in Russia, headed by the Grand Duke, who wanted Sazonov to take a more aggressive attitude and who were continually trying to exert pressure on the peace-loving

21 Szápáry to Berchtold, July 21, A.R.B., I, 45.
22 E.g. in the Albanian crisis in November, 1913; see also below, ch. viii, at note 85, Sazonov's remark to Szápáry on July 26, that he "had no sympathy at all for the Balkan Slavs," and his apparently momentary inclination to abandon them, if he could reach a compromise settlement with Austria which would save Russia's prestige.

Tsar. The war spirit and "champagne mood" which was stirred by the presence of the French guests is well described by Paléologue in his account of the banquet which Grand Duke Nicholas gave in Poincaré's honor on the evening of July 22, after a military review at Krasnoe Selo. Paléologue arrived a few minutes early and found the Montenegrin Princesses, Anastasia and Melitza, wives of Grand Duke Nicholas and Grand Duke Peter respectively, decorating the tables; they both began to talk to him excitedly:

> "Do you know that we are passing through historic days, blessed days! Tomorrow, at the review, the bands will play nothing but the *Marche Lorraine* and *Sambre et Meuse*. Today, I had a telegram from my father in the proper style; he tells me we shall have war before the month is out. What a hero, my father! He is worthy of the Iliad. Here, look at this little box—it never leaves me; it has Lorraine soil in it, yes, Lorraine soil, which I collected beyond the frontier when I was in France two years ago with my husband. And now look at that table of honor! It is decorated entirely with thistles; I would not have any other flowers put on it. Now then! They are thistles from Lorraine! I picked a few stalks on the territory annexed [by Germany]; I brought them here and had the seeds sown in my garden. Melitza, talk to the Ambassador some more; tell him all this day means to us, while I go and receive the Tsar."

> During the meal I sat next the Grand Duchess Anastasia and the dithyrambics continued, mixed with prophecies: "War is going to break out. Nothing will be left of Austria. You will get Alsace-Lorraine back. Our armies will meet in Berlin. Germany will be annihilated."

> Then suddenly—"I must control myself, the Tsar is looking at me." [23]

Late that same night, at 4 A. M., Sazonov sent off to the Russian Chargé d'Affaires at Vienna the warning telegram

[23] Paléologue, I, 14 f.

which before Poincaré's visit he had told Schilling was unnecessary:

> Please point out in a friendly but firm manner the dangerous consequences of any Austrian action of a character inacceptable to the dignity of Serbia. The French and English Ambassadors are trusted to give councils of moderation.[24]

Poincaré completely approved of this, and the French Ambassador at Vienna was instructed accordingly.[25] But the British Foreign Office realized the danger of a veiled threat of this kind. Sir Eyre Crowe noted: "Any such communication at Vienna would be likely to produce intense irritation, without any benefical other effect." Sir Arthur Nicolson was "afraid that it is not a judicious move." And Sir Edward Grey decided to postpone any action until next day.[26]

This Franco-Russian move to head off Austria from making demands on Serbia, however, came to nothing, because the Russian Chargé d'Affaires in Vienna did not receive his instructions until 3 P. M. on July 23. He went at once to the Ballplatz, but was told that Berchtold was very busy and could not see him until next morning. In

[24] Sazonov to Kudashev, Tg. 1475 (much condensed); July 22 [23], 4 A. M.; Schilling's *Diary*, pp. 27; and p. 85 for unabridged text; also L.N., II, 275. Renouvin says (p. 77) Sazonov sent this telegram "during the night on July 21-22 about 4 A.M.," but he is in error; it was really sent on July 23 at 4. A. M., as is clear from the serial number (1475 is close to 1487 sent on July 24; *cf. Krasnyi Arkhiv*, IV, p. 45), and from the fact that it was received in Vienna at 3 P. M. on July 23 (Schilling's *Diary*, p. 38), that is, within the 10-12 hours which was the normal interval for telegrams between St. Petersburg and Vienna. To be sure, the telegram is dated "July 22, 4 A. M.," but this is evidently one of the many cases in which telegrams written late in the evening and not put on the wire until after midnight, were stamped at the telegraph office with an early morning *hour* which had the misleading effect of antedating by 24 hours the *day-of-the-month* date which the writer of the telegram had correctly put upon it before he went to bed. [25] F.Y.B., 22, 23.

[26] Minutes on Buchanan's tg. to Grey, which was received July 23, 3 P.M.; B.D., 84.

the meantime the ultimatum was presented at Belgrade at 6 P. M. on July 23.[27] Even had the instructions arrived earlier, they would almost certainly have failed to deter Berchtold, especially in view of England's do-nothing attitude and of the Vienna Cabinet's firm determination.

Meanwhile in Russia the final festivities of the Poincaré visit took place in blissful ignorance of the fact that Austria had already presented her demands at Belgrade, and that the Franco-Russian move to prevent it would prove abortive. In the farewell toast on board the *France*, the President thanked the Tsar for the warmth of his reception, which afforded "an emphatic affirmation of the indissoluble alliance which unites Russia and my native France"—two countries which would continue to coöperate in the future as in the past, because "both have many times experienced the advantages accruing to each from the regular coöperation, and because they are both animated by the same ideal of peace combined with strength, honor and dignity." The words were acclaimed with tumultuous enthusiasm, and made on all present a vivid and lasting impression of Poincaré's complete determination to stand firmly behind Russia. A few days later Paléologue cited them to the Under-Secretary, as an evidence of such perfect Franco-Russian accord that they would bluff Germany out of making war in support of Austria.[28]

The result of Poincaré's visit, as the English Ambassador was confidentially informed by Sazonov and Paléologue next morning, had been to establish the following points:

[27] Kudashev to Sazonov, July 26; Schilling's *Diary*, p. 38 f. The French Ambassador did not receive his instructions until July 24, so that the "observations intended to prevent presentation of the Note or to cause its terms to be modified would now be out of place;" Bunsen to Grey, July 24, 7:50 P.M., B.D., 97. Renouvin is in error (p. 79) in speaking of the Franco-Russian move as "made at Vienna on July 22."

[28] Schilling's *Diary*, p. 32; Paléologue, I, 16 ff.

at Berlin, its severe demands and intransigent tone made a painful impression and caused the most serious misgivings.

Sir Edward Grey called it "the most formidable document he had ever seen addressed by one State to another that was independent." But he did not care to discuss the merits of the dispute between Austria and Serbia; that was not England's concern. It was solely from the point of view of the peace of Europe that he would concern himself with the matter, and he would wait to hear the views of the other Powers.[30] After talking with the French and German Ambassadors, he began to make a series of proposals for preserving the peace of Europe which will be discussed later.

In Paris, M. Bienvenu-Martin, Minister of Justice, who was Acting-Minister of Foreign Affairs during the absence of Poincaré and Viviani, was completely nonplussed. He did not know what to do, beyond informing the absent President and Minister of the new developments and giving Serbia some cautious advice.[31] But he soon received instructions sent by wireless from the *France,* where Poincaré and Viviani had learned by a radiogram from Russia the substance of the ultimatum. Viviani had at once sent wireless messages to St. Petersburg, London, and Paris, "that, in his opinion, (1) Serbia should immediately offer all the satisfaction compatible with her honor and independence; (2) that she should request an extension of the twenty-four hour [*sic*] time-limit within which Austria demanded a reply; (3) that England, Russia and France should agree to support this request; and (4) that the Triple Entente should see whether it would be possible to substitute an international investigation in place of an

---

[30] Grey to Bunsen and the other British Ambassadors, July 24, 1 P. M.; B.D., 91; *cf.* also B.D., 98, 99, 100; A.R.B., II, 14, 15; K.D., 157; and F.Y.B., 32.

[31] *Cf.* F.Y.B., 21-34.

Austro-Serbian investigation." [32] Bienvenu-Martin proceeded to take some steps accordingly, but they came too late to produce any positive results.

It was in St. Petersburg, however, that the ultimatum caused the greatest excitement and alarm. The Russian Ministers and Entente Ambassadors did not get to bed until long past midnight, after the *France* had steamed away under the stars carrying Poincaré down the Gulf of Finland. They had not yet recovered from the fatiguing festivities and bountiful banquets, when they were rudely awakened toward 7 A. M.,[33] after very few hours of sleep, by the news of a telegram from Belgrade telling of the ultimatum. During the succeeding fortnight of almost sleepless days and nights, the fatigue and mental demands were far greater than during Poincaré's visit. Not only in St. Petersburg, but everywhere in the Foreign Offices of Europe, responsible officials now began to fall under a terrible physical and mental strain of overwork, worry, and lack of sleep, whose inevitable psychological consequences are too often overlooked in assessing the blame for the events which followed. But if one is to understand how it was that experienced and trained men occasionally failed to grasp fully the sheaves of telegrams put into their hands at frequent intervals, how their proposals were sometimes confused and misunderstood, how they quickly came to be obsessed with pessimistic fears and suspicions, and how in some cases they finally broke down and wept, one must remember the nerve-racking psychological effects of continued work and loss of sleep, combined with the conscious-

32 Poincaré, *Les Origines de la Guerre*, p. 213; this and the other important wireless messages to and from Poincaré and Viviani on board the *France* are suppressed from the *French Yellow Book.*

33 Paléologue, I, 22 f.; Sazonov, *Fateful Years*, p. 152, says that, having learned during the night of July 23-24 of the presentation of the ultimatum, he left Tsarskoe Selo next morning to return to St. Petersburg.

ness of the responsibility for the safety of their country and the fate of millions of lives.

"*C'est la guerre Européenne,*" were the words with which Sazonov greeted Baron Schilling, on arriving from Tsarskoe Selo at the Russian Foreign Office about 10 A. M. on Friday morning. He at once telephoned the news to the Tsar, who exclaimed, "This is disturbing," and gave orders that he be kept informed as to further developments.[34]

A few minutes later Szápáry arrived to read the full text of the ultimatum and to explain and justify Austria's action. Sazonov, who had not yet had time to consult with the other Russian Ministers or to learn how far England would back him up, received Szápáry by saying that he knew what brought him, but could not state what Russia's attitude would be. Szápáry then read aloud the ultimatum, but was frequently interrupted by Sazonov's questions and objections to its statements. At the mention of the *dossier*, which was to place the full Austrian evidence against Serbia before the Powers, Sazonov asked why Austria bothered with it, when she had already sent an ultimatum, showing she wanted war and not an impartial investigation; as things were, after the ultimatum, he said, he was not at all curious to see the *dossier*. "The fact is, you want war, and have burned your bridges." When Szápáry protested that Austria was peace-loving, and merely wanted security for her territory against foreign revolutionary agitation and for her dynasty against bombs, Sazonov remarked sarcastically, "One sees how pacific you are, now that you are setting Europe on fire." There followed a long discussion for an hour and a half. Sazonov sought to defend Serbia against the Austrian charges, and criticized the form and severity of the demands, especially the shortness of the time-limit. He kept saying from time to time:

[34] Schilling's *Diary*, p. 28 f.

"I know what it is. You want to make war on Serbia!
I see what is happening, the German newspapers are egging you on. You are setting fire to Europe. It is a great
responsibility you are assuming; you will see the impression
this will make here and in London and Paris and perhaps
elsewhere. They will consider this an unjustifiable aggression." He recalled the scandals of the Friedjung trial, but,
contrary to Szápáry's expectation, Sazonov did not argue
about the pressure from Russian public opinion, Slavdom,
or Greek Orthodoxy. He spoke rather of England, France
and Europe, and the effect which the ultimatum would have
outside Russia. Szápáry got the impression that the Russian Minister was more dejected than excited, and was
being careful not to say anything which would prejudice
Russia's future action. On the whole he thought Sazonov
"relatively calm." [35]

Sazonov, however, was more excited and disturbed than
Szápáry appeared to think. Of a naturally mercurial temperament, he was now particularly indignant at Berchtold's
methods. The short time-limit, the withholding of the
dossier, and the humiliating demands on Serbia, all seemed
to him to indicate that Austria was determined on war at
once with Serbia. It was particularly deceitful on Austria's
part to have pretended for three weeks that the demands
would be mild, such as Serbia could surely accept, and then
to face the little kingdom with an ultimatum which seemed
to indicate that Austria wanted war and would soon cross

[35] Szápáry to Berchtold, July 24, 3:35, 8:00 and 8:25 P.M.; A.R.B.,
II, 16, 17, 18. The *Austrian Red Book* of 1915 condenses these three
telegrams into one and suppresses seven passages. On this interview between Sazonov and Szápáry, see also Pourtalès to Bethmann, July 24;
K.D., 148. For Berchtold's simultaneous interview with Kudashev, the
Russian Chargé d'Affaires in Vienna, in which Berchtold sought to be as
conciliatory as possible, saying that he had no desire to humiliate Serbia
but only to require necessary guarantees of security for Austria, and that
he had no intention of annexing Serbian territory but only of maintaining the *status quo*, see A.R.B., II, 23; and Schilling's *Diary*, p. 39 f.

the frontier into Serbian territory. Moreover, Poincaré and the French Prime Minister had left Russia only a few hours previously. They were now out on the Baltic, where it was difficult for him to get into touch with them. Furthermore, he suspected that much that Szápáry said was not true. Therefore Russia must be prepared for war, or at least a strong diplomatic bluff, and he must make sure of British and Rumanian support. Accordingly, while he had been talking with Szápáry, he had Baron Schilling notify the Ministers of War,[36] Navy, and Finance of the course of events and summon them to a Council of Ministers at 3 P. M. Schilling warned Izvolski and Shebeko to return to their posts at Paris and Vienna, and recalled Neratov, Prince Trubetzkoi and other Foreign Office advisers from their leaves of absence. He also pointed out to the Finance Minister the necessity of withdrawing without delay as far as possible all State deposits in Germany.[37]

Sazonov himself consulted with General Ianushkevich, the Chief of the General Staff, and proposed preparations for a partial mobilization of the Russian army, directed exclusively against Austria, the announcement of which might serve as a warning to Germany and an effectual bluff to stop Austria from attacking Serbia. This at any rate seems to be the conclusion to be drawn from the following narrative of General Dobrorolski.[38] Dobrorolski was Chief

[36] Sukhomlinov later denied that he took part in the Council of Ministers on July 24 (cf. Wegerer, in Pol. Sci. Quart., XLIII, 204 f., June, 1928), but we seriously doubt whether his post-War denial is trustworthy.

[37] Schilling's Diary, p. 29.

[38] Sergei Dobrorolski, "Mobilizatsia russksoi Armii v 1914 G.," in the Belgrade Voennii Sbornik, I, pp. 91-116; Aug.-Sept., 1921; German translation, Die Mobilmachung der russischen Armee, 1914, Berlin, 1922; and French translation, "La Mobilisation de l'Armée Russe en 1914," in Revue d' Histoire de la Guerre Mondiale, I, April-July, 1923.

Other valuable material on Russian military preparations and mobilization in 1914 may be conveniently noted at this point. Among the memoirs of Russian Generals: V. A. Sukhomlinov, Erinnerungen, Berlin, 1924, more valuable on his army reforms before 1914, than on July, 1914, in which he minimizes his part. I. Danilov, Russland im Weltkriege,

of the Mobilization Section of the General Staff in 1914, and therefore in a position to know authoritatively all the technical details and preparations of Russia's mobilization measures. Driven into exile by the Bolshevist revolution, and writing his narrative in Belgrade in 1921 without access to his notes and papers, he made a few minor slips of memory. But his remarkable frankness, authoritative information, and general accuracy is confirmed by all the

Jena, 1925 (Russian ed. Berlin, 1925; and French trans., Paris, 1927), chs. i-vi; Danilov was Quartermaster General from 1909-1914, and supplements Dobrorolski's account at certain points in an article in *Rev. d'Hist. de la Guerre Mondiale*, I, 259-266, Oct., 1923. V. I. Gurko, *Russia, 1914-1917*, N. Y., 1919, pp. 1-24; A. S. Lukomski, *Vospominaniia* [Memoirs], 2 vols., Berlin, 1922. A. A. Polivanov, [Memoirs containing extracts from his diaries, in Russian] ed. A. M. Saiontschovski, Moscow, 1924.

Very illuminating are the numerous Russian mobilization telegrams and other military documents captured by the Germans during the war, published and analyzed by R. Hoeniger, *Russlands Vorbereitung zum Weltkrieg*, Berlin, 1919; and more completely by G. Frantz, *Russlands Eintritt in den Weltkrieg*, Berlin, 1924 (quoted hereafter as "Frantz"). B. von Eggeling, *Die russische Mobilmachung und der Kriegsausbruch*, Berlin, 1919, is the first-hand account of the German Military Attaché in St. Petersburg in 1914.

Sazonov's memoirs, *Fateful Years* (N. Y., 1928) cannot be relied on.

The contradictory testimony and confused newspaper reports of the famous Sukhomlinov Trial of 1917 were summarized by the present writer in his third article in the *Amer. Hist. Rev.*, XXVI, 225-254, Jan., 1921, together with the other literature then available; extracts from the Russian newspaper reports of the trial are also given by R. Hoeniger, in the *Deutsche Rundschau*, April, 1918, pp. 15-80; in an anonymous pamphlet, *Suchomlinow, Die russische Mobilmachung im Lichte amtlicher Urkunden und der Enthüllungen des Prozesses*, Bern, 1917; and by P. Renouvin, in *Rev. d'Hist. de la Guerre* Mondiale, II, 49-69, April, 1924; but this testimony from the Sukhomlinov Trial is now of relatively small value.

For more recent accounts, see the military histories in Russian by I. K. Zichovich (Moscow, 1922), and N. N. Golovine (Prague, 1925); H. von Kuhl, *Der deutsche Generalstab in Vorbereitung und Durchführung des Weltkrieges*, Berlin, 1919, 2nd ed. 1920; G. Frantz, *Russland auf dem Wege zur Katastrophe*, Berlin, 1926; Michael T. Florinsky, "The Russian Mobilization of 1914," in *Pol. Sci. Quart.*, XLII, 203-227, June, 1927; the reply to this by A. von Wegerer, *ibid.*, XLIII, 201-228, June, 1928; the articles by Danilov, Demartial, Dobrorolski, Frantz, Montgelas, Sukhomlinov, and von Wegerer, in KSF, I, 97-104; II, 18-21, 78-98, 205-207, 225-231; III, 27-38, 753-762; IV, 207-219, 430-435; by Montgelas, in the *Deutsche Rundschau*, May, 1922, pp. 113-124, and July, 1922, pp. 1-6; and by G. Frantz, in *Current History*, March, 1927, pp. 852-858.

documents which have since come to light, as well as by talks which the present writer was privileged to have with him in 1923. Dobrorolski writes:

On July 11 [N. S., 24], St. Olga's Day, between 11 o'clock and noon, the Chief of the General Staff, General Ianushkevich, called me on the service telephone and told me to come immediately to his office.

"The situation is very serious," he said as I entered. "Austria has delivered a wholly unacceptable ultimatum to the Serbian Government and we cannot remain indifferent. It has been decided to announce this publicly and decisively. Tomorrow there will appear in the *Russkii Invalid* a short official warning, saying that all Russia is following with close attention the course of the negotiations between the Austro-Hungarian and the Serbian Governments, and will not remain inactive if the dignity and the integrity of the Serbian people, our blood brothers, are threatened with danger.[39] Have you everything ready for the proclamation of the mobilization of our army?"

Upon my replying in the affirmative, the Chief of the General Staff said to me, "In an hour bring to me all the documents relative to preparing of our troops for war, which provide, in case of necessity, for proclaiming partial mobilization against Austria-Hungary only. This mobilization must give no occasion to Germany to find any grounds of hostility to herself."

I pointed out that a partial mobilization was out of the question. But General Ianushkevich ordered me anew to make a detailed report to him after an hour in accordance with his decision already made. . . . The absolute impossibility of a partial mobilization of the army was evident. By what motives was our strategy to be guided? By political considerations. [Dobrorolski then explains that on account of the system of alliances Russia was convinced that a war between Austria and Russia would inevitably

[39] For the text of the announcement as actually made on July 25, see R.O.B., 10.

involve Germany, and therefore no mobilization plan had been worked out for war against Austria alone.]

What then could be the purpose of any partial mobilization against Austria-Hungary alone? A threat which was not supported by a convincing evidence of one's own power would give rise to an attempt to despise this threat. A partial mobilization of our forces would have had exactly the opposite consequences of those which we reckoned upon.

From a strategic point of view the partial mobilization was simply folly. It was the intention to mobilize four Military Districts: Kiev, Odessa, Moscow and Kazan. In the territory covered by these military districts thirteen army corps had their standing peace quarters.[40]

Dobrorolski goes on to explain all the technical dangers and difficulties of any such partial mobilization as was proposed. After mobilization the troops of these four districts would necessarily advance to the frontier, but to strike at Austria effectively from the East and North, it was necessary for some of them to advance through the Warsaw District. Yet in order not to alarm Germany the Warsaw District was to remain untouched! And if no preparations were made in the Warsaw District, the part of it which bordered on Austria would remain uncovered and unprotected. Moreover, if a general mobilization should follow the partial mobilization, the utmost confusion would take place, because the reservists for the Warsaw District were drawn partly from the Moscow and Kazan Districts, where partial mobilization would already have taken place. These dangers and difficulties were not apparently, however, at first fully grasped by Sazonov, or even by Ianushkevich, who had been in office only a few months, and, as we shall see, this plan of partial mobilization was proceeded with, to the utter dismay of the military technicians like Dobrorolski and General Danilov.

[40] Dobrorolski, pp. 99-101 (German trans., pp. 17-19).

After his interview with Szápáry and his arrangement with Ianushkevich, Sazonov hurried to the French Embassy, where he lunched with Paléologue and Buchanan. Diamandi, the Rumanian Minister, was also invited to join them, because "it was of the greatest advantage for us that Rumania should be drawn in on our side, while for Rumania it was manifestly flattering to participate as an equal in the diplomatic steps taken by the Great Powers." [41] Sazonov said that "the step taken by Austria meant war," and he hoped that England would proclaim her solidarity with France and Russia. He said that Austria's conduct was "immoral and provocative," that some of her demands were absolutely inacceptable, and that she never would have acted as she had done without first having consulted Germany. He told Buchanan of the perfect agreement of views which had been established between France and Russia during Poincaré's visit,[42] and Paléologue added, "France would not only give Russia strong diplomatic support, but would, if necessary, fulfil all the obligations imposed on her by the alliance." Buchanan replied that he could not speak for England, but would telegraph Grey all that they had said; he personally could hold out no hope that England would make any declaration of solidarity that would entail armed support of France and Russia; England had no direct interest in Serbia, and public opinion in England would never sanction a war on her behalf. Sazonov replied that the Serbian question was but part of the general European question and that England could not efface herself; that he personally thought Russia would have to mobilize, but no decision would be taken until a Council of Ministers had been held. Buchanan then suggested bringing influence to bear on Austria to extend the time-limit, but Paléologue "replied that time did not permit of this; either Austria was bluffing, or had made up her mind to act

[41] Schilling's *Diary*, p. 30.   [42] See above, at note 29.

at once. In either case a firm and united attitude was our only chance of averting war." As Sazonov and Paléologue both continued to press Buchanan for a declaration of complete solidarity, he said he would telegraph a full report to Sir Edward Grey. He even went so far as to express his personal opinion that Grey, "might be prepared to represent strongly at Vienna and Berlin the danger to European peace of an Austrian attack on Serbia, . . . and that if war became general it would be difficult for England to remain neutral." Sazonov remarked that if war did break out, England would be sooner or later dragged into it, and if she did not make common cause with France and Russia she would have rendered war more likely, and would not have played a "beau rôle." Buchanan concluded from Paléologue's language that "it almost looked as if France and Russia were determined to make a strong stand even if we declined to join them." [43]

Sazonov, disappointed at being unable to secure England's immediate declaration of Entente solidarity which he had hoped might give pause to Austria, still avoided seeing the German Ambassador. He was not yet ready to indicate to him what Russia's policy would be. Moreover, he wished first to consult his ministerial colleagues. Accordingly, on leaving the luncheon conference at the French

[43] Buchanan to Grey, July 24, 5:40 P.M.; B.D., 101; cf. also Sir George Buchanan My Mission to Russia (2 vols., London, 1923), I, 189 ff.; and Paléologue, I, 23 f., where it is clear that the French Ambassador was exerting all his influence to make Sazonov stand firm, even if it led to war, and where a very different impression is given from that in his telegram of July 24 as published in F.Y.B., 31; one suspects that here also the editor of the *French Yellow Book* has used the blue pencil very generously. In the original serial form in which Paléologue published this part of his memoirs (*Rev. des Deux Mondes*, Jan. 15, 1921, p. 248), he represents Buchanan as saying regretfully at this luncheon meeting, "Ah! if only the Conservative Party [in England] were in power now, I am sure that they would understand what the national interest now so clearly imposes on us;" but he discreetly omitted this and several other passages when he published his memoirs in book form. Buchanan (I, 210) takes exception to some of Paléologue's statements.

Embassy about 3 P. M., he proceeded to the meeting of the Ministerial Council. Here he set forth the diplomatic situation and probably argued at length to persuade the reluctant military authorities to accept his partial mobilization plan. We have no precise and satisfactory record of the discussion, but after several hours the Council adopted the following resolutions: (1) to get into touch with the other Powers to request Austria to extend the time-limit, and so give them time to become acquainted with and to investigate the *dossier* of Sarajevo documents which Austria had declared she would communicate; (2) to advise Serbia not to offer armed resistance, if Austria should invade her territory but to announce that she was yielding to force and entrusting her fate to the judgment of the Great Powers; (3) to authorize the Ministers of War and Marine to ask the Tsar's consent to announce, depending on the course of events, mobilization in the four Military Districts of Kiev, Odessa, Moscow and Kazan, and of the Baltic and Black Sea Fleets; (4) to fill up immediately the stocks of war-supplies, and (5) to recall instantly state funds in Germany and Austria.[44]

Thus, an effort was to be made to have the Great Powers examine the merits of the Austro-Serbian question—to "Europeanize" it, instead of "localizing" it, as Austria and Germany wished; and, if this was unsuccessful, to arrange that much of the Austrian army would be tied up in Serbia at the moment Russia should finally have to take up arms. Sazonov accordingly telegraphed to Belgrade that "if the helpless situation of Serbia is indeed such as to leave no doubt as to the outcome of an armed conflict with Austria," it would be better not to make resistance, but retreating, let Austria occupy territory without a fight and appeal to

[44] Journal of the Council of Ministers, July 24, approved by the Tsar, July 25; printed from the copy in the Hoover War Library by Robert C. Binkley, in *Current History*, Jan., 1926, p. 533; *cf.* also Schilling's *Diary*, p. 30.

the Powers to intervene.[45] He also sent a circular telegram
to the Powers urging an extension of the time-limit, so
that, if Austria enabled the Powers to acquaint themselves
with the results of the Sarajevo investigation, they would
be in a position to give Serbia corresponding advice.[46]

As these efforts might not be successful, the Council
had also decided "in principle" in favor of Sazonov's
"partial mobilization" plan, that is, the mobilization of
1,100,000 men—thirteen army corps in the four southern
districts near Austria; this was only to be announced, however, when Sazonov should decide it was necessary, and
this decision of the Council was not final until approved
by the Tsar next day.[47]

All these arrangements were made by Sazonov before he
received Pourtalès and heard Germany's views on the
ultimatum and policy of "localization." Pourtalès had been
told in the morning that Sazonov could not receive him
after Szápáry, because he must go to a meeting of the
Council of Ministers,[48] whereas in reality he had gone to
the luncheon conference at the French Embassy. It was
not until toward 7 P. M. that Pourtalès was finally
admitted. When he attempted, in accordance with the
instructions given to him and the other German Ambassadors,[49] to justify Austria's action and to urge that the
Austro-Serbian conflict should remain "localized," Sazonov,
"who was very much excited and gave vent to boundless

45 Sazonov to the Russian Chargé d'Affaires in Belgrade, July 24;
Schilling's *Diary*, pp. 33, 86. Cf. Crackanthorpe to Grey, July 28 (B.D.,
221): Serbian Government expected immediate attack on Belgrade
on departure of Austrian Minister and so removed at once. Plan of
campaign is now to draw into interior as large a portion as possible
of Austrian army so as to weaken Austria elsewhere. Under-Secretary
of State tells me that Russian support is assured."

46 Schilling's *Diary*, pp. 33, 40; R.O.B., 4, 5; B.D., 125.

47 *Cf.* Buchanan to Grey, July 25; B.D., 125; and statement of a
former Russian Minister of War to the present writer.

48 Pourtalès to Bethmann, July 24, 6:10 P.M.; K.D., 148.

49 K.D., 100

reproaches against Austria-Hungary, stated in the most determined manner that it would be impossible for Russia to admit that the Austro-Serbian quarrel could be settled between the two parties concerned." He argued shrewdly that the Serbian promises of 1909, to which Austria made reference in the ultimatum, were given, not to Austria alone, but to the Powers; consequently, the question whether Serbia had lived up to these promises was a European one; it was for Europe to examine the *dossier*, and see whether Austria's charges were well founded.[50] Moreover, Austria could not be both prosecutor and judge.

Pourtalès replied that it was not practical to submit the question for adjudication by the six Great Powers, because the general political attitude of the Powers and their allied grouping would be the decisive factor in their judgment of the case. What would be the practical use of such a "judicial procedure," if the political friends of Austria took one side, and her opponents the other? Who would decide in such a case? He promised, however, to report Sazonov's idea to Berlin, but "he doubted whether Germany would expect her ally to lay the results of her investigation before a European Areopagus. Austria would refuse, as any Great Power must, to subject to arbitration a question in which her vital interests were at stake." Pourtalès then urged "monarchical solidarity" and the danger of countenancing regicides, but Sazonov quickly shifted the conversation to the broader political ground that a whole Government and Nation could not be held responsible for the act of an individual, and that Austria's charges were by no means convincing. He launched into

[50] Sazonov's argument was shrewd and technically quite correct, because, as Szápáry regretted (A.R.B., II, 19), in the ultimatum itself, Serbia was accused, in failing to live up to the promises of 1909, of "acting in opposition to the will of Europe," and because a copy of the ultimatum had been sent "to all the other Signatory Powers" who were interested in any modifications of the Treaty of Berlin.

such unrestrained accusations against Austria that Pour-talès expressed the fear that he was blinded by his hatred of Austria. "Hate," replied Sazonov, "is foreign to my nature. I do not hate Austria; I despise her." Finally he exclaimed: "Austria is seeking a pretext to gobble up Serbia; but in that case Russia will make war on Austria." Pourtalès sought to calm him by expressing his conviction that, at most, Austria was only intending to inflict a de-served chastisement on Serbia, and was far from thinking of making territorial gains. But Sazonov shook his head doubtingly: "First Serbia would be gobbled up; then will come Bulgaria's turn; and then we shall have her on the Black Sea." [51]

The interview was a tense one, and served only to accentuate more sharply the conflict between two views which were now coming into dangerous conflict—should the Austro-Serbian question remain "localized," or be "Euro-peanized." As Pourtalès was leaving Sazonov's office, Paléologue was waiting to come in and learn the decisions taken by the Ministerial Council and the outcome of the interview with Pourtalès, but his reports as published do not give a satisfactory account of what passed between him and the Russian Foreign Minister.[52]

WARLIKE PORTENTS AT KRASNOE SELO, JULY 25

On Saturday, July 25, the wave of midsummer heat which had been hanging over St. Petersburg for a month seemed to reach its climax. The trains were crowded with peace-loving people pouring out for the summer holidays. Out on the sun-baked plain at Krasnoe Selo, the Tsar and all St. Petersburg's high society were gathered to witness

[51] Pourtalès to Bethmann, July 25, 1:08 A.M., and detailed report later in the day; K.D., 160, 204. *Cf.* also Szápáry to Berchtold, July 25, 2:30 A.M.; A.R.B., II, 19; and Schilling's *Diary*, p. 31.

[52] Paléologue to Bienvenu-Martin, July 25 [24?]; F.Y.B., 38; Palé-ologue, I, 24-26; and Schilling's *Diary*, p. 31 f.

the summer review of the Russian troops. Late in the forenoon an important Ministerial Council was held at which the Tsar presided. It lasted so long that the maneuvers had to be postponed an hour. Even when they finally took place, they were cut short, and an unusual military excitement pervaded all the officers. The foreign Military Attachés got the impression that the Ministerial Council had considered mobilizing the Russian army, and perhaps had even decided to order it, at least in the four Southern Military Districts facing Austria.[53]   General Adlerberg, the Governor of St. Petersburg, by a slip of the tongue, in talking with the German General Chelius, actually spoke of measures "for mobilization." Baron Grünwald, the Tsar's chief equerry, sitting next to Chelius at the banquet that evening, said to him, "The situation is very serious. What was decided this noon, I am not permitted to tell you. You yourself will soon learn it. But take it from me, it looks very serious." He touched glasses with Chelius and drank his health with the words, "Let us hope we shall see each other again in better times!"[54]

[53] Major Eggeling, German Military Attaché, in the *Nordd. Allg Zeitung*, No. 261, Oct. 21, 1917; Eggeling, *Die Russische Mobilmachung*, pp. 23-25.

[54] Chelius to the Kaiser, July 26; K.D., 291. Chelius was Emperor William's personal representative at the court of the Tsar. For many years "Willy" and "Nicky" had each kept at the court (*à la suite*) of the other such a personal representative, in addition to the regular ambassadors, consuls, and military and naval attachés. They were accorded special intimacy, and served to keep the two autocrats in closer personal touch with each other. Owing to their privileged position and their intimate contact with the Sovereign's entourage, they were often able to get a closer view of the currents of feeling and the personages of influence than the regular formal diplomatic representatives. Chelius, who gives the best account of these events on July 25, gives evidence here and elsewhere of this close touch. Tatishchev, the Tsar's representative at the Kaiser's court, happened during these critical days to be in Russia. On July 30, 1:20 A.M., the Tsar telegraphed to the Kaiser: "Am sending Tatishchev this evening with instructions," but apparently this emissary of peace was stopped by Sazonov at the railway station just as he was departing for Berlin; R. Rosen, *Forty Years of Diplomacy* (London, 1923).

After the military review had been held, in an unusually curtailed form, it was announced that the maneuvers at Krasnoe Selo and in the whole Empire were to be broken off, and that the troops were to return at once to their standing quarters, as they would have to do in case of war.

The idea that mobilization and war were imminent was increased by the immediate promotion that same evening of the St. Petersburg Military Academy cadets to the position of regular officers in the army, instead of later in the year as customary. At the banquet following the Tsar's address to these new appointees, says the German Military Attaché, "young officers openly expressed their joy to me that now at last they were starting something 'against Austria.' Others aired their rage against 'Austrian presumption.' Even Prince Peter of Montenegro, who was present just at this time, thought he had to tell me that in his country there reigned a distinct enthusiasm for war, and that mobilization was in full progress. Not a man seemed to recollect that we [Germans] were in alliance with Austria!"[55]

Following the banquet there was a theatrical performance, which, under the leadership of the Grand Duke Nicholas, was made the occasion of a great demonstration for war. On this same evening St. Petersburg was startled out of its stillness by the unexpected sound of the hoofbeats of the Imperial Guards hurrying back through the mist to the capital, although they were to have been quartered out at Krasnoe Selo for another month.[56] "At seven o'clock," writes Paléologue, "I go to the Warsaw Railway

II, 171; Schilling's *Diary*, p. 64 ff.; K.D., 390, 399; and details by A. Bach in KSF, II, 508 ff., Nov., 1924.

[55] Eggeling, in *Nordd. Allg. Zeitung*, No. 261, Oct. 17, 1917.

[56] On the events at Krasnoe Selo on this fateful Saturday, July 25, see K.D., 194, 291; Eggeling, *Die Russische Mobilmachung*, pp. 22-27; A.R.B., II, 37, 60, 61; Meriel Buchanan, *The City of Trouble* (New York, 1918), pp. 10-12.

Station to say good-bye to Izvolski, who is returning to his post in haste. On the platforms, there is lively animation: the trains are crowded with officers and soldiers. This already looks like mobilization. We exchange rapidly our impressions, and come to same conclusion, '*Cette fois, c'est la guerre.*'"[57] Next day Princess Paley, who was in close touch with the Grand Dukes, sent an urgent telegram to her mother and daughter who were at Bad Kissingen in Germany to leave immediately for Switzerland or Italy;[58] and General Danilov, who had been hurriedly recalled from a tour in the Caucasus, telegraphed to his family in Podolia near the Austrian frontier begging them to return at once to St. Petersburg.[59]

THE RUSSIAN "PERIOD PREPARATORY TO WAR"

What took place on July 25 at this important Ministerial Council (often incorrectly called a Crown Council) in the presence of the Tsar to cause all these impressions of impending war? Again we have no precise record of what was said by each person present, but we know the final decisions taken. We may surmise that a conflict took place between Sazonov, who adhered to his "partial mobilization" plan, and the military leaders, led by the Grand Duke Nicholas, who feared that the technical and political difficulties of a partial mobilization would be disastrous.[60]

General Sukhomlinov, Minister of War, later claimed to have taken a passive attitude during the July crisis,[61] but his *apologia* is not convincing. General Danilov, speaking of the Ministerial Council, says: "It is easy to understand the decision of those members of the Council who had little knowledge of purely military problems and were

[57] Paléologue, I, 27 f.
[58] Princess Paley, "En Russie à la veille de la guerre," in *La Revue de Paris,* Nov. 15, 1923, p. 592.   [59] Danilov, p. 16.
[60] *Cf.* Dobrorolski, as quoted above at note 40.
[61] Sukhomlinov, *Erinnerungen,* pp. 357-379.

not acquainted with the technical side of mobilization. They were solely guided by the natural desire of safeguarding the honor of Russia and of avoiding at the same time anything that could suggest a hostile attitude towards Germany. But how can it be explained that General Sukhomlinov, who took part in the Council, deemed it possible to agree even without a word of protest to a decision which put Russia in a very dangerous position? Was it mere negligence or utter incompetence?" [62] Whether General Ianushkevich was now fully aware of the dangers of a partial mobilization, or whether he still had to be convinced that it was folly, is not certain. In any event the military leaders felt that a war between Austria and Serbia was necessarily a war between Austria and Russia, and therefore between Russia and Germany. They had no doubt that Austria was about to begin the invasion of Serbia as soon as the time-limit expired. In fact, later in the day, a Russian officer looking at his watch at six o'clock, remarked to General Chelius, "The cannon on the Danube will have begun to fire by now, for one doesn't send such an ultimatum except when the cannon are loaded." [63] They were probably convinced that war was "inevitable," and that here was Russia's heaven-sent opportunity to have her final reckoning with Germany, and to acquire that control of Constantinople and the Straits, which had been so seriously considered at the secret conference on February 8/21, 1914, and for which preparations had been ordered, in order that, when a crisis should break out, Russia should be able to secure her historic aims at the Bosphorus.[64] Therefore the sooner general mobilization was declared the better.[65]

[62] Danilov, p. 15.
[63] Chelius to the Kaiser, July 26; K.D., 291.
[64] Cf. above, I, ch. v, "Balkan Problems," at notes 309-311.
[65] For indications of the conflict of opinions among the various Ministers on the question of military measures, see K.D., 130, 194, 203.

It is quite possible that one of the arguments at the Ministerial Councils on Friday and Saturday was the dangerous domestic situation. St. Petersburg and all the larger cities in Russia were in the throes of an extensive workingmen's strike. By a strange irony of fate, at the same moment when the Russian military bands, in the camp at Krasnoe Selo, had been welcoming Poincaré with the *Marseillaise*, the Cossacks in the suburbs of St. Petersburg had been striking down working-men for singing this same martial anthem.[66] An apparently well-informed Russian sympathizer, writing at length in the *Gazette de Lausanne* of September 7 and 8, 1917, in comment upon the Sukhomlinov trial, asserts that in 1914 general mobilization was strongly urged as a salutary measure against this internal industrial and revolutionary danger, rather than as a necessary military precaution against German attack; it would also counteract, it was urged, the feared autonomous and separatist agitation among the non-Slavic elements in the Russian Empire. The idea of a foreign war to avert domestic troubles is, of course, a very familiar one in the history of many countries.[67] The militarists may quite probably have believed that the leading forth of the specter of threatening internal revolution and anarchy would serve as a good bogey with which to persuade the peace-loving Tsar to consent to a general mobilization, and they were ready to assure him that, in case of mobilization

204, 338; A.R.B., II, 60, 61, 73, III, 19, 71; Dobrorolski, Danilov, and Sukhomlinov, *passim;* Nekliudov, *Diplomatic Reminiscences,* pp. 284-285.

[66] Pourtalès to Bethmann, July 23; K.D., 130; *cf.* also V. A. Wroblewski, "Die russischen Arbeiterunruhen im Juli, 1914," in KSF, III, 325-331, May, 1925.

[67] *Cf.* Jules Cambon's similar suspicions about Germany in his report to Pichon, July 30, 1913 (F.Y.B., 5): "Some want war . . . for social reasons, i.e., to provide the external interests which alone can prevent or retard the rise to power of the democratic and socialist masses . . . This social class [the Junkers], which forms a hierarchy with the King of Prussia as its supreme head, realizes with dread the democratization of Germany and the increasing power of the Socialist Party."

and war, the strikes would offer no serious obstacle,[68] as in fact proved to be the case.

At any rate, whatever the arguments used at this Council, Sazonov prevailed in maintaining his plan for "partial mobilization." But a concession was made to the militarists in the adoption of a series of preparatory military measures which would facilitate a "general mobilization" when the Tsar should finally be persuaded to consent to it. In all, five decisions were taken by the Ministerial Council. The details of the fifth, and most important, of these were kept very secret. The others were soon evident, or were communicated to Paléologue and Buchanan at once, and to Pourtalès a little later.

What were these five decisions?

1. The Tsar's approval of the decision "in principle" for contingent "partial mobilization" against Austria—the decision which had been reached at the Ministerial Council of the preceding afternoon. This was reported to the French Government in Paris, which was able to inform Poincaré on July 26 on his voyage homeward:

> At the Ministerial Council on the 25th, which was held in the presence of the Tsar, the mobilization of thirteen army corps, intended in case of need [*eventuellement*] to operate against Austria was considered; this mobilization, however, would only be effective if Austria were to bring armed pressure to bear on Serbia, and not until notice had been given by the Minister of Foreign Affairs, upon whom falls the duty of fixing the day, liberty being left to him to go on with the negotiations, even if Belgrade should be occupied. Russian opinion makes it clear that it is both

[68] Pourtalès to Bethmann, July 25 (K.D., 205): "From a trustworthy source I hear that in the Ministerial Council here yesterday [July 24] the question of first consideration discussed was whether the present internal condition of Russia is such that the country could face external complications without trouble. The majority of the Ministers present are said to have expressed themselves to the effect that Russia need not hesitate before such complications on account of the internal situation."

politically and morally impossible for Russia to allow Serbia to be crushed.[69]

This decision in favor of partial mobilization, in case of need, to bluff Austria, is confirmed by the testimony of Ianushkevich at the Sukhomlinov trial in 1917: "At first it had been decided to proclaim a partial mobilization— the four districts—to frighten off Austria-Hungary."[70] It was welcome to Sazonov because he hoped it would check Austria, and give a turn to the diplomatic negotiations which would result in a settlement acceptable to Serbia and Russia. It avoided the danger of the "general mobilization," which was desired by the military leaders, but which would probably lead Germany to retaliate with a counter-mobilization, and so bring on a general European war. It would also gain time for diplomatic negotiations, during which wide-reaching measures preparatory to war could be carried on under cover of a secret "Regulation concerning the Period Preparatory to War," to be mentioned a little later.

In 1912, at the height of the Balkan Wars, at a diplomatic crisis with Austria in many respects similar to that of 1914, a secret Russian Military Commission, in annulling for technical reasons the order that "the proclamation of mobilization is equivalent to the declaration of war," had stated significantly:

[69] Bienvenu-Martin's summary to Viviani on board the *France,* July 26; F.Y.B., 50. Paléologue's telegram on which this summary is supposed to be based is suppressed from F.Y.B.; it may have been his telegram of July 26, at 1:55 P. M., which M. Bourgeois, though he had access to the French archives, has published in two variant and evidently garbled forms; Bourgeois et Pagès, pp. 39, 137. *Cf.* also Buchanan to Grey, July 25, 8 P. M.; Sazonov told us "this morning Emperor had sanctioned drafting of Imperial Ukase, which is only to be published when Minister of Foreign Affairs considers moment come for giving effect to it, ordering mobilization of 1,100,000 men. Necessary preliminary preparations for mobilization would, however, be begun at once;" B.D., 125 (but also suppressed from B.B.B.).

[70] As reported in the *Novoe Vremia,* No. 14,852, Aug. 13 [26], 1917.

It will be advantageous to complete concentration without beginning hostilities, in order not to deprive the enemy irrevocably of the hope that war can still be avoided. Our measures for this must be masked by clever diplomatic negotiations, in order to lull to sleep as much as possible the enemy's fears.[71]

Thus, if the announcement of partial mobilization should not after all succeed in checking Austria, it could at least be used conveniently to explain and screen the measures of the "Period Preparatory to War," which it was decided were to take place over the whole empire and which would therefore greatly facilitate the general mobilization against Germany as well as against Austria, if eventually necessary. Sazonov believed that he now had the trump cards in his hand. He could continue to negotiate, and he held in his hand the threat of force to strengthen his bluff; but at the same time military preparations would be going on preparatory to a general mobilization if his bluff of partial mobilization was called. Also the militarists in Russia could not get out of control, because a decision as to mobilization was dependent on the course of the diplomatic negotiations, which were also in his hands. Sazonov was highly delighted with this arrangement. He was also agreeably surprised to find that Austria did not attack Serbia at once after the expiration of the time-limit and the rupture of Austro-Serbian diplomatic relations on this same Saturday afternoon. During the next three days (July 26-28) of "direct conversations" with Vienna, he appeared to be much more conciliatory and optimistic, so much so, in fact, that it was specially remarked by a number of persons.[72] But this optimism was not shared by the Russian

[71] Protocol of the Special Military Commission of Nov. 8 [21], 1912, quoted by Hoeniger, p. 34 f., and by Frantz, p. 236.

[72] By Pourtalès, "I found Sazonov much quieter and more conciliatory today" (July 26, 3:15 P.M.; K.D., 217); by Buchanan, "I found Sazonov this afternoon very conciliatory and more optimistic" (July 27, 8:40

military authorities, and came to a sudden end with the news of the Austrian declaration of war on Serbia on July 28.[73]

2. The second of the decisions taken by the Ministerial Council of July 25 was the recall of the troops to their standing quarters.[74]

At the moment of the Sarajevo murder and during the following weeks, the Russian troops throughout the empire were dispersed in camps for maneuvers and summer training, often at a considerable distance from their regular standing quarters. It was in these standing quarters that was kept the full equipment, which was necessary for war, and which the soldiers must have before they could start for the front. It was necessary therefore that they should be recalled as quickly as possible to the point at which they would be given their full equipment and be ready for transportation to the designated area of concentration on the frontier. This is why the camp at Krasnoe Selo was broken up at the close of the maneuvers on Saturday afternoon, as has already been indicated. Ianushkevich lost no time in putting this decision into operation also for all the rest of the troops in the empire. At 4:10 P.M. he had the General Staff send out secret cipher telegram No. 1547:

P.M.; B.D., 198); by Paléologue, "Sazonov has used conciliatory language to all my colleagues" (July, 27; F.Y.B., 64); and especially by Szápáry, the Austrian Ambassador, as will be indicated later in connection with the "direct conversations" between St. Petersburg and Vienna.

[73] Cf. Dobrorolski, p. 104 (German trans., p. 22 f.); "The unlucky idea of a partial mobilization was not yet dropped. It had its adherents, but not in the military departments. . . . Among the optimists was Sazonov. By this optimism only can one explain the fact that he persistently advocated a partial mobilization, and supported at Peterhof [to the Tsar] confidence in its success. . . . On July 15 [28], the day of the Austro-Hungarian declaration of war on Serbia, Sazonov suddenly abandons his optimism. He becomes filled with the idea that a general war is inevitable, and calls the attention of Ianushkevich to the necessity of not delaying any longer the [general] mobilization of our army."

[74] Dobrorolski, p. 102 (German trans., p. 20); Sukhomlinov, p. 360; K.D., 194, 339; A.R.B., II, 60; Eggeling, p. 25.

St. Petersburg, July 12 [25], 1914, 4:10 P.M.

Prepare quickly transport plans and provisions for the return of all troops to their standing quarters. Time for the completion of the work: twenty-four hours. 1547.

[Signed] General Dobrorolski.[75]

This was followed later the same night by telegram No. 1557:

St. Petersburg, July 12 [25], 1914, 11:59 P.M.

His Majesty commands that upon the arrival of this telegram the troops are to return from their camps to their standing quarters. If their simultaneous return involves difficulties, the Staffs and Administrations of the Corps, Divisions, and independent formations are to have precedence. The troop divisions close to their standing quarters can remain there and do not need to return to their winter barracks. 1557.

[Signed] Bieliaiev.[76]

This breaking off of maneuvers and return of the troops to their standing quarters was not, however, in any way equivalent to mobilization. It was, to be sure, a necessary preliminary to mobilization, but was not in any way a menacing or hostile act.[77] Nevertheless, the execution of the unexpected order which began on Sunday, July 26, involved the movement of more than a million men throughout the empire, and gave rise to military excitement

[75] Telegram to the Chief of Staff of the Warsaw District, captured later by the Germans, and published by Hoeniger, p. 80, and by Frantz, p. 258.

[76] Hoeniger, p. 80; Frantz, p. 259.

[77] Similar orders for the return of troops to their standing quarters were given in France as early as July 27 (K.D., 341, note 3), but in Germany not until July 28 for the nine corps to be "hastily" mobilized, and not until July 29, between 1 and 1:30 P.M., for the greater number of remaining corps (*Investigating Commission*, II, p. 68. Anlage 17, and p. 69, Anlage 20); for the best detailed analysis of the French and German preliminary military measures, based on a study of the French official General Staff History of the War, which show in every case that the French preparations considerably antedated the German, see M. Montgelas, "Das französische Generalstabwerk," in KSF, V, 1206-1220, Dec., 1927.

among Russian officers everywhere similar to that which had prevailed at Krasnoe Selo on the preceding evening. It also naturally led to disturbing reports being sent to Berlin and Vienna from German and Austrian agents in Russia.

3. The promotion of cadets to be officers.[78]

The Russian army lacked in 1914, even on a peace footing, some 3000 younger officers. These were being trained in the St. Petersburg Military Academy and similar schools, but the cadets would normally not be graduated and made officer until later in the year. To fill this deficiency as far as possible at once, it was decided to make the promotion immediately. The cadets of the St. Petersburg Academy were advanced to the rank of officer at Krasnoe Selo just before the banquet on Saturday evening; the Tsar himself made them an address, saying, "Believe in God, as well as in the greatness and glory of our country. Seek to serve Him and Me with all your strength." The promotions in the other military schools followed almost immediately.[79] Also the organizations in which officers were receiving practical training were dissolved so that they should be free to take active command. These measures not only created a large number of much-needed subaltern officers, but also freed for active service in the field many mature officers who had hitherto been detailed on educational work. But in spite of these efforts, one of the most serious defects in the Russian army, as the War was soon to show, was the inadequacy of the officers, both as to quality and quantity.

4. The proclamation of the "state of war" in towns containing fortresses and in the frontier sectors facing Germany and Austria.

---

[78] Dobrorolski, pp. 102, 114; K.D., 194, 291; A.R.B., II, 60, 77; Paléologue to Bienvenu-Martin, July 26; Bourgeois et Pagès, p. 39.

[79] Cf. Paumgartner in Odessa to Berchtold, July 27; "Reserve officers who were to have been let go, have been retained; also school cadets have already been enrolled; in Odessa alone 390. Great excitement among officers;" A.R.B., II, 77.

The order for this was sent out by Gen. Ianushkevich still later this same night, i.e., at 1 A.M. on July 26.[80] That the order was speedily obeyed on the frontier toward Germany is indicated by the proclamation of the Commander of the fortress of Kovno: "In accordance with the command of the Tsar and of General Rennenkampf's order No. 13,482, July 26, I declare the fortress and district of Kovno placed in a 'state of war.' " [81] The purpose of this proclamation was to give the local military commanders full powers, as under martial law, to take all actions necessary to secure the success of mobilization, and to prevent trouble from spies or other hostile-minded persons. It also forbade the newspapers to publish any news in regard to military and naval preparations, such as the movements or provisioning of troops or naval vessels, the recall of officers on leave, military transportation, or the collection of merchant ships in harbors.[82]

One incident which grew out of the order shows the desire for peace and friendly relations between Russia and Germany which was sincerely held by the Tsar and by Pourtalès, the German Ambassador. The *Prinz Eitel Friedrich,* a German merchant ship lying in the harbor near the fortress of Kronstadt, aroused the suspicions of the commander of the fortress, because she had a wireless outfit and was observed to be sending radiograms. As a "state of war" had been proclaimed in the fortress sector and the wireless outfit might be used for espionage purposes, the

---

[80] General Staff tg. no. 1566; printed by Hoeniger, p. 80; and by Frantz, p. 242; *cf.* also Paléologue to Bienvenu-Martin, July 26; Bourgeois et Pagès, pp. 39, 137.

[81] E. Mueller-Meiningen, *Diplomatie und Weltkrieg* (Berlin, 1917), p. 930. Bülow, German consul at Kovno, was able to telegraph from Eydkuhnen in East Prussia on July 27, at 5:35 P.M., presumably having heard the news many hours earlier: "Kovno has been placed in a state of war;" K.D., 264. For similar orders of July 26 for other fortresses, see Frantz, pp. 243-250.

[82] Dobrorolski, pp. 102, 104 (German ed., pp. 21, 23); Hoeniger, pp. 66-67.

На подлинномъ Собственною Его Император-
скаго Величества рукою начертано: „Согласенъ",
въ Красномъ Селѣ, 12 Іюля 1914 года.

Скрѣпилъ: Предсѣдатель Совѣта Министровъ,

Статсъ-Секретарь *Горемыкинъ.*

ОСОБЫЙ ЖУРНАЛЪ СОВѢТА МИНИСТРОВЪ

12 Іюля 1914 года.

О приведеніи въ дѣйствіе Высочайше утвержденнаго, 17 Февраля 1913 года, Положенія о подготовительномъ къ войнѣ періодѣ.

Вашему Императорскому Величеству благо-
угодно было, 12 сего Іюля, Высочайше утвердить
особый журналъ Совѣта Министровъ 11 Іюля 1914 года,
по заявленію Министра Иностранныхъ Дѣлъ о послѣд-
нихъ выступленіяхъ Австро-Венгерскаго Правитель-
ства въ отношеніи Сербіи. Журналомъ этимъ, между
прочимъ, предоставлено Военному и Морскому Мини-
страмъ, по принадлежности, испросить Высочайшее
Вашего Императорскаго Величества соизволеніе
на объявленіе, въ зависимости отъ хода дѣлъ, моби-
лизаціи четырехъ военныхъ округовъ—Кіевскаго,
Одесскаго, Московскаго и Казанскаго, Балтійскаго и
Черноморскаго флотовъ, а также незамедлительно
ускорить пополненіе запасовъ матеріальной части
арміи.

Нынѣ, въ соотвѣтствіи съ современнымъ оборотомъ
дипломатическихъ переговоровъ и въ цѣляхъ приня-

к. 11516.

FACSIMILE OF THE MINUTES OF THE RUSSIAN COUNCIL OF
MINISTERS OF JULY 25, 1914
See note 87

commander of the fortress reported the case to the Grand
Duke Nicholas who commanded the whole Petrograd Military District, including Kronstadt. The Grand Duke at
once ordered the German captain to be arrested, the wireless apparatus to be seized, and the ship forbidden to leave
the harbor. As Germany and Russia were still at peace, this
arbitrary action led Pourtalès to make a vigorous protest
to Neratov at the Foreign Office. As a result, the Tsar, the
same day, sent an autograph letter to the Grand Duke
ordering him to set the captain free and not detain the ship,
and expressing condemnation of the measures taken against
the ship of a friendly state. Sazonov also telephoned in a
friendly way, and apologized for the Grand Duke's action.
Pourtalès then said that he considered the incident closed,
and would say nothing of it to the Government at Berlin.[83]

5. The secret orders for the "Period Preparatory to
War."

Though the decision for contingent partial mobilization
may have been regarded by Sazonov and the Tsar seriously,
as a satisfactory military measure in case of need, it was
by no means so regarded by the militarists and the General
Staff. Besides the technical and political difficulties and
the total lack of perfected plans, what would Russia's ally
think of such a measure? In the negotiations for the
Franco-Russian alliance in 1892, General Obruchev, the
Russian Chief of Staff at the time, had energetically denied
the possibility of a partial mobilization against Austria;
Russia must and would order general mobilization, even in
case of a war with Austria alone.[84] And General Vannovski,
the Minister of War, had likewise declared to General

[83] There is therefore nothing about it in the *Kautsky Documents*,
but the details are given by Dobrorolski, and by Pourtalès, *Am Scheideweg*,
p. 34.

[84] "En ce qui concerne la Russie, il lui est absolument impossible,
en cas de guerre avec l'Autriche, de faire une mobilisation partielle. Il
leur faut faire et ils feront une mobilisation générale;" Aug. 10, 1892;
Livre Jaune: L'Alliance Franco-Russe, p. 68.

Boisdeffre, the French Chief of Staff: "You tell me in this case [of an attack by Austria alone] to make a partial mobilization, but this is absolutely impossible for us, because the troops which we shall assemble in Poland come from all the points of the Empire and are mixed together. Beside this being impossible, in making a partial mobilization, we should expose ourselves to too great dangers with the menace of a rapid attack from Germany." [85]   This point of view was as true in 1914 as in 1892.

For all these reasons the Russian General Staff regarded this partial mobilization project as the height of folly; nevertheless, since the Ministerial Council and the Tsar had decided in favor of it, they hurriedly began to work out plans for it, secretly hoping, however, that it would never be carried out.[86]   But at the same time, as a measure of far greater importance and safety, they persuaded the Tsar to approve the putting into operation of the wide-reaching measures preparatory to general mobilization comprised in the very secret "Regulation Concerning the Period Preparatory to War." [87]   The Regulation was to become effective

[85] *Livre Jaune: L'Alliance Franco-Russe*, p. 73.

[86] Dobrorolski, p. 102 f. (German trans. p. 21).

[87] For the facsimile of the Council's decision, approved by the Tsar on July 25, the writer is indebted to the courtesy of the Hoover War Library. This reads: Copy
                                                                    Confidential

On the original is written in His Imperial Majesty's own hand: "Agreed to," at Krasnoe Selo, July 12 [25], 1914.

Countersigned: President of the Council of Ministers,
                            Secretary of State Goremykin.

Special Journal of the Council of Ministers, July 12 [25], 1914.

Concerning the bringing into effect of the Regulations Concerning the Period Preparatory to War, sanctioned by His Majesty on February 17 [March 2], 1913.   [The first paragraph mentions the Tsar's approval of the recommendation of the Council of July 24 for partial mobilization, already published by Mr. Robert C. Binkley from the same volume in the Hoover War Library, and summarized above at note 44].

Today, in accordance with the present trend of the diplomatic negotiations and with the aim of taking measures necessary in all departments for preparing and guaranteeing the success of the mobilization of the Army, Navy, and Fortresses, and the concentration of the armies at

on July 26, and Ianushkevich lost no time in putting it into force, as is seen from two secret cipher telegrams, numbers 1566 and 1575, which he sent out from the General Staff before dawn on Sunday morning, July 26, to the commanders of the troops in the Warsaw Military District:

St. Petersburg, July 13 [26], 1 A.M.

His Majesty commands all the fortresses of the District to be placed in a state of war. It is ordered to begin with the works which are indicated in Lists 1 and 2 attached to the Regulation Concerning the Period Preparatory to War, approved by His Majesty on February 17 [March 2], 1913. 1566.

[Signed] Lieut.-Gen. Ianushkevich.[88]

St. Petersburg, July 13 [26], 3:26 A.M.

His Majesty commands that July 13 [26] is to be reckoned as the beginning of the Period Preparatory to War in the whole territory of European Russia. You are to take, in accordance with Lists 1 and 2 of the Regulation Concerning the Period Preparatory to War, all the measures which are to be carried out under the direction of the District Staffs, Provisioning Boards, Corps Commanders, Fortress Commanders, Troop Divisions, and Administrative Bureaus. The Regulation was sent on March 22 [April 4], 1913 under No. 813. 1575.

[Signed] Lieut.-Gen. Ianushkevich.[89]

the frontiers of our possible enemies, the Council of Ministers declares that the time has come for bringing into effect, beginning with July 13 [26] in all lands of the Empire the Regulations Concerning the Period Preparatory to War, for both lists; and authorizes moreover the Minister of War to request the supreme consent of Your Imperial Majesty for the taking by the War Department of these and other measures not provided for in the aforesaid lists, which he shall duly consider necessary according to circumstances, and which shall be reported to the Council of Ministers. . . .

[88] Captured Russian telegram, printed by Hoeniger, p. 80; and by Frantz, p. 243; for the execution of the order concerning the fortresses, see above, at notes 80-81.

[89] Hoeniger, p. 81; Frantz, p. 243. It is to be noted that this telegram shows that the "preparatory measures" were to be carried out "in the whole territory of European Russia." This proves the incorrectness of

What is the significance of this cryptic "Period Preparatory to War" with its "Lists 1 and 2"?

One of Russia's greatest handicaps to the successful beginning of war had been the relative slowness of mobilization. Owing to her vast areas, inadequate railway systems,
and somewhat inefficient local military authorities, the Russian mobilization machine had not been able in the past to
work with anything like the speed of the German, or even
the Austrian, military machine. To remedy this defect as
far as possible had been the aim of one of Sukhomlinov's
reforms. It had been discussed as early as the spring of
1912, and was finally solved at a secret conference in February, 1913, sitting under the presidency of General Lukomski, and containing representatives of the Navy and
Interior Departments as well as of the War Department.
This conference drafted, and the Tsar approved on March 2,
1913, a very secret "Regulation Concerning the Period
Preparatory to War." [90]

According to this Regulation,

"Period Preparatory to War" means the period of diplomatic complications preceding the opening of hostilities, in
the course of which all Boards must take the necessary

the commonly made assertion (e.g. by Recouly, p. 157, and by Paléologue,
I, 28) that measures preparatory to war were ordered only in the Military Districts of Kiev, Odessa, Kazan and Moscow.

[90] Dobrorolski, p. 102 f. (German trans. p. 21 f.); Sukhomlinov, p.
343 f., Hoeniger, 8-12, 17-20; Frantz, pp. 22-24. Dobrorolski speaks of this
as the "Pre-mobilization Period" (*Predmobilizatsennoe Period*), but the
official journal given in facsimile above and the captured Russian telegrams regularly speak of it as the "Period Preparatory to War." Ordered
before dawn on July 26 for the whole Russian Empire, it may very
roughly be compared with the Austrian "Alarmierungstag" (ordered on
the night of July 25-26, for five of the eight corps which were to operate
against Serbia and for two others—one on the Rumanian front and one
for the protection of the Danube bridges; *Investig. Comm.*, II, pp. 19, 83;
Conrad, IV, 122); with the French *"alerte"* (ordered July 30; Poincaré, *Les Origines de la Guerre*, p. 255; Recouly, p. 76; Montgelas, in
KSF, V, p. 1214, Dec., 1927); and with the German *"Drohender Kriegsgefahrzustand"* (ordered *ca.* 1 P. M., July 31; K.D., 479, 499).

measures of preparation for security and success at the mobilization of the Army, the Fleet, and the Fortresses, as well as for the march of the Army to the threatened frontier.[91]

These preparatory measures are grouped under two headings, known as "List 1" and "List 2." Under "List 1" are the measures which are to be taken at once, upon the order of the Minister of War, as soon as the Tsar has approved the recommendation of the Ministerial Council in favor of putting into effect the Regulation Concerning the Period Preparatory to War. The expenditures incurred are to be paid for out of the ordinary funds assigned to the local Boards. According to "List 1," in the districts on Russia's Western frontier, it is decreed:

> Upon the order of the Minister of War [not upon that of the Tsar] the reservists and the territorial reserve are to be called up for reserve exercises in such a way that the reservists may be assigned as far as possible according to the existing mobilization plan among the frontier troop divisions. Out of the territorial reserve will be formed troops for securing the frontiers, the lines of communication, the telegraph system, and other objects of military importance. The expenditures incurred are to be labelled in the accounts under the head of funds granted for reservist training and for "trial mobilization." [92]

[91] Quoted by Hoeniger, p. 17; and by Frantz, p. 189.

[92] Hoeniger, p. 19; Frantz, p. 195. The Belgian Minister in St. Petersburg reported on March 27, 1914, that the Duma committee on national defense had approved almost without exception the credits demanded, and that the extraordinary credits for military purposes would amount to the enormous sum of 450 million rubles (*Investig. Comm.*, II, pp. 98-99). On these "trial mobilizations," which often took place in time of peace for local areas, see Hoeniger, pp. 58-66; and Dobrorolski, p. 114: "Beside these 'control mobilizations' or *'povyerochnie mobilizatsii'*, there existed another form of mobilization practice—'trial mobilization' [*opitnia mobilizatsia*], including the calling up of reservists and the furnishing of horses by the population. Sufficient money was granted for these, and this practice had a double advantage: They were instructive both for the troops and the reservists, as well as for the local

Detailed regulations under "List 1" also explained that the frontier posts are to be made ready for mobilization, are to be completely armed for the campaign in the field, and are to guard the frontier. All orders for mobilization, for advance to the concentration area, and for protecting this advance are to be carefully examined. The troops are to be instructed as to the uniforms and probable dispositions of the enemy. Horses are to be reshod. No more furloughs are to be granted, and officers and men on furlough or detailed elsewhere are to return at once to their troop divisions. Espionage suspects are to be arrested. Measures to prevent the export of horses, cattle, and grain are to be worked out. Money and valuable securities are to be removed from banks near the frontier to the interior. Naval vessels are to return to their harbors and receive provisions and full war equipment.[93]

"List 2" represents a still further stage in preparatory measures. According to it, upon the order of the Minister of War, "the calling up of reservists and the territorial reserve takes place to an extent which exceeds the funds of the current year fixed for training and trial mobilization. It also includes in the frontier districts the buying of horses and wagons for the baggage trains, and the transport of baggage to its destination. Officers' families receive free transportation from the frontier to places of safety in the interior. Freight cars having the standard gauge of European railways (4 ft. 8½ in. instead of the Russian 5 ft. gauge) are no longer to be allowed to leave Russia. The harbors are to be closed by the setting of mines, and Rus-

authorities charged with the registration and the calling up of the reservists and horses. Just two months before the actual mobilization [in July, 1914], a trial mobilization of this kind took place in the Odessa Military District, for the 34th Artillery Brigade at Ekaterinoslav. Experience showed that one need not worry about the mobilization of our field troops."

[93] Frantz, pp. 190-198.

sian merchant ships destined for military or naval uses are to be detained in port.[94]

One important elastic clause in the Regulation also provided: "The Ministerial Council will further decide the question whether still other measures in addition to those set forth in the 'Lists' are to be carried out during the Period Preparatory to War." [95]

Thus, under cover of "trial mobilizations" and the "Period Preparatory to War," military measures could be ordered by the Minister of War, which did not require the approval of the Tsar or a public announcement of mobilization, but which nevertheless were almost equivalent to mobilization in the frontier districts. Such a "trial mobilization" had been undertaken on a wide scale in the fall of 1912 close to the German frontier, and had called forth a strong protest from the German Chief of Staff, Moltke—a protest which Sazonov, at that time, appeared to admit was well founded.[96]

Highly significant is Dobrorolski's own admission that the militarists and the General Staff, at least, on July 25, already regarded war as a settled matter; and also that the local authorities on the frontier, in their zeal or nervousness, may have even gone further than the Regulation properly permitted. This is what he says:

> The following days [after Sazonov had been informed of the Austrian ultimatum] are well known to everybody through the "colored books" and documents published by the European Governments. The war was already a settled matter ["*Voina byla uzhe predrieshena*"], and the whole flood of telegrams between the Governments of Russia and

[94] Frantz, pp. 190-192, 198-200. *Cf.* Pourtalès to Bethmann, July 27, 7:17 P.M. (K.D., 274): "Swedish consul at Riga reports mouth of the Düna closed by mines. In Riga all the freight cars have been unloaded and placed at the service of the military administration."
. [95] Frantz, p. 190.
[96] G.P., XXXIII, 128-9 in footnote, 316 f.; 407 f.; Hoeniger, p. 25; *Deutschland Schuldig?*, pp. 141-142.

Germany represented merely the stage setting [*mise en scène*] of a historical drama.

The postponement of the final moment of decision was, to be sure, very useful for the preparatory measures, but it augmented the tension on both sides of the frontier.

The establishment of the Pre-Mobilization Period, as it had been defined, did not give authority to undertake measures having the character of mobilization; but it was evident that in the frontier zones, where the population and the officials were nervous, it was possible that they would allow themselves to be drawn into taking measures which went beyond instructions, in order to insure the safety of mobilization.

Especially was this naturally the case on the German frontier, where there was the danger that the requisitioning of horses and the calling up of the reservists would be exploited by an enterprising neighbor.

In the Suwalki Government [near East Prussia] there were actually cases where horses were prematurely brought together at the concentration points, which gave the German Ambassador at St. Petersburg, Count Pourtalès, occasion to address protests to our Government, and especially to the Minister of War, through the Military Attaché. Sukhomlinov denied in the most categorical manner that any mobilization measures had been taken on our side; but one cannot guarantee that not a single frontier military commander would not take such measures on his own initiative, when the Pre-mobilization Period was once decreed. Frontier incidents are indeed always possible, and all the more so at such a moment.[97]

There was thus the danger that the Russian military authorities would take such wide-reaching "preparatory measures" that Germany would become alarmed and resort to counter-measures, which in turn would lead to a general European war. The German Foreign Office in fact received, as the *Kautsky Documents* show, between the morning of

[97] Dobrorolski, p. 103 (German trans. p. 21 f.).

July 26 and the evening of July 30 twenty-eight reports of Russian military preparations, no less than sixteen of which related to the Russian frontier against Germany; and the German General Staff and Navy Department received many more such reports.[98] But in spite of this, Germany refrained from corresponding preparatory measures (*Drohender Kriegsgefahrzustand*) until she received on July 31 official news that Russia had taken the final military step of openly announcing by placards throughout the streets of St. Petersburg a general mobilization of the whole Russian army and navy. These secret "preparatory measures," which had been decided on at the Ministerial Council on the afternoon of the 25th, and ordered before dawn of the 26th, enabled Russia, when war came, to surprise the world by the rapidity with which she poured her troops into East Prussia and Galicia.

DIPLOMATIC NEGOTIATIONS AND MILITARY PREPARATIONS

Though the military authorities had objected very strenuously to "partial mobilization," to be undertaken only "in the four southern districts toward Austria," they found it a very convenient form of camouflage by which to attempt to mislead the Germans as to the secret "preparatory measures," which General Ianushkevich had ordered "in the whole territory of European Russia" on July 26 at

[98] *Cf.* especially K.D., 216, 230, 242, 255, 264, 274-276, 291, 294, 296, 310a, 327, 330, 331, 333, 335a, 338, 339, 343, 344, 348, 349, 365, 365a, 370, 372, 375a, 390, 401, 410, 412, 422, 429, 431a, 445; *Investig. Comm.*, II, p. 28 f., and note 8; Eggeling, *Die Russische Mobilmachung*, pp. 25-28; and compare also Bogitchevitch, p. 83: "On July 28, in company with several Serbian officers, I arrived at Warsaw [from Berlin]. As far as the German frontier, not the slightest indications were seen of military measures. But immediately after crossing the German frontier [into Russian Poland], we noticed mobilization steps being taken on a grand scale (assembly of freight cars in the several stations, military occupation of the railway stations, massing of troops in the several cities, transport of troops at night, mobilization signalling). When we arrived at Brest-Litovsk, July 28, the state of siege had already been proclaimed."

3:26 A.M.,[99] and which were taking place while Sazonov was carrying on his diplomatic negotiations. This does not necessarily imply, as many Germans believe,[100] that "partial mobilization" was deliberately and primarily agreed upon as a ruse to deceive the Germans or that Sazonov's diplomatic negotiations for a peaceful solution were pure hypocrisy, "war being already a settled matter," as Dobrorolski says. There seems little doubt, as indicated above, that the partial mobilization plan was seriously regarded by Sazonov and the Tsar, if not by the General Staff, as a good means of checking Austria without provoking Germany. And if it provoked Germany, Russia would wait for Germany to declare war or attack first, and thus be branded before the world as the aggressor.[101]   There seems equally little doubt that between July 26 and 28 Sazonov honestly carried on diplomatic negotiations with the optimistic hope, not shared by the Russian military authorities, of securing a peaceful solution satisfactory to Russia.[102]   Pourtalès, however, like Buchanan,[103] had become very apprehensive as to the danger of even a partial mobilization against Austria.   He was clear-minded enough to realize that it would be an exceedingly dangerous means of exerting diplomatic pressure.   If Russia should attempt a bluff of this kind, he feared that the militarists everywhere would gain an increased influence, and soon take the question beyond

[99] See above, at note 89.

[100] Hoeniger, 44-54; Eggeling's comment on the German edition of Dobrorolski, pp. 39-48; and Frantz, in *Current History*, March, 1927, p. 855.

[101] *Cf.* Sukhomlinov's statement to Paléologue: "The Minister of War has repeated his wish to leave to Germany the eventual initiative of the attack," Paléologue to Bienvenu-Martin, July 26; Bourgeois et Pagès, p. 39.

[102] It is noteworthy that Pourtalès has always maintained this view of Sazonov's honesty of purpose; see his comment on the German edition of Dobrorolski, p. 38.

[103] For Buchanan's apprehensions, see his despatches to Grey on July 24, 25 and 27 (B.D., 101, 125, 170); and *My Mission to Russia*, I, 192 ff.

the control of the diplomatists, by the purely technical and strategic arguments which they knew so well how to urge.[104] He had also received from Bethmann-Hollweg the following telegram:

> After Count Berchtold has declared to Russia that Austria does not aim at any territorial acquisitions in Serbia, but only wishes to secure repose, the maintenance of the peace of Europe depends on Russia alone. We trust in Russia's love of peace and in our traditional friendly relations with her, that she will take no step which would seriously endanger the peace of Europe.[105]

Accordingly, on Sunday evening, July 26, having heard many rumors of Russian preparatory mobilization measures, Pourtalès deemed it wise to give Sazonov a friendly but firm warning, "concerning the news current among the foreign Military Attachés, according to which it is supposed that mobilization orders have been issued to several Russian Army Corps on the Western Frontier." He "called his attention to the great danger of such measures, which might easily call forth counter-measures." Sazonov "replied that he could guarantee that no mobilization order of the sort had been issued; that, on the contrary, in the Ministerial Council it had been decided to delay with any such order until Austria-Hungary adopted a hostile attitude toward Russia. M. Sazonov admitted that there had already been taken 'certain military measures in order not to be taken by surprise.' " [106]

Sazonov evidently felt that he had been rather vague in his assurance that the mobilization order "would be de-

---

[104] Pourtalès, *Am Scheideweg*, pp. 24-26.

[105] Bethmann to Pourtalès, July 26, 1:35 P.M.; K.D., 198.

[106] Pourtalès to Bethmann, July 26, 9:30 P.M., K.D., 230; *cf.* also A.R.B., II, 61. The German General Staff, though doubting the sincerity of these assurances, telegraphed to the German Military Attaché in St. Petersburg that no military measures were contemplated by Germany, but he was to observe and report the Russian measures; K.D., 267a.

layed until Austria-Hungary adopted a hostile attitude toward Russia." Did he mean partial or general mobilization? Did "hostile attitude toward Russia" mean an Austrian invasion of Serbia, or an Austrian mobilization in Galicia facing against Russia? He must have realized that his admission about "certain military measures in order not to be taken by surprise" was hardly calculated to have a very reassuring effect upon the German Ambassador. He may also well have had a somewhat uneasy conscience in view of what we know about the wide-reaching measures of the "Period Preparatory to War" which were already in full swing on the western frontier toward Germany as well as toward Austria. He therefore decided it would be well to have a more definite statement made, and telephoned to the Minister of War. He asked Sukhomlinov to make it plain to the German Military Attaché, as one military man speaking to another, that nothing was contemplated except measures preparatory to a contingent partial mobilization against Austria. Accordingly, late on Sunday evening, Eggeling was invited to an interview with Sukhomlinov, which Eggeling thus reports, with his own shrewd conclusions:

> Sazonov requested him to enlighten me on the military situation. The Minister of War gave me his word of honor that no sort of mobilization order had yet been issued. For the present merely preparatory measures were being taken. Not a horse had been recruited, not a reservist called in. If Austria crossed the Serbian frontier, such Military Districts as are directed against Austria, *viz.* Kiev, Odessa, Moscow, Kazan, would be mobilized. Under no circumstances those on the German front, Warsaw, Vilna, St. Petersburg. Peace with Germany, he said, was earnestly desired.
>
> Upon my inquiry as to the object of the mobilization against Austria, he shrugged his shoulders and indicated the

diplomats. . . . I got the impression of great nervousness and anxiety. I consider the wish for peace genuine; military statements in so far correct, that complete mobilization has probably not been ordered, but preparatory measures are very far-reaching. They are evidently striving to gain time for new negotiations and for continuing their armaments. Also the internal situation is unmistakably causing serious anxiety. The general feeling is: hope from Germany and for the mediation of His Majesty [the Kaiser].[107]

Pourtalès also communicated these dubious assurances of Sazonov and Sukhomlinov to his Austrian colleague. Szápáry reported them in turn to Vienna, with conclusions which well sum up the situation:

Although the direct informing of the German Military Attaché [by Sukhomlinov] indicates nervousness on Sazonov's part, and although mobilization against Austria only in case the Serbian frontier is crossed appears rather to reveal the purpose of exerting diplomatic pressure, it must not be left out of account that, in addition to the lack of veracity in the assurances here, there is a lack of harmony between the doings of the diplomats and the militarists, as well as the importance of gaining time for Russian mobilization.

The character of the military preparations now in progress seems specially suited to the mentality of the Tsar, Nicholas, since, though avoiding regular war measures, which to him particularly are repugnant, a certain preparedness is nevertheless arrived at.[108]

SUMMARY OF THE RUSSIAN DANGER

The Russian danger lay in the fact that Sazonov natu rally felt bound to protect Serbia, whose hopes and aspirations Russia had encouraged in the past, and whom she

107 Eggeling's report, sent by Pourtalès to Bethmann, July 27, 1 A.M.; K.D., 242.

108 Szápáry to Berchtold, July 26 (telegraphed July 27, 4:30 A. M.); A.R.B., II, 61.

could not abandon now without loss of prestige to herself
and the Triple Entente. Still more, he was determined to
prevent Austria from gobbling up Serbian territory and upsetting the *status quo* in the Balkans. He had jumped to
the conclusion that this was the meaning of the Austrian
ultimatum, and that an Austrian invasion of Serbia was
likely to begin immediately upon the expiration of the
48-hour time-limit. He was strongly encouraged by the
French Ambassador to stand firm in protecting Serbia and
in checking Austria. Therefore on July 24, even before
hearing the German Ambassador's justification of Austria
and plea for "localization," Sazonov had decided to take the
side of Serbia, if necessary, even if it should involve war.
He adopted the plan of "partial mobilization," which was
a dangerous method of exerting diplomatic pressure. At
the luncheon conference with Paléologue and Buchanan,
"he personally thought that Russia would have to mobilize." To be sure, he desired to avert war, and he made
several proposals which he hoped might avert it. He
begged Buchanan for an English declaration of Entente
solidarity, which Buchanan did not feel able to give. And
he proposed to extend the time-limit and give the European
Powers an opportunity to pass upon the Austro-Serbian
question, a proposal which was met evasively at Berlin and
negatively at Vienna.

Then, on July 25, even before Austria had broken off
diplomatic relations with Serbia, Sazonov and the Tsar
conceded to the Russian militarists the putting into effect
of various military measures, including those of the "Period
Preparatory to War," which roused anticipations of war
among the Russian officers, and gave an impression, as
Dobrorolski puts it, that "war was already a settled matter." Henceforth the army leaders, recognizing that partial mobilization was folly on account of the technical and
political difficulties involved in it, exerted steadily increas-

ing pressure for general mobilization; and the danger was that Sazonov would accept their views, and add the weight of his pressure to that of the General Staff in persuading the Tsar to consent to the final military step which would probably make a general war inevitable. Even on Saturday evening, July 25, Sazonov himself, in spite of his hopes to the contrary, seems to have thought war likely, and to have been ready to resort to it if his partial mobilization bluff did not work. Meeting again with Paléologue and Buchanan, he told them of his partial mobilization plan, and again received active encouragement from Paléologue, as we now know from the interesting parts of Buchanan's dispatch which were suppressed or altered when published in 1914:

> French Ambassador said he had received a number of telegrams from the Minister in charge of the Ministry of Foreign Affairs, that no one of them displayed the slightest sign of hesitation, and that he was in a position to give his Excellency [Sazonov] formal assurance that France placed herself unreservedly on Russia's side.
>
> [After thanking Paléologue, Sazonov turned to the British Ambassador with the question, "And your Government?" Buchanan replied that Sir Edward Grey did not yet despair of the situation, and that the great thing was to gain time. He repeated that] England could play the rôle of mediator at Berlin and Vienna to better purpose as a friend who, if her counsels of moderation were disregarded, might one day be converted into an ally, than if she were to declare herself Russia's ally at once. Sazonov said that unfortunately Germany was convinced that she could count upon our [British] neutrality. . . . He did not believe that Germany really wanted war, but her attitude was decided by ours. If we took our stand firmly with France and Russia there would be no war. If we failed them now, rivers of blood would flow and we would in the end be dragged into war

French Ambassador remarked that French Government would want to know at once whether our fleet was prepared to play part assigned to it by Anglo-French Naval Convention. He could not believe that England would not stand by her two friends, who were acting as one in this matter.

[Buchanan urged prudence on Sazonov and warned him, if Russia mobilized, Germany would not be content with mere mobilization, or give Russia time to carry out hers, but would probably declare war at once. Sazonov repeated that] he did not wish to precipitate a conflict, but unless Germany can restrain Austria, I can regard the situation as desperate. Russia cannot allow Austria to crush Serbia and become predominant Power in Balkans, and, secure of support of France, she will face all the risks of war.[109]

At the close of this meeting between the representatives of the Triple Entente, Sazonov threatened England with a point on which Sir Edward Grey and his advisers were very sensitive. "For ourselves," Buchanan reported, "the position is a most perilous one, and we shall have to choose between giving Russia our active support, or renouncing her friendship. If we fail her now, we cannot hope to maintain that friendly coöperation with her in Asia, that is of such vital importance to us." [110]

Sazonov's fears as to Austrian intentions were partly owing to Szápáry's failure to make at once the declaration

[109] Buchanan to Grey, July 25, 8:00 P.M.; B.D., 125; cf. B.B.B., 17, where much is suppressed, and where the paraphrase of the last sentence altered materially the meaning by adding the words, "if she feels," so that it read, "if she feels secure of the support of France, she [Russia] will face all the risks of war." Whether Paléologue actually received "a number of telegrams," as he asserted, does not appear from F.Y.B.; but his remarks here and elsewhere, and his inquiry about the British fleet, leave no doubt that Sazonov felt "secure of the support of France." Until the French documents are published in full, we shall not know how much this feeling was the result of Poincaré's assurances during his visit, how much it may be that Paléologue went beyond his instructions in encouraging Russia and failed to keep his own government sufficiently informed, and how much Sazonov exaggerated the nature of Paléologue's assurances.   [110] B.D., 125.

—which had been promised to Tisza should be made [111]—
that Austria intended no territorial gains at Serbia's expense.[112] It was not until after he had been assured of
Austria's territorial disinterestedness by Pourtalès and
later by Szápáry,[113] and until after he had been agreeably
surprised to find that the expiration of the time-limit was
not immediately followed by an Austrian attack on Serbia,
that Sazonov was visibly eased in his mind and became
again somewhat optimistic. Thereupon, from July 26 to
28, he carried on conciliatory diplomatic negotiations, while
at the same time the Russian military authorities were
secretly making wide-reaching military preparations which
would facilitate an eventual "general," as well as a "partial," mobilization. Rumors of these preparations began
to cause alarm in Germany. This situation continued until
the news of Austria's declaration of war on Serbia on July
28 put an abrupt end to Sazonov's optimism and gave a new
and fatal turn to the Russian danger. But before discussing this, we must consider the Serbian reply to the Austrian
ultimatum, and various proposals offered by the Powers
for a peaceful solution of the question.

[111] See above, ch. v, at notes 104-106.
[112] *Cf.* A.R.B., II, 19, 40.
[113] By Pourtalès on the evening of July 24 (K.D., 204; A.R.B., II,
19), and again on July 26 (K.D., 198, 230); and by Szápáry on July 26
(K.D., 238; A.R.B., II, 73).

CHAPTER VII

THE SERBIAN REPLY

THE first reports of the Sarajevo assassination which reached Belgrade caused the gravest consternation among Government officials. Mr. Pashitch, the Prime Minister, went to bed to give undisturbed thought to the problem, and remarked to his first visitor, "It is very bad. It will mean war." [1] Mr. Ljuba Jovanovitch, the Minister of Education, "overwhelmed with grave anxiety," did not doubt for a moment that Austria-Hungary would make this the occasion for war on Serbia.[2] Hartwig, the Russian Minister in Belgrade, is said to have exclaimed, "In Heaven's name! Let us hope that it was not a Serbian." [3]

The Serbian Government at once realized that in view of all the anti-Austrian propaganda in the past and of the fact that the plot had been prepared in Belgrade, the Austrian Government would be likely to hold the Serbian agitation, if not the Serbian Government, responsible, and use

[1] H. F. Armstrong, "Three Days in Belgrade," in (N. Y.) *Foreign Affairs*, V, 267-275, Jan., 1927, gives a very interesting account, largely based on conversation with Serbian officials, of the presentation of the Austrian ultimatum and the composition of the Serbian reply, July 23-25.

[2] See above, ch. ii, at note 14.

[3] Gooss, p. 72; K.D., 10. He did not, however, cancel a quiet bridge-party which he had arranged for that same evening, and later, during the requiem mass for the murdered couple, it was charged that he did not follow the example of the other Legations in placing his flag at half-mast. He claimed on the other hand that he had done so, and that the flag had unfortunately become twisted about so that it did not show plainly. It was after a discussion with the Austrian Minister, Giesl, on this point that he suddenly fell dead from a heart attack in the Austrian Legation on July 11—an incident that gave rise to a wild unfounded rumor that he had been poisoned. *Cf.* Baron Wladimir Giesl, *Zwei Jahrzehnte im nahen Orient*, Berlin, 1927; and B.D., 48, 62.

it as a pretext for war. The Serbian Government therefore sought to preserve as correct an attitude as possible. It cancelled the festivities which were celebrating Vidov Dan, published in the official paper a severe condemnation of the crime, expressed proper condolences, and declared its readiness to hand over to justice any subjects who might be shown to have been guilty of complicity. It did not, however, take any proper steps to make an inquiry of its own as to the origins of the plot in Belgrade; on the contrary Dr. Grouitch, the Secretary General of the Serbian Foreign Office, told the Austrian Chargé d'Affaires on July 1 "that up to the present nothing had been done, and that the matter did not concern the Serbian Government." [4] It waited to see how much Austria would be able to discover and what accusations she would bring forward.

Nor did the Serbian Government take any effective steps to curb the violent attacks on Austria in the Belgrade Press, whose comments on the Sarajevo assassination, according to the British Ambassador in Vienna, contained "expressions amounting almost to condonation and even approval of the dastardly outrage." [5] Pashitch took the attitude that he was unable to prevent these provocative polemics, seeing that the Serbian Constitution guaranteed complete freedom of the press and prohibited all censorship or seizure of newspapers.[6] The Serbian attacks, to be sure, were in part provoked by the equally bitter and insulting attacks of the Austro-Hungarian Press, which now took special pains to reprint selections from the more outrageous Serbian newspaper articles, with the aim of circulating them in Europe and turning public opinion against the Belgrade

[4] Griesinger to Bethmann, June 30, July 2; K.D., 10, 12; and Crackanthorpe to Grey, July 2; B.D., 27.

[5] Bunsen to Grey, July 4; B.D., 34. Even the Serbian Minister in Vienna found it necessary to warn his Government to moderate the tone of the Press (Jovan Jovanovitch to Pashitch, June 30, July 1; S.B.B., 2, 9).

[6] Pashitch to the Serbian Legations abroad, July 14, 19; S.B.B., 20, 30.

Government. There thus developed during the three weeks after the Archduke's murder an intensely bitter press campaign of vilification between Austria and Serbia, which whipped up the war spirit among the masses on both sides of the frontier. It was the psychological preparation for war.[7]

The propaganda of the Austrian newspapers, which enjoyed a wider circulation, was on the whole much more successful at first than that of Serbia in influencing public opinion in Europe, especially in England. On July 16 the London *Times* denounced "the reckless and provocative language which a good many Serbian newspapers are alleged to have used, both before and after the crime that has shocked Europe." It issued the warning that "Serbia ought herself, and of her own motion, to make the inquiry, which she has reason to suppose that Austria-Hungary will call upon her to make, and lay the full report of the proceedings before the Powers." Next day the influential *Westminster Gazette* justified Austria's desire to clarify her relations with Serbia, after a crime believed to have its origins in Belgrade and to be part of a deliberate attempt to tear away the Serb provinces of the Dual Monarchy; Austria "cannot be expected to remain inactive; and Serbia will be well advised if she realizes the reasonableness of her great neighbor's anxiety, and does whatever may be in her power to allay it, without waiting for a pressure which might involve what Count Tisza calls 'warlike complications.'" This attitude on the part of powerful English papers gave great encouragement to Austrian hopes that England would remain inactive toward a "localized" Austro-Serbian conflict. But they caused a correspondingly

[7] *Cf.* B.D., 29, 34, 35, 46, 55, 64, 70, 81; S.B.B., *passim;* Appendix ix of the Austrian *dossier* (A.R.B., II, 48), giving choice extracts culled from the Serbian Press; H. Kanner, *Kaiserliche Katastrophenpolitik* (Vienna, 1922), pp. 309-327; and J. F. Scott, *Five Weeks: the Surge of Public Opinion on the Eve of the Great War* (N. Y., 1927), pp. 20-98.

great uneasiness and nervousness on the part of Serbia; and were made the subject of some diplomatic protest and many comments.[8]

Pashitch finally became seriously alarmed at the attitude of the Austrian, German and British Press, at the ominous silence of Vienna, and perhaps also at the news of Berchtold's intentions which had leaked out through Count Lützow to the British authorities on July 16.[9] This news had been at once passed on to the British resident in Belgrade,[10] and may have been hinted to the Serbian Minister in London, who telegraphed to Pashitch on July 17: "The Austrian Embassy is making great efforts to win over the English Press against us, and to induce it to favor the idea that Austria must give a good lesson to Serbia. . . . No reliance should be placed in the ostensibly peaceable statements of Austro-Hungarian official circles, as the way is being prepared for diplomatic pressure upon Serbia, which may develop into an armed attack." [11]

The despatches from the Serbian Minister in Vienna were also alarming, as to the incitement of public opinion by the Austrian Press Bureau and the secret steps which were probably being taken. "Austria has to choose between two courses: either to make the Sarajevo outrage a domestic question, inviting us to assist her to discover and punish the culprits; or to make it a case against the Serbians and Serbia, and even against the Jugoslavs. After taking into consideration all that is being prepared and done, it appears

---

[8] *Cf.* B.D., 58, 61, 73, 80, 125, 153, 156; K.D., 55, 92. Shortly after the *Times* article of July 16, Mr. Wickham Steed used his great influence to swing the *Times* around to an anti-Austrian and anti-German attitude (*cf.* Steed, *Through Thirty Years*, I, 402-412), but the greater part of the English Liberal Press remained sympathetic to Austria and severe on Serbia, until after Austria declared war on Serbia (*cf.* J. F. Scott, pp. 206-246; and Irene Cooper Willis, *England's Holy War*, N. Y., 1928, Part I.

[9] See above, ch. v, at note 95.

[10] B.D., 50, "Repeated to Belgrade."

[11] Boshkovitch to Pashitch, July 17; S.B.B., 27.

to me that Austria will choose the latter course. Austria-Hungary will do this in the belief that she will have the approval of Europe . . . and that she will thus raise her prestige internally as well as externally." [12] All this appears to have made the Belgrade Cabinet nervous as to the wisdom of their passive waiting policy and their neglect to search for and arrest accomplices in Serbia.

On July 18, when the British Chargé d'Affaires at Belgrade alluded to the *Times* article that the wisest course for Serbia would be to undertake herself an enquiry into the conspiracy on Serbian soil, Dr. Grouitch of the Serbian Foreign Office replied that, when the Sarajevo investigation was completed, Serbia would be ready to comply with any requests, compatible with international usage, for a further investigation. But until then she could not act. He then tried to deceive the British as to the Serbian Government's knowledge of the assassins. "Of Princip the Serbian Government knew nothing," he said,[13] a statement manifestly untrue in view of the admission of the Serbian Minister of Education that he was personally acquainted with Princip and had twice examined him,[14] and also in view of what has been said above in the chapters on the assassination plot and the responsibility for it. Grouitch added that, "should it come to the worst and Austria declare war, Serbia would not stand alone. Russia would not remain

[12] Jovanovitch to Pashitch, July 15; S.B.B., 25; *cf.* also 15-17 and 22-24.

[13] Crackanthorpe to Grey, July 18; B.D., 80. A few days later the Serbian Minister in London similarly tried to deceive the British as to the other conspirator, Chabrinovitch, repeating the false statement current in Belgrade newspapers, that "the Serbian authorities, considering him [Chabrinovitch] suspect and dangerous, had desired to expel him, but on applying to the Austrian authorities, the latter had protected him and said that he was a harmless and innocent individual" (B.D., 87). For the details as to the extent to which this was false, see A. von Wegerer, "Die angebliche Bürgschaft der k. u. k. Regierung für Chabrinovitch," and "Wie Serbien England täuschte," in KSF, IV, 330-332 (May, 1926), and V, 238-249 (March, 1927).

[14] Ljuba Jovanovitch, *Krv Slovenstva*, p. 10.

quiet, were Serbia wantonly attacked, and Bulgaria would be immobilized by Rumania."

Next day Pashitch sent a long telegram of a similar tenor to the Serbian Ministers abroad, denouncing the activities of the Austrian Press, which, he said, were to blame for such excesses as appeared in the Serbian newspapers. He instructed his diplomatic representatives to impress upon the Governments to which they were accredited Serbia's "desire to maintain friendly relations with Austria-Hungary," and her willingness, if requested, "to subject to trial in our independent courts any accomplices in the outrage who are in Serbia—should such, of course, exist. But," he added, "we can never comply with demands which may be directed against the dignity of Serbia, and which would be inacceptable to any country which respects and maintains its independence." [15] Shortly after this, Pashitch departed from Belgrade on an electioneering campaign caused by the dissolution of the Skupshtina which had been brought about by his conflict with the "Black Hand" over the "priority question." He was therefore absent from the capital at the moment that the Austrian Minister, Baron Giesl, presented the Austrian ultimatum on the afternoon of July 23.

FRAMING THE SERBIAN REPLY

Berchtold had taken care that Serbia should not evade giving a reply punctually within the 48 hours required. Neither the absence of Pashitch, nor the possible resignation of his Cabinet, was to be allowed as an excuse for delay, because a resigning Cabinet was to be regarded as responsible for the carrying on of business until a new one

[15] Pashitch to the Serbian Legations abroad, July 19; S.B.B., 30. In London, Boshkovitch, acting on these instructions, was advised that Serbia should "meet the Austrian requests in a conciliatory and moderate spirit" (B.D., 87); in Berlin, the Serbian Chargé d'Affaires begged the German Government to use its influence in reconciling Austria and Serbia, but was told that, in view of Serbia's attitude, it could well understand that Austria might take energetic measures (K.D., 86, 91, 95).

was formed. To make certain that there would be someone to receive the ultimatum when it was presented, and to enable Pashitch to be recalled quickly, Giesl notified the Belgrade Foreign Office on the morning of July 23 that he would have an important communication to make between 4 and 5 o'clock that afternoon. At the appointed hour Dr. Grouitch and the three Cabinet Ministers who happened to have remained in Belgrade met in anxiety at the Foreign Office. They had already dispatched a telephone message to Pashitch and arranged for a special train to hurry him back to the capital. But Giesl did not appear. Instead he sent a secretary, begging to say that he would come instead at 6 o'clock. His delay was caused by an eleventh hour instruction from Vienna. Berchtold, upon further information from Berlin as to Poincaré's movements, wanted to make doubly sure that the French President be well out on the Baltic before the news of the ultimatum could reach Russia, and therefore Giesl was to postpone delivery for an hour.[16]

Finally at 6 o'clock Giesl arrived, handed in the Note, and said, "Unless a satisfactory reply is given on all points by 6 o'clock on Saturday, the day after tomorrow, I shall leave Belgrade with all the personnel of my Legation." He was told that it would be difficult to answer so important a communication in so short a time, especially in the absence of several Cabinet Ministers. He replied that in this age of railways, telegraphs and telephones, in a country as small as Serbia, this need be only a matter of a few hours, and that he had already suggested in the morning the desirability of Pashitch's return. Without any further discussion Giesl then departed, leaving the dismayed Ministers to study the Note which still lay unread upon the table.[17]

[16] Berchtold's instructions to Giesl, July 21 and 23; A.R.B., I, 36, 62, 63; see also K.D., 110, 112, 127; and ch. v, notes 75-76.

[17] Giesl to Berchtold, July 23; A.R.B., I, 64, 65, 67; and H. F. Armstrong, op. cit., pp. 268-272.

The Serbian Ministers then began to go through the fateful document. Their emotion grew as its tenor and object became clear. Nobody cared to be the first to speak. At last Ljuba Jovanovitch got up, and said, "Well, there is nothing to do but die fighting." [18] Obviously the first thing to do was to telegraph the news of Giesl's action to the Serbian Ministers in foreign countries, stating that "the demands are such that no Serbian Government could accept them in their entirety." [19] The representatives of the Powers at Belgrade were similarly notified at once. A special appeal for help was instantly dispatched to Russia,[20] reaching Sazonov and Paléologue, as we have seen, very early next morning before they had slept off the fatigue of the Franco-Russian festivities. This was followed by a moving plea from the Prince Regent of Serbia to the Tsar: "We are unable to defend ourselves and beg your Majesty to come to our aid as soon as possible. The much-appreciated goodwill which your Majesty has so often shown toward us inspires us with the firm belief that once again our appeal to your noble Slav heart will not pass unheeded." [21] The King of Italy also was invoked, to use his good offices to induce his Austrian ally to prolong the time-limit and moderate the demands.[22]

Meanwhile the Cabinet Ministers who were away, taking part in the electoral campaign, had been summoned back in all haste to the capital. Pashitch arrived within a few hours at 5 o'clock on Friday morning, July 24. At 10 o'clock the Cabinet began a long and gloomy session, but no decision as to an answer was reached. It met again in the evening, and still again on Saturday morning, knowing that an answer of some kind must be given before 6 P.M.

[18] Armstrong, p. 272.

[19] Pachu to the Serbian Ministers abroad, July 23; S.B.B., 33.

[20] Russian Chargé d'Affaires at Belgrade to Sazonov, July 23; R.O.B., 1, 2.

[21] S.B.B., 37; R.O.B., 6.   [22] B.D., 96.

Pashitch saw the Montenegrin and Greek Ministers. The former assured him emphatically that Montenegro would march side by side with Serbia. But the Greek Minister was uncertain what attitude his Government would take; M. Venizelos, the Premier, was absent from Athens, but telephoned from Munich to Berlin next morning that if Bulgaria took advantage of an Austro-Serbian conflict to attack Serbia, Greece would oppose such Bulgarian interference.[23] Far more important, however, was the attitude which the Triple Entente Powers would take.

Unfortunately for Serbia, it happened that these three Great Powers were not represented at Belgrade at this moment by regular Ministers. Hartwig, the energetic Russian Minister and strong champion of Serbia, had dropped dead a few days previously when talking with Giesl, and his successor had not arrived. No British Minister was on the spot, though Mr. des Graz was on his way from London to Belgrade. The French Minister was suffering from a nervous breakdown and was invisible; his successor, M. Boppe, was only just arriving from Constantinople and was unacquainted with his new post. So the Chargés d'Affaires of the Entente Powers could do little for Serbia except report home the news of Austria's unacceptable demands, and await instructions. These were slow in coming, so slow, in fact, that they were probably too late to have had any decisive influence on Serbia's decision.

Sazonov talked with the Serbian Minister on Friday evening about 7 o'clock, and is said to have "advised extreme moderation in respect to the Serbian reply." [24] But no such advice appears in the Serbian Minister's account of this conversation. On the contrary, as he was leaving Sazonov, he met the German Ambassador, and told him "he

23 Giesl to Berchtold, July 24; A.R.B., II, 3, 4; Russian Chargé d'Affaires in Berlin to Sazonov, July 25; Krasnyi Arkhiv, I, p. 166.
24 Schilling's Diary, p. 31.

would see before long that this was not a question merely between Serbia and Austria, but a European question." [25] Later in the evening, Sazonov telegraphed to his Chargé d'Affaires in Belgrade that if the Serbians felt helpless in case of an Austrian invasion, they had better offer no resistance, but retire without fighting and appeal to the Powers for protection.[26]   But whatever advice Sazonov gave is said not to have reached Belgrade until after the Serbian reply had been handed to Giesl at 6 o'clock on July 25.[27]

Sir Edward Grey telegraphed on Friday at 9:30 P.M. that "Serbia ought certainly to express concern and regret that any officials, however subordinate, should have been accomplices in murder of the Archduke, and promise, if this is proved, to give fullest satisfaction;" for the rest, "to reply as they consider the interests of Serbia require;" and, in order to avert military action by Austria, "to give a favorable reply on as many points as possible within the limit of time, and not to meet Austria with a blank negative." He added, with an eye to preserving Entente solidarity, "Consult with your Russian and French colleagues as to saying this to Serbian Government.   Serbian Minister here implores us to give some indication of our views, but I cannot take responsibility of giving more advice than above, and I do not like to give that without knowing what Russian and French Governments are saying at Bel-

[25] Spalajkovitch to Pashitch, July 24; S.B.B., 36. If Spalajkovitch or Sazonov may have sent other messages to Belgrade while the Serbian reply was being framed, either advising moderation or promising Russian support, they have not been published. The Serbian Minister at Vienna, however, stated "that active exchange of telegrams is taking place between Belgrade and St. Petersburg, and that, in his opinion, reply of Serbian Government will depend on result of this correspondence" (Bunsen to Grey, July 24, 1:30 P.M.; B.D., 93).

[26] Tg. 1487, July 24; Schilling's *Diary*, pp. 33, 86.   See also B.D., 125; and B.D., 221, quoted in preceding chapter, note 45.

[27] Seton-Watson, p. 257 note; *cf.* also Crackanthorpe to Grey, July 25, 12:30 P. M.: "My Russian colleague and new French Minister . . . are as yet without instructions" (B.D., 111).

grade." [28]　This advice also came too late materially to influence the Belgrade Cabinet. Crackanthorpe replied at 12:30 P.M. next day that his colleagues were still without instructions; in view of this, and of the proposed conciliatory terms of the Serbian reply, of which Dr. Grouitch had already given him an advance summary, he had abstained from offering Grey's advice to the Serbian Government.[29]

M. Berthelot, the Political Director at the Quai d'Orsay, advised the Serbian Minister in Paris on July 24 that Serbia should "try to gain time," by offering satisfaction on all the points not inconsistent with her dignity and sovereignty, and by asking for further information on others; above all, Serbia should "attempt to escape from the direct grip of Austria by declaring herself ready to submit to the arbitration of Europe." [30]　Whether this advice arrived at Belgrade in time to influence the Serbian reply is uncertain. The fact that Serbia's reply did substantially follow the line Berthelot suggested makes it seem likely.

In any case, however, Pashitch and his colleagues, rather than any of the Great Powers, must be given the main credit for the cleverness with which they met a difficult situation. They framed a reply which not only won the approval and sympathy of all the Powers except Austria, but which also commanded the admiration of the man who framed the Austrian ultimatum itself, "as the most brilliant example of diplomatic skill which I have ever known." [31] They had instantly decided that "no Serbian Government could accept the Austrian demands in their entirety." [32]

[28] B.D., 102.

[29] Crackanthorpe to Grey, July 25; 12:30 P.M.; B.D., 111, 114.

[30] Bienvenu-Martin's circular telegram, July 24; F.Y.B., 26; cf. also A.R.B., II, 11.

[31] Musulin, Das Haus am Ballplatz, p. 241. Berchtold, reporting to Francis Joseph on July 28, spoke of "the very cleverly composed reply of the Serbian Government, which however is wholly worthless in content, though yielding in form" (A.R.B., II, 78).

[32] Pachu to the Serbian Ministers abroad. July 23, S.B.B., 33.

Such being the case, they now concluded that Austria would treat any reply they could make as unsatisfactory, and make war. Therefore they "would appeal to the Governments of the friendly Powers to protect the independence of Serbia. If war was inevitable, Serbia would carry it on." [33] Since Austria would evidently reject any reply which did not yield on all points, they could afford to give their reply a very conciliatory form, apparently yielding on many points, and even suggesting submitting the question to the arbitration of the Hague Tribunal. This kind of a conciliatory reply would help gain the sympathy and protection of the Powers, and tend to place Austria in the wrong when she rejected it. It was, however, more yielding in form than in substance, and it is significant that two or three hours before they handed it to Giesl at the expiration of the time-limit, they had already ordered the general mobilization of the whole Serbian army.[34] In fact they had at once begun to make such frantic military preparations for defence and for the transport of the Government archives, treasure and officials from an exposed position in Belgrade to the interior,[35] that the German Minister was misled into telegraphing his Government at 11:50 P.M. on Friday night, "Mobilization is already in full swing." [36]

This ordering of Serbian mobilization before handing in the conciliatory reply, which was regarded more as a diplomatic gesture than a serious effort to satisfy Austria, had another advantage. Serbian hatred against Austria had been so stimulated by the newspaper campaign, and Serbian military officers of the "Black Hand" group were so eager for war and ready to overthrow Pashitch, that if he had

[33] Pashitch to Spalajkovitch, July 24; S.B.B., 34.

[34] At 3 P.M., July 25, according to Giesl, A.R.B., II, 23.

[35] Cf. Giesl to Berchtold, July 25, 1 P.M.; A.R.B., 22; and Armstrong, p. 272 f.

[36] K.D., 158. The Austrian Chief of Staff also received news late on Friday night from an officer near the frontier that mobilization had been proclaimed at Shabats in Serbia at 4 P.M. on July 24 (Conrad, IV, 109).

made his conciliatory reply involving some humiliating concessions, there might have been danger of a military revolt
against the civil Government. Even before the presentation of the ultimatum, Serbian officials had pointed out the
danger from the excited national feeling in their country,[37]
and the German Minister reported that Pashitch's "position is a very difficult one, in view of the coming elections
and of the agitation that has arisen throughout the country. Every concession to the neighboring Monarchy will be
charged against him by the united Opposition as weakness.
In addition to that, is the fact that military circles, blinded
by their megalomania and chauvinism, are forcing him to
roughness which is otherwise wholly opposed to his conciliatory nature." [38] This became even more true after the
ultimatum became known. "The military categorically
demand the rejection of the Note and war." "In case of
the proclamation of the Order of the Day [which Austria
demanded should be published in the official Bulletin of
the Army], a military uprising is feared." [39] But the preparations for war and the proclamation of mobilization, before making known that the Government had yielded to
some of the Austrian demands, satisfied the military officers
and averted this danger.

The main points of the Serbian reply were substantially threshed out at the long Cabinet meeting on Saturday
morning. The representatives of the friendly Powers were
given an advance summary of it and informed that "it
will be drawn up in most conciliatory terms and will meet
Austrian demands in as large measure as possible." [40] The
actual wording was drafted mainly by Stojan Protitch, the
Minister of Interior, but every phrase was discussed and
re-discussed by the other Ministers, and changes made up

[37] F.Y.B., 19; B.D., 27, 40.
[38] Griesinger to Bethmann, July 21; K.D., 137.
[39] Griesinger to Bethmann, July 24; K.D., 158, 159.
[40] Crackanthorpe to Grey, July 25, 12:30 P.M., B.D., 114.

to the last moment. The final Serbian text, as handed over to Grouitch for translation into French and typing, was so full of erasures and corrections that only one who had been working on it could decipher the sense. As he was dictating the translation to the typist and the minutes were flying by, the only remaining typewriter broke down, and in the end the text was copied out in a rather shaky hand by a secretary. It was then given to Pashitch, who started off a little before six o'clock to deliver it in person to the Austrian Minister.[41]

THE SUBSTANCE OF THE SERBIAN REPLY

The Serbian reply was more conciliatory in form than in substance. To make this clear the Austrian authorities delayed making it public until they had time to make comments upon it. These they published in parallel columns with the Serbian reply, showing that the concessions at many points were so guarded with limitations and conditions as to be virtually worthless as guarantees of security for the future, as well as failing to be the complete assent which they had demanded. But they were not able to publish this annotated edition of the Serbian reply until July 28, and it then came too late to have the effect in Europe for which they had hoped.[42] Meanwhile Serbia had circulated her reply and the advance summary of it, and created the good impression which she had hoped for.[43]

[41] Armstrong, *op. cit.*, pp. 273-275; Mr. Armstrong gives a facsimile of a part of the Serbian reply and of other interesting Serbian documents connected with the July Crisis, in *Current History*, Oct., 1927.

[42] Berchtold did not inform even Germany of the Serbian reply for more than two days. Berlin telegraphed for it in vain on July 26 (K.D., 226), and again on July 27 (K.D., 246): "Please telegraph text of the Serbian reply immediately." Finally on July 28 at 1:45 A.M. (K.D., 280) Tschirschky telegraphed that he had urgently requested the text of the reply, but had only just received it in printed form with the Austrian annotations; as it was being given to the Press and was a long document, he dispensed with sending it by telegraph.

[43] *Cf.* B.D., 114, 115, 171; K.D., 271, 293.

A summary of the Serbian reply, and of the Austrian parallel comments which are here indicated by brackets, follows.

"Convinced that their reply will remove any misunderstanding which may threaten to impair the good neighborly relations" between the two countries, the Serbian Government protest that at no time since their promises of 1909 have they or their agents attempted to change the political and legal state of affairs created in Bosnia and Herzegovina. [This was trying to shift the argument, since the ultimatum did not maintain that the Serbian Government or their official agents had attempted to change the situation created in 1909, but that in failing to suppress the movement directed against Austria, they had not lived up to their promise to adopt a friendly and neighborly attitude].

The Serbian Government "cannot be held responsible for manifestations of a private character, such as articles in the press and the peaceable work of societies. . . . They are prepared to hand over for trial any Serbian subject, without regard to his situation or rank, of whose complicity in the Sarajevo crime proofs shall be forthcoming." They also agree to publish on the first page of the *Journal Officiel* the declaration condemning all propaganda "which may be" directed against Austria-Hungary, and regretting that, "according to the communication from the Imperial and Royal Government," certain Serbian officers and functionaries participated in the above-mentioned propaganda. [In altering the declaration from the form demanded by Austria, by the insertion of the quoted phrases, the Serbian Government were insincere in implying that no such propaganda existed, or that they were not aware of it].

Coming to the ten Austrian demands, the Serbian Government then undertook:

1. "To introduce at the first regular meeting of the

Skupshtina a provision into the Press law providing for the most severe punishment of incitement to hatred and contempt of the Austro-Hungarian Monarchy," and also proposing a modification of the Constitution which would permit the confiscation of newspapers. [This was unsatisfactory—it did not assure a definite result within a given time, and if the bills were rejected by the Skupshtina everything would be as it was before].

2. "To dissolve the *Narodna Odbrana* and every other society which may be directing its efforts against Austria-Hungary," although the Serbian Government possesses no proof, and Austria furnishes none, that the members of these societies have committed criminal acts. [Austria could not admit the reservation in the last clause; nor did Serbia comply with Austria's further demands that the means of propaganda possessed by these societies should be confiscated, and that their reëstablishment under other names be prevented].

3. "To eliminate without delay from public instruction in Serbia everything that serves, or might serve, to foment the propaganda against Austria-Hungary, whenever facts and proofs are furnished." [Serbia asks proofs when she must know that the school books contain objectionable matter, and that many of the teachers are enrolled in the *Narodna Odbrana*].

4. To remove from the military service all persons proved by a judicial inquiry to be guilty of acts directed against Austria-Hungary, after information had been furnished by the latter. [This confined removals to officers convicted by a judicial inquiry of crimes punishable by law, but Austria demanded removal of officers who fomented propaganda, a proceeding which was not generally punishable by law in Serbia].

5. As to the demand to accept the collaboration in Serbia of Austrian representatives for the suppression of

subversive propaganda, the Serbian Government "do not clearly grasp the meaning and scope of the demand . . . but will admit such collaboration as agrees with the principles of international law, criminal procedure, and good neighborly relations." [The reservation is vague and calculated to lead to insurmountable difficulties in reaching an arrangement].

6. The Serbian Government "consider it their duty to open an inquiry [*enquête*], against all such persons as are, or eventually may be, implicated in the plot"; but "as regards the participation in this inquiry of Austro-Hungarian agents, cannot accept such an arrangement, as it would be a violation of the Constitution and of the law of criminal procedure." [Serbia has misinterpreted Austria's clearly expressed demand which was for two distinct things: (1) the opening of a judicial inquiry [*enquête judiciaire*], in which, of course, no Austrian collaboration was expected: and (2) Austrian collaboration in the preliminary police investigations [*recherches*] for the collection and verification of evidence, for which numberless precedents exist].

7. The Serbian Government arrested Tankositch the very evening the ultimatum was delivered, but has not been able to arrest Ciganovitch. [The Prefect of Police at Belgrade contrived the departure of Ciganovitch, and then declared that no man of the name existed in Belgrade].[44]

8. The Serbian Government will take measures to prevent the smuggling of arms and explosives across the frontier, and will severely punish the frontier officials who allowed the Sarajevo assassins to cross over.

9. The Serbian Government will gladly give explanations as to the remarks in interviews made by their officials in Serbia or abroad, alleged to be hostile to Austria, as soon as Austria specifies the passages and it is shown they were

[44] On Serbian complicity in Ciganovitch's sudden disappearance, see above, ch. iii, at notes 44-45 and 55-58.

actually made. [The interviews in question must be well known to the Serbian Government; their request for details and proof indicate unwillingness to comply seriously with this demand].

10. The Serbian Government will inform Austria of the execution of the above measures as soon as each has been carried out.

If Austria is not satisfied with this reply, the Serbian Government "are ready, as always, to accept a peaceful agreement, by referring this question either to the decision of the International Tribunal of the Hague, or to the Great Powers which took part in drawing up the declaration made by the Serbian Government on March 31, 1909." [45]

Though some of the Austrian comments are pettifogging in character, they show that it is by no means true, as often stated, that Serbia virtually yielded to all the Austrian demands except one. Nos. 1, 2, and 3 were accepted to a very reasonable extent, and Nos. 8 and 10 completely. But Nos. 4, 5, and 9 were answered evasively or with serious reservations. No. 7 contained an implication concerning Ciganovitch which was untrue. No. 6 concerned the collaboration in Serbia of Austrian officials in searching out (though not in trying and judging) Serbian accomplices in the assassination plot; this was refused, though most important, either because Pashitch and his colleagues misunderstood it, deliberately or unconsciously; or because it seemed to infringe upon Serbia's sovereignty; or because they feared it would lead to inconvenient discoveries concerning the complicity of the "Black Hand" and other Serbian officials, as well as concerning the Serbian Government's cognizance of a plot which they had failed to prevent.

The general impression, however, made upon contemporaries by the Serbian reply was favorable. At the British Foreign Office Sir Eyre Crowe noted: "The answer is

[45] S.B.B., 39; A.R.B., II, 96; B.D., Appendix B.

reasonable. If Austria demands absolute compliance with
her ultimatum, it can only mean that she wants war." [46]
The German Emperor, after reading it on the morning of
July 28, jotted down at the end of it, "A brilliant performance for a time-limit of only 48 hours. This is more than
one could have expected! A great moral success for Vienna;
but with it every reason for war drops away, and Giesl
ought to have remained quietly in Belgrade! After such a
thing, *I* should never have ordered mobilization!—W." [47]

Giesl, however, was justified by his instructions in rejecting it as unsatisfactory. One cannot accept, on the other
hand, the arguments sometimes made by Austrians, that
the rejection of the Serbian reply was justifiable on the
ground that it did not give Austria adequate guarantees of
security; because it was not primarily guarantees which
Austria aimed at in her ultimatum, but an excuse for weakening Serbia and putting an end to the Greater Serbia
danger by making war on her.

THE DIPLOMATIC BREAK BETWEEN AUSTRIA AND SERBIA

The time-limit was to expire at 6 P. M. on Saturday
afternoon, July 25. A few minutes before six, Pashitch
arrived at the Austrian Legation and handed in the Serbian
reply. Giesl said he would have to compare it with his
instructions, and that he would then give an immediate
answer. As he knew that Serbia had already ordered mobilization, he had little expectation that the reply would be
wholly satisfactory, and had probably written his answer
to it before he saw it. He now hurriedly glanced at it to
make sure that Serbia had not completely yielded on every
point, and that, as Berchtold desired, he could reject it as
unsatisfactory and break off diplomatic relations. Pashitch

---

[46] Minute on Serbian Reply, July 28; B.D., 171.
[47] K.D., 271. See also his letters to Jagow and to Moltke (K.D.,
293) quoted below, ch. ix, at note 56.

had hardly returned to his office in the Ministry of Foreign Affairs, when he received a note from Giesl, that as the time-limit "has now expired and as I have not received a reply which is satisfactory, I have the honor to inform your Excellency that I am leaving Belgrade tonight together with the Staff of the Imperial and Royal Legation; . . . that from the moment this letter reaches your Excellency the rupture in the diplomatic relations between Serbia and Austro-Hungary will have the character of a *fait accompli*." [48] So great was Giesl's speed that he and his whole staff were able to catch the 6:30 P. M. train from Belgrade. He certainly established the speed record for the rupture of diplomatic relations.

In order that the measures for Austrian partial mobilization against Serbia might follow the diplomatic break as quickly as possible, Berchtold had made elaborate preparations to get the news from Giesl with the utmost promptness. After leaving Belgrade at 6:30 P. M., Giesl was to arrive at Semlin across the frontier at 6:40 P. M., and there to use the railway telephone which would be held open for him to inform Tisza at Budapest, who in turn would forward the message at once to Vienna. [49] Berchtold himself had gone to Ischl to attend an early dinner which Emperor Francis Joseph was giving to the Duke and Duchess of Cumberland. Toward noon he received an urgent telegram from the Russian Chargé d'Affaires begging an extension of the time-limit, on the grounds that the Powers had been taken by surprise and had not yet had an opportunity to study the *dossier* of Sarajevo evidence which Austria had promised them. But Berchtold replied that he could not grant any such extension. He added, however, that even after diplomatic relations with Serbia should have been broken off, a peaceful settlement could be brought about

[48] Giesl to Pashitch, July 25; S.B.B., 40.
[49] Berchtold to Giesl, July 24, 1:30 P.M.; A.R.B., II, 1.

afterwards by Serbia's complete acceptance of the Austrian demands. But in such a case Austria would expect to be indemnified by Serbia for the expenses incurred in military preparations.[50] It was clear that he counted confidently on a diplomatic break with Serbia to be followed by military measures against her.

In the evening Berchtold sat impatiently in the Emperor's Cabinet at Ischl waiting for the expected message, and finally went out to take a turn in the air. At quarter to eight the telephone rang. Count Kinsky took the message at Vienna and repeated it to Ischl:

> Minister Giesl telephones from Semlin to Budapest: two minutes before six P.M. answering note delivered; since unsatisfactory on several points, Baron Giesl has broken off relations and left. At 3 P.M. general mobilization was ordered in Serbia. The Government and Diplomatic Corps left for Kragujevatch.[51]

Baron Margutti jotted down the message on a slip of paper and ran with it to Francis Joseph. The old man took the paper in trembling hands, and sank into his chair, muttering in a choked unaccustomed voice, *"Also doch!"* ["So it has come after all"], as if he had hoped and believed to the last that a rupture might be avoided. Then, after staring at the paper for a while, lost in thought, he remarked, half to himself, "Well, the rupture of diplomatic relations still does not mean war." [52]

Meanwhile Berchtold had been quickly called in, and was closeted with the Emperor. He had been urged by Tisza, by Conrad, and by the Austrian Ambassador in Berlin, that Austria ought to order mobilization against Serbia at once; any delay or hesitation would be regarded

---

[50] A.R.B., II, 27-30.

[51] A.R.B., II, 26. Pashitch (S.B.B., 41) gives 5:45 P.M., and not "two minutes before six," as the time at which he handed the Serbian reply to Giesl.   [52] Margutti, p. 404.

as a sign of weakness and increase the likelihood of Russian intervention.[53] Using these arguments, it did not take him long to persuade his aged Emperor of the necessity of ordering immediately the partial mobilization contemplated in case of war against Serbia and Montenegro alone. The Kaiser's assent reached the Chief of Staff at 9:53 P. M., and was at once put into execution: July 27 was ordered as the "alarm" day, and July 28 as the first day of actual mobilization.[54]

The task of the Austrian Staff was a very difficult one. If there was to be war merely with Serbia and Montenegro, the situation was simple. It was calculated that the mobilization of about half the Austrian army—8 Army Corps with 20 infantry divisions—would be sufficient to secure a satisfactorily quick victory over the 12 Serbian and 4 Montenegrin infantry divisions. But if Russia made war, either before Serbia, or simultaneously, or after Serbia, it was all important that Austria should throw as great a mass of troops as possible toward the northeast, into the main theater of war in Galicia, leaving only a minimum number in the Balkan theater. Serbia's fate would be decided by the outcome of the fighting against Russia; moreover, Germany wanted Austria to send as many troops as possible against Russia, to relieve the Russian pressure on eastern Germany, while the bulk of the German Army was attempting to crush the French in the west.

Conrad and Berchtold were uncertain whether Russia would intervene or not. They hoped of course that she would not, and that the war with Serbia would be "localized." There is much evidence that this was also their expectation, though they were ready to risk the danger that Russia might move.[55] To provide as far as possible for the uncertainty whether Austria could fight Serbia without

[53] A.R.B., II, 21, 22, 32; Conrad, IV, 109 ff.
[54] Conrad, IV, 122.   [55] *Cf.* Conrad, IV, 110-124; 266 ff.

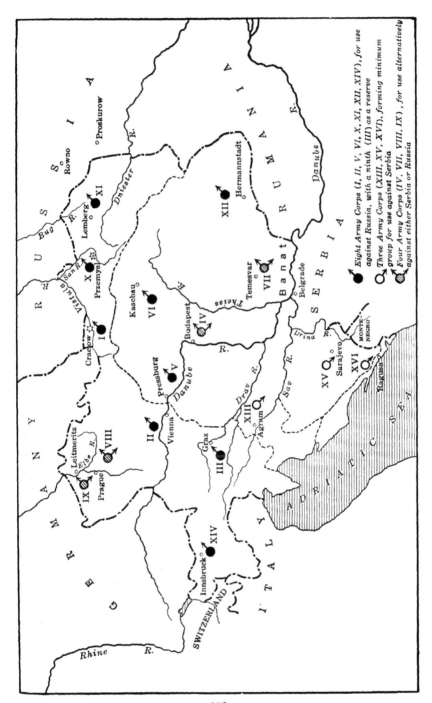

Eight Army Corps (I, II, V, VI, X, XI, XII, XIV), for use against Russia, with a ninth (III) as a reserve ●

Three Army Corps (XIII, XV, XVI), forming minimum group for use against Serbia ○

Four Army Corps (IV, VII, VIII, IX), for use alternatively against either Serbia or Russia ◐

fighting Russia, or *vice versa*, Conrad had worked out mobilization plans which divided the Austrian forces into four groups: (1) a minimum Balkan group, consisting of three Army Corps—the XVth and XVIth in Bosnia and Herzegovina, and the XIIIth at Agram; (2) a group of eight Army Corps for use against Russia and if necessary against Rumania—I, Cracow; X, Przmysl; XI, Lemberg; XII, Hermannstadt, all near the Northeast Frontier; and II, Vienna; V, Pressburg; VI, Kaschau; and XIV, Innsbruck; (3) an alternative group of four Army Corps—IV, Budapest; VII, Temesvar; VIII, Prag; and IX, Leitmeritz— which could be used either against Serbia or Russia; in case of war with Serbia alone this group would roll toward the Danube to attack Belgrade and Serbia from the north while the first group were attacking from the west; but if Russia made war before it had become engaged on the Danube, it could be shifted north to the Galician front; and (4) the IIIrd Army Corps at Graz, to be held as a reserve, which could also be used either against Serbia or Russia. These strategic arrangements made it possible to mobilize half the Austrian army without mobilizing any troops near the Russian frontier, thus avoiding as far as possible giving Russia grounds for alarm. The eight Army Corps, accordingly, to which Conrad issued mobilization orders on the evening of July 25, were those comprised in groups (1), (3), and (4) above.[56]

As Austria and Serbia had now broken off diplomatic relations and were mobilizing against one another, the Great Powers began to put forward a variety of proposals for preserving peace.

[56] Conrad, IV, 122 ff., 266 ff.; R. Kiszling, "Die österreichisch-ungarischen Kriegsvorbereitungen und die Mobilisierungsmassnahmen gegen Russland 1914," in KSF, IV, 365-377, June, 1926; and the Diary Notes of General F. Demus-Morau, *ibid.*, IV, 549-552, Aug., 1926.

CHAPTER VIII

PROPOSALS FOR PRESERVING PEACE

EVERYWHERE it was anticipated that the Sarajevo assassination would tighten dangerously the long-standing tension between Austria and Serbia. Numerous proposals were therefore made by all the Great Powers to prevent this tension from developing into an armed conflict between the two exasperated countries, and, if this did break out, to prevent it from involving the other Powers in a general European conflagration. Some of these proposals—such as Sir Edward Grey's suggestion for "direct conversations" between Austria and Russia, Germany's plan of "localization," and the Poincaré-Sazonov move to head off an Austrian ultimatum—were made prior to the publication of Berchtold's demands on Serbia. After the stiff ultimatum became known, and especially after the diplomatic break and commencement of mobilizations in Serbia and Austria, the proposals for preserving peace came in a flood, sometimes running parallel and sometimes counter to one another. They were often confused, and not always kept perfectly clear and distinct even in the minds of their authors. Sir Edward Grey, for instance, both in writing his memoirs and in July, 1914, did not grasp clearly the importance of the distinction between mediation between Austria *and Russia* and between Austria *and Serbia*.

Sazonov also, in his nervousness, put forth in rapid succession so many suggestions that they became bewildering: a suggestion to head off an Austrian ultimatum,[1] to

[1] See above, ch. vi, at notes 24-27.

extend the time-limit,[2] to have Serbia appeal to the Great Powers,[3] to have England and Italy collaborate with Austria to end the tension,[4] to have Austria modify her ultimatum, even after it had been presented and answered,[5] to have the Great Powers institute a kind of informal international supervision over Serbia to prevent anti-Austrian plots in the future,[6] and above all to have England restrain Austria and Germany by proclaiming unmistakably her solidarity with France and Russia.[7] No wonder that at the British Foreign Office Sir Arthur Nicolson complained on July 27: "This is confusing. In three consecutive days M. Sazonov has made one suggestion and two proposals all differing from each other. . . . One really does not know where one is with M. Sazonov, and I told Count Benckendorff so this afternoon." [8]

Germany's main solution, until she read the conciliatory Serbian reply and began seriously to realize that Russia would not remain quiet, was the "localization" of the conflict which she had been urging for a week. But this was absolutely unacceptable to Russia and France, and therefore to England. As Sir Arthur Nicolson wrote to Buchanan: "The talk about localizing the war merely means that all the Powers are to hold the ring while Austria quietly strangles Serbia. This to my mind is quite preposterous, not to say iniquitous." [9]

Italy, embarrassed by her obligations to both groups of Allied Powers, and therefore especially desirous of preventing a European war, hoped to work with England to this end. On July 27 and 28 she made an excellent proposal.

[2] R.O.B., 4, 5; Schilling's *Diary*, 33, 40; B.D., 117, 118; A.R.B., II, 27-30.

[3] See above, ch. vi, at note 45; and B.D., 125, 221.

[4] B.D., 170.

[5] See below on "Direct Conversations" at notes 84-87.

[6] B.D., 198, 203.   [7] B.D., 101, 125.   [8] Minute, B.D., 179.

[9] July 28; B.D., 239; and Minute, B.D., 249. See also below, ch. ix, "Germany's Belated Peace Efforts."

If the Powers would give the advice, even after the diplomatic break of July 25, Serbia might be induced even still to accept the Austrian demands in their entirety; Austria would then be satisfied; Serbia would save her face by yielding to Europe and not to Austria alone; and the Powers could adjust the details by which Serbia would carry out the demands of Austria. The proposal seemed to be substantially acceptable to the Serbian Minister in Rome. But in the end it came to nothing, largely because it was not taken very seriously by the Entente Powers and was crowded aside by their other proposals, and because Austria quickly complicated the situation by declaring war on Serbia.[10]

To attempt to give an account of all these numerous proposals for preserving peace in July, 1914, would be tedious and futile. But it will be useful to review briefly at this point a few of those which were made before July 28, and which were of special significance, or seemed to have the greatest prospect of being successful, or have often been not clearly understood. They are the various proposals of Sir Edward Grey, and the so-called "Direct Conversations" between Vienna and St. Petersburg.

ENGLAND'S KEY POSITION

In most of the peace proposals, England was generally recognized as holding the key to the situation, for several reasons. Her direct interests in the Balkans were less than those of the other Great Powers, and, as Grey reiterated, the merits of the Austro-Serbian dispute were not his concern; it was only from the point of view of the peace of Europe that he would concern himself with the

[10] B.D., 202, 231, 276, 328; F.Y.B., 72; K.D., 249, 357, 432; Dirr, p. 152 f.; an anonymous article [by the French Ambassador in Rome, Barrère?], "L'Italie et les Responsabilités Austro-Allemandes de la Guerre," in *Rev. des Deux Mondes*, Oct. 1, 1927; M. Morhardt, *Les Preuves* (Paris, 1924), pp. 249-274.

matter, and about this he felt great apprehension. Now, just as during the Balkan Wars, he was looked to as the man most impartial and best able to take steps toward calling an international conference or providing some other means of preventing the two groups of Great Powers from coming into conflict. Moreover, England was not bound by any formal alliance with either group. And finally, it was realized that with her great sea-power she would probably be able to exercise a decisive pressure, by whatever attitude she might assume, both upon Franco-Russian and Austro-German, as well as upon Italian, policy. Therefore Russia and France besought Grey to preserve peace by indicating energetically to Germany that if war came, England would support them. And Germany besought him to preserve peace by putting pressure on Russia to remain quiet.

But Grey was unwilling, early in the crisis, to warn Germany energetically, because his Cabinet was divided on the question of England's eventual intervention; he could not make a threat which he might not be able to carry out; and he was fearful of saying anything which might encourage France and Russia to let themselves in for war, counting on support which the British Cabinet and Parliament might not be willing to render when the ordeal came. It was only very gradually that he acceded to the urgings of Russia and France, seconded by his own Secretaries, Crowe and Nicolson, and gave warning hints to Germany in the shape of announcements concerning the British Fleet, and later in plainer terms to the German Ambassador. Nor, on the other hand, was he willing to put restraint upon Russia, for fear it might break down the solidarity of the Triple Entente, cause "misunderstandings," and possibly wreck the Anglo-Russian Entente concerning the Middle East.

In the early summer of 1914, before the Sarajevo trag-

edy, and even during the days immediately following it,
English minds were far more absorbed as to what might
happen in Ireland than in the Balkans. The eternal Irish
question threatened at last to reach a tragic culmination.
Ulster was arming, and openly defying the Asquith Government to apply force through Sir John French's army. The
Irish Nationalist Volunteers had also begun to arm. Ireland seemed on the verge of civil war. Hardly anyone in
England appeared to realize how the European situation
might be seriously menaced by a double murder in far-
away Bosnia. Only a few men who had closely followed
Continental politics, like Sir Arthur Nicolson and Sir Eyre
Crowe, and perhaps Sir Edward Grey, at the Foreign Office,
or who were responsible for the safety of the British Empire,
like Lord Haldane at the War Office and Winston Churchill
at the Admiralty, became somewhat apprehensive. Yet
Lord Haldane had created a little standing army ready to
be sent across the Channel at a moment's notice, and had
been organizing a larger territorial force for the protection
of England herself. And Winston Churchill had assembled
for maneuvers at Portsmouth what he proudly but justly
calls "incomparably the greatest assemblage of naval power
ever witnessed in the history of the world. The King
himself was present and inspected ships of every class. On
the morning of the 19th [July] the whole Fleet put to
sea for exercises of various kinds. It took more than six
hours for this armada, every ship decked with flags and
crowded with bluejackets and marines, to pass, with bands
playing and at 15 knots, before the Royal Yacht, while
overhead the naval seaplanes and aeroplanes circled continuously. Yet it is probable that the uppermost thought
in the minds both of the Sovereign and those of his Ministers there present, was not the imposing spectacle of British
majesty and might defiling before their eyes, not the oppressive and even sultry atmosphere of Continental politics,

but the haggard, squalid, tragic Irish quarrel which threatened to divide the British nation into two hostile camps. One after another the ships melted out of sight beyond the Nab. They were going on a longer journey than any of us could know." [11]

Aside from the fact that Sir Edward Grey's time and attention were largely absorbed at this time in Parliamentary affairs and the acute Irish situation, there were many reasons why he at first felt no serious alarm for the peace of Europe. In spite of the persistent and fundamental undercurrent of friction caused by Germany's naval policy, his relations with Germany were on the whole better than they had been for many months. The treaties concerning the Bagdad Railway and the Portuguese colonies had been completed and initialed; they awaited only the final signature, which was delayed owing to the fact that Germany had to complete some arrangements with Turkey concerning the railway, and Sir Edward wanted to publish the secret Anglo-Portuguese Guarantee Declaration of 1899 along with the new German treaty, while Germany wished to delay publication.[12] Sir Edward Grey hoped that the signing of these two treaties, settling two longstanding sources of irritation, would do much to produce a better political atmosphere between Germany and England.

Another happy augury for more cordial relations was the visit of the British Fleet at Kiel. Though it was unfortunately interrupted by the tragic news of Sarajevo, this Kiel visit, according to the British Naval Attaché, was a great success, all the more so because of its non-political character. The Germans were honestly glad to see their guests and were looking forward eagerly to a return visit to an English port, being sick to death of the sight of

[11] Churchill, *The World Crisis* (London, 1923), p. 190 f.
[12] G.P., XXXVII, 96 ff., 452 ff.; Grey, I, 293, note; Gooch, *Camb. Hist. of Brit. Foreign Policy*, III, 477-481; B.D., p x.

Heligoland, round which their monotonous naval work centered. One surprise for the British was the fact that they were beaten in football and the other sports, in which they had always supposed they had a monopoly of superiority.[13] Altogether the utmost good fellowship prevailed between officers and men on both sides, and the comments of the Press were less acrid and irritating than usual.

Also, the alarm and suspicion which had been aroused in Germany by the "leak" of the secret negotiations for an Anglo-Russian naval convention, intended to strengthen the solidarity of the Triple Entente and to satisfy Russia and France as an offset to England's Bagdad and Portuguese settlements with Germany, seemed to have been relieved, if not entirely dispelled, by Grey's denials in Parliament. Lichnowsky assured him that his statement in Parliament "had given great satisfaction in Berlin and had had a reassuring effect," and that Bethmann hoped that, if new developments or emergencies arose in the Balkans, they would be discussed as frankly between Germany and England as during the last Balkan crisis.[14] Grey agreed cordially, so that when Lichnowsky left for Kiel and a ten days' vacation in Germany, the two countries seemed to be on unusually good terms. Grey believed that he could successfully continue the main aims of his foreign policy: the cultivation of more intimate relations with France and Russia as a protection against Germany; the smoothing out of causes of friction with Germany; and at the same time the preservation of the peace of Europe by preventing any questions which arose from throwing the two systems of alliance into opposition.

13 Captain Henderson's report, July 3; B.D., 7.

14 Grey to Goschen, June 24; B.D., 4; Grey I, 293. *Cf.* also Jagow's statement a week earlier to Goschen, that he had so much confidence in Grey's "loyalty and straightforwardness that his mind was now completely at rest;" Grey, I, 283. For German alarm at the negotiations for an Anglo-Russian Naval Convention, see G.P., XXXIX, 591 ff.

It has often been said that war could have been avoided in 1914 if a Conference of the Powers could have met and discussed the Austro-Serbian quarrel. This is quite probable. As none of the responsible statesmen wanted a European war, it is possible, even probable, that a way out of even this most difficult Balkan conflict might have been found in a Conference, as it had been found during the crises of the Balkan Wars. The Conference which Sir Edward Grey proposed in 1914, however, it may be noted, was of four Powers—England, France, Germany and Italy —while the Conference which had succeeded in averting a general European conflagration during the Balkan Wars was of the six Great Powers, Russia and Austria being also included.

It is also commonly asserted by Entente writers that Sir Edward Grey did his utmost to bring about a Conference, but that Germany vetoed it, and that her veto places on her shoulders a further responsibility for the World War. This is the impression which Viscount Grey gives in his memoirs. He devotes most of a chapter to this question of "the Conference." Sazonov was ready, he says, "to let the Conference have its chance, if Austria would hold her hand. France and Italy were ready to coöperate. Germany did not raise the objection I had feared, but, while agreeing in principle, vetoed the Conference. . . . They [Bethmann and von Jagow] vetoed the only certain means of peaceful settlement without, as far as I knew, even referring it to Austria at all. . . . I remember well the impulse to say that, as Germany forbade a Conference, I could do no more, and that it was on Germany that the responsibility must rest if war came." [15] But this explanation is too simple, and is far from being wholly true. Viscount Grey does not adequately indicate all vicissitudes which his Conference idea met with, arising from various

[15] Grey, I, 308, 311.

other actions of his own, and from the objections and hesitations with which it was received by Russia and France, as well as by Germany and Austria. He did not in fact stick steadily to any one clearly defined Conference proposal, but, in his genuine desire to do anything and everything to avert a European war, made a variety of suggestions. Some of these, before being examined more in detail, may be summarized as follows:

(1) An early suggestion for "direct conversations" between Vienna and St. Petersburg, which was vetoed by President Poincaré. The "direct conversations" which did take place between Austria and Russia, July 26-28, which Grey and Nicolson regarded as "the best method," and which the Russian and German Governments both thought preferable to a Conference, were the consequence of a suggestion, not by Grey, but by the German Ambassador at St. Petersburg.

(2) A proposal for mediation between Austria *and Russia* by the four less directly interested Powers, "accepted in principle" by Germany, but disliked by Russia and France.

(3) A proposal for mediation between Austria *and Serbia* in a Conference of Ambassadors, made under the influence of Russia and M. Paul Cambon, at first rejected by Germany and Austria, but later accepted in modified form and *bona fide* by Germany, though not by Austria.

GREY'S PROPOSAL FOR "DIRECT CONVERSATIONS" BETWEEN
VIENNA AND ST. PETERSBURG

In the intervals of the Irish trouble Sir Edward Grey had conversations with Prince Lichnowsky on July 9, 15, and 20.[16] The German Ambassador urged England to exercise restraint upon Russia. But Sir Edward Grey became more cautious and more regardful of Russia's point of

16 B.D., 41, 68; K.D., 30, 52, 92.

view. It would all depend, he told Lichnowsky, on what kind of measures Austria might take. "Should a tremendously excited feeling arise in Russia as a result of Austrian military measures, he would not be in a position to hold Russian policy in check, and, in view of the vexation existing at the moment in Russia against England,[17] he would have to have some regard for Russia's sensitive feelings."[18] He gently hinted that "the more Austria could keep her demand within reasonable limits, and the stronger the justification she could produce for making any demand, the more chance there would be of smoothing things over." And, he added, he "hated the idea of a war between any of the Great Powers, and that any of them should be dragged into a war by Serbia would be detestable."[19] Lichnowsky, on his part, remained pessimistic as to his own Government's intentions, but optimistic as to Grey's efforts for peace and belief that "a peaceful solution would be found." To his hope that Russian and English influence would persuade Serbia to agree to justifiable demands, Grey replied that "everything would depend on the form of satisfaction demanded. . . . He [Grey] hoped that the quarrel might be settled and localized, for the idea of a war between the Great Powers of Europe must be repelled under all circumstances."[20]

Meanwhile, however, the vituperations of the Austro-

[17] This vexation arose from British irritation at the aggressive conduct of Russian consuls in Persia, and from Russian irritation at the Anglo-Persian Oil Agreement of 1913, which secured to the British Admiralty oil monopolies at the head of the Persian Gulf in the "neutral sphere;" these were valued at $200,000,000, and would provide fuel for the newest and largest type of English naval vessels which Winston Churchill had just decided should be equipped as oil-burners (*cf.* Churchill, pp. 129-135; B.D., p. x.). To smooth away this vexation and to strengthen the solidarity of the Triple Entente was one of President Poincaré's objects in his visit to Russia at this time (*Cf.* Poincaré, *Les Origines de la Guerre*, pp. 201 f.; B.D., 49, 75, 164, 318).

[18] Lichnowsky to Bethmann, July 15; K.D., 52.

[19] Grey to Rumbold, July 20; B.D., 68.

[20] Lichnowsky to Bethmann, July 20; K.D., 92.

Serbian Press campaign became more bitter and dangerous, and the reports from the Balkans more alarming.[21] Official reports reached Sir Edward Grey from Vienna, based on confidential information from Count Lützow, formerly Austrian Ambassador in Rome and now an intimate associate of Count Berchtold, which foreshadowed a very stiff ultimatum.[22] From Paris Grey received militaristic clippings from the *Matin* and the *Temps;* the latter was publishing a series of very chauvinistic articles from their Russian correspondent, setting forth Russia's great increase in military strength and preparedness for war with Germany.[23] And from St. Petersburg Buchanan reported in no uncertain terms Sazonov's statement that "anything in the shape of an Austrian ultimatum at Belgrade could not leave Russia indifferent, and she might be forced to take some precautionary military measures." [24]

Noting these more stormy indications on the sinking political barometer, Sir Edward Grey deemed it opportune to throw out a cautious peace proposal. Acceding neither to Lichnowsky's desire that he should put restraining pressure on Russia, which he knew would be resented by the two other members of the Triple Entente, nor to the desire of Russia for restraining pressure upon Austria,[25] which he feared would be equally resented at Vienna and at Berlin,[26] Sir Edward Grey chose a more cautious middle course. He made the confidential suggestion to Sir George Buchanan in Russia of what were later called "direct conversations" between Vienna and St. Petersburg:

> It is possible that the Serbian Government have been negligent, and that proceedings at the trial at Sarajevo will

[21] B.D., 43, 45, 53, 55, 61, 62.
[22] B.D., 50, 55, 56; quoted above, ch. v, at note 95.
[23] B.D., 52, 66.
[24] Buchanan to Grey, July 18; B.D., 60.
[25] B.D., 39, 60.
[26] *Cf.* Minutes on B.D., 76.

show that the murder of the Archduke was planned on Serbian territory. If Austrian demands in Serbia are kept within reasonable limits, and if Austria can produce justification for making them, I hope every attempt will be made to prevent any breach of the peace. It would be very desirable that Austria and Russia should discuss things together if they become difficult. You can speak in this sense if occasion seems to require it.[27]

A couple of days later Sir Edward Grey set forth his idea for "direct conversations" more fully to the Russian Ambassador in London, who evidently did not relish it, and to Buchanan:

> I spoke to Count Benckendorff to-day of the apprehension felt about Austria and Serbia. . . . I said it was very desirable that the Russian Government should communicate directly with the Austrian Government. . . . Count Benckendorff spoke of the difficulty of making a friendly communication in Vienna; at present there was nothing to go on.
>
> I said I had been thinking what might be done if I were in M. Sazonov's place. It might be possible for M. Sazonov to send for the Austrian Ambassador in St. Petersburg; to refer to the statements in the press that Austria was going to make some demand on Serbia; to emphasize the strength of pro-Serb feeling in Russia, and how strong and irresistible this feeling might become if there was a crisis; and then to ask the Austrian Government to take Russia into their confidence by telling them exactly the extent and nature of their grievance against Serbia, and what they felt it necessary to ask. It might be then possible for the Russian Government to get the Austrian demand kept within reasonable limits.
>
> I also said that I had told Mr. des Graz, who was proceeding to Belgrade at the end of this week as our Minister there, that it was not our business to take violent sides in this matter, and that what he could say in Belgrade must depend on what case the Austrians presented. If they

[27] Grey to Buchanan, July 20; B.D., 67.

proved that the plot to assassinate the Archduke Franz
Ferdinand had been prepared and organized on Serbian
territory, and that Austria had real grounds of complaint
against Serbia, it would be possible for him to urge in Belgrade that the Serbian Government really ought to give
to Austria the utmost assurances they could for the preven-
tion of such plots against Austria being carried on in Serbia
in future.[28]

This suggestion of Sir Edward Grey's was an excellent
one, but it met with instant and emphatic condemnation
from President Poincaré, when Buchanan proposed it to
him during the visit to St. Petersburg:

> His Excellency [President Poincaré] expressed opinion
> that a conversation *à deux* between Austria and Russia
> would be very dangerous at the present moment, and seemed
> favorable to moderating counsels by France and England at
> Vienna.[29]

"Very dangerous" to have Austria and Russia converse
with a view to coming to a friendly and peaceful solution
of the Austro-Serbian conflict?   One rubs one's eyes to see
if one has read aright.   Very dangerous to what?   Certainly
not to the peace of Europe.   But perhaps to M. Poincaré's
policy of having the Triple Entente stand as a solid block
in opposition to Germany and Austria, refusing conciliatory
arrangements with either of them, and preparing to force
them to accept diplomatic defeat or fight against superior
forces.   For more than two years he had sought to tighten
the Triple Entente in every way possible, and to prevent
separate understandings by any one of its members with
Germany or Austria.   He had repudiated M. René's efforts

[28] B.D., 79.   For Grey's proposals to the Austrian Ambassador for
"direct conversation," see B.D., 86; and A.R.B., I, 59.

[29] Buchanan to Grey, July 22; B.D., 76 (omitted from B.B.B.).   Poincaré (IV, 252) merely alludes to this in a couple of sentences, and gives
an incorrect reference in his footnote ("73" for "75").

at conciliation by greater autonomy to Alsace-Lorraine.[30] When M. Crozier, the French Ambassador at Vienna, sought to establish better relations between Austria and Russia and France, and the listing of Austrian securities on the Paris Bourse, M. Poincaré thwarted his efforts; then he recalled him and replaced him by M. Dumaine, a less capable man, but a more docile instrument of his own policies. And in his memoirs he seeks to discredit M. Crozier by heaping ridicule upon his "Olympian thoughts," "vague suggestions which he mistook for ideas," and "cloudy vaporings." [31] According to Izvolski, M. Poincaré claimed also to have prevented the success of the Haldane Mission and the Anglo-German negotiations for a naval understanding.[32] During the Balkan Wars he never wanted Sazonov to enter upon any separate negotiations without first concerting a policy with the two other members of the Triple Entente.

M. Poincaré's contemporary telegrams and his later memoirs continually reiterate the desire to have the Triple Entente always concert together their line of action before any one of them approached Germany or Austria.[33] So now, in the more serious crisis of July, 1914, quite in keeping with his whole policy since he became Minister of Foreign Affairs in January, 1912, he thought "a conversation à deux between Austria and Russia would be very dangerous."

After Poincaré's decisive disapproval of "direct conversations" it is doubtful whether Buchanan even mentioned the idea to Sazonov, since his telegram to Grey, quoted above, does not speak of it, but continues:

[30] Cf. Bourgeois et Pagès, p. 343 f.; Poincaré, I, 125 ff, 138 ff.; and the retraction which he was forced to make in the Rev. des Deux Mondes, Feb. 15, 1926, p. 885 ff.

[31] Cf. Poincaré, I, 238-274; Ph. Crozier, "L'Autriche et l'avant-guerre," in La Revue de France, April 1 to June 1, 1921.

[32] Izvolski to Sazonov, Dec. 5, 1912; M.F.R., p. 309; L.N., I, 365; Stieve, II, 377; cf. also Poincaré, I, 165 ff.

[33] See above, Vol. I, chs. IV, V, passim.

I also spoke to the Minister of Foreign Affairs, whom I met later in the day. His Excellency said that if Austria could prove plot had been hatched in Serbia there was no objection to her asking Serbian Government to institute judicial inquiry, and this, he believed, Serbia was ready to do. He thought, however, it would be advisable for three Governments [Russia, France and England] to counsel moderation at Vienna. This should be done in friendliest manner, and should not take the form of any collective action. He begged me to telegraph to you in this sense, and said he would speak to the President of the Republic to-day on the subject.[34]

These telegrams from Sir George Buchanan show that both Poincaré and Sazonov wanted to have Russia, France and England put pressure on Austria, which would force her to abandon her plans at the behest of the Triple Entente. And in fact, before President Poincaré's departure from Russia, Sazonov told Buchanan that the Russian Ambassador in Vienna was being instructed to concert with his French and British colleagues "with a view to giving friendly counsels of moderation," and hoped that Grey would give similar instructions. But the British Foreign Office Secretaries disapproved the suggestion and Grey decided not to act on it until next day.[35] Next morning he was informed of the text of the ultimatum which had already been presented at Belgrade the night before. Since England had delayed to fall in with the Poincaré-Sazonov plan and the ultimatum had already been presented, the French and Russian Ambassadors at Vienna made no use of their instructions to have the Triple Entente give Austria the intended warning.[36]

Thus Sir Edward Grey's first peace proposal for "direct

[34] Buchanan to Grey, July 22; B.D., 76.
[35] Buchanan to Grey, July 23, and Minutes; B.D., 84; for the details of this abortive move, see above, ch. vi, at notes 24-27.
[36] Bunsen to Grey, July 24; B.D., 97.

conversations" between Vienna and St. Petersburg fell to the ground, owing to Poincaré's decisive disapproval and desire to substitute in its place Triple Entente pressure at Vienna. The direct conversations which Sazonov consented to undertake later, July 26-28, after Poincaré had left Russia and no longer exercised such an immediate influence on the Russian Minister of Foreign Affairs, were owing to the initiative, not of Sir Edward Grey, but of the German Ambassador in St. Petersburg.[37]

GREY'S PROPOSAL FOR MEDIATION BETWEEN AUSTRIA AND RUSSIA

On the morning of Friday, July 24, Count Mensdorff called at Downing Street to communicate the Austrian Note to Serbia and the reasons for it. Sir Edward Grey's report of the interview shows his alarm for the peace of Europe:

> I said . . . that I thought it a great pity that a time-limit, and such a short time-limit, had been introduced at this stage, and the note seemed to me the most formidable document I had ever seen addressed by one State to another that was independent. . . .
>
> I was not, however, making these comments in order to discuss the merits of the dispute between Austria-Hungary and Serbia; that was not our concern. It was solely from the point of view of the peace of Europe that I should concern myself with the matter, and I felt great apprehension.
>
> I must wait to hear the views of other Powers, and no doubt we should consult with them to see what could be done to mitigate difficulties.[38]

This was a very busy and harassing day for Sir Edward. The Buckingham Palace Conference had just broken down and failed to bring about any solution of the Irish question.

[37] See below, at notes 80-83.
[38] Grey to British Ambassadors in Europe, July 24, 1:30 P.M.; B.D., 91. Confirmed by Mensdorff to Berchtold, July 24, 2:50 P.M.; A.R.B., II, 14.

A Cabinet Meeting was to be held on it in the afternoon. On top of this problem now came Mensdorff's news of the ominous Austrian ultimatum. Grey had to talk with M. Cambon and Prince Lichnowsky, and he naturally took the French Ambassador first. Grey proposed to him mediation between Austria *and Russia* by the four less directly interested Powers—Germany and Italy representing the Triple Alliance, and England and France representing the Triple Entente. As this might mean that France would be expected to exert a moderating influence on her ally, Cambon did not like the idea. He preferred mediation between Austria *and Serbia,* which would probably mean that Austria would have to back down in some of her demands upon Serbia and accept a diplomatic defeat. How Cambon subtly tried to shift Sir Edward Grey over from mediation between Austria *and Russia* to mediation between Austria *and Serbia* may be seen in Grey's despatch to the British Ambassador in Paris:

> I told M. Cambon that this afternoon I was to see the German Ambassador, who some days ago had asked me privately to exercise moderating influence in St. Petersburg. I would say to the Ambassador that, of course, if the presentation of this ultimatum to Servia did not lead to trouble between Austria and Russia, we need not concern ourselves about it; but, if Russia took the view of the Austrian ultimatum, which it seemed to me that any Power interested in Serbia would take, I should be quite powerless, in face of the terms of the ultimatum, to exercise any moderating influence. I would say that I thought the only chance of any mediating or moderating influence being exercised was that Germany, France, Italy, and ourselves, who had not direct interests in Serbia, should act together for the sake of peace, simultaneously in Vienna and St. Petersburg.
>
> M. Cambon said that, if there was a chance of mediation by the four Powers, he had no doubt that his Government would be glad to join in it; but he pointed out that

we could not say anything in St. Petersburg till Russia had expressed some opinion or taken some action. But, when two days were over, Austria would march into Serbia, for the Serbians could not possibly accept the Austrian demand. Russia would be compelled by her public opinion to take action as soon as Austria attacked Serbia, and therefore, once the Austrians had attacked Serbia, it would be too late for any mediation.   ·

I said that I had not contemplated anything being said in St. Petersburg until after it was clear that there must be trouble between Austria and Russia. I had thought that if Austria did move into Serbia, and Russia then mobilised, it would be possible for the four Powers to urge Austria to stop her advance, and Russia also to stop hers, pending mediation. But it would be essential for any chance of success for such a step that Germany should participate in it.

M. Cambon said that it would be too late after Austria had once moved against Serbia. The important thing was to gain time by mediation in Vienna. The best chance of this being accepted would be that Germany should propose it to the other Powers.

I said that by this he meant a mediation between Austria and Serbia.

He replied that it was so.

I said that I would talk to the German Ambassador this afternoon on the subject.[39]

In short, Grey said: mediation at Vienna *and St. Petersburg,* but only "after it was clear that there must be trouble between Austria *and Russia."* Cambon said: intervene with mediation *at Vienna* between Austria *and Serbia at once,* and get Germany to propose it.

Cambon's account of this interview with Grey, however, supposing it is correctly given in the *French Yellow Book,* never mentioned Grey's mediation proposal in the form Grey really made it to him. Already, earlier that same

[39] Grey to Bertie, July 24; B.D., 98.

morning, Cambon had heard of the Austrian ultimatum from the Serbian Minister in London, and had hastened to get into touch with Benckendorff:

> In consultation with my Russian colleague, who thinks it extremely difficult for his Government not to support Serbia, we have been asking ourselves what intervention could avert the conflict. As Sir Edward Grey has summoned me for the afternoon, I propose to suggest that he ask for the semi-official intervention of the German Government at Vienna to prevent a sudden attack.[40]

Cambon did in fact urge upon Grey mediation at Vienna to prevent an Austrian attack on Serbia, as is seen from Grey's long despatch to Bertie quoted above. But Cambon either failed to get the point of Grey's own original suggestion as to mediation between Austria *and Russia,* or he purposely Cambonized it to fit in with what he had already agreed with the Russian Ambassador, as we see from his own account of his interview with Grey:

> Sir Edward Grey having discussed with me his desire to leave no stone unturned to avert the crisis, we agreed in thinking that the British Cabinet might ask the German Government to take the initiative in approaching Vienna with the object of offering mediation between Austria and Serbia, of the four Powers which are not directly interested. If Germany agrees, time will be gained, and this is the essential point.
>
> Sir Edward Grey told me he would discuss with Prince Lichnowsky the proposal I have just explained. . . . [After the interview with Grey, Cambon again talked with his Russian colleague]. Count Benckendorff thinks it right to attempt the *démarche* upon which I have agreed with Sir Edward Grey.[41]

[40] P. Cambon to Bienvenu-Martin, July 24; F.Y.B., 33.

[41] P. Cambon to Bienvenu-Martin, July 24; F.Y.B., 32; evidently this telegram, which the editors of the *Yellow Book* print under No. 32 should follow, not precede, that printed under No. 33, and quoted just above.

Cambon then departed from London to Paris this same Friday afternoon or evening, and did not return until late Monday night, July 27.[42]   What his purpose was in going thither, or what he did there, is not revealed by any of the documents in the *French Yellow Book*. Perhaps it was merely to give aid and counsel to Bienvenu-Martin, who was inexperienced in foreign affairs and somewhat at sea as to his bearings, with a storm gathering and the pilot and captain of the French ship still absent somewhere in the Baltic. The temporary withdrawal of Cambon's strong personality and influence on Sir Edward Grey seriously worried the Russian Ambassador who wrote to Sazonov on Sunday: "Unfortunately Cambon is away, and will not return until Tuesday morning. I have asked that he be begged to speed his return. I fear that Grey is not sure of his public opinion, and he doubts if he will be supported, if he engages himself any further." [43]

On Friday afternoon, after his interview with Cambon, and after a long and wearisome Cabinet on the Irish question, Sir Edward Grey saw Prince Lichnowsky. After the latter had given him the German *communiqué* defending Austria's action and urging a "localization" of the conflict, Sir Edward Grey replied that if the ultimatum did not lead to trouble between Austria and Russia, he "had no concern with it." But he was apprehensive of the view Russia might take. Referring to Lichnowsky's previously

---

[42] The next despatch from the French Embassy in London, reporting Grey's Friday evening interview with Lichnowsky (F.Y.B., 37), is signed, not by Cambon, but by Fleuriau, the French Chargé d'Affaires. Fleuriau continued to sign despatches (F.Y.B., 40, 63, 66, 68, 69, 71) for the next three days, and on July 27 informed the British Foreign Office (B.D., 173): "M. Cambon returns at 11 this evening." His presence in Paris is indicated in F.Y.B., 53, and B.D., 183. In telling his story of the tragic days before the War to M. Recouly, Cambon says nothing of his Paris visit, and does not begin his narrative until the events of July 31; Recouly, *Les Heures Tragiques d'avant Guerre*, ch. ii, "A Londres—Récit de M. Paul Cambon."

[43] Benckendorff to Sazonov, July 26; L.N., II, 329.

expressed hope that he would exercise moderating influence at St. Petersburg, he said that now, in view of the extraordinarily stiff character of the Austrian Note, he "felt quite helpless as far as Russia was concerned." He then made his own mediation proposal, and added to it Cambon's plan for restraining Austria:

> The only chance I could see of mediating or moderating influence being effective, was that the four Powers, Germany, Italy, France and ourselves, should work together simultaneously at Vienna and St. Petersburg in favor of moderation in the event of the relations between Austria and Russia becoming threatening.
>
> The immediate danger was that in a few hours Austria might march into Serbia and Russian Slav opinion demand that Russia should march to help Serbia; it would be very desirable to get Austria not to precipitate military action and so to gain more time. But none of us could influence Austria in this direction unless Germany would propose and participate in such action at Vienna.[44]

Next day, having heard from Buchanan that M. Sazonov "thought that Russia would at any rate have to mobilize," [45] Sir Edward Grey made to Russia his proposal for mediation between Austria and Russia by the four less directly interested Powers.[46]

In view of the sweeping statement often made that Germany blocked all Sir Edward Grey's peace proposals, it is interesting to note the attitude of Germany, and compare it with that of Russia and France.

Germany at once expressed approval. On Saturday

[44] Grey to Rumbold, July 24, 7:45 P.M.; B.D., 99. For Lichnowsky's account of this conversation see K.D., 157, and A.R.B., II, 15. Grey's telegram was also sent to British Ambassadors in Paris, St. Petersburg, Vienna, and Rome for their information.

[45] B.D., 101.

[46] He explained it directly to Count Benckendorff in London (B.D., 132), and telegraphed it to Buchanan in St. Petersburg (July 25, 2:15 P.M.; B.D., 112).

morning, July 25, when the British Chargé at Berlin presented it, the German Foreign Office was still optimistic that the conflict could be localized. It had been informed that Berchtold had told the Russian Ambassador in Vienna that "Austria-Hungary had no intention of seizing Serbian territory." It thought that this assurance might exercise a calming effect at St. Petersburg, but if not—if the relations between Austria and Russia became threatening— then Germany "was quite ready to fall in with your [Grey's] suggestion as to the four Powers working in favor of moderation at Vienna and St. Petersburg." [47] Meanwhile, in London, before the arrival of this, Sir Edward Grey and the German Ambassador again discussed the proposal for mediation between Austria and Russia. Prince Lichnowsky said "he thought Austria might with dignity accept it, and expressed himself personally favorable." Grey endorsed this, and said that "between Serbia and Austria I [Grey] felt no title to intervene, but as soon as it was a question between Austria and Russia, it was a question of the peace of Europe, in which we must all take a hand. . . . The participation of Germany would be essential to any diplomatic action for peace." [48] In response to Lichnowsky's report of this conversation and urgent advice to coöperate with England, the German Foreign Office immediately reaffirmed its approval of mediation between Austria and Russia, should "localization" become impossible:

> Sir E. Grey's distinction between Austro-Serbian and Austro-Russian conflict entirely to the point. In the former we do not want to interfere any more than England; as hitherto we hold that the question ought to remain localized through the non-interference of all the Powers. . . . Should

[47] Rumbold to Grey, July 25, 3:16 P.M.; B.D., 122.
[48] Grey to Rumbold, July 25, 3 P.M.; B.D., 116. *Cf.* Lichnowsky to Bethmann, July 25, 2:02 P.M. (K.D., 180), and his letter to Jagow (K.D., 179).

an Austro-Serbian strife arise, we are ready, reserving our known treaty obligations, to have mediation begin between Austria and Russia.[49]

After receiving this, Lichnowsky informed Grey, who was out of town, in a written note: "My Government accepts your suggested mediation à quatre." [50]

What was the attitude of Russia and France toward the British mediation proposal? The Russian Ambassador objected to it, as we learn from a despatch of Grey to Buchanan which was suppressed from the British Blue Book of 1914:

> I told Count Benckendorff to-day of what I had said to the German Ambassador this morning as to the possibility of Germany, Italy, France and ourselves work'ng together in Vienna and St. Petersburg to secure peace after Austria and Russia had mobilized.
>
> Count Benckendorff was very apprehensive that what I said would give Germany the impression that France and England were detached from Russia.[51]

[49] Jagow to Lichnowsky, July 25, 11:05 P.M.; K.D., 192.

[50] B.D., 145. Some writers, to prove that Germany blocked Grey's proposal, point to the fact that it was wirelessed to the Kaiser in Norway, who made the marginal note: "This is superfluous! Austria has already explained to Russia, and Grey cannot propose anything else. I will not join in—unless Austria expressly requests it, which is not likely. In questions of honor and vital interests one does not consult others" (K.D., 157). This marginal note, like so many of the Kaiser's annotations, is interesting for a study of his psychology. But it exercised no practical influence upon the actual course of events as far as this mediation proposal of Grey's was concerned; because the German Government had already expressed their approval through Lichnowsky, and, by the time the marginal note reached the German Foreign Office on July 27 (ibid., note 13), the situation had already essentially changed, and Grey had made another proposal. On this same day, July 27, the Kaiser himself returned to Potsdam, and was very soon ready, as indicated later, to accept mediation on the basis of the Austrian occupation of Belgrade.

[51] Grey to Buchanan, July 25; B.D., 132, and note. The note, however, is misleading in saying that, while Benckendorff demurred to Grey's proposal, "M. Sazonov according to No. 125, was prepared to accept the idea;" Sazonov, in B.D., 125, was talking about mediation between Austria and Serbia, not between Austria and Russia. This letter of Grey's

France also, like Russia, took a negative attitude toward Sir Edward Grey's proposal for mediation between Austria *and Russia.* As has been indicated above, it was made to Cambon around mid-day on Friday, July 24; but it made little or no impression on him, owing perhaps to his eagerness to impress upon Grey the plan for mediation between Austria *and Serbia,* which he and Count Benckendorff had agreed upon together. Nor did Cambon report it to his Government. Sir Edward waited in vain for any reply from the French. He had to admit next day to Lichnowsky that "he did not yet know whether France would participate. He had talked with Cambon, but had so far received no reply. He counted firmly on the assent of France, although he did not know how far she was already committed to Russia." [52]

Thus, it was not so much Germany, as Russia and France, who failed to give approval to Sir Edward Grey's proposal for mediation by the four Powers if Austria and Russia should mobilize.

GREY'S PROPOSAL FOR A CONFERENCE OF AMBASSADORS, JULY 26

On Saturday evening, July 25, the European situation had taken a decided turn for the worse. Austria had broken off diplomatic relations at Belgrade, and Austria and Serbia had ordered mobilization against each other. In Russia war excitement and the military party were in the ascendant, the Tsar had sanctioned provisionally the mobilization of 1,100,000 men, and measures of the "Period Preparatory to War" were about to be put into effect. But the news of these ominous events had not yet reached London, where a more hopeful tone prevailed than the day before,

of which a part is here quoted, was at first included in the draft copy of the *Blue Book* of 1914 as No. 28, but then deleted by Sir Edward Grey's direction, and No. 28 was marked *"Nil."*

[52] Lichnowsky to Bethmann, July 25; K.D., 180; *cf.* also B.D., 116.

upon the first news of the Austrian ultimatum. There came a rumor—untrue as it turned out—that Serbia had accepted the Austrian demands. Germany had expressed approval of mediation by the four Powers at Vienna and St. Petersburg, if "localization" failed and the situation between Austria and Russia became threatening. As the situation seemed more hopeful, some of the British Cabinet left London for Sunday in the country. Winston Churchill, who had arranged to spend the day with his family at Cromer, decided not to alter his plan, and went peacefully to bed with a feeling that things might blow over. Sunday morning he went down to the beach and played with his children, damming up the little rivulets which trickled down to the sea as the tide went out. Sir Edward Grey, for his part, went down for Sunday rest to Itchen Abbas and his beloved birds and woods. Sir Arthur Nicolson was left in charge at the Foreign Office.

But on Sunday morning, those who had remained in London began to realize that the danger was greater than ever. At noon, Winston Churchill was called up from the Admiralty, and decided to return to London that evening. Without waiting for him, but with his approval, the Admiralty sent out at 4 P. M. the secret and significant order that the fleet was not to disperse for maneuvers as hitherto intended, but was to remain concentrated at Portland.[53] At the Foreign Office Sir Arthur Nicolson found much bad news which had come in overnight. Austria and Serbia had severed diplomatic relations. Serbia had ordered mobilization and removed the Government from Belgrade to Nish. From Vienna Bunsen reported that "war is thought to be imminent." It was reported that the German fleet had received orders to concentrate off the Norwegian coast and that the Kaiser had given up his northern cruise and was returning direct to Kiel, a step which the German

[53] Churchill, p. 199 ff.; Corbett, *Naval Operations*, I, 24.

Foreign Office regretted as likely to cause speculation and excitement.[54]   From Buchanan in St. Petersburg came a long telegram:

> [Sazonov] thought that, in the event of an Austrian attack, Serbian Government would abandon Belgrade and withdraw their forces to the interior, while they would at the same time appeal to Powers to help them. His Excellency was in favor of such an appeal. . . . Were Serbia to appeal to Powers, Russia would be quite ready to stand aside and leave question in hands of England, France, Italy and Germany.
>
> [After telling of the Tsar's approval of the contingent mobilisation of 1,100,000 men, Paléologue's "formal assurance that France placed herself unreservedly on Russia's side," and his inquiry "whether the British fleet was prepared to play part assigned to it by Anglo-French Naval Convention," Buchanan continued:] His Excellency [Sazonov] assured me once more that he did not wish to precipitate a conflict, but unless Germany can restrain Austria I can regard situation as desperate. Russia cannot allow Austria to crush Serbia and become predominant Power in the Balkans, and, secure of support of France, she will face all the risks of war. For ourselves position is a most perilous one, and we shall have to choose between giving Russia our active support or renouncing her friendship. If we fail her now we cannot hope to maintain that friendly coöperation with her in Asia that is of such vital importance to us.[55]

This telegram, indicating that "Russia, secure of support of France, will face all the risks of war," might well have prompted Sir Edward Grey to the conclusion that it

[54] For all this bad news, see B.D., 130-138.

[55] Buchanan to Grey, July 25, 8 P.M., received 10:30 P.M.; B.D., 125. *Cf.* B.B.B., 17, in which the paraphrase of 1914 alters the meaning in the second sentence of the last paragraph by adding three words to read, "*if she feels* secure of support of France, she [Russia] will face all the risks of war." See also above, ch. vi, at note 109, for important passages omitted from the *British Blue Book* of 1914.

was high time to attempt to exercise a moderating influence at St. Petersburg—if he preferred to place the preservation of the peace of Europe above the maintenance of the Triple Entente. But he did not. Although Buchanan at St. Petersburg in the early part of the crisis attempted to exercise restraint upon Russia, no such effort was made from London. The British Foreign Office took the stand expressed in a minute by Sir E. Crowe on July 25:

> The moment has passed when it might have been possible to enlist French support in an effort to hold back Russia.
>
> It is clear that France and Russia are decided to accept the challenge thrown out to them. Whatever we may think of the merits of the Austrian charges against Serbia, France and Russia consider that these are the pretexts, and that the bigger cause of Triple Alliance versus Triple *Entente* is definitely engaged.
>
> I think it would be impolitic, not to say dangerous, for England to attempt to controvert this opinion, or to endeavor to obscure the plain issue, by any representation at St. Petersburg and Paris. . . .
>
> Our interests are tied up with those of France and Russia in this struggle, which is not for the possession of Serbia, but one between Germany aiming at a political dictatorship in Europe and the Powers who desire to retain individual freedom.[56]

England expected Germany to exercise restraint upon Austria not to move against Serbia, but unless Germany did so England was unwilling to exercise any restraint upon her Entente friends. Here was the evil of the system of alliances. On neither side was a Power willing to put out a restraining hand upon its ally or friend for fear of destroying the alliance or friendship. Instead, therefore, of dispatching a moderating telegram to St. Petersburg, England now merely decided to make a new peace proposal. Sir

[56] B.D., 101.

Arthur Nicolson, noting Sazonov's suggestion to Buchanan quoted above, wrote to Sir Edward Grey at Itchen Abbas:

> I think that the only hope of avoiding a general conflict would be . . . that you should telegraph to Berlin, Paris, Rome, asking that they shall authorise their Ambassadors here to join you in a Conference to endeavour to find an issue to prevent complications and that abstention on all sides from active military operations should be requested of Vienna, Serbia, and St. Petersburg pending results of conference.[57]

Grey at once approved, and on July 26, at 3 P. M., this proposal for a Conference of Ambassadors of the four Powers was dispatched to Paris, Berlin and Rome. It was also repeated to the British representatives at St. Petersburg, Nish and Vienna with instructions to endeavor to prevent active military operations pending the results of a Conference, as soon as they had received similar instructions from their Italian, French and German colleagues.[58]

This proposal for a Conference of Ambassadors at London at first sight seemed a good one and was certainly made with sincerity. A similar Conference of Ambassadors at London under Sir Edward Grey's leadership had functioned successfully during the Balkan Wars to prevent that cancerous trouble from spreading to the rest of Europe. Incidentally, however, its decisions had exasperated the authorities in Vienna and made the very word "Conference" anathema to them.[59] But the Ambassadorial Conference during the Balkan Wars was not quite the same thing as that which Grey was now proposing. The London

[57] B.D., 139.
[58] Grey to Bertie and others July 26, 3 P.M.; B.D., 140, 141.
[59] A.R.B., III, 79. Sir Francis Bertie also gathered from the German Ambassador in Paris "that Austrians are particularly suspicious of words 'intervention,' 'mediation' and 'conference,' and suggested therefore that care should be taken to speak of conversations, moderating advice, etc.;" Bertie to Grey, July 27; B.D., 183.

Conference of 1912-13 had been composed of the Ambassadors of all the Great Powers of Europe, who represented the two opposing groups into which Europe was divided, instead of four only, as Grey had proposed. All the members of the London Conference, except perhaps Austria, had at that time, been genuinely anxious to preserve the peace of Europe. In 1912-13, Russia was not ready for war; France did not want a war over Balkan questions; and Germany did not want to be dragged into a war because of Austria's difficulties. But in 1914 these Powers were, for various reasons, less disinclined for war than in 1912-13. Moreover, the London Conference of 1912-13 had merely been called upon to settle differences between Turkey and the Balkan states, and among the Balkan states themselves. Though Austro-Russian rivalry had been strong, the London Conference had not been compelled to decide vital questions at issue between these two Great Powers.

But now in 1914, Grey was proposing the far more delicate task of attempting to decide a question which involved the prestige of the Triple Alliance and Triple Entente. He was virtually proposing a tribunal which was ostensibly fair and possible, being composed of two allies of Austria (Germany, Italy), and two friends of Russia (England and France). But, in view of Italy's nationalist hostility to Austria, of her ambitions in the Balkans which conflicted with those of Austria, and of her secret agreements with France (in 1900 and 1902) and with Russia (at Racconigi in 1909), it was likely that Italy would be more inclined to side with the Entente than with her ally.[60]

---

[60] At this moment, July 26, the British Ambassador in Rome was telegraphing to Grey: "I gather . . . that inasmuch as Austria did not consult Italy before delivering Note, and inasmuch as by her mode of attack on Serbia she would be constructively provoking Russia, the *casus foederis* contemplated by Alliance would not arise" (B.D., 148). See also Flotow to Bethmann, July 24 (K.D., 156) quoted below, ch. ix, at note 18; and Bethmann-Hollweg, *Betrachtungen zum Weltkrieg*, I, 133, 144.

In the proposed Conference, therefore, the "four less directly interested Powers" would be likely to stand three to one against Austria and Germany, instead of being evenly balanced two to two. This fact probably explains in large part Germany's ultimate rejection of this European "Areopagus." To Germany, the proposal had the additional objection that, though "active military operations" were to be suspended pending the result of the Conference, Russia could still continue her "preparatory measures," and so deprive Germany of her advantage of being able to mobilize much more quickly than Russia.

Whether purposely or not, in wording his draft, Nicolson had avoided indicating whether he intended that the Conference of the four Ambassadors should mediate between Austria *and Serbia*, which would be unpalatable at Berlin and Vienna, or between Austria *and Russia*, which would be equally unpalatable at Paris and St. Petersburg. Essentially, however, it was bound to mean intervention between Austria *and Serbia*, in order to prevent Austria from invading Serbian territory. This was clear from the way it was explained, to the German Ambassador in London:

> I have just spoken with Sir A. Nicolson and Sir W. Tyrrell. . . . Both men look at Sir Edward Grey's proposal to hold a Conference à *quatre* here as the only possibility of avoiding general war; and they hope it will secure full satisfaction to Austria, since Serbia would be more ready to yield to the Powers and give way to their joint wishes than to the threats of Austria, but the absolute condition for the success of the conference and the maintenance of peace would be that no military movements should take place. Should the Serbian boundary once be crossed, all would be lost, for the Russian Government could not tolerate this. . . . The localization of the conflict hoped for in Berlin, they said, was wholly impossible and must be discarded from practical politics.[61]

[61] Lichnowsky to Bethmann, July 26, 8:25 P.M.; K.D., 236.

In other words, Grey's new proposal was the kind of mediation which Paul Cambon had been desiring from the outset—mediation between Austria *and Serbia*. Though it was made with sincerity, Nicolson was not at all hopeful, as he wrote to Grey a little later on Sunday afternoon: "It seems to me the only chance of avoiding a conflict— it is I admit a very poor chance—but in any case we shall have done our utmost. Berlin is playing with us. . . . I am not hopeful. Still no chance should be neglected." [62]

What was the attitude of each of the Powers towards Sir Edward Grey's new proposal for a Conference of Ambassadors at London?

Italy immediately "welcomed the proposal," just as she had already welcomed the earlier proposal for mediation between Austria and Russia.[63]

Lichnowsky in London was in favor of accepting Grey's proposal, believing that the "localization" hoped for by Germany was no longer practicable and should be dropped. If, however, Germany should coöperate with Grey in preserving the peace of Europe, "German-English relations would be placed on a firm foundation for time everlasting." If not, everything would be doubtful, and it was necessary "to spare the German nation a struggle in which it has nothing to gain and everything to lose." [64]   But when the proposal was made at Berlin, Bethmann telegraphed to Lichnowsky:

> We could not take part in such a conference, as we should not be able to summon Austria before a European court of justice in her case with Serbia. Sir Edward Grey

[62] B.D., 144.

[63] Rodd to Grey, July 26; B.D., 154. *Cf.* also B.D., 133, 189; F.Y.B., 72.

[64] Lichnowsky to Bethmann, July 26, 8:25 P.M.; K.D., 236; *cf.* also his despatches of July 27 (K.D., 258, 265, 266). The British proposal was formally made in Berlin on the morning of July 27 by an *Aide Mémoire* from Goschen to Bethmann; K.D., 304.

makes a sharp distinction, as Your Excellency has expressly reported, between Austro-Serbian and Austro-Russian conflict, and is concerned about the former just as little as ourselves. Our mediation activities must be confined to a possible Austro-Russian clash. In regard to the Austro-Serbian conflict, the method of a direct understanding between St. Petersburg and Vienna . . . appears to me to be feasible. I therefore request you most urgently to advocate in London the necessity and the possibility of localization.[65]

Similarly Sir Edward Goschen, the British Ambassador to Germany, who had just returned to his post and talked with Jagow, reported:

Conference you [Grey] suggest would practically amount to a court of arbitration and could not, in his opinion, be called together except at the request of Austria and Russia. He could not therefore, desirous though he was to cooperate for the maintenance of peace, fall in with your suggestion. . . . He added that the news he had just received from St. Petersburg showed that there was an intention on the part of M. Sazonov to exchange views with Count Berchtold. He thought that this method of procedure might lead to a satisfactory result, and that it would be best, before doing anything else, to await outcome of the exchange of views between the Austrian and Russian Governments.[66]

Germany rejected Grey's conference proposal for several reasons. She had not quite yet abandoned her hope, though she was to do so in a few hours, that the Austro-Serbian conflict could be treated as one to be "localized." She hoped, as Jagow told Goschen, that the "direct conversations" which were being opened between St. Petersburg and Vienna, might prove a more satisfactory method of averting trouble between these two countries. She knew also that a Conference would not be palatable to her ally,

[65] K.D., 248.
[66] Goschen to Grey, July 27, 6:17 P.M.; B.D., 185.

for Austria retained bitter memories of the decisions of the London Conference during the Balkan Wars, and of its impotency in enforcing its decisions against Serbia. Bethmann naturally feared that in such a Conference of four Powers as Grey proposed, Germany would inevitably be in a minority of one to three; Italy would side with the Triple Entente rather than with her own nominal allies, and so Germany at the Conference would stand alone in representing Austria's point of view against England, France and Italy.[67] Furthermore, from a military point of view, a conference of ambassadors might work to Germany's disadvantage; its decisions would be likely to drag out for days or weeks; but meanwhile Russia was making active military preparations; if the Conference should break down and war come eventually, Germany would be deprived of much of the military advantage which she enjoyed in being able to mobilize more rapidly than Russia, an advantage which she counted on partly to offset the superior numbers of the French and Russian armies. A final, and probably decisive, reason for the rejection of Grey's conference proposal was the fact that the German Foreign Office had received simultaneously a strongly worded annotation from Emperor William emphatically rejecting Grey's earlier proposal for mediation between Austria and Serbia.[68]

Though there are thus many reasons which made it natural for Germany to reject Grey's conference proposal, and though she herself a few hours later abandoned her "localization" plan, accepted the idea of mediation, and began to put pressure on Austria also to accept it, her

[67] Bethmann-Hollweg, *Betrachtungen zum Weltkriege,* I, 133, 144 f. Jagow, *Ursachen,* p. 118 f.

[68] For the Kaiser's annotation, which reached Berlin by wireless from on board the *Hohenzollern* at 12:07 A.M. on July 27, (K.D., 157, final note), see above, note 50. Lichnowsky's despatch containing Grey's proposal was also received July 27, 12:07 A.M. and when ultimately submitted to the Kaiser, "His Majesty disapproved of Lichnowsky's point of view" (K.D., 236, note 2).

rejection of the Conference was a grave political mistake. It was another stupid blunder, comparable to giving Austria a free hand at Potsdam on July 5, and to endorsing and justifying the Austrian ultimatum when urging "localization" on July 24. It strengthened the suspicion among the Entente Powers that Germany was not sincere in protesting that she desired to maintain the peace of Europe. It unfortunately made them doubt her sincerity, when, a little later, she genuinely tried to restrain Austria and induce her to accept mediation. As Sir Eyre Crowe noted, on hearing Jagow's negative reply to the conference proposal: "So far as we know, the German Government has up to now said not a single word at Vienna in the direction of restraint or moderation. If a word had been said, we may be certain that the German Government would claim credit for having spoken at all. The inference is not reassuring as to Germany's goodwill." [69] It was suspicion of this kind which largely contributed to the ultimate catastrophe.

France is also generally stated by Entente writers to have "sent in at once a completely favorable answer." [70] But as a matter of fact France appears to have hesitated. On the following day, July 27, the French Chargé d'Affaires in London twice called attention to the proposal, adding that it "ought, I think, to be supported." [71]

On July 26, the German Ambassador, at Paris, Baron von Schoen, had stated to Bienvenu-Martin, that "Austria has declared to Russia that she does not desire territorial acquisitions . . . but only to secure peace and quiet and

[69] Minute, July 28, on B.D., 185.

[70] Oman, *The Outbreak of the War of 1914-1918* (London, 1919), p. 48; Headlam, *The History of Twelve Days* (London, 1915), p. 106; Poincaré, *Les Origines de la guerre,* p. 223 ff.

[71] Fleuriau to Bienvenu-Martin, July 27, F.Y.B., 68, 69. *Cf.* also Mensdorff to Berchtold, July 26, 5:55 P.M. (A.R.B., II, 58): "Sir A. Nicolson to whom I spoke in Grey's absence is very much disturbed. . . . He has as yet practically no news from Paris."

exercise police supervision, and consequently it rests with Russia to prevent war. Germany is at one with France in her ardent desire to preserve peace, and she sincerely hopes that France will exercise a moderating influence at St. Petersburg." Bienvenu-Martin pointed out that Germany on her part might well act on similar lines at Vienna, especially in view of the conciliatory spirit displayed by Serbia. Schoen replied that this was not possible, owing to the decision not to intervene in the Austro-Serbian dispute. Bienvenu-Martin "then asked whether the four Powers— Great Britain, Germany, Italy and France—could not make representations at St Petersburg and Vienna, for that the matter amounted, in effect, to a dispute between Austria and Russia. The Ambassador alleged that he had no instructions. Finally, the Minister refused to agree to the German proposal, since the Prime Minister is absent. Berthelot unfortunately was not present at this interview." Berthelot, the Director of the Political Department of the Ministry for Foreign Affairs, believed that Schoen "aims at intimidating France and at securing her intervention at St. Petersburg. All things taken together, and considering the whole attitude of Germany and Austria-Hungary, he [Berthelot] inclines to the view that these Powers are seeking a brilliant diplomatic victory, but not war at any price, although in the last instance they would not shrink from it. He regards an emphatic and energetic action by England at Berlin as useful." [72]

France in fact had no more desire to exert pressure for peace on her Russian ally, than did Germany on her Austrian ally. Such pressure might have tended to sow distrust between two allies just at the moment when they most

[72] Sevastopulo to Sazonov, July 26, tgs. nos. 187, 188; M.F.R., p. 514; Romberg, pp. 12-15; *Livre Noir*, II, p. 278; R.O.B., 28, 29, where parts are suppressed. For Schoen's account, see K.D., 200, 235, 240 and 241; and *The Memoirs of an Ambassador* (London, 1922). p. 181 ff.

M. BIENVENU-MARTIN (left) Acting-Minister for Foreign Affairs
in July, 1914; M. PHILIPPE BERTHELOT (rear), Political Director of
the French Foreign Office; FREIHERR VON SCHOEN (right), German
Ambassador in Paris, 1910-1914.

needed to stand together, and would not have been welcome in the capital where it was exerted. In the case of France and Russia this is seen from paragraphs in despatches of Izvolski and Sazonov which were suppressed from the original *Russian Orange Book*. On July 27, immediately after his return from St. Petersburg, Izvolski telegraphed to Sazonov:

> "Directly after my return to Paris, I discussed the situation with Bienvenu-Martin, in the presence of Berthelot and Abel Ferry. They confirmed the details of the steps taken by the German Ambassador, of which you have been informed by Sevastopulo's telegrams nos. 187 and 188. . . . Schoen laid especial emphasis on the expression of solidarity of Germany and France. According to the conviction of the Minister of Justice [Bienvenu-Martin], these steps on the part of Germany are taken with the evident object of disuniting Russia and France, of inducing the French Government to make representations at St. Petersburg, of thus compromising our ally in our eyes, and, finally, in case of war, of throwing the responsibility not on Germany, who is ostensibly making every effort to maintain peace, but on Russia and France. . . . Altogether, I am surprised how correctly the Minister of Justice and his colleagues understand the situation, and how firm and calm is their determination to give us the most complete support, and to avoid the slightest appearance of disunity between us." [73]

Fortunately for the French point of view, Sir Edward Grey's proposal was capable of being interpreted as including mediation between Austria and Serbia, as well as between Austria and Russia, for it spoke of "Vienna, Belgrade, and St. Petersburg." This was seen by Viviani, who informed Bienvenu-Martin from on board the *France*, "The action of the four less interested Powers cannot . . . be

[73] Izvolski to Sazonov, July 27; M.F.R., p. 516; Romberg, pp. 22-23; *Livre Noir*, II, p. 281-282; *cf.* also R.O.B., 35.

exerted only at Vienna and St. Petersburg. In proposing to exert it also at Belgrade, which means in fact between Vienna and Belgrade, Sir Edward Grey grasps the logic of the situation; and, in not excluding St. Petersburg, he offers on the other hand to Germany a method of withdrawing with perfect dignity from the *démarche* by which the German Government have caused it to be known at Paris and London that the affair was looked upon by them as purely Austro-Serbian and without any general character." [74]

Without waiting, however, for Viviani's reply, the French Foreign Office, on July 27, upon the repeated urging from London, finally accepted Grey's proposal, but did not want it acted upon until Germany had exerted pressure at Vienna: "Ministry for Foreign Affairs thinks that it would be dangerous for *Entente* Ambassadors to speak at Vienna, until it is known that the Germans have done so with some success." [75] It is, therefore, hardly true, as Professor Oman says, that "Paris sent in at once a completely favorable answer." [76]

When Grey's proposal was presented at St. Petersburg, Russia did not favor it. Sazonov had already entered upon "direct conversations" with Vienna, by which he hoped to induce Austria to accept modifications in her demands on Serbia. If Sazonov could accomplish this by conciliatory negotiations conducted at the same time that extensive military preparations were taking place in case they failed, he would have secured a great diplomatic triumph by his own efforts directly for Russia, without having to accept a solution of the crisis brought about by a conference of the Powers or by moderating counsels from France. So he at first preferred to pursue his "direct conversations," rather than have Sir Edward Grey take the initiative in calling a

[74] Viviani to Bienvenu-Martin, July 28; F.Y.B., 76.
[75] Bertie to Grey, July 27, 2:45 P.M.; B.D., 183; also 194, 211; and F.Y.B., 61, 70, 71.   [76] Oman, p. 48.

conference of Ambassadors. If the former failed, he could always fall back on the latter. This explains his negative answer to Sir Edward's proposal:

The British Ambassador, upon instructions from his Government, asked me whether Russia would agree that England should take the initiative in convoking a conference in London of the representatives of England, France, Germany and Italy, in order that they might examine *à quatre* the possibility of a way out of the present situation.

I replied to the Ambassador that I have begun direct conversations with the Austro-Hungarian Ambassador favorably; but I have not as yet received any reply as to the proposal made by me for revising the note by the two Cabinets. If our direct explanations with the Vienna Cabinet lead to no result, I should be ready to accept the English proposal, or any other, which would bring about a peaceful solution of the conflict.

I wish, however, from this day forth, to put an end to a misunderstanding which slipped into the answer [of Bienvenu-Martin to Schoen]. In case it is a question of exercising a moderating influence at St. Petersburg, we reject it in advance, because we have from the beginning taken a stand which we cannot at all alter, since we have already met all the demands of Austria-Hungary which are acceptable.[77]

To this Izvolski replied reassuringly:

According to my conversation yesterday at the Quai d'Orsay, the Acting Minister of Foreign Affairs does not for a minute admit the possibility of exercising a moderating influence in St. Petersburg, but only replied to the German Ambassador that it was not Russia, but Austria, that was

[77] Sazonov's tg. No. 1521 to Izvolski in Paris and Benckendorff in London, July 27, *Krasnyi Arkhiv*, I, p. 174; Romberg, p. 16; *Livre Noir*, II, p. 279. The first part of this telegram was also communicated to the Russian Ambassadors in Berlin, Vienna and Rome; the last paragraph, significantly enough, was suppressed from R.O.B., 32, but found its way in a curtailed form into B.B.B., 53; for an explanation of this curtailment, see B.D., 206, note.

menacing the peace of Europe; and that, in any case, if there was a question of any moderating influence, this should be exercised not only in St. Petersburg, but first of all in Vienna. As a result of his conversation with Baron Schoen, the Minister declined to accept the German proposal.[78]

The last paragraph of Sazonov's telegram and the whole of Izvolski's reply, both of which were suppressed from the *Russian Orange Book* along with other passages which did not square with the Russian thesis that Germany was to blame and that Russia had done everything possible to avert war, throw a new light on Russian diplomacy in the July crisis. Russia and her French ally were insisting that Berlin exercise a moderating influence at Vienna, while Russia herself refused from the outset to accept any such influence, and was supported in this by France. In this respect Russia was pursuing an uncompromising attitude, threatening to the peace of Europe, exactly analogous to that of Germany from July 5 to 28, who had been insisting that France and England should exercise a moderating influence at St. Petersburg, while she herself refused to do likewise at Vienna. But there was soon a difference: by July 28 Germany had abandoned her hitherto uncompromising attitude, as we shall see later, and really began to attempt to exercise an increasingly strong moderating influence at Vienna; but France and England continued to refrain from restraining Russia, and Russia proceeded to the general mobilization, which she had been warned would make a European War inevitable.

Since none of the Powers, except Italy, gave an immediate and unconditional acceptance to his conference proposal, and since Russia and Germany decidedly preferred to await first the success of the "direct negotiations," Grey

[78] Izvolski to Sazonov, tg. no. 198, July 28; M.F.R., p. 517; Romberg, p. 30; *Livre Noir*, II, p. 283.

willingly put his own proposal aside for the moment. "I entirely agree," he telegraphed to Goschen, "that direct exchange of views between Austria and Russia is the most preferable method of all, and as long as there is a prospect of that taking place I would suspend every other suggestion. . . . It will no doubt relieve the tension and make the situation less critical." [79]

What were these "direct conversations" between Sazonov and Szápáry at St. Petersburg which originated simultaneously and moved parallel with Grey's conference proposal, and were partly responsible for its being dropped?

DIRECT CONVERSATIONS BETWEEN VIENNA AND ST. PETERSBURG, JULY 26-28

It is said by most writers that it was Sazonov who originated the attempt to find a peaceful solution of the crisis by direct negotiations between St. Petersburg and Vienna.[80] As a matter of fact, the idea had occurred to Sir Edward Grey at the outset, but had been put aside and lost to sight. It was the German Ambassador in St. Petersburg, Count Pourtalès, who was really responsible for bringing this peace proposal into practical operation.

On Sunday morning, July 26, after the break-up of the maneuvers at Krasnoe Selo and the other military decisions on the preceding afternoon,[81] Count Pourtalès and M. Sazonov happened to meet on the platform of the rail-

[79] July 28, 4:00 P.M., B.D., 218. Nicolson also, "puzzled by the fresh proposals which Sazonov makes almost daily," believed his last proposal to open up conversations direct with Vienna "seems the best procedure" (letter to Buchanan, July 28; B.D., 239); see also above, at notes, 1-9.

[80] Cf. Headlam, pp. 107, 117; Oman, p. 51. This is also stated by Paléologue to Bienvenu-Martin, July 27, (F.Y.B., 54) and is implied by Buchanan to Grey, July 27, (B.D., 179); but cf. Buchanan to Grey, July 29 (B.D., 271, suppressed from B.B.B.): Sazonov "does not wish reference to be made to the fact that it was at the suggestion of the German Ambassador that he had proposed direct conversation with Austria." [81] See above, ch. vi, last part.

way station at Krasnoe Selo. They entered the same carriage and traveled up to St. Petersburg together.

Pourtalès, finding Sazonov much less excited than the day before, took advantage of this informal opportunity again to urge that Austria had no hostile intentions toward Russia, and was only seeking measures of safety to protect herself from the Serbian danger on her borders. Sazonov replied that Russia likewise had no desire for war; a bridge must therefore be found, on the one hand, to satisfy the demands of Austria, the legitimacy of which he recognized so far as they related directly to the instigators of the crime; and, on the other hand, to make their acceptance possible to Serbia; some of the demands would have to be toned down, and he urged joint action by all the Powers, including Germany, to bring this about. Pourtalès then urgently advised him to have a frank and friendly talk with Szápáry, the Austrian Ambassador at St. Petersburg, with whom Sazonov had had no words since the excited interview of Friday, when first confronted with the Austrian ultimatum. On arriving at St. Petersburg, Pourtalès then went to see Szápáry, told him of Sazonov's calm and conciliatory state of mind, and gave him the same good advice to seek a frank and friendly direct conversation with the Russian Minister.[82]

Acting on the German Ambassador's suggestion, Szápáry at once went to see Sazonov and had the friendly conversation for which Pourtalès had thus prepared the way. We have five accounts of the conversations: the first-hand accounts by Szápáry to Berchtold, and by Sazonov to the Russian Ambassadors at Vienna and London; and the reports by Pourtalès, Buchanan, and Paléologue as they heard it from the two principals.[83] It is worth while to

---

[82] Pourtalès's diary in K.D., IV, p. 161; Graf Pourtalès, *Am Scheidewege zwischen Krieg und Frieden* (Berlin, 1919) p. 19; Pourtalès to Bethmann, July 26, 3:15 P.M., arrived at Berlin 7:01 P.M., and immediately forwarded to Tschirschky at Vienna; K.D., 217.

give Szápáry's account, although it is long, partly because his narrative is more detailed than those of the others, partly because the most interesting parts of it were suppressed in the original *Austrian Red Book* of 1915, and partly because it throws very interesting light on Sazonov:

Have just had a long conversation with M. Sazonov. The German Ambassador had already told me in the forenoon that early today, he had found the Minister [Sazonov] much calmer and more conciliatory. He had advised him to seek a conversation with me, for he knew that I was filled with the best intentions toward Russia, and how greatly I regretted that our action against Serbia met with so little understanding in St. Petersburg. Sazonov received me very cordially, in contrast to his decidedly piqued attitude on Friday. He spoke to me of his above-mentioned conversation with Count Pourtalès, and said that if I myself had not already come to him of my own accord, he would have begged me to visit him in order to have a chance to speak frankly with me. Last Friday, he had been somewhat taken by surprise and had not controlled himself so much as he had wished; besides, at that time, our conversation was a purely official one.

I replied that I also had wished to have the opportunity to speak frankly with him, since I had the impression that mistaken ideas in regard to the character of our action were prevalent in Russia. We seem to be suspected of wishing to push forward into Balkan territory and to begin a march to Salonica or even to Constantinople. Others indeed went so far as to describe our action as the starting point of a preventive war against Russia, which had been planned by Germany. All these suppositions, I said, were partly erroneous and partly absolutely unreasonable. The aim of our action was self-preservation and self-defense against hostile propaganda of word, writing, and deed, which threat-

[83] A.R.B., II, 73; R.O.B., 25; K.D., 238; B.D., 170, 179, 207-209; F.Y,B., 54.

ened our existence. It would occur to no one in Austria-Hungary to threaten Russian interests, or indeed to pick a quarrel with Russia. Yet we are absolutely determined to attain the aim we have set before ourselves, and we consider the path which we have chosen the most practicable. As, however, the action under discussion was an act of self-defense, I would not conceal from him that every consequence which might arise had been considered by us. Nevertheless, I was quite clear, I said, that if a conflict between the Great Powers arose, the consequences would be most fearful, and then the religious, moral, and social order of the world would be at stake. In glaring colors I set forth, as Sir Edward Grey also has probably done here, a notion of what might follow if a European war broke out.

Sazonov agreed with me thoroughly and seemed uncommonly pleased with the purport of my explanations. He began assuring me that in Russia, not only he, but the whole Ministry, and, what is of the greatest importance, his Sovereign, were filled with similar feelings toward Austria-Hungary. He could not deny, he said, that in Russia there were old grievances against Austria; he admitted that he had had them too, but this belonged to the past and must not interfere with practical politics; and as far as the Slavs were concerned—though indeed he ought not to say this to an Austro-Hungarian Ambassador, he said—he had no sympathy at all for the Balkan Slavs. In fact, they were a heavy burden for Russia, and we could hardly imagine what Russia had already had to suffer from them.

Our aim, he said, as I had described it to him, was an entirely legitimate one, but he considered the path we were pursuing to attain it was not the safest way. He said the Note which we had presented was not happy in its form. He had been studying it meanwhile, and, if I had time, he would like to look it through once more with me. I remarked that I was at his service, but was not authorized either to discuss the text of the Note with him nor to interpret it. His remarks, however, would of course be of interest. The Minister then went through all the points of

the Note, and today found seven of the ten points acceptable without great difficulty; only the two points [5 and 6]
dealing with the collaboration of Austro-Hungarian officials
in Serbia, and the point [4] dealing with the removal of
officers and civil servants to be designated *ad libitum* by us
seemed to him to be unacceptable in their present form;
with regard to Point 5 I was in a position to give an authentic interpretation in the sense of your Excellency's telegram
No. 172 of July 25; [84] with regard to the other two points,
I said I did not know how my Government interpreted
them, but that they were both necessary demands.   M.
Sazonov thought that one might for instance have in mind
consular intervention at the legal proceedings; and concerning the dismissal of officials, proofs of the guilt of the
persons accused would still have to be produced.   Otherwise,
King Peter would run the risk of being killed at once.   I
replied that this view of the case by the Minister made
the best justification of our action in Serbia.   M. Sazonov
said that we ought to remember that the Karageorgevitch
family would, without doubt, be the last dynasty in Serbia.
Did we want to set up on our frontier an anarchistic
witches's caldron?   Surely not!   I replied that we certainly had an interest in the maintenance of the monarchical
form of government, but also, that the last remark of the
Minister again proved how necessary firm action on our
part in Serbia was.

By way of summing up what had been said, the Minister declared that in the matter of the Note, it was really
merely a question of phraseology, and that perhaps a more
acceptable way for us could be found, by which these difficulties could be gotten over.   Would we accept, he said,
the mediation of our ally, the King of Italy, or that of the

[84] Berchtold to Szápáry, telegram no. 172, July 25, 1 P.M., A.R.B.,
II, 38: "By point 5 we mean 'collaboration' in the creation of a secret
'*bureau de sûreté* in Belgrade, which would function like the analogous
Russian creations in Paris and Berlin, and would coöperate with the
Serbian police and administrative boards." It must be remembered that
at the time of this interview Sazonov and Szápáry were not yet aware of
the text of the Serbian reply (*cf.* B.D., 207-209).

King of England? I replied that I was not in a position to express an opinion; that I did not know what dispositions my Government had already taken; that matters had already begun to move; and that certain things could not be retracted when once they had been started. Moreover, the Serbians had already mobilized yesterday [Saturday, July 25], and what else had happened since then, I did not know.

At the close of the conversation, M. Sazonov again in the warmest words expressed his pleasure at the explanations which I had given and which had materially calmed him. He would also, he said, make a report of our conversation to Tsar Nicholas, whom he would see day after to-morrow [Tuesday, July 28], which was his day for being received in audience.

Russian policy has traveled a long distance in two days —from the first rude rejection of our procedure and from the proposition for a judicial investigation of our *dossier*, making a European question out of the whole affair; and from that point on again to a recognition of the legitimacy to our claims and to a request for mediators. Nevertheless, we must not overlook the fact that along with this backing-water policy on the part of the diplomatists, there is setting in a lively activity on the part of the militarists, as a result of which Russia's military, and therefore also her diplomatic, situation threatens daily to become less favorable for us.

P.S. Incidentally in the course of the conversation, M. Sazonov asked whether I could let him see our *dossier;* upon my replying that I was not in possession of a copy, he asked whether it could not be shown to M. Shebeko [Russian Ambassador] in Vienna.[85]

[85] Szápáry to Berchtold, July 27, 2:15 P.M. [July 26, 2:15 P.M., or July 27, 2:15 A.M.]; A.R.B., II, 73. This telegram is also dated '27' instead of '26' by Gooss, p. 206, and in the *Austrian Red Book* of 1915. That 'July 27, 2:15 P.M.' is incorrect is evident from the fact that it bears the serial number '165,' and must therefore be prior to number '168,' which was dispatched on July 27 at 4:30 A.M. The other accounts make it clear that this interview took place around noon or a little later on July 26. As it is doubtful whether such a long telegram could have been put into cipher by 2:15 P.M. on Sunday,

Pourtalès' Sunday advice to Sazonov and Szápáry thus seemed likely to bear good results by opening admirably the way to "direct conversations," and for it he was warmly thanked by both when he saw them later in the day.

In the evening, after talking with both men again, he reported: •

> Count Szápáry had an extended interview this afternoon with Sazonov. Both men, with whom I talked after it, were favorably impressed by it. . . . [Here follows a summary of the interview, similar to Szápáry's account.] The Minister begged me urgently to tell him whether I could not make some sort of a proposal. In reply I emphasized the fact that I was not authorized to make any proposals, and therefore could only express my personal views; but that the following way seemed to me perhaps practicable. In case the Vienna Cabinet should consent to modify somewhat the form of its demands, as the expressions of Count Szápáry seemed to indicate was not altogether out of the question, perhaps an attempt could be made, with this in view, to get into touch with Austria directly. Should an agreement result from this, then . . . [cipher group lacking] Serbia could be advised by Russia to accept the demands of Austria on the basis agreed upon between Russia and Austria, and to let the Austrian Government know this through the mediation of a third Power.
>
> Sazonov, upon whom I again strongly impressed the fact that I did not speak in the name of my Government, declared that he would at once telegraph to the Russian Ambassador in Vienna along the lines of my proposal.[86]

Accordingly on Sunday evening Sazonov telegraphed to the Russian Ambassador in Vienna informing him of the

one may conclude that it was probably dispatched on July 27 at 2:15 A. M., 'P. M.' being a misprint for 'A. M.' It arrived at Vienna at 4:30 P. M., which would be about 16 hours or the normal period of transmission between Vienna and St. Petersburg at this congested time.

[86] Pourtalès to Bethmann, July 26, 10:10 P. M., arrived July 27, 12:45 A.M.; K.D., 238.

interview with Szápáry. He instructed him to ask Berchtold to authorize Szápáry to discuss at St. Petersburg a redrafting of certain points in the ultimatum which would satisfy Austria's main demands and yet be acceptable to Serbia.[87] Thus was opened the way for "direct conversations," which Berlin preferred to Grey's conference proposal, which the British Foreign Office approved, and which Paléologue also "believed preferable to any other procedure and likely to succeed;" as he summed it up, Sazonov proposed to Austria: "Take back your ultimatum; modify its form; and I will guarantee you the result." [88]

Unfortunately, however, all these hopes were misplaced, owing to Berchtold's obstinacy and determination to proceed with his plan of military action against Serbia. Proposals for preserving peace, instead of being accepted by him, decided him to forestall them by presenting Europe with the *fait accompli* of an Austrian Declaration of War on Serbia.

SUMMARY

Such were a few of the more important proposals for preserving peace, prior to July 28; they all came to nothing.

Grey's original suggestion for "direct conversations," vetoed by Poincaré as "very dangerous," was quickly dropped and completely lost to sight.

The Entente efforts to have Austria extend the time-limit were either directly rejected by Vienna, or rendered impossible by the shortness of the time within which the Powers had to act.

Grey's proposal for mediation between Austria and Russia, accepted in principle by Germany, was not immediately accepted by France, who wanted mediation between Austria and Serbia, nor by the Russian Ambassador in Lon-

---

[87] Sazonov to Shebeko, July 26; R.O.B., 25.

[88] Paléologue to Bienvenu-Martin, July 26; F.Y.B., 54; *cf.* also Paléologue, I, 28.

don who was "very apprehensive" that it would encourage Germany in the impression that the Triple Entente was lacking in solidarity.

Grey's proposal for a conference of the Ambassadors of four Powers, rejected for various reasons by Germany, not accepted immediately by France, and put aside by Russia in favor of "direct conversations," was quickly suspended by its author, who also agreed that "the direct exchange of views between Vienna and St. Petersburg is the most preferable of all."

But these "direct conversations," suggested by the German Ambassador in St. Petersburg, and taken up by Sazonov, were thwarted by Berchtold's refusal to consent to any modification of his demands, and by his declaration of war on Serbia with the deliberate purpose of forestalling any kind of mediation which might prevent Austrian military action against Serbia.

As it took many hours for telegrams to come and go, and as the situation changed rapidly from day to day, it was essential for the success of these various peace proposals that they should be accepted immediately. But they were not so accepted. With the exception of England and Italy, the different Powers, for one reason or another, in the case of each proposal, either preferred other methods, or delayed immediate acceptance, or gave a negative reply. So the proposals for preserving peace made prior to the Austrian Declaration of War on Serbia fell to the ground. After Austria had faced Europe with the *fait accompli,* it was more difficult than ever to get satisfactory peace proposals accepted.

CHAPTER IX

GERMANY'S BELATED PEACE EFFORTS

U<small>NTIL</small> Monday, July 27, Bethmann and his colleagues at Berlin had adhered consistently to their policy of hoping and insisting that the Austro-Serbian conflict could and should be localized. Early on Sunday afternoon, July 26, having heard of some of the Russian military decisions at Krasnoe Selo and that "all preparations are being made for mobilization against Austria," [1] Bethmann again stated Germany's attitude and sought to dissuade Russia from taking mobilization measures which might endanger the peace of Europe:

> Since Count Berchtold has stated to Russia that Austria wishes to make no territorial acquisitions in Serbia, but only to bring about quiet, maintenance of European peace depends on Russia alone. Confiding in Russia's love of peace and in our long-established friendly relations, we trust that she will take no step that will seriously endanger the peace of Europe. [2]

At the same time, in similar telegrams to London and Paris, Bethmann urged England and France to exercise a

[1] Pourtalès to Bethmann, July 25, received July 26, 3:28 A.M., K.D., 194.

[2] Bethmann to Pourtalès, July 26, 1:35 P.M.; K.D., 198. Later in the evening (7:15 P.M.; K.D., 219) he made a stronger appeal, indicating his willingness "to support Russia's desire not to have the integrity of the Serbian Kingdom placed in question." Both communications "made a very good impression" on Sazonov, who said "a way must be found of giving Serbia her deserved lesson while sparing her sovereign rights," as might be done if Germany would coöperate in influencing Austria, to moderate some of her demands (Pourtalès to Bethmann, July 28; K.D., 282).

moderating influence at St. Petersburg. But these failed completely of their desired effect.[3]

Similarly on Monday morning, July 27, after rejecting Grey's conference proposal in favor of "direct negotiations," Bethmann telegraphed to Paris: "We cannot mediate in the conflict between Austria and Serbia, but possibly later between Austria and Russia." This suggestion of mediation between Austria and Russia hints at the beginning of a change in his attitude—the first sign of an eventual abandonment of "localization," and the possible adoption of some mediatory rôle to secure an agreement between Vienna and St. Petersburg. Pourtalès's telegrams, with the news of "direct conversations," were at once forwarded, with slight omissions and without comment, to Tschirschky at Vienna.[4] And Jagow told the Russian Chargé d'Affaires "that he could not advise Austria to give way, but that the very fact of Pourtalès's telegram being transmitted to Vienna means that he rather recommended such a way out of the situation." [5] By Monday evening there were further signs that Bethmann was beginning to waver in his mind as to the wisdom of his "localization" policy.

GERMAN DOUBTS AS TO "LOCALIZATION"

An important factor in Germany's immediate decisions was the hurried return of the Kaiser to Potsdam on the afternoon of July 27.[6] "The Foreign Office," Jagow was

[3] K.D., 199, 200. Lichnowsky could not see Grey, who had gone out of town over Sunday; but from talks with Nicolson and Tyrrell he concluded that "localization" must be abandoned in favor of Grey's mediation proposal (K.D., 218, 236). In Paris Bienvenu-Martin at first seemed ready to exercise moderation at St. Petersburg, after Germany had shown that she was exercising it at Vienna (K.D., 235, 240, 241, 252). But Berthelot and Sazonov were emphatically opposed to any pressure being put upon Russia (see above, p. 391 f.).

[4] K.D., 217, 238, notes.

[5] Bronevski to Sazonov, July 27; *Krasnyi Arkhiv*, I, p. 172; the last clause is suppressed from R.O.B., 38.

[6] At 3:00 P. M. according to Moltke (*Erinnerungen*, p. 381,) who had a conference with him shortly afterwards.

reported to have said, "regret this step which was taken on His Majesty's own initiative. They fear that His Majesty's return may cause speculation and excitement." [7] During his northern cruise he had been furnished by Bethmann with scanty but fairly optimistic reports, calculated to keep the Kaiser calm and deter him from giving any orders to the German Fleet which might cause alarm.[8] But Bethmann had been unsuccessful. Hearing from the Admiralty that the Kaiser, on the strength of a Wolff telegram, had directed the Fleet to make preparations to return home, Bethmann "ventured most humbly to advise that Your Majesty order no premature return of the Fleet." Upon this the Kaiser made the characteristic annotation:

> Unbelievable assumption! Unheard of! It never entered my mind!!! This was done on report of my Minister about the mobilization at Belgrade! This *may* cause mobilization of Russia; *will* cause mobilization of Austria. In this case I must keep my fighting forces by land and sea *collected*. In the Baltic there is not a single ship!! Moreover, I am not accustomed to take military measures on the strength of one Wolff telegram, but on that of the general situation, and that situation the *Civilian* Chancellor does not yet grasp.[9]

The Kaiser had also been irritated while still at sea, because it was through a newspaper agency, and not officially through Bethmann, that he had first learned the terms of Austria's demands on Serbia.[10] As the Kaiser neared Berlin, Bethmann sent him another optimistic summary of the situation, and prepared a sheaf of the latest

---

[7] Rumbold to Grey, July 26; B.D., 147.

[8] K.D., 67, 116, 125, 182, 191, 197, 221.

[9] July 25; K.D., 182. The Minister at Belgrade had reported on the evening of July 24: "Mobilization is already in full swing" (K.D., 158); the news was premature when sent, but true when it reached the Kaiser on July 25 at 3:45 P. M.

[10] Kaiser to Foreign Office, July 26; K.D., 231.

telegrams, which had poured into the Foreign Office, to be given him upon his arrival at Potsdam.[11]

The military and naval leaders had also returned to Berlin by the afternoon of July 27. Moltke, before the crisis arose, had planned to return from his cure at Karlsbad on July 25, but delayed a day.[12] On his arrival he talked with Bethmann and agreed that an attitude of calm should prevail, but took also the precaution of sending to the Foreign Office a draft in his own hand of the ultimatum to be sent to Belgium in case of war.[13] After talking with Bethmann again next morning, the 27th, he wrote to his wife: "The situation continues to be decidedly not clear. Not very quickly will it clear up; it will be some fourteen days before one can know or say anything definite." [14]

Admiral Tirpitz had been requested by Bethmann on July 24 not to return from his summer home in Switzerland, in order to avoid arousing alarming comment which might embarrass the Foreign Office in its "localization" policy. Nevertheless, on his own responsibility, the Grand Admiral also returned to Berlin on July 27, convinced that Bethmann was pursuing a perilous path in allowing such tension to develop with Russia in the foolish hope that an Austro-Serbian conflict could be localized, and that even in case of war on the Continent England would remain neutral. "The Chancellor," he had written to a subordinate just before leaving Switzerland, "is absolutely on the wrong track, wrapped up in his idea of winning the favor of perfidious Albion. . . . We must, at all costs, come to an understanding with Russia, and play the Bear and the Whale against each other." [15]

[11] Bethmann to Kaiser, July 27, 11:20 A.M.; K.D., 245.

[12] K.D., 74, 197.   [13] K.D., 376, note 1.

[14] Moltke, *Erinnerungen*, p. 381. This indicates that he still supposed Austria would not declare war on Serbia until Conrad had completed the concentration of the Austrian forces calculated for August 12.

[15] Tirpitz, *Erinnerungen* (Berlin, 1920), p. 150; *cf.* also pp. 213 f. and 236 f. Tirpitz, according to his later memoirs, would have liked to see

The Kaiser and his officials, who were now back in Berlin, were all vexed at the way in which the Chancellor had kept them absent from the capital and insufficiently informed. They were seriously alarmed at the way Bethmann had allowed Berchtold to draw so heavily upon the blank check of July 5. They had been told that, in order to secure the successful "localization" of the Austro-Serbian dispute, calm was necessary; but they were doubtless of the same mind as the Kaiser, who, while at sea, pencilled ironically on one of Bethmann's admonitions to calmness in spite of rumors of Russian mobilization: "To remain calm is the citizens' first duty! just keep calm, always keep calm!! A calm mobilization is something new, indeed!" [16]

They saw that a serious crisis was very rapidly developing for which no special military preparations had been made, and for which the diplomatic situation began to look unfavorable. Russia, drawing encouragement from France and England, was making louder objections and more wide-reaching military preparations than had been anticipated. Lichnowsky's reports from London were pessimistic: "Since the appearance of the Austrian demands, nobody here believes in localizing conflict. . . . Consider moment arrived to start mediation along lines suggested by Sir Edward Grey"; Grey's secretary "pointed out to me, repeatedly and with emphasis, the immense importance of Serbia's territory remaining unviolated until the question of the conference had been settled, as otherwise every effort would have been in vain and the world war would be inevitable. The localization of the conflict as hoped for in Berlin

Bethmann ousted from the Chancellorship, and his incompetent subordinate, Jagow, replaced by some strong and able man like Hintze, who unfortunately, however, at the moment was sitting in Mexico. But though the Kaiser was irritated at Bethmann, he declared on July 29 that "he could not part with this man, because he enjoys the confidence of Europe" (ibid., p. 237)   [16] K.D., 197.

was wholly impossible, and must be dropped from the calculations of practical policies." [17]

The Italian Foreign Minister, San Giuliano, had declared that, since Austria had not consulted her ally "before entering upon a move so portentously aggressive, . . . Italy could not consider herself bound in connection with the further consequences. . . . The Austrian Note was worded so aggressively and so ineptly, that the public opinion both of Europe and of Italy would be against Austria—no Italian Government could stand against it. . . . The Triple Alliance compact was an obligation in connection with a defensive war; Austria was now proceeding aggressively; and Italy, therefore, even in the event of Russian intervention, would not be further obligated." [18]

So it began to look as if Bethmann's optimism and "localization" policy might prove a frightful blunder.[19]

At a conference at Potsdam late on Monday afternoon, July 27, between the Kaiser, Bethmann, Jagow, Moltke, and some other officials,[20] in spite of the irritation at the Chancellor, there still seems to have been substantial solidarity of opinion that he was correct in his view that a peaceful solution for the crisis could be found; and no important military orders were issued.[21] "Localization" apparently still remained the German program.

[17] Lichnowsky to Bethmann, July 26; K.D., 218, 236.

[18] Flotow to Bethmann, July 24; K.D., 156, 168. For other disquieting reports received by July 27 concerning Italy, arising from Berchtold's failure to respect Italy's feelings as an ally and to purchase her loyalty by satisfactory compensations, see K.D., 46, 109, 119, 136, 211, 244; and above, ch. v., at notes 119-128.

[19] Lichnowsky had already realized this (cf. his reports *passim* and especially his letter to Bethmann of July 16, and Jagow's reply; K.D., 62, 72); Tirpitz and Helfferich, writing their recollections with the advantage of hind-sight, also claim to have quickly realized it; but Bethmann, with a less clear perception of what Bismarck used to call the "imponderabilia" has always asserted that he steered the only available course.

[20] Moltke, *Erinnerungen*, p. 381; Tirpitz, *Politische Dokumente*, II, 2, says that he and the Minister of War, Falkenhayn, were not present.

[21] *Investigating Commission*, II, pp. 8 f., 15; and Montgelas, in KSF, V, 1208 ff., December, 1927.

GERMAN ADVICE TO AUSTRIA

But on returning from Potsdam to Berlin, Bethmann and Jagow found a handful of new telegrams which showed that the situation was becoming more serious, and which indicated the doubtful wisdom of continuing to adhere rigidly to the policy of strict "localization." Germany must pay more heed to mediation proposals and advise Berchtold to give them consideration. She must attempt, but without giving Austria offense or doubt as to her continued support, to take back into her own hands that freedom of action in the Serbian question which she had so unwisely abandoned on July 5. Instead of saying at Vienna, as she had done three weeks earlier, that the Kaiser "naturally cannot take any stand in the questions between Austria and Serbia, for they are beyond his competence," [22] Germany must assume the rôle of mediator, and advise Austria to consider the English and Russian peace proposals. Otherwise, there would be an increase in the suspicion which was being circulated by the French Ambassadors [23] that Germany was egging Austria on, knew the text of the ultimatum from the beginning, wanted war, and was acting *mala fide* in pretending to desire peace. Moreover, England would be dangerously antagonized and might not, in case of a continental war, preserve the neutral attitude, for which Germany hoped and which she believed had just been promised by King George to Prince Henry of Prussia.[24]

One of the telegrams which Bethmann and Jagow found was the full text of the Serbian reply which had been

[22] See above, ch. v, at note 37.

[23] F.Y.B., 15, 32, 38, 41, 43, 48, 67, 74; K.D., 215, 415, 485.

[24] "King of Great Britain said to Prince Henry of Prussia that England would maintain neutrality in case war should break out between Continental Powers" (German Naval Attaché in London to German Naval Office, July 26; K.D., 207; *cf.* also K.D., 201 and 374).

handed in at the Foreign Office by the Serbian Legation early in the afternoon.[25]

Though Bethmann had already been given to understand that it "agreed to nearly all the points," [26] the reading of the text showed him definitely how conciliatory it was, and how far Serbia had yielded to the demands. He may well have been irritated at Berchtold for not having even yet sent a copy of it to Berlin.[27]

There were four new telegrams telling of Russian military preparations along the German frontier: Kovno put in a state of war; the mouth of the Düna barred with mines; and troop movements at several points.[28]

A telegram from Vienna announced Austria's sudden decision "to issue the official declaration of war tomorrow, or the day after tomorrow at the latest, primarily in order to cut the ground from every attempt at intervention," [29] instead of adhering to the plan, already notified to Berlin, of waiting until about August 12, when the concentration of the troops would be completed.

A telegram from Lichnowsky indicated the disturbing

[25] It was dispatched from Belgrade to the Serbian Legation in Berlin on July 25, 7:40 P. M.; arrived July 26, 8:58 P. M.; and was handed over in a hardly legible form by the Serbian Chargé d'Affaires to the Berlin Foreign Office next day, but at what hour is not precisely indicated (K.D., 271, note 3). Bethmann, telegraphing to the Kaiser July 27, at 11:20 A. M., speaks of "Serbia's answer to the ultimatum, the text of which we have not yet been able to get hold of" (K.D., 245); and ten minutes later he telegraphed to Vienna: "Please telegraph text of the Serbian reply immediately" (K.D., 246). It was evidently not in hand at the conference at Potsdam, since it was sent to the Kaiser by special messenger at 9:30 P. M.; but did not arrive in time for him to read it that night (K.D., 270, note 2; 293). Jules Cambon seems to be mistaken in saying that the Serbian Chargé d'Affaires gave it to Jagow "this morning" (July 27; F.Y.B., 74).

[26] K.D., 245.

[27] Berchtold delayed forwarding it until he had time to annotate it; see above, ch. vii, note 42.

[28] K.D., 264, 274-276; see also above, ch. vi, "The Russian Danger."

[29] Tschirschky to Berlin, July 27, 3:20 P. M.; arrived 4:37 P. M.; sent to the Emperor the same night, and to the Army and Navy Staffs next morning; K.D., 257, see also below, at notes 42-54.

fact that Sir Edward Grey was losing patience with Germany. Grey had just read the text of the Serbian reply, and found that "Serbia had agreed to the Austrian demands to an extent he would never have believed possible." Should Austria reject it as a foundation for negotiations, or occupy Belgrade, "Russia could not regard such action with equanimity, and would have to accept it as a direct challenge. The result would be the most frightful war Europe had ever seen, and no one could tell to what such a war would lead." Grey therefore requested Germany to use her influence to get Vienna to accept the Serbian reply, either as satisfactory or as a basis for conferences. He was convinced that it lay in Germany's hands to settle the matter by proper representations. "I found the Minister vexed for the first time," Lichnowsky added; "he spoke with great seriousness and seemed absolutely to expect that we should successfully make use of our influence to settle the matter. . . . I am convinced that if war should come after all, we should no longer be able to count on British sympathy or British support, as every evidence of ill-will would be seen in Austria's procedure." [30]

In view of all this serious news, Bethmann decided that the time had come to accede to Grey's request to act as mediator. He telegraphed to Tschirschky at Vienna the text of Lichnowsky's telegram with its warning and its proposal from Grey that the Serbian Note be accepted as a basis for a settlement, and added:

> Since we have already refused one English proposal for a conference, it is impossible for us to waive *a limine* this English suggestion also. By refusing every proposal for mediation, we should be held responsible for the conflagration by the whole world, and be set forth as the original

[30] Lichnowsky to Bethmann, July 27, 1:31 P.M., received 4:37 P.M.; forwarded to Vienna 11:50 P.M.; and to the Kaiser by messenger July 28 at 5 A.M.; K.D., 258, 277, 283.

instigators of the war. That would also make our position impossible in our own country, where we must appear as having been forced into war. Our situation is all the more difficult, inasmuch as Serbia has apparently yielded to a very great degree. Therefore we cannot refuse the mediator's rôle, and must submit the English proposal to the consideration of the Vienna Cabinet, especially as London and Paris continue to make their influences felt in St. Petersburg. I request Count Berchtold's opinion on the English suggestion, as likewise his views on M. Sazonov's desire to negotiate directly with Vienna.[31]

But by the time Tschirschky presented this communication to Berchtold, the Austrian Minister replied that "now, since the opening of hostilities on the part of Serbia and the ensuing [Austrian] declaration of war, England's move was made too late." [32] Berchtold had faced his ally, as well as Europe, with the *fait accompli* of war with Serbia, and so "cut the ground from any attempt at intervention."

There has been much discussion as to the sincerity of Bethmann's action in this matter. On this same evening the Austrian Ambassador at Berlin, Szögyény, telegraphed to Berchtold at 9:15 P. M.:

[1] The Foreign Secretary [Jagow] very decisively informed me in strict confidence that the German Government would shortly acquaint Your Excellency with possible English proposals of mediation.

[2] The German Government give the most positive assurance that they do not identify themselves in any way with the proposals, they are even decidedly against their being considered, and they only forward them, in compliance with the English request.

[3] In doing so they are guided by the view that it is of the utmost importance that England should not make

[31] Bethmann to Tschirschky, July 27, 11:50 P. M.; arrived at the Embassy in Vienna at 5:30 A.M.; K.D., 277.
[32] Tschirschky to Bethmann, July 28, 4:55 P.M.; K.D., 313.

common cause with Russia and France at the present moment. Consequently everything must be avoided that would break down the wire between Germany and England which has hitherto worked so well. If Germany were to tell Sir Edward Grey plainly that she would not forward the request to Austria-Hungary, which England thinks more likely to be considered if it comes through Germany, this would lead to the very state of affairs it is so essential to avoid.

[4] Moreover, the German Government at every single English request of the kind in Vienna, would declare to her [*bei jedem einzelnen derartigen Verlangen Englands in Wien demselben erklären*] most emphatically that it would in no wise endorse to Austria-Hungary such attempts at intervention, and only passed them on in compliance with England's wish.

[5] Yesterday, as he said, the English Government had approached him [Jagow], through the German Ambassador in London and directly through their representative here, to persuade him to support England's request concerning our modification of the Note to Serbia. He, Jagow, had replied that he would indeed comply with Sir Edward Grey's wish to forward England's request to Your Excellency, but he himself could not endorse it, since the Serbian conflict was a question of prestige for the Austro-Hungarian Monarchy, in which Germany also was concerned.

[6] He, the Secretary of State, had therefore forwarded Sir Edward Grey's note to Herr von Tschirschky, but without instructing him to submit it to Your Excellency; he had then been able to inform the British Cabinet that he did not directly reject the English wish, but had even passed it on to Vienna.

[7] In conclusion the Secretary of State repeated his attitude, and begged me, in order to avoid any misunderstanding, to assure Your Excellency that his having acted as intermediary in this instance does not at all mean that he is in favor of the English proposal being considered.[33]

[33] Szögyény to Berchtold, July 27, 9:15 P.M., arrived at Vienna

Several observations may be made upon this Szögyény telegram, which is somewhat confused, inaccurate, and repetitious.

(1) In the 4th paragraph it is not at all clear whether *"demselben"* means "to England" or "to Vienna." The two ablest French and German experts, Renouvin and Montgelas, interpret it to mean "to England"; but if so, Szögyény was contradicting the essential notion expressed in his first three paragraphs. If it means "to Vienna," Szögyény's statement is contradicted by the fact that the German Government never declared in Vienna "that it would in no wise endorse to Austria-Hungary such attempts at intervention."

(2) In the 5th paragraph it is not clear to what Szögyény refers. England expressed no wish for "the modification of the *Note to Serbia"* on July 26 ("Yesterday"). This may be a confusion in Szögyény's mind with Grey's request. of July 25 (not "Yesterday"), received in Berlin the same day, that Germany "may feel able to influence the Austrian Government to take a favorable view of it," i.e., of the *Serbian reply;* this request, as Szögyény states in his 6th paragraph, was in fact forwarded at once to Tschirschky in Vienna, and England was so informed.[34] Szögyény can hardly have been thinking of the English proposal for a conference of Ambassadors, made at London to Lichnowsky on July 26 and at Berlin by Goschen on July 27 (both cannot be *"Yesterday"),* which Germany frankly rejected at once,[35] because he sent a report about that later.[36]

July 28, 9:00 A.M.; A.R.B., II, 68; Gooss, p. 173 ff. The American Delegation at the Versailles Peace Conference cited only the first two paragraphs of this telegram, which, taken by themselves, give a false impression. For different interpretations of this famous Szögyény despatch, see, among others, H. Delbrück, in *Preussische Jahrbücher*, vol. 176, pp. 487-490, June, 1919; Renouvin, pp. 121-126; Montgelas, *Leitfaden,* p. 176 f.

[34] B.D., 115, 149; K.D., 186, notes to 186, and 191a.

[35] See above, ch. viii, at notes 58-69.

[36] Szögyény to Berchtold, July 28, 7:40 P.M., (some *thirty hours after the event!*); A.R.B., II, 84: "The English mediation proposal according to which Germany, Italy, England and France should come together in

(3) No evidence exists that Jagow told England "the Serbian dispute was a question of prestige for the Austro-Hungarian Monarchy, in which Germany also was concerned," as Szögyény alleged at the end of the 5th paragraph.

(4) Szögyény was at this time so old a man, that his recall had already been decided upon and his successor selected. His age and the nervous strain of these days would explain the confusion and inaccuracy of this telegram, and make it doubtful whether it can be completely relied on, especially as this was not the only instance of his inaccuracy and unreliability in this crisis.[37]

(5) Finally, and most important, it has usually been assumed that when Szögyény announced in the 1st paragraph that "the German Government would shortly acquaint Your Excellency with possible English proposals of mediation," he was referring to Lichnowsky's telegram proposing mediation on the basis of the Serbian reply, and forwarded with Bethmann's comment, which has been quoted above at notes 30-31. If this was actually the case, and if Szögyény's telegram is trustworthy (which is open to doubt), it would throw a sinister light upon the sincerity of Bethmann's action. But it is quite possible that it was not Lichnowsky's telegram referred to above, but the British proposal for a Conference of the Four Powers, which Szögyény understood from Jagow might soon be passed on to Vienna. Jagow frankly and emphatically rejected the proposal, and there was nothing underhanded or deceitful in his telling Szögyény that the German Government was decisively opposed to its being considered, and only passed it on in compliance with England's wish. It may be objected that Jagow does not appear to have forwarded the

a conference in London, to find a way for the settlement of the present difficulties, has been rejected by Germany on the ground that a conference would not be the suitable means for accomplishing the aim."

[37] K.D., 324. See above, ch. v, note 43.

Conference proposal to Vienna. But this is easily explained. During the morning of July 27, Berlin had only an indefinite and informal knowledge of the Conference proposal contained in a telegram sent by Lichnowsky on Sunday evening.[38] Szögyény may have been told that Germany disapproved of this, and that if she forwarded it to Vienna it would not mean that she in any way endorsed it. Later in the day Goschen made the formal request for a Conference; this was rejected,[39] but Jagow and Bethmann, in hurrying out to Potsdam, neglected to forward it to Vienna. When they returned from Potsdam, read the text of the Serbian reply, and found Lichnowsky's telegram with a a good mediation proposal, they forwarded the latter instead of the Conference proposal. Another objection which might be raised to this view that Szögyény was thinking of a Conference proposal which Berlin might soon forward to Vienna is the fact that his telegram was sent at 9:15 P. M., and would hardly apply to a conversation around noon. But he was often many hours late in getting information at the German Foreign Office and in forwarding it to Vienna; such a delay of some nine hours would be nothing unusual for him.[40] Furthermore, it is very doubtful whether Bethmann and Jagow could have returned from Potsdam early enough to read Lichnowsky's telegram, tell Szögyény they disapproved it but were forwarding it to please the English, and

[38] In reply to this telegram of Lichnowsky's (K.D., 236; see above at note 17) Bethmann telegraphed to him at 1:00 P.M. (K.D., 248): "No knowledge here up to present of Sir Edward Grey's proposal to hold a conference à quatre there. We could not take part in such a conference, as we should not be able to summon Austria before a European court of justice."

[39] Goschen to Grey, July 27, 6:17 P.M.; B.D., 185.

[40] For instance, Germany requested from Vienna the text of the Serbian reply at 11:30 A.M. (K.D., 246), and Szögyény does not report the news until 5:50 P.M. Similarly, Goschen reported the rejection of the Conference proposal on Monday at 6:17 P.M. (B.D., 185), and Szögyény did not report it until more than twenty-four hours later on Tuesday at 7:40 P.M. (A.R.B., II, 84).

still leave time for Szögyény to put it all into cipher by 9:15 P. M.

It would seem, therefore, that there are good grounds for thinking that the Szögyény telegram referred to the Conference proposal, which was openly and frankly rejected, and not to the later mediation proposal forwarded by Bethmann toward midnight.

One may conclude that Bethmann was sincere, on the evening of July 27, in assuming the rôle of mediator to the extent of calling upon Berchtold to consider the proposals of Sir Edward Grey and of Sazonov for finding a settlement, in which Austria should accept the Serbian reply as a sufficiently satisfactory basis for further discussions. No doubt Bethmann was largely influenced by his desire not to antagonize England. But if this had been his only motive in forwarding the British proposal, as one school of interpreters of the Szögyény telegram believe, there was no need for him to have included Sazonov's "direct conversations" among the proposals which Berchtold was asked to consider. No doubt also Bethmann ought to have given stronger advice, if he wanted to make certain of restraining Austria, but he did not wish to offend her or raise doubts as to Germany's loyalty as an ally.[41] But even had he spoken in stronger terms, it would not have prevented the Austrian declaration of war on Serbia, because Berchtold had already decided on this step in order "to cut the ground from any attempt at intervention." When Tschirschky presented Bethmann's communication he was told that, since Austria and Serbia were already at war, "England's move was made too late."

---

[41] It is significant that in forwarding Lichnowsky's telegram to Vienna he omitted the last sentence which might seem to imply that Austria was under Germany's thumb: "The key to the situation is to be found in Berlin, and, if peace is seriously desired there, Austria can be restrained from prosecuting, as Sir E. Grey expresses it, a foolhardy policy" (K.D. 258, 277).

THE AUSTRIAN DECLARATION OF WAR ON SERBIA, JULY 28

There had been a general fear in Europe that Austria would quickly follow her diplomatic break with Serbia by a declaration of war or an opening of hostilities. This also had at first been the expectation and advice of Germany, in order to secure "localization" and by quick action reduce the likelihood of Russian intervention.[42] When this did not take place, there was some feeling of relief, and the prospects for the success of "direct conversations" seemed good. The reason that military action did not follow the diplomatic break at once was that the first day of Austria's partial mobilization was not to be until July 28, and the armies would not be concentrated for action until about two weeks later. Conrad did not want war until his armies were concentrated. Tschirschky was informed of this about noon on July 26. Berlin learned of it on the morning of July 27, and was therefore not expecting a declaration of war or the opening of hostilities until about August 12.[43]

But when Pashitch's advance summary of the Serbian reply began to make a favorable impression,[44] and when Berlin transmitted Grey's hope that Vienna would take a favorable view of it,[45] Berchtold began to doubt the wisdom of so long a delay. "When do you want a declaration of war?" he asked Conrad toward noon on July 26. "About August 12," the Chief of Staff replied. "The diplomatic situation will not last as long as that," said Berchtold.[46] However, no change in Conrad's plans was made at the moment. The Vienna authorities still believed that Russia would not move, and that there was no need for haste in

[42] Szögyény to Berchtold, July 25, 2:12 P.M.; A.R.B., II, 32; and Tschirschky to Bethmann, July 26, 4:50 P.M.; K.D., 213.

[43] Conrad, IV, 131 f. Tschirschky to Bethmann, July 26, 4:50 P.M.; K.D., 213. Dirr, p. 148. Moltke, *Erinnerungen*, p. 381. Szögyény to Berchtold, July 27, 5:50 P.M.; A.R.B., II, 67.

[44] B.D., 114, 115.   [46] Conrad. IV, 131 .

[45] K.D., 186; A.R.B., II, 57.

dealing with Serbia. But on July 27, when the news of the Krasnoe Selo military preparations and demonstrations came in,[47] they "decided to issue the declaration of war tomorrow, or at latest day after tomorrow, in order to cut the ground from every attempt at intervention." [48]

Such an intervention seemed even more likely, in the course of the evening, with the arrival of Szápáry's despatch proposing "direct conversations" [49] and news of Grey's proposal for a Conference.[49a] Berchtold therefore instructed Szápáry that he might converse with Sazonov, but "without entering into any kind of a binding engagement." [50] At the same time a declaration of war against Serbia was drawn up, together with a memorandum to persuade Emperor Francis Joseph to authorize its being sent "early tomorrow morning."   It contained two main arguments. First, since the Serbian reply was cleverly worded and conciliatory in form but wholly worthless in substance, the Entente Powers might make an attempt to reach a peaceful settlement, "unless a clear situation is brought about by a declaration of war."   And second, the Serbians had opened hostilities by firing on Austrian troops at Temes-Kubin on the Danube. Berchtold then went to Ischl. By using these two arguments he won the Emperor's assent, telephoned the news to Vienna, and the Austrian declaration of war was then dispatched to Nish a little before noon on July 28, in an uncoded telegram in French.[51]

[47] July 27, 7 and 8 A.M.; A.R.B., II, 49, 60; see also above, ch. vi, "The Russian Danger."

[48] Tschirschky to Bethmann, July 27, 3:20 P.M.; K.D., 257. *Cf.* also Berchtold to Szögyény, July 27, 11:10 P.M. (A.R.B., II, 69), where he says the declaration of war will be issued "in a few days" [*in den nächsten Tagen*], even though active military operations could not begin until a couple of weeks later, when Conrad had concentrated the troops.   [49] Received July 27, 4:30 P.M.; see above ch. viii, at note 85.

[49a] Mensdorff to Berchtold, July 27, received 6:30 P.M.; A.R.B., II, 71.   [50] Berchtold to Szápáry, July 27, 10:20 P. M.; Gooss, 210.

[51] A.R.B., II, 78; S.B.B., 45-47. B.D., 225, 233. Mr. H. F. Armstrong, to whom the present writer is indebted for the accompanying facsimile,

FACSIMILE OF THE AUSTRO-HUNGARIAN DECLARATION OF
WAR ON SERBIA

The telegram, sent from Vienna July 15/28 at 11:10 A.M. and received
at Nish at 12.30 P.M., runs in translation as follows:

The Royal Serbian Government not having answered in a satisfactory
manner the note of July 23, 1914, presented by the Austro-Hungarian Minister at Belgrade, the Imperial and Royal Government are themselves
compelled to see to the safeguarding of their rights and interests, and, with
this object, to have recourse to force of arms. Austria-Hungary consequently considers herself henceforward in a state of war with Serbia.

The Austro-Hungarian Minister for Foreign Affairs,

COUNT BERCHTOLD.

Berchtold had now "brought about a clear situation" by his *fait accompli*. When the Russian Ambassador came to propose "direct conversations," Berchtold told him that he could not accept the Serbian reply as a basis for discussion, "because war on Serbia has been declared today." [52] Similarly Berchtold informed Germany and England that Grey's proposal for a conference came "too late," and, "in view of the state of war already existing, has been outstripped by events"; [53] and also that Austria "would have to decline any suggestion of negotiations on basis of Serbian reply. Prestige of the Dual Monarchy was now engaged, and nothing could prevent conflict." [54]

The precipitate declaration of war by Austria thus forestalled the English and Russian proposals for taking the Serbian reply as a basis for negotiations. It created a new situation. To meet this new situation, several new proposals for preserving the peace of Europe, and at the same time satisfying Austria and Serbia, were quickly forthcoming from Germany and England (but no longer from Russia). One of these in fact was outlined by the Kaiser several hours before he was aware that Austria had declared war. It is commonly known as the "pledge plan" or "Halt in Belgrade" proposal.

gives an interesting history of it in *Current History*, Oct., 1927, p. 95. As telegraph connections with Belgrade were broken off, it was sent *via* Czernowitz and Bucharest.

The first draft of the declaration of war gave, as one of the grounds for war, the Serbian provocation at Temes-Kubin, but as this was not confirmed, it was omitted from the final declaration of war. Some writers believe that the Temes-Kubin rumor was invented to deceive and persuade Francis Joseph, and it is significant that Conrad makes no mention of it. Berchtold explained to the Emperor next day, July 29, that the Temes-Kubin conflict had been too insignificant to include in the Declaration to Serbia as a ground for war; Gooss, p. 218.

[52] Berchtold to Szápáry, July 28, 11:40 P.M.; A.R.B., II, 95.

[53] Berchtold to Szögyény, July 28, 11:00 P.M.; and to Mensdorff, July 29, 1:00 A.M.; A.R.B., II, 81, 90.

[54] Bunsen to Grey, July 28, 1:10 P.M.; B.D., 227; *cf.* also 226, 230; K.D., 313; and A.R.B., II, 82.

THE KAISER'S "PLEDGE PLAN"

When the Kaiser awoke on Tuesday morning, July 28, he had before him the text of the Serbian reply and many of the other documents which had led Bethmann the night before to ask Berchtold to consider the British and Russian peace proposals. The Kaiser was greatly impressed with the conciliatory and yielding character of the Serbian reply and the diplomatic success which Austria had achieved, as appears from his annotation on it:

> "A brilliant performance for a time-limit of only 48 hours. This is more than one could have expected! A great moral success for Vienna; but with it every reason for war drops away, and Giesl ought to have remained quietly in Belgrade! After such a thing, *I* should never have ordered mobilization." [55]

He therefore wrote at once to Jagow: "I am convinced that on the whole the wishes of the Danubian Monarchy have been acceded to. The few reservations that Serbia makes could be settled by negotiation. It contains the announcement *orbi et urbi* of a capitulation of the most humiliating kind, and as a result, *every cause for war* falls to the ground. Nevertheless, the piece of paper, like its contents, is of little value so long as it is not translated into *deeds*. The Serbians are Orientals, therefore lying, deceitful, and masters in evasion. In order that these beautiful promises may be converted into reality and deeds," and "in order to give the army, now mobilized *to no purpose* for the third time, the external *satisfaction d'honneur* of an ostensible success," Austria should be given temporary military occupation of Belgrade as a pledge. "I propose that we say to Austria: Serbia has been forced to retreat in a very humiliating manner, and we offer our congratulations;

[55] K.D., 271.

naturally, as a result, *no more cause for war exists;* but a *guarantee* that the promises *will be carried out,* is probably necessary; that could probably be secured by a *temporary* military occupation of a portion of Serbia, similar to the way we left troops in France in 1871 until the billions were paid. *On this basis* I am ready to *mediate for peace* with Austria. . . . Submit a proposal to me, along the lines sketched out, to be communicated to Vienna." [56]

Thus the Kaiser was ready at last to yield to England's request that he act as a mediator and advise Vienna to abandon the idea of war with Serbia. But while Sir Edward Grey had urged that Austria be dissuaded from any military action, the Kaiser was ready to permit it to the extent of having Austria secure a tangible pledge that the Serbian promises would be really carried out. Before the Kaiser's proposal could be embodied in a despatch and communicated to Austria, the latter, as we have seen, had already declared war on Serbia. It then remained to be seen whether Austria, and especially Russia, would be willing to accept the Kaiser's mediation proposal, which was sincerely calculated to avert a European war.

Before the Kaiser's autograph letter to Jagow had been brought from Potsdam to Berlin and put in the form of a concrete proposal to Vienna, Bethmann had received irritating news concerning Berchtold's attempt to rattle the German sword, his persistent neglect of Germany's advice to satisfy Italy, and his secret intention to partition Serbia. Bethmann had understood on July 5 that he was agreeing to support Austria in her vital interest of putting an end to the dangerous Greater Serbia propaganda; that danger was now taken care of by the Serbian reply, if its promises were duly carried out. He did not understand, and he did

---

[56] William II to Jagow, July 28, 10:00 A. M.; and a similar note by his secretary to Moltke, "who is entirely in accord with my views;" K.D., 293, and note 6 of new edition. Italics are the Kaiser's.

not intend, that Germany should be forced to follow Berchtold in secret plans which Austria had withheld from her
ally, and which might involve the rupture of the Triple
Alliance by Italy's withdrawal from it, and even the rupture of the peace of Europe in such a way that Germany
and Austria would seem to be responsible. He would not
permit that Russia and the Pan-Slav Press should back up
Serbia in a continuance of the Greater Serbia menace, but
on the other hand, he thought Austria ought to satisfy the
Russian desire that Serbia be not subjected to a partition.[57]

Bethmann therefore refused to allow Berchtold to rattle
the German sword. Berchtold and Conrad had asked
Tschirschky that Berlin warn St. Petersburg that the military preparations against Austria were so threatening that
counter-measures would have to be taken.[58] Instead of
acceding to this suggestion, Bethmann tried to calm and
restrain the Vienna authorities by telling them: "Military
reports concerning Russia, so far as known here, are only
rumors, and are not yet confirmed. Even according to
General Moltke's view, a categorical declaration at St.
Petersburg would seem today to be premature." [59] And
at the same time, in reply to Sazonov's admission that "a
way must be found of giving Serbia her deserved lesson
while sparing her sovereign rights," [60] he instructed Pourtalès: "Please tell Sazonov that I am grateful for his communication and for its conciliatory spirit, and further hope
that Austria's declaration of disinterestedness will satisfy
Russia and serve as a basis for further agreement." [61]

Bethmann also heard that Berchtold was persisting in

[57] Cf. Bethmann to the Prussian Ministers at the Federated German
States, July 28; K.D., 307; and also his telegrams to Vienna quoted below.
[58] Tschirschky to Bethmann, July 27 [July 28, 1:45 A. M., received
4 A.M.]; K.D., 281.
[59] Bethmann to Tschirschky, July 28, 3:20 P.M.; K.D., 299.
[60] See above, note 2.
[61] Bethmann to Pourtalès, July 28, 3:35 P.M.; K.D., 300.

his neglect to follow German advice in regard to satisfying Italy's hopes for compensation.[62] The German Ambassador in Rome had reported San Giuliano as insisting that "the existence of Serbia is an unconditional necessity for Italy. This barrier against Austria cannot be allowed to disappear." [63] Instructions had therefore been sent from Berlin to Vienna that the Kaiser "considers it absolutely necessary that Austria should come to an understanding in time with Italy about Art. VII and the compensation question"; an immediate conference between Berchtold and the Italian Ambassador is "urgently necessary." [64]

Most irritating of all was the news from London concerning Austria's doings. Though Berchtold had disclaimed any intention to annex Serbian territory [65] and had declared Austria's "territorial disinterestedness," the Austrian Ambassador in London had confided to Lichnowsky that Serbia was to be "beaten to the earth," and "it was the intention to present portions of Serbia to Bulgaria and presumably also to Albania." [66] These were secret intentions which had been expressed at the Austrian Ministerial Council of July 19,[67] but which were contrary to Bethmann's expectations and contrary to what he had been sincerely stating to the Powers. He therefore noted indignantly: "This duplicity of Austria's is intolerable. They refuse to give us information as to their program, and state expressly that Count Hoyos's statements which suggested a partition of Serbia were purely personal; at St. Petersburg they are lambs with not a wicked thought in their hearts, and in

[62] See above, at note 18, and also ch. v, at notes 119-128.

[63] Flotow to Bethmann, July 27, 2:40 P.M.; K.D., 261.

[64] Jagow to Tschirschky, July 27, 9 P.M., and 9:30 P.M.; K.D., 267, 269.

[65] In conversation with the Russian Chargé d'Affaires in Vienna on July 24 (A.R.B., II, 23), but this disclaimer had not been confirmed by Szápáry in St. Petersburg.

[66] Lichnowsky to Bethmann, July 28, 12:58 P. M., received 3:45 P.M.; K.D., 301.   [67] See above, ch. v, at notes 104-106.

London their Embassy talks of giving away portions of Serbian territory to Bulgaria and Albania." [68]

It was thus with some justifiable irritation at Austria that Bethmann took up the Kaiser's offer to mediate on the basis of the "pledge plan" and embodied it in the following telegram to Vienna:

[Aside from a declaration to Russia that it intends no territorial acquisition in Serbia] the Austro-Hungarian Government, in spite of repeated questions as to its purposes, has left us in the dark. The reply now at hand of the Serbian Government to the Austrian ultimatum makes it evident that Serbia has in fact met the Austrian demands in so wide-reaching a manner that if the Austro-Hungarian Government adopted a wholly uncompromising attitude, a gradual revulsion of public opinion against it in all Europe would have to be reckoned with. . . . [Russia will presumably be satisfied] if the Vienna Cabinet repeats in St. Petersburg the definite declaration that territorial acquisitions in Serbia lie far from its purpose, and that its military measures aim solely at a temporary occupation of Belgrade and other definite points of Serbian territory in order to compel the Serbian Government to a complete fulfilment of the demands, and to serve as guarantees for future good behavior, to which Austria-Hungary unquestionably has a claim after her experiences with Serbia. The occupation could be regarded like the German occupation in France after the Peace of Frankfort, as security for the demand of the war indemnity. As soon as the Austrian demands were fulfilled, a withdrawal would follow. . . . You are immediately to express yourself emphatically in this sense to Count Berchtold and have him take the proper step in St. Petersburg. You are carefully to avoid giving the impression that we wish to hold Austria back. It is solely a question of finding a method which will make possible the accomplishment of Austria's purpose of cutting the vital nerve of Greater Serbian propaganda without at the same

[68] K.D., 301, note.

time unchaining a world war, and in the end, if this is unavoidable, of improving as far as practicable the conditions
under which it is to be waged. Wire reply.[69]

This telegram of Bethmann's was a step in the right
direction. It was well adapted to the new situation created
by the fact that Austria was already at war with Serbia,
which he had just learned. It was aimed to make the Austrian armies "halt in Belgrade." But its language was not
sufficiently vigorous to compel immediate assent from
Berchtold. Nor did it correspond precisely with the Kaiser's
more decisive instructions that Vienna was to be told that
"no more cause for war exists." Bethmann was too much
afraid of offending Austria. He was too much concerned
with preventing the odium of responsibility for a war from
falling on Germany and Austria, rather than with preventing such a war altogether. However, he also at once informed Russia that he was striving to persuade Vienna to
have a frank discussion with St. Petersburg and to make
plain in an unobjectionable and satisfactory manner the
purpose and extent of Austria's procedure.[70] He likewise
told the British Ambassador that "he was doing his very
best both at Vienna and at St. Petersburg to get the two
Governments to discuss the situation directly with each
other and in a friendly way. He had great hopes that such
discussion would take place and lead to a satisfactory result." He reiterated his desire to coöperate with England,
and his intention to do his utmost to maintain the general
peace. His last words to Goschen were: "A war between the

[69] Bethmann to Tschirschky, July 28, 10:15 P.M., K.D., 323. Cf.
A.R.B., III, 24, and Gooss, pp. 243-244. Bethmann also telegraphed to
Tschirschky Pourtalès' account of Sazonov's more conciliatory attitude
and his admission that a means must be found for giving Serbia her
"deserved lesson" and building a bridge upon which Austria could retreat,
K.D., 282, 309.

[70] Bethmann to Pourtalès and the other German Ambassadors abroad,
July 28, 9 P.M.; K.D., 315.

Great Powers must be avoided." [71]   But neither to Russia
nor to England did he indicate the exact terms of the
"pledge plan," as he wished to learn first whether it would
be acceptable to Austria. On this point he was to be kept
in nerve-racking suspense for sixty critical hours, and
finally answered in the negative!

THE "WILLY-NICKY" TELEGRAMS

Besides informing Sazonov through the usual diplomatic
channels that Germany was mediating at Vienna to bring
Austria to a direct and satisfactory agreement with Russia,
Bethmann decided on this same evening of July 28 to have
recourse to a direct exchange of telegrams between the
Kaiser and the Tsar. In times past this "Willy-Nicky"
correspondence had often done much to cement the tra-
ditional friendship and good relations between Prussia and
Russia. It might be a help in the present time of trouble.
Accordingly, a draft telegram was drawn up in the Foreign
Office, submitted to the Kaiser, who made several changes
in it, and sent from Berlin at 1:45 A. M. on July 29:

> It is with the gravest concern that I hear of the impres-
> sion which the action of Austria against Servia is creating
> in your country. The unscrupulous agitation that has been
> going on in Servia for years has resulted in the outrageous
> crime, to which archduke Franz Ferdinand fell a victim.
> The spirit that led Servians to murder their own king and
> his wife still dominates the country. You will doubtless
> agree with me that we both, you and me, have a common
> interest as well as all Sovereigns to insist that all the persons
> morally responsible for the dastardly murder should receive
> their deserved punishment. In this case politics play no
> part at all.
> On the other hand I fully understand how difficult it is

[71] Goschen to Grey, July 28, midnight; B.D., 249; this last sentence
was suppressed from B.B.B., 71, in 1914. Cf. also Bethmann to Lichnowsky, July 28, 8:40 P.M.; K.D., 314.

for you and your Government to face the drift of your public opinion. Therefore, with regard to the hearty and tender friendship which binds us both from long ago with firm ties, I am exerting my utmost influence to induce the Austrians to deal straightly to arrive to a satisfactory understanding with you. I confidently hope you will help me in my efforts to smooth over difficulties that may still arise.

Your very sincere and devoted friend and cousin
Willy [72]

The same idea had occurred almost simultaneously to the Tsar and the little group of advisers around him who were sincerely anxious to prevent the Austro-Serbian conflict from developing into a Russo-German war. Prince Trubetzkoi told Chelius, the Kaiser's personal representative at the side of the Tsar, that Serbia's answer and readiness to submit the question to arbitration ought to make it possible to avoid a European war. "We do not love the Serbs at all," he told Chelius, "but they are our Slavic blood-brothers, and we cannot leave our brothers in the lurch when they are in trouble. Austria can annihilate them, and that we could not permit." He hoped that the Kaiser would advise Austria not to over-stretch the bow, but to recognize Serbia's conciliatory promises and accept the arbitration of the Hague Tribunal. "The return of your Kaiser has made us all feel easier, for we trust in His Majesty and want no war, nor does Tsar Nicholas. It would be a good thing if the two Monarchs should come to an understanding by telegraph." [73]

The suggestion that the Austro-Serbian conflict be submitted to arbitration at the Hague, which Pashitch had already appended to the Serbian reply, possibly at Russian

[72] K.D., 335; *Krasnyi Arkhiv*, IV, p. 18; Schilling's Diary, p. 45.
[73] Chelius to the Berlin Foreign Office, July 28, received July 29, 3:42 A.M. (K.D., 337), a couple of hours after the Kaiser had sent his first telegram to the Tsar.

suggestion,[74] was a favorite one with the Tsar. The Hague
Tribunal owed its origin to him. On July 27 he had written
to Sazonov:

> I will receive you tomorrow at six o'clock. An idea has
> come to me and, not to lose time which is golden, I am
> communicating it to you. Why do we not try, after coming
> to an understanding with France and England, and after-
> wards with Germany and Italy, to propose to Austria that
> she submit her conflict with Serbia to the examination of
> the Hague Tribunal? Perhaps the moment is not yet lost
> before irreparable events occur. Try to take this step
> today, before your report [to me tomorrow] in order to gain
> time. In me hope for peace is not yet extinct.[75]

This letter of the Tsar's is one of many evidences of his
sincere desire to use every means for preserving peace. But
Sazonov paid no attention to it. Instead, he was counting
on bluffing Austria into a diplomatic retreat by the threat
of partial mobilization, and at the same time carrying on
the extensive measures of the "Period Preparatory to War"
which would facilitate a more speedy general mobilization.
While the Tsar was making this proposal of the Hague
Tribunal, his Minister of Foreign Affairs was instructing his
agents abroad to telegraph all information about troop
movements, was rejecting in advance any moderating influence to be exercised at St. Petersburg, and was assuring
Montenegro that Russia would not be indifferent to Serbia's
fate and therefore Montenegro should coördinate her policy
with that of Serbia.[76] But there is no likelihood that, even
if he had taken the step requested by the Tsar, it would
have had any success. Austria would certainly have rejected it, and the Kaiser's note on it in Chelius's report
was: "Nonsense." A little later, "Nicky" seeing that Sazo-

---

[74] See above, ch. vii, at notes 30 and 45.   [75] *Livre Noir*, II, 283.
[76] Sazonov's telegrams, July 27, nos. 1504, 1514, 1521, 1522, 1523;
Krasnyi Arkhiv, IV, pp. 48-50.

nov had taken no steps in this direction, telegraphed direct to "Willy," apparently without Sazonov's knowledge: "It would be right to give over the Austro-Serbian problem to the Hague conference (*sic*)." [77] But this merely met with an exclamation point from the Kaiser and a line from Bethmann: "The idea of the Hague Conference will be naturally excluded in this case." [78] The fact is that, from the beginning of the crisis, Pashitch's offer to submit to an arbitral tribunal such a portentous political question, involving vital interests and national honor, was never taken seriously by any of the leading statesmen of Europe.

The Tsar also, like Trubetzkoi and Bethmann, pinned hopes on a direct exchange of telegrams with the Kaiser. At 1 A. M. on July 29, he sent an appeal to Potsdam. It crossed on the wires with that sent by the Kaiser. It was cordial, but it revealed his own weakness in the face of the pressure which was being put upon him by the Russian militarists to order a general mobilization:

> Am glad you are back. In this most serious moment, I appeal to you to help me. An ignoble war has been declared to a weak country. The indignation in Russia shared fully by me is enormous. I foresee that very soon I shall be overwhelmed by the pressure brought upon me and be forced to take extreme measures which will lead to war. To try and avoid such a calamity as a European war I beg you in the name of our old friendship to do what you can to stop your allies from going too far.[79]

Replying to this, the Kaiser stated that he shared the Tsar's wish to preserve peace. He pointed out, however, as Bethmann had already done, that Austria aimed at no territorial gains at Serbia's expense, but ought nevertheless

[77] Tsar to Kaiser, July 29, 8:20 P.M.; K.D., 366; Schilling's Diary, p. 54; Paléologue, I, 36.

[78] Bethmann to Pourtalès, July 30, 2:40 A.M.; K.D., 391.

[79] K.D., 332; K.A., IV, p. 19; Schilling's Diary, p. 46.

to have a guarantee that the Serbian promises would be carried out. He added:

> I think a direct understanding between your Government and Vienna possible and desirable, and as I already telegraphed to you, my Government is continuing its exertions to promote it. Of course military measures on the part of Russia which would be looked upon by Austria as threatening would precipitate a calamity we both wish to avoid and jeopardize my position as mediator which I readily accepted on your appeal to my friendship and my help.[80]

This peace effort on the Kaiser's part made a deep impression on the Tsar. It was successful, as will appear later, to the extent of causing him to suspend the order for Russian general mobilization which had been pressed from him by the Chief of Staff and which was on the point of being dispatched over the wires. The Tsar had taken new hope and telegraphed back:

> Thank you heartily for your quick answer. Am sending Tatishchev this evening with instructions. The military measures which have now come into force were decided five days ago for reasons of defence on account of Austria's preparations. I hope from all my heart that these measures won't in any way interfere with your part as mediator which I greatly value. We need your strong pressure on Austria to come to an understanding with us.[81]

But the news of Russia's wide-reaching military preparations and partial mobilization against Austria, now admitted by the Tsar to have been "decided five days ago for reasons of defence on account of Austria's preparations,"

[80] Kaiser to Tsar, July 29, 6:30 P.M., received 9:40 P.M.; K.D., 359; K.A., IV, p. 24; Schilling's Diary, p. 55.

[81] Tsar to Kaiser, July 30, 1:20 A.M., received 1:45 A.M.; K.D., 390; Schilling's Diary, p. 56. On Tatishchev's mission, and his being stopped by Sazonov, see above, ch. vi, note 54.

when Austria had carefully avoided preparations against Russia, roused the Kaiser's indignation. He had been sincerely trying to mediate and bring Austria to accept the "pledge plan" and satisfy Russia by direct negotiations; but meanwhile Russia had been getting a five days' start in military preparations. "I cannot agree to any more mediation," he noted, "since the Tsar who requested it has at the same time secretly mobilized behind my back. It is only a manoeuvre, in order to hold us back and increase the start they have already got. My work is at an end!" [82]

So the German effort to preserve peace by the old means of direct telegrams between the two monarchs came to nothing, owing to Austria's declaration of war on Serbia and to the consequent Russian partial mobilization, as well as to the other secret military measures of the "Period Preparatory to War" which the Tsar had ordered at Krasnoe Selo on July 25. Several more telegrams were exchanged between "Willy" and "Nicky," but they had no chance of success, because Russia's general mobilization, ordered about 6 P. M. on July 30, had made a general European war virtually inevitable.

BETHMANN'S PRESSURE AT VIENNA

As we have seen above, Bethmann sent off the "pledge plan" to Vienna on the evening of July 28, with instructions to Tschirschky to express himself "emphatically" to Berchtold and to "wire reply." [83] At the same time he had notified England and Russia that he was doing his best to persuade Vienna to come to a frank and friendly discussion with St. Petersburg, and that he wished to coöperate to maintain the general peace. "A war between the Great Powers must be avoided," he had told the British Ambassador. But he now began to be seriously embarrassed because he received no reply from Berchtold to the proposed

[82] K.D. 390.   [83] See above, at note 69.

"pledge plan." All the following day he waited in vain for an answer, though telegrams even at this time of crowded wires ordinarily were transmitted between Berlin and Vienna within three or four hours. He was embarrassed at Berchtold's silence for several reasons: because the German military authorities were beginning to urge that Germany ought to take precautionary military measures in view of the news from Russia, as will be indicated later; because he could give no answer at London and St. Petersburg as to the success of his mediatory efforts at Vienna; because of the bad impression which Austria's declaration of war had meanwhile made; and because of the reports which he had received from the other capitals which seemed to indicate bad faith or stupidity on the part of his ally.[84] Therefore on the evening of July 29 he sent off three more urgent telegrams to Tschirschky, partly to inform him of these reports concerning Austria's actions and partly to get an immediate answer in regard to the "pledge plan." In the first he forwarded Lichnowsky's despatch concerning the remarks of the Austrian Ambassador in London, and added in severe disapproval of Austria:

> These expressions of the Austrian diplomats must be regarded as indications of more recent wishes and aspirations. I regard the attitude of the Austrian Government and its unparalleled procedure toward the various Governments with increasing astonishment. In St. Petersburg it declares its territorial disinterestedness; us it leaves wholly in the dark as to its programme; Rome it puts off with empty phrases about the question of compensation; in London Count Mensdorff hands out part of Serbia to Bulgaria and Albania and places himself in contradiction with Vienna's solemn declaration at St. Petersburg. From these contradictions I must conclude that the telegram disavowing Hoyos [who, on July 5 or 6 at Berlin, had spoken unofficially of Austria's partitioning Serbia] was intended

84 See above at notes 62-68.

for the gallery, and that the Austrian Government is harboring plans which it sees fit to conceal from us, in order to assure itself in all events of German support and to avoid the refusal which might result from a frank statement.[85]

The second telegram, sent uncoded, said: "Answer by wire immediately whether telegram 174 of yesterday [concerning the 'pledge plan'] has arrived"; and the third: "I await immediate carrying out of telegram 174." [86]

Tschirschky had already on the morning of July 29 promptly carried out his original instructions in telegram 174 concerning the "pledge plan," but had been met with a dilatory and evasive answer: Berchtold was ready to repeat his declaration of territorial disinterestedness, but "as to the further declaration concerning military measures, Count Berchtold says that he is not in a position to give me a reply at once. In spite of my representations as to the urgency of the matter, I have up to this evening received no further communication." [87]

On this same day, Wednesday, July 29, while still waiting in vain for a reply from Berchtold as to the "pledge plan," Bethmann had already taken up two more peace proposals which had been suggested, and supported both energetically at Vienna. One was the suggestion from Sazonov for "direct conversations" between Vienna and St. Petersburg.[88]

Bethmann had already handed this propitious suggestion on to Vienna without comment as soon as it had been

[85] Bethmann to Tschirschky, July 29, 8:00 P.M.; K.D., 361. This was for Tschirschky's personal information, but he was instructed to call Berchtold's attention to the advisability of avoiding suspicion as to his declarations to the Powers with regard to the integrity of Serbia, and to his failure to satisfy Italy.

[86] Bethmann to Tschirschky, July 29, 10:18 and 10:30 P.M.; K.D., 377 and note.

[87] Tschirschky to Bethmann, July 29, 11:50 P.M., received July 30, 1:30 A.M.; K.D., 388. [88] K.D., 238, 282.

received by him on July 27. But it had been evaded and then rejected by Berchtold, because Sazonov had intended that the direct conversations should take up modifications of the terms of Austria's ultimatum. Berchtold was determined not to enter into any negotiations which might touch the local issues existing purely between Austria and Serbia. As an additional reason for his refusal to "converse directly" on Austro-Serbian relations, he pointed out that the time for a peaceful settlement of those relations was passed, since the declaration of war and the opening of hostilities had already taken place. Consequently, "direct conversations" between Vienna and St. Petersburg had come to a halt, with the result that Sazonov was much incensed.[89] Sazonov concluded, though mistakenly, that because Berchtold flatly refused to discuss Austro-Serbian relations, he was also unwilling to converse at all with Russia.

To reopen "direct conversations" Bethmann now sent three more telegrams to Vienna very late on Wednesday night. After mentioning the hopeful interchange of telegrams which had begun between the Kaiser and the Tsar, he passed on Sazonov's information that Russia had decided to mobilize in her four southern districts, but added, calmingly, that this was "far from meaning war"; the Russian army might be a long time under arms without crossing the frontier, and Russia wanted to avoid war if in any way possible. It had been pointed out to Sazonov that Austria would probably take counter-measures and thus start the ball rolling. Sazonov was complaining that "direct conversations" were making no headway. "Hence we must urgently request, in order to prevent a general catastrophe, or at least to put Russia in the wrong, that Vienna inaugu-

---

[89] For this abortive result of the proposals for "direct conversations," see A.R.B., II, 73, 95; III, 16, 17, 19, 20; and above ch. viii, at notes 80-88, and below ch. x, at note 4.

rate and continue conversations according to telegram 174,"
—that is, according to the "pledge plan." [90]   Having heard
from Sazonov that Berchtold had given a "categorical refusal" to direct conversations, and fearing there had been
some misunderstanding, Bethmann telegraphed still more
emphatically to Vienna a couple of hours later:

> The refusal of every exchange of views with St. Peters-
> burg would be a serious mistake, for it provokes Russia
> precisely to armed interference, which Austria is primarily
> interested in avoiding. We are ready, to be sure, to fulfill
> our obligations as an ally, but must refuse to allow our-
> selves to be drawn by Vienna into a world conflagration
> frivolously and in disregard of our advice. Please say this
> to Count Berchtold at once with all emphasis and with
> great seriousness.[91]

The other plan which Bethmann also cordially took up
late Wednesday night was Grey's proposal for mediation
between Austria and Russia, either by the four Powers, or
by Germany alone, on the basis of Serbia's reply. News
had come from Rome that she was now ready, "on condition
of certain interpretations, to swallow even articles 5 and 6,
that is, the whole Austrian ultimatum." [92]   This proposal
of Grey's was eagerly welcomed by Bethmann as a possible
happy solution. In sending it on to Vienna, he genuinely
again "pressed the button," by adding:

> "Please show this to Berchtold immediately and add that
> we regard such a yielding on Serbia's part as a suitable
> basis for negotiation along with an occupation of a part of
> Serbian territory as a pledge." [93]

[90] Bethmann to Tschirschky, July 30, 12:10 and 12:30 A.M.; K.D.,
383, 385.

[91] Bethmann to Tschirschky, July 30, 3 A.M.; K.D., 396.

[92] Lichnowsky to Bethmann, July 29, 2:08 P.M.; K.D., 357; on this
"Italian proposal," see above, ch. viii, note 10.

[93] Bethmann to Tschirschky, July 30, 12:30 A.M.; K.D., 384.

But Berchtold was still deaf to the button; he merely made the characteristic reply that, though the integral acceptance of Austria's note would have been satisfactory before hostilities had begun, "now after the state of war has begun, Austria's conditions must naturally take another tone." [94]

Grey's proposal was all the more eagerly welcomed by Bethmann, partly because Grey quickly supplemented it by embodying the two very points which Germany herself had already been urging at Vienna and St. Petersburg in her "pledge plan," viz., a new statement by Austria of her intentions in Serbia which would satisfy Russia, and a pledge in the shape of the temporary military occupation of Belgrade which would satisfy Austria; and partly because he was alarmed at Grey's first "warning" that England could not be counted upon to remain neutral in case of a general war. As Lichnowsky reported his conversation with Grey:

> To him [Grey] personally a suitable basis for such mediation seemed to be that Austria, after the occupation perhaps of Belgrade or other places, should announce her conditions. Should Your Excellency [Bethmann], however, undertake the mediation as I was able to propose to him early this morning as a possibility, this would, of course, suit him just as well. . . . [At the close of the conversation Grey] said he wanted to make me a friendly and private statement. . . . It would be possible for her [England] to stand aside so long as the conflict is limited to Austria and Russia. But if we and France should be drawn in, then the situation would immediately be a different one, and the British Government under the circumstances would be forced to rapid decisions. In this case it would be impossible to stand aside for long and to wait; "if war breaks out, it will be the greatest catastrophe that the world has ever seen." He was far from wishing to utter any kind of

[94] Tschirschky to Bethmann, July 30, 3:20 P.M.; K.D., 432.

threat; he merely wanted to save me from being misled, and himself from reproach of insincerity, and, therefore, chose the form of a private explanation.[95]

Upon hearing of this alarming possibility, so contrary to his expectations and hopes, that England might not remain neutral, Bethmann immediately transmitted the whole Grey-Lichnowsky conversation to Vienna, and proceeded to "press the button" very vigorously:

If Austria refuses all negotiations, we are face to face with a conflagration in which England will be against us; Rumania and Italy according to all indications will not be for us, and we shall stand two against four Powers. Through England's opposition the main blow will fall on Germany. Austria's political prestige, the military honor of her army, as well as her just claims against Serbia, can be adequately satisfied by her occupation of Belgrade or other places. Through her humiliation of Serbia, she will make her position in the Balkans as well as in her relation to Russia, strong again. Under these circumstances we must urgently and emphatically urge upon the consideration of the Vienna Cabinet the adoption of mediation in accordance with the above honorable conditions. The responsibility for the consequences which would otherwise follow would be, for Austria and for us, an uncommonly heavy one.[96]

To this urgent request by Germany for Austria's acceptance of a solution, which perhaps even yet might have avoided the conflagration of Europe, Berchtold gave no definite or frank answer. Bethmann's telegram, inclosing Lichnowsky's conversation with Grey, after being deciphered was handed to Tschirschky, Thursday, July 30,

[95] Lichnowsky to Bethmann, July 29, 6:39 P.M.; arrived 9:12 P.M.; K.D., 368. *Cf.* also Grey's report to Goschen of the same conversation, in a letter which was printed in the *British Blue Book* of 1914 (no. 89) as if sent, but which now appears to have remained in the British Archives marked, "Not sent—War" (B.D., 286).

[96] Bethmann to Tschirschky, July 30, 2:55 A.M.; K.D., 395. *Cf* also Goschen to Grey, B.D., 329; and Gooss, pp. 233-246.

while he was at lunch with Berchtold. "Berchtold listened, pale and silent, while they were read through twice; Count Forgách took notes; finally Berchtold said he would at once lay the matter before the Emperor." After Berchtold had departed to put on another suit of clothes in which to present himself before His Majesty, Tschirschky spent a good part of the afternoon setting forth long and earnestly to Forgách and Hoyos all of Bethmann's arguments. It was useless. Instead, he was cynically informed by these two intimate advisers of Berchtold that "in view of the feeling in the army and in the people, any checking of the military operations in progress was out of the question. . . . Conrad von Hötzendorf [Austrian Chief of Staff] would lay before the Emperor this evening the order for general mobilization, as a reply to the measures already taken." He was also finally told that Berchtold could not give any answer until the following morning, for the reason that Tisza, who would not be in Vienna until then, must be consulted.[97]

By this time, the evening of July 30, Russia had ordered general mobilization, though the official news of it was not known at Berlin and Vienna until next day. But Germany had repeatedly given Russia to understand that this measure, directed against Germany as well as against Austria, and generally understood by the military authorities everywhere to mean a decision for war, would necessarily lead to German mobilization and consequently to war. So Bethmann's efforts at mediation failed. They came too late, and were not sufficiently vigorous to compel his ally to come to a timely understanding with Russia. Nor were they taken very seriously by the Entente Powers, whose faith in the sincerity of Germany's desire for peace had already been shaken by her apparent support of Austrian policy hitherto, and by the failure of her belated pressure at Vienna to produce any tangible results.

[97] Tschirschky to Bethmann, July 31, 1:35 A.M.; K.D., 465.

CHAPTER X

THE RUSSIAN MOBILIZATION

At the Council of Ministers, held at Krasnoe Selo on the afternoon of July 25, as we have seen above in the chapter on "The Russian Danger," the Tsar's ministers had decided on a number of preparatory military measures. They included the wide-reaching preparations of the "Period Preparatory to War" which were intended to facilitate a Russian general mobilization against Germany as well as against Austria; they had been ordered before dawn on July 26, had been going on actively ever since, and had caused increasing alarm at Berlin in spite of the beguiling assurances of Sazonov and Sukhomlinov that no mobilization measures against Germany were intended. The decisions of July 25 also included a contingent partial mobilization against Austria, to be put into operation when Sazonov should decide that the diplomatic situation required it. It was hoped that the knowledge of this decision would prove a successful diplomatic bluff in frightening Vienna out of military action against Serbia. In the meantime, from July 25 to 28, while these military preparations had been going on to enable Russia to overcome her relative slowness in mobilization in case war became inevitable, Sazonov had appeared optimistic and been ready to carry on "direct conversations" with Vienna, with a view to finding a compromise settlement between the Austrian demands and the Serbian reply.

But on Tuesday, July 28, Sazonov's optimism received several rude shocks. He was disappointed and indignant that his proposal for "direct conversations," made two days previously, had as yet met with no response from Berchtold.

439

He was also unfavorably impressed by the fact that Szápáry could not give him the *dossier* which Austria had promised. His optimism began to change to pessimism. He began to conclude that Austria was fully determined on war with Serbia, and was therefore unlikely to listen to mediation proposals until punishment had been inflicted on her. Finally, he was thrown into great excitement late in the afternoon of July 28 by the arrival of the news that Austria had just declared war on Serbia. His optimism evaporated completely. He became thoroughly pessimistic, jumped nervously to the conclusion that a European conflict was probably inevitable, and that Russia should order mobilization; the only question was, should it be *partial* or *general* mobilization? This somersault in his attitude is revealed in the series of interviews and conferences which he crowded into the afternoon and evening of this busy Tuesday.

Early in the afternoon Sir George Buchanan called at the Russian Foreign Office. He found that Sazonov had received disquieting news [1] from Vienna—but not yet the

1 What this "disquieting news" was is not clear. It may possibly have been one of three things:

(1) News received in Moscow on July 28 about 1:00 P.M. that Austrian reservists living in Moscow were urgently instructed to report themselves at the Consulate (*Investig., Comm.*, II, 87, Anlage 49).

(2) A telegram from the Russian Ambassador in Vienna: "The order for general mobilization has been signed" (R.O.B., 47). Even if this telegram is genuine, the information was unquestionably false, because, as will be indicated later, it is certain that the order for Austrian general mobilization was not signed until three days later—shortly before noon on July 31. But there are reasons for thinking that this telegram is not genuine: Sazonov does not cite it, but rather the Austrian declaration of war, as the ground for Russian partial mobilization; nor is it mentioned in Schilling's Diary; nor is it cited by the Russian General Staff or by Dobrorolski or by Danilov in their summaries of the situation on July 28. Montgelas and Stieve, *Russland und der Weltkonflikt*, p. 150 f., and Renouvin, p. 147, think this R.O.B. document is a Russian forgery. Paléologue, however, claims (I, 35) to have heard a rumor of it on July 29.

(3) The news of the Austrian declaration of war against Serbia. However, as this did not reach Nish until 12:30 P.M. one may doubt whether it could have arrived from there at St. Petersburg by 3:00 P.M., which was about the time Buchanan and Sazonov had their interview. Moreover,

report of the Austrian declaration of war on Serbia—and was already taking a "pessimistic view of the situation." Buchanan asked him whether he would not be satisfied with Austrian assurances in regard to Serbia's independence and integrity; England would welcome any arrangement to avert a European war, "but it was important that we should know the real intentions of the Imperial Government"—a phrase which suggests that Buchanan did not think that Sazonov was being completely frank with him. Sazonov replied that "no engagement which Austria might take on these two points [Serbia's independence and integrity] would satisfy Russia, and that on the day Austria crossed the Serbian frontier, order for mobilization against Austria would be issued." He added that there was no need to fear internal disturbances in Russia, and that, "in the event of war, the whole nation would be behind the Government." Buchanan suggested that as a last resort the Tsar should make a personal appeal to Francis Joseph to restrict Austria's action within limits which Russia could accept. But Sazonov again insisted that the only way to avert war was for England to let it be clearly known that she would join France and Russia. Buchanan got the impression that Russia "was thoroughly in earnest," and that Russia would fight if Austria attacked Serbia.[2]

if Sazonov had been aware of it, it seems almost certain that it would have found an important place in their conversation. It was apparently still unknown to Sazonov when he talked with Szápáry later in the afternoon, for it formed no part of their discussion, and Szápáry, in his later report of their conversation, added that the declaration of war on Serbia, "which has since taken place," will perhaps disclose Russia's real intentions (A.R.B., III, 16).

[2] Buchanan to Grey, July 28, 8:45 P.M.; B.D., 247. *Cf.* also Paléologue, I, 30-32. According to Paléologue, who was waiting in the ante-chamber, Buchanan reported that he "had just begged Sazonov not to consent to any military measures which Germany could interpret as a provocation. One must leave to the German Government all responsibility and all initiative in an attack. English opinion would not countenance the idea of participating in the war unless the aggression unquestionably came from Germany." Buchanan's despatch contains nothing of all this.

After talking with Buchanan, Sazonov saw Pourtalès, and tried to convince him that Serbia's reply was satisfactory, and that Germany therefore should join in urging mediation at Vienna. But he met with little encouragement from the German Ambassador, who still adhered to his Government's "localization" policy, and did not yet know of the pressure which Bethmann was about to put on Vienna to accept the "pledge plan." On the contrary, Pourtalès complained of the hostile tone of the Russian Press and of the fact that reliable reports made it clear to Germany that Russia's military preparations were extending far beyond what Sukhomlinov had stated to the German Military Attaché on the evening of July 26. He had also learned that the military authorities had put out of commission the wireless apparatus on a German merchant ship, the *Eitel Fried-* *rich,* in the harbor of St. Petersburg in defiance of international law. He had protested against this and the matter had been set right by the direct orders of the Tsar. But the incident gave Pourtalès further reason for expressing diplomatically to Sazonov the fear that the Russian militarists "were perhaps carrying the preparations for which they were responsible further than was intended" by Sazonov. He therefore warned Sazonov of the very serious danger which might arise in the existing critical situation from wide-reaching Russian military preparations.[3]

Either he did not report fully to Sir Edward Grey, or, more probably, Paléologue is fathering upon the British Ambassador views which he alleges (I, 33 f.) he himself expressed to Sazonov a little later and which will be discussed below.

[3] Pourtalès to Bethmann, July 28, 8:12 P.M.; K.D., 338; Szápáry to Berchtold, July 28 (dispatched July 29, 1:15 A.M.), A.R.B., II, 94. Pourtalès in his later memoir (*Am Scheideweg,* pp. 32-37) indicates that he had two interviews with Sazonov on the afternoon of July 28, a stormy one before the *Eitel Friedrich* incident, and a more peaceful one after it. Paléologue (I, 33) gives the impression that Pourtalès was so overcome with emotion at the danger of war that he could scarcely speak. On the *Eitel Friedrich* incident, see Dobrorolski, p. 104 (German ed., p. 23), and Pourtalès, *Am Scheideweg,* pp. 34-37.

Sazonov then received the Austrian Ambassador, but was disappointed that Szápáry had received no answer to the proposal of two days earlier for "direct conversations." Sazonov said that boded no good, and that the situation was serious. He again requested urgently a copy of the *dossier,* which Austria had promised to lay before the Powers, but had not yet delivered at St. Petersburg; he wanted to see it, he said, before war against Serbia should begin; otherwise, it would be too late to examine it. He and Szápáry repeated their old arguments about the Austrian ultimatum and the Serbian reply in a calm and friendly way, but without coming to any satisfactory conclusion. Szápáry then took his departure, "because the Minister had an appointment with his Imperial Master at Peterhof." [4]

Sazonov, however, apparently did not go out to Peterhof at once. He first talked with Paléologue, and communicated with the Chief of Staff concerning the ordering of mobilization in Russia in view of the news of the Austrian declaration of war on Serbia which had just arrived.

PALÉOLOGUE'S DECLARATION OF FRENCH SUPPORT

Paléologue, who says he had purposely waited until Sazonov had talked with the other ambassadors, was then closeted with the Russian Minister of Foreign Affairs in an interview of which we have two very different versions. Baron Schilling, who usually noted accurately every evening

[4] Szápáry to Berchtold, July 29, 10:00 A.M.; A.R.B., III, 16. Though dated July 29, the first part of this telegram no. 173 refers to July 28. On July 28 at 11:40 P.M., Berchtold finally telegraphed Szápáry that he was unwilling to discuss the Serbian reply as a basis for "direct conversations," because it had been rejected as unsatisfactory, and, moreover, war had already been declared (A.R.B., II, 95). Szápáry did not receive this message until the following afternoon at some time roughly between 2:00 P.M. and 6:00 P.M.; for Pourtalès reported on July 29 at 1:58 P.M. (K.D., 343) that up to that time Sazonov had received no reply from Berchtold; but at 6:10 P.M., (K.D., 365) Pourtalès reported that Vienna had finally "replied with a categorical refusal."

the substance of Sazonov's most important interviews, says:

> "The French Ambassador, upon instructions of his Government, informed the Minister of Foreign Affairs of the complete readiness of France to fulfil her obligations as an ally in case of necessity." [5]

This declaration of Paléologue's was of such extreme importance to Russia just at this juncture that it evidently overshadowed everything else in Baron Schilling's mind on July 28, because it is the only entry made in his diary for that day, aside from his usual summary of telegrams.[6] That Paléologue did make such a declaration, and that it gave further encouragement to Sazonov to stand firm and presently to approve Russian mobilization is confirmed by the fact that next day, Sazonov, in notifying Izvolski of his decision "to hasten our armaments and to assume that war is probably inevitable," added:

> "Please express to the French Government our sincere gratitude for the declaration, which has been officially made to me in its name by the French Ambassador, that we can count fully upon the assistance of our ally, France. In the existing circumstances, this declaration is especially valuable to us." [7]

Paléologue, however, in his memoirs, gives an altogether different version. He says not a word of this important declaration. Instead, after an account, perhaps more picturesque than accurate, of Pourtalès' nervousness and Sazonov's coolness, he enlarged upon his own importance as

[5] Schilling's *Diary*, p. 43.

[6] Possibly, however, the brevity of Schilling's *Diary* for July 28 is to be explained by the fact that one or two pages for this day were misplaced or lost.

[7] Sazonov to Izvolski and to the other Russian Ambassadors, tg. no. 1551, July 29; M.F.R., p. 520; L.N., II, 289; R.O.B., 58; reported to Viviani at Paris between 2 and 3 A.M. on July 30; B.D., 373; Viviani, *Réponse au Kaiser,* p. 149; Poincaré, IV, 383.

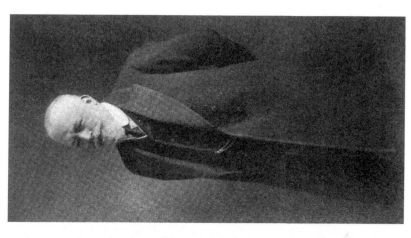

COUNT POURTALÈS

M. PALÉOLOGUE

representative of a country which was temporarily decapi-
tated by Poincaré's absence and the very intermittent means
of communicating with him. In view of the resulting great
responsibility resting upon himself as the Ambassador of
France, he alleges that he begged Sazonov to be very cautious about taking any military measures which might
jeopardize English support; that Sazonov said he was having great difficulty in restraining the Russian General Staff;
and that he, Paléologue, then got him to promise to accept
all the measures which France and England should propose
to preserve peace, and to authorize him to telegraph this
promise to Paris.[8] It is, however, very doubtful whether
Sazonov would have been willing to make any such blanket
promise, and if he did, he did not keep it, for he speedily
approved at least partial mobilization, which can hardly be
regarded as a measure proposed by France and England
to preserve peace. In the account of this Paléologue-Saz-
onov conversation, Baron Schilling was presumably correct,
and Paléologue was probably giving a free rein to his post-
War imagination.

Whether Paléologue, in making his declaration of
Franco-Russian solidarity to Sazonov, was really acting "on
instructions from his Government" as Schilling says, or was
saying what was not true, or was incorrectly reported by
Schilling and Sazonov, must remain uncertain until the
French finally make a complete publication of their documents for this period.[9] Perhaps his declaration was his way

[8] Paléologue, I, 33. A brief telegram to this effect does in fact appear
in F.Y.B., 86, but it may well be questioned whether it was not sent to
conceal from France, and especially from England, the fact that the
Russian militarists were pressing hard for a *general mobilization,* of which
Paléologue's telegram says not a word.

[9] A similar doubt as to Paléologue's veracity arises in connection with
his statements on July 25, as reported by Buchanan (B.D., 125), that
"he had received a number of telegrams" from Bienvenu-Martin and "was
in a position to give formal assurance that France placed herself unre-
servedly on Russia's side;" and that the "French Government would
want to know at once whether our [British] fleet was prepared to play

of carrying out a telegram sent to him by Viviani on July 27, which said: "Please say to M. Sazonov that France, appreciating like Russia the high importance for both countries of affirming their perfect understanding in regard to other Powers and of not neglecting any effort with a view to a solution of the conflict, is ready to support completely, in the interests of general peace, the action of the Imperial Government." [10] In any case, Paléologue's declaration was in keeping with the assurances which President Poincaré himself had given a week before upon his visit to Russia, and also with Izvolski's telegram from Paris on July 27: "I was surprised how well the Acting Minister for Foreign Affairs and his colleagues understand the situation, and how firm and quiet is their decision to give us fullest support and to avoid even the smallest suspicion of a disagreement with us." [11]

THE NEWS OF THE AUSTRIAN DECLARATION OF WAR ON SERBIA

In the course of the afternoon of July 28, news reached Russia of the Austrian declaration of war on Serbia. It may have arrived while Sazonov was in conversation with Paléologue and been partly the reason for the latter's declaration of French support. The news dissipated any remnants of optimism in Sazonov's mind. It made him fear that Austria would soon invade Serbia, and confirmed his growing conviction that Germany was standing behind Austria and would continue to do so, unless he made it clear that Russia was determined to threaten Austria with force in order to protect Serbia. He came to the conclusion that the time had come to order the partial mobilization which had been approved "in principle" on July 25. He therefore

part assigned to it by the Anglo-French Naval Convention." There is nothing in the *French Yellow Book*, as published, to substantiate these statements. [10] Poincaré, IV, 335, 385 ff.

[11] Tg. no. 195; M.F.R., p. 516; L.N., II, 282; suppressed from R.O.B., 35.

announced in the various European capitals: "In view of the declaration of war by Austria against Serbia, my direct conversations with the Austrian Ambassador are obviously useless!" [11a]

In other words, he abandoned "direct conversations" as a peaceful solution many hours before he heard of Austria's "categorical refusal," which he did not learn until the following afternoon.[12] He also instructed his ambassadors abroad to inform the Governments that, in consequence of Austria's declaration of war, Russia had decided to order next day partial mobilization in the four Southern Military Districts of Odessa, Kiev, Moscow and Kazan; but added: "Russia entertains no aggressive intentions against Germany." [13]

These telegrams seem to leave no doubt that Sazonov wished to give Europe the impression that he was now merely carrying out the means of pressure upon Austria which had already been decided upon at Krasnoe Selo on July 25 and several times stated to the Powers, and that the reason for it was the Austrian declaration of war on Serbia. Pourtalès is also of the opinion that Sazonov's change in attitude "took place only on the 28th, when it

[11a] Sazonov to Benckendorff and other Russian Ambassadors, tg. no. 1538, July 28; K.A., p. 52; Schilling's *Diary*, p. 44; *cf.* R.O.B., 48, where phrases are altered, omitted, and added. In this telegram he also urged immediate English mediation to prevent Austria from crushing Serbia; B.D., 258.

[12] See above, note 4. In his memoirs (*Fateful Years*, p. 185 ff.), Sazonov pretends that he was informed of Berchtold's refusal on July 28, before authorizing partial mobilization.

[13] Sazonov to Bronevski in Berlin and other Russian Ambassadors, tgs. nos. 1539, 1540; K.A., I, p. 178; L.N., II, 283; Schilling's *Diary*, p. 44. Bronevski did not inform Jagow of this until after 5:00 P.M. on July 29 at the moment Jagow learned it with consternation from Pourtalès (Schilling's *Diary*, pp. 103, 106; K.D., 343). Izvolski informed the French Foreign Office at 11:15 A.M. on July 29, just before Poincaré's arrival in Paris (Poincaré IV, 373). Benckendorff informed Nicolson some time on July 29 (B.D., 258). Sazonov did not communicate this important decision to the foreign ambassadors in St. Petersburg until the morning of July 29 (K.D., 343; B.D., 276; *cf.* Paléologue, I, 35).

became known that the threatening attitude of Russia had not sufficed to prevent Austria from declaring war on Serbia. Undoubtedly the change in Sazonov's feeling was primarily brought about by this step on the part of the Vienna Cabinet." [14]

But it is quite possible that Sazonov's change of attitude went even further than a decision to put into effect a partial mobilization—that he now reluctantly accepted the view of the military authorities that a European war had become inevitable and that a general, instead of a partial, mobilization should be adopted. This is the view of Dobrorolski, who says:

> On July 28, the day of the Austrian declaration of war on Serbia, Sazonov's optimism vanishes at a stroke. He is filled with the idea that a general war is inevitable, and informs Ianushkevich that one must no longer delay with the mobilization of our army, . . . that he was even astonished that it had not begun sooner.[15]

To be sure, Sazonov was aware that any precipitate general mobilization on Russia's part, directed against Germany as well as against Austria, might have a bad effect upon public opinion in France and England if it should become known; but, on the other hand, he had just received from Paléologue the renewed declaration of French support, and there was the encouraging news from Sir Edward Grey that the British fleet had been ordered to remain concentrated instead of dispersing to its normal peace-time positions.[16] Sazonov also knew that a Russian general mobilization would almost certainly lead to a German general

---

[14] Comment of Pourtalès on the German edition of Dobrorolski, p. 38.

[15] Dobrorolski, p. 104 (German ed. p. 23). In his own memoirs Sazonov says (p. 188) that the Russian Government and public opinion was now convinced on July 28 that war was "inevitable." Chelius likewise telegraphed to the Kaiser on July 29 (K.D., 344) that "in the *entourage* of the Tsar . . . since the declaration of war, they consider a general war almost inevitable."   [16] B.D., 177, 247.

mobilization, and so to a European war. A partial mobilization, on the contrary, was less likely to call forth immediate counter-measures from Germany.[17] But even this would probably lead to Austrian general mobilization and so place European peace in serious jeopardy. But whether consciousness of these facts outweighed in his mind the arguments of the military technicians as to the folly and impossibility of a partial mobilization is not clear. He decided that the time had come for some mobilization and so informed Ianushkevich. In any event the four districts of Odessa, Kiev, Moscow and Kazan were to be mobilized, in accordance with the announcement which he was making to the Powers. He left it to Ianushkevich to argue next morning with the Tsar in favor of general mobilization.[18]

[17] *Cf.* Izvolski to Sazonov tg. no. 197, July 27: "Jules Cambon telegraphs from Berlin that, in answer to his question of what attitude Germany would take towards a partial mobilization in Russia, Jagow stated that such a mobilization would not be followed by German mobilization; but that, if Russia attacked Austria, Germany would at once reply by an attack on Russia" (M.F.R., p. 516; L.N., II, 282). Similarly also Bronevski to Sazonov, July 27, quoting Jagow as saying: "We shall mobilize if Russia mobilizes on our frontier, or if Russian troops advance on Austrian soil" (*Krasnyi Arkhiv*, I, p. 173).

[18] In *Fateful Years* Sazonov says (p. 188): "The Council of Ministers, with the Tsar presiding, decided to mobilize at once the four military districts." But there is no other substantial indication of any such Council of Ministers on July 28, and it is most unlikely. He may be confusing in his mind the Councils of July 24 and July 25. Recouly to be sure, says (p. 158) that the question of partial or general mobilization was "long discussed on Wednesday, July 28" at 5:00 P. M. at a conference between Ianushkevich, Sukhomlinov, Sazonov and Neratov. But Recouly's statement is open to three objections: (1) July 28 was not "Wednesday" but Tuesday; (2) Sazonov was so occupied with the conversations noted above on the afternoon of July 28 that he would hardly have had time for a "long discussion" before going out for his audience at Peterhof; (3) Recouly says General Danilov gave him the details of this conference, but Danilov himself in his memoirs (*Russland in Weltkrieg*, Berlin, 1925, pp. 16-22), while giving the same arguments in favor of general mobilization as those repeated by Recouly, does not mention Sazonov or Neratov as being present at any such conference; he mentions beside himself only the military specialists, Ianushkevich, Dobrorolski, and Ronzhin, the head of the Department of Military Transportation. Renouvin (p. 133 ff.), however, it may be noted, accepts Recouly's account without question.

After his conversations with the Ambassadors and his decision for partial mobilization in any event, Sazonov went out to Peterhof and reported to the Tsar on the Austrian declaration of war and the general situation. Whether he advocated the view of Ianushkevich that the time had come for general mobilization, or whether he still advised the Tsar merely in favor of his own former partial mobilization plan is not certain. We have no record of what he said to the Tsar. Presumably he gave a gloomy picture of the situation. The only evident consequence of his visit was the telegram which the Tsar sent to the Kaiser late that same night: ". . . An ignoble war has been declared to a weak country. The indignation in Russia, fully shared by me, is enormous. I foresee that very soon I shall be overwhelmed by the pressure brought upon me, and be forced to take extreme measures which will lead to war. . . ."[19] Was this "pressure" which the Tsar feared would overwhelm him, exerted only by the military leaders, or by his entourage, or perhaps by Sazonov himself?

THE TSAR'S ASSENT TO RUSSIAN GENERAL MOBILIZATION

The views of Dobrorolski and the military leaders as to the folly of a partial mobilization were strengthened by the return of Quartermaster-General Danilov. He had been on a tour of inspection in the Caucasus, but had been hastily recalled to St. Petersburg on July 26. He now used all his influence to have general mobilization ordered in place of partial mobilization. In his memoirs he sets forth at length, and in as convincing a manner as Dobrorolski, all the technical and political difficulties of a partial mobilization. The latter would provide only 13 army corps, whereas 16 were calculated as necessary for the successful blow against Austria. If the Warsaw District was left untouched, it would

---

[19] July 29, 1:00 A.M.; K.A., IV, p. 19; Schilling's *Diary,* p. 46; K.D., 332.

be impossible to concentrate for an attack on Austria in Galicia as planned, and a wholly new scheme of campaign would have to be suddenly improvised. Worst of all, if a general mobilization should eventually follow a partial mobilization, the confusion would be intolerable, inasmuch as the Warsaw District had to draw some of its reservists from the four Districts already dislocated by partial mobilization. Owing to the greater density of population in the southwestern part of the Empire, Russia had not worked out a mobilization plan by which each Military District drew its recruits exclusively from within its own borders. This technical difficulty would mean that in case a general mobilization followed a partial mobilization, Russia would not be able to fulfil the expectation of her French ally in quickly bringing satisfactory forces against Germany.[20]

For all these and other technical reasons, therefore, Danilov insisted on the holding of a military council in which the arguments against the partial mobilization plan of July 24 and 25 were again considered. It probably met on the afternoon or evening of July 28, and was attended by Ianushkevich, Dobrorolski, Danilov, and Ronzhin, the head of the Department of Military Transportation. As a result, Ianushkevich was convinced that every effort must be made to persuade the Tsar to approve general mobilization. When therefore he heard from Sazonov that mobilization ought no longer to be delayed, he prepared two imperial ukases, one for the partial, and the other for the general, mobilization. The first was to be used if the Tsar persisted in adhering to the plan of July 25; his assent to the second was to be secured if possible.[21]

With these two draft orders in his portfolio, Ianushke-

[20] Danilov, *Russland im Weltkriege*, pp. 16-22. See also similarly Dobrorolski, pp. 96-103 (German ed. pp. 14-22), and above, ch. vi, at notes 40, 73.

[21] Danilov, p. 16 f.; Dobrorolski, p. 104 f. (German ed. p. 23 f); Sukhomlinov, *Erinnerungen*, p. 361 f.

vich went out to Peterhof on the morning of July 29. Apparently without much difficulty, he certainly secured the Tsar's signature to the ukase for general mobilization, and probably also to that for partial mobilization; the latter to be used in case there might come a turn for the better in the diplomatic situation.

It was one of the greatest weaknesses of Nicholas II, of which all his ministers complained from time to time, that he was too apt to assent to the minister who last happened to have his ear. This weakness was all the more disastrous because of the unfortunate Russian system of lack of Cabinet solidarity, and of the practice of separate ministerial reports to the Tsar for his supreme approval or disapproval. Ianushkevich was so confident in this weak trait in his Monarch's character, and of his own ability to win him over, that even before going out to Peterhof, he sent secret word to Zhilinski, the commander of the Warsaw Military District, and presumably to all the Military Districts, stating that "general mobilization" was imminent:

> July 17 [30] will be announced as the first day of our general mobilization. The announcement will follow upon the agreed telegram. 1785. [Signed] Lieutenant-General Ianushkevich.[22]

Some hours earlier Danilov had also asked the Warsaw Military Commander about arrangements for unloading cavalry divisions which were being pushed forward toward

22 Tg. no. 1785, Ianushkevich to Zhilinski, July 29, *ca.* 7:20 A.M.; captured by the Germans later and quoted by Höniger, pp. 100 f. and by Frantz, p. 265. This is confirmed by Zhilinski's telegram next day, after the Tsar had changed his mind and suspended general, in favor of partial, mobilization: "The Chief of the General Staff telegraphed yesterday [July 29] that July 30 would be announced as the first day of mobilization, but since this has not taken place I conclude that changes have taken place in the political situation. Would it not be possible to inform me of the changes which have taken place in this matter? 1954;" Zhilinski to Sukhomlinov, July 30, 2:25 P.M.; quoted by Höniger, p. 110, and by Frantz, p. 266.

the German frontier.[23] One can imagine how the receipt of these telegrams would lead the Russian commanders at Warsaw and at other posts along the German frontier to strain every nerve toward preparing for war, short of a public announcement of mobilization. Aware of this fact, Danilov was also conscious that Russian troops, expecting at any moment the publication of the imminent general mobilization, might commit some act of hostility on the frontier which would give Germany grounds for ordering mobilization, and which also might compromise Russia with her allies, by making Russia seem to be the aggressor. He therefore quickly telegraphed explicitly that, upon the announcement of mobilization, the opening of actual hostilities was not to take place except upon a special telegram, and the frontier troops were to be warned, "in order that no irremediable mistakes shall occur." [24] These telegrams make it clear that the military authorities confidently expected general mobilization would be approved by the Tsar and ordered on July 29, but wished to avoid as far as possible having Russia seem the aggressor.

Returning from Peterhof with the ukase for general mobilization signed by the Tsar in his pocket, Ianushkevich summoned Eggeling, the German Military Attaché. He told him that he had just come from the Tsar, but that everything was just as Sukhomlinov had said it was a couple of days before.[25] "He gave me his word of honor in the most solemn manner and offered me written confirmation that up to that moment, 3:00 P.M., nowhere had there been mobilization, i.e., the calling up of a single man or horse. He could give no guarantee for the future, he said, but would assure me most emphatically that His Majesty, now as before, did not desire mobilization on the fronts along

[23] Tg. no. 1746, July 28, 11:58 P. M.; Höniger, p. 105; Frantz, p. 245.
[24] Tg. no. 1754, July 29, 1:10 A. M.; Höniger, p. 105; Frantz, p. 241.
[25] See above, ch. vi, at notes 107, 108.

our borders." In view of the many reports concerning the
calling of reservists, including the Warsaw and Vilna districts toward Germany, Eggeling said that this statement
puzzled him. "Ianushkevich replied that, on the word of
an officer, such reports were mistaken; it was simply a case
of a false alarm here and there." [26] Eggeling was forced to
conclude that Ianushkevich was attempting to mislead him,
and the historian can hardly escape the same conclusion.

While Ianushkevich was perhaps within the letter of the
truth in saying that the Tsar did not desire mobilization
on the German front, he knew that he had in his pocket [27]
the Tsar's order for a mobilization of this very kind, and
that he was going to put it into effect just as soon as he
could get the necessary signatures of three other ministers.

The Tsar's signature to the mobilization ukase was not
sufficient to allow it to be ordered forthwith. In order to
maintain a check on the military authorities, Russian law
provided that the mobilization order must also be countersigned by the Ministers of War, Marine and Interior.[28]
Ianushkevich therefore handed over the mobilization order
to Dobrorolski who was to get the three signatures. This
officer has left a vivid and essentially accurate account of
his part in the events of this most important day in his
life, except that he places some of the events an hour or
two too early.[29] He went first to Sukhomlinov, the Minister

[26] Pourtalès to Bethmann, July 29, 7 P.M.; K.D., 370; Eggeling,
pp. 27-41; Höniger, "Untersuchungen zum Suchomlinow-Prozess," in
Deutsche Rundschau, April, 1918, pp. 32-33.

[27] At the Sukhomlinov Trial in 1917, referring to his statement to
Eggeling, Ianushkevich declared, "I considered myself justified in offering
him such a written declaration, because, as a matter of fact, at this
moment, mobilization had not yet been announced. I still had the ukase
for mobilization in my pocket" (Novoe Vremia, No. 14,852, Aug. 13/26,
1917).

[28] Dobrorolski, p. 105 (German ed. p. 24); Sukomlinov, p. 361; Frantz,
p. 66.

[29] Dobrorolski, pp. 105 ff. (German ed. pp. 24 ff.), and his supplementary statment in KSF, II, 78-89, April, 1924. He says that he
received the document from Ianushkevich "in the morning, that is

of War, whom he found tired, depressed and apparently regretful of his recent bellicose newspaper article, "Russia is ready, France must be also." Nevertheless Sukhomlinov signed the document, though with a heavy heart, realizing now too late, says Dobrorolski, that Russia was plunging into a war for which she was not fully prepared and which was beyond her strength. In these last days it was Ianushkevich, the Chief of Staff, and not Sukhomlinov, who was most active in pressing for general mobilization.

The Minister of Marine, Grigorovich, was not to be found at the Admiralty; his adjutant said he would not return home till toward seven o'clock. Going on to the Ministry of the Interior, Dobrorolski found alarm at the danger of internal revolution. "With us," said Maklakov, "the war cannot be popular deep down among the masses of the people, among whom revolutionary ideas mean more than a victory over Germany. But one cannot escape one's fate . . ."; and crossing himself, Maklakov signed the mobilization order. These visits took two or three hours, after which Dobrorolski returned to the General Staff Office, to wait for the return of the Minister of Marine. Later in the evening he finally secured his signature also, and then was able to go to the Central Telegraph Office to dispatch the order throughout the Empire. Dobrorolski has left a vivid account of it:

> The Chief Director of the Post and Telegraph had been notified beforehand that a message of extraordinary importance was to be sent out. After I had entered the cabinet of the St. Petersburg Telegraph Office, I handed him the telegram, and waited to be present personally at the transmission of the telegram to the four corners of the Russian Em-

about noon," but it was probably not until after three in the afternoon—after Ianushkevich's interview with Eggeling. He also says it was at 9:30 P.M. that he was on the point of sending out the mobilization order over the wires, when he was suddenly recalled; but it must have been a little later, since the Kaiser's telegram which occasioned the recall of the order did not arrive until 9:40 P.M.

pire. In my presence they proceeded to click off the telegram
on several typewriters in order to send it at the same moment
by all the wires which connected St. Petersburg with the
principal centres of the Empire, from which the despatch
would be transmitted to all the towns in the governments
and territorial districts. There existed a special instruction
for the sending of the mobilization telegram. During its
transmission no other telegrams of any sort could be sent.

The imposing room of the St. Petersburg Central Telegraph Office with its telegraph keys, to the number of some
dozen, was ready to receive the mobilization telegram.

But at this moment—about 9:30 P.M.—General Ianushkevich called me on the telephone and ordered me to hold
back the telegram until the arrival of a Captain in the
General Staff, Tugan-Baranovski. He entered and told me
that he had hurried after me through the city to bring me
a special order from the Tsar not to send out the telegram
for general mobilization. General mobilization was to be
suspended, and in its place, by order of the Tsar, partial
mobilization was to be adopted in accordance with the plan
previously arranged.

I at once took back the telegram for general mobilization which I had delivered to the telegraph office and all the
copies of the telegram. I notified the head of the telegraph
office of the withdrawal which had taken place, and rode
away.[30]

Before explaining this sudden eleventh-hour change of
decision, we must glance back for a moment to see what
Sazonov and the ambassadors had been doing while Ianushkevich had been out at Peterhof and Dobrorolski had been
getting the necessary signatures for the general mobilization
order.

On the morning of July 29 about 11 o'clock Pourtalès
called upon Sazonov to make an "agreeable communication"
—that Austria had renewed her declaration that she did not

[30] Dobrorolski, p. 107 (German ed. p. 25 f).

intend to take Serbian territory and that Germany was striving to persuade her to come to a frank discussion with Russia and satisfy her as to the purpose and extent of her procedure in Serbia. But Sazonov replied that, since he had had no answer to his proposal for "direct conversations" and Austria had declared war on Serbia, Austria's good faith was questionable. Russia therefore had decided to mobilize the military districts on the Austrian frontier and the order would be given that very day; this did not mean war; "the Russian army would doubtless remain under arms for weeks to come without crossing the frontier." Pourtalès pointed out the peril that the General Staffs of Russia's neighbors would press for counter-measures.[31]

In notifying Pourtalès that Russia was about to order partial mobilization against Austria only, Sazonov was not necessarily acting insincerely, because he did not yet know whether Ianushkevich had persuaded the Tsar to sign the ukase for general as well as partial mobilization. But, after lunch, in his interview with the British Ambassador, he can hardly be said to have been completely frank, because he gave Buchanan to understand that "the order for partial mobilization was signed today," and that "it had been decided not to order the general mobilization which the military authorities had strongly recommended."[32] Had Sazonov by this time heard from Ianushkevich the result of his visit to Peterhof? If not, how could he say "the order for partial mobilization was signed today?" If he had heard from Ianushkevich, as is probably the case, he knew that the order for general mobilization also had been signed, and it was not true that "it had been decided not to order the general mobilization." In either case he gave Buchanan an impression of definiteness about the Russian military de-

[31] Pourtalès to Bethmann, July 29, 1:58 P.M.; K.D., 343; Schilling's *Diary*, p. 47 f.

[32] Buchanan to Grey, July 29, 8:40 P.M.; B.D., 276.

cisions which was not in accordance with the facts. His purpose, of course, was obvious—he wished to avoid alarming and alienating British opinion. Therefore he coupled his information about partial mobilization with the statement that mobilization would take a week or more, and that Russia would not precipitate war by immediately crossing the frontier, and he hoped England could meanwhile find some satisfactory peaceful solution.

In the middle of the afternoon, Pourtalès had a second interview with Sazonov, who sent for him to tell him the news, evidently just received from the Russian Ambassador in Vienna,[33] that Berchtold had replied with a "categorical refusal" to the request for "direct conversations." Sazonov therefore, "grasping at every straw," wished now to return to Grey's proposal for a conference of ambassadors. Pourtalès, however, said he did not know his Government's attitude on this, but "could not help feeling that the order of Russian mobilization, in case it were really impending, was a great mistake. . . . Sazonov did not deny the imminence of mobilization, but stated that Russia was compelled by Austria to take this step; mobilization, however, was far from meaning war." [34]

Sazonov next received a call from the Austrian Ambassador, who came "to clear up apparent misunderstandings." Having just received Berchtold's telegram refusing to discuss the text of the Austrian ultimatum, Szápáry had to admit that Austria was unwilling to carry on direct conversations on this subject, but was quite ready to converse on the broader basis of Austro-Russian relations; that she had no wish to injure Russian interest, was seeking no territory, and did not intend to interfere with Serbia's sovereignty.

Sazonov replied that though Austria might not take Ser-

[33] *Cf.* Berchtold to Szápáry, July 28, 11:40 P.M.; A.R.B., II, 95.
[34] Pourtalès to Bethmann, July 29, 6:10 P.M.; K.D., 365; *Am Scheideweg*, 41 f.

bian territory, she was nevertheless attacking Serbian sovereignty by virtually reducing her to a vassal state. This would upset the balance of power in the Balkans, and consequently injure Russian interests. There followed a long fruitless discussion in a *circulus vitiosus*. Finally Sazonov said "a ukase would be signed today ordering a mobilization of a fairly wide extent; but he could assure me most officially that their troops were not meant to attack us; they would only stand ready with arms grounded in case Russia's Balkan interests were endangered; a *note explicative* would confirm this." (No such note, however, was ever issued.)

The responsibility for this order Sazonov sought to put wholly on the military authorities, according to Szápáry's report. When Szápáry mentioned that he had heard Russia was alarmed because Austria had mobilized eight corps against Serbia, "Sazonov confirmed to me that it was not he, who knew nothing of this, but Tsar Nicholas who, upon the information of the Chief of Staff, had expressed this alarm." Szápáry pointed out that even a child in military matters ought to see the mobilization of Austria toward the south could not threaten Russia, and urged that if peace were to be preserved, a quick end should be put to the machinations of the military authorities who on the basis of false news were in danger of taking matters into their own hands. "Sazonov remarked very characteristically that he could say this to the Chief of Staff, because the latter was seeing His Majesty every day. He himself, however, in a time like the present, only went for his usual Tuesday audience, and then learned for the first time from His Majesty what the militarists had been urging upon him."

"While we were thus engaged in a confidential exchange of views," Szápáry continued, "Sazonov heard by telephone that we had bombarded Belgrade. He became like a changed man [*wie ausgewechselt*]. He sought to take up

again all his previous arguments in a way which flew in the
face of all logic, and said he saw now that the Tsar was
right. 'You only wish to gain time by negotiations, but
you go ahead and bombard an unprotected city!' " He went
on to denounce Austria in the most excited fashion. Whereupon Szápáry took his leave.[35] The exact hour of this interview is uncertain, but it was probably in the later part of
the afternoon, after Sazonov had heard from Ianushkevich
that the Tsar had signed the ukase for general mobilization.
This may explain why he spoke of "a mobilization of fairly
wide extent," instead of the "partial mobilization," which he
had indicated to Pourtalès and Buchanan earlier in the day.

A little later, between six and seven o'clock, while Sazonov was still in a very excited state, Pourtalès called again
at the Russian Foreign Office to carry out instructions just
received from Berlin. Alarmed by the rumors of wide-
reaching Russian military preparations—but not of the decision for Russian partial mobilization of which he did not
hear until a little later [36]—Bethmann had telegraphed to
Pourtalès: "Kindly call M. Sazonov's serious attention to
the fact that further continuation of Russian mobilization
measures would force us to mobilize, and in that case a
European war could scarcely be prevented." [37]

[35] Szápáry to Berchtold, July 29, 11:00 P.M.; A.R.B. III, 19. Pourtalès, in a telegram sent at 8:00 P.M. (K.D., 378), says: "Sazonov has
admitted to Szápáry that mobilization is impending, and added that a
note explicative would be published." This indicates that the Sazonov-
Szápáry interview took place prior to Pourtalès's "warning," to be mentioned in a moment. Schilling's *Diary*, p. 49, is therefore inaccurate in
placing the news of the bombardment of Belgrade *after* Pourtalès's warning.
Curiously enough, Schilling makes no mention of this Sazonov-Szápáry
interview—possibly because it was the aim of the Russians (and especially
of the French) to shift the responsibility in the final days as much as
possible from Austria to Germany.

[36] From Sverbeiev after 5:00 P.M. (Schilling's *Diary*, pp. 103, 106);
and from Pourtalès in a telegram received at 1:58 P.M. (K.D., 343).

[37] Bethmann to Pourtalès, July 29, 12:50 P.M.; received at St.
Petersburg at 4:35 P.M.; K.D., 342; Schilling's *Diary*, p. 48. Allowing time
for decodification, and for the codification of Pourtalès' reply which was

In stating this to Sazonov, Pourtalès said "it did not imply a threat, but simply a friendly opinion." But Sazonov received it "in a state of great excitement" and said he would report it to the Tsar.[38] Sazonov, however, appears to have interpreted it as a threat, and replied sharply: "Now I have no further doubt as to the true cause of Austria's intransigence." Pourtalès jumped up from his seat in protest, and the two parted coolly.[39]

Sazonov then informed the Tsar by telephone of the communication just made by Pourtalès. The Tsar directed him to discuss with Ianushkevich and Sukhomlinov the question of general mobilization at once, while he himself telegraphed to the Kaiser: "Thanks for your telegram conciliatory and friendly, whereas official message presented today by your Ambassador to my Minister was conveyed in a very different tone. Beg you to explain this divergency. It would be right to give over the Austro-Serbian problem to the Hague Conference. Trust in your wisdom and friendship." [40]

The news of the bombardment of Belgrade, followed by Pourtalès's warning that the further continuation of Russian mobilization measures would lead to German mobilization and war, removed any last doubts which Sazonov may have had as to need of immediate general mobilization. In the discussion with Ianushkevich, he agreed that, as war with Germany was probably unavoidable, it would be a mistake to postpone longer the general mobilization

sent at 8:00 P.M. (K.D., 378), it is clear that this third Pourtalès-Sazonov interview took place between 6 and 7 P. M., as Pourtalès correctly states in his memoir (*Am Scheideweg*, p. 45 f.). Schilling's *Diary*, p. 48, is inaccurate in placing it "at 3:00 P. M."; Schilling perhaps confused it with the second Pourtalès interview, mentioned above at note 34, which did take place about 3:00 P. M.

[38] Pourtalès to Bethmann, July 29, 8:00 P.M., K.D., 378; *cf.* Schilling's *Diary*, p. 48.   [39] Schilling's *Diary*, p. 48 f.

[40] Tsar to Kaiser, 8:20 P.M.; received 8:42 P.M.; K.D., 366; Schilling's *Diary*, p. 54. On the Tsar's Hague Tribunal idea, see preceding chapter, at notes 74-78.

or to interfere with its successful execution by first ordering
a partial mobilization. This decision "was telephoned to
the Tsar who authorized taking steps accordingly." It was
also, according to Baron Schilling, "received with enthusiasm by the small circle of those acquainted with what was
in progress." [41]

Dobrorolski, who had meanwhile collected the three necessary signatures, started for the Central Telegraph Office
to send out the general mobilization order. And Sazonov
dispatched a telegram to the Russian Ambassadors in Paris
and London, which hardly stated fully and frankly either
the communication of Pourtalès or the momentous step
which Russia was on the point of taking:

> The German Ambassador informed me today of the de-
> cision of the German Government to mobilize its armed
> forces, if Russia did not stop her military preparations.
> Now, in point of fact, we only began these preparations in
> consequence of the mobilization of eight army corps already
> undertaken by Austria, and owing to her evident unwilling-
> ness to accept any means of arriving at a peaceful settle-
> ment of her dispute with Serbia.
>
> As we cannot comply with the wishes of Germany, we
> have no alternative but to hasten on our own armaments
> and to assume that war is probably inevitable.[42]

If we put confidence in the complete sincerity of the
telegram just quoted, and in the accuracy of Schilling's
Diary as to the crowded events of July 29, as some writers

41 Schilling's *Diary*, p. 50.

42 Sazonov to Izvolski and Benckendorff, tg. 1551, July 30; L.N., II,
289; B.D., 300. R.O.B., 58, omits the words, "of eight army corps;" and
it was not true that Russia only began her military preparations in consequence of the mobilization already undertaken by Austria; she began
them on the night of July 25-26, before she had heard of the Austrian partial mobilization against Serbia. Sazonov's telegram to Izvolski goes on
to thank France for Paléologue's declaration of French support, "in the
existing circumstances very valuable to us," and to urge that England
should at once join Russia and France (see above, at notes 5-11).

are inclined to do,[43] it would appear that it was the warning from Pourtalès which caused the Russian decision to order general mobilization instead of partial mobilization. But it was naturally Sazonov's aim, in order to secure British aid, to make it appear that it was a German menace, and not Austria's upsetting of the balance in the Balkans, which caused Russia to "hasten her armaments," as Sazonov euphemistically referred to Russia's imminent general mobilization. And as to Schilling's *Diary*, it is clearly inaccurate in several respects: in placing the warning from Pourtalès at 3:00 P.M., instead of between 6 and 7 P.M.; in putting the news of the bombardment of Belgrade *after* the warning of Pourtalès, instead of earlier during the long Szápáry-Sazonov interview; and in saying not a word of the latter. Moreover, Dobrorolski's narrative makes no mention of the warning of Pourtalès as having any decisive influence, or of there being any hesitation or delay after Ianushkevich returned from Peterhof with the signed ukase, except the delay caused by getting the signatures of the three ministers. To be sure, Dobrorolski was a military officer, more likely to be informed in regard to what was being done by the General Staff than by the Foreign Office.

From the somewhat divergent accounts of Schilling's *Diary* and Dobrorolski's narrative, and from the summary of the activities of the Russian diplomatic and military officials given above, one may conclude that the Tsar in signing the ukases for general and partial mobilization was still hesitating in his mind between the two, and expected Ianushkevich to confer with Sazonov before sending out the order for either. Ianushkevich, however, took the Tsar's assent to general mobilization as an authorization to proceed with it directly. On returning from Peterhof to St.

---

[43] *Cf.* M. T. Florinsky, "The Russian Mobilization of 1914", in *Political Science Quarterly*, XLII, 215 ff., June, 1927; Poincaré, IV, 397; Renouvin, p. 135 ff., however, is more cautious and critical

Petersburg, he informed Sazonov of his success in persuading the Tsar. He did so shortly before he talked with Eggeling about 3 P.M.,[44] and before Sazonov talked with Szápáry. Ianushkevich then went ahead getting Dobrorolski to secure the signatures for the order for general mobilization, prior to the warning from Pourtalès and without being influenced by it. Meanwhile Sazonov, not having been consulted by the Tsar, made no effort to interfere in a military matter outside his province, and acquiesced in what Ianushkevich was doing. Then came his interview with Szápáry, and his third talk with Pourtalès between 6 and 7 P.M. He now believed that Berchtold had given a "categorical refusal" to direct conversations, that Belgrade had been bombarded, and that Germany had warned that she would mobilize if the Russian military preparations did not cease. This accumulation of hostile indications, on the part of both Austria and Germany, put to flight any remaining inclination on his part in favor of his earlier partial mobilization plan. Toward 8 P.M., when he told the Tsar over the telephone of the warning from Pourtalès, and the Tsar thereupon authorized him to talk with Ianushkevich concerning mobilization at once, he agreed with the Chief of Staff that it should be ordered immediately. The decision was "received with enthusiasm" by the little circle at the Foreign Office, who now "assumed that war was almost inevitable."

It was mainly the pressure of the Russian militarists, not the warning of Pourtalès, that almost started the general mobilization order over the wires. Then the Tsar changed his mind.

[44] At the Sukhomlinov Trial in 1917, Ianushkevich declared that the Tsar had instructed him to assure Pourtalès that the mobilization was no hostile act against Germany. He communicated this to Sazonov. But Sazonov feared that Pourtalès would interpret this in his own way, and advised Ianushkevich instead to give the assurance to Eggeling, the German Military Attaché. Ianushkevich, accordingly acted on this advice (Ianushkevich's testimony as reported in the *Novoe Vremia;* quoted by Oman, *The Outbreak of the War,* p. 67; and by Höniger, in the *Deutsche Rundschau,* April, 1918, p. 33).

THE TSAR'S CANCELLATION OF GENERAL MOBILIZATION

At 9:40 P.M. Nicholas II received at Peterhof a second telegram from the Kaiser. In it William II insisted that "Serbian promises on paper are wholly unreliable," and, in the dominating tone which he had so often found successful in the past with the Tsar, told him warningly:

> It would be quite possible for Russia to remain a spectator of the Austro-Serbian conflict without involving Europe in the most horrible war she ever witnessed. I think a direct understanding between your Government and Vienna possible and desirable, and as I already telegraphed you, my Government is continuing its exertions to promote it. Of course, military measures on the part of Russia which would be looked upon by Austria as threatening would precipitate a calamity we both wish to avoid, and jeopardize my position as mediator which I readily accepted on your appeal to my friendship and my help.[45]

The Kaiser apparently judged correctly the effect of this tone on the weak and changeable "Nicky," for the Tsar, ruminating on the situation, began to think he had made a mistake in signing the ukase for general mobilization. He now decided immediately and on his own initiative [46] to cancel the order for general mobilization, and to substitute in its place the apparently less dangerous partial mobilization.

The Tsar therefore called up Ianushkevich, and there followed a three-cornered telephone conversation between the Tsar, Sukhomlinov, and Ianushkevich, in which the two military men tried to convince the Tsar that he was making a terrible mistake; that there was no guarantee that the Kaiser's mediation at Vienna would be successful; that it was clear from Germany's and Austria's conduct that a

[45] Kaiser to Tsar. July 29, 6:30 P.M., received 9:40 P.M.; K.D., 359; Schilling's *Diary*, p. 55.   [46] Paléologue, I, 37.

general war had become inevitable; and that to suspend the
general mobilization would only give the enemy a chance
to mobilize more quickly than Russia. But for once the
Tsar remained firm. Ianushkevich in despair found himself compelled to recall Dobrorolski from the telegraph office
where he was on the point of sending out the order for
general mobilization. In its place, toward midnight of July
29, the order for partial mobilization was dispatched over
the wires.[47]

At the famous Sukhomlinov Trial in 1917, the Minister
of War declared that he had disobeyed the Tsar and had
persisted with the general mobilization on the night of July
29.[48] But it is now clear from the accounts of Dobrorolski
and other evidence that he was lying, and in his own later
memoirs he no longer insisted on this version of the events
of the night of July 29.

Sazonov was at once informed by Ianushkevich of the
Tsar's change of mind and of the substitution of partial
for general mobilization. He had already sent one of the
Secretaries, M. Basili, to inform Paléologue that it had been
decided to issue orders that very night for partial mobilization, but to commence general mobilization in secret. Paléologue says he was quite taken aback: "Would it not
be possible, for the moment, to be content with partial
mobilization?" "No," said Basili, "the question has just
been thoroughly examined by our highest military authorities." [49]

Basili then suggested that, as the Germans might decipher a French telegram, it would be better for Paléologue

[47] It was received and acted upon by the Moscow military authorities
before 12:01 A. M. on July 30; Frantz, p. 262.

[48] See the present writer's extracts from the Russian Press reports of
the trial in *American Historical Review*, XXVI, 246-250 (Jan., 1921); the
excellent arrangement of extracts by M. Renouvin in the *Revue d'Histoire de la Guerre Mondiale*, II, 49-69 (April, 1924); and the summaries by
Höniger, in *Deutsche Rundschau*, XLIV, 15-80 (April, 1918).

[49] Paléologue, I, 36.

to notify his Government of this very secret information by a telegram sent in Russian cipher via the Russian Foreign Office to Izvolski. Paléologue accepted the suggestion. But before the telegram had been put into cipher he and Basili received word of the Tsar's change of mind. So Paléologue said nothing to his Government of the momentous decision for general mobilization which Russia had been about to order. He merely repeated the account of the warning from Pourtalès, and said that the tone in which it had been made "has caused the Russian Government at once to order the mobilization of thirteen army corps which are intended against Austria-Hungary." [50]

After midnight Sazonov again had a long interview with Pourtalès, in which the difference between the Russian and German point of view became more clearly defined. Sazonov wanted Germany to press Austria to drop those demands of the ultimatum which infringed the *sovereignty* of Serbia: Russia's vital interests could not allow that Serbia should sink to a vassal state of Austria—"become a Bokhara"—by the acceptance of demands which infringed her sovereign rights. Pourtalès, on the other hand, wanted Russia to accept Austria's declaration of willingness to respect the *territorial integrity* of Serbia as sufficient. Neither man would yield to the other. Pourtalès pointed out that Germany had already gone far in putting pressure on Vienna, and that the situation now had been made very much more difficult by the fact that Russia had decided to order partial mobilization. But Sazonov flatly refused to be satisfied merely with an Austrian declaration of territorial disinterestedness in regard to Serbia.[51]

---

[50] Paléologue to Viviani, July 30, 1 A.M.; F.Y.B., 100; and Basili's account as reported by Recouly, p. 160 ff. This is another case in which Paléologue failed to keep his government fully and promptly informed as to events in St. Petersburg.

[51] Pourtalès to Bethmann, July 30, 4:30 A.M. and 9:30 A.M.; K.D., 401, 412.

Sazonov's insistence on this question of Serbian sovereignty was further brought to the front on the forenoon of July 30, when Pourtalès finally begged him to formulate in writing a statement which would satisfy Russia and yet have at least a prospect of being a successful solution. Sazonov then wrote out the following "formula:"

> If Austria, recognizing that the Austro-Serbian question has assumed the character of a question of European interest, declares herself ready to eliminate from her ultimatum points which violate the sovereign rights of Serbia, Russia engages to stop her military preparations.[52]

This "formula," however, represented hardly any concession on Sazonov's part, except that it did not demand the immediate halt of the Austrian operations against Serbia. Nor was it likely to prove acceptable to Austria, even after it was modified at Sir Edward Grey's suggestion, so as to provide for an Austrian occupation of Belgrade, and for intervention by the Great Powers. But neither the original nor the modified formula had any serious chance of success. It was overtaken by the very rapid course of events arising from the pressure of the militarists, and especially by the fact that a few hours after proposing his formula, Sazonov secured from the Tsar a second change of mind and final consent to general mobilization.

RUSSIAN GENERAL MOBILIZATION ORDERED

It was with dismay and despair that the Russian Chief of Staff and Minister of War had been forced by the Tsar to cancel general mobilization on the night of July 29. But they were determined not to rest until they had per-

---

[52] Pourtalès to Bethmann, July 30, 1:01 P.M.; K.D., 421. *Cf.* also R.O.B., 60; and Paléologue, I, 37 f., who says this formula proposal was made at 2:00 P.M. on July 30; but Paléologue is mistaken; it was made earlier, either at 2:00 A.M., as Sazonov stated to Buchanan and Paléologue (B.D., 302; F.Y.B., 103), or more probably in the late forenoon, as Pourtalès insists (*Am Scheideweg*, pp. 51 ff.).

suaded him to change his mind a second time and again to consent to the general mobilization which they considered indispensable.   On the morning of July 30 they conferred again with Sazonov and found that he was wholly in agreement with them.   They called the Tsar on the telephone and tried to persuade him to return to his resolution of the day before, and allow general mobilization to begin.   The Tsar at first resolutely rejected their request, and finally announced curtly that he was breaking off the conversation.   Ianushkevich, who held the telephone, could only inform him that Sazonov was there also, and begged permission to say a word to him.   A certain silence followed, after which the Tsar expressed his consent to listen.   Sazonov requested His Majesty to receive him immediately for a report which could not be delayed.   After another silence the Tsar asked, "Is it all the same to you if I receive you at the same time with Tatishchev at 3 o'clock, because otherwise I have not a minute of free time today?" Sazonov thanked the Tsar, and said that he would arrive at the appointed hour.[53]

Ianushkevich then adjured Sazonov not to fail to get from the Tsar a renewed assent to general mobilization. He reiterated the technical arguments of the great danger that Russia would not be ready for war with Germany, which he believed inevitable, if there was further delay; because later general mobilization would be very seriously dislocated by the partial mobilization already ordered; this dislocation could only be avoided by an immediate general mobilization.   As a further means of putting pressure on the Tsar he suggested that Sazonov use a political argument: Russia's French ally would be displeased and would regard Russia as failing to live up to the obligations of her alliance; the Kaiser would coax out of the French a promise of neutrality; and he would then fall upon Russia

[53] Schilling's *Diary*, p. 63. *Cf.* also Sazonov, *Fateful Years*, p. 199 ff.

when she was entangled in the midst of her partial mobilization.[54] Finally, he begged Sazonov, the moment he was
successful in persuading the Tsar, to inform him at once
by telephone from Peterhof, so that he could take immediately the necessary measures, and, before it was too late,
convert the partial into a general mobilization. "After
this," added the Chief of Staff, "I will retire from sight,
smash my telephone, and generally take all measures so
that I cannot be found to give any contrary orders for a
new postponement of general mobilization." [55]

Sazonov agreed completely, and Ianushkevich telephoned to Dobrorolski: "There is hope for an improvement
of the situation; be ready to come to me with all the documents immediately upon my telephone call in the afternoon." [56]

Sazonov then talked with Buchanan and Paléologue,
telling them of an interview with Pourtalès, at which the
German Ambassador, "seeing that war was inevitable,
broke down completely and appealed to Sazonov to hold
out a last straw and to make some suggestion which Pourtalès could telegraph to his Government." Whereupon
Sazonov had drawn up the "formula" mentioned above.
Sazonov then said in substance to the two Ambassadors:
"If Austria rejects this proposal, preparations for a general mobilization will be proceeded with, and European
war will be inevitable. For strategical reasons Russia can
hardly postpone converting partial into general mobilization, now that she knows Germany is preparing, and excitement in the country has reached such a pitch that she
cannot hold back if Austria refuses to make concession." [57]
Buchanan evidently made no effort to deter Sazonov from

[54] Dobrorolski, p. 108 (German ed., p. 28).

[55] Schilling's *Diary*, p. 64.

[56] Dobrorolski, p. 108 (German ed., p. 27).

[57] Buchanan to Grey, July 30, 1:15 P.M.; received 3:15 P.M.; B.D.
302; *cf.* also F.Y.B., 103; and above, at notes 51, 52.

his purpose of converting partial into general mobilization; his failure to do so must have been an encouragement to the Russian Minister.

Paléologue, at the time of this interview, had received a dispatch from Viviani, repeating that France was ready to fulfil the obligations of the Alliance, but instructing him to advise Sazonov to avoid military measures which might offer Germany a pretext for mobilization. Paléologue telegraphed back that he had carried out these instructions.[58] But in his memoirs, and very probably at the time, he placed much more emphasis on the first part of Viviani's message assuring French loyalty to the Alliance, than upon the last part suggesting caution in mobilization measures. Moreover, Izvolski had telegraphed to Sazonov that Margerie, an official in the French Foreign Office, had said that the French Government, without wishing to interfere in Russian military preparations, thought they should be carried on in the least open and provocative manner; and that the French Minister of War advised Russia to strengthen her military preparations, but to avoid as much as possible the appearance of doing so.[59]

Sazonov then lunched with Basili and Krivoshein, the Minister of Agriculture, who also besought him to wring from the Tsar a consent to general mobilization. After lunch Sazonov went out to Peterhof with Tatishchev at 2:00 P.M. He found the Tsar pale and nervous, now fully conscious of the awful seriousness of the responsibility resting upon him. "Think of the responsibility which you are advising me to take!" said the Tsar. "Think of the thousands and thousands of men who will be sent to their death!" In reply Sazonov tried to prove to him that he

[58] Poincaré, IV, 399 ff.; Paléologue, I, 39 f. Perhaps misled by the fact that in F.Y.B., 102, two of his despatches have been garbled into one, Paléologue incorrectly places this interview at 6:00 P. M. instead of in the forenoon. See also below, ch. xi, at note 6.

[59] Izvolski to Sazonov, July 30; M.F.R., p. 521; L.N., II, 290.

would have nothing with which to reproach his conscience, if war broke out, because it had clearly become inevitable. Diplomacy had .finished its work.   It was time for His Majesty to think of the safety of his Empire.   To fail to order general mobilization would only dislocate the whole Russian military organization, and disconcert Russia's allies. "It only remains to do everything necessary to meet war fully armed and under the conditions most favorable for us.   Therefore it is better without fear to call forth a war by our preparations for it, and to continue these preparations carefully, rather than out of fear to give an inducement for war and be taken unawares." [60]

For almost an hour the Tsar's firm desire to avoid war at all costs made him hesitate to adopt measures which, however indispensable from a military point, were calculated, as he clearly saw, to hasten the catastrophe.   The tenseness of feeling which he lived through in these minutes expressed itself among other ways in the irritability, unusual for him, with which he snubbed General Tatishchev. The latter, who had taken no part in the conversation, remarked in a moment of silence: "Yes, it is hard to decide." The Tsar replied in a sharp and displeased tone: "I will decide," and gave his decision for an immediate general mobilization.   Sazonov thereupon hurried to the telephone on the ground floor of the palace, notified Ianushkevich, who was waiting impatiently for the news, and added: "Now you can smash the telephone.   Give your orders, General, and then—disappear for the rest of the day." [61]

Ianushkevich immediately summoned Dobrorolski, who quickly gathered again the three necessary signatures from the ministers who at the moment were gathered in extraordinary session.   His mobilization order had been so

---

[60] Schilling's *Diary*, p. 65; and Paléologue, I, 39.
[61] Schilling's *Diary*, p. 65 f.; and Dobrorolski, p. 109 (German ed ┌ 28); Sazonov. p. 202 ff.

planned that the first day of general mobilization was set for July 31, and so made to coincide with the day on which the troops in the four Southern Districts were actually to be called up and transportation was to begin; thus was avoided all confusion which might have resulted if general mobilization had been delayed a day longer. With the new signed ukase Dobrorolski hurried again, as the night before, to the Central Telegraph Office. "Every operator was sitting by his instrument waiting for the copy of the telegram, in order to send to all the ends of the Russian Empire the momentous news of the calling up of the Russian people. A few minutes after six, while absolute stillness reigned in the room, all the instruments began at once to click. That was the beginning moment of the great epoch." [62]

Dobrorolski waited for the confirming reply telegrams. They began to come in about 7:00 P.M., and made it certain that all the places in direct telegraph connection with St. Petersburg, which comprised all the more important cities in European and Asiatic Russia, were receiving the order promptly and correctly.[63] In the Warsaw Military District, for instance, bordering on Germany, various Russian commanding officers received the mobilization telegrams at 7:55 P.M., 8:02 P.M., 8:15 P.M., and acted upon them at once.[64]

In a remote Siberian village an English traveller was awakened a few hours later, at 4:00 A.M., by a great commotion outside his window, and was asked by an excited peasant: "Have you heard the news? There is war." [65]

During the night the red mobilization placards, calling men to the colors, had been posted up everywhere on the street corners. No further change of mind on the part of the Tsar was now possible. Russia was committed to the

[62] Dobrorolski, p. 109 f. (German ed., p. 28 f.).
[63] Dobrorolski, p. 110.
[64] Frantz, pp. 68, 265; cf. Höniger, pp. 114-118.
[65] Stephen Graham, *Russia and the World* (New York, 1915), p. 1 f.

step which military men everywhere, just as the Siberian peasant, understood meant war.

What were the reasons for this fatal decision to order general mobilization? The Entente Powers, in their efforts to excuse and justify it, have often alleged various reasons —which are false.

One story is that the Russian decision was brought about by a telegram from Sverbeev, the Russian Ambassador in Berlin, stating: "The order for the mobilization of the German army and navy has just been issued." It was occasioned by the publication of news to this effect soon after one o'clock by an "extra" of a Berlin newspaper, the *Lokal-Anzeiger*. This, it is said, was a trick on the part of the Germans to precipitate general mobilization in Russia and so make her seem to be the aggressor. But the news had been immediately contradicted by the German Foreign Office and the "extra" had been suppressed. The Russian Ambassador had thereupon quickly sent a second telegram, unciphered, cancelling the first, and followed it by a third, ciphered, explaining the circumstances.[66] It has now been conclusively established that none of these three telegrams reached St. Petersburg until *after* the Tsar had given his decision. They could therefore have had no influence in causing it. Nor did Sazonov or any of the Russian authorities at the time, in July, 1914, allege this *Lokal-Anzeiger* episode as an excuse for the Russian general mobilization. It was a later invention, first given notoriety by Sir Edward Grey in 1916.[67]

[66] *Krasnyi Arkhiv,* I, pp. 179 f. *The Russian Orange Book,* Nos. 61, 62, published the first and third telegrams in a falsified form, and suppressed the second.

[67] For the detailed facts, see Montgelas, in the *Deutsche Rundschau,* May, 1922, pp. 113-124; and in his *Leitfaden,* 215 ff. We have not repeated them at length here, because all careful historical scholars, like M. Renouvin (pp. 183 ff.), now follow Montgelas in rejecting this *Lokal-Anzeiger* explanation of Russian general mobilization as a legend. Even M. Sazonov, shortly before his death, admitted that "it did not cause our mobilization" (Florinsky, in *Pol. Sci. Quart.,* June, 1927, p. 222 f).

Another reason, alleged by the French Ambassador at St. Petersburg in his somewhat untrustworthy memoirs, is that the decision was caused by a menacing telegram from the Kaiser. According to this legend, Sazonov, on arriving at Peterhof, found that the Tsar "had received a very bad impression from a telegram sent him the night before in an almost menacing tone: 'If Russia mobilizes against Austria, my rôle as mediator, which I accepted at your express prayer, will be endangered, if not ruined. The whole weight of the decision lies on your shoulders now, who have to bear the responsibility for peace or war.' Having read and reread this telegram, Sazonov made a gesture of despair," and proceeded to urge general mobilization upon the Tsar, on the grounds that war was already inevitable and Germany was only pretending to mediate in order to gain time to complete secretly her preparations for attack. After hesitation, continues Paléologue, the Tsar reluctantly yielded and gave his decision. "The clock marked exactly 4:00 P.M." [68] But this telegram from the Kaiser [69] was not sent until 3:30 P.M., and was not received at Peterhof until 6:30 P.M. Being received more than two hours *after* the Tsar's decision, and half an hour *after* Dobrorolski had actually begun to send the general mobilization order over the wires, it can no more have been the cause of Russia's general mobilization than the *Lokal-Anzeiger* "extra." Either Sazonov gave Paléologue an untrue account of his audience with the Tsar; or, more probably, the French Ambassador was again drawing upon his lively imagination.

Still another reason alleged for the Russian general mobilization is that it was caused by Austria's general

[68] Paléologue, I, 38 f. Sazonov (p. 202 ff.) repeats the legend. Possibly the Tsar's decision was made two or three hours earlier (*cf.* Dobrorolski, in KSF, II, 87, April, 1924), but not later than 4 P.M. Schilling's *Diary*, p. 63 ff. says Sazonov's audience began at 3 P.M., and lasted nearly an hour, which would also place the Tsar's decision at 4 P.M.

[69] K.D., 420; Schilling's *Diary*, p. 67.

mobilization and by mobilization measures taken secretly but continuously by Germany for the past six days. This legend was perpetuated by the falsified form in which the *French Yellow Book* published the belated telegram in which Paléologue finally notified his Government of Russia's fatal step. The original and falsified forms may be seen side by side.[70]

Original text:	Falsified text, F.Y.B., 118:
The general mobilization of the Russian army has been ordered.	As a result of the general mobilization of Austria and of the measures for mobilization taken secretly, but continuously, by Germany for the last six days, the order for the general mobilization of the Russian army has been given, Russia not being able, without most serious danger, to allow herself to be further out-distanced; really she is only taking military measures corresponding to those taken by Germany. For imperative reasons of strategy the Russian Government, knowing that Germany was arming, could no longer delay the conversion of her partial mobilization into a general mobilization.

As the greater part of this document in the *French Yellow Book* is now admitted by the French authorities to be a pure fabrication, it is hardly necessary to note that

70 Paléologue to Viviani, via Bergen, July 31, 10:43 A. M., received 8:30 P. M.; printed in its original form by Renouvin, p. 181 f., and in its falsified form in F.Y.B., 118. *Cf.* also Poincaré, IV, 455-458, for the delay in deciphering and bringing it to his notice.

[Even

the Austrian general mobilization was not ordered until eighteen hours after that of Russia, and that there is no truth in the statement that Germany had for six days been taking secret mobilization measures.[71]   That the officials of the French Foreign Office who edited the *Yellow Book* in 1914 should have thought it necessary to resort to such a deliberate distortion of the truth, suggests that they were conscious of how fatal Russia's action was, and how largely Paléologue and France were responsible for it, and therefore sought to excuse and justify it even by falsifying documents.

Was Sazonov, shortly before going out to Peterhof, strengthened in his determination to persuade the Tsar to order general mobilization by the conversation which he had with Buchanan and Paléologue, and by the telegram from Izvolski?[72]   Or, as M. Renouvin ingeniously suggests,[73] did this conversation and telegram merely cause him, upon his return from Peterhof after securing the order for general mobilization, to inform Paléologue, with an economy of truth hardly usual toward one's own ally, that the Russian Government "was resolved to proceed secretly with the preliminary measures [*premières mesures*] of general mobilization."[74]   One would not know with certainty from this ambiguous phrase that the Russian Government had already ordered full mobilization, and it is the claim of Renouvin and Poincaré that the Cabinet at Paris was not aware of the Russian general mobilization, so far as any information had come from Paléologue, until more than a whole day after it had been ordered, that is, until the arrival

---

[71] On Bethmann's restraint on Moltke and the German military authorities, and on Austrian general mobilization, see below, ch. xi.

[72] See above, at notes 57-59.   [73] Renouvin, pp. 186 ff.

[74] Paléologue to Viviani, July 30, 9:15 P.M., received 11:30 P.M.; part of this telegram is printed in F.Y.B., 102, but the passage quoted was suppressed; what appears to be the complete text is given by C. Appuhn and P. Renouvin, *Introduction aux Tableaux d'Histoire de Guillaume II*, (Paris, 1923), p. xcv.

at 8:30 P.M. on July 31 of the telegram that Paléologue sent via Bergen at 10:43 A. M.[75]

If Renouvin and Poincaré are correct, then Paléologue's telegram had deceived his Government. Who was the guilty author of the deceit? Did Sazonov mislead Paléologue, who innocently passed on the misinformation to Paris? Or did Paléologue know the truth from Sazonov or others, and conceal from Paris the plain fact that the order for general mobilization had been sent out over the wires three hours before he sent his own ambiguous message that Russia "was resolved to proceed secretly with the preliminary measures of general mobilization"? One cannot say with certainty. M. Renouvin makes Sazonov the author of the deceit. But one of Buchanan's telegrams leads one to think that it may have been Paléologue—that again the French Ambassador knew important information which he concealed from his Government. Buchanan apparently telegraphed on July 30 at 6:40 P.M. correctly and unambiguously: "It has been decided to issue orders for general mobilization." [76] Since Buchanan and Paléologue were in such close and constant touch with each other, is it not highly probable that Paléologue knew as well as Buchanan soon after 6:00 P.M. on July 30 that general mobilization had been decided upon? And if so, he should have sent a clear and unambiguous message to that effect, instead of one which misled his Government at Paris. Paléologue's rôle during the July crisis is one of the questions which most needs clearing up through complete and satisfactory edition of the French documents.

Thus it is not the *Lokal-Anzeiger* "extra," nor the Kaiser's telegram, nor Austrian mobilization which can explain or excuse the Russian general mobilization. What

[75] *Cf.* Renouvin, p. 190, note 3: "The French Government did not interpret M. Paléologue's message as the announcement of general mobilization;" and Poincaré, IV, 403 f., 408, 452 ff.

[76] B.D., 347, and explanatory note.

influence Buchanan and Paléologue had upon Sazonov on July 30 is uncertain. The Russian general mobilization was caused by the fact that Sazonov and the military officers on July 30 simply held the same views as on the evening of July 29, when they would have sent out the order for general mobilization had not the Tsar changed his mind. The situation had not changed essentially in the meantime, except that the partial mobilization, already ordered on the night of July 29, made the military authorities demand even more insistently an immediate general mobilization, because of technical military considerations.

"MOBILIZATION MEANS WAR"

By ordering general mobilization about 6:00 P.M. on July 30, Russia had now taken the step which military men everywhere clearly understood almost certainly meant war. This was also clearly understood by Sazonov and the Tsar, as appears from Schilling's account of their conversation at Peterhof and the Tsar's long hesitation to assume the terrible responsibility. Partial mobilization might be undertaken by a Great Power without leading to war, as had happened on several occasions in Russia and Austria in the preceding years. But general mobilization by a Great Power was generally understood to mean that it had only resorted to this final step of putting the great military machine in motion, with the automatic movement of the troops to the frontier with the greatest despatch, when it had finally concluded that war could no longer be avoided.

"Mobilization means war." This was a political maxim which for years had been widely accepted by military men on the Continent everywhere. It had been plainly hinted at by Pourtalès to Sazonov during the July crisis. It was stated by the French and Russian Chiefs of Staff, and accepted by the Tsar, as far back as 1892, as is seen from the records of the negotiations for the Franco-Russian Alliance:

> "General Obruchev emphasized finally the necessity of the immediate and simultaneous mobilization of the Russian and French armies at the first news received by either of the two countries of a mobilization of the forces of the Triple Alliance. He understands further that this mobilization of France and Russia would be followed immediately by positive results, by acts of war, in a word would be inseparable from an 'aggression.' " [77]

Similarly, General Boisdeffre, in talking with the Tsar the day after the Military Convention had been approved, remarked:

> "The mobilization is the declaration of war. To mobilize is to oblige one's neighbor to do the same. Mobilization involves the carrying out of strategic transportation and concentration. Otherwise, to leave a million men on one's frontier, without doing the same simultaneously, is to deprive oneself of all possibility of moving later; it is placing oneself in the situation of an individual who, with a pistol in his pocket, should let his neighbor put a weapon to his forehead without drawing his own." [To which Alexander III replied], "That is exactly the way I understand it." [78]

In a Russian secret order approved by the Tsar on March 12, 1912, at the moment Russia helped to secure the

[77] Report of the French Military Attaché in St. Petersburg, July 16, 1892; *L'Alliance Franco-Russe*, p. 56.

[78] Report of General Boisdeffre; *ibid.*, p. 95 f. M. Renouvin, p. 309, has argued that in these negotiations the principle that "Mobilization means war" was understood to apply only to the adversaries of France and Russia, and not to a Russian mobilization. Though no doubt, in the passage just quoted, Boisdeffre had in mind mobilization by the enemies of France, he was stating a general principle, endorsed by all military men. It would be an illogical and one-sided argument to maintain that mobilization by Germany or Austria means war, and that mobilization by Russia or France does not mean war. Moreover, Obruchev speaks expressly of the mobilization of France and Russia as involving immediate acts of war: "Il entend du reste que cette mobilisation de la France et de la Russie soit suivie immédiatement d'effets actifs, d'actes de guerre, en un mot soit inséparable d'une 'aggression;' " *ibid.*, p. 56.

signing of the Serbo-Bulgarian Treaty which was to lead to the Balkan Wars, it was expressly stated that "the telegram announcing mobilization is also at the same time to be effective as the Tsar's order for the opening of hostilities against Germany and Austria." [79] Though this order, for technical and political reasons, was later cancelled, and the telegrams for mobilization and the opening of hostilities were to be issued separately, it still represented the conception of military men that general mobilization means war. Dobrorolski, for instance, speaking of the Russian mobilization of 1914, says explicitly: "The whole plan of mobilization is worked out ahead to its end in all its details. When the moment has been chosen, one only has to press the button, and the whole state begins to function automatically with the precision of a clock's mechanism. . . . The choice of the moment is influenced by a complex of varied political causes. But once the moment has been fixed, everything is settled; there is no going back; it determines mechanically the beginning of war." [80]

[79] Quoted by Frantz, pp. 46, 234.
[80] Dobrorolski, p. 92 (German ed., p. 9 f.).

CHAPTER XI

OTHER MOBILIZATIONS AND DECLARATIONS OF WAR

IN following the Russian diplomatic and military steps to the point where general mobilization was ordered on the afternoon of July 30, we have outrun the narrative of events in the other capitals of Europe. In Paris, London, and Berlin also, hopes of peace and fears of imminent war had brought into opposition the activity of the diplomats and the pressure of the military authorities. The former still worked to save the situation, or at least, if that proved impossible, to make it appear that they and their allies were not responsible for the impending catastrophe. The latter pressed for military measures which they regarded as imperative to secure strategic advantages in the war which they were increasingly convinced was inevitable.

FRANCE AND THE 10-KILOMETER WITHDRAWAL

President Poincaré and M. Viviani, who landed at Dunkirk on the morning of July 29, reached Paris about noon. They were quickly informed of the precautionary military measures in anticipation of war which the Cabinet and M. Messimy, the Minister of War, had been taking in their absence since the evening of July 25. The measures included the return to their standing quarters of troops in training, the recall of officers on leave, and provision for the transportation from Morocco of all possible troops.[1]

[1] Poincaré, IV, 360-369; Recouly, pp. 61 ff., giving Messimy's narrative; and for the detailed military measures, see the French General Staff History, *Les Armées Françaises dans la Grande Guerre* (Paris, 1923),

These were all approved. They also learned of Austria's persistently intransigent attitude and of her declaration of war; of Germany's apparent complete support of Austria; of various visits which the German Ambassador had made to the French Foreign Office which did not inspire confidence as to Germany's desire for peace; of Sir Edward Grey's unwillingness definitely to commit himself as to England's future course; and of Sazonov's announcement that Russia was about to order partial mobilization.[2]   At a Cabinet meeting in the afternoon Poincaré says he found all the ministers "closely united in the resolution to do the impossible to avoid war and also to neglect no preparations for defense."[3]

Late that night, or rather between 2 and 3 A.M. on July 30, Izvolski communicated to the French Minister of Foreign Affairs and the Minister of War a most important telegram just received from St. Petersburg, indicating the imminence of war. "Not being able to accede to Germany's desire [that Russia cease her military preparations], it only remains for us to hasten our armaments and regard war as imminent," Sazonov telegraphed. After expressing gratitude for Paléologue's declaration of complete French support, "especially precious to us in the present circumstances," Sazonov added: "It would be extremely desirable that England also, without losing time, should join France and Russia, for only in this way can she prevent a dangerous rupture of the European balance of power."[4]

Viviani and Messimy at once held a conference at the Elysée with Poincaré, who had gone to bed. They ap-

passim; and the analysis of it by Montgelas in KSF, V, 1206-1220, Dec. 1927; Montgelas indicates that the French measures regularly preceded the corresponding German ones, sometimes by as much as two or three days. *Cf.* also the report of the British Military Attaché in Paris on July 29; B.D., 321.

[2] Poincaré, IV, 371-378; F.Y.B., 56-85.   [3] Poincaré, IV, 371.
[4] For this tg. no. 1551 from Sazonov, see above, ch. x, at note 42.

proved a telegram from Viviani to Paléologue, which was at once communicated to Izvolski, put into cipher, and sent to St. Petersburg and London at 7 A.M. on July 30. It began with a reference to Viviani's telegram of July 27 from on board the *France*, which stated the French Government's wish to support efforts for a peaceful solution of the conflict, but which, Poincaré asserts, led Paléologue to make the declaration of French support which Sazonov found "especially precious." [5] It then continued:

> France, however, is resolved to fulfil all the obligations of the Alliance.
>
> But I think in the interests of general peace and in view of the conversation pending between the less interested Powers, that it would be opportune that, as regards the precautionary and defence measures which Russia believes it necessary to adopt, she should not take immediately any step which might offer to Germany a pretext for a total or partial mobilization of her forces." [6]

What the French Government had in mind is more clearly stated in another telegram which Izvolski hastened to send to Sazonov:

> Margerie, whom I have just seen, told me that the French Government, without wishing to interfere in our military preparations, would consider it extremely desirable, in view

[5] Poincaré, IV, 335, 385. See also above, ch. X, at notes 5-11.

[6] This wording represents the present writer's approximation of the probable true original text of this passage, which is given in three quite different forms; (a) by the editors of the F.Y.B., 101; (b) by Poincaré, IV, 385 f.; and (c) by Izvolski, L.N., II, 290; (b) and (c) make no mention of Sazonov's telegram to Izvolski nor of a visit by Schoen, which form the first and last parts of (a); (a) says nothing of Viviani's telegram of July 27 from the *France*, which is mentioned in (b) and (c). Poincaré makes the last sentence read that Russia should not take immediately any steps toward a partial or total mobilization *of her own forces;* but Poincaré has misquoted his document, as is obvious from his own paraphrases on pp. 399 and 408, and from F.Y.B., 102, which indicate that Russia should not take any step which would offer *Germany* a pretext for mobilization. This tg. no. 208, from Izvolski to Sazonov, is also printed in M.F.R., p. 520, and in Romberg, p. 50 f., but was suppressed from R.O.B.

of the negotiations still pending for the preservation of peace, that these preparations should be carried on in the least open and least provocative manner. The Minister of War, on his part, expressing the same idea, told Count Ignatiev [Russian Military Attaché in Paris] that we could declare that, in the higher interests of peace, we were willing to slow down temporarily our mobilization measures, which would not hinder us from continuing and even strengthening our military preparations, while refraining, as much as possible, from the transportation of masses of troops.[7]

From these two telegrams from Paris to St. Petersburg, it appears that the French Government was anxious that Russia should not precipitate a European war, but should still continue measures in preparation for it, since it appeared inevitable. Poincaré must also have been aware that his renewal of the promise of full French support was likely to encourage Russia to defy Germany, and so lead to war. He did not wish to seem to interfere in Russian mobilization measures. Nevertheless, for diplomatic reasons, he did not want France or her ally to take any open and provocative military measures, which might seem aggressive, or might give Germany a pretext for mobilizing or—most important of all—which might make an undesirable impression on England and Italy. Apparently convinced that war was now inevitable,[8] and remembering the French mistake of being the formal aggressor in 1870,

[7] Izvolski to Sazonov, tg. no. 210, July 30; M.F.R., p. 521; L.N., II. 290. *Cf.* also Poincaré, IV, 386 f. This idea of strengthening military preparations but avoiding the appearance of doing so by refraining from troop movements *en masse* or by special trains, was immediately adopted by Messimy himself for the French corps near the German frontier, as will be seen in a moment in connection with the "10-kilometer withdrawal."

[8] *Cf.* Bertie to Grey, July 30 (B.D., 320): "The Spanish Ambassador says that the President of the Republic told a friend this morning that he considers war inevitable." This conviction would be natural in view of Sazonov's telegram and of the reports which the highly suspicious French Ambassador in Berlin had been pouring into Paris (*cf.* F.Y.B., 30, 35, 41-43, 47, 67, 73, 74, 92; and Poincaré, IV, 319 ff., 349, 414 ff.).

he did not intend to have any similar mistake made in 1914;
Russia and France should wait for Germany to take the
initiative and thereby incur the odium of responsibility.[9]
Events were to prove his shrewdness, for Bethmann soon
made the formal mistake of declaring war, which Ollivier
had made in 1870. Therefore, for the present, while diplomatic negotiations were still pending, Russia should conceal as far as possible "the precautionary and defensive
measures which she considered it necessary to adopt."

If President Poincaré had expressed himself with his
usual vigor and clarity—if he had said unmistakably to
Russia: "Do not order general mobilization for the present
while diplomatic negotiations are going on"—if he had even
spoken as vigorously as Bethmann was speaking to Vienna
—there is a possibility that war might still have been
avoided. Russian general mobilization had not yet been
ordered. Viviani's telegram reached Paléologue toward
noon on July 30 before Sazonov went out to Peterhof to
secure the Tsar's renewed assent to general mobilization.
If Poincaré had given a vigorous warning, and if Paléologue had repeated it to Sazonov, there was still time for the
Russian Minister to secure the further postponement of
Russian general mobilization until the "Halt in Belgrade"
proposal or some other form of mediation might have kept
the Powers back from the abyss.

But Poincaré was by now more concerned in securing
England's aid and in taking military precautions in France,
than in holding back Russia. "It would be extremely desirable that England also, without losing time, should join
France and Russia, for only in this way can she prevent a

---

[9] *Cf.* J. Cambon to Poincaré, tg. no. 225, July 30, 4:52 P.M., received
8:10 P.M. After mentioning the *Lokal-Anzeiger* episode, Cambon says:
"It is important not to publish in France the mobilization measures until
after they have certainly been decided in Berlin, in order that English
public opinion which can play so great a rôle in events, shall not attrib-
ute to us any initiative tending toward war" (Poincaré, **IV, 420**).

dangerous rupture of the European balance of power,"
Sazonov had telegraphed. Poincaré agreed. Several steps
which he took on July 30, and page after page of his memoirs, indicate that henceforth his great aim was to get
England definitely to announce that she would give France
armed support.

Early on the morning of July 30 Paul Cambon in London was informed of Sazonov's telegram indicating war as
imminent and of the French reply to it. Cambon was instructed to tell Grey, and remind him of the letters exchanged in 1912, by which each had agreed, if peace was
threatened, immediately to discuss with the other whether
both Governments should act together, and, if so, what
measures they would be prepared to take in common.[10]
Cambon was also to furnish Grey with a long list of military preparations which Germany was alleged to have made,
"showing that the German military preparations were more
advanced and more on the offensive upon the frontier than
anything France had yet done." It was to let Grey "see
that though France was resolute, it was not she who was
taking aggressive measures." [11]

But when M. Cambon reminded Sir Edward Grey of
the 1912 exchange of letters, and "said that the peace
of Europe was never more seriously threatened than
now," he met with disappointment. Though he acted with
extreme caution and tact, not asking Grey to say directly
that England would intervene, but only what he would
do in certain circumstances, such as an aggression by Germany on France, Sir Edward would only say he would see

[10] Poincaré, IV, 386; Grey, I, 94-96, 328-331.

[11] B.D., 319 and enclosure. This was only one of several similar documents, exaggerating German military preparations and frontier aggressions,
and minimizing those of France, which Cambon furnished to Grey during
these critical days when Poincaré was trying to get from England a definite promise of support; cf. B.D., 338, 364, 473; Poincaré, IV, 435. For
doubt as to their accuracy, see the analysis of the French General Staff
History of the War by Montgelas, in KSF, V, 1206-1220, Dec., 1927.

him again next day after the Cabinet had met.[12] Cambon also talked with Sir Arthur Nicolson, but found little encouragement. English public opinion, said Nicolson, was indifferent to the Austro-Russian Balkan rivalry; it was not yet time to consider British intervention; German financial interests were influential in the "City" and with some of the Cabinet; Asquith did not at present dare take a resolute attitude; but Nicolson himself was "personally a partisan of intervention." [13]

On the evening of July 30 Poincaré himself spoke more bluntly and pressingly to Sir Francis Bertie, the British Ambassador in Paris. He argued very urgently that if England would make an immediate declaration of her intention to support France, "there would be no war, for Germany would at once modify her attitude, . . . and even if it did not prevent war, British aid to France at the outbreak of hostilities would assist in the maintenance of the balance of power in Europe. Aid given later might be too late, and if England remained neutral and Germany became omnipotent on the Continent, the position of England would be entirely altered to her detriment as a Great Power." Bertie replied that the doubtful attitude of the House of Commons made it difficult to make any such declaration, and that anyway the orders to the British fleet not to disperse must be a pretty clear indication to Germany of England's attitude.[14] But in his private comment to Grey, Bertie observed: "The French, instead of putting pressure on the Russian Government to moderate their zeal, expect us to give the Germans to understand that we mean fighting if war breaks out. If we gave an assurance of armed assistance to France and Russia now, Russia would become more exacting and France would follow in her wake." [15]

12 Grey to Bertie, July 30; B.D., 319.
13 P. Cambon to Viviani, July 30, 8:30 P. M.; Poincaré, IV, 434.
14 Bertie to Grey, July 30; B.D., 373; cf. also 318.   15 B.D., 320.

Since Sazonov's telegram had said that he was hastening Russia's military measures and considered war imminent, Poincaré, and especially the French Minister of War, wanted to take measures for increasing the frontier troops as fully and quickly as possible, and yet avoid the appearance of making military preparations which might lead to frontier encounters or which might make an unfavorable impression on England. This conflict between efforts to satisfy strategic and diplomatic interests was the origin of the famous "10-kilometer withdrawal."

At the meeting of the French Cabinet on the morning of July 30, after the arrival of Sazonov's telegram, the French Minister of War urged that *couverture* should be adopted at once. This meant that the covering troops should take up their places on the frontier, and involved the mobilization of five army corps and all the French cavalry. But there was the diplomatic objection that this might seem to give France the rôle of aggressor and endanger the hoped-for British support and Italian neutrality. To reconcile the conflicting interests of strategy and diplomacy it was decided in principle to adopt a compromise. *Couverture* was to take place, but with restrictions. The covering troops were to move up toward the frontier, so far as was possible by moving on foot and horse; reservists were not to be summoned; horses were to be bought instead of requisitioned; and the troops were to keep back a short distance from the actual frontier. This would lessen the danger of unfortunate incidents, which at this time of excitement and suspicion might be exaggerated into "aggressions" and "acts of war." As Viviani said in the Chamber of Deputies in 1919, replying to his critics who charged that the 10-kilometer order had enabled Germany to get an initial advantage and seize the French iron-ore districts: "We realized that everything might turn on some chance incident. A patrol might get on the wrong road and run up against an enemy patrol, a sergeant or a corporal might lose his head, a soldier might think himself in danger and fire off his rifle." [16]

In the *French Yellow Book* Viviani is represented as telegraphing to Paul Cambon in London on July 30: "We have held back our troops 10 kilometers from the frontier, forbidding them to approach nearer. . . . In thus delivering a strip of territory undefended to the sudden aggression of the enemy, the Government of the Republic hopes to prove that France does not bear, any more than Russia, the responsibility for the attack." [17]

As a matter of fact, however, no limit of precisely 10 kilometers was fixed at all. Neither in the telegram which Viviani really sent to Paul Cambon on July 30, nor in the order which Messimy issued to five corps commanders at 4:45 P.M., is there any mention of "10-kilometers." Viviani's telegram to Paul Cambon instructed him to call Sir Edward Grey's attention to the French and German military preparations. "England will see from them that, though France is resolute, it is not she who is taking aggressive measures. Draw Sir Edward Grey's attention to the decision taken by the Cabinet this morning. Although Germany has taken up covering positions some hundreds of meters or some kilometers from the frontier, on the whole frontier from Luxembourg to the Vosges, and placed her covering troops in their war positions, we have not done so—although our plan of campaign, conceived for the offensive, contemplates that the war positions of our covering troops shall be as near the frontier as those of the Germans. We have thus left a strip of national territory

---

[16] *Débats parlementaires*, January 31, 1919.

[17] F.Y.B., 106. In this document the editors have merged two telegrams (*cf.* B.D., 319, 338) into one, and the date of the second, just quoted, is falsified from July 31 to July 30. The curious reason for this falsification is given in B.D., 319, note. Poincaré (IV, 424 f., 435), either unconsciously or deliberately, repeats the falsifications.

without defense open to sudden attack. We have not done this for any other reason than to show the British Government and public opinion that France, like Russia, will not be the first to fire." Then follows a list of German frontier and other military preparations.[18]   Messimy's order to the corps commanders instructed them to carry out the order of 1909 concerning mobilization of the frontier troops; those which could march on foot were to take up their positions, and those to go by rail were to be ready to entrain. "However, for diplomatic reasons, it is indispensable that no frontier incident shall be caused by us. Consequently no troops or patrols under any pretext are to approach the frontier or go beyond the line," which was then designated by naming some fifty towns and villages near the frontier.[19]

Thus, there was no line drawn exactly ten kilometers from the frontier everywhere. At numerous points it was only four or five kilometers from the frontier, as Messimy stated to the Briey Committee in 1920.[20]   General Joffre even "asked that he should not feel obliged to carry out the order in absolute strictness," and the Government granted his request.[21]   Nevertheless, the fact that the French Government did hold back its covering troops a few kilometers from the frontier was a wise measure. It did tend to prevent unfortunate "incidents" which might have precipitated a war. But it would be a mistake to regard it mainly as a proof of Poincaré's love of peace. Rather it

---

[18] Viviani to P. Cambon, July 30; communicated to Grey, B.D., 319.

[19] Messimy to the Commanders of the 2nd, 6th, 7th, 20th and 21st Army Corps, July 30, 4:55 P.M.; *Les Armées Françaises*, Tome I, Vol. I, Annex No. 15.   Even when France ordered general mobilization on August 1, since Grey had not yet promised military support, Messimy again telegraphed the Commanders: "With a view to assuring ourselves of the support of our English neighbors, it is still essential not to have patrols or detachments cross the general line fixed by the telegram of July 30, except in case of a clearly established attack" (*ibid.*, No. 25). This was reiterated by President Poincaré himself a few hours later at 10:30 P.M. (*ibid.*, No. 26).

[20] Renouvin, p. 215.   [21] Renouvin, p. 215.

was a measure primarily calculated to win British approval and military support, and to minimize the fact that France was taking an important military measure preparatory to war.

THE BRITISH FLEET AND WARNINGS TO GERMANY

In England the strategic problem was different from that of the military authorities on the Continent. By arrangements made many weeks earlier, England was fortunate in having her fleet already concentrated in the most powerful naval force which the world had ever seen. There was therefore no question of feverish haste to prepare it as quickly as possible to meet the enemy, but merely of whether orders should be given to keep it concentrated, instead of allowing it to disperse again to its normal positions as in time of peace.

On Saturday, July 25, Grey and his advisers learned from Buchanan that Sazonov "thought that Russia would at any rate have to mobilize," and that Poincaré's visit had established between France and Russia a "perfect community of views" and a "solemn affirmation of the obligations imposed by the alliance." Upon this Sir Eyre Crowe commented: "We should decide *now* to mobilize the fleet as soon as any other Great Power mobilizes, and we should announce this decision without delay to the French and Russian Governments." Even at this early date he believed: "The moment has passed when it might have been possible to enlist French support in an effort to hold back Russia." The mobilization of the fleet might also, he thought, serve as a warning to Germany. But Sir Edward Grey, who had just been told by Winston Churchill, the First Lord of the Admiralty, that the fleet could be mobilized in twenty-four hours, thought it premature to make any statement as yet to France and Russia.[22] He still pre-

[22] B.D., 101, and "Minutes" by Crowe and Grey on July 25.

ferred to keep a non-committal attitude, neither encouraging the Russians and French, nor threatening the Germans.

But next day, after the arrival of more alarming news from Austria and Serbia, Winston Churchill and the First Sea Lord, on their own authority, decided that the fleet should not disperse. Grey approved, and a public announcement of the fact that the fleet was to remain concentrated appeared in the British papers on the morning of July 27.[23] Grey intended this as a warning to dispel the current impression in Germany and Austria that England would remain neutral. The announcement did help to dispel the anxieties of the Russian Ambassador, Count Benckendorff, and was received "with great satisfaction" by his colleague, Paul Cambon.[24] But in Austria and Germany it did not make as effective an impression as the British Foreign Office appears to have expected. In mentioning it to the Austrian Ambassador, Grey himself rather minimized its significance: "I had explained that we should not have thought of calling up reserves or taking any step of a menacing character; but that, our naval force having been collected for manœuvres, we could not, when there was a possibility of a European conflagration, choose this moment for dispersing it."[25] And in Germany it was at first regarded as less important than the assurance which Prince Henry of Prussia had just brought from King George that England would remain neutral.[26]

On July 28 the feeling at the British Foreign Office became more pessimistic. The officials were puzzled by the fresh proposals which Sazonov kept making almost daily. Sir Edward Grey's own mediation proposals, as well as the "direct conversations" between Vienna and St. Petersburg,

[23] Churchill, *The World Crisis*, pp. 197 ff.

[24] B.D., 177, 238, 239.

[25] Grey to Bertie, July 28; B.D., 238; *cf.* Mensdorff to Berchtold, July 27; A.R.B., II, 72.

[26] See below, at notes, 40, 41.

which he had accepted as a substitute, seemed to be making no headway in view of the Austro-German thesis that the Serbian dispute should be "localized." As Sir Arthur Nicolson summarized the situation in a letter to Buchanan: "I can quite understand Russia not being able to permit Austria to crush Serbia. I think the talk about localizing the war merely means that all the Powers are to hold the ring while Austria quietly strangles Serbia. This to my mind is quite preposterous, not to say iniquitous. I do not understand after the very satisfactory way in which Serbia has met the Austrian requests, how Austria can with any justification proceed to hostile measures against her. If she deliberately provokes war with Serbia . . . she must know very well that such an action on her part would in all probability lead to a general European conflagration, with all its untold disastrous consequences. Germany has not played a very straight game—at least so far as we are concerned— in all this business." He noted, however, with satisfaction, the orders given to keep the British fleet together, and the change in tone of the British Press, which at first in the days immediately after Sarajevo had been sympathetic toward Austria; these two facts, he thought, had made it perfectly clear to Germany and Austria that they could not count with any certainty upon England remaining neutral.[27]

Finally on July 29, after the news of the Austrian declaration of war on Serbia, which made Sazonov regard "direct conversations" as illusory and state that partial mobilization would soon take place in Russia, officials in the inner circle in England came to regard a European war as almost inevitable. "What is the use of exchanging views at this juncture?" asked Sir Arthur Nicolson. "I am of the opinion that the resources of diplomacy are, for the present, exhausted."[28] Four of Sir Edward Grey's des-

---

[27] Nicolson to Buchanan, July 28; B.D., 239.
[28] Minute on B.D., 252.

patches, dated July 29, though published in the *British Blue Book* of 1914 as if sent, are now revealed in the archives marked, "Not sent—War." [29] Mr. Asquith stated in the House of Commons that the situation was one "of extreme gravity."

In fact, on the previous afternoon, July 28, at 5 P.M., Winston Churchill had ordered that the fleet was to proceed during the night at high speed and without lights through the Straits of Dover from Portland to its fighting base at Scapa Flow. Fearing to bring this order before the Cabinet, lest it should be considered a provocative action likely to damage the chances of peace, Mr. Churchill had only informed Mr. Asquith, who at once gave his approval. On July 29, the official "warning telegram" was dispatched from the Admiralty. The British Fleet was now ready, whatever happened, to meet and control the situation.[30]

On the morning, July 29, Sir Edward Grey at last decided to give Germany a more definite warning, as Russia and France had been continually urging. Quite characteristically he first told Cambon of what he was going to say to Lichnowsky, but at the same time reiterated that his warning to Germany would not mean that England had yet made up her mind what she would do if France and Germany became involved. England was "free from engagements," and would "have to decide what British interests required." [31] To Lichnowsky Grey then repeated Sazonov's statement that after the Austrian declaration of war Russia would no longer be in a position to negotiate with Austria direct and desired a return to the British mediation proposals. Accordingly Grey suggested it would be "a suitable basis for mediation, if Austria, after occupying Belgrade, for example, or other places, should announce

[29] *Cf.* B.D., 282-286.

[30] Churchill, p. 207 ff; Julian S. Corbett, *History of the Great War; Naval Operations* (London, 1920), I, 25 ff.

[31] Grey to Bertie, July 29; B.D., 283.

her conditions." Grey then gave to Lichnowsky, in the form of a friendly and private communication, the warning that, as long as the conflict remained confined to Austria and Russia, England could stand aside; but if Germany and France should be involved, then the situation would be immediately altered and the British Government would be forced to rapid decisions.[32]

But before Grey's warning was deciphered and known in Berlin, Bethmann took a step which caused the British Foreign Office to believe that Germany had practically determined to go to war, violate Belgium, and crush France.

BETHMANN AND MOLTKE

In Berlin, as in Paris and London, the situation was regarded as very critical on Wednesday, July 29.

Bethmann had urged Austria to accept the "Halt in Belgrade" mediation plan, but had received no answer from Vienna. Such silence on the part of his ally was extremely irritating and embarrassing to the German Chancellor.[33] Because of it, he was unable to show the Entente Powers that his pressure at Vienna was meeting with success and would bring a satisfactory solution of the crisis.

Furthermore, the German military authorities, like the General Staffs everywhere, were pressing for early military measures to insure the safety of their country and the success of their strategic plans, in case the diplomatists could not preserve peace.

Helmuth von Moltke, who bore the name but lacked the genius of his more famous uncle, was now Chief of the German General Staff, having accepted that difficult office reluctantly in 1906 in succession to Count Schlieffen. In

---

[32] Lichnowsky to Bethmann, July 29, 6:39 P.M., received 9:12 P.M.; K.D., 368; cf. also B.D., 286.

[33] See above, ch. ix, "Germany's Belated Peace Efforts."

a long summary of the political situation on July 29, Moltke now pointed out the dangerous sequence of mobilizations which would probably take place, in case Russia carried out her announced intention of ordering partial mobilization in her southern districts if Austria advanced into Serbia. Russia, he said, had been making military preparations on the frontier against Germany, as well as against Austria, so that she would be able to move her armies forward in a very few days when she actually issued her mobilization orders. France also, according to his information, appeared to be taking measures preparatory to general mobilization. The situation thus was becoming daily more unfavorable to Germany, and might lead to fateful consequences if Germany, by a collision between Austria and Russia, should be forced to mobilize and fight on two fronts. Therefore, he concluded, "it is of the greatest importance to ascertain as soon as possible whether Russia and France intend to let it come to a war with Germany." [34]

Bethmann, however, was still hoping that the "pledge plan" of "Halt in Belgrade" might bring a satisfactory solution. He therefore insisted on waiting for a reply from Vienna. He was vigorously opposed to taking any decisive military measures which might jeopardize his diplomatic efforts.

According to the information or rumors gathered by the Bavarian Military Attaché in Berlin on this day, Moltke "is exerting all his influence in favor of taking advantage of the exceptionally favorable opportunity for striking a decisive blow," pointing out the momentary military embarrassment of France, the over-confidence of Russia, and the good time of year with the harvests mostly gathered and the annual training period of recruits completed. Bethmann, on the other hand, "is putting on the brakes with all his might, and is anxious to avoid everything which

[34] K.D., 349.

might lead to similar measures in France and England
and start the ball rolling." [35]

These opposing views were set forth to the Kaiser at
Potsdam on the afternoon and early evening of July 29 in
separate reports by the military and civilian authorities.
But there was no "Potsdam Council," nor any decision in
favor of German mobilization, such as was incorrectly reported next day by the suspicious French Ambassador and
has been commonly assumed by later writers.[36] Bethmann
was successful in "putting on the brakes," as is seen from
his summary of the situation at the Prussian Council of
Ministers at noon next day: "The military authorities had
expressed the desire that a 'state of threatening danger of
war' be proclaimed, but he had successfully defended before
His Majesty the objections." Such a proclamation meant
mobilization, and mobilization meant war; mediation proposals had been made at Vienna, and the answer to these
must be awaited before one abandoned hope and efforts for
peace; "one could not conveniently carry on military and
political activities at the same time." Accordingly, "His
Majesty had consented that before any further decisions
were arrived at, the move at Vienna, previously explained,
should be brought to a conclusion." [37] The only precautionary military measures ordered by the evening of July
29 were the protection of railways and valuable buildings,
the recall of officers and men on leave, the reinforcement
of frontier fortresses, and other minor measures similar to,
but less extensive than, those which had been going on in

[35] Wenninger to the Bavarian Minister of War, July 29; Dirr, p. 221.
For the controversy between Hermann Lutz and Theobald von Schäfer as
to the trustworthiness of Wenninger's despatch, see KSF, V, 1107-1125,
Nov. 1927.

[36] Cf. F.Y.B., 105; Bourgeois et Pagès, pp. 95, 132; Viviani, Réponse
au Kaiser, p. 153; Oman, p. 73. For the facts concerning the separate
reports made to the Kaiser, see A. von Wegerer, "Der angebliche 'Kron-
rat' vom 29. Juli 1914," in KSF, I, 8-12, July, 1923; and Tirpitz.
Politische Dokumente (Hamburg and Berlin, 1926), II, 2-5.

[37] Protocol of the Prussian Council of Ministers. July 30; K.D., 456

HERR VON JAGOW

German Secretary for Foreign Affairs, 1913-1916

GENERAL MOLTKE

German Chief of Staff, 1906-1914

Russia since July 26 and which had already been ordered in France.[38]

While Bethmann thus succeeded in holding back the military authorities from any decisive and irreparable step, he made a number of important diplomatic moves on July 29, some with a view to averting war, others with a view to securing advantages if war proved inevitable.

Shortly after noon he sent his warning through Pourtalès to Sazonov, that "further continuance of Russian mobilization measures would force us to mobilize." Later, at 6:30 P.M., after the arrival of the announced decision of Russian partial mobilization, the Kaiser sent the second telegram to the Tsar which led the latter to cancel the order for general mobilization which was on the point of being dispatched over the wires. These two efforts to deter Russia from the fatal step of ordering mobilization have been discussed in the preceding chapter.

On returning from Potsdam to Berlin, and finding still no answer from Vienna to his "pledge plan," Bethmann telegraphed to Tschirschky in order to secure confirmation of its arrival and an immediate reply.[39]

Then he sent for the British Ambassador to secure certainty on a question which had been very much discussed at Potsdam, and was of the greatest importance to Germany in case of a possible European War—the question of British neutrality. Bethmann had been optimistically hoping for this. He had therefore been anxious to avoid all measures which might antagonize England. On July 25 and 26 he had telegraphed to the Kaiser at sea, advising that the German fleet remain quietly away in Norwegian waters, inasmuch as reports from London indicated that the dispersal

[38] *Investigating Commission*, II, 8-11; Montgelas, in KSF, V, 1206-1214, Dec., 1927; and above, ch. vi. the section on the Russian "Period Preparatory to War."

[39] Bethmann to Tschirschky, July 29, 10:18 and 10:30 P.M.; K.D., 377 and note.

of the British fleet and the discharge of reservists was going on according to schedule. "For the present, at least, Sir E. Grey is not considering direct participation by England in a possible European War." [40]   But the Kaiser had not followed the advice, and had ordered the German fleet to return to its base at Kiel.   Bethmann's optimism had been strengthened by news that the Kaiser's brother, Prince Henry, on a visit to England, had been assured by King George on July 26: "We shall try all we can to keep out of this, and shall remain neutral."   But meanwhile the announcement on the 27th that the British fleet was *not* to be dispersed made it doubtful whether King George's statement could still be relied on.   Prince Henry, who came to Potsdam on the afternoon of July 29, was "convinced that this statement was made in all seriousness," and that England would remain neutral at the start, but whether she would do so permanently he doubted, "on account of her relations with France." [41]

It was about 10:30 P.M. that Bethmann sent for Goschen and "made the following strong bid for British neutrality in the event of war."   Provided Great Britain remained neutral, Germany was ready to give every assurance that she aimed at no territorial acquisitions at the expense of France in Europe, though she could give no such assurance concerning the French colonies.   Germany would respect the neutrality of Holland, but as regards Belgium, Bethmann "could not tell to what operations Germany might be forced by the action of France, but he could state that, provided that Belgium did not take sides against Germany, her integrity would be respected at the conclusion of the war."   But he trusted that British neutrality, in case of a war which might possibly arise from the

40 K.D., 182, 221.
41 Prince Henry to the Kaiser from Kiel, July 28; K.D., 374.   King George's assurance had at once been telegraphed to Berlin by the German Naval Attaché in London on July 26; K.D., 207.

present conflict, might form the basis for a future neutrality agreement between England and Germany, which had been the object of his policy ever since he had been Chancellor.[42]

Bethmann's bid for British neutrality was a most unfortunate and foolish blunder. It made the worst possible impression in London. Sir Eyre Crowe noted: "The only comment that need be made on these astounding proposals is that they reflect discredit on the statesman who makes them." He concluded that "Germany practically admits the intention to violate Belgian neutrality," and "is practically determined to go to war."[43] Sir Edward Grey, after securing the approval of Mr. Asquith, but without waiting to lay his answer before the Cabinet, replied to Goschen that the Chancellor's proposals "cannot be entertained for a moment." England's material interests made it impossible to allow France to be so crushed as to lose her position as a Great Power, even though Germany should not take territory from France as distinct from her colonies. "But apart from that, for us to make this bargain with Germany at the expense of France would be a disgrace from which the good name of this country would never recover." Nor could England bargain away her obligation and interest as regards the neutrality of Belgium. England must preserve full freedom to act as circumstances should require.[44] In his memoirs also Grey reveals the "feeling of despair" with which he read Bethmann's dishonoring proposal, which was "like a searchlight lighting up an aspect of the situation which had not yet been looked at."[45] Next day he asked the French and German Governments each for an assurance to respect the neutrality of

[42] Goschen to Grey, July 30, 1:20 A.M., received 9 A.M.; B.D., 293. Bethmann had spoken from typewritten notes (cf. K.D., 373) and Goschen, to insure accuracy, made on the spot a draft of the Chancellor's statement and read it to him for his approval before sending it to Grey (B.D., 677).   [43] Minute on B.D., 293.

[44] Grey to Goschen, July 30, 3:30 P.M.; B.D., 303.

[45] Grey, I, 316 ff.

Belgium, so long as no other Power violated it.[46] Bethman greatly regretted having made the bid for British neutrality. Nor would he have spoken as he did, had he known of Grey's warning to Lichnowsky [47] which reached Berlin at 9:12 P.M.[48], but which apparently had not been deciphered or handed to the Chancellor before his conversation with Goschen.

Another step taken on July 29, probably as a result of the conferences at Potsdam, was Jagow's despatch of a message in a sealed envelope to the German Minister at Brussels. It was carried by a messenger, instead of being telegraphed in cipher, because there was no immediate haste, and because it was not desirable to reveal even to the Minister himself a demand on Belgium which after all it might never be necessary to make. On opening the envelope, the Minister merely found instructions to keep safely locked up another sealed document which he would find enclosed, but which he was to open only if subsequently instructed by telegram from Berlin. The inner envelope contained an ultimatum to Belgium, based on a draft which Moltke had written with his own hand on July 26. It stated the German intention to march through Belgium, if possible with the friendly consent of Belgium; but if Belgium offered opposition, "Germany would be obliged, to her regret, to regard the Kingdom as an enemy." [49]

These two steps—the bid for British neutrality and the forwarding of the sealed ultimatum to Brussels—indicate how seriously the German authorities contemplated on the evening of July 29 the probability of war. They show that Bethmann had found himself forced to yield to Moltke's

---

[46] B.D., 348.

[47] So Jagow explained somewhat apologetically to Goschen next morning. Goschen says he is sure Bethmann and Jagow, or at all events Jagow, were dreadfully put out that the neutrality proposal had ever been made, and never alluded to Grey's answer to it; B.D., 677.

[48] K.D., 368.   [49] K.D., 375, 376; cf. also 648, 735.

view of strategic necessity and to the violation of Belgium, *if war should come.* But they do not prove that Bethmann had yet yielded to the view that war was already inevitable, or that any decision for war had been reached.

On the contrary, the Chancellor redoubled his efforts to preserve peace by putting increased pressure on Austria. After the interview with Goschen, though thoroughly tired out by his long and difficult day, Bethmann consulted with Jagow concerning the fresh telegrams which had meanwhile poured in. Among them was the Tsar's personal suggestion to the Kaiser that the Austro-Serbian problem be given over to the Hague Conference. But just as Sazonov had paid no attention to the Tsar's instructions two days earlier to take steps in this direction, so now it was decisively rejected in Berlin.[50]

A telegram from Lichnowsky told of Grey's approval of the Italian suggestion of mediation by the Great Powers on the basis of Serbia's reported willingness at last to accept even Points 5 and 6 of the Austrian ultimatum.[51] Pourtalès told of Sazonov's indignation at Vienna's "categorical refusal" to enter upon direct conversations, and of his desire to return to Grey's conference proposal; but this was coupled with the grave news that "Sazonov did not deny the imminence of mobilization," though stating that this "was far from meaning war."[52] Bethmann sent on to Vienna the substance of both of these telegrams, as well as those just exchanged between the Kaiser and the Tsar. He again "urgently requested" the acceptance of the "pledge

[50] See above, ch. ix, at notes 73-78; Kaiser's marginal note, and Bethmann to Pourtalès, July 30, 2:40 A.M.; K.D., 366, 391. In *Fateful Years* (pp. 194 f., 203), M. Sazonov condemns Germany for neglecting the Tsar's "excellent suggestion" of the Hague Tribunal, but omits to mention that he himself completely neglected it two days previously. Does this indicate candor and honesty on his part?

[51] Lichnowsky to Bethmann, July 29, 2:08 P.M., received 5:07 P.M.; K.D., 357.

[52] Pourtalès to Bethmann, July 29, 6:10 P.M., received 8:29 P.M.; K.D., 365.

plan" of "Halt in Belgrade," and the inauguration and continuance of direct conversations between Vienna and St. Petersburg in order to satisfy Sazonov.[53]

Meanwhile Lichnowsky's later telegram had been deciphered, telling of Grey's suggestion of mediation on the basis of an Austrian occupation of Belgrade, and also of Grey's private and friendly warning that England might find it impossible to stand aside. As Grey's suggestion was very similar to Bethmann's own "Halt in Belgrade" plan, and as the warning put an end to all illusions as to the possibility of British neutrality, Bethmann welcomed Grey's suggestion as supporting his own efforts, and forwarded it to Vienna. In commenting on it, he pointed out in strong terms how dangerous it would be for Austria to refuse all negotiations, and added: "Under these circumstances we must urgently and emphatically urge upon the consideration of the Vienna Cabinet the adoption of mediation in accordance with the above honorable conditions." [54]

Then, finally, before catching a little sleep, he sent telegrams to St. Petersburg and London which he hoped would help to prevent war and secure mediation. To Pourtalès he telegraphed: "Please tell Sazonov that we are continuing to mediate; condition, however, would be the suspension for the time being of all hostilities against Austria on the part of Russia"; and to Lichnowsky: "Kindly thank Sir E. Grey for his frank explanation and tell him that we are continuing to mediate in Vienna and are urgently advising the acceptance of his proposal." [55]

On the morning of July 30 Bethmann at last received a reply from Vienna to his "Halt in Belgrade" mediation plan, but the reply was wholly unsatisfactory and non-com-

[53] Bethmann to Tschirschky, July 30, 12:10 and 12:30 A.M.; K.D., 383, 385.

[54] Bethmann to Tschirschky July 30, 2:55 A.M.; K.D., 395.

[55] Bethmann to Pourtalès and to Lichnowsky, July 30, 2:55 A.M.; K.D., 392, 393.

mittal on one of the essential points. Berchtold was ready
to repeat the declaration concerning Austria's territorial
disinterestedness, but "so far as the further declaration
with reference to military measures is concerned, Count
Berchtold says that he is not in a position to give me a
reply at once. In spite of my representations as to the
urgency of the matter, I have up to this evening received
no further communication." [56]

Accordingly, in his summary of the situation to the
Prussian Ministry of State about noon, Bethmann gave an
account of his efforts to bring about an understanding between Vienna and St. Petersburg, seconded by Grey's proposal of mediation based on the Austrian occupation of
Belgrade, but had to admit that the result of his efforts was
still uncertain. The Kaiser had consented, however, that
no decisive steps toward mobilization should be taken until
the move at Vienna had been brought to a conclusion. Nor
would he himself give up his hope and efforts to maintain
peace, as long as it had not been repelled.[57]

Late in the afternoon he learned that Berchtold rejected
the Italian suggestion that Serbia might at last be willing
to accept Points 5 and 6 of the ultimatum; such an acceptance might have sufficed, if Serbia had manifested her willingness earlier; but "now, since a state of war had super-
vened, Austria's conditions would naturally be different."
Berchtold had, however, instructed Szápáry to begin conversations with Sazonov at St. Petersburg on Austro-
Russian (but not Austro-Serbian) relations. He himself
would explain to the Russian Ambassador in Vienna that
Austria had no idea of making any territorial acquisitions
in Serbia, and that, after the conclusion of peace, the occupation of Serbian territory would be merely temporary to

---

[56] Tschirschky to Bethmann, July 30, 11:50 P. M., received July 30,
1:30 A.M.; K.D., 388.

[57] Protocol of the Prussian Ministry of State, July 30; K.D., 456.

secure the fulfilment of Austrian demands; to the extent that Serbia fulfilled the conditions of peace, evacuation would follow. But as to accepting Grey's suggestion for a mediation by a conference of the Powers, involving the cessation of hostilities, he could not give an answer until next day after an audience with Francis Joseph.[58]

In order to find out what Vienna was intending to do, the Berlin Foreign Office resorted to the telephone,[59] but Tschirschky's reply indicated that Berchtold was not likely to yield to the mediation proposals which Bethmann had been so constantly urging; in any case Berchtold would not give a definite reply until he had consulted Tisza who would not be back in Vienna until early the following morning.[60]

Meanwhile the Kaiser, also impatient, had finally telegraphed personally to Francis Joseph: "I should be honestly obliged to you if you would favor me with your decision as soon as possible." [61]

While Bethmann had thus been trying in vain to get an answer from Vienna, Moltke had become increasingly nervous over the situation. On the morning of July 30 he was still willing to abide by the decision of Bethmann and the Kaiser, that Russia's partial mobilization did not necessitate Germany's mobilization, for he wrote out for Captain Fleischmann, whom Conrad had sent to Berlin as *liaison* officer, the following telegram for the Austrian Chief of Staff:

> Russia's mobilization is not yet a cause for mobilization. [Moltke meant for *Germany's* mobilization, but Conrad seems to have understood for *Austria's* mobilization.] Not until state of war exists between Austria and Russia. In contrast to the mobilizations and demobilizations which have been customary in Russia, Germany's mobilization

[58] Tschirschky to Bethmann, July 30, 2:30 P.M.; received 5:25 P.M.; K.D., 433.

[59] *Cf.* K.D., 441.

[60] K.D., 440.

[61] July 30, 7:15 P.M.; K.D., 437

would unconditionally lead to war. Do not declare war on Russia, but await Russia's attack.[62]

Moltke seemed to be convinced that Russia was forcing Europe into war, and, in order to make it clear that Russia was the aggressor, he believed that the initiative in the declaration of war should come, not from Austria or from Germany, but from Russia—a point of view exactly analogous to that of Poincaré, Paléologue and Jules Cambon, who were convinced that Germany was forcing Europe into war and that the odium of the initiative must be carefully left to her.

In the afternoon, however, after hearing that Sazonov had said that it was impossible to stop the Russian mobilization, and that the Tsar admitted that the preparatory measures had been going on for five days, Moltke became much excited and believed that the danger to Germany and Austria was critical. He talked with Bienerth, the Austrian Military Attaché, who then telegraphed to Conrad:

> Moltke said that he regards the situation as critical if the Austro-Hungarian Monarchy does not mobilize immediately against Russia. Russia's announced declaration concerning mobilization she has ordered makes necessary counter-measures by Austria-Hungary, and must also be cited in the public explanation. Thereby there would arise the *casus foederis* for Germany. With Italy make some honorable agreement by promising compensations, so that Italy will remain actively in the Triple Alliance; in fact, do not leave a man on the Italian frontier. Decline the renewed

[62] Fleischmann to Conrad, July 30; Conrad, IV, 151 f. For Fleischmann's *letter* to Conrad, sent July 30 and received July 31, which gave a fuller account of Moltke's statements, see Theobald von Schäfer, "Generaloberst von Moltke in den Tagen vor der Mobilmachung und seine Einwirkung auf Oesterreich-Ungarn," in KSF, IV, 522 f., Aug., 1926; this valuable article of Schäfer's (KSF, IV, 514-549) contains important hitherto unpublished material from the Vienna War Archives, which throws new light on the documents published by Conrad, and which was unknown to Mr. Heinrich Kanner when he wrote *Der Schlüssel zur Kriegsschuldfrage* (Munich, 1927).

advances made by England for the maintenance of peace. The standing firm in a European war [*Durchhalten des europäischen Krieges*] is the last chance of saving Austria-Hungary. Germany will go with her unconditionally." [63]

In speaking thus, Moltke exceeded his authority and improperly gave *political* advice, which belonged exclusively within the functions of the Chancellor. He exemplified one of the great evils of militarism: the danger in time of crisis of interference by the military officials in civilian affairs. Moltke had no authority to interpret the alliance, or to say that the Russian mobilization furnished the *casus foederis* for Germany. It belonged to the Chancellor alone to interpret Germany's treaty obligations; and just the night before, Bethmann had told Moltke and Falkenhayn, the Prussian Minister of War, that Russian partial mobilization did not constitute the *casus foederis,* and that there was therefore not yet any occasion for Germany to mobilize. To this Moltke had objected "mildly, very mildly." [64]

In saying that Austria ought to give satisfactory compensations to Italy, Moltke was, to be sure, merely reiterating what the Berlin Foreign Office had been urging unsuccessfully upon Berchtold for many days past. But his suggestion that Austria decline the British peace proposal ran directly counter to the very thing Bethmann had been striving for. If any excuse for Moltke's remarks is to be found, one may perhaps say that he was merely expressing his personal opinions to the Austrian Military Attaché, rather than offering Austria official advice, since nothing is

[63] Bienerth to Conrad, July 30, 5:30 P.M., received and deciphered during the night at Vienna; Conrad, IV, 152; Schäfer, p. 525 f. The Austrian Ambassador, Szögyény, in two telegrams to Berchtold (5:30 P.M. and 7:40 P.M., received 7:20 P.M. and 10:20 P.M. (A.R.B., 32, 34) mentions Bienerth's conversation with Moltke, and emphasizes the importance of satisfying Italy, but says nothing of declining the British proposal.

[64] Falkenhayn's notes in H. v. Zwehl, *Erich v. Falkenhayn* (Berlin, 1926), p. 57.

said of the *casus foederis* or declining the British proposal in the Austrian Ambassador's report of Moltke's remarks, nor in the following laconic telegram which Moltke himself is believed to have sent direct to Conrad later:

> Stand firm to Russian mobilization [*Russische Mobilisierung durchhalten*]. Austria-Hungary must be preserved. Mobilize at once against Russia. Germany will mobilize. Bring Italy, by compensations, to her alliance obligations.[65]

Moltke feared that, through Austria's delay in mobilizing against Russia, Germany would be left to bear the brunt of the Russian attack. In his conversations and correspondence with Conrad ever since 1909 Moltke had always urged that, in case of danger from an Austro-Serbian war developing into a general European War, Austria should send only a minimum force against Serbia, and make her maximum effort against Russia in Galicia, in order to relieve the Russian pressure against East Prussia. Germany could then deliver her crushing blow against France in the West. Conrad, on the other hand, had always argued that Moltke should send a considerable force against Russia, in order to relieve the Russian pressure against Austria in Galicia. Each Chief of Staff had thus quite naturally represented the selfish interests of his own country, and they had never reached that perfect harmony of a "military convention,"

---

[65] The "Moltke telegram" is nowhere to be found in the German Archives, or in the Vienna War Archives, or among Conrad's papers, says Schäfer, p. 526. It is printed in Conrad, IV, 152, as being received on July 31 at 7:45 A. M. When it was sent cannot be ascertained; quite possibly late in the evening after Moltke had received two reports of the Russian general mobilization, mentioned below. He feared lest Conrad, intent on his campaign against Serbia, would not mobilize quickly against Russia.

For accounts in English giving two views of this Moltke telegram and its significance, see R. Grelling, "Moltke, the Man Who Made the War," in *Current History*, Sept., 1926, pp. 916-925; and Count Montgelas, "Justifying Germany in 1914," *ibid.*, April, 1927, pp. 77-80. *Cf.* also Kanner, *Der Schlüssel zur Kriegsschuldfrage*, p. 40 ff.; and Renouvin, p. 194 f. (Eng. trans., 213 ff.).

fixing the precise number of troops which each was to employ against Russia, which Dr. Kanner regards as the "key" to the question of war responsibility.[66] On the contrary, this Moltke telegram, and other evidence to be cited below in connection with Austrian general mobilization, betray an extraordinary, though brief, lack of confidence and understanding on the part of these two Chiefs of Staff toward each other, such as was quite lacking on the part of the Russian and French Chiefs of Staff.

In the course of the evening of July 30, probably about 11:00 P.M., Moltke talked again with Bethmann. A little later—shortly after midnight—Moltke told Major Haeften that he had received "two reliable reports from independent sources, stating that mobilization of all Russia's armed forces had already been ordered." [67] This was altogether likely, as Russian general mobilization had been ordered at 6 P.M., and the orders had been quickly transmitted to the Warsaw District on the German frontier.[68]

Whether Moltke had already heard these "two reliable reports" when he talked with Bethmann is uncertain, but quite probable. For he caused Bethmann to waver momentarily in his hope to avoid war and his determination to keep "putting the brakes" on the military authorities.

At 9:00 P.M. the Chancellor had sent an "urgent" telegram No. 200, to Tschirschky at Vienna, recalling Grey's proposal which Austria was reported as likely to reject, and informing him of Grey's promises to work for peace at Paris and St. Petersburg. He added the emphatic warning and advice:

[66] *Cf.* Dr. Heinrich Kanner, *Der Schlüssel zur Kriegsschuldfrage,* Munich, 1926, *passim;* and the present writer's review of it, with Dr. Kanner's rejoinder, in *Amer. Hist. Rev.,* XXXII, 317-319, 942-946, Jan., July, 1927.

[67] Note by Haeften, Aug. 2, 1914; printed in Schulthess, *Europäischer Geschichtskalender,* 1917, II, p. 996 ff.; and quoted by Montgelas, *Leitfaden,* p. 137.

[68] See above, ch. x, at notes 62-65.

If England's efforts succeed, while Vienna declines every-thing, Vienna will be giving documentary evidence that it absolutely wants a war, into which we shall be drawn, while Russia remains free from responsibility. That would place us, in the eyes of our own people, in an untenable position. Thus we can only urgently advise Austria to accept the Grey proposal, which preserves her status for her in every way. Your Excellency will at once express yourself most emphatically on this matter to Count Berchtold, perhaps also to Count Tisza.[69]

Then, after hearing what Moltke had to say, Bethmann telegraphed again to Tschirschky at 11:20 P.M.: "Please do not carry out instructions No. 200 for the present." [70] His reason appears in a draft telegram which, however, was quickly replaced by another telegram and was never sent to Tschirschky. In the unsent draft telegram Bethmann said: "I cancelled the order of instructions in No. 200, as the General Staff just informs me that the military prepa-rations of our neighbors, especially in the East, will force us to a speedy decision, unless we do not wish to expose our-selves to the danger of surprise." [71] This indeed looks as if Bethmann had at last yielded to Moltke. But hardly had this telegram been drafted, when the Chancellor learned of the following telegram from the King of England to Prince Henry of Prussia:

So pleased to hear of William's efforts to concert with Nicky to maintain peace. . . . My Government is doing its utmost suggesting to Russia and France to suspend further military preparations, if Austria will consent to be satisfied with occupation of Belgrade and neighboring Serbian terri-tory as a hostage for satisfactory settlement of her demands, other countries meanwhile suspending their war prepara-tions. Trust William will use his great influence to induce

[69] Bethmann to Tschirschky, July 30, 9:00 P.M., received July 31, 3:00 A.M.; K.D., 441.
[70] K.D., 450.   [71] K.D., 451.

Austria to accept this proposal, thus proving that Germany and England are working together to prevent what would be an international catastrophe. Pray assure William that I am doing and shall continue to do all that lies in my power to preserve peace of Europe.[72]

This telegram gave Bethmann new hope. Instead of sending the draft telegram, with Moltke's alarming news which would have tended to make Austria decide for general mobilization, Bethmann sent on to Vienna King George's friendly message. explaining that its arrival had caused the cancellation of No. 200. He directed Tschirschky to communicate King George's telegram to Berchtold "without delay," and again added: "A definite decision in Vienna during the course of the day is urgently desired." [73]

These telegrams seem to show that Bethmann for a brief moment wavered and gave up hope. But they do *not* show, as has sometimes been maintained, that he definitely and completely changed his attitude, yielded to Moltke's pressure, and decided to send an ultimatum to Russia several hours before he learned of the Russian general mobilization.[74] On the contrary, after a brief delay he again put forward at Vienna the British proposal in the shape of King George's telegram, though he did not renew his emphatic warning in telegram No. 200.[75] His momentary wavering was caused by Moltke's news about Russian military preparations. But as this was not definite, he still refused to agree to Germany's sending an ultimatum to Russia or to ordering the "Threatening Danger of War," which was the preliminary step to German mobilization. He was determined to wait still further, until he received the answer from Vienna to the "Halt in Belgrade" proposal, or until the news

[72] George V to Prince Henry, July 30, 8:54 P. M., received 11:08 P. M.; K.D., 452.
[73] Bethmann to Tschirschky, July 31, 2:45 A.M.; received 9:00 A.M.; K.D., 464.   [74] *Cf.* Kanner, *Der Schüssel*, p. 41 f.
[75] Renouvin, (Eng. trans., p. 191) emphasizes this point.

of Russian general mobilization was definitely confirmed, as it was confirmed in a despatch from Pourtalès which arrived at 11:40 A.M. next day. He hoped soon to have certainty on these two points. As Moltke and Falkenhayn were pressing for an early decision, Bethmann consented that it should be made next day, July 31, at noon.[76] No decision therefore was taken on the night of July 30. And Moltke, shortly after his conversation with Bethmann, stated to Haeften very pessimistically that he did not know how it would all end. "Tomorrow noon comes the decision for peace or war. The Chancellor, the Minister of War, and I have an audience together with His Majesty." Though he had two reliable reports concerning Russian general mobilization, Moltke added: "Before advising His Majesty to mobilize, I wish to await a third confirmation of the news about Russian mobilization." [77]

About 7 A.M., July 31, Moltke received a telephone message from a Staff Officer at Allenstein in East Prussia, stating that the frontier had been completely closed by the Russians and that the red placards ordering mobilization had already been posted up. Moltke replied: "It is necessary that you procure one of these posted orders. I must have certainty as to whether they are really mobilizing against us. Before having that certainty, I am not able to elicit a mobilization order." [78] In other words, Moltke himself admits that Bethmann was unwilling to agree to a decision until Germany had conclusive and absolute evidence of the Russian general mobilization which was suspected and which in fact had been ordered some twelve hours earlier. This evidence was finally supplied in the telegram from Pourtalès at 11:40 A.M. Had Bethmann not received it—had the Tsar not yielded to Sazonov and the Russian militarists

---

[76] Zwehl, *E. v. Falkenhayn*, p. 57.
[77] Schulthess, *Europäischer Geschichtskalender,* 1917, II, p. 996.
[78] Schulthess, *Europäischer Geschichtskalender,* 1917, II, p. 1000.

—it is probable that Bethmann would still have held out
against Moltke and Falkenhayn, and a further breathing-
space been given for consideration of the "Halt in Belgrade" proposal, or for Sazonov's "formula," or for other
negotiations toward a peaceful solution.   This is not to say,
however, that, in this late stage of the crisis, it is probable
that a peaceful solution would have been found.   But at
any rate it would have given the civilian officials in St.
Petersburg and Berlin further opportunity to try to find a
solution, and the arguments of military necessity would have
had less of a hearing in both capitals.

However, as the events actually took place, it was the
precipitate Russian general mobilization, and not any "military convention" between Moltke and Conrad such as Dr.
Kanner imagines, which determined Germany's decision
for "Threatening Danger of War," followed by her ultimatums and mobilization, in view of the European War which
even Bethmann recognized was made inevitable by Russia's
step.

AUSTRIAN GENERAL MOBILIZATION, JULY 31

In Vienna Berchtold and Conrad were dominated more
by a determination to carry out a campaign against Serbia
than by a fear of war with Russia.   Hence the Austrian ultimatum, the partial mobilization exclusively against Serbia
with careful avoidance of provocative measures in Galicia,
and the declaration of war on Serbia, all of which have already been described.

Even after moving against Serbia and bombarding Belgrade, Conrad had still assumed that Russia would not resort to armed intervention.   He had therefore sent no troops
to the Galician front.   But upon Sazonov's announcement
that Russia would mobilize in her southern districts if Austria crossed the Serbian frontier,[79] Conrad began to realize

[79] Szápáry to Berchtold, July 29, 4:26 P.M., received 10 P.M.; A.R.B.
III, 18.

that the Galician front was in danger. He regarded as grotesque Sazonov's assurance that Russian troops once mobilized would stand idle on the frontier with arms stacked. He at once resolved that Austria ought to mobilize, both as a defensive measure of safety against superior Russian forces, and as a counter-bluff which he somewhat illogically seemed to think might frighten Russia off.[80]   Early on July 30, the German Ambassador in Vienna noted: "Here they are resolved to mobilize, as soon as Germany approves; firmly resolved to permit no further Russian mobilization. Proposal: say to St. Petersburg and eventually to Paris, that if the mobilization continues, general mobilization will begin in Austria and Germany." [81]   That is, Berchtold and Conrad proposed to rattle the German sword, by having Bethmann threaten Russia and France with general mobilization by the Central Powers, unless Russian mobilization measures ceased.

But when the Austrian Ambassador in Berlin tried to persuade Germany to take such a step,[82] Germany refused. She had already gone as far in this direction as she deemed prudent in the "warning" given by Pourtalès to Sazonov on July 29. Szögyény was therefore informed by Jagow that since Germany had already pointed out in a friendly spirit at St. Petersburg the dangerous consequences of Russian mobilization, she could not again take the same step. She advised Austria to make representations at St. Petersburg on her own account.[83]

But Conrad did not wait for the arrival of this discouraging answer. Nor did he and Berchtold give serious heed to Bethmann's renewed urgent advice to accept Grey's peace

---

[80] Conrad, IV, 145-147.

[81] Tschirschky's short-hand note on a telegram (K.D., 385) which he received July 30 at 6:00 A.M.; *Investigating Commission*, I, 98.

[82] Memoranda of Szögyény and Jagow, July 30; K.D., 427, 429.

[83] Jagow to Tschirschky, July 30, 9:00 P.M.; K.D., 442. Szögyény to Berchtold, July 31, 12:38 A.M.; A.R.B., III, 51.

proposal, which Tschirschky says he presented "most impressively" after lunch on July 30. Berchtold, "who listened pale and silent," merely said he would report to the Emperor about it at once, and went to change his clothes in order to appear in the correct garb for an audience. From Berchtold's subordinates, Hoyos and Forgach, Tschirschky learned that "the restriction of the military operations [now in progress against Serbia] was, in their opinion, out of the question, in view of the feeling in the army and among the people. Count Tisza will appear in Vienna early tomorrow. His opinion must be obtained on this far-reaching decision." Tschirschky learned also that Conrad was about to submit to Francis Joseph the order for Austrian general mobilization as the reply to the measures already taken by Russia.[84]

In spite of Bethmann's advice which had just been urged by Tschirschky, Berchtold and Conrad, at their audience with Emperor Francis Joseph later in the afternoon, persuaded the aged monarch to approve the following decisions. War against Serbia was to be carried out; Grey's proposal was to be answered very politely in form but without accepting it in substance. General mobilization in Austria was to be ordered on August 1, with August 4 as the first day of mobilization; but this question would be discussed again next day.[85]

The final reservation, providing for discussion again next day of the date of mobilization, was probably mainly owing to the necessity of getting Count Tisza's approval. It may have also been partly owing to the arrival of Fleischmann's telegram from Moltke: "Russia's mobilization is not yet a cause for mobilization," [86] and to Bethmann's continued urgent advice to accept Grey's mediation proposal. In fact,

[84] Tschirschky to Bethmann, July 30, 5:20 P. M., received 5:56 P. M.; and July 31, 1:35 A.M., received 4:35 A.M.; K.D., 434, 465.

[85] Conrad, IV, 151.

[86] Conrad, IV, 152; and see above, at note 62.

says Conrad: "While Emperor Francis Joseph, at this hardest moment of his life, was taking with deep solemnity and calm resolution the step whose heavy consequences were as clear to him as its inevitability, it seemed as if Emperor William was thinking of retreat, and as if the feeling in Berlin had changed on account of Italy's jumping out." [87] Nevertheless, in spite of Berlin's attitude, Conrad seems to have concluded after the audience that the Austrian general mobilization was a settled question as soon as it should have Tisza's approval early next morning. He was even resolved that it should be ordered *next day*, July 31, instead of August 1, as agreed at the audience with the Emperor. Therefore at 7:30 P.M., he wrote out a telegram, to be sent to Berlin at 8:00 A.M. on July 31, which stated: "According to His Majesty's decision it is resolved: to carry through the war against Serbia; to mobilize the rest of the army and to concentrate it in Galicia; first day of mobilization, August 4. Mobilization order will be issued today, July 31." [88] The telegram was, in fact, sent off as directed at 8:00 A.M. on July 31.

Meanwhile, in the course of the night, had come Bienerth's telegram, and at 7:45 A.M. Moltke's own telegram urging Austria to mobilization at once.[89] These telegrams did not cause Austrian mobilization, except in the sense that they removed any hesitation on Conrad's part concerning the order he had written the previous evening, and confirmed Berchtold in the decision taken in the audience with the Emperor the day before to reject the substance of Grey's proposal while appearing to yield to it in form.

[87] Conrad, IV, 151.

[88] Schäfer, p. 536. Conrad also gave Tschirschky to understand that he had resolved on Austrian mobilization, for Tschirschky noted on a telegram received July 30 at 10:00 A.M. (K.D., 396), that Conrad would discuss general mobilization with the Emperor in the afternoon and then tell the Russian Ambassador that it meant "no hostility, no conflict; precaution, no threat, still less any idea of attack" (*Investigating Commission*, I, 99).   [89] See above, at notes 63, 65.

When Conrad took Moltke's telegram to Berchtold and the other Ministers, Berchtold exclaimed: "Who is in charge? Moltke or Bethmann?" After reading aloud Emperor William's telegram to Francis Joseph, urging the "Halt in Belgrade" proposal, Berchtold turned to the others and said: "I called you together because I had the impression that Germany was drawing back; now I have the most satisfactory assurances from the highest military authority." [90]

Francis Joseph's final assent was thereupon secured to an order for general mobilization, fixing August 4 as the first day of mobilization. The order reached the Ministry of War on July 31 at 12:23 P.M., and was immediately published. It did not, however, immediately remove all misunderstandings between Conrad and Moltke in the course of the afternoon. Conrad, in ordering general mobilization, did not at first expect war with Russia. He had not yet heard of Russian general mobilization and believed he could still carry through the war against Serbia, as he had telegraphed to Moltke at 8:00 A.M. on July 31. Upon receiving this, Moltke had immediately begged Conrad "not to divert strong forces from the main struggle, which in his opinion ought to be waged against Russia, by an undertaking against Serbia. The main force must be held ready against Russia, because the German rear covering-forces are inadequate against a decisive Russian advance." [91] At 6:00 P.M. he telephoned to Vienna: "Is Austria going to leave us in the lurch?" [92]

Conrad telephoned in reply at 9:30 P.M., asking for a definite statement whether he was to reckon with certainty on war with Russia taking place immediately; he did not know whether Russia was only bluffing, and therefore he did not want to be diverted from his action against Serbia.

---

[90] Conrad, IV, 153. Berchtold was referring to Moltke.
[91] Fleischmann to Conrad, July 31, 11:15 A.M., received 6:05 P.M.; Schäfer, p. 540.   [92] Schäfer, p. 541.

It was not until late in the evening of July 31 that he was convinced by Moltke and by the Kaiser's next telegram to Francis Joseph that Germany expected that her ultimatums to Russia and France would be rejected, and that Austria's main effort ought therefore to be directed against Russia and not against Serbia.[93]

The Austrian general mobilization was not a decisive factor in the final chain of events causing the war. It was not ordered until eighteen hours after the Russian general mobilization had been ordered, and did not contribute to the steps which Germany took in answer to the Russian mobilization.

After securing Francis Joseph's final approval of Austrian general mobilization, Berchtold now deceived Europe by the pretense of adopting a more conciliatory attitude, which is contradicted by his real intentions as revealed in the minutes of the secret Ministerial Council held about noon. With the Russian Ambassador in Vienna he took up conversations again in a most friendly manner, and to all the Powers he pretended that Austria was ready to "approach nearer" Grey's proposal.[94] To the British Ambassador he gave the impression, as Bunsen later wrote to Grey, that

> Austria, in fact, had finally yielded, and that she herself had at this point good hopes of a peaceful issue is shown by the communication made to you on the 1st of August by Count Mensdorff to the effect that Austria had neither "banged the door" on compromise nor cut off the conversations. . . . Unfortunately these conversations at St. Petersburg and Vienna were cut short by the transfer of the dispute to the more dangerous ground of a direct conflict between Germany and Russia. Germany intervened on the 31st July by means of her double ultimatums to St. Peters-

[93] Schäfer, pp. 541-544.
[94] A.R.B., III, 62, 65, 66, 78, 94; *Krasnyi Arkhiv*, I, p. 186; Schilling's *Diary*, p. 72; B.D., 360, 412; Poincaré, IV, 465 ff.

burg and Paris. The ultimatums were of a kind to which only one answer is possible, and Germany declared war on Russia on the 1st August, and on France on the 3rd August. A few days' delay might in all probability have saved Europe from one of the greatest calamities in history.[95]

How far Berchtold was, however, from the slightest intention of really and honestly yielding to mediation and stopping the Austrian advance in Serbia is now unmistakably revealed in the protocol of the minutes of the Ministerial Council. After stating Grey's last proposal and Bethmann's strong urging that it be accepted, Berchtold pointed out that experience showed that mediatory Powers always tried to reach a compromise by forcing one Power to pare down the conditions it had made:

> It was probable that they would attempt this now also, when in the present conjuncture France, England, and Italy also would represent the Russian standpoint, and we [Austria] should have a very doubtful support in the present German Ambassador in London. From Prince Lichnowsky everything else was to be expected except that he would represent our interests warmly. If the action should end now merely with a gain of prestige, it would in my opinion have been undertaken wholly in vain. From a mere occupation of Belgrade we should gain absolutely nothing, even if Russia should give her consent to it. All this would be mere tinsel [*Flitterwerk*]. Russia would come forward as the savior of Serbia, and especially of the Serbian army. The latter would remain intact, and in two or three years we should again have to look forward to the attack of Serbia under much more unfavorable conditions.

He had therefore had an audience with Francis Joseph. His Majesty had at once declared that there could be no check placed upon military operations, but accepted the plan "that we should carefully avoid accepting the English proposal in

[95] Bunsen to Grey, Sept. 1, 1914; B.D., 676.

actual substance, but that in the form of our answer, we should pretend to be ready to meet it. . . ." [96]

Berchtold's colleagues agreed with him or went even further. Tisza, who had now completely changed his attitude, made no opposition. To Stürgkh, "the very thought of a mediatory conference was so odious that he preferred to avoid even the pretense of accepting one." Bilinski was equally hostile to a conference, because "the course of the London Conference was so horrible to recall to memory, that all public opinion would reject the repetition of such a spectacle." [97]

There is therefore no substantial truth in the widely accepted Entente version that Austria was at last ready to yield, when Germany intervened with her ultimatum and declaration of war, and so precipitated the general European War. Germany did intervene because of the Russian general mobilization. But Austria had no genuine intention of yielding to Grey's idea, or of abandoning the campaign against Serbia and being content with the occupation of Belgrade or even neighboring territory. One reason that Austria refused to be satisfied with the occupation of Belgrade was military necessity. Her plan of campaign did not make possible an immediate occupation of Belgrade, but provided that her main attack on Serbia should come from Bosnia from the southwest, and not directly upon Belgrade from the north across the Danube. [98]

"THREATENING DANGER OF WAR" IN GERMANY, JULY 31

Bethmann had restrained Moltke from taking any irremediable military steps until a decision should be made at noon on July 31 at a meeting between themselves and the

[96] A.R.B., III, 79; repeated in slightly less bald language, *ibid*, III, 80. *Cf*. Gooss, pp. 234-243, 301-306.

[97] Minutes of the Ministerial Council, July 31; A.R.B., III, 79.

[98] *Cf*. R. Kiszling, "Die praktische Undurchführbarkeit eines Handstreiches auf Belgrad," in KSF, V, 231-238, March, 1927.

Kaiser.[99]   By that time it was hoped that an answer would
at last have come from Vienna as to the "Halt in Belgrade"
plan, and that there would be definite information as to the
military situation in Russia.   A favorable answer from
Vienna might open the way for peace.   A confirmation of
the reports of general mobilization in Russia would force
Germany to take steps to protect herself against the danger
of a war on two fronts.

In anticipation of a peaceful settlement the Kaiser at
Potsdam had written out in his own hand on the morning
of July 31 a long statement for the Admiralty Staff summar-
izing the telegrams exchanged with the Tsar, and enclosing
the one to Prince Henry from George V: "His proposals
are similar to mine, which I suggested to the Vienna Cabinet, which has left us for six days without an answer. . . .
Diplomatic conferences have at last commenced between
Vienna and Peterhof, and Peterhof has also begged London
for intervention." [100]   While in the midst of this, the Kaiser
received a telephone message from Berlin announcing beyond the slightest doubt that general mobilization was in
progress in Russia.   Without waiting to consult his Foreign
Office, he telegraphed to King George:

> Many thanks for your kind telegram.   Your proposals
> coincide with my ideas and with the statements I got this
> night from Vienna which I have had forwarded to London.
> I just received news from Chancellor that official notifica-
> tion has reached him that this night Nicky has ordered the
> mobilization of his whole army and fleet.   He has not even
> awaited the results of the mediation I am working at and
> left me without any news.   I am off for Berlin to take
> measures for ensuring safety of my eastern frontiers where
> strong Russian troops are already posted.[101]

[99] Moltke's   statement   to   Haeften   after   midnight,   July   30-31;
Schulthess, *Europäischer Geschichtskalender*, 1917, II, 996 f.

[100] K.D., 474.

[101] Kaiser to George V, July 31, 12:55 P.M.; K.D., 477.

The definite news of the Russian general mobilization, ordered about 6:00 P.M. on July 30, was surprisingly late in reaching Berlin.

In St. Petersburg neither Pourtalès nor the German Military Attaché, Eggeling, knew anything of it until the morning of July 31, after the news had already been printed in the newspapers and been posted up in the streets for hours. As soon as Eggeling learned of it, he hurried to Pourtalès, who sent off a telegram at 10:20 A.M.:

> General mobilization of the army and navy ordered. First mobilization day, July 31.[102]

Bethmann telephoned the news to Potsdam. The Kaiser motored at once to Berlin. A conference took place with Bethmann, Moltke and other officials. About 1:00 P.M. it was decided to proclaim "Threatening Danger of War" [*drohende Kriegsgefahr*]. This proclamation set in motion a number of precautionary measures preparatory to actual mobilization, and was somewhat similar to the Russian "Period Preparatory to War." It did not necessarily and inevitably involve mobilization, but it meant that the German Government expected it would be followed by mobilization within at least forty-eight hours, and mobilization would mean war. As Bethmann telegraphed to Vienna, in order to persuade Austria to divert her main effort against Russia instead of against Serbia:

> After the Russian total mobilization we have proclaimed "Threatening Danger of War," which will presumably be followed within forty-eight hours by mobilization. The latter inevitably means war. We expect from Austria an immediate *active* participation in the war against Russia.[103]

102 Pourtalès to Bethmann, July 31, 10:20 A. M., received 11:40 A. M.; K.D., 473.

103 Bethmann to Tschirschky, July 31, 1:45 P.M.; received 4:20 P.M.; K.D., 479. Moltke also said the same more emphatically to Conrad in telephone conversations in the course of the afternoon and evening

It is often said that had the German Government really wanted peace, even after learning of the Russian general mobilization, it should have contented itself with declaring German mobilization and then standing on the defensive; that Sazonov would have lived up to his promises that the Russian army would make no attack but stand with arms grounded; and that this would have again given the diplomatists a chance to find a peaceful solution. It is said, in a word, that the proper answer to mobilization is counter-mobilization and not war. But this argument leaves out of view the fact that in St. Petersburg and Paris, as well as in Berlin, the maxim had long been accepted by military men, and by the highest political authorities like Tsar Alexander III,[104] that "mobilization means war." It had been clearly hinted by Pourtalès to Sazonov on the afternoon of July 29 before Russia ordered general mobilization.[105] It was obviously clear to the Tsar on July 30 in view of his hesitation to yield to Sazonov's arguments and to accept the solemn responsibility which he realized would send thousands and thousands of men to their death.[106] And it was explicitly stated by Bethmann to the Prussian Council of Ministers on July 30: "The declaration of 'Threatening Danger of War' meant mobilization, and this under our conditions—mobilization toward both sides—meant war." [107]

The argument also leaves out of view the fact that in the plans of the General Staffs everywhere on the Continent mobilization was inextricably bound up with the "plan of campaign," which provided not only for the march to the frontier but in most cases the crossing of the frontier in order to get the advantage of the offensive and the waging

(Schäfer, pp. 538-543) and Emperor William made a similar appeal to Emperor Francis Joseph at 4:40 P.M. (K.D., 503).

[104] See above ch. x, at notes 77-80.

[105] See above ch. x, at note 37.

[106] See above, ch. x, at notes 53, 60, 61.   [107] K.D., 456.

of war in the enemy's country. Mobilization started the military machine in motion, and once in motion, for technical reasons, it was virtually impossible to halt it without dislocation of the long-prepared and minutely worked out plan of campaign. Though the civilian authorities might want to stop the machine at the frontier, and might promise that they would do so, as the Tsar promised the Kaiser, it was doubtful whether they would be able to do so, owing to the insistent arguments of the military authorities that any interference with the carefully prearranged schedule would be disastrous. Even the Kaiser, whose authority in civil and military matters was not least among monarchs, on understanding from Lichnowsky that England might guarantee the neutrality of France, for a moment on August 1, thought he could halt the German army, once in motion, from crossing the frontier into Luxemburg. But even he was quickly overborne by Moltke and by the news that Lichnowsky had made a "mistake," and made to realize that it was impossible.[108] And, as a matter of fact, at this very moment, a detachment of German soldiers appeared already to have crossed the frontier and violated the neutrality of Luxemburg.[109]

Furthermore, the argument leaves out of view the fact, just suggested, that when mobilizations have taken place, "military necessity" tends to prevail over the diplomatic considerations of the civilians. This was particularly true in Germany. It was perfectly recognized in St. Petersburg and Paris, as well as in Berlin, that as Germany would have to fight a war on two fronts, and as she was threatened by the superior number of troops which Russia and France could bring against her, she would have to strike her main blow first at one and then at the other. She could not divide

[108] K.D., 562, 570, 575, 578, 579, 596, 603, 612, 630, 631; B.D., 419, 453, 460; and the dramatic narrative of Moltke, *Erinnerungen*, pp. 19-23.

[109] Protest of Eyschen, Minister of the Grand Duchy of Luxemburg, to Jagow, Aug. 1, 9:30 P.M.; K.D., 602.

her main forces and face both fronts at once. Taking advantage of the fact that she could mobilize more rapidly than Russia, she would have to make her first attack on France, in the West, while the Russian forces were slowly gathering in the East. She must equalize her inferiority in numbers by the greater speed of her military machine. For Germany merely to have answered mobilization by counter-mobilization, and to have stood on the defensive while diplomatic negotiations (probably futile) proceeded, would have meant that she would lose all her advantage in speed. The Russian armies would have had time gradually to mobilize and to concentrate on the East Prussian frontier, in overwhelming numbers, thus compelling Germany either to divide her forces and face superior numbers, simultaneously East and West, or to open her eastern territory to Russian invasion while she made her main effort against France in the West. These were military considerations, convincing to the German civilian as well as military authorities,[110] and recognized by the military authorities in Russia and France, which made it obviously impossible for Germany merely to answer Russian general mobilization by counter-mobilization. It was not Germany's lack of desire for peace, but her "plan of campaign," arising from her inferior numbers and her double frontier, which compelled her, after proclaiming "Threatening Danger of War," followed by mobilization, to move at once beyond her frontier.

Germany's plan of campaign also contemplated going through the relatively flat and less strongly fortified territory of Belgium, in defiance of international law and of Prussia's guarantee of Belgian neutrality. Only in so doing, the militarists believed, could Germany strike and crush

[110] Bethmann, *Betrachtungen* (Berlin, 1919), I, 164 ff.; H. v. Kuhl, *Der deutsche Generalstab in Vorbereitung und Durchführung des Weltkrieges* (2nd ed., Berlin, 1920), p. 98 ff.; W. Groener, *Das Testament des Grafen Schlieffen* (Berlin, 1927), pp. 10 ff., 195 ff.; R. Kann, *Le Plan de Campagne allemand de 1914 et son Exécution* (Paris, 1923), p. 26 ff.

the French forces quickly, so that she could then turn against Russia. By going through Belgium it was calculated that a decisive victory—a "Cannae"—could be won within six weeks. On the other hand, to attempt to reach the French armies by striking straight west, without touching the neutralized territories of Luxemburg and Belgium, would take months, on account of the hilly country, the rising escarpments,[111] and the strong lines of defensive forts which France had built since 1870.

Bethmann, with his juristic training and upon the advice of a legal expert in the Foreign Office, wished to keep within the requirements of the Hague Convention of 1907, which declared that hostilities must not commence without previous warning, either in the form of a reasoned declaration of war or an ultimatum with a conditional declaration of war. Compelled to accept the German plan of campaign which provided for an ultimatum to Belgium, demanding passage across her territory, he desired to regularize it by a previous formal declaration of a state of war between Germany and Russia, in case Russia did not accede to an ultimatum to demobilize at once. Falkenhayn, and especially Tirpitz, were opposed to such a declaration of war against Russia. They thought it an unnecessary, foolish and clumsy mistake in diplomatic technique, which would make an unfortunate impression on public opinion and brand Germany before the world as the aggressor.[112] Pourtalès also was of this opinion. The course of events showed that he was right. But, at the moment, Bethmann and Jagow seemed to have believed that

[111] Cf. W. M. Davis, Handbook of Northern France (Cambridge, 1918), p. 27 ff.

[112] Cf. Zwehl, Erich v. Falkenhayn, p. 58; Tirpitz, Politische Dokumente, II, 11-12; and the communications of H. E. Barnes and B. E. Schmitt, in the Amer. Hist. Review, XXXIII, 456-459, January, 1928. Moltke appears to have been indifferent on this question; Bethmann (Betrachtungen, I, 156) is correct in saying that Falkenhayn opposed a declaration of war on Russia, but incorrect in saying that he himself was persuaded to it by Moltke.

a violation of Belgian neutrality prior to Germany's being formally at war with Russia would affect world opinion more adversely than a German initiative in declaring war. So Bethmann decided at once to send an ultimatum to Russia and another to Russia's ally.

Pourtalès was therefore informed that Russia's mobilization of her entire army and navy, undertaken while negotiations were still pending, and before Germany had taken any mobilization measures, had compelled Germany to proclaim "Threatening Danger of War." "Mobilization must follow in case Russia does not suspend every war measure against Austria-Hungary and ourselves within twelve hours and make us a distinct declaration to that effect. Please inform Sazonov of this, and telegraph the hour of your communication." [113]

Pourtalès received this message shortly after 11:00 P.M., deciphered it, and delivered it to Sazonov at midnight. Sazonov replied to him, as the Tsar had done, that for technical reasons it was impossible to suspend the mobilization measures.[114]

As the time-limit for Russia's final answer did not expire until noon on August 1, Pourtalès made an effort in another direction. Taking advantage of his personal friendship with Count Fredericks, the Tsar's Minister of the Household, he sent him a letter entreating him to use his influence with the Tsar to prevent the catastrophe of war before it should be too late. The Count saw the Tsar, but Nicholas II could only assure him, as he had assured the Kaiser, that Russian mobilization did not mean war and that he hoped German mobilization did not mean so either.[115]

In the ultimatum to Paris, Baron Schoen was instructed

---

[113] Bethmann to Pourtalès, July 31, 3:30 P.M., received 11:10 P.M.; K.D., 490.
[114] Pourtalès to Bethmann, Aug. 1, 1:00 A.M.; K.D., 536; Pourtalès, *Am Scheideweg*, pp. 74-76.
[115] K.D., 539, 546; Pourtalès, *Am Scheideweg*, pp. 76-81.

to inform France of the demands which were being made at St. Petersburg, and to say that German mobilization would inevitably mean war. He was to "ask the French Government if it intends to remain neutral in a Russo-German war. Answer must be given within eighteen hours." If, contrary to expectation, France declared its intention to remain neutral, the Ambassador was to demand the turning over of the fortresses of Toul and Verdun to be held as a pledge of neutrality and returned after the completion of the war with Russia.[116]

At 7:00 P.M., when Baron Schoen went to the Quai d'Orsay to carry out these instructions, the French Government had already learned from the French Ambassador in Berlin that Germany had declared "Threatening Danger of War" in consequence of the Russian general mobilization, and that Schoen was about to ask what France's attitude would be.[117] Viviani therefore had had time to consult with Poincaré how he should evade a direct answer. In reply to Schoen's question he simply said: "Let me hope that extreme decisions can be avoided, and permit me to take time to reflect." He promised to give an answer at the expiration of the eighteen hours, that is, on Saturday, August 1, at 1:00 P.M.[118]

Next day, when Schoen came before the expiration of the eighteen hours to repeat his question whether France would remain neutral, Viviani replied: "France will act in accordance with her interests." As he made no promise of neutrality, Schoen naturally said nothing of his secret in-

[116] Bethmann to Schoen, July 31, 3:30 P.M.; K.D., 491.

[117] Jules Cambon to Viviani, July 31, 3:50 P.M., received 4:25 P.M.; omitted from F.Y.B., but printed by Poincaré, IV, 446 f.

[118] Schoen to Bethmann, July 31, 8:17 P.M., received Aug. 1, 12:30 A.M.; K.D., 528. Viviani, *Réponse au Kaiser*, pp. 192 f. Poincaré, IV, 448-451. According to Schoen, Viviani said he had no news of any general mobilization in Russia, only of precautionary measures. According to Viviani, Schoen talked of asking for his passports. The interview was painful but courteous

structions to ask for Toul and Verdun. The French did not learn of this German intention until they succeeded during the war in deciphering the German telegrams exchanged in July, 1914.[119]

The proclamation of "Threatening Danger of War" had been urged by Moltke and Falkenhayn since the evening of July 29. But Bethmann had held out against it until receiving definite news that Russia had ordered general mobilization. As the Russian order had been given because Sazonov and Ianushkevich had persuaded the Tsar that war was inevitable, so now the Russian mobilization was the decisive fact which at last convinced the civil as well as the military authorities in Germany that war was inevitable. News of the Russian step caused military considerations everywhere (except in England) to take precedence over political considerations, and rendered futile and illusory all the later diplomatic efforts. Some of these efforts were made sincerely but without serious expectation of success; some were only diplomatic gestures calculated to give an appearance of pacific intentions and to throw the odium of responsibility upon the opposing side. Thus, neither the Russian "formula" which Sazonov had proposed to Pourtalès,[120] nor the personal appeal which Pourtalès made in a visit on his own initiative to the Tsar at Peterhof,[121] nor the final exchange of telegrams between "Willy" and "Nicky," [122] nor Berchtold's pretense of being at last ready to make some concessions,[123] could have any chance of success. As these last diplomatic efforts were futile and illusory, they need not be set forth in detail.

[119] Schoen to Bethmann, Aug. 1, 1:05 P. M., received 6:10 P. M.; K.D., 571; cf. also 543, 598; Viviani, p. 204; Poincaré, IV, 478 f.

[120] See above, ch. x, at note 52.

[121] On the early afternoon of July 31; K.D., 535; Pourtalès, Am Scheideweg, pp. 64-73.

[122] K.D., 480, 487, 546, 600; Schilling's Diary, pp. 72 ff., 81 f.

[123] See above, at note 94.

MOBILIZATION IN FRANCE AND GERMANY, AUGUST 1

Shortly after Schoen had made his first communication concerning the Russian mobilization and the steps that Germany was forced to take in consequence, the French Government finally received, on July 31, at 8:30 P.M., Paléologue's belated telegram announcing it.[124] This left no doubt that the news of it, which had already come from German sources through Jules Cambon, Schoen, and a telegraph agency, was correct. This news, coupled with that of the German "Threatening Danger of War" received from Cambon, left little doubt in the minds of the French Cabinet that a European War was inevitable. General Joffre demanded the complete mobilization of the eastern army corps. "Every delay of twenty-four hours in calling up reservists and sending the telegram for *couverture* means a retardation of the concentration forces, that is, the initial abandonment of fifteen to twenty kilometers of territory for every day of delay." At 5:00 P.M., therefore, before Schoen came to ask Viviani about French neutrality, the Cabinet decided to order that *couverture,* which had been already ordered with limitations on July 30 in connection with the "10-kilometer withdrawal," should now take place in its fullest extent.[125]

A little later at 1:00 A.M., the Russian Military Attaché at Paris reported to St. Petersburg:

> The French Minister of War has declared to me in a tone of hearty enthusiasm the firm decision of the French Government for War, and begged me to confirm the hope of the French General Staff that all our efforts will be directed against Germany, and that Austria will be treated as a *quantité négligeable.*[126]

[124] See above, ch. x, at note 70.

[125] Poincaré, IV, 458.

[126] Izvolski to Sazonov, July 31 [Aug. 1], 1:00 A.M.; M.F.R., 522; L.N., II, 294.

In the evening occurred the tragic assassination of Jean Jaurès, the veteran socialist leader who had long opposed the policies of M. Poincaré which he feared would some day lead his country into war.[127] There came also the secret assurance from Rome that the Italian Government considered itself freed by Austria's conduct from its Triple Alliance obligations.[128] But Sir Edward Grey continued in a non-committal attitude which was most distressing to Paul Cambon in London and to the French Cabinet in Paris.[129]

Early next morning, Saturday, August 1, General Joffre, surmising that Germany was proceeding to full mobilization under cover of "Threatening Danger of War," declared that he could no longer assume the responsibility of command unless France ordered general mobilization. The Cabinet then authorized the Minister of War to order it before 4 P.M.[130] In view of Schoen's communication and Viviani's answer to it, and in view of a telegram from Paléologue announcing Germany's ultimatum to Russia, it seemed certain that Germany would soon mobilize, even if, as Joffre surmised, she was not already doing so. About 3:45 P.M., after the Minister of War handed over the mobilization order to an officer of the French General Staff, it was immediately telegraphed throughout France in time so that the mobilization could begin next morning.[131]

The telegram from Pourtalès reporting that Sazonov had replied that it was impossible for technical reasons to suspend Russian mobilization had been received in Berlin on August 1 at 12:30 A.M. The time-limit for any further reply expired at noon. Schoen's telegram giving Viviani's final answer, "France will act in accordance with her inter-

127 Cf. F. Gouttenoire de Toury, Jaurès et le Parti de la Guerre, Paris, 1922. Poincaré, IV, 474 f.
128 Poincaré, IV, 473.
129 Cf. Poincaré, IV, 475-478, 486-494.
130 Recouly, p. 81 ff.; Poincaré, IV, 479 f.
131 Recouly, p. 85. Les Armées françaises, Tome I, Vol. I, Annexe. No. 21.

ests," did not reach Berlin until 6:10 P.M. But his earlier telegrams made it seem almost certain, as Germany expected, that France would not remain neutral, and certainly not hand over Toul and Verdun to German occupation. Germany therefore ordered mobilization August 1 at 5:00 P.M., quarter of an hour later than France.[132] Germany was the last of the Great Powers to take this final and supreme military measure.

Expecting that Sazonov would maintain his view that Russia could not suspend mobilization and would fail to comply with the ultimatum, Bethmann forwarded to Pourtalès a declaration of war. The Ambassador, receiving it about 6:00 P.M. went at once with it to Sazonov. Three times, with increasing signs of emotion at his painful duty, he asked the Russian Minister of Foreign Affairs whether he could not give him a favorable answer to his request of the day before. Three times Sazonov answered in the negative. "In that case, Sir," said Pourtalès, drawing from his pocket a folded paper, "I am instructed to hand you this note," and gave him the declaration of war.[133] Then losing self-control, the Ambassador went to the window and wept, saying: "I never could have believed that I should quit St. Petersburg under these conditions." He then embraced Sazonov and went away, asking that he be informed at the Embassy concerning his passports and arrangements for his departure, as he was not capable at the moment of talking about anything.[134]

The German declaration of war on France was not made

[132] K.D., 554. French mobilization at 3:45 P.M., French time, was 4:45 P.M. according to German or Central European time.

[133] Bethmann to Pourtalès, August 1, 12:52 P.M.; K.D., 542. Pourtalès to Bethmann, Aug. 1, 8:00 P.M.; K.D., 588; Pourtalès, *Am Scheideweg*, pp. 81-85. The declaration had been drawn up in two alternative forms to accord with Sazonov's possible replies. By an oversight Pourtalès left both forms in the Foreign Minister's hands, as an *aide-mémoire*, but in their agitation neither of the men noticed this fact at the moment.

[134] Schilling's *Diary*, p. 76-78.

until 6:15 P.M. on August 3. It alleged several hostile
French acts: French troops had crossed the frontier in the
Vosges. "A French aviator, who must have flown across
Belgium territory, was shot down yesterday in an attempt
to wreck the railroad at Wesel. . . . Yesterday, French air-
men dropped bombs on the railroads near Karlsruhe and
Nuremberg. Thus France has forced us into war." Schoen
was therefore instructed to communicate the foregoing
to the French Government, ask for his passports, and
turn over the Embassy to the charge of the American
Ambassador.[135]

The alleged hostile acts were based on false information which the German Government, in its haste, had
taken no care to verify. Furthermore, the despatch to
Schoen reached him in a very mutilated form, so that much
of it was unintelligible. Though the declaration of war
and the grounds for it were such a very serious matter,
Schoen did not feel justified in taking the necessary time to
get from Berlin a complete and exact text of the mutilated
document. He had been told to deliver the declaration at
6:00 P.M. Bethmann again wished to be formally correct
in notifying a state of war before the German forces crossed
the frontier into France, as they were about to do in accordance with the pre-arranged and all-important plan of campaign.

Schoen therefore put together, as best he could, a
declaration of war based on his mutilated telegram, and
handed it in to Viviani. It contained the untrue allegations
as to the French aviators over Wesel, Karlsruhe and
Nuremberg.[136]

135 Bethmann to Schoen, Aug. 3, 1:05 P.M., received 4:15 P.M. (German time, 5:15 P.M.); K.D., 734.
136 K.D., 734, a, b. Poincaré, IV, 520 ff. Montgelas, *Leitfaden*, p
182 f. Renouvin, pp. 237-248 (Eng. trans., pp. 264-276).

ENGLAND AND BELGIUM

In spite of Paul Cambon's appeal to Grey on July 30, recalling their exchange of notes in 1912,[137] and in spite of a personal entreaty which President Poincaré sent by special messenger to King George on the afternoon of July 31,[138] the British Foreign Secretary still remained unwilling to give any pledge to France. As Grey notified the British Ambassador in Paris:

> I went on to say to M. Cambon that though we should have to put our policy before Parliament, we could not pledge Parliament in advance. Up to the present moment, we did not feel, and public opinion did not feel, that any treaties or obligations of this country were involved. Further developments might alter this situation and cause the Government and Parliament to take the view that intervention was justified. The preservation of the neutrality of Belgium might be, I would not say a decisive, but an important factor, in determining our attitude. . . .
>
> M. Cambon expressed great disappointment at my reply. He repeated his question of whether we would help France if Germany made an attack on her.
>
> I said that I could only adhere to the answer that, as far as things had gone at present, we could not take any engagement. *The latest news was that Russia had ordered a complete mobilization of her fleet and army. This, it seemed to me, would precipitate a crisis, and would make it appear that German mobilization was being forced by Russia.*[139]

Sir Arthur Nicolson and Sir Eyre Crowe, however, were strongly urging that "the whole policy of the Entente can

[137] See above, at notes 11-13.

[138] *Cf.* B.D., 366; and Poincaré, IV, 437-440.

[139] Grey to Bertie, July 31; B.D., 367; and Paul Cambon's reports, in Poincaré, IV, 440-442, 475-478. The words in Italics were suppressed from the *British Blue Book* of 1914 (No. 119). They show that Grey realized the truth, but allowed it to be suppressed in order to support the Franco-Russian effort to minimize the importance of Russia's step.

have no meaning if it does not signify that in a just quarrel England would stand by her friends. This honorable expectation has been raised. We cannot repudiate it without exposing our good name to grave criticism." [140]

Sir Edward Grey knew that the Cabinet was still sharply divided on the question of British participation in a European War. He was therefore taking care to be extremely cautious in avoiding any commitments to France until opinion in the Cabinet and in Parliament should be brought more decisively to the side of France by some new fact, such as a German ultimatum to France or a refusal to respect the neutrality of Belgium. This latter possibility had been revealed to him in connection with Bethmann's "bid" for British neutrality, lighting up "like a searchlight" a new aspect of the situation.[141]

On Friday, July 31, the day after receiving Bethmann's "bid," Grey decided to clarify the Belgian question by addressing to the French and German Governments a request asking each for an assurance that it would respect the neutrality of Belgium so long as no other Power violated it.[142] He also informed the Brussels Government of this step, and added: "I assume that Belgium will to the utmost of her power maintain neutrality, and desire and expect other Powers to observe and uphold it." [143]

France at once gave an unqualified assurance in the affirmative.[144] But at Berlin Jagow told the British Ambassador that he could not possibly reply without consulting Bethmann and the Kaiser. "He rather doubted whether

---

[140] Crowe's memorandum, July 31; B.D., 369; cf. also 368, and Minutes on 382, 383.   [141] See above, at notes 42-45.

[142] Grey to Bertie and Goschen, July 31, 5:30 P.M., B.D., 348. This step was decided upon at a Cabinet meeting in the morning, before he heard of the Russian mobilization and the consequent German "Threatening Danger of War"; cf. Cambon to Viviani, July 31, 8:40 P.M. (Poincaré, IV, 442).

[143] Grey to Villiers, July 31, 6:15 P.M.; B.D., 351.

[144] Bertie to Grey, Aug. 1, 1:12 A.M., received 2:15 A.M., B.D., 382.

they could answer at all, as any reply they might give could not fail, in the event of war, to have the undesirable effect of disclosing to a certain extent part of their plan of campaign."[145]

Already, however, on this same Friday, before hearing the dubious German reply in regard to Belgium, Sir Edward Grey determined in his own mind, in agreement with Nicolson and Crowe, that England's obligation of honor to France and her own material interests made it imperative for her to intervene on the Franco-Russian side. In the morning he had told the German Ambassador that if Germany could get any reasonable proposal put forward which made it clear that Germany and Austria were striving to preserve European peace, he would support it and go to the length of saying that, if France and Russia would not accept it, he would have nothing more to do with the consequences. "But, otherwise," he warned Lichnowsky, "if France became involved, we should be drawn in." [146] He told Cambon confidentially of this statement to Lichnowsky, but carefully explained that this "was not the same thing as taking an engagement to France," and that he could not pledge Parliament in advance.[147] Cambon could only inform Paris that Grey, "who is a partizan of immediate intervention," would discuss the matter again with the Cabinet next morning.[148]

On August 1, Cambon, knowing of Germany's ultimatums and of the French intention to order mobilization,[149] renewed his appeals to Grey. He urged very strongly the British obligation to help France, both on account of the withdrawal of the French fleet to the Mediterranean, leaving the northern coast undefended except for British assis-

[145] Goschen to Grey, Aug. 1, 2 A.M., received 3:30 A.M.; B.D., 383
[146] Grey to Goschen, July 31, 2:45 P.M.; B.D., 340; cf. K.D., 489, 496, 497. [147] Grey to Bertie, July 31; B.D., 367. Poincaré, IV, 440 f.
[148] Cambon to Viviani, July 31, 8:40 P.M.; Poincaré, IV, 442.
[149] Poincaré, IV, 486.

tance, and on account of British interest. "If we [English]
do not help France," Cambon said, "the Entente would disappear; and, whether victory came to Germany, or to
France and Russia, our situation at the end of the war
would be very uncomfortable." But Grey replied there was
no obligation. That if France were forced into a war
against her wish, it was because of her alliance with Russia.
England had purposely kept clear of alliances in order not
to be involved in this way. "This did not mean that under
no circumstances would we assist France, but it did mean
that France must take her own decision at this moment
without reckoning on an assistance that we were not now
in a position to promise." Cambon answered in dismay
that he could not transmit this reply to his Government,
and asked to be authorized to answer that the British Cabinet had not yet come to any decision. To mitigate Cambon's disappointment, Grey then said that the appearance
of a German fleet in the English Channel and an attack
on the French coasts, or a violation of Belgium might alter
public opinion in England, and that he would bring these
questions before the Cabinet next morning. Meanwhile
Cambon might report that no decision had been taken.[150]

August 2 was the "Sunday of Resolve" for England.
The Cabinet sat almost continuously all day. In the morning it was still too uncertain as to British opinion and too
divided against itself to come to a decision. Until luncheon-
time the danger that a considerable minority would resign
from the Cabinet and thereby greatly weaken the Government at a critical moment, still caused the majority to hesitate, in spite of the arrival of news that German troops had
entered Luxemburg.[151] The neutrality of Belgium, as Grey

[150] Grey to Bertie, Aug. 1, 8:20 P.M., and letter Aug. 1; B.D., 426,
447. Cambon to Viviani, Aug. 1; Poincaré, IV, 487.
[151] Villiers to Grey, Aug. 2, 10:50 A.M., received 11:45 A.M.; B.D.,
465; cf. also 466-468, 472. P. Cambon appears to have received the news
at 8:00 A.M., but did not discuss it with Grey until 3:00 P.M. (cf. C. F

told Cambon in the afternoon, "was a much more important matter" [152] than the neutrality of Luxemburg. The violation of the latter did not of itself bring a decisive change in the attitude of the Cabinet. The decisive fact was that about noon a letter was brought from Mr. Bonar Law, the leader of the Unionist Party, assuring the Cabinet of support of his followers in Parliament. Such support had already been intimated unofficially to Winston Churchill in a letter three days earlier from another prominent Unionist, Mr. F. E. Smith, later Lord Birkenhead.[153] But Mr. Bonar Law's letter might be regarded as official, and represented the expressed view of a number of most important Unionist leaders, including Lord Lansdowne, who had hurried up to London to make his influence felt. Mr. Bonar Law's letter was as follows:

2nd August, 1914.

Dear Mr. Asquith,—Lord Lansdowne and I feel it our duty to inform you that, in our opinion, as well as in that of all the colleagues whom we have been able to consult, it would be fatal to the honor and security of the United Kingdom to hesitate in supporting France and Russia at the present juncture; and we offer our unhesitating support to the Government in any measures that they may consider necessary for that object.[154]

Roux, in *Revue des Deux Mondes*, Aug. 15, 1926. The violation of Luxemburg was regarded by Sir Edward Grey as a much less important matter than that of Belgium, partly because Luxemburg did not lie on the English channel, and partly because Luxemburg's neutrality was secured by a "collective guarantee," and Belgian neutrality by an "individual guarantee." In the case of the former, a breach of the guarantee by one of the guarantors might be regarded as liberating the other guarantors from their obligations; not so, in the case of an "individual guarantee," in which each guarantor remained obligated independently of the action of the others. (*cf.* Grey, II, 3-10; and E. C. Stowell, *The Diplomacy of the War of 1914* (Boston, 1915), pp. 376 ff., 422 ff., 600 ff.).

[152] Grey to Bertie, Aug. 2, 4:45 P.M.; B.D., 487.

[153] Churchill, *The World Crisis*, I, p. 215 f.

[154] First published in the London *Times*, Dec. 15, 1914, with some explanatory remarks by Mr. Bonar Law; *cf.* also Lord Loreburn, *How the War Came*, p. 210; and Mr. L. J. Maxse, in *The National Review*, Aug. 1918.

Upon the receipt of this promise of support Grey and the Cabinet determined to give Cambon the assurance concerning the north coast of France about which he had asked the day before. So, about 3 P.M., Grey informed the French Ambassador that "if the German fleet comes into the Channel or through the North Sea to undertake hostile operations against the French coasts or shipping, the British fleet will give all the protection in its power." [155] This assurance was still subject to approval by Parliament, Grey added, and did not mean that England would send troops to France. It was merely a promise to make war against Germany, contingent upon a hypothetical action by the German fleet. It looked, however, like war, and led Lord Morley and Mr. John Burns to resign from the Cabinet. It gave also much comfort to the French, even though it did not go as far as they had hoped. The assurance was given before Germany presented her ultimatum to Belgium, news of which did not reach London until the morning of August 3.

About 7 P.M. on August 2 the German Minister at Brussels had handed to Mr. Davignon, the Belgian Minister of Foreign Affairs, the German demands drawn up by Moltke on July 26 and forwarded from Berlin on July 29 in a sealed envelope within a sealed envelope. [156] It stated that Germany "is in receipt of reliable information relating to the proposed advance of French armed forces along the Meuse, route Givet-Namur. They leave no doubt as to France's intention to advance against Germany through Belgian territory." As it was to be feared that Belgium would be unable, unaided, to resist the French advance, and as "it is for Germany a dictate of self-preservation that she anticipate the hostile attack," Germany regretted that she would be forced to enter upon Belgian soil. She con-

---

[155] Grey to Bertie, Aug. 2, 4:45 P.M.; B.D., 487.
[156] See above at note 49.

templated no hostile activities against Belgium. If the Kingdom adopted "a benevolent neutrality toward Germany," the German Government promised at the conclusion of peace to guarantee Belgium's sovereign rights and independence, to evacuate the territory, to buy for cash all the necessities required by her troops, and to make good every damage which they might cause. But should Belgium oppose German troops, or destroy railroads and tunnels, "Germany would be obliged, to her regret, to regard the Kingdom as an enemy." An unequivocal reply was demanded within twelve hours.[157]

Mr. Davignon instantly notified King Albert. A Cabinet meeting was called and sat till past midnight. It was unanimous that Belgium's honor and interests demanded the rejection of the German demand. No German "strategic interest" could justify "a violation of international law." "The Belgian Government, if it were to accept the proposals submitted to it, would sacrifice the honor of the nation and at the same time betray its duty toward Europe." It was therefore "firmly resolved to repel by all means in its power every attack upon its rights." Such was the brave reply which the little Kingdom gave to the German Minister at 7 A.M. on August 3.[158]

Mr. Davignon on the morning of August 3 at once notified the Powers of Germany's ultimatum and its rejection, but did not immediately appeal to the Guaranteeing Powers for support.[159] He was not at first convinced, according to

[157] Jagow to Below, July 29 and Aug. 2; K.D., 376, 648. The German Minister at Brussels was instructed to make certain changes in the original ultimatum, omitting the clause that Germany "will even be prepared to favor with the best of good will any possible claims of the Kingdom for territorial compensation at the expense of France," shortening the time-limit for an answer from twenty-four to twelve hours, and post-dating the ultimatum to make it appear that it had just been received.

[158] B.G.B. [*Belgian Gray Book*], 22; and K.D., 779.
[159] B.G.B., 23, 24; B.D., 521, 551, 562.

the British Minister,[160] that there was real danger from Germany, and wished, in case of aggression, to show that the Belgians were able to defend themselves. Accordingly, on August 3, King Albert merely appealed to King George for "diplomatic intervention" to safeguard the neutrality of Belgium.[161]

The news of the German ultimatum to Belgium and its categorical rejection reached Sir Edward Grey toward noon on Monday, August 3,[162] shortly before he was to make his speech in Parliament announcing the British decision to oppose by force any German attack on the north coast of France. It enabled him to bring forward more effectively the question of Belgian neutrality, which he knew would be one which would strongly affect British public opinion toward the policy which he himself was already convinced in his own mind that England ought to follow. He had little time, in the midst of reading telegrams and hurried interviews with Ambassadors and others, for composing a formal speech.[163] But what he said in the House of Commons on the afternoon of August 3 is eloquent in its simplicity and in the tragic seriousness of the subject.

Sir Edward Grey began his speech with the question of Britain's obligations to France, sketching the development of the system of alliances from the time of the first Morocco Crisis, and giving the House its first knowledge of the Anglo-French military and naval conversations and the exchange of notes in 1912. He insisted that "whatever took place between the military and naval experts, they were not binding engagements upon the Government." "We do not construe anything which has previously taken place in our diplomatic relations with other Powers in this matter as

160 Villiers to Nicolson, Aug. 12; B.D., 670.   161 B.G.B., 25.
162 Villiers to Grey, Aug. 3, 9:31 A.M., received 10:55 A.M.; B.D., 521.
163 Cf., Grey, II, 10-18; the speech is reprinted, ibid., pp. 308-326. For trenchant criticisms, see H. Lutz, Lord Grey and the World War, and Count Montgelas, British Policy under Sir Edward Grey, N. Y., 1928.

restricting the freedom of the Government to decide what attitude they should now take, or restrict the freedom of the House of Commons to decide what their attitude should be." He then spoke of the transfer of the French fleet to the Mediterranean to take the place of the British fleet transferred to home waters, and of the assurance given to M. Cambon the day before.

Finally he came to the question of Belgian neutrality. He referred very effectively to Germany's refusal to give an unequivocal promise to respect it, to the German ultimatum to Belgium and its rejection, and to the appeal of King Albert for "diplomatic intervention." If Belgium lost her independence, then Holland and Denmark would lose theirs; and if France were beaten to her knees and lost her position as a Great Power, England would be faced by the "unmeasured aggrandizement" of Germany. Forestalling the argument that England might stand aside, husband her strength, and intervene at the end to protect her interests, he added:

> If, in a crisis like this, we run away from those obligations of honour and interest as regards the Belgian Treaty, I doubt whether, whatever material force we might have at the end, it would be of very much value in face of the respect that we should have lost. . . . I do not believe, for a moment, that at the end of this war, even if we stood aside and remained aside, we should be in a position, a material position, to use our force decisively to undo what had happened in the course of the war, to prevent the whole of the West of Europe opposite to us—if that had been the result of the war—falling under the domination of a single Power, and I am quite sure that our moral position would be such as to have lost us all respect. I can only say that I have put the question of Belgium somewhat hypothetically, because I am not yet sure of all the facts, but, if the facts turn out to be as they have reached us at present, it is quite clear that there is an obligation on this country to do its

utmost to prevent the consequences to which those facts will lead if they are undisputed.[164]

Grey did not ask the House of Commons for definite endorsement of any precise measures. He was merely skilfully informing them of what he had done so far, assuring them that his hands were still free and that it was for Parliament to decide; but at the same time he persuasively placed before them his own conviction that England ought not to stand aside. The applause with which his speech was greeted left no doubt that Parliament would support him. After the speech and the Cabinet meeting in the evening, Grey confided to Cambon that the Cabinet had decided next morning to send instructions to the British Ambassador in Berlin to demand that the German ultimatum to Belgium be withdrawn. "If they refuse," added Grey, "there will be war."[165]

The Cabinet's decision was strengthened next day, August 4, by news that the Germans had actually violated Belgian territory. At 2 P.M. Sir Edward Grey sent the ultimatum to Berlin. He mentioned Germany's ultimatum to Belgium and the report that "Belgian territory has been violated at Gemmenich." "In these circumstances, and in view of the fact that Germany declined to give the same assurance respecting Belgium as France gave last week in reply to our request," Grey repeated his request, and asked that a satisfactory reply be received in London by midnight. Otherwise, Sir Edward Goschen was to ask for his passports, and the British Embassy was to be turned over to the care of the American Ambassador.[166]

Sir Edward Goschen took the ultimatum to the German Foreign Office about 7 P.M. Jagow told him that no such assurance as requested could be given. He had already

164 Grey II, 321-322.
165 Cambon to Viviani, Aug. 4, 12:17 A.M.; Poincaré, IV, 519 f.
166 Grey to Goschen, August 4, 2 P.M. and 5 P.M.; B.D., 594, 615

explained to Goschen earlier in the day that Germany had been compelled by strategic necessity to go through Belgium to reach France in the quickest and easiest way—that it was a matter of life and death for her. Goschen then said he should like to go and see the Chancellor as it might be his last opportunity. Goschen's narrative continues:

I found the Chancellor very agitated. His Excellency at once began a harangue which lasted for about 20 minutes. He said that the step taken by His Majesty's Government was terrible to a degree, just for a word "neutrality" a word which in war time had so often been disregarded—just for a scrap of paper, Great Britain was going to make war on a kindred nation who desired nothing better than to be friends with her. All his efforts in that direction had been rendered useless by this last terrible step, and the policy to which, as I knew, he had devoted himself since his accession to office, had tumbled down like a house of cards. . . . I said that in the same way as he and Herr von Jagow wished me to understand that for strategical reasons it was a matter of life and death to Germany to advance through Belgium and violate her neutrality, so I would wish him to understand that it was, so to speak, a matter of "life and death" for the honor of Great Britain that she should keep her solemn engagement to do her utmost to defend Belgium's neutrality if attacked. That solemn compact simply had to be kept, or what confidence could anyone have in engagements given by Great Britain in the future? The Chancellor said "But at what price will that compact have been kept. Has the British Government thought of that?" I hinted to his Excellency as plainly as I could that fear of consequences could hardly be regarded as an excuse for breaking solemn engagements, but his Excellency was so excited, so evidently overcome by the news of our action and so little disposed to hear reason, that I refrained from adding fuel to the flame by further argument. As I was leaving he said that the blow of Great Britain joining Germany's enemies was all the greater that almost up to the last moment he and his Government had been working with us and supporting our efforts to maintain peace between Austria and Russia. I admitted that that had been the case, and said that it was part of the tragedy which saw the two nations fall apart just at the moment when the relations between them had been more friendly and cordial than they had been for years.[167]

As the clock struck midnight and no satisfactory answer had been given to Goschen, Germany and England were at war.

The Sarajevo spark had started the fire which had now spread over Europe. Serbia and the Great Powers were involved in a life and death struggle.

[167] Goschen to Grey, Aug. 6; B.D., 671; see also 666, 667.

CHAPTER XII

CONCLUSION

NONE of the Powers wanted a European War. Their governing rulers and ministers, with very few exceptions, all foresaw that it must be a frightful struggle, in which the political results were not absolutely certain, but in which the loss of life, suffering, and economic consequences were bound to be terrible. This is true, in a greater or less degree, of Pashitch, Berchtold, Bethmann, Sazonov, Poincaré, San Giuliano and Sir Edward Grey. Yet none of them, not even Sir Edward Grey, could have foreseen that the political results were to be so stupendous, and the other consequences so terrible, as was actually the case.

For many of the Powers, to be sure, a European War might seem to hold out the possibility of achieving various desired advantages: for Serbia, the achievement of national unity for all Serbs; for Austria, the revival of her waning prestige as a Great Power, and the checking of nationalistic tendencies which threatened her very existence; for Russia, the accomplishment of her historic mission of controlling Constantinople and the Straits; for Germany, new economic advantages and the restoration of the European balance which had changed with the weakening of the Triple Alliance and the tightening of the Triple Entente; for France, the recovery of Alsace-Lorraine and the ending of the German menace; and for England, the destruction of the German naval danger and of Prussian militarism. All these advantages, and many others, were feverishly striven and intrigued for, on all sides, the moment the War actually broke out, but this is no good proof that any of the statesmen mentioned deliberately aimed to bring about a war to secure these advantages. One cannot judge the motives which actuated men before the War, by what they did in an absolutely new situation which arose as soon as they were overtaken by a conflagration they had sought to avert. And in fact, in the case of the two Powers between whom the immediate conflict arose, the postponement or avoidance of a European War would have facilitated the accomplishment of the ultimate advantages aimed at: Pashitch knew that there was a better chance for Serbian national unity after he had consolidated Serbian gains in the Balkan Wars, and after Russia had completed her military and naval armaments as planned for 1917; and Berchtold knew that he had a better chance of crushing the Greater Serbia danger and strengthening Austria, if he could avoid Russian intervention and a general European War.

It is also true, likewise, that the moment war was declared, it was hailed with varying demonstrations of enthusiasm on the part of the people in every country—with considerable in Serbia, Austria, Russia and Germany, with less in France, and with almost none in England. But this does not mean that the peoples wanted war or exerted a decisive influence to bring it about. It is a curious psychological phenomenon that as soon as a country engages in war, there develops or is created among the masses a frenzy of patriotic excitement which is no index of their pre-war desires. And in the countries where the demonstrations of enthusiasm were greatest, the political influence of the people on the Government was least.

Nevertheless, a European War broke out. Why? Because in each country political and military leaders did certain things, which led to mobilizations and declarations of war, or failed to do certain things which might have prevented them. In this sense, all the European countries, in a greater or less degree, were responsible. One must abandon the dictum of the Versailles Treaty that Germany and her allies were solely responsible. It was a dictum exacted by victors from vanquished, under the influence of the blindness, ignorance, hatred, and the propagandist misconceptions to which war had given rise. It was based on evidence which was incomplete and not always sound.[1] It is generally recognized by the best historical scholars in all countries to be no longer tenable or defensible. They are agreed that the responsibility for the War is a divided responsibility. But they still disagree very much as to the relative part of this responsibility that falls on each country and on each individual political or military leader.

Some writers like to fix positively in some precise mathematical fashion the exact responsibility for the war. This was done in one way by the framers of Article 231 of the Treaty of Versailles. It has been done in other ways by those who would fix the responsibility in some relative fashion, as, for instance, Austria first, then Russia, France and Germany and England. But the present writer deprecates such efforts to assess by a precise formula a very complicated question, which is after all more a matter of delicate shading than of definite white and black. Oversimplification, as Napoleon once said in framing his Code, is the enemy of precision. Moreover, even supposing that a general consensus of opinion might be reached as to the relative responsibility of any individual country or man for immediate causes connected with the July crisis of 1914, it is by no means necessarily true that the same relative responsibility would hold for the underlying causes, which

[1] For a recent analysis of the evidence laid before the Commission on Responsibility for the War at the Paris Peace Conference, and the untenability of the conclusions based upon it, see A. von Wegerer, "Die Wiederlegung der Versailles Kriegsschuldthese," in *Die Kriegsschuldfrage*, VI, 1-77, Jan., 1928; also his article, with replies to it, in *Current History*, Aug., 1928, pp. 810-828.

for years had been tending toward the creation of a dangerous situation.

One may, however, sum up very briefly the most salient facts in regard to each country.

Serbia felt a natural and justifiable impulse to do what so many other countries had done in the nineteenth century—to bring under one national Government all the discontented Serb people. She had liberated those under Turkish rule; the next step was to liberate those under Hapsburg rule. She looked to Russia for assistance, and had been encouraged to expect that she would receive it. After the assassination, Mr. Pashitch took no steps to discover and bring to justice Serbians in Belgrade who had been implicated in the plot. One of them, Ciganovitch, was even assisted to disappear. Mr. Pashitch waited to see what evidence the Austrian authorities could find. When Austria demanded coöperation of Austrian officials in discovering, though not in trying, implicated Serbians, the Serbian Government made a very conciliatory but negative reply. They expected that the reply would not be regarded as satisfactory, and, even before it was given, ordered the mobilization of the Serbian army. Serbia did not want war, but believed it would be forced upon her. That Mr. Pashitch was aware of the plot three weeks before it was executed, failed to take effective steps to prevent the assassins from crossing over from Serbia to Bosnia, and then failed to give Austria any warning or information which might have averted the fatal crime, were facts unknown to Austria in July, 1914; they cannot therefore be regarded as in any way justifying Austria's conduct; but they are part of Serbia's responsibility, and a very serious part.

Austria was more responsible for the immediate origin of the war than any other Power. Yet from her own point of view she was acting in self-defence—not against an immediate military attack, but against the corroding Greater

Serbia and Jugoslav agitation which her leaders believed
threatened her very existence. No State can be expected
to sit with folded arms and await dismemberment at the
hands of its neighbors. Russia was believed to be intriguing
with Serbia and Rumania against the Dual Monarchy. The
assassination of the heir to the throne, as a result of a plot
prepared in Belgrade, demanded severe retribution; otherwise Austria would be regarded as incapable of action,
"worm-eaten" as the Serbian Press expressed it, would sink
in prestige, and hasten her own downfall. To avert this
Berchtold determined to crush Serbia with war. He deliberately framed the ultimatum with the expectation and
hope that it would be rejected. He hurriedly declared war
against Serbia in order to forestall all efforts at mediation.
He refused even to answer his own ally's urgent requests to
come to an understanding with Russia, on the basis of a
military occupation of Belgrade as a pledge that Serbia
would carry out the promises in her reply to the ultimatum.
Berchtold gambled on a "local" war with Serbia only,
believing that he could rattle the German sword; but rather
than abandon his war with Serbia, he was ready to drag
the rest of Europe into war.

It is very questionable whether Berchtold's obstinate
determination to diminish Serbia and destroy her as a
Balkan factor was, after all, the right method, even if he
had succeeded in keeping the war "localized" and in temporarily strengthening the Dual Monarchy. Supposing that
Russia in 1914, because of military unpreparedness or lack
of support, had been ready to tolerate the execution of
Berchtold's designs, it is quite certain that she would have
aimed within the next two or three years at wiping out this
second humiliation, which was so much more damaging to
her prestige than that of 1908-09. In two or three years,
when her great program of military reform was finally completed, Russia would certainly have found a pretext to

reverse the balance in the Balkans in her own favor again. A further consequence of Berchtold's policy, even if successful, would have been the still closer consolidation of the Triple Entente, with the possible addition of Italy. And, finally, a partially dismembered Serbia would have become a still greater source of unrest and danger to the peace of Europe than heretofore. Serbian nationalism, like Polish nationalism, would have been intensified by partition. Austrian power and prestige would not have been so greatly increased as to be able to meet these new dangers. Berchtold's plan was a mere temporary improvement, but could not be a final solution of the Austro-Serbian antagonism. Franz Ferdinand and many others recognized this, and so long as he lived, no step in this fatal direction had been taken. It was the tragic fate of Austria that the only man who might have had the power and ability to develop Austria along sound lines became the innocent victim of the crime which was the occasion of the World War and so of her ultimate disruption.

Germany did not plot a European War, did not want one, and made genuine, though too belated efforts, to avert one. She was the victim of her alliance with Austria and of her own folly. Austria was her only dependable ally, Italy and Rumania having become nothing but allies in name. She could not throw her over, as otherwise she would stand isolated between Russia, where Panslavism and armaments were growing stronger every year, and France, where Alsace-Lorraine, Delcassé's fall, and Agadir were not forgotten. Therefore, Bethmann felt bound to accede to Berchtold's request for support and gave him a free hand to deal with Serbia; he also hoped and expected to "localize" the Austro-Serbian conflict. Germany then gave grounds to the Entente for suspecting the sincerity of her peaceful intentions by her denial of any foreknowledge of the ultimatum, by her support and justification of it when it was published, and by her refusal of Sir Edward Grey's conference proposal. However, Germany by no means had Austria so completely under her thumb as the Entente Powers and many writers have assumed. It is true that Berchtold would hardly have embarked on his gambler's policy unless he had been assured that Germany would fulfil the obligations of the alliance, and to this extent Germany must share the great responsibility of Austria. But when Bethmann realized that Russia was likely to intervene, that England might not remain neutral. and that there was danger of a world war of which Germany and Austria would appear to be the instigators, he tried to call a halt on Austria, but it was too late. He pressed mediation proposals on Vienna, but Berchtold was insensible to the pressure, and the Entente Powers did not believe in the sincerity of his pressure, especially as they produced no results.

Germany's geographical position between France and Russia, and her inferiority in number of troops, had made necessary the plan of crushing the French army quickly at first and then turning against Russia. This was only possible, in the opinion of her strategists, by marching through Belgium, as it was generally anticipated by military men that she would do in case of a European War. On July 29, after Austria had declared war on Serbia, and after the Tsar had assented to general mobilization in Russia (though this was not known in Berlin and was later postponed for a day owing to the Kaiser's telegram to the Tsar), Bethmann took the precaution of sending to the German Minister in Brussels a sealed envelope. The Minister was not to open it except on further instructions. It contained the later demand for the passage of the German army through Belgium. This does not mean, however, that Germany had decided for war. In fact, Bethmann was one of the last of the statesmen to abandon hope of peace and to consent to the mobilization of his country's army. General mobilization of the continental armies took place in the following order: Serbia, Russia, Austria, France and Germany. General mobilization by a Great Power was commonly interpreted by military men in every country, though perhaps not by Sir Edward Grey, the Tsar, and some civilian officials, as meaning that the country was on the point of making war,—that the military machine had begun to move and would not be stopped. Hence, when Germany learned of the Russian general mobilization, she sent ultimatums to St. Petersburg and Paris, warning that German mobilization would follow unless Russia suspended hers within twelve hours, and asking what would be the attitude of France. The answers being unsatisfactory, Germany then mobilized and declared war. It was the hasty Russian general mobilization, assented to on July 29 and ordered on July 30, while Germany was still trying to bring Austria to accept mediation proposals, which finally rendered the European War inevitable.

Russia was partly responsible for the Austro-Serbian conflict because of the frequent encouragement which she had given at Belgrade—that Serbian national unity would be ultimately achieved with Russian assistance at Austrian expense. This had led the Belgrade Cabinet to hope for Russian support in case of a war with Austria, and the hope did not prove vain in July, 1914. Before this, to be sure, in the Bosnian Crisis and during the Balkan Wars, Russia had put restraint upon Serbia, because Russia, exhausted by the effects of the Russo-Japanese War, was not yet ready for a European struggle with the Teutonic Powers. But in 1914 her armaments, though not yet completed, had made such progress that the militarists were confident of success, if they had French and British support. In the spring of 1914, the Minister of War, Sukhomlinov, had published an article in a Russian newspaper, though without signing his name, to the effect, "Russia is ready, France must be ready also." Austria was convinced that Russia would ultimately aid Serbia, unless the Serbian danger were dealt with energetically after the Archduke's murder; she knew that Russia was growing stronger every year; but she doubted whether the Tsar's armaments had yet reached the point at which Russia would dare to intervene; she would therefore run less risk of Russian intervention and a European War if she used the Archduke's assassination as an excuse for weakening Serbia, than if she should postpone action until the future.

Russia's responsibility lay also in the secret preparatory military measures which she was making at the same time that she was carrying on diplomatic negotiations. These alarmed Germany and Austria. But it was primarily Russia's general mobilization, made when Germany was trying to bring Austria to a settlement, which precipitated the final catastrophe, causing Germany to mobilize and declare war.

The part of France is less clear than that of the other Great Powers, because she has not yet made a full publication of her documents. To be sure, M. Poincaré, in the fourth volume of his memoirs, has made a skilful and elaborate plea, to prove *"La France innocente."* But he is not convincing. It is quite clear that on his visit to Russia he assured the Tsar's Government that France would support her as an ally in preventing Austria from humiliating or crushing Serbia. Paléologue renewed these assurances in a way to encourage Russia to take a strong hand. He did not attempt to restrain Russia from military measures which he knew would call forth German counter-measures and cause war. Nor did he keep his Government promptly and fully informed of the military steps which were being taken at St. Petersburg. President Poincaré, upon his return to France, made efforts for peace, but his great preoccupation was to minimize French and Russian preparatory measures and emphasize those of Germany, in order to secure the certainty of British support in a struggle which he now regarded as inevitable.

Sir Edward Grey made many sincere proposals for preserving peace; they all failed owing partly, but not exclusively, to Germany's attitude. Sir Edward could probably have prevented war if he had done either of two things. If, early in the crisis, he had acceded to the urging of France and Russia and given a strong warning to Germany that, in a European War, England would take the side of the Franco-Russian Alliance, this would probably have led Bethmann to exert an earlier and more effective pressure on Austria; and it would perhaps thereby have prevented the Austrian declaration of war on Serbia, and brought to a successful issue the "direct conversations" between Vienna and St. Petersburg. Or, if Sir Edward Grey had listened to German urging, and warned France and Russia early in the crisis, that if they became involved in war, England would remain neutral, probably Russia would have hesitated with her mobilizations, and France would probably have exerted a restraining influence at St. Petersburg. But Sir Edward Grey could not say that England would take the side of France and Russia, because he had a Cabinet nearly evenly divided, and he was not sure, early in the crisis, that public opinion in England would back him up in war against Germany. He could resign, and he says in his memoirs that he would have resigned, but that would have been no comfort or aid to France, who had come confidently to count upon British support He was determined to say and do nothing which might encourage her with a hope which he could not fulfil. Therefore, in spite of the pleadings of the French. he refused to give them definite assurances until the probable German determination to go through Belgium made it clear that the Cabinet, and Parliament, and British public opinion would follow his lead in war on Germany. On the other hand, he was unwilling to heed the German pleadings that he exercise restraint at Paris and St. Petersburg, because he did not wish to endanger the Anglo-Russian Entente and the solidarity of the Triple Entente, because he felt a moral obligation to France, growing out of the Anglo-French military and naval conversations of the past years, and because he suspected that Germany was backing Austria up in an unjustifiable course and that Prussian militarists had taken the direction of affairs at Berlin out of the hands of Herr von Bethmann-Hollweg and the civilian authorities.

Italy exerted relatively little influence on the crisis in either direction.

Belgium had done nothing in any way to justify the demand which Germany made upon her. With commendable prudence, at the very first news of the ominous Austrian ultimatum, she had foreseen the danger to which she might be exposed. She had accordingly instructed her representatives abroad as to the statements which they were to make in case Belgium should decide very suddenly to mobilize to protect her neutrality. On July 29, she placed her army upon "a strengthened war footing," but did not order complete mobilization until two days later, when Austria, Russia, and Germany had already done so, and war appeared inevitable. Even after being confronted with the terrible German ultimatum, at 7 P.M. on August 2, she did not at once invite the assistance of English and French troops to aid her in the defense of her soil and her neutrality against a certain German assault; it was not until German troops had actually violated her territory, on August 4, that she appealed for the assistance of the Powers which had guaranteed her neutrality. Belgium was the innocent victim of German strategic necessity. Though the German violation of Belgium was of enormous influence in forming public opinion as to the responsibility for the War after hostilities began, it was not a cause of the War, except in so far as it made it easier for Sir Edward Grey to bring England into it.

In the forty years following the Franco-Prussian War, as we have seen, there developed a system of alliances which divided Europe into two hostile groups. This hostility was accentuated by the increase of armaments, economic rivalry, nationalist ambitions and antagonisms, and newspaper incitement. But it is very doubtful whether all these dangerous tendencies would have actually led to war, had it not been for the assassination of Franz Ferdinand. That was the factor which consolidated the elements of hostility and started the rapid and complicated succession of events which culminated in a World War, and for that factor Serbian nationalism was primarily responsible.

But the verdict of the Versailles Treaty that Germany and her allies were responsible for the War, in view of the evidence now available, is historically unsound. It should therefore be revised. However, because of the popular feeling widespread in some of the Entente countries, it is doubtful whether a formal and legal revision is as yet practicable. There must first come a further revision by historical scholars, and through them of public opinion.

INDEX

Made in the USA
San Bernardino, CA
22 January 2018